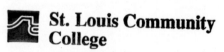

Private Action and the Public Good

Private Action
and
the
Public Good

Edited by Walter W. Powell and Elisabeth S. Clemens

YALE UNIVERSITY PRESS / NEW HAVEN & LONDON

Printed in the United States of America.

Library of Congress Cataloging-in-Publication Data

Private action and the public good / edited by Walter W. Powell and Elisabeth S. Clemens.

p.   cm.

Includes bibliographical references and index.

ISBN 0-300-06449-7 (alk. paper)

1. Public interest.   2. Common good.   3. Nonprofit organizations.
I. Powell, Water W.   II. Clemens, Elisabeth Stephanie, 1958–   .
JC330.15.P75   1998
361.7'63'0973 — dc21   97-26367

A catalogue record for this book is available from the British Library.

The paper in this book meets the guidelines for permanence and durability of the Committee on Production Guidelines for Book Longevity of the Council on Library Resources.

10 9 8 7 6 5 4 3 2 1

For Jim Wood

Contents

Acknowledgments

Although any edited volume is a collaborative project, the list of those who have helped us to produce *Private Action and the Public Good* is particularly long. Our special thanks go to James Wood, director of the Program on the Governance of Nonprofit Organizations, and Robert Payton, past executive director of the Indiana University Center on Philanthropy. Many of the initiatives of the center, including this volume, have been generously funded by the Lilly Endowment, and we are extremely grateful for the endowment's support. For four years, Jim and Bob orchestrated a series of meetings that brought together doctoral students, young faculty, and senior scholars in warm, lively, and constructive debates. These gatherings in Indianapolis contributed to much of the work represented in this volume and, in the process, created lasting ties among the many fellows whose careers have been enhanced by the program. We are also indebted to Dwight Burlingame, associate director of the Center on Philanthropy, and to Warren Ilchman, who assumed the office of executive directive at the time of the conference. To the center staff, who made possible all the program meetings as well as the final conference, our gratitude is heartfelt. We would also like to acknowledge all our colleagues who participated in the program's final conference and, in many ways, enriched the papers included in this volume: Avner Ben-Ner, Ken Dauber, Paul DiMaggio, Peter Dobkin Hall, Cheryl Hyde, Kathleen McCarthy, Debra Minkoff, Jayendu Patel, Robert D. Putnam, David Smith, Melissa Middleton Stone, Miriam Wood, Dennis Young, Mayer Zald, and Richard Zeckhauser, as well as all the doctoral and young faculty fellows. Finally, the entire volume has benefited greatly from Carrie Rothburd's close readings of each chapter and her fine editorial skills.

Introduction

To the casual observer, the realms of business, government, and nonprofit organizations seem separate and distinct, with the different sectors performing different functions. Business and government are often seen as antagonists and, in many nations, the role of government is being reduced and more activities turned over to the market, purportedly in order to enhance efficiency and responsiveness. But markets have a harsh side and a sharp edge to them; consequently, nonprofit associations are held up as a softer and more compassionate alternative. Such a portrait is, of course, a crude simplification of the contemporary organizational landscape. But it is rather close to the views held by many citizens, pundits, and politicians as well as by champions of the marketplace and civil society alike. A deeper look at the institutional division of labor, however, not only reveals strong interconnections and interdependencies among the three sectors of government, business, and nonprofits, but also documents that common organizational problems and constraints are found across sectors. The issues of governance — how organizations are controlled, how they relate to their various constituents, and whether organizational interests are consistent with broader societal goals — cut across all three sectors.

Drawing on organizational, legal, and economic analyses, as well as concern for the congruence of organizational behavior with societal goals, the study of governance not only bridges but transforms often disparate discussions about the roles of business, government, and nonprofits. Questions about the power and responsibilities of boards of directors, rules governing mergers and acquisitions, the role of institutional investors and the pay of corporate executives, have been widely debated in the business and legal communities in recent years (see Roe 1994; Blair 1995). The focus of the corporate governance discussion is basically on the ground rules of governance: what constraints and requirements should be imposed on the executives who manage publicly traded corporations, and what influence and recourse should be afforded to the various constituents: employees, stockholders, and communities. Viewed more broadly, corporate governance entails more than the private sector, raising questions about the array of legal, institutional, and cultural practices that shape what different institutional forms are allowed to do, and define who controls organizations and how that control is exercised. Interestingly, although the discussion of corporate governance is quite specific at the level of the firm, it is murky at the macro level, where questions about the alignment of organizational and managerial interests with societal goals are largely unresolved. In contrast, there is much more clarity with respect to how the goals of nonprofit organizations should mesh with the interests of society. Indeed, both the purpose and tax-exempt status of nonprofit organizations are ostensibly dependent on the delivery of goods and services that benefit the larger society. But at the level of the individual nonprofit organization, governance issues again become murky. For the nonprofit organization, what is the yardstick that assesses how organizational actions best meet broad societal goals? Thus, discussions of governance must proceed on two levels — organizational and societal — and much more insight and understanding are needed as to how these levels either cohere or conflict. A fundamental question, then, for the private, public, and nonprofit sectors is whether the goals and interests of organizations and their leaders and managers are congruent with the interests of the larger society such that the activities of the organizations — be they generating profits or providing services — increase the collective well-being of society. Grappling with these thorny questions of governance provided the impetus for this book.

ORIGINS OF THE GOVERNANCE PROGRAM

The roots of this volume go back to 1988 and the launching of a program on the governance of nonprofit organizations at the Indiana University Center on Philanthropy. The program, guided by James Wood, a sociologist, brought together faculty and graduate students from a wide range of social science disciplines for biannual discussions of the many goals pursued by nonprofit organizations. The program originated in a series of conversations about the meanings and applicability of the concept of governance. Wood assembled a group of scholars to facilitate these conversations, faculty with strong research interests in nonprofits — Burton Weisbrod and Dennis Young from economics, Barry Karl from history, John Baker from law, Melissa Stone from organizational behavior, David Smith from philosophy, and Jerry Hage, Woody Powell, and Mayer Zald from sociology. This advisory board was joined by Charles Beibel, affiliated with the Lilly Endowment, and Bob Payton and Dwight Burlingame of the Center on Philanthropy.

The program's aims were expansive. We sought to offer financial support and intellectual guidance to a select group of advanced graduate students and young faculty doing research on issues of governance in the nonprofit sector. Our goal was to create an interdisciplinary community drawn together by common scholarly interests. The research agenda was framed to account for the growth in the importance of the nonprofit sector in the United States and abroad and to survey the wide range of activities pursued under the nonprofit rubric. The startling array of activities performed by nonprofits around the globe made arriving at a common definition of what constitutes a nonprofit quite difficult. But rather than trying to establish a single definition or pursue a particular theoretical approach, we chose an avowedly exploratory agenda.

Over its five-year history, the governance program funded some four dozen young scholars conducting research on topics as varied as the effects of U.S. tax policy on charitable giving, the role of neighborhood associations in the civic life of low-income housing projects, the effects of corporate philanthropy on art museum exhibits, the contribution of voluntary associations to the "velvet" revolutions in Eastern Europe, and the role of nongovernmental organizations in the economic and political development of newly emerging nations. Recognizing the heterogeneity of activities that are labeled nonprofit, our aim was to understand more fully the diverse political, economic, and historical circumstances that have given rise to the nonprofit sector here and abroad. This broad interpretation of governance was guided by the recognition that the nonprofit sector has routinely played a critical role in which competing visions of social, economic, and institutional arrangements are debated and tried out (see Hall 1992). The most salient common feature of nonprofits may be neither an organizational trait nor legal status but the conditions under which they are typically founded. Indeed, Michael O'Neill (1989) has suggested that one of the chief roles of the nonprofit sector has been to move into areas of social ambiguity and remain there until it becomes clearer what the issues, needs, and problems are.

Regardless of their origins, however, nonprofits are organizations in which individuals somehow manage to act collectively. In every sector and society in which we sponsored research, there was a persistent tension between acting in the public interest and pursuing private interests. Moreover, as nonprofit organizations grow and the sector expands, there are strong pressures to modify activities in the direction of increasing similarity with governmental and for-profit organizations, at times endangering the societal goals celebrated in mission statements and origin stories (DiMaggio and Powell 1983). Because organizations cannot survive on good intentions alone, nonprofits must grapple with issues of fiscal solvency, competition, regulation, and accountability. An unintended consequence of these tensions is that questions of efficiency, cost-effectiveness, and practicality dominate much of the discussion of nonprofits, obscuring real debate about larger collective values. The issues of performance and the changing role and mix of market, state, and association are critical, but we did not want to lose sight of the contribution that nonprofits may or may not make to the collective good. Consequently, the theme of private action and the public good became an organizing motif for the governance project. We recognized that the idea of the public good is indeed vexed and contested and that researchers need to ask questions like Which public? and For whose good?

When the initial five-year funding for the program was dispensed, we chose not to institutionalize the project as an ongoing operation. Much of the enjoyment and contribution of the program stemmed from the success of creating a responsive community drawn from many universities and multiple disciplines, assembled regularly with minimum fanfare for the purpose of sharing ideas. Rather than create a permanent program, we opted instead to pay tribute to the accomplishments of the project with a culminating conference featuring the research of some of the many participants in the program. As editors of this volume, we were the primary organizers of the conference, drawing on our long involvement with the governance program.[1]

GROWTH AND SCALE OF THE NONPROFIT SECTOR

The growing range and richness of research on nonprofits reflect the dramatic increase in nonprofits worldwide. In the United States, the nonprofit sector has grown explosively since World War II. Hall (1995) reports that the commissioner of the Internal Revenue Service testified before Congress in 1953 that no more than fifty thousand charitable tax-exempt organizations were registered with his agency. By the mid-1970s, this number exceeded seven hundred thousand and by the mid-1980s was nearly one million (Weisbrod 1988). But the expansion in the number of nonprofits is by no means confined to the United States. In 1990, nonprofit hospitals provided 15 percent of patient days of hospital care in France and 42 percent in Germany; the corresponding figure for the United States is 67 percent (Weisbrod 1995). In the child day care field, nonprofits cared for 35–39 percent of the children in Germany, Japan, and France and 82 percent in the United Kingdom; in the United States the figure is 56 percent (Salamon and Anheier 1994; Hansmann 1995). Figures on the employment side are equally robust. In the service sector, nonprofits account for 6 percent of total employment in Italy, 9–10 percent in Japan, the United Kingdom, France, and Germany; the figure is 15 percent in the United States (Salamon and Anheier 1994, 33).

The causes underlying the spread of the nonprofit sector vary widely around the globe, but two factors stand out. First, nonprofits are an institutional hybrid that combines public service with private initiative. Consequently, in many areas, public sector services may be initiated by, transferred to, or assumed by nonprofits. Governments have divested themselves of numerous activities that have been supplanted by either private provision or voluntary associations (Smith and Lipsky 1993). In the United States, fire services, indigent health care, and even prisons are examples. Governments also contract with nonprofits to provide public services. Indeed, in many domains — the arts and education, for example — the dominant model of service provision involves private nonprofit organizations operating largely with federal monies. Finally, we find industries such as health care and day care in which there is extensive competition among different organizational forms, and such sectoral competition appears to have further stimulated nonprofit growth. The range of experimentation with "third party government" (Salamon 1987) is broad and has resulted in complex gradations of public, private, and nonprofit.

In developing nations, nongovernmental organizations

(NGOs) also play a considerable role in service provision and in international aid and development. But equally critical has been the growing advocacy role played by NGOs in support of human rights and improving the status of women and children. Moreover, this advocacy role is by no means limited to emerging nations. The rise of specialized advocacy movements is the second major cause of nonprofit expansion. The industrial democracies have witnessed very rapid proliferation of special interest, nonprofit advocacy groups (Jenkins 1987). In contrast to older political groups that sought to redistribute wealth and political power, advocacy groups articulate collective interests, for example, a cleaner environment or the expansion of citizenship rights, by relying on appeals directed as much at the general public as at those in the corridors of power.

The expansion of nonprofit organizations as both service providers and advocates for reform has spurred scholarly efforts to explain why this form of organization varies in its prevalence and grows at different rates cross-nationally. Estelle James (1987) has argued that the size of nonprofit sectors varies with the degree of social, religious, and linguistic heterogeneity of a society. Burton Weisbrod (1975; 1988), perhaps the most sophisticated theorist of the "third" sector, has argued that the more homogeneous the society, the less need there is for the nonprofit form. But when citizens' preferences are broadly heterogeneous, a government that meets only the desires of a majority will leave many undersatisfied, willing to pay more for collective services but unable to secure them from government. As diversity increases and dissatisfaction with existing institutional arrangements increases, nonprofits are created as both a response and a complement to public and private enterprise.

NONPROFITS AND CIVIL SOCIETY

In recent debates, attention to the ways in which nonprofits provide public services has been joined by the contention that nonprofits are a public good in their own right. As a form of voluntary association, nonprofits have been linked to the idea of a public sphere, existing outside of the realm of government and large-scale private enterprise. Commentators across the political spectrum have sought to recapture the Enlightenment concept of civil society — that society exists prior to ruling authorities, and while authority is founded on contract, society rests on an individual's natural freedom of association (Bell 1989; Taylor 1990; Walzer 1991). The rediscovery of a public sphere has many sources; indeed, there are a welter of competing definitions as to what constitutes civil society. Daniel Bell (1989) suggests that "the demand for a return to civil society is the demand for a manageable scale of social life" — one based on participation in voluntary associations, church, and community. Charles Taylor (1990) offers a vision of a public sphere that stresses self-government at the local level and a direct involvement in civic life. Present in both of these accounts are metaphors of scale

---

1. Walter Powell served as a member of the advisory board of the governance project from its inception, and Elisabeth Clemens was a Young Faculty Fellow in 1990–91 and subsequent participant in program meetings.

and space. The public sphere is a local arena between individuals and large-scale organizations. Voluntary associations play a critical role in almost every conception of civil society. Consider, for example, the comprehensive account offered by Jürgen Habermas (1992, 453):

> The institutional core of civil society is constituted by voluntary unions outside the realm of the state and the economy and ranging from churches, cultural associations, and academies to independent media, sport and leisure clubs, debating societies, groups of concerned citizens, and grass-roots petitioning drives all the way to occupational associations, political parties, labor unions, and "alternative institutions."

But do nonprofit organizations represent a more authentic and independent alternative to the market or the state? Some scholars have questioned whether the growth of nonprofits really contributes to social connectedness and the kind of civic engagement that makes democracy work (Putnam 1993). Many U.S. nonprofits, such as the Sierra Club and the American Association of Retired Persons, are mailing list organizations, a kind of checkbook community in which members are tied to common ideologies and policies but not to one another (Putnam 1996). Moreover, most prominent nonprofits, such as the Ford Foundation, the Metropolitan Museum of Art, and Harvard University, are large bureaucracies and hardly qualify as secondary associations. The debate over civic engagement, however, is healthy in its own right and has attracted numerous rebuttals contending that there are a host of new alternative secondary associations that involve personal contact and generate mutual trust (Lemann 1996; Portes and Landolt 1996; Schudson 1996; Skocpol 1996).

PURPOSE AND MISSION

The debate over civic engagement, whether in the United States or elsewhere, reflects in part the considerable difficulty in defining what constitutes a nonprofit organization. Indeed, two of the leading scholars of international research on nonprofits, Lester Salamon and Helmut Anheier (1994), note that the nonprofit sector is but one possible embodiment of a society's caring tradition. They recognize the terminological tangle that plagues efforts to define and distinguish among charitable activities, the independent sector, the voluntary sector, tax-exempt 501(c)3 organizations, nongovernmental organizations, and the private, nonprofit sector. Even in the United States, which has the most well defined nonprofit sector, many citizens do not recognize clearly the difference between nonprofits, for-profits, and government agencies. Indeed, there is ample evidence for the argument that the nonprofit designation is little more than an accident of history and tax laws (Simon 1987). More broadly, there are fundamental differences in the scope and structure of the nonprofit sector cross-nationally. Salamon and Anheier (1994, 2) observe that "few societies have anything approaching a coherent notion of a distinct private nonprofit sector, and those that do often include entities that would be unrecognizable to U.S. scholars."

But even though the term *nonprofit* has little in the way of consistent transnational or transhistorical meaning, there are broad similarities that can be cobbled together to produce a useful definition of nonprofit status (Hall 1987; DiMaggio and Anheier 1990; Salamon and Anheier 1993). Recognizing that nonprofits vary from shoestring operations to large, powerful entities with assets exceeding those of some nations, one can find a common feature in negation. Nonprofits are subject to a nondistribution constraint — they cannot distribute profits to members, and in return for agreeing to this constraint, they receive special tax, legal, and regulatory treatment (Hansmann 1980). There are also several common elements of nonprofit mission. Hall (1987) suggests that nonprofits exist either to provide a service or to further a cause. They may perform public tasks, either delegated by the state or for which there is public demand but no public provision. Nonprofits also arise to influence the direction of public policy. In their comparative work on the nonprofit sector around the globe, Salamon and Anheier (1993; 1994) have identified five characteristic features: nonprofits are formally organized, organizationally separate from government, constrained from redistributing earnings, self-governing, and voluntary.

These definitional debates are not just a sterile scholarly exercise. Around the globe there are organizations that appear to be neither commercial nor governmental; whether they should be tax-exempt, are autonomous from government, independent of the control of a few key members, and provide services that benefit the public good are issues of great concern to donors, policymakers, and governments everywhere. The difficulties in identifying what a nonprofit is stem from the multiple purposes such organizations serve: providers of social services, advocates for social change, or alternatives to commercial entities. The broad missions of nonprofits are ostensibly justified by the expectation that nonprofits will produce public goods that would go underproduced in their absence or on the grounds that production exclusively through the marketplace would exclude some members of society.

The task of this book, then, is to attempt to clarify our understanding of nonprofit mission and performance. We begin with discussions of the meaning of such terms as *the public good, civil society, altruism,* and *other-regarding entrepreneurialism.* We then turn to an analysis of nonprofit behavior to see whether nonprofits operate differently from other organizational forms. We next examine the dramatic changes taking place in the relations between nonprofits and government. Recognizing that the goals of service provision, advocacy, managerial effectiveness, and fiscal solvency may be in conflict, we focus on how nonprofit organizations maintain their mission in the face of complex challenges that threaten their viability. Our goal is not to produce a comprehensive treatment of the nonprofit sector; other books do this effectively. Instead, our aim is to clarify the meanings of the public good, enhance our understanding of the division of institutional labor, and broaden the focus of research on organizational goal attainment.

OVERVIEW OF THE BOOK

The chapters in part I begin with philosophical concerns as an entry point to questions of institutional mix. Building on enduring debates over the relation of the public good to private interest, Jane Mansbridge contends that public and private need not be conceived as mutually exclusive. Instead, she identifies institutional forms that "nest public spirit within a return to self-interest," an apt description of many nonprofit enterprises. She offers a broad-ranging review and critique of the Western philosophic tradition as well as more utilitarian economic theories, concluding that the public good is more than the summation of private interests. Craig Calhoun cautions, however, that there are dangers in an overly enthusiastic embrace of the public good, a concept that is contested not only philosophically, as Mansbridge argues, but also politically by the multiple communities that constitute the public of modern societies. Rejecting communitarian visions of restored and unproblematic unity, Calhoun urges an appreciation and strengthening of the ability of disparate communities to foster the capacity necessary for participation in an authentic debate over the nature of the public good. He reminds us of the difficulty of finding a single public good in a pluralist society.

Alan Wolfe joins the discussion by examining the literature on the predominance of egoism over altruism in human behavior. He contends that individualist explanations, rooted in either psychology or economics, do not adequately account for the altruistic actions observed both in laboratory experiments and throughout history. Wolfe argues instead that while altruistic behavior may have diverse causes, "environmental altruism" — those beliefs and institutions that "insist that the decisions we take be made in light of their consequences for others" — is crucially important. Consequently, societies may vary both in the level of altruism they encourage and in the extent to which altruism is located in individual motives or social structure. Mark Chaves explores the role of religious beliefs as a source of altruism, or, to use his term, "other-regarding entrepreneurialism." Challenging interest-driven arguments that depict religious organizations as motivated by a drive to secure adherents or to provide selective incentives to members, Chaves suggests that religion may be regarded as a public good insofar as it produces commitments to "doing good" or "standing by the poor" that in turn promote involvement in altruistic organizational projects. In his view, religious activism is a kind of public good that facilitates identity formation.

In part II, we move from the general themes concerning nonprofit mission to careful analyses of nonprofit perfor-

mance. The chapters in this section bring sophisticated empirical evidence to bear on the questions: Does institutional form matter? Do nonprofits provide such public services as health care and day care better than other types of organizations? One of the innovative features of Burton Weisbrod's analysis is that he separates religious and secular nonprofits. Weisbrod examines nursing homes and facilities for the mentally handicapped, finding that church-related nonprofits administered fewer sedatives to older patients and employed more full-time staff than either secular nonprofits or for-profit entities. Consumer satisfaction was higher with church-related nonprofits. In addition, religious facilities tended to charge less and have longer waiting lists. This chapter brings a much-needed new dimension to the research literature, illuminating important differences between secular and religious organizations.

The next three chapters pursue the analysis of the relationship between institutional form and organizational performance. Marc Schlesinger, in an important contribution to the literature on institutional form, recognizes that ownership-related differences depend very much on the environment in which an organization operates. External influences vary markedly from one region to another and across industries. The critical feature of his analysis of psychiatric hospitals in the United States is that he examines how organizational form and the broader political and economic context interact. Many researchers have made the plausible argument that the more substantial the external constraints (for example, competition and regulatory oversight), the smaller the differences between nonprofits and for-profits. Schlesinger suggests, however, that external influences may operate in different ways, nonprofits being more sensitive to regulation and for-profits more attuned to competitive rivalry. Indeed, he finds that where community groups, state regulators, and medical professionals wield strong influence, nonprofits treat more state-financed patients, as well as patients without insurance, and more patients with chronic conditions. But in environments with less regulatory oversight and monitoring, nonprofits are much more similar in performance to for-profits. In areas with low levels of competition, nonprofits are more substantially involved in the treatment of the poor. Schlesinger's chapter is a reminder of how complex the issues of ownership are and an excellent guidepost for future research.

In regard to day care, ownership effects continue to be important but often in unexpected ways. Michael Krashinsky examines day care in Canada and finds variability in the quality of both nonprofit and for-profit care. On average, nonprofits evince somewhat higher quality. But government intervention in the industry on behalf of the nonprofit sector has had the effect of pushing for-profit entrepreneurs to incorporate as nonprofits. Government support, intended to bolster the ostensibly better-performing organizational form, may well have the unintended effect of creating "pseudo-nonprofits." Krashinsky warns that particularly with respect to small organizations, it may be very hard to tell whether a nonprofit is "real" or operating in disguise. In her careful study of day care in Wisconsin, Elizabeth Mauser looks at whether nonprofits provide higher quality care and whether they are less likely to take advantage of informationally disadvantaged consumers. She, too, finds variability in the quality of both nonprofit and for-profit care. But, like Weisbrod, she notes that religious nonprofits stand out with higher quality and less variability. She also finds support for the idea that nonprofits are perceived as more trustworthy. In the most competitive regions, the nonprofit status is an important signal to parents.

We continue the analysis of the sectoral division of labor in part III, turning from the comparison of nonprofit organizations with for-profit firms to an assessment of changes in the relationship between nonprofits and government, both in the United States and in Europe. These chapters involve qualitative surveys of new developments rather than detailed empirical analyses. Kirsten Grønbjerg examines the administration of social service and community development programs in the United States. She argues that nonprofits, for-profits, and public agencies are not simply substitutes for one another but exist in complex and often contradictory relations of interdependence. For-profits impose market criteria of exchange on nonprofits, and state agencies increasingly depend on a nonprofit infrastructure to provide public services.

The changing relations between government and nonprofits throughout Europe are the subject of the next three chapters. Lester Salamon and Helmut Anheier compare social welfare policies in the United States and Germany, contending that the ideologically charged opposition of market-based versus state-centered welfare provision obscures their many common elements. The authors discern the building blocks for a "third route . . . [that] makes it possible to capture the benefits of the two respective sectors while minimizing their respective drawbacks." Claire Ullman's analysis of French welfare provision reveals that the strong state-centered tradition that has long dominated French politics is being gradually displaced by a new partnership between state agencies and nonprofit organizations. The initiative for this greater role for nonprofits was taken by the Socialist government. In France the growth of nonprofits is not, as in the United States and Britain, a part of an effort to curtail the power of government. But before readers assume there is a general convergence on a mixed institutional model of welfare provision, Helmut Anheier and Wolfgang Seibel's survey of East Germany, Poland, and Hungary illustrates the wide diversity of arrangements that nonprofits are involved in. Contrasting the emergence and growth of a nonprofit sector in these three nations since 1989, they find that the scope and scale of the nonprofit sector are shaped by the prior strength of civic associations and religious institutions and by the extensiveness of the underground economy.

In the last two parts of the book, we move from broad comparisons of economic and political arrangements to more fine-grained portraits of nonprofit organizations. The chapters in part IV address the politics of sponsorship—the tensions that exist among the interests of organizations, of those that provide financial support to them, and of those whom they serve. Nancy Robertson examines the relations between blacks and whites in American women's associations during the early twentieth century. Echoing Craig Calhoun's concern with how particular communities join to construct and pursue an understanding of a public good, in this case "racial uplift," Robertson demonstrates that genuinely altruistic intentions did not neutralize the power of advantaged white women to define a common "women's interest" as a public good. The difficulties entailed in sponsorship of the powerless by the powerful are also central to J. Craig Jenkins' chapter on foundation patronage of social movement organizations. Drawing on his analyses of social movement philanthropy since the 1950s, he examines how foundations negotiate the tension between funding nonprofits that pursue some public good and the legal restrictions against philanthropy serving political purposes. He also illustrates the power of sponsors to channel nonprofits into "safer," more broadly accepted courses of action. The next two chapters extend the analysis of sponsorship, drawing international and cross-national comparisons. Considering the experience of both North American and European nonprofits operating in developing countries, Brian Smith argues that differences in their organizational goals (economic development for the former, social transformation for the latter) are minimized by the constraints of the political circumstances of the recipient nations. Any connection between NGO activities and political transformation, he concludes, is likely to be indirect and mediated by the social and economic empowerment of the disadvantaged. His message is reinforced by David Brown's comparison of state-NGO cooperation in development projects in Bangladesh, Indonesia, Pakistan, and Zimbabwe. Building on the concept of social capital (that is, those "institutional arrangements—social trust, norms of reciprocity and tolerance, and networks of informal association—that foster voluntary cooperation among individuals"), Brown contends that NGOs are potentially a significant force in remedying inequalities in power due to their capacity as "bridging organizations" to build stocks of social capital by fostering grassroots involvement.

The four chapters in part V bring the book full circle. Each focuses on organizational behavior in nonprofits to address the broad political-economic themes raised by the authors in the opening chapters. Considering the changing meanings of *volunteer* and *professional*, Barry Karl argues that whereas volunteer-dominated charitable groups once formed an important alternative to the expanding modern state, a voluntary sector increasingly dominated by professionals who donate their time may still serve to enrich our civic culture. Surveying recent research on feminist organizations, Catherine Alter considers how feminist commitments to participatory democracy shape the functioning of agencies and activist groups. She goes on to assess the extent to which feminist organizations offer a viable alternative to modern bureaucratic forms. Victoria Alexander draws on recent work in organizational theory to revisit questions raised by Chaves and Weisbrod. As nonprofit organizations operate in increasingly complex and uncertain environments, how are organizational goals formed and under what circumstances do organizational actions serve their altruistic statements of mission as opposed to more self-interested ends of organizational preservation? Finally, Jerald Hage reflects on how nonprofits negotiate the "institutional cusp" between the field of oppositional politics (which requires emotional commitment and esprit de corps) and the rationalized, business world of service provision. Drawing on both social movement theory and organizational analysis, he uses the tension between the emotional demands that elicit commitment and the efficiency requirements that organize business as a lens for tracing the evolution of nonprofits over time and through changing political climates.

Nonprofit organizations have long existed in a gray area, straddling government and the marketplace. Nonprofits are partially sheltered from market forces and subsidized in part by government funding. Although somewhat buffered from the winds of competition, they nevertheless face complex, contradictory pressures and demands that threaten their mission and survival. Illuminating those pressures and demands is a key task of this book.

REFERENCES

Bell, Daniel. 1989. "American Exceptionalism Revisited: The Role of Civil Society." *Public Interest* 95:38–57.

Blair, Margaret M. 1995. *Ownership and Control: Rethinking Corporate Governance for the Twenty-First Century.* Washington, D.C.: Brookings Institution.

DiMaggio, Paul, and Helmut Anheier. 1990. "The Sociology of Nonprofit Organizations." *Annual Review of Sociology* 16: 137–59.

DiMaggio, Paul, and Walter W. Powell. 1983. "The Iron Cage Revisited: Institutional Isomorphism and Collective Rationality in Organizational Fields." *American Sociological Review* 48(2):147–60.

Habermas, Jürgen. 1989 (1962). *The Structural Transformation of the Public Sphere.* Cambridge: MIT Press.

Hall, Peter Dobkin. 1987. "A Historical Overview of the Private Nonprofit Sector." In *The Nonprofit Sector: A Research Handbook,* ed. Walter W. Powell, 3–26. New Haven: Yale University Press.

———. 1992. *Inventing the Nonprofit Sector and Other Essays on Philanthropy, Voluntarism, and Nonprofit Organizations.* Baltimore: Johns Hopkins University Press.

———. 1995. "Theories and Institutions." *Nonprofit and Voluntary Sector Quarterly* 24(1):5–13.

Hansmann, Henry. 1980. "The Role of Nonprofit Enterprise." *Yale Law Review* 89:835–99.

———. 1987. "Economic Theories of Nonprofit Organization." In *The Nonprofit Sector: A Research Handbook,* ed. Walter W. Powell, 27–42. New Haven: Yale University Press.

———. 1995. "The Changing Roles of Public, Private, and Nonprofit Enterprise in Education, Health Care, and Other Human Services." Yale Law School, working paper.

James, Estelle. 1987. "The Nonprofit Sector in Comparative Perspective." In *The Nonprofit Sector: A Research Handbook,* ed. Walter W. Powell, 397–415. New Haven: Yale University Press.

Jenkins, J. Craig. 1987. "Nonprofit Organizations and Policy Advocacy." In *The Nonprofit Sector: A Research Handbook,* ed. Walter W. Powell, 296–320. New Haven: Yale University Press.

Lemann, Nicolas. 1996. "Kicking in Groups." *Atlantic Monthly* (April): 22– 26.

O'Neill, Michael. 1989. *The Third America: The Emergence of the Nonprofit Sector in the United States.* San Francisco: Jossey-Bass.

Portes, Alejandro, and Patricia Landolt. 1996. "The Downside of Social Capital." *American Prospect* 26:18–21, 24.

Putnam, Robert D. 1993. *Making Democracy Work: Civic Traditions in Modern Italy.* Princeton: Princeton University Press.

———. 1996. "The Strange Disappearance of Civic America." *American Prospect* 24:34–48.

Roe, Mark J. 1994. *Strong Managers, Weak Owners: The Political Roots of American Corporate Finance.* Princeton: Princeton University Press.

Salamon, Lester, and Helmut Anheier. 1993. "Mapping the Nonprofit Sector Cross-Nationally: A Comparative Methodology." *Voluntas* 4(4):530–54.

———. 1994. *The Emerging Sector.* Baltimore: Johns Hopkins University Institute for Policy Studies.

Schudson, Michael. 1996. "What If Civic Life Didn't Die?" *American Prospect* 25:17–20.

Simon, John. 1987. "Tax Treatment of Nonprofit Organizations." In *The Nonprofit Sector: A Research Handbook,* ed. Walter W. Powell, 67–98. New Haven: Yale University Press.

Skocpol, Theda. 1996. "Unraveling from Above." *American Prospect* 25:20–25.

Smith, Stephen R., and Michael Lipsky. 1993. *Nonprofits for Hire.* Cambridge: Harvard University Press.

Taylor, Charles. 1990. "Modes of Civil Society." *Public Culture* 3(1):95–118.

Walzer, Michael. 1991. "The Idea of Civil Society." *Dissent* 38(2):293–305.

Weisbrod, Burton. 1975. "Toward a Theory of the Voluntary Nonprofit Sector in a Three Sector Economy." In *Altruism, Morality, and Economic Theory,* ed. E. S. Phelps, 171–95. New York: Russell Sage.

———. 1988. *The Nonprofit Economy.* Cambridge: Harvard University Press.

———. 1995. "The Economic and Social Importance of Nonprofit Organizations." Northwestern University, working paper.

Part One

Philanthropy and the Public Good

1

JANE MANSBRIDGE

On the Contested Nature of the Public Good

The public good — unendingly contestable, dangerous in the extreme, inevitably manipulated by elites: This is the value I want to make more central to American democratic institutions and Americans' lives. Its contestability, danger, and manipulability have quite reasonably brought it into disrepute. These vices cannot be cured. But learning to live with them — mitigating the danger and manipulability while welcoming the contest — helps us retrieve the public good from platitude, disdain, and justifiable mistrust to rebuild it as a centerpiece of American politics.

A CONTESTED CONCEPT

Congruence or Opposition?
The meaning of the concept "the public good" is so disputed that we cannot even say for sure whether it is congruent with or contrasts with each person's private good.

The moral language of the Western tradition has typically contrasted the public good with private goods. In this tradition, which may have reached its height in the Christian Middle Ages, we praise individuals for serving the public good and criticize them for neglecting it.

I would like to thank Mayer Zald for his public comments on an earlier draft and acknowledge the support in writing this chapter of the Institute for Policy Research at Northwestern University.

Yet since Plato, Western thinkers have also suggested that the opposition between public good and private benefits so prominent in ordinary language might conceal a deeper congruence. Plato argued that what was good for the polity was by nature also good for the individual. Plato's argument required changing the ordinary understanding of individual benefit, so that what appeared on the surface to be selfless behavior could be understood, after scrutiny, as truly good for the individual. In the eighteenth century, Adam Smith made the reverse argument — that what was good for the individual in a narrow sense was also good, through the "invisible hand," for the polity. Smith's argument required changing the ordinary understanding of what was good for the polity, so that what appeared on the surface to be the clash of selfish interests could be understood, after scrutiny, as contributing to economic prosperity.

Plato, Smith, and the tradition of conflict between public and private goods are each right. Human beings derive great satisfaction from acting on principle, making commitments to others, and taking part in cooperative endeavors. In part because these commitments often directly promote the public good, social arrangements must not diminish and should actively encourage the satisfactions individuals take in their commitments to principle and to others. At the same time, human beings are also narrowly self-interested. Efficient social arrangements must therefore also make it possible for

3

action motivated by narrow personal aggrandizement to promote the public good indirectly, as in the economic market. Finally, when a conflict between private and public goods appears, bolstering support for the public good requires yet a third set of social arrangements, in which material and normative sanctions reward acts of public spirit and punish selfishness.

These contradictory conceptualizations produce strong but sometimes resolvable tensions within the concept of the public good. The tension between the Platonic effort to argue that acting justly (a public good) will produce happiness (a personal benefit) and the medieval Christian conviction that individuals must choose between good (the public good) and evil (selfish, private ends) can be partially resolved by postulating, as Plato did in the parts of his work most compatible with Christianity, higher and lower parts of the self. Fulfilling the higher parts gives the deepest satisfaction, is what God desires, and furthers the public good. Yet this move does not fully resolve the tension, because the two normative systems produce different and somewhat conflicting emphases. The Platonic system suggests that self-knowledge is the route to right action and the Christian system insists that knowledge can take one only so far; the crucial issue is then one of will, choosing the good even if it brings one pain.

Christian dualism also conflicts, again not completely, with the Smithian idea, developed in the seventeenth and eighteenth centuries, that acting in one's narrow self-interest for personal self-aggrandizement actually furthers the public good. One can partially resolve this conflict by specifying spheres in which acting in one's narrow self-interest furthers the public good and spheres in which it does not. Some tension lingers, however, for the spheres have no natural and obvious points of demarcation. Moreover, the moral permission to act self-interestedly in one sphere spreads easily to other spheres, contributing at the very least to a lack of clarity about what morality dictates in those spheres.

Contest, Danger, and Manipulability

In addition to these analytic tensions, which leave mixed messages about the public good, nineteenth- and twentieth-century deliberations have produced three reasonable conclusions that undermine appeals to act for that good.

First, we now realize that we can never know with certainty what the public good is in any particular case. The public good will probably always be, and should be, a contested concept.[1] Debating how we ought to act, both collec-

tively and individually, often requires debating the meaning of the public good. The unsettled, contested nature of the concept is part of the unsettled, contested nature of politics itself. This conclusion undermines a philosophical agenda whose goal is settled knowledge, either of self or of polity. It also undermines a moral agenda that, appealing to a choosing will, assumes the good and evil that the will addresses to be relatively knowable.

Second, we now recognize the danger inherent in the emotional bases of appeals to the public good. Love (or some feeling of empathy or affinity with a group or individual) and duty (or some form of commitment to principle) are the two known forms of altruism, of which public spirit is a subset (Mansbridge 1990b). In spite of the efforts of Immanuel Kant and others to base morality on pure reason, appeals to both love and duty are most likely to succeed if they have some emotional resonance. We activate commitment even to principle in part by appealing to people's emotional attachments to the aspects of their identity most linked to that principle.

Yet emotional evocation opens the door to demagoguery. Orators asking for sacrifice in the name of a public good call up visual images of the homeland, chords of anger against a hated enemy, yearnings for a settled peace, and self-images of righteousness. We have little philosophical guidance for negotiating the emotions, including those connected with public spirit. I know of only a few such guidelines. Reflecting in tranquility on a decision based on an emotional appeal makes that decision more reliable (hence the resistance to speed connoted by *deliberation*). Similarly, interpersonal contact in tranquility between individuals makes it possible, with good will, to sort through some of the emotions that a collective presence often exacerbates or distorts. Finally, some reliability derives from being able to subject facts and insights in a deliberation to the usual cognitive tests. If one feels awkward bringing up a fact or causal analysis that runs counter to prevailing sentiment, the ratio of emotion to cognition is probably too high.[2] The goal in deliberation ought not to be to "keep emotions out of it." Because we evoke love and duty at least in part through the emotions, interpreting the ideal of reasoned or rational deliberation to delegitimate the use of emotion in deliberation makes it almost impossible to appeal for selfless behavior. Yet, after Hitler and Freud, the present generation's heightened sensitivity to the

---

1. W. B. Gallie has argued that in political and social life some concepts are "essentially contested." That is, part of the function of these concepts is to serve as the site of conflicts over ideas, the way a baseball diamond serves as the site for the contest in a baseball game. In Gallie's argument, essentially contested concepts are "concepts the proper use of which inevitably provokes endless disputes about their proper uses on the part of their users" (1955–56, 169). Gallie suggests five conditions of an essentially contested concept — that it be apprais-

ive, internally complex, initially variously describable, open, and understood to be contested — conditions met by the concept of the public good. The disputes to which essentially contested concepts give rise are amenable to demonstrations of evidence, cogency, and rational persuasion. When a concept is essentially contested, however, these elements of deliberation may result not in conversion but in the different parties refining their understandings and seeing more clearly their points of conflict with others.

2. Emotion and cognition are not, of course, dichotomies; each capacity interpenetrates and requires the other (Rorty 1985; Nussbaum 1995).

dangers of drawing on the emotions tends to undermine appeals to public spirit or the public good.

Third, we now realize that in the conditions of uncertainty created by ongoing contest over issues in which settled knowledge is hard or impossible to come by, the dominant groups in any society have a great advantage in constructing the reigning understanding of a concept. The cultural and intellectual hegemony of an elite has the greatest effect when most people cannot easily test the propositions in question against their everyday experience. Because of this inherent advantage of elites, members of subordinate groups and those members of dominant groups who want justice for subordinate groups must subject any reigning understanding of the public good to deliberative scrutiny before assuming that sacrifices ought to be made on its behalf. Our heightened recognition of the power of elites to shape the dominant understanding of the public good also undermines attempts to induce cooperative behavior through moral appeals to that good.

All three conclusions from the last two centuries — that the public good is essentially contested, that its evocation is open to demagogic exploitation, and that its meaning in any given case is likely to be heavily shaped by the interests of dominant groups — are reasonable and, I believe, correct. All three make the public good suspect. In the present climate, I can say to myself, "I can't *know* what I ought to do, so I might as well serve myself. This 'public good' stuff is dangerous. These appeals usually just mask the interests of a ruling class. And anyway, this society runs on the principle that all its members work only in their self-interest."

But if enough people take this view for any of these reasons, a society will not be able to produce efficiently a large number of goods that require subtle and complex forms of human cooperation. Such forms of cooperation, which range from not littering, voting, and obeying the law all the way to volunteering for combat, depend not only on self-interest but also on many individuals acting in the public good on the basis of primarily internal rewards. A normative structure resulting from the large-scale practice of narrowly self-interested behavior would degrade the lives of everyone, perhaps especially the poorest and least powerful. Modern-day generations thus face the contrast between the growing weight of reasons to act only in one's narrow self-interest and the growing necessity, in an increasingly interdependent world, for sophisticated forms of cooperation that require a leaven of public spirit.

Surviving Contest, Danger, Manipulation — Even Mixed Messages

Logically and within the realm of practical experience, it is possible to act in the public good without knowing for sure precisely what that good is, just how much it is contaminated by demagoguery, or exactly how free it is from the imprint of dominant interests. One does one's best to understand the situation, both individually and with others; one makes one's best guess; and one acts accordingly. The choice to take a lower salary for a job that has a greater chance of helping others, to pick up a piece of litter, or to give blood does not require absolute certainty about the nature of the public good to produce either internal satisfaction or justifiable social approbation.

The provisional quality of any commitment to the public good need not be stronger than the internal qualifier an educated layperson today attaches to almost any theoretical or practical conclusion. We act upon the study that shows we should eat margarine until another study shows it is no better than butter. We plan to stay in hotels that we know only through their brochures. The "satisficing" (making do, not "optimizing") nature of our knowledge does not keep us from acting. It should not therefore keep us from trying to act well.

Logically and within the realm of practical experience, it is also possible to teach human beings to get deep satisfaction from helping others and following normative principles while at the same time in some realms pursuing their narrow self-interests. We need to learn better how to let the engine of self-interest do its useful work without infecting the motivation to do good.

As the inheritors of an intellectual legacy that began before Plato and has become increasingly refined in the past two hundred years, today's theorists and practitioners face two urgent tasks: promoting the public good and guarding against the worst misuses of the concept.

To promote the public good, we need to envision, create, recognize, and advocate whatever forms of constitutional design reasonably teach the internal satisfactions of furthering what we believe, provisionally, to be the public good; we need to encourage self-interest when we believe that self-interested action promotes public ends; and we need to marshall normative and material rewards and punishments to support forms of behavior that we think will advance the public good when it conflicts with private interests.

To guard against the greatest misuses of the concept, we need to work toward bringing about societies constituted on relatively just principles, societies in which we can come to trust more thoroughly the dominant conceptions of the public good. We need to envision, create, recognize, and advocate deliberative forms that, no matter how just we believe a particular society to be, raise the awkward questions of who benefits from what understandings of the public good. We need to ask what may be the full effects, particularly on the disadvantaged, of any system of rewards and punishments designed to promote the public good. And we must try to understand what, in any instance, the effects of undermining support for the public good might be. The trick is to sustain a critique of ongoing mystifications sufficient to prevent the worst abuses of elite power without promoting a cynicism about the public sphere so thorough as to induce privatization.

Theorists and practitioners of deliberative democracy are working on designing institutions to improve the quality of public debates about the public good.[3] The continuing contest over defining what *public good* should mean, so important in criticizing potential domination, sometimes encourages individuals and groups to talk past one another, as each group clings to its meaning, oblivious to the interpretations of others. That continuing contest over definition can discourage deliberation because few busy citizens are interested in endeavors that do not lead to resolution. But the contest also keeps alive the problems and dangers inherent in any specific definition, generates alternatives, and prompts creativity in reaching for solutions.

Theorists and practitioners of game theory, rational choice analysis, and economic sociology are working on other questions of constitutional design.[4] The analytic tools that game theorists have developed in the last half of the twentieth century have clarified for the first time some central internal relations concerning the nature of the public good. Although a few such theorists study narrowly self-interested motivation (see critiques in Mansbridge 1990b, 1995), the larger analytic approach reveals dramatically how concern for the public good contributes to cooperation and consequently to productivity. In this framework, I argue that we must add to the Platonic and Smithian forms of congruence and to medieval Christian opposition a fourth relation between self-interest and the public good. In this new relation, concern for the public good must "nest" within sufficient returns to material self-interest so that such a concern can survive.

In the following sections on the historical and contemporary meanings of the public good, I preserve the commendatory force of *the public good,* a posture of general approval toward those who try to promote the public good, and the conceptual distinction between individual, or private, goods and the public good. At the same time, I argue against definitional fiat. What is public, what is good, and what is the public good will probably always be, and should be, contested. Because arguing about what words mean is one way of arguing about how we should act, trying to legislate definitions of contested concepts is like trying to legislate an end to political, moral, and conceptual debate. In the case of the public good and similarly contested normative concepts, the laudable attempt to achieve scholarly precision works against the way that people who disagree on how we ought to act also disagree about the public good itself.

HISTORICAL MEANINGS

In the late fifth and early fourth centuries B.C., Plato argued, some think tautologically, that the good (*agathon*) is what

"every soul pursues and for its sake does all that it does."[5] Plato and many other ancient Greek thinkers assumed that certain states of being were good by nature and that humankind could come to know at least in part the character of that good. In politics, Plato developed an ideal in which this knowledge generated political agreement, which produced unity, "the greatest blessing for a state" (*Republic* 464b).

In trying to criticize our era's understanding of the public good, some of the best political theorists have misinterpreted the ancient Greeks. Richard Flathman, for example, has written that one theory of the public good "argued with unequaled force and beauty by Plato, holds that the words 'public interest' (or 'common good,' as Plato would prefer it) refer to or stand for a body of substantive truths or principles."[6] But in the *Republic* and his other works, Plato never used the words *koinon agathon*, or common good. Because Plato believed so strongly in the ideal of unity for the polis, in which all citizens would "rejoice and grieve alike at the same births and deaths" and "utter in unison such words as 'mine' and 'not mine'" (*Republic* 462b-c; also 464a and *Laws* 739d), his use of *koinon*, "common," might be thought to imply *agathon*, "good," and his use of *agathon* to imply *koinon*. But we cannot look to Plato for a theory of what the phrase *koinon agathon* should mean politically because in none of his works did he use that phrase in a political sense.[7]

In a highly influential work, Sheldon Wolin has stressed a contrast between the Greek ideal of the good (as in the public good) and today's comparatively debased concept of interest (as in the public interest), a word that entered the language with the advent of capitalism in the sixteenth and seventeenth centuries. The introduction of the phrase *public interest* did indeed mark a distinct departure from the earlier *common good.* As I read the historical record, however, the starkest

---

3. See, inter alia, Barber 1984; Cohen 1989; Cohen and Rogers 1992; Schmitter 1992; Young 1990, 1992; Sunstein 1988; Besette 1994; Boyte 1989; Mansbridge [1980] 1983, 1993.

4. See, inter alia, Taylor [1976] 1987; North 1981, 1990; Hardin 1982; Levi 1988; Shepsle 1989; Ostrom 1990, 1992; Coleman 1990; Sabel 1993; Granovetter 1994.

5. *Republic* 506a. See also Aristotle, *Nicomachean Ethics* 1094a: the good (*agathon*) is "that at which all things aim." For commentary, see the excellent account of the public good in Held 1970, esp. 136 ff. on Plato. While disagreeing with her ultimate conclusion, I have found her analysis, her sources, and her criticisms of others' analyses unfailingly helpful. I have been guided by her selections and interpretations at several points in this chapter. Other useful sources on the meanings of the public good are Friedrich, ed. 1962, Flathman 1966, and Dahl 1989, and works cited therein.

6. Flathman 1966, 53. See also 56, n. 5: "Plato's conclusion is that 'public interest' and 'common good' are concepts which would be appropriately employed only by philosopher-kings in discussion with other philosopher-kings"; and 57: "Plato sought objectivity and timelessness of content for 'public interest'." Each of Flathman's formulations implies, incorrectly, that Plato was explicitly concerned with exploring the meaning and use of the concept of the public interest or common good.

7. For help with the Ibycus search for these references in the work of Plato and Aristotle, I thank John Kirkpatrick. For their considerable help with the Greek translations, I thank Ronald Mansbridge and Sara Monoson. Any errors in interpretation are mine.

contrast is not with ancient Greece but with the Christian Middle Ages.[8]

The Greeks did not, by and large, either glorify the common good or stress its difference from material advantage. Plato, as is well known, had a particular concern for the soul. His search for the meaning of the good (*agathon*) was far deeper than Aristotle's and had a mystical element that would inspire the Neoplatonists and early Christians. Aristotle, who did not share this bent, nevertheless also had a conception of the political good that was far from crassly material. He argued that the *polis* was, by nature, "directed to the most supreme of all goods" (1252a6) and was "designed to make citizens virtuous and just" (1280b13). He explicitly contrasted that aim with a mere "alliance for mutual defence against injury by anybody [or] for the sake of trade and of business relations" (1280a34–35).

Yet when Aristotle joined *koinon* with *agathon* in the phrase "the common good," he seems to have included material interests in this deep complex of aims. Moreover, in the *Politics* Aristotle used the phrase *koinon agathon* only twice (1268b31 and 1284b6–7). Far more often he joined *koinon* with *sumpheron*, "advantage" or "profit," in phrases now usually translated as "common advantage" and "common interest." In his famous passage on tyranny, describing the corruption of the common good in monarchies, oligarchies, and democracies, Aristotle used not *koinon agathon* but

koinon sumpheron and even *koinon lusiteloun, lusiteloun* meaning "profit, gain, or advantage" (1279b7–10).[9] Both standard Greek lexicons and the context in which Aristotle wrote make it clear that by *sumpheron* he implied material benefit, advantage, and interest as much as more intangible forms of good.

In Rome, in the first century B.C., when Cicero wrote of magistrates that "salus populi suprema lex esto" (the good of the people shall be their chief law) (*De Legibus* III, iii, 8), he used a word, *salus*, that also meant "health" or "soundness" as well as "safety, welfare, and well-being," and thus in its original connotations implied more than an instrumental, material good (although health in its narrow sense is a material good). But in his famous definition of a republic, Cicero used the phrase *utilitatis communione*, "community of interest," not *bonum commune*, "common good."[10]

In at least some influential Greek and Roman writers' understanding of the public good, then, material well-being played an important role. At the same time, these thinkers did not emphasize the conflict between private and public goods. Eric Havelock ([1957] 1964, 391) goes so far as to claim that "a basic split between the moral or ideal and the expedient or selfish did not develop until Christian other-worldly influences had begun to affect the vocabulary and the mind of the West."

Medieval Christianity, from Augustine through Aquinas, saw a flowering of concern with the common good, especially in contrast to private benefit. For Augustine, "the highest and truest common good" was God (*Letters*, cited in

---

8. For Wolin's argument, see Wolin 1960, esp. 280. The word *interest* came into use, with its French and Italian cognates, *intérêt* and *interresse*, in the second half of the sixteenth century. It originally meant the amount of money a lender charged for the use of monetary capital. As usury gradually became legal and started to be called merely lending, the word *interest* emerged as a neutral designation for various forms of profit. It soon evolved to mean the interest one had in, or piece one owned of, a business or other profit-making concern. From this meaning it evolved to connote also the permanent, stable, and fundamental goods for any individual, as opposed to the transient, unstable, and surface "passions." It also stood for those fundamental goods based on the drives for self-preservation and self-aggrandizement that were thought to motivate (or thought should motivate) a state or an individual (see Hirschman 1977, esp. 35).

Writers in the sixteenth and seventeenth centuries interpreted the public good in a more material way than their medieval predecessors (substituting "common interest" for "common good," habitually translating *salus* as "safety" in the phrase *salus populi suprema lex esto*, and stressing the preservation of property as the end of the state). The contrast between sixteenth- and seventeenth-century usages and those of the Middle Ages should not, however, lead one to read medieval meanings of the public good back into the Greeks and Romans, thereby underestimating their concern for material advantage (e.g., Douglass 1980).

Today the word *interest* is used in two different theoretical senses. Many Continental and English theorists (e.g. Hirschman [1986] 1992, Barry 1965) use it to mean only narrow self-interest. Many American theorists (e.g., Flathman 1966, Held 1970, Mansbridge [1980] 1983) use it to mean the full range of goods that individuals can want or make their own, including other-regarding and public-regarding interests. For the evolution of meanings in the word *interest*, see Hirschman [1986] 1992.

9. "Tyranny is monarchy ruling in the interest (*sumpheron*) of the monarch, oligarchy government in the interest (*sumpheron* implied) of the rich, democracy government in the interest (*sumpheron*) of the poor, and none of these forms governs with regard to the profit of the community (*to koino lusiteloun*)" (*Politics* 1279b). *Koinon sumpheron* appears in the *Politics* at 1276a13, 1278b21–23, 1279a29–39 (four times in this passage), and 1282b18. At least at one point (*Politics* 1279a13–14) Aristotle seems to use *sumpheron* and *agathon* interchangeably. At another point he writes that what is "good (*agathon*) in the political field, that is, the general advantage (*koine sumpheron*), is justice" (*Politics* 1282b17–18). This passage reveals a characteristic refusal to distinguish between "advantage," with some material overtones, and normative good.

10. The definition reads, in Keyes's translation: "A commonwealth [*res publica*, literally "public things" or "public affairs"] is the property of a people [*res publica res populi*]. But a people is not any collection of human beings brought together in any sort of way, but an assemblage of people in large numbers associated in an agreement with respect to justice and a partnership for the common good [*utilitatis communione*]" (*De Republica* I, 25). Others translate *utilitatis communione* "a community of interest." Augustine quoted this description of a republic in his *City of God* (II, 22), and Thomas Aquinas subsequently quoted it from Augustine in his *Summa Theologica* (II-II, Q 42, A 2), both repeating the words *utilitatis communione*. Yet in distinguishing between the existing "earthly city," based on force, and the City of God, based on the love of God, the true *bonum commune*, Augustine associated Cicero's words with the City of God (Lavere 1983).

McCracken 1981, lxii). For Aquinas, the *bonum commune* became identical with natural law (Lewis 1940) and the preservation of order (Froelich 1989). Nevertheless, when in the Middle Ages the Roman term *res publica* became not only the English "republic," but also the "common weal" or "common wealth," the word "wealth" in that translation continued to capture the implication of material benefit or advantage that inheres in the Greek *sumpheron* and the Latin *utilitas*. Even Thomas Aquinas, who as we shall see substituted the phrase *bonum commune* for *koinon sumpheron* in paraphrasing Aristotle's comments on tyranny, quoted earlier medieval writers who used *communi utilitate*.[11] Modern capitalists were thus not the first to impute material benefit to the public good by speaking of the public interest.

The contrast between public and private good developed strength in the Middle Ages. Throughout this period, theologians contrasted kings who sought their private good to those who sought the good of the people. "A tyrannical government," Aquinas wrote, in a much-quoted paraphrase of Aristotle, "is directed not to the common good [*bonum commune*], but to the private good [*bonum privatum*] of the ruler, as the Philosopher says."[12] Medieval theologians constantly urged kings to seek "the welfare of each and all" and "the advantage of the commonwealth"[13] in contrast to their own private goods. They also extended this exhortation to commoners. Ewart Lewis concludes that "the emphasis which medieval writers placed on the superiority of the common good to private good was a response to the real medieval problem of persuading arrogant individualism to give way to community consciousness" (1954, 214).

Sixteenth-century writers continued to paint the contrast between public and private goods. Thomas More stressed the duties of commoners, lamenting that men "speak still of the common wealth; but every man procureth his own private wealth."[14] In the seventeenth century, even Thomas Hobbes wrote scathingly of kings that, when their care for "the common interest" or "publique interest" conflicted with their "private good," they usually preferred the private ([1651]

1947, 157). Two decades or so later, in his treatise justifying revolution, John Locke returned to the medieval preoccupation with kingly duties, concluding that a king should use his prerogative only for the "publick good" ([1679–89] 1965, II, s.156, p. 418; s.158, p. 420; s.160, p. 422; s.164–66, pp. 424–25), and that when the king used his power not "to do good" but to "promote an Interest distinct from that of the publick," he gave the people the right to limit his power.[15]

Yet in the seventeenth century, a new argument — one presaging that of Adam Smith — entered the English debate. Although some economic writers of the time argued traditionally that "private advantages are . . . impediments of publick profit,"[16] others wanted to lift time-honored trade restrictions on the grounds that "the advancement of private persons will be the advantage of the publick."[17] Picking up a version of this theme, Hobbes joined other royalists in arguing that when reason prevailed, kings would see that their private interests and the public interest were identical, because "the riches, power and honour of a monarch arise only from the riches, strength and reputation of his subjects" ([1651] 1947, 158; see Wolin 1961, 279–80; Gunn 1969, 62–79).

These new arguments for the congruence of private and public good derived much of their significance from breaking with the medieval tradition of contrast. The stress on congruence grew in popularity during the seventeenth century. By the eighteenth century, such mainstream theorists as the Earl of Shaftesbury, Joseph Butler, Francis Hutcheson, and John Maxwell in England and Claude-Adrien Helvétius and the Marquis Luc de Clapiers de Vauvenargues in France were insisting on the harmony of self-interest and social interest (Myers 1983; Lovejoy 1961, 45).[18] Alexander Pope

11. See *Summa Theologica* (I-II, Q. 90. A. 2), quoting Isidore of Seville's *Etymologiae*: "laws are enacted for no private profit [*privato commodo*], but for the common benefit [*communi utilitate*] of the citizens." See also II-II, Q. 42, A. 2: "the benefit of the people, which is a manifest good" (*utilitati multitudinis, quae est manifeste bonum*).

12. *Summa Theologica* II-II, Q. 42, A. 2. See note 9 above for Aristotle's original, using *sumpheron* and *lusiteloun*.

13. John of Salisbury, quoted in Lewis 1954, 170, 172. "The welfare of each and all" has an aggregative implication.

14. [1518, trans. 1551] 1895, 299, spelling modernized. The Latin reads "*publico . . . commodo.*" In his *Dialogue between Cardinal Pole and Thomas Lupset* (1536–38), Thomas Starkey argued that in the "very and true commonweal" the needs of each individual would be the needs of the commonwealth, with each "ever having before his eyes the common weal, without regard of his own vain plesures, frail fantasies and singular profit" (quoted in Allen [1928] 1960, 146, original spelling retained).

15. II, s.164, p. 424. When the king breaches his trust "in not preserving the Form of Government agreed on, and in not intending the end of government it self, which is the publick good and preservation of Property," subjects, Locke concluded, had the right to rebel (II, s.239, p. 474). It was probably in this context, contrasting the public good to the private good of the ruler(s), that Locke concluded, "The *Legislative Power* . . . is limited to the publick good" (II, s.135, p. 403; s.222, p. 461). Note the interchangeable use of "interest" and "good," along with the link between the public good and the preservation of property.

16. Samuel Fortrey, *England's Interest* (1663), quoted in Appleby 1978, 108.

17. Joseph Lee, "A vindication of a regulated enclosure" (1656), quoted in Appleby 1978, 62.

18. None of these individuals had a philosophy that simply espoused narrow self-interest. Hutcheson, indeed, saw congruence as deriving from the direction of Providence, which created in humankind (1) a moral sense urging benevolence and (2) a mental and emotional constitution in which "true happiness" derives from exercising that benevolence. In this way for each person, "His constant pursuit of publick Good is the most probable way of promoting his own Happiness" (Hutcheson, "Essay on the Nature and Conduct of the Passions," 3d ed. 1742, cited in Taylor 1989, 261). This route to congruence has a greater affinity to Plato's logic than to that of the invisible hand. Moreover, Adam Smith both insisted on the social cultivation of benevolence and stressed the semipermanent nature of conflicts of interest, particularly

summed up the sentiment in verse: "Thus God and Nature link'd the gen'ral frame, / And bade Self-love and Social be the same"("An Essay on Man," Epistle III, ll. 317–18, in Pope [1733] 1966). Thomas Jefferson, instructing his overseer of slaves to protect his long-run property interests in slave children by excusing their mothers from fieldwork in their last days of pregnancy, concluded piously, "In this as in all other cases, providence has made our interests and our duties coincide perfectly" (Jefferson [1774–1826] 1953, 43). Arguments like these did not give up the appeal to duty. But strictly speaking, the actions they commended no longer required that appeal. Those actions could now be justified solely by appeals to reason, or long-run self-interest.

CONTEMPORARY MEANINGS

Today, the contrast between public and private good retains, rightly, a strong normative thrust.[19] When we say, "Mary is an exemplary citizen," we mean in part that we approve of her giving to the collective what she could have given to herself. We would lose a moral relation of great importance to both individuals and the public if we could no longer draw on such forms of commendation. Cooperative arrangements require institutions that not only reward cooperative behavior materially but also facilitate the moral approbation of communal acts and the condemnation of selfish ones. The decline of the Soviet Union was assured when calling an individual "a hero of the socialist state" lost all moral meaning.

To preserve the normative contrast between public good and private benefit, however, a polity does not need a precise and uncontested definition of the public good. The contrast can continue fruitfully even when some, for example, define the public good as a sum of individual goods and others define it more organically, as deriving from the function of the collective.

Aggregative Meanings: Good for Everyone and Good for Most. Since the seventeenth century, some thinkers have seen the public as no more than an aggregate of its individual members. Locke was among the first to define the public in the *public good* as an aggregate. In a sentence that also stressed the contrast between the public good and the king's private good, Locke wrote that government is "for the public good, i.e., the good of every particular Member of that Society, as far as by common Rules, it can be provided for; the Sword is not given the Magistrate for his own good alone" ([1679–89] 1965, I, s.92, p. 247). If we were to take Locke's

parenthetical definition literally, which he surely did not intend, we would assume that a community could have no public good unless the proposed policy were good for every one of its members.

Various versions of the good-for-everyone formulation have been popular over the years. Against political scientists who contended that no policy could be literally good for everyone in a polity as large as a modern nation-state, Brian Barry (1965, 195) argued that it is, after all, in the interests of literally every single person in the United States not to have the Strategic Air Command take off and drop all its bombs on the United States. Among economists, the criterion of Pareto-optimality, which defines situations in which at least one person is better off and no one is hurt, was devised to provide an operational definition of a public good that was, at least in a weak sense, literally good for everyone.

A more frequent form of a public good that is good for everyone is the kind portrayed in collective action problems. This is a good that, once provided, cannot feasibly be withheld from any member of a group. Examples are clean air, common defense, common grazing lands, fisheries and forests, higher salaries negotiated by a union (a "public good" for members of the union), and higher prices negotiated by a cartel (a "public good" for members of the cartel). In cases in which goods are public in this sense, that is, indivisible, it always pays each member to consume the good without paying for it, that is, to "free ride" on others' provision of that good. In these cases, every member of the public benefits from the good *qua* member of the public, but it is also in everyone's interest *qua* individual to benefit even further by not contributing to that good (therefore undermining the good by free riding).[20] In other cases, when we praise someone for

---

between merchants and the rest of the community (see Holmes 1990, 284, 345 n, 105).

19. The normative thrust of the concept is one of the central points in Flathman 1966, 3, 4, 8, and passim. See also Cassinelli 1989 and Frankel 1962, 200, cited in Held 1970, 216–17; Braybrooke 1989, 130; Banfield and Meyerson 1955, 322. The Oxford English Dictionary even defines "public" as "in general, and in most of the senses, the opposite of private" (1989, 12:778).

20. Olson [1965] 1971. Jean-Jacques Rousseau's much-debated "general will" can be best understood as applying only to those goods which are good for every single individual in the polity. Taken literally, Rousseau suggested that government simply cannot apply to other goods (see Held 1970 and Mansbridge [1980] 1983). Brian Barry proposed the formulation in which the public interest should mean "those interests which people have in common *qua* members of the public" (1965, 190), that is, "those interests which people have in their capacity as members of the public" (223). We can understand this point best in the context of the kind of analysis Olson provides of public goods. (For more on this definition of public goods, common pools, and prisoners' dilemmas, see below, esp. n. 24 and accompanying text.) For a critique of Barry, see Held 1970, 117–18; for a defense, see Douglass 1980. On theories in which the common good means the good for literally everyone, see Held 1970, chap. 4. Robert Goodin (1996) shows that commitment to a separation of powers which produces deadlock by institutionalizing multiple sources of veto can be explained by a logic that (1) defines the public good as good-for-everyone (the least common denominator) and (2) blocks government action not meeting that criterion for the public good. Some framers of the U.S. Constitution have held a good-for-everyone definition, but none plausibly held a mixture of meanings (some aggregative and some unitary), assumed that the public good was knowable and relatively transparent, and gave sufficient weight to the status quo that they favored blocking any government

acting in the public good against her private good, we assume that the public good does *not* promote the narrow self-interest of the individual in question. We thus implicitly define the public good in a way that does not mean good for everyone.

Jeremy Bentham proposed a different aggregative standard when he proclaimed, "The interest of the community then is, what? — the sum of the interests of the several members who compose it" ([1780] 1907, 3). Benthamite utilitarianism simply sums individual pleasures and pains, using the preponderance of pleasure to define the public good. Bentham even fantasized that on assuming office all legislators would be required to take an oath always to choose the policy that produced the most pleasure and least pain summed over all individuals. In a Benthamite summation, the pleasure of 51 percent would count as the public good even if that pleasure resulted in a like degree of pain for 49 percent.

To make Bentham's calculus accord more with ordinary usage, one might say that a policy is a little in the public interest or very much in the public interest depending on how large a majority the policy favored. Or, to use a formulation that Kenneth Arrow later developed, we could tell a legislator to choose "the social state yielding the highest possible social welfare within the environment."[21]

The problem with Bentham's pure summing is that in our moral discourse we sometimes contrast what a mere majority wants with the public good. The Supreme Court of the United States, for example, insists that legislation be justified not merely by having passed by a majority vote in the legislature but also by having a "public purpose" (Sunstein 1984). This language would not make sense if "public" meant only "what a majority wants."

In spite of their problems, some combination of these aggregative meanings forms a large part of what contemporary Americans mean, most of the time, by the public good. Countless individuals have acted as good citizens in order to promote what they roughly consider to be the greatest good of the greatest number. Yet aggregative understandings of the public good are less likely than functional or collective understandings to inspire extreme sacrifice.

Processual Meanings. One can, of course, simply *define* the public good as the product of a particular process, such as a democratic process. This definitional move, however, makes it impossible to criticize that process as not producing a public good.[22]

One can also assume that the public good is knowable, and that some process will reveal it. "The public interest," wrote Walter Lippmann, "may be presumed to be what men would choose if they saw clearly, thought rationally [and] acted disinterestedly and benevolently" (1956, 40). In actual politics, however, clear-thinking, rational, disinterested, and benevolent people can and do disagree on what is in the public good. Sometimes the problem is only that some are misinformed. Sometimes groups have different causal analyses — one group thinks that one means will bring about a commonly desired end while another group thinks another means will bring about that end. Most often, however, disinterested disagreements over the public good derive from groups giving different weights to different values. They have varying conceptions of what would be good for the polity.

Increasing political participation through decentralization, for example, sometimes conflicts with increasing material equality. The more local the democracy, the less money its members usually spend on helping the poor. Highly decentralized systems also allow rich communities to spend a great deal on their needs, leaving poor communities with little to spend on theirs. When participation conflicts with equality in these ways, some groups and individuals will favor more participation, some more equality — producing a rational and often even disinterested disagreement on the public good.

Functional or Collective Meanings. When aggregative and processual meanings fail, we may also think of the public good as what would be good for the enterprise to which a group of individuals belong, rather than what would be good for the individuals in that enterprise. Although this way of thinking has led to many evils throughout human history, it is not itself flawed. The evils committed in the name of a higher good can be condemned as evil without condemning the concept of a higher good or the concept of an entity with a function different from the functions of its component parts. Just as a circle composed of unconnected dots is more than just a sum of the dots, so organizations and political bodies can have functions that are more than aggregations of the desires of the individuals in them.

For example, when we think of one political science de-

action that was neither good for everyone nor congruent with a more unitary understanding of the public good. Bentham's move to aggregation by summing utilities reversed the previous presumption in favor of inaction. Because in no actual polity do existing social or political arrangements maximize utility, utilitarianism demands change.

21. Arrow [1951] 1964, 22, cited in Held 1970, 71. On theories in which the common good means the good of a "preponderance" of the public, see Held 1970, chap. 3.

22. Stanley Benn and R. S. Peters suggest another processual defini-

tion. To say that the state should seek the common good, they write, "is to say only that political decisions should attend to the interests of its members in a spirit of impartiality" (1959, 321; see commentary in Held 1970, 130). Most users of the word, however, mean something far more substantive than this. Moreover, "impartial" is another highly contested term, particularly among recent feminist writers, e.g., Young [1987] 1988, 61–62; Benhabib [1987] 1988, 81; Minow 1987, 75–76; Friedman 1991. Adam Smith might also be thought to have suggested a procedure, free competition, designed to produce a public good. The problem here is that free market competition does not always produce the public good, as in the cases of externalities or prisoners' dilemma dynamics leading to mutually destructive outcomes.

partment as being better than another, we do not usually mean only that it meets its members' individual needs better. We also mean that it does better the jobs that we agree a political science department is supposed to do — it produces more useful research, say, and better-educated students. When we ask individual professors to sacrifice some of their private interests for the good of the department, we usually ask them to do so in order that the department can do better the job it is designed to do. Although I have never heard of such a case, it is not inconceivable that a chair might ask a member to resign for the good of the department. Imagine now a university getting an increase in income so large that it could hire the very best scholars in the field, if only the slots were available. It is inconceivable practically, but not hypothetically, to imagine a dean asking everyone in the department to resign, and every member actually doing so, taking a permanent personal loss, for the good of the department. Similarly, a whole high school team might be willing to be replaced by better players in order to win the big game against a traditional rival. In each case, the good of the department and of the team would have a standing separate from the good of the individuals composing it.

In cases like these, we say that members of a collective make the good of the collective their own. In economists' terms, they encompass the utility of the collective in their own utility function. When they do this, the utility they make their own can be not the combined utility of a collection of other individuals, but rather the good of an entity that differs to some degree from the good of the individuals in it. One makes the good of a collective one's own in this sense either by adopting an ideal, such as the development of good political science, that an organization or collective can pursue and that is worth personal sacrifice, or by developing feelings of loyalty to a collective entity — a football team, a high school, a nation, or even a business.

Commitments to an ideal and loyalty to a group are the kinds of public good that inspire the heaviest sacrifice, for example, risking one's life in a war. They are more sacred, more powerful, and more dangerous than commitments to an aggregative public good.

Meanings of Good *and* Public. What is good for any citizen or group of citizens is always a matter of debate. Sometimes preferences are all that one needs to demarcate the good. At other times, because of failures in information, an individual or public may prefer what is not good for it. Because individuals usually are the best judges of their own goods, it is always dangerous to act against the preferences of individuals or groups to promote what is good for them. But although dangerous, taking action for the public good against the preferences of a majority of the public may be justified in areas in which the public is least informed.[23]

23. For the highly contested debate on this issue, see inter alia Burke [1774] 1925, Mill [1859] 1947, Pitkin 1967, Balbus 1971, Connolly

What we mean by the public is just as contested as what we mean by good. Existing power holders often take for granted the boundaries of their public. When I wrote above of the good of an academic department and its members, my words implied that *members* meant the tenure-track (possibly even only the tenured) faculty of the department. But what about the non-tenure-track faculty? Is the public good to be estimated without them? What about teaching fellows? Graduate students? Undergraduates? The administrative staff? Including the material interests of these groups in an aggregative conception of the public good would change its meaning. Including these groups' understandings of the function of the department would usually change that meaning too.

In a nation-state, the public good might appear as, quite obviously, the good of its citizens. But that good was once defined to exclude slaves, Blacks, and women. And today, what about noncitizens and guestworkers? Perhaps the public good should be seen as the good of all residents rather than only citizens. What about unborn children?

In the Middle Ages, writers on politics often quoted the saying, "That which affects all should be decided by all." In recent times in the United States, both the Students for a Democratic Society (1962) and later President Richard Nixon, in a State of the Union address, argued that people should have "a bigger voice in deciding for themselves those questions that so greatly affect their lives" (Nixon, 1971, cited in Cook and Morgan 1971). If being affected by a decision places one in the relevant public for that decision, the U.S. government should include the citizens of China as part of the public in making decisions on trade restrictions (see Dahl 1989, 291–93).

The boundaries of some publics exclude the members of other publics. Smaller communities often want to exclude and resist interference by the larger publics in which they are embedded. Is one of these publics the true public and another the false one? More likely both have claims to consideration as a public. The boundaries of any democratic polity are always contested. As those boundaries are contested, so is the nature of the public good.

Feminist theorists have recently pointed out that male power-holders have often drawn the line between public and private in ways that exclude from the public sphere concerns of great importance to women. The phrase "the public good" means not only whatever is good for all or most members of the polity or whatever furthers the goal of the polity, but also whatever the dominant speakers of the current language call public. Women must struggle to get the prevention of rape in

1972. When constitution-makers and populace make a reasonable guess that more informed decisionmakers will act (to a greater degree than in most matters) in the interests of those for whom they make decisions (perhaps because they have relatively similar interests), they are willing to grant greater autonomous power, as to the commander in chief and the members of the Supreme Court (Mansbridge [1980] 1983).

marriage considered a public good, not only because the goal does not yet command complete consensus but, more important, because dominant norms and usage place marriage in the private as opposed to public realm. Dominant norms — whether male, capitalist, or other — influence the kinds of things that appear in the language as public goods. In the contest over these categories, individual contestants have far from equal power.

Craig Calhoun argues in this book that we cannot take as given the definition of the public in whose good we are interested. The public good, he points out, must be "forged," not simply "found." I would add that sometimes, on some issues, a genuine consensus on the public good can be forged through deliberation. On other issues, a genuine consensus can be forged over time only by changing the political, economic, and social conditions that created the grounds for conflict. But on some issues, no genuine consensus can be forged. On these issues, the public good is often best served by trying to equalize the ability to exert force and threaten sanctions, then decide the issue through as fair a procedure as possible. Because inequalities in power cannot be eliminated, both deliberative and procedural methods for forging an understanding of the public good must continually be open to criticism.

Calhoun also rightly points out that the public good must be constructed discursively, that this construction is always partial, and that the public by and for whom it is constructed consists of different individuals sometimes bound together by mere practical circumstances. He does not say, but I shall add, that massive differences in, among other things, information, contacts, verbal skills, and feelings of potential efficacy produce great inequalities among the participants in most deliberations. When we praise individuals using one construction of the public good, we often implicitly exclude or partially exclude other constructions of that good and the individuals who act according to those meanings. Symbolic, affective, and moral ties that go beyond the bonds of practical circumstances make possible the praise and blame every complex society needs. At the same time, however, every social and moral norm, every foundation for praise and blame, creates inequalities among groups of individuals who comply to a greater and lesser degree with that norm. The answer is not to eliminate norms, and thus the possibility of our telling one another what we think we ought to do, but to preserve the possibility of contest, remain sensitive to the myriad forms inequality can take, and work to make discursive and power resources more equal.

Two Functions of the Contested Concept. I am not arguing here in favor of any one of the meanings of the public good that I have just surveyed. Neither am I urging that we turn our backs on the conflicts inherent in the phrase and leave the issues to the philosophers. The worst outcome of my portrayal of the public good as a site of contest would be that

deadly undergraduate conclusion, "There's no point in thinking (or fighting) about it; it's only different opinions." We need to continue to struggle over these meanings because in doing so we articulate more clearly what we want the public and ourselves to be.

Most of us, however, cannot wage this struggle every day. Rather, we often hold many conflicting connotations together when we think of the public good. Contemporary Americans, for instance, often understand the public good as primarily an aggregation of individual goods that is more than a majority and less than the totality of all individuals in the public, but add to this picture a thread or two of certain ideals or goals associated with the nation as a whole.

As political theorists, as social scientists, and as laypeople, we can usually live with the uncrystalized conflict that is the public good. Although to pursue a set of logical philosophical entailments or to operationalize a term for behavioral research we may want to choose only one from the set of competing meanings, in practical political life we often do not need to choose. It is often not necessary to be analytically clearer than the ordinary language once we accept that in its contested state, without final determination, the concept of the public good still serves two linked functions. One function of the term is to serve as a site for normative contestation over what is public and what is good. Another is to signify approval, especially in contrast with private interests.

The question, Is airline deregulation in the public good? exemplifies the first function, serving as a site for contestation. Some say deregulation is a public good because it will decrease fares, thus benefiting the consumer. Everyone is a consumer, therefore fare decreases benefit the public. But in fact not everyone consumes airline tickets, and among consumers not everyone consumes at an equal rate. Perhaps decreased fares only transfer benefits from airline employees to airline users. What if deregulation reduces service to small towns and cities? Does hurting important parts of the public make it less of a public good? These are conceptual questions as well as questions about the effects of specific policies. In the deliberation involving these conceptual questions, different policies contend for the label the public good. The process of deliberation should air these questions and let the public struggle with them. When people formulate their views and test their arguments against others, they are more likely to see how strongly they feel about what, and why, coming eventually to some individual determinations, and perhaps a set of different collective determinations, about what they mean by the public good. In this sharing, winnowing, and confronting, the phrase *the public good* serves as a site for analytically fruitful contestation.

The process of open, critical deliberation becomes even more vital when we recognize that any concept of the public good will inevitably contain hidden assumptions about the legitimacy, even the superiority, of an existing system.

In the second function — that of serving as approbation,

particularly in contrast with private interests — it often seems not to matter in many cases what precise meaning we give the public good. Everyone has the experience that, in general, if each person takes from a common pool without replenishing it, the common pool deteriorates to everyone's eventual detriment. Because we know from experience that it is more pleasant to live with someone who voluntarily helps clean up the house or in other ways contributes to the common pool, and we know more broadly that voluntary cooperation for public-spirited reasons is a highly efficient form of solving commons dilemmas, we are likely to approve in general of public-spirited behavior in others, and by extension in ourselves. To take this general stance of approval, we do not have to specify the meaning of the public good more precisely.

Managers of nonprofit enterprises, for example, often take lower salaries than their counterparts in the private sector. They do so in part because they are willing to make some sacrifice to do work they consider in the public good. That good does not have to be Pareto-optimal. It does not have to be good for everyone. It can be aggregative, though it usually has to be good for more than a bare majority. Yet it need not be aggregative. It can be the good of a collective or an ideal that perhaps a majority would not endorse. Some unprecise combination of these meanings goes into the meaning of public good when individuals make their decisions to act in the public good rather than in their narrow self-interest. It is not usually necessary to be more precise.

NEW TOOLS, NEW SOLUTIONS: "NESTING" PUBLIC SPIRIT WITHIN A RETURN TO SELF-INTEREST

Around 1950, mathematical theorists introduced an heuristic thought experiment entitled the prisoners' dilemma (Luce and Raiffa 1957; Hardin 1982). In this two-person dilemma, the rewards are arranged so that it always pays each person to act so as to reduce the reward for the other player (to "defect") no matter what the other does; but if both players defect (as it is individually "rational" for them to do), both get rewards lower than if both had cooperated.[24] In one fre-

quently cited example, the "tragedy of the commons," it is individually rational for each self-interested person to put as many cows as possible to graze on the common land, but if all do so, the commons become overgrazed and the cows all starve (Hardin 1968). In another example, it is individually rational for self-interested individuals to avoid contributing to the common defense and thus to "free ride" on others' efforts because once anyone provides such defense, the free riders will benefit without contributing. If everyone takes this stance, however, no one provides for defense and all suffer (Olson [1965] 1971).

The conceptual tool of the prisoners' dilemma makes possible a major analytic advance beyond traditional theories that simply asserted an enlightened self-interest congruent with the public good. Even in the thirteenth century, when Thomas Aquinas stressed the conflict between private and public goods, he concluded in some passages that individual good and common good were essentially congruent: "He who seeks the common good of the multitude consequently seeks his own good . . . because one's own good cannot exist without the common good" ([1266–73], quoted in Lewis 1954, 212). Arguments of this form, repeated through the seventeenth century (examples in Gunn 1969), make the faulty assumption that simply because an individual is part of the public, contributions to that public are to the individual's own benefit.

In the eighteenth century, David Hume argued that cooperation was in each person's "remote interest" (Hume [1739–40] 1978, 545). A century later, Alexis de Tocqueville made a similar argument for "self-interest rightly understood," a doctrine postulating that "it is in the interest of every man to be virtuous" ([1835–40] 1954, 2:129 ff.).[25] Yet by not specifically requiring virtue (or, failing virtue, institutions to reward cooperation and punish defection), such arguments were analytically incoherent. They did not and could not explain exactly how an individual motivated only by

---

24. In the classic prisoners' dilemma, a district attorney offers, in confidence, each of two prisoners release from jail if they give evidence that will convict the other. If one remains silent ("cooperates" with his partner in prison) but the other gives evidence ("defects" on his partner), the prisoner who remains silent will receive a heavy jail term (big negative payoff), but his comrade, who squealed, will be released (big positive payoff). If both remain silent, they will both get only a short term in jail (small negative payoff). If both give evidence against one another, they will both get heavy terms. For each, the best strategy is to give evidence on the other ("defection" is the individually rational "dominant strategy") no matter what the other does, but if both do this, they will each be worse off than if they had kept quiet. For a more thorough explanation, see Axelrod (1984, 8), who orders the payoffs more subtly. "Common pool" dilemmas have a similar structure, in

which every individual has an incentive to give nothing and take a share of the pool to which others have contributed (the pool increases with each contribution beyond the extent of that contribution). But everyone acting on this incentive reduces the pool to zero.

25. Hume postulated, for example, a "remote" interest in "the preserving of peace and order in society" ([1739–40] 1978, 545). He also spelled out implicitly the dynamic of the prisoners' dilemma in his famous example of the two farmers who would not help each other harvest their corn, both losing their harvests "for want of mutual confidence and security" (ibid., 520–21). Tocqueville described the doctrine of self-interest rightly understood as "The personal advantage of each member of the community [may] consist in working for the good of all" ([1835–40] 1954, 2:129). Tocqueville advanced this argument not as his own, but as that of many Americans he had met, commenting with a reporter's detachment, "They endeavor to prove that it is the interest of every man to be virtuous. I shall not here enter into the reasons they allege, which would divert me from my subject; suffice it to say that they have convinced their fellow countrymen" (130; see also 132).

narrow self-interest would come to see cooperative behavior as being in that self-interest. It is in neither one's "remote self-interest" nor one's "self-interest rightly understood" to cooperate in a situation structured like a prisoners' dilemma if one's self-interest does not encompass the good of others or adherence to principles, if one's own behavior will not influence others' behavior, and if voluntary selection or other institutions do not reward cooperative behavior. When there are opportunities to free ride on others' efforts, simply being a member of a community that benefits from its members' contributions does not provide sufficient incentive for a narrowly self-interested individual to contribute.

The structure of the prisoners' dilemma clarifies these dynamics. In such a structure, producing an outcome in the common good — in this case an outcome that is relatively good for both prisoners or for all in a larger public — requires changing in some way the individual consequences of cooperation or defection. As Hobbes realized implicitly in the seventeenth century, one solution to such dilemmas is to set up a sovereign with the power to punish defectors (Hobbes [1651] 1947).[26]

We now know, however, that the prisoners' dilemma can be solved by any human contrivance that changes the payoffs in the matrix so that each person has sufficient incentive to cooperate. That incentive can be based on public-spirited motivations as well as on narrow self-interest. When American college students are allowed to talk to one another for ten minutes before interacting in a group situation structured like a prisoners' dilemma, they discuss the issues and promise one another to cooperate (and eventually about 85 percent usually do cooperate) against their individual self-interest. The dilemma will not be repeated and the students' actions are anonymous, so that anyone can defect, earn ten or fifteen dollars more than the others, and walk away both richer and free from sanction. The cooperation of these students against their self-interest seems to stem from a combination of "we-feeling" with the others in the group and conscience about the promises they have made and the behavior they consider right (Dawes et al. 1990; Mansbridge 1990b).

Further experiments with prisoners' dilemmas reveal that when some people in a group defect, those defections quickly undermine the others' cooperative impulses (Isaac, McCue, and Plott 1985). Another's defection causes a cooperator to lose not only material rewards but probably some self-esteem as well, resulting from being exploited and taken for a "sucker."

In contrast to most laboratory and computer simulations, in the real world the choice of whether or not to enter a prisoners' dilemma–like interaction is often voluntary. One can join — or invest oneself in — one enterprise or another, become friends with one person or another, or even choose to live in one community rather than another. If some individuals have, for whatever reasons, a greater empathy for others that leads to greater cooperation or a moral character whose integrity requires adherence to certain principles of cooperation, and if reputation or other markers of potential cooperation are relatively discernable among individuals, potential cooperators will seek out other likely cooperators with whom to interact, avoiding the potential defectors. The rewards of mutual cooperation will accrue to the cooperators, and the defectors will be left with the dregs of mutual defection (Frank 1990).

Voluntary selection in this way acts to provide self-interested returns to those who may be cooperating for purely non-self-interested reasons. Other institutions can also create sufficient self-interested returns to altruistic action so that the altruistic actor will not be put out of business in the course of competition, and the altruistic motive, whatever its source, will not be extinguished in the course of social learning.[27]

I call this process "nesting" altruism within a return to self-interest. It adds a fourth relation between self-interest and altruism to the earlier ideas of Platonic congruence, Smithian congruence, and medieval Christian opposition. In this relation, the motives of altruism and self-interest remain distinct, but the material benefits that meet self-interested desires or needs facilitate altruistic actions. In a simple case, Mother Theresa needs to eat. Continued existence is in her material self-interest; and goods such as food, by maintaining her material existence, also maintain her altruism. Less simply, among nonsaints, discovering that one can do well by doing good encourages doing good. Rewards for altruistic action that meet the altruist's material needs or desires provide an ecological niche, or protective nest, in which altruistic behavior can flourish. The logic of the nesting process does not assume that people act empathetically or in accordance with principle in order to further their material self-interest. Daniel Batson (1991), whose experiments Alan Wolfe cites in this book, is right, I believe, in his demonstrations that people sometimes act from motives that have no source other than pure altruism. The logic of nesting altruism or public spirit protectively in some return to self-interest is compatible with theories that see empathy as an innate human instinct or that see the human psyche as having a deep structure attuned to the perception of justice and injustice.

---

26. One can also set aside collateral that will be lost if one defects (Schelling [1960] 1971); devise selective benefits for cooperation (Olson [1965] 1947); exchange rights of control over the others' moves (Shild 1971 and Hernes 1971, cited in Coleman 1990); or in an iterated game respond with a tit-for-tat strategy to the others' cooperating and defecting moves (Axelrod 1984; for the more effective "generous tit-for-tat," see Nowak and Sigmund 1992 and Godfray 1992).

27. In Plato's *Republic,* Glaucon offers the common wisdom that a reputation for justice is likely to produce the material goods of "first office and rule in the state . . . , then a wife from any family he chooses, and the giving of his children in marriage to whomsoever he pleases, dealings and partnerships with whom he will" (362b). Glaucon's question, which forms the starting point for the central reasoning of the *Republic,* is why it would not be best of all to have the reputation for justice but in fact be unjust.

The logic of nesting only shows that in certain institutional conditions, behavior that derives from empathic or principled motivations can receive sufficient return to narrow self-interest so as not to be extinguished. When the high cost of an altruistic action would keep most people from indulging their altruistic motivations, some self-interested return to the action allows the altruism to flourish. The self-interested return thus provides an ecological niche in which that altruism can nest (Mansbridge 1990b).

Recent work on industry compliance with government regulation has yielded results congruent with this logic. The most effective regulatory strategy, these studies indicate, combines a foreground appeal to concern with the public good with a background structure of certain, graduated, and potentially strong sanctions. The sanctions, on which an analysis based on narrow self-interest would focus, prove relatively ineffective alone, inspiring pervasive and inventive strategies for cheating. Appeals to public spirit are far more efficient. When regulations are reasonable and congruent with what the regulated themselves consider the public good, fairly high percentages of the regulated want to comply with them, for what seem to be genuinely altruistic, or public-spirited, reasons. But the cooperators fear competition from those who do not comply. By reducing the profits of the defectors, governmental sanctions make it possible for the majority of the regulated to cooperate from public-spirited motives with little or no material loss (Ayers and Braithwaite 1992).

Consider a corporation whose business will benefit if the business community in general acts for some public good (say, creating a system of post–high school training for young people), even though such an action has material costs for each contributor. If each institution or individual cares only for its long-run narrow self-interest, the corporations who will benefit from the training program must set up some institution that materially rewards those who contribute to the program (cooperation) and punishes noncontribution (defection); only then can they keep one or more of their number from free riding on the good of training, thus getting better employees but not contributing to the cost, while with the ensuing savings lowering the price of its product and undercutting the survival capacity of the others.

The corporations' directors may, however, be more than narrowly self-interested. They may care for their community or have principles that make them believe they ought to take public-spirited action. In this case, any institution they devise to produce cooperation can be far more efficient than their accepting a situation in which everyone is acting from narrow self-interest, because now the institution can rely primarily on public spirit for participation, resorting to punishment for the few defectors infrequently and mostly in small doses. Yet even in this case, so long as there are any defectors at all, if the corporations cannot set up an institution that will reward cooperation and punish defection, the cooperators will lose in competition with the defectors.

In the United States today, where few if any corporations have devised the kinds of institutions I have described, businesses contribute to the public good primarily when an informal monopoly or oligopoly allows the business to pass all costs on to the consumer or when the contribution is so small as not to affect the competitive environment. In some contexts, however, the public-spirited contribution can bring a material return. For example, a corporation may find part or all of the cost of its public-spirited action repaid in reputational effects. Sending a "costly signal" (a signal that has negative consequences for the sender and is thus a greater guarantor of good faith than mere words) about its public-spirited ways of doing business may produce profitable cooperative responses in other entities with which the corporation has to deal — other corporations, legislatures, and consumers.

When interactions are voluntary and have a prisoners' dilemma structure, cooperators will look around for other cooperators with whom to interact and will pay attention to costly signals. Indeed, when prisoners' dilemma interactions produce habits of looking for other cooperators with whom to interact, those habits may spill over into interactions that do not have such a structure or into interactions whose structure is uncertain.

When situations have the structure of a prisoners' dilemma, fostering "self-interest rightly understood" thus requires not just moral exhortation and public spirit but also the discovering and creating of business situations — for example, "conspiracies in restraint of trade," other forms of protected markets, or reputational returns to worthiness — in which public-spirited impulses can survive. This kind of calculus lies behind some recent experiments in neocorporatism, in which business and labor elites, together with government representatives of more diffuse consumer and environmental interests, make agreements on what they believe to be the public good; these agreements take on the force of law, and the state dispenses the small doses of sanction required to keep potential defectors in line (see Cohen and Rogers 1993).

Nonprofit enterprises afford another way of nesting public-spirited impulses within some return to self-interest. Most nonprofits depend, to a greater or lesser degree, on the impulses of their workers and external contributors to do good. Their workers' frequent willingness to accept salaries lower than what they would be in private business, as well as the affiliations of nonprofits with churches and other groups whose livelihood depends on their reputations, can serve as a costly signal that as agents these actors will act as their contributors desire. The agents may thus not have to engage in other costly procedures to reassure the principals. If public decisionmakers knew, for example, that the directors of a shelter for the homeless had made their own the interests of those they sheltered, the decisionmakers could allow those directors more discretion and thus enable them to act more efficiently than directors who were working entirely for profit.[28] Nonprofit enterprises also may function more efficiently than their for-profit competitors because their internal organization can rely more heavily on public spirit.

Nesting public-spirited motivations within some return to self-interest entails the great risk — much like the risks in mixing market transactions with other kinds of transactions — of self-interested motivation driving out other motivations. In studies of work, extrinsic motivation has been shown to drive out intrinsic motivation. That is, once you are paid for doing something you used to do for love of the work itself, you begin to do it only for the pay. But extrinsic motivation does not drive out intrinsic when material rewards are designed to look as if they are acknowledging the intrinsic motivation, not paying directly for the behavior (Deci and Ryan 1985; Frey 1994). An effective institutional design would nest public-spirited behavior within some material return in such a way that the material return publicly acknowledged and praised the public-spirited motivation. Reputational returns to public-spirited behavior, for example, act as forms of acknowledgment, not pay. In a regulatory system run primarily on public spirit, the small sanctions for first offenses (for example, cheating on the regulations or other forms of defection) thus usually serve as a public expression of disapproval more than a sufficient material deterrent in themselves.

In a complex, highly interdependent society many interactions, large and small, contain some component structured like a prisoners' dilemma.[29] A host of environmental problems, such as pollution, water shortage, and overfishing, have one form of prisoners' dilemma structure. So do such everyday goods as queuing for tickets or any scarce good, contributing to public radio, voting, avoiding negative campaign tactics, not carrying guns to school, and not being rude to strangers. Escalating global interdependence urgently demands understanding how we now cooperate, and finding new ways to cooperate, in prisoners' dilemma and similar interactions.

In this quest, we need intellectual inspiration from wherever we can find it. Seventeenth- and eighteenth-century theorists made it clear that many mutually profitable exchanges and the public good arising from those exchanges need little more than the motivations of narrow self-interest. More recently, we have recognized that any elaborate system of exchange requires some form of reliable external sanction for the enforcement of contracts. We also now realize that most complex, efficient systems of exchange require some inter-

nalized sanctions, in which individuals blame themselves for noncooperative behavior even when the likelihood of their being caught is small. Few institutions other than the market can work efficiently with a mix of motivations that includes a relatively high proportion of narrow self-interest.

Our generation has the analytic task of sorting out which institutional arrangements in which contexts work most efficiently like an ideal market, based on a high proportion of narrow self-interest, and which work better with other mixes of motivations. For any given problem several different institutional arrangements and mixes may be equally efficient, and both context and the availability of different cultural resources make universal solutions improbable. Our job is to make good contextually based guesses, which can then be tested in practice.

In many contexts, efficient outcomes require a leaven of what I have been calling public spirit, or concern for the public good. But the public to whom one's loyalty or principles apply may range from all humanity to the members of one's in-group. The fierce loyalties — based on kin, gang, ethnicity, religion, or ideology — that in-groups command may have remained functional because they helped solve prisoners' dilemma interactions within the group.

For any so-called public good, whether directed at good ends or bad, encouraging public spirit requires stressing one form of congruence. It requires helping individuals broaden their goals and satisfactions so that they can take some pleasure in the goods of others, find some satisfaction in working for collective ends, and feel fulfilled in acting according to principles that they have made their own. Encouraging public spirit also requires stressing one form of conflict. It requires establishing norms, models of behavior, and practices of moral exhortation rooted in the assumption of an opposition between private and public good, so that when individuals experience such conflicts they can turn to those norms, models, and practices for guidance and inspiration. In spite of the many ways in which past Western cultures differ from the modern American one and in spite of the withering or disappearance today of many cultural and moral resources on which past thinkers could draw, we can still learn both from Plato's comments on self-knowledge and from the Christian stress on the conflict between personal desires and the common good.[30] We are now more skeptical, however, of the good that these earlier traditions assumed to be, to some degree, discoverable.

The examples of urban gangs, ethnic wars, genocide, religious inquisitions, and ideological bloodbaths make it clear that encouraging action in the public good requires strong,

28. This is one reason, among many less benign reasons, for the growth in contracting government services to nonprofits (Lipsky 1993).

29. For simplicity I have focused here on prisoners' dilemma interactions. Other games, such as the "assurance game," can also be solved more easily if one has morally based as well as materially based reasons for believing, say, that others will keep their promises. The problems of positional goods are one form of prisoners' dilemma, broadly speaking (the first to stand at a football game see better, but then everyone has to stand, so that at the end all are worse off).

30. For example, saying that we must protect the exercise of public-spirited behavior so that the motivation to cooperate will not be undermined by excessive material costs ("nesting" that motivation in a context of some return to material self-interest) has some relation to the otherwise very different point that one can be just only in a well-ordered republic.

deliberative scrutiny to monitor the commonality and the goodness of the public good toward which these efforts are bent. For understandable reasons, one seventeenth-century English royalist, anticipating Burkean criticisms of the French Revolution, wrote scathingly, "From such as still aim at the public's good, / . . . From a reformation founded in blood, / Libera me" (Anon. 1659, cited in Gunn 1969, 85).[31] Or as one rational choice theorist put it recently, "Whenever I hear the words 'the public good,' I reach for my wallet [to make sure it has not yet been picked]" (Anon. 1994, private conversation).

Any scrutiny of the public good must ask, Whose good? It must also address questions of justice. Sometimes a society may have to pay off a ruling class for having, in particular historical circumstances, solved the collective dilemmas that make cooperation possible. Even institutions and norms that may seem extortionate in comparative perspective may be relatively acceptable in circumstances in which there is no more egalitarian way to produce cooperation. But constitutional design should aim, among other things, at reducing to their functional minima the rewards to elites for helping establish and maintain cooperative institutions and norms.

CONCLUSION: LIVING WITH CONTEST

I conclude that we need not share the dismay of the political scientists of this century who, faced with the impossibility of pinning down an exact meaning of the public good, fantasized about abolishing the term altogether. In the 1950s Frank Sorauf wrote, "Perhaps the academicians ought to take the lead in drawing up a list of ambiguous words and phrases that 'never would be missed.' For such a list I would have several candidates, but it should suffice here to nominate the 'public interest.' "[32]

As I have argued, the public interest can have several different relations with private interests — relations of congruity,

contrast, and a form of compatibility in which the one nests inside the other. The phrase can also have several different meanings — aggregative, procedural, and functional. Common to all these relations and meanings, however, we find at least two meanings in use. First, the phrase serves as a site for contest over what is public and good. Second, it serves to direct approbation to those who act in the public good, especially in contrast to promoting their private interests.

Although the present state of imprecision is not necessarily better than a precise definition would be, at least one of the present functions, serving as a site for contest, would be destroyed by narrowing and fixing forever the meaning of the public good. The other function, that of signaling approbation, also is not greatly damaged by lack of precision. We can praise people for acting in the public good and in so doing encourage more people to act that way, without answering the questions I have raised in this chapter about the precise meaning of that phrase. Yet we must continue to ask the questions, while recognizing that they cannot be answered definitively.

The public good is a dangerous concept. Asking people to act in the public good and not in their self-interest asks them to leave a terrain in which their everyday experience gives them relatively reliable messages on what is good for them and to enter a terrain in which, because uncertainty is far greater, authoritative others play a far greater role in suggesting what the public good should be. In the continuing conflict over meaning, two sources of influence have greater weight than they should: individuals and groups who appeal to the exclusivity and hatred that may be part of group loyalty and individuals and groups whose privileged social positions allow them to use force and the threat of sanction as well as unequal deliberative resources to promote their opinions and interests.

Yet neither the dangers nor the necessity of ongoing contest over the very meaning of the words should lead us to discard appeals to the public good. We need to make those appeals as much as we need to guard against their misuse. The possible influence of demagogues playing on the emotions of group loyalty and the inevitable greater influence of the powerful create an imperative to keep alive the possibility of conflict over meanings and application. The dangers can be monitored and reduced through lively, open deliberation. But some reduced version of those dangers ultimately must be accepted as part of the costs of cooperation. In an extraordinarily large number of contexts, human beings need, in order to cooperate, some concept of a public good. We must learn to live with, even welcome, a concept that remains continually in contest.

31. Adam Smith reported in *The Wealth of Nations* (1776) that he had "never known much good done by those who affected to trade for the public good." Ten years earlier another economist, James Steuart, concluded, "Were everyone to act for the public, and neglect himself, the statesman would be bewildered . . . were a people to become quite disinterested, there would be no possibility of governing them. Everyone might consider the interest of his country in a different light, and many might join in the ruin of it, by endeavoring to promote its advantages" (*Inquiry into the Principles of Political Oeconomy,* 1761). At the time of the framing of the American Constitution, Alexander Hamilton concluded, "The safest reliance of every government is on man's interests. This is a principle of human nature on which all political speculation, to be just, must be founded" ("Letters from Phocion," 1784, all cited in Hirschman 1992). For the implications of safe predictability in the common seventeenth-century maxim, "Interest will not lie," see Gunn 1969, 36–44; Mansbridge 1990a). For a contemporary consideration, see Barry 1965.

32. 1962, 186. See also David Truman: "We do not need to account for a totally inclusive interest because one does not exist" (1951, 51). For analysis, see Held 1970, 9, 79–81.

REFERENCES

Allen, J. W. [1928] 1960. *A History of Political Thought in the Sixteenth Century.* London: Methuen.

Appleby, Joyce Oldham. 1978. *Economic Thought and Ideology in Seventeenth- Century England*. Princeton: Princeton University Press.

Aquinas, Thomas. [1266–73] 1966. *Summa Theologiae*. Blackfriars trans. London: Eyre and Spottiswoode.

Aristotle. [336–22 B.C.] 1944. *Politics*. H. Rackham, trans. Cambridge: Harvard University Press/Loeb Classical Library.

Arrow, Kenneth. [1951] 1963. *Social Choice and Individual Values*. New York: Wiley.

Augustine. [413–26] 1981. *City of God*. George E. McCracken, trans. Cambridge: Harvard University Press/Loeb Classical Library.

Axelrod, Robert. 1984. *The Evolution of Cooperation*. New York: Basic Books.

Ayers, Ian, and John Braithwaite. 1992. *Responsive Regulation: Transcending the Deregulation Debate*. New York: Oxford University Press.

Balbus, Isaac D. 1971. "The Concept of Interest in Pluralist and Marxian Analysis." *Politics and Society* 1:151–77.

Banfield, Edward, and Martin Meyerson. 1955. *Politics, Planning and the Public Interest*. Glencoe, Ill.: Free Press.

Barber, Benjamin R. 1984. *Strong Democracy: Participatory Politics for a New Age*. Berkeley: University of California Press.

Barry, Brian. 1965. *Political Argument*. New York: Humanities Press.

Batson, Daniel. 1991. *The Altruism Question*. Hillsdale, N.Y.: Lawrence Erlbaum Associates.

Benhabib, Seyla. [1987] 1988. "The Generalized and Concrete Other." In *Feminism as Critique: On the Politics of Gender*, ed. Seyla Benhabib and Drucilla Cornell. Minneapolis: University of Minnesota Press.

Benn, Stanley, and R. S. Peters. 1959. *The Principles of Political Thought*. New York: Free Press, 1959.

Bentham, Jeremy. [1780] 1907. *Introduction to the Principles of Morals and Legislation*. Oxford: Oxford University Press.

Bentley, Arthur. [1908] 1949. *The Process of Government*. Evanston, Ill.: Principia Press.

Bessette, Joseph M. 1994. *The Mild Voice of Reason: Deliberative Democracy and American National Government*. Chicago: University of Chicago Press.

Boyte, Harry C. 1989. *Commonwealth: A Return to Citizen Politics*. New York: Free Press.

Braybrooke, David. 1989. "The Public Interest: The Present and Future of the Concept." In *The Public Interest: NOMOS V*, ed. Carl J. Friedrich. New York: Atherton.

Burke, Edmund. [1774] 1925. "To the Electors of Bristol." In *Selections,* ed. L. N. Broughton. New York: Scribners.

Cassinelli, C. W. 1989. "The Public Interest in Political Ethics." In *The Public Interest: NOMOS V,* ed. Carl J. Friedrich. New York: Atherton.

Cicero. [54–52 B.C.] 1928. *De Re Publica*. Clinton Walker Keyes, trans. Cambridge: Harvard University Press/Loeb Classical Library.

Cohen, Joshua. 1989. "Deliberation and Democratic Legitimacy." In *The Good Polity*, ed. Alan Hamlin and Phillip Petit. Oxford: Blackwell.

Cohen, Joshua, and Joel Rogers. 1992. "Secondary Associations and Democratic Governance." *Politics and Society* 20:393–472.

Coleman, James S. 1990. *Foundations of Social Theory*. Cambridge: Harvard University Press.

Cook, Terence E., and Patrick M. Morgan, eds. 1971. *Participatory Democracy*. San Francisco: Canfield Press.

Dahl, Robert A. 1989. *Democracy and Its Critics*. New Haven: Yale University Press.

Dawes, Robyn, Alphons J. C. van de Kragt, and John M. Orbell. 1990. "Cooperation for the Benefit of Us — Not Me, or My Conscience." In *Beyond Self-Interest*, ed. Jane J. Mansbridge. Chicago: University of Chicago Press.

Deci, Edward L., and Richard M. Ryan. 1985. *Intrinsic Motivation and Self-Determination in Human Behavior*. New York: Plenum.

Douglass, Bruce. 1980. "The Common Good and the Public Interest." *Political Theory* 8:103–17.

Flathman, Richard E. 1966. *The Public Interest*. New York: Wiley.

Frank, Robert H. 1990. "A Theory of Moral Sentiments." In *Beyond Self-Interest*, ed. Jane J. Mansbridge. Chicago: University of Chicago Press.

Frankel, Charles. 1962. *The Democratic Prospect*. New York: Harper.

Friedman, Marilyn. 1991. "The Practice of Partiality." *Ethics* 101:818–35.

Friedrich, Carl J., ed. 1989. *The Public Interest: NOMOS V*. New York: Atherton.

Froelich, Gregory. 1989. "The Equivocal Status of Bonum Commune." *New Scholasticism* 62:38–57.

Gallie, W. B. 1955–56. "Essentially Contested Concepts." *Proceedings of the Aristotelian Society* 56:167–98.

Godfray, H. C. J. 1992. "The Evolution of Forgiveness." *Nature* 355:206–07.

Granovetter, Mark. 1994. "The Economic Sociology of Firms and Entrepreneurs." In *The Economic Sociology of Immigration*, ed. Alejandro Portes. Princeton: Russell Sage and Princeton University Press.

Goodin, Robert E. 1996. "Institutionalizing the Public Interest: The Defense of Deadlock and Beyond." *American Political Science Review* 90:331–43.

Gunn, J. A. W. 1969. *Politics and the Public Interest in the Seventeenth Century*. London: Routledge and Kegan Paul.

Hardin, Garrett. 1968. "The Tragedy of the Commons." *Science* 162:1243–48.

Hardin, Russell. 1982. *Collective Action*. Baltimore: Johns Hopkins University Press.

Havelock, Eric A. [1957] 1964. *The Liberal Temper in Greek Politics*. New Haven: Yale University Press.

Held, Virginia. 1970. *The Public Interest and Individual Interests*. New York: Basic Books.

Hirschman, Albert O. 1977. *The Passions and the Interests*. Princeton: Princeton University Press.

——. [1986] 1992. "The Concept of Interest: From Euphemism to Tautology." In *Rival Views of Market Society*. Cambridge: Harvard University Press.

Hobbes, Thomas. [1651] 1947. *Leviathan*. London: J.M. Dent and Sons.

Holmes, Stephen. 1990. "The Secret History of Self-Interest." In *Beyond Self-Interest*, ed. Jane J. Mansbridge. Chicago: University of Chicago Press.

Hume, David. [1739–40] 1978. *A Treatise of Human Nature*. 2d ed. Ed. L. A. Selby-Bigge and P. H. Nidditch. Oxford: Oxford University Press.

Isaac, R. Mark, Kenneth F. McCue, and Charles R. Plott. 1985. "Public Goods: Provision in an Experimental Environment." *Journal of Public Economics* 26:51–74.

Lavere, George. 1983. "The Problem of the Common Good in Saint Augustine's *Civitas Terrena*." *Augustinian Studies* 14:1–10.

Levi, Margaret. 1988. *Of Rule and Revenue*. Berkeley: University of California Press.

Lewis, Ewart. 1940. "Natural Law and Expediency in Medieval Political Theory." *Ethics* 50:144–63.

———. 1954. *Medieval Political Ideas*. London: Routledge and Kegan Paul.

Lippmann, Walter. 1956. *The Public Philosophy*. New York: Mentor.

Locke, John. [1679–89] 1965. *Two Treatises of Government*. Ed. Peter Laslett. Cambridge: Cambridge University Press.

Loeb, James. 1981. "Introduction." In *Augustine's* City of God, ed. James Loeb. Cambridge: Harvard University Press.

Lovejoy, Arthur O. 1961. *Reflections on Human Nature*. Baltimore: Johns Hopkins University Press.

Luce, R. D., and H. Raiffa. 1957. *Games and Decisions: Introduction and Critical Survey*. New York: Wiley.

Mansbridge, Jane J. [1980] 1983. *Beyond Adversary Democracy*. Chicago: University of Chicago Press.

———. 1990a. "The Rise and Fall of Self-Interest in the Explanation of Political Life." In *Beyond Self-Interest*, ed. Jane J. Mansbridge. Chicago: University of Chicago Press.

———. 1990b. "On the Relation of Altruism and Self-Interest." In *Beyond Self-Interest*, ed. Jane J. Mansbridge. Chicago: University of Chicago Press.

———. 1992. "A Deliberative Theory of Interest Representation." In *The Politics of Interests: Interest Groups Transformed*, ed. Mark Petracca. Boulder: Westview Press.

———. 1994. "Rational Choice Gains by Losing." *Political Psychology* 16:137–55.

McCracken, George E. 1981. "Introduction." In *Augustine*, City of God, trans. George E. McCracken. Cambridge: Harvard University Press/Loeb Classical Library.

Meyers, Milton L. 1983. *The Soul of Modern Economic Man: Ideas of Self-Interest, Thomas Hobbes to Adam Smith*. Chicago: University of Chicago Press.

Mill, John Stuart. [1859] 1947. *On Liberty*. New York: Appleton-Century-Crofts.

Minow, Martha. 1987. "Justice Engendered: Foreword to the Supreme Court 1986 Term." *Harvard Law Review* 101:10–95.

More, Thomas. [1516] 1895. *Utopia*. Trans. Ralph Robynson. 1551. Oxford: Oxford University Press.

Nussbaum, Martha Craven. 1995. "Emotions and Women's Capabilities." In *Women, Culture, and Development*, ed. Martha Craven Nussbaum and Jonathan Glover. Oxford: Oxford University Press.

North, Douglass C. 1981. *Structure and Change in Economic History* New York: Norton.

———. 1990. *Institutional Change and Economic Performance*. Cambridge: Cambridge University Press.

Nowak, Martin A., and Karl Sigmund. 1992. "Tit for Tat in Heterogeneous Populations." *Nature* 355:250–52.

Olson, Mancur. [1965] 1971. *The Logic of Collective Action*. Cambridge: Harvard University Press.

Ostrom, Elinor. 1990. *Governing the Commons*. Cambridge: Cambridge University Press.

———. 1992. *Crafting Institutions for Self-Governing Irrigation Systems*. San Francisco: ICS (Institute for Contemporary Studies) Press.

The Oxford English Dictionary. 1989. J. A. Simpson and E. S. C. Weiner, eds. Oxford: Oxford University Press.

Pitkin, Hanna Fenichel. 1967. *The Concept of Representation*. Berkeley: University of California Press.

Plato. [412–348 b.c.] 1963. *Republic*. In *The Collected Dialogues*, ed. Edith Hamilton and Huntington Cairns, trans. Paul Shorey. Princeton: Princeton University Press.

Rorty, Amélie Oksenberg. 1985. "Varieties of Rationality, Varieties of Emotion." *Social Science Information* 24:343–53.

Sabel, Charles. 1993. "Studied Trust: Building New Forms of Cooperation in a Volatile Economy." In *Explorations in Economic Sociology*, ed. Richard Swedberg. New York: Russell Sage.

Schelling, Thomas C. [1960] 1963. *The Strategy of Conflict*. Cambridge: Harvard University Press.

Schmitter, Philippe C. 1995. "The Irony of Modern Democracy and the Viability of Efforts to Improve its Practice." In *Associations and Democracy,* ed. Joshua Cohen and Joel Rogers.

Shepsle, Kenneth A. 1989. "Studying Institutions: Some Lessons from the Rational Choice Approach." *Journal of Theoretical Politics* 1:131–49.

Smith, Steven Rathgeb, and Michael Lipsky. 1993. *Nonprofits for Hire: The Welfare State in the Age of Contracting*. Cambridge: Harvard University Press.

Sorauf, Frank. 1962. "The Conceptual Muddle." In *The Public Interest: NOMOS V*, ed. Carl J. Friedrich. New York: Atherton.

Students for a Democratic Society. 1962. "The Port Huron Statement." Reprinted in James Miller, *Democracy Is in the Streets*. New York: Simon and Schuster, 1987.

Sunstein, Cass R. 1984. "Naked Preferences and the Constitution." *Columbia Law Review* 84:1689–1732.

———. 1988. "Beyond the Republican Revival." *Yale Law Journal* 97:1539–90.

Taylor, Charles. 1989. *Sources of the Self*. Cambridge: Harvard University Press.

Taylor, Michael. [1976] 1987. *The Possibility of Cooperation*. Cambridge: Cambridge University Press.

Tocqueville, Alexis de. [1835–40] 1954. *Democracy in America*. Trans. Henry Reeve and Phillips Bradley. 2 vols. New York: Vintage.

Truman, David. 1951. *The Governmental Process*. New York: Knopf.

Wolin, Sheldon S. 1960. *Politics and Vision*. Boston: Little, Brown.

Young, Iris Marion. [1987] 1988. "Impartiality and the Civic Public." In *Feminism as Critique: On the Politics of Gender*, ed. Seyla Benhabib and Drucilla Cornell. Minneapolis: University of Minnesota Press.

———. 1990. *Justice and the Politics of Difference*. Princeton: Princeton University Press.

———. 1995. "Social Groups in Associative Democracy." In *Associations and Democracy,* ed. Joshua Cohen and Joel Rogers.

2
CRAIG CALHOUN

The Public Good as a Social and Cultural Project

A good deal of ink has been spilled in arguments over whether the public good is distinct from the sum of private goods, and if so, how. Broadly utilitarian approaches have been pervasive not just in economics but in legal reasoning and politics. By contrast, parts of both conservative and radical traditions have long stressed that the goods that unite people cannot be reduced to individual interests. Individuals are not independent, and their interests are always shaped and reshaped through social life rather than fixed in advance. Accordingly, we cannot explain social life nontautologically in terms of individual interests alone. Instead of summation of individual interests, such theorists have asserted alternative conceptions of the public good, starting with classical ideas of moral virtue. In recent years, a number of theorists have tried to build on this heritage and to offer a "communitarian" alternative to conventional political and economic discourse. This would restore moral language and ethical reasoning to public discourse alongside more utilitarian understandings of interests. Although I am sympathetic to much of the communitarian effort and wish to appropriate parts of it, I want to call attention here to issues that make it more problematic than most communitarians take it to be. In particular, I suggest that in considering the public good we need to think more clearly of the public as a realm or realms of discourse and contestation within which both identities and interests are constituted. The public good cannot be discovered independently of this public process, by communitarians any more than utilitarians.

The language of community can be misleading, first of all, because it elides the important differences between webs of personal relations rooted in face-to-face interaction and large-scale societal organization dependent on complex organizations, markets, and various other forms of indirect relationships and representation through cultural categories rather than personal networks. Second, communitarians too commonly present the public good as though it could be assessed objectively and externally, as though they could offer a form of cost-benefit analysis alternative to one based on economic interests. This happens mainly when the public good is seen ahistorically in substantive terms — for example, as rooted in communities that always already exist or in Aristotelian virtues — rather than in terms of historically specific human action. This draws attention away from the continuous reshaping of the identity of any public and of communities within it as well as of the goods which different actors pursue. Third, communitarian thought often neglects to ask questions like Which public? and Whose good? The community as a whole is too easily assumed to be unitary or

This is a revised version of a keynote presentation to a Lilly Foundation conference, Indianapolis, November 1993. I am grateful for comments from Lis Clemens, Woody Powell, and Jonathan Sher.

at least differentiated only into equivalent subsidiary communities and thus the potential bearer of a single good.

In each of these three senses, communitarian thought often militates against seeing the public good as a social and cultural project. It presumes a unity that needs to be examined precisely and sometimes questioned and that in any case can exist only to the extent that it has been constructed by various actors. Modifying *good* with the term *public* ought to signal to us the importance of discourses across lines of difference and the creation of settings in which the project of relating different goods (and different communities) to each other can be pursued. To see the public good as a simple unity would generally be misleading with regard to small-scale local communities but is necessarily so with regard to countries of hundreds of millions of highly diverse citizens.

The issue is not whether to accept exclusive reliance on utilitarian individualism, but how to go beyond it. The communitarian strategy stresses substantive conceptions of the common good. Community is an aspect of the common good; at the same time, a particular social whole — the community — is seen as the bearer of this common good. This, however, closes off in advance what should be the active and never-ending process of constituting and reconstituting both collective and individual identities. I want to argue instead that even if we accept community as an important positive value (as indeed I do), we need to distinguish that generic characteristic of life together or mode of social organization from actual, historically specific communities. The latter are more arbitrary and more subject to changing constitutions than communitarian theory generally recognizes. At the same time, we need to distinguish community from public life and see public life as a process, one often involving multiple discourses or institutional bases for discourse, in which individual and collective identities are reshaped through communication and interaction and in which alternative conceptions of what is good are brought to the fore. This argument necessarily leaves the actual constitution of any collective identities or claims on individuals indeterminate and open to social, political, and cultural construction and contest.

As befits a southerner and a preacher's son, let me use a story, a parable, to illustrate this indeterminacy of concrete communities and collective goods identified with them. It is an especially appropriate story because it concerns Indianapolis, where the Lilly Foundation brought scholars together to inquire into "private action and the public good," thus initiating the proximate chain of events leading to this book.

WHICH PUBLIC, WHOSE GOOD?

Through the first half of the twentieth century, Indianapolis had a thriving African-American population, with industry, a nationally important jazz scene, and a sense of identity. Spatially compact, partly because of forced segregation, this population formed two communities, northwest of downtown and on the near eastside. They were internally diverse and included their own public institutions like churches and theaters, their own commercial establishments, and both prosperous and depressed sections.

Like many African-American communities, those in Indianapolis were hit hard by the Great Depression. After World War II, economic recovery was only partial, and the cohesiveness of the communities was undermined both by new opportunities for individual mobility that drew many talented young people away and by the penetration of large-scale business organizations replacing local establishments. Each community nonetheless survived, maintained in significant part by close-knit webs of interpersonal relationships and mutual support and also by shared knowledge of important local traditions. But to outsiders and to some of Indianapolis's black elite, the communities appeared mainly as depressed and as public problems. They were finally destroyed in the name of community development.

Earlier efforts to improve the lot of impoverished African Americans had presumed that they would stay more or less where they were. Public housing was thus constructed in the midst of the existing communities. In this context, the public housing projects became relatively stable socially. But the new thinking did not see maintenance of community as a value in and of itself and instead sought to disperse what had been the concentrations of African Americans in traditionally black communities and to bring in new economic resources by removing so-called eyesores and building new buildings for new uses. A centerpiece in this effort was the construction of the Indiana University-Purdue University at Indianapolis campus near the center of what had been an African-American community. Public housing projects, among the country's oldest, were razed to make way for university student housing. Thousands of people were forced to move.

Developers championing revitalization were aided by well-intentioned philanthropists and urban planners. They sought to make a better Indianapolis community, conceptualizing this community on the level of the city as a whole, rather than seeing Indianapolis as a public realm within which many communities and diverse groups might need to maintain distinctive identities or want to contest their relationship to the whole. They built office complexes that made downtown Indianapolis look more and more the same as other American cities and that simultaneously left streets full of cars and empty of pedestrians, deprived the great downtown department stores of their markets, and dispersed African Americans from what had been real, centered communities into a mix of suburbs and more impoverished urban districts.

The older black communities had also been bases for public participation. They housed a wide variety of voluntary associations and public institutions: major and vital churches, the Indianapolis *Leader,* the Flanner Guild, the Twentieth Century Literary Society (and many others), the Woman's Improvement Club of Indianapolis, and the Afro-American

Council. The African-American communities were prominent enough to lure national organizations like the Knights of Pythias and the Anti-Lynching League to hold meetings there (Ferguson 1988; Specht 1989). They were politically organized and indeed began to shift allegiance from Republican to Democratic parties in 1924, eight to twelve years before the main national realignment of black voters, because of their own effective mobilization as well as because of the reactionary leadership of the Indiana Republicans, who were linked to the Ku Klux Klan (Griffin 1983).

The black communities were also centers of employment and business development. Most famously, one was the base for Madame C. J. Walker, the first African-American woman to become a millionaire entrepreneur. Madame, as she was known, employed three thousand people in the manufacture of cosmetics and hair products, with a payroll of about two hundred thousand dollars by 1917 (Doyle 1989). Beyond party politics and business, her community had been a center of artistic and cultural activity. It had remained a community not just because of jobs, but because of a sense of cultural continuity — something we might consider a public value in itself.

But most black kids in Indianapolis today do not know that J. J. Johnson, Freddie Hubbard, and other jazz greats were born there. Johnson in fact moved back, but in four years did not play publicly in Indianapolis, complaining that there was simply not the audience that existed, say, in Chicago. Madame C. J. Walker became a lady an isolated theater is named after — if she is remembered at all.[1] The solidarity and continuity of the Indianapolis African-American community were reduced in nearly every aspect of the public realm.

The moral to my story is this: public life depends on communities — multiple and diverse — but not on the presumption of or attempt to create a single larger community. Even on the scale of Indianapolis, let alone on the scale of America, to think of the public good as equivalent to the good of *a* community can lead us to underestimate the workings of power and large-scale economic forces in reshaping the very communities in which we live. It is also apt to divert attention from the diverse, concretely interpersonal communal settings within which people are knit together in favor of focus on larger categories of common identity. And it inhibits concentration on the problem of how members of such communities — and in general, people who are different from each other — might enter into the project of public discourse about what would be good to do. Positing *a* community as the basis of *the* public good is apt to obscure contests over collective identity and disempower those whose projects are not in accord with those of dominant groups.

1. Madame Walker is, of course, celebrated in some teaching of African-American history on a national scale. But her legacy has become general and abstract, not rooted in locality or everyday life.

IS THE PUBLIC A COMMUNITY?

In recent years, American politics has become visibly focused on struggles over self-definition and collective identity. African Americans, Asians, Hispanics, women, gay men and lesbians, and a host of other groups have sought both to constitute their own collective identities as meaningful for each other and to win for themselves positive recognition in the broader public and sometimes various material benefits.[2] This has meant confronting internal differences as well as differences from "mainstream America." Does one speak of Hispanics, thus, or of Puerto Riqueños, Cubans, and both Chicanos and Chicanas?

These struggles feel newly challenging, but the politics of identity is not new; it is a part of all politics insofar as actors contest the identities under which they are incorporated into political processes and the identity of the broader political field itself. The politics of identity is at stake when Muslims debate their loyalty to secular states, nations without states, and international Islam. It is at stake when workers are urged to identify with the labor movement rather than with their employers, their local communities, their ethnic groups, their crafts, or their religions. Social movements, political action, and public life all depend on the constitution of certain identities as salient and in turn open participants to processes of struggle over and possible reformulation of identities at both collective and individual levels. As the name "Evangelical Christian" has become a potent public identity in recent years, for example, it has changed not just political processes but personal lives and local communities.

The politics of identity often appears as an assertion of difference.[3] In response, many of us grow angry over what we take as rejections of our community by one another, refusals to acknowledge the priority of the common good over the various separate claims of identity and interest. One-sided articulation of differences can indeed be a problem. But we commonly fail to see that the whole is an ideological construct, that it privileges certain constituent identities over others. This is a tendency not just in everyday discourse but in otherwise more sophisticated social and political theory. The public is a realm in which differences are articulated and notions of the public good constituted; it is poorly grasped by the language of community, especially when the community is assumed to be preexisting and relatively fixed.

In facing up to a divided America and an even more divided world, we face problems that have developed not just because of what we do not share, but because of something we do share. We share an idea that really strong public life

2. For discussion of the substantial literature on these processes, see Calhoun ed. 1994 and Calhoun 1995.

3. It is of course equally true that every assertion of difference between groups involves a corresponding claim to identity (and thus implicit sameness) within groups. See discussion in Calhoun 1995, esp. chap. 7.

depends on agreement as to basic values and identities. When speaking of the public good, in other words, we tend to emphasize an image of our similarity as members of a category — Americans, *the* public — rather than the more differentiated relations we may have as members of concrete social networks and interdependent social systems.[4] The image of categorical similarity ironically shapes the thinking of both those who lay claim to the language of the public good and those who see it as repressive. The former seek to identify the underlying commonalities that constitute the public as a category of similar persons. The latter charge that such commonalities and apparent agreements must be coerced, a product of repression of some more essential difference. Both sides miss the possibility that what makes a public is not agreement among interlocutors but a discussion in which each party gives reasons for and attempts to understand views that may be quite divergent.[5]

The result is that the idea of public in the phrase *public good* is generally either taken for granted as a sum of what we share or rejected out of hand in the name of what we do not. But we are not in this situation because of these new conflicts; they simply reflect and exacerbate an old problem. We have by several routes been drawn into an impoverished and static way of thinking and speaking of the collectivities whose interests or welfare we describe as public.

Consider, for example, changes in the way religion appears in public discourse. Americans have not by any means given up religion or even denied it entrance to the public square, as Peter Berger and Richard Neuhaus once asserted (1978). Rather, we have reduced religion to an interest group, reduced religious thought to clichés, and made of religion something to be invoked, not argued over.[6] It is not the same to have Billy Graham or Pat Robertson speak *for* Christians as to have manifold and diverse arguments carried out *among* Christians (and adherents of other religions) in terms of their faith as well as their perceptions of the world — as was the case, for example, in the era of the Founding or the Second Great Awakening. When politicians today invoke the biblical language of covenant, to take one example, they are making an appealing gesture but seldom either taking theology very seriously or expecting us to introduce the language of covenant into our daily conversations. It is now a word for ceremonial speeches, and so, I am afraid, are most other religious terms that enter public discourse. Soul and sin and redemption, meanwhile, either remain closeted in the putatively private discourse of religious communities or make us shudder

by the manner of their attempted introduction into public discourse. We have, in short, lost the ability to carry out political arguments in or with relationship to religious terms, and because so much of America's political culture drew on religious vocabulary — even when speakers were militant freethinkers and deists — in the absence of an equally rich replacement, this impoverishes our discourse.

At the same time, attempts to renew religious discourse are as apt to obscure as to address the underlying issues of what sort of communities and what sorts of public life we have and want. Many such attempts, for example, introduce the language of community uncritically as a reference to a global whole rather than a means to differentiate among practical clusters of concrete social relations. With or without religious language, we also need sociological and political language that does justice to societal complexity and provides adequately for contestation in public discourse. It is on these points that I raise questions about — or try to supplement — the work of a number of so-called communitarians. I have in mind thinkers like Robert Bellah, Amitai Etzioni, Charles Taylor, and Alasdair MacIntyre. I want to walk with these communitarians through the valley of utilitarian despair, but on emerging I shall insist that although their challenge to atomistic, interest-based individualism is powerful and their communitarian program in part attractive, the ideals of community remain deeply insufficient as a basis for thinking about and trying to bring about the public good.

The problem is the result of too much emphasis on the word *good* and not enough on the word *public*. Keeping the theme of private action for the public good very much in mind, I challenge the distinction of public from private on which it relies — which, alas, is the same one that allows us to imagine that giant corporations are best understood as creatures of private agreements among individuals and thus deserve to be granted protections from the public gaze. My contention, in a phrase, is that an important task for the so-called voluntary sector is to focus less exclusively on finding and serving the good — the utilitarian interests or the Aristotelian virtues — of a postulated public and more on building the conditions of public life so that publics always in the process of making themselves might also make themselves good.

One key to this effort is to keep the distinction between a community and a public meaningful. The binding interpersonal commitments that make up community are important in themselves and for the individual members of such communities. John Rawls, for example, is right to see the necessity of such immediate, largely face-to-face associations within a larger society and to qualify the individualism of his theory of justice with reference to such "social unions" (Rawls 1971, 421–22). But although these social unions are significant potential bases for participation in public life, reference to them as preexisting social units does not provide an adequate basis for reckoning the interests of a public. In the first place, while society may be in part, as Rawls puts it, a

---

4. On the analytic language of category and network, see White 1992 and Nadel 1954, 1957.

5. See discussion in Calhoun 1995, especially chapters 2 and 3 and the conclusion, of how communication across lines of difference involves processes of change, not merely translation into a metalanguage that can express underlying agreement.

6. See Carter 1993, though his argument is stated in somewhat tendentiously strong terms.

union of diverse social unions, it is not only that. Societal integration in any modern country is accomplished not only in the manner of the personal relationships that establish community but through markets, bureaucracies, and other large-scale and largely impersonal mechanisms.[7] This means that public issues are not only the sum of the directly interpersonal relations of communal life; public discourse must include attempts to address the workings of these more impersonal social systems. Moreover, if the social unions of Rawls's image are really diverse, then any attempt to achieve voluntary relations among them must depend on a public discourse that is qualitatively different from that which takes place within the purview of more or less binding communal relationships. While public discourse may itself be voluntary, it is not about solely voluntary interpersonal relationships. It is also about large-scale patterns of power and systemic organization. Although public life may depend on relationships and capacities formed in private, the public good is not the sum of any preexisting private or particular interests or a compromise among them. A public, in any large contemporary society, is constituted largely among strangers and among people differing in deep and influential ways. The public good needs to be seen as dynamic, as a project in which varied actors participate, speaking through different cultural understandings, never altogether agreeing on just what the public is, yet producing it continuously if incompletely through their very discourse.

MORE THAN ONE ROAD BEYOND ATOMISM AND SELF-INTEREST

Showing the limits to individualism is central to communitarianism. In many versions, perhaps most famously in *Habits of the Heart,* this argument is presented as a critique of American or modern culture (Bellah et al. 1985). In other, more theoretical guises, the communitarian argument is presented not against "ordinary culture" so much as against pernicious philosophies. MacIntyre (1981, 1988), for example, writes sometimes as though history were made directly by philosophers, who have only to think an idea for it to wreck havoc. In both versions, the central ideas communitarians challenge have been the atomism and instrumentalism of the liberal tradition. Jeremy Bentham is perhaps the paradigmatic philosopher of such instrumental individualism (though sharply to the progovernment side of a divided liberalism). "The community is a fictitious *body,*" he wrote, "composed of the individual persons who are considered as constituting as it were its *members.* The interest of the community then is, what? — the sum of the interests of the several

members who compose it" (Bentham 1970, 12). Community, for Bentham, is an aggregate of autonomous individuals, not a creature of intersubjectivity or social relations.[8]

Communitarians offer three main sorts of objections to this view: (1) it is impossible to make sense of individuals as creatures so radically prior to community or social life; (2) community itself bears value distinct from the values or interests of current members of communities; and (3) the ways in which individual interests coalesce into collective interests is not a matter of mere addition but involves some internal social and cultural relations or interdependence.

Individualism, communitarians argue persuasively, requires certain social and cultural conditions. The idealized self-sufficiency of much modern individualist ideology — notably in America — is not simply exaggerated but based on illusions and failure to recognize the actual contributions of a variety of communal relations to the creation and nurturance of individuals. The ideal of radical self-sufficiency was probably illusory in this way even on the nineteenth-century frontier; rugged individualists often depended on each other's support in tight-knit communities. This ideal is still more illusory in the 1990s world of giant corporations, global trade, and electronic media. As Taylor (1989) has asked: doesn't the radical prioritization of the individual self depend on some basic misunderstandings about what it means to be an individual, including the need to participate in the shared community of speakers of a language and the way in which our individual thoughts and actions depend on a background of practices, institutions, and understandings that we do not create as individuals? If we treat communities only as sums of individuals, how do we account for the genesis of these individuals: their nurturance as children, their reliance on shared culture — including the culture of individualism — and their psychical as well as social dependence on interpersonal relations and institutions? It is not just that behind every great corporate leader stands a secretary, a father and mother, and a board of directors, but that the very heroic individualism of these corporate leaders depends on the institutional availability of the roles they inhabit, the regimes of private property they dominate, the fiction of the corporation as a legal individual.

If individuals are not altogether and radically prior to community and social life, should we not see community as bearing value in itself, not only expressing the value inherent in the summed interests of community members? Taylor and many other communitarians have set out to articulate notions that some goods are irreducibly social. They belong to us only as members of communities or societies, not purely as individuals. This may be true in the thin sense of many of the so-called collective goods of economists and rational choice

---

7. Following Talcott Parsons, Jürgen Habermas (1984, 1988) identifies these large-scale modes of societal integration with the "nonlinguistic steering media" of money and power because their basic organizations are not established through the intentions and meaningful interaction of individuals.

8. See Mansbridge, "On the Nature of the Public Good" (in this volume), for a related discussion of the issue of aggregative vs. holistic concepts of the public good.

theorists, but most communitarians wish to describe a much thicker sense in which our goods are irreducibly social. Thus Taylor writes,

> As individuals we value certain things; we find certain outcomes positive. But these things can only be good in this way, or satisfying or positive after their particular fashion, because of the background understanding which has developed in our culture. Thus I may value the fulfillment which comes from a certain kind of authentic self-expression or the experience which arises from certain works of art, or outcomes in which people stand with each other on a footing of frankness and equality. But these things are only possible against the background of a certain culture. . . .
>
> If these things are goods, then other things being equal, so must the culture be which makes them possible. If I want to maximize these goods, then I must want to preserve and strengthen this culture. But the culture as a good, or more cautiously as the locus of some goods (for there might be much that is reprehensible in it as well), is not an individual good. (Taylor 1995)

Taylor's argument is, I think, a sensible one and, coupled with Amartya Sen's famous analysis of "welfarism," shows that a completely utilitarian notion of the public good cannot be adequate.[9] Such a notion suggests among other things that what is good about any social state of affairs can be decomposed into goods for members considered as individuals. But this runs directly counter to recognizing either (a) the way in which shared culture makes possible the very constitution of certain phenomena as goods (for example, the appreciation of abstract art or the enjoyment of Mexican food), and (b) the way in which membership in particular social associations (that may indeed confer benefits on individuals) also commits individuals to particular understandings of their common good such that their welfare functions can no longer be assessed as prior to the collectivity.

In general, communitarians do not suggest that we simply fail to value community or that in our individualism we have no common values. Rather, the point is that we are inhibited in giving adequate weight to the communitarian values we already hold, partly because our reliance on utilitarian individualist thinking makes it hard for us to articulate our values on community. We talk a great deal about making our communities safe, we ask which suburbs will make good communities for our children, we talk nostalgically about the good old days when community was strong. But we have trouble translating this talk into the right sort of action, communitarians suggest, as when we move from one town

to another rather than striving to make the first a stronger community.

This is not entirely because our talk of community is mere lip service. Observant communitarian critics see that Americans (or should I say, *even* Americans?) are deeply invested in ideals of community. These ideals have informed Americans' high rates of participation in churches and other religious organizations, in voluntary associations and public service groups, in private charitable activities, in the founding of private colleges and universities, and in democratic self-governance. Rather, the problem lies, according to many communitarians, in the difficulty we have giving weight to community when faced with competing goods.[10] At the heart of the argument is the sound point that in discourses from politics to law to economics to ethics to personal well-being we have lost our ability to articulate the value of community.[11] And this loss is partly due to the proliferation of individualism in philosophies and legal doctrines as well as to the slightly less sophisticated theories of talk show hosts.

It is important, however, to ask just how we should understand community in such an argument. Is it a general term for social relations as distinct from the illusion of autonomous individuals? If so, it problematically lumps together very different kinds and arrangements of social relations. Is it a reference to a specific mode of being together — for example, to feeling at one with each other? If so, it runs the risk of imposing one categorical idea about the whole community on constituent groups and individuals. Is community a term for unchosen bonds among human beings or for those forged in conscious discourse, choice, and interaction? It is not

9. Sen (1979, 468) defines *welfarism* as the utilitarian position that "the judgment of the relative goodness of alternative states of affairs must be based exclusively on, and taken as an increasing function of, the respective collections of individual utilities in these states."

10. The current flowering of a political communitarianism is particularly American, and arguments about individual and community have a special salience in American history (a point noted by Phillips 1993 in his sustained, if tendentious, critique of communitarianism). Nonetheless, the broad outlines of the current communitarian position are shared among a wide variety of thinkers in many countries. Many of these have been conservatives, and part of what is distinctive about the current communitarian politics in America is that it is for the most part a branch of the Left. This is not unique, however, as a moment's reflection on nineteenth-century Europe reminds us (remember communism?). The individualism/communitarianism debate did not start with John Rawls and his critics or with the rise of neo-Aristotelianism or even with the rediscovery of classical republicanism. It has been with us throughout the modern era.

11. Thus the political arguments of Alasdair MacIntyre and Charles Taylor are equally moral ones. Taylor has stressed the importance of being able to articulate community as one of what he calls our "strong moral sources." Kai Erikson has tried to show how legal proceedings value economic goods but not the less tangible goods of community; Wendell Berry has argued in a different genre but a similar vein about how we accidentally lose community because we don't recognize its value in a host of decisions we make under the influence of industrial culture. Amitai Etzioni has set out to show the importance of community to the development of a policy analysis adequately sensitive to moral and human issues. The list could go on.

enough, in other words, to know that human beings are social as much as individual or that community has a value. It is crucial to know how to differentiate varying kinds of appeals to social values that may constitute the public good.

Communitarian arguments move us on the path to understanding the public good as a social and cultural project because they show us why the public good must be understood in terms of social relations and culture. At the same time, they inhibit further progress in two ways. First, the communitarian discourse obscures the extent to which different sorts of social relations figure in different kinds and scales of collectivities. I would prefer to keep the terms *community* and *public* distinct to signal one aspect of this and at the same time to counterpose both to systemic social organization that takes place outside either communal organizations of interdependent social relations or culturally differentiated and discursively mediated publics. Second, the communitarian discourse obscures the extent to which social collectivities are forged rather than found. It is not enough to assert that the public good is more than the sum of individual interests or that a community is more than the sum of individual members. This leaves open a crucial variable: the extent to which people experience their social relations as "primordial," or given immutably to them by the past or external forces, and the extent to which they are able to reconstitute their social and cultural lives together through their conscious action and communication with each other.

Something of the second issue is signaled in the passage quoted above from Taylor, in which he speaks very confidently of "this culture" and "the culture," in ways that suggest that he imagines them to be rather strongly integrated and bounded. This singular and integral notion of culture invites poststructuralist critiques and the assertion of innumerable claims to subcultural autonomy. Taylor's terms keep us from recognizing that the sort of cultural context or background that makes possible both collective and individual goods is always plural, always in process, and never altogether coherent. There is never a single tradition to be preserved and strengthened by itself, but always a field within which multiple traditions contend, each weaving into the fabric of the others even if they maintain recognizable distinction. This multiculturalism is not always happy but rather rent through with power and violence as well as excitement and mutual influence. But neither is it merely some new ideal; it is the inextricable condition of life, varying in extent but present throughout world history. Even Confucian China, paradigm case of a self-declared integrated culture, was simultaneously Buddhist and Taoist China, was home to iconoclastic schools of painting and poetry that sometimes drew more eyes and ears than the putative mainstream, and was superimposed, in a sense, as an elite project on numerous and often regionally distinct folk cultures. So it is with America: capitalist, democratic nation of immigrants, "lifestyle enclaves," youth culture, and the opposition of Main Street to both Wall Street and the Beltway.

Taylor's invocation of the common culture as substance rather than discourse was an aspect of another argument; he might revise it on further reflection. In any case, his is hardly an extreme example.[12] But the tendency to speak of the culture that enables us to constitute our public goods as though it were or could be unitary is a problem, and it is worth noting that from this perspective it is all too easy for cultural diversity to come to seem a problem, and not the normal condition of at least large-scale social life. The theme of unitary culture, moreover, is linked to the problematic notion of national community.[13]

COMMUNITY OF THE WHOLE?

Communitarian theory coincides with certain habits of ordinary speech in trying to describe what knits together the country as a whole (and sometimes even international collectivities) through the language of community. As we have seen, this exaggerates the extent to which very large scale societal organization is accomplished through directly interpersonal relationships. Even where it is acknowledged that community may not always be harmonious, communitarian language tends to emphasize a sense of mutuality and reciprocity and the notion that the large-scale polity can be an equally beneficent totality for all. The polis, as MacIntyre (1988, 200) puts it, "is directed at achieving all the goods of its citizens." It is no accident, likewise, that this formulation treats the citizens' goods as existing (if not necessarily known) in advance of public life rather than as established within individual and collective projects.

Questions about whether America is really a large, internally integral and homogenous community are at least as long-standing as the debates between Federalists and Antifederalists.[14] Early in the nineteenth century, as Americans began to develop national celebrations and myths, the notion

12. Taylor (1992) has, for example, distanced himself from MacIntyre's Aristotelian claim to locate an enduringly compelling substantive definition of the good life.

13. The idea that cultures appear as discrete and internally integrated is a compelling one throughout modern social science, but it may itself be a reflection of nationalist assumptions more than empirical observation or historical analysis (see Calhoun 1995, chaps. 3, 8). In their different ways, both structuralism and functionalism have run into this problem. The tradition of writing history within national boundaries has reinforced the problematic sense of cultural unity, though this has been challenged by some writers of comparative sociology and world history; not least Pitirim Sorokin (1957).

14. This was a manifest issue *between* Federalists and Antifederalists but also a hidden issue on occasion because the habit of not distinguishing national from local community was widespread. Madison, for example, uses the term *community* throughout the *Federalist Papers* in ways that do not distinguish the local and the national (or for that matter the small national elite from the larger national populace). For example, from *Federalist* 49: "The most rational government will not find it a superfluous advantage, to have the prejudices of the community on its side" (Madison 1961, 315).

was widely promulgated that Americans should imagine themselves spiritually descended from the *community* that landed at Plymouth Rock. The language of a single, large national community became ingrained in American speech partly through political rhetoric and partly through the mythologizing of American history carried out by popular historians like Charles Beard, especially in the wake of the Civil War. But this mythology did not take root evenly or everywhere. The South found such myths less compelling, for example, even before the Civil War began to be foreshadowed. Jamestown never became the basis for a comparable story. After the War between the States, the fabric of the nation was rewoven so effectively that, ironically, twentieth-century southerners feel generally more American than most others.

The notion of a unified national history combined with the elision between a small face-to-face community (the Pilgrims) and the larger subsequent nation support the illusion that scale doesn't matter. This illusion (and the mythic narrative that supported it) suppressed discourse on differences; each act of recalling the Founding — as in the pageants of grade school classes throughout the country — was also an act of forgetting that some came to America as slaves, that some were already here as indigenes, that others came as transported criminals, and that still others came as refugees from famine and political rather than religious repression. Differences in the way each group fit into American society were likewise forgotten in the reconstituting of the nation as a single community. As Ernst Renan wrote of France, "Forgetting, I would even go so far as to say historical error, is a crucial factor in the creation of a nation, which is why progress in historical studies often constitutes a danger for [the principle of] nationality. Indeed, historical enquiry brings to light deeds of violence which took place at the origin of all political formations, even those whose consequences have been altogether beneficial. Unity is always effected by means of brutality" (1990, 11).

The American ideology of being a national community — a city on the hill — has inspired not only high ideals but lower realities of prejudice against those who do not fit the model and fear of those in our midst who have seemed different in their ideals, cultures, or characters. This has worked on scales smaller than the nation as a whole. Recall Indianapolis and the way in which the positive venture of overall community improvement was linked with a failure to recognize the existing African-American communities.

Not only has national mythology encouraged the dominant culture's belief in a singular whole with little place for actively different minorities, but many minority groups have adopted similar ideologies of internal unity in the forging of their own identities and the forgetting of intranecine clashes — the solidarity of black nationalism, for example, rather than the tensions between black Muslims and black Christians, or black men and black women. Minority identities are forged not just in and for themselves, however, but in inter-

action with the broad processes of identity politics.[15] Sojourner Truth, for example, is remembered for words quoted on posters throughout America: "Ain't I a Woman?" Yet these are almost certainly not words she uttered, but rather the reconstruction of a white observer who heard her speak and rendered her words as he thought a Negro ought to have spoken. Sojourner Truth spoke Dutch as her first language and presumably an Afro-Dutch dialect as an adult. She passed her childhood in slavery, but in New York State, not in the South, and in the city, not the countryside. She taught herself to be a brilliant orator, but she did not speak in any presumptively singular black American dialect, neither that of the transcriber's imagination nor that of popular memory.[16] The internal diversity of African Americans, in other words, is as prone to be overlooked or denied as the diversity of the country as a whole.

The problem of relying on purely communitarian imagery to approach political culture becomes more acute in our present age of very large scale social integration, of mass media and giant corporations, and big government. The face-to-face communities in which we invest so much of our faith and hope appear to us as separate from the large-scale world of bureaucracies and the abstract images of various threatening categories of people whom we never meet in ordinary sociable interaction: the residents of inner city ghettos, the advocates of unpopular political positions, the adherents of alternative lifestyles, religious extremists. Within face-to-face communities, we recognize and deal with difference in terms of the individuals involved and our specific relations to them. Beyond this level, however, we are apt to think mainly in terms of categories — identities within which we regard individuals as essentially similar.[17] Thus Indianapolis leaders saw the city's African Americans in a relatively undifferentiated way and chose to eradicate the functioning commu-

15. As E. P. Thompson (1992, 7) has written with regard to eighteenth-century England, "Generalisations as to the universal of popular culture become empty unless they are placed within specific historical contexts. The plebeian culture which clothed itself in the rhetoric of 'custom' . . . was not self-defining or independent of external influences. It had taken form defensively, in opposition to the constraints and controls of the patrician rulers." And equally, there was not simply one plebeian culture, but a range of locally distinct ones.

16. See Donna Haraway's (1992) interesting discussion of this. By contrast, the speeches of white southerners and Yankees alike were generally transcribed in standard English even when their accents were thick and their grammar tended toward dialect.

17. The difference between such directly interpersonal relationships and reliance on categorical identities motivates attempts to try to achieve more and better interpersonal connections across racial lines. On the small scale of shared worship and summer camps, these have been a staple of religious groups' efforts to confront the issue of race. Some such groups have tried more substantial and long-term efforts — like relocating African Americans from Chicago's South Side to small towns in Indiana, where not only their economic prospects are better, but also their prospects for directly interpersonal relations across racial lines. See Paul Schnorr (1993).

nities along with the "social problems" that attracted outsiders' attention. Categorical identities are also at stake in the imagined community of the nation. The nation itself is often understood as one large category of essentially similar members rather than as a highly differentiated web of relationships among diverse people and groups. Minorities within the nation gain recognition mainly as categories — African Americans, Asians, Hispanics — not as parties to concrete relationships. This is partly the result of large scale, not an easily altered matter of attitude, but even so we need to keep in mind the implications of scale and not cultivate the illusion that the kinds of actions appropriate and adequate within face-to-face communities automatically translate into effective policies on a national scale.[18] We cannot solve problems like the deep racial divisions of American society simply by tending to the racial problems in our local communities. However commendable and valuable such actions may be, they cannot speak to the problems of the South Bronx and the South Side of Chicago, to the ghettoization and hypersegregation that guarantee that many blacks and whites will not see each other as neighbors in a community but as categories of threatening or simply distant strangers.

When we think that unity must be founded on sameness, then difference immediately arouses anxiety. The idea that we can be Americans only by being the same as each other actually makes our American identity very vulnerable. This sameness seems under attack from new waves of immigration, from new ideas about gender, from new claims by gay men and lesbians. How can we still be a community, we wonder, when we are so different from each other?

I do not mean to suggest that we have in the past always handled our problems well or enjoyed a better national community. We would be mistaken to think that all our problems are new or that in the past we had some perfect basis for national unity — some essential shared ingredient of the American soul which, now lost, can never be replaced. The idea that a once clearly common culture is only now threatened by diversity is simply false. Our American unity has always been a fabric subject to tears and reweaving; different cultures have long contended. So it is today.

But today, problems of diversity within the polity are exacerbated. In the first place, we have seen a change in political culture that makes it difficult — at least explicitly — to advocate simple repression of difference; we have developed a society based crucially on consent (even though consent may be engineered or coerced). Second, we have come to recognize and include in explicit ways within our political culture (and corresponding organizations) various categori-

cal identities — blacks, Asians, women, gun owners — that are highly effective in the mobilization of interest groups and social movements as well as salient objects of discourse. To offer a language of national community without explicitly recognizing the illegitimacy of repression and the diversity of legitimate identities within the polity is either to be naive or to attempt a performative erasure of actual conditions. Community — specific webs of dense and multiplex social relations — remains powerful as a way of achieving integration across lines of difference without repression. But it does this not at the level of the country as a whole but in numerous local constructions, crossings of specific boundaries, and mixing of specific identities. Some communities bring together people of different races, thus, but only within a common class. Others bring together people of different classes, but only within a common religious orientation, and so forth. The adding up of these multiple, cross-cutting connections is crucial to the achievement of social solidarity, but in itself it does not account for any whole or afford a basis for speaking of the public good.

Public discourse is a crucial means of achieving connections across the categorical divisions of the population, of which race is perhaps the most obvious. Yet the media and other institutions segment such discourse as much as unify it — identifying and even constituting group-specific markets — but also reproducing within various groups some of the same issues that beset the larger polity. There is, thus, a genuine nationwide black public sphere in America today.[19] It transcends locality and incorporates diverse African-American voices. It works through newspapers and radio talk shows, self-help programs, black Muslim preaching, and black feminist writing. While it may sometimes employ the language of a singular black community, discourse in this realm is public in the sense that it may be entered by members of many communities and addresses issues that cut across them; within it, various ideas of African-American identity and of the public good are formed and changed, not just reflected.

At the same time, however, African Americans have differential access to this public discourse, to its component discourses, and to the goods which it thematizes. Their everyday lives are grounded in communities of varying strength, for example, and communities which offer them varying social, economic, psychic, and intellectual resources for participation in the broader black public sphere (let alone in any cross-racial public spheres). Perhaps even a deeper threat than the division of America into communities that have a hard time speaking to each other is the division into those whose lives are rooted in supportive communities and those whose lives are not. The destruction of the Eastside community in Indianapolis, for example, both undercut black participation in public life by removing a communal base and radically

18. One of Ronald Reagan's famous lines was the argument in a television broadcast that balancing the federal budget was just the same as balancing the family checkbook. However reassuring such imagery, it is false and misleading. Such elisions of the distinction between large-scale systems of societal integration and immediate practices of the lifeworld is a basic source of much populist politics; see Calhoun (1988).

19. See the discussion of the Black public sphere in the special issue of *Public Culture* (Winter 1994).

reduced the intersections among groups of African Americans: middle-class professionals and unemployed youths, teenage mothers and political activists, passionate churchgoers and drug-users, jazz musicians and their audiences.

The social problems concentrated in African-American inner city ghettos seem as apt to produce despair as constructive action partly because of the seeming failures of previous attempts to integrate the American community conceived as a singular whole. To have tried to address racial inequality — however half-heartedly — and to have failed has changed the basic sense of what is possible for many Americans, including many well-intentioned liberal Americans. This pessimism cuts across racial lines. In Cornel West's (1993, 15) words, "The major enemy of black survival in America has been and is neither oppression nor exploitation but rather the nihilistic threat — that is, loss of hope and meaning. . . . The self-fulfilling prophecy of the nihilistic threat is that without hope there can be no future, that without meaning there can be no struggle."

The worry is spreading that America's history of racial abuse and oppression can no longer be redeemed. But the very way we talk about the public good may be part of the problem. By approaching it as a matter of ascertaining either the greatest good for the greatest number or the one right good for the community as a whole, we systematically prejudice our discourse against competing visions of the good affirmed by minorities. When we affirm universalistic accounts of the public good that turn out in practice to be based on taking the positions of the dominant culture as universal, we remove credibility from the public discourse that might help us deal with difference. This has been the problem with bourgeois individualist ideas that represented the universal man as a property owner, and with discourses of human rights that represented the universal human as a man. It is a pressing issue with regard to cultural diversity in America today because the majority discourse has so radically lost credibility in relation to some minority discourses and because commonplace attempts to redress imbalances (as through multicultural curricula in schools) too often amount to essentializations of particular minority identities. We need something more to foster a dynamic discourse about differences and the public good.

In a way, thinking of the race issue in the terms of the civil rights era has become ironically comforting for white Americans. We can view television representations of the bad old days — like the recent series "I'll Fly Away" — with a sense of progress that pulls our attention away from the continuing crisis (and that also implies that the main issue is whether *we* white people choose to accept black people). African Americans may no longer be excluded in the same ways from full participation in predominantly White communities or national public life, though such racism does continue. But the issue of race has been changed by the fact that for many Americans (including whites and others but especially blacks), poverty and oppression are not any longer primarily

experienced within strong communities offering members mutual support and sustenance. They are in many cases experienced in relative isolation by members of deeply damaged social groups, reproduced in a cycle of deepening crisis by troubled families and social institutions, amidst spreading violence as well as racism. As West (1993, 16) puts it, we have to face up to the "shattering of black civil society." This shattering has been produced in part by drugs and crimes and other familiar ills, but it was produced also by well-intentioned actions like the destruction of Eastside.

If problems of race (and closely correlated problems like drugs and AIDS and teenage pregnancy) are too commonly grasped in contemporary discourse as problems of individuals — individuals allegedly lacking morality or intelligence, for example, communitarian discourse tends to a symmetrical error. It turns our attention away from the large-scale political economic sources of these problems and toward a new discourse about "the deserving poor." White liberals delight in novels by black women that describe their strong families, but the attraction is partly rooted in the contrast to pervasive images of a very different kind of life in many of America's black ghettos. Reading Toni Morrison is too often linked to a fantasy — not her fantasy, but that of readers drawn to the illusion that simply opening the boundaries of implicitly white American community life will solve the problem of race that troubles our conscience.[20] But an end to racism doesn't mean merely letting nice, middle-class black families live unmolested in suburban neighborhoods. Nor is tolerance the solution to teenage pregnancy. To redeem ourselves, we need to reach for new moral (and political-economic) resources, ones that will reach *beyond* community to produce basic social structural transformations. Without such transformation, talk of community will remain illusory even at the local scale and especially at the national.

PUTTING THE PUBLIC BACK IN PUBLIC GOOD

A strengthening of local communities — and for that matter of "communities without propinquity" — is all to the good and may provide important bases for public life, but in and of itself it is no substitute for invigorating the public sphere.[21] While communitarian discourse has the rhetorical advantage that community sounds intuitively good to almost all

20. Compare Nancy Robertson's account (in this volume) of the ways in which white northern women active in the YWCA thought about racial equality and their correspondingly ambivalent relationship to Black women.

21. "Communities without propinquity" was Melvin Webber's evocative phrase for those important affiliations that bind moderns across spatial distances: professional networks, for example, play some of the role for many of us that local communities played for our ancestors. We should not underestimate, however, the differences in sense of what community means that are implied by supralocal affiliations. Bonds are less likely to be multiplex and more likely to be single purpose, for example, and networks are likely to be less dense. See discussion in Calhoun (1980, 1987).

Americans, we do not seem to have the unambiguously positive sense of *public* that we do of *community*.

Discussion of public life tends to evoke a basic cynicism.[22] We have to a very large extent lost faith in our public institutions. Public opinion polls now present data not on whether we have more respect for politicians or press or police, but for which group we have *less*. Moreover, many of us seem to doubt the very idea that through public discourse and political participation we can make a difference.[23] This may be one reason community appeals so widely as a political concept; it places our attention in a realm in which we have more confidence that we can act efficaciously. Ironically, though, the turn to communitarian language may itself be undermining appreciation for the various virtues of the public sphere.

We may make different demands on communities and publics because they represent two different modes of organizing social life. Community is present in the familiarity of dense networks of social relationships, in the intensity of sharing and commitment that comes from frequent multiplexity in those relationships, and in the cohesion of cultural systems that organize such relations (Calhoun 1980). Public life, by contrast, requires us to engage and care about the needs of strangers. It calls for us to grasp our interdependence with people to whom we are connected only indirectly, through markets, governments, communications media, and similar large-scale organizations and systems. It calls for us to recognize, respect, and communicate with each other when many of our basic cultural values or categories of understanding are not shared.

We are misled in this regard by the excessive idealization of the classic Athenian polis in much political theory. Athens was small, its citizenry a narrow elite that could gather in a single public square of modest size and communicate without microphones or amplifiers, let alone television. This model of the public sphere emphasized a distinctive mode of interaction and discourse among people who were also connected to each other (albeit in varying degrees) by the bonds of community. In complex, large-scale modern societies, we do not have the luxury of resting public life on such communal foundations (and most of us would in any case decry the slavery and exclusion of women and immigrants also fundamental to Athenian democracy).

A public is not a category of essentially similar people. It is a differentiated body joined, at least in part, by the capacity of its members to sustain a common discourse across their lines of difference. As Jürgen Habermas has argued, one of the crucial conditions of the modern polity was the creation of a sphere of public discourse based on but transcending private identities and economic foundations and engaging the state without being contained within it (Habermas 1989). This discursive realm helped to constitute the collective good as the public good — that is, the good identified by (at least potentially) rational-critical subjects through their discourse with each other. The public was a self-producing body, and self-aware through its discourse, rather than being defined merely by common subjection to a monarch or common implication in systems of bureaucratic power or economic exchange.

Following Habermas's classic exploration can help us understand the relationship of civil society to cultural diversity and public discourse. The basic question guiding his exploration of the public sphere was, To what extent can the wills or opinions guiding political action be formed on the basis of rational-critical discourse? This is a salient issue primarily where economic and other differences give actors discordant identities and conflicting interests.

For the most part, Habermas took it as given that the crucial differences among actors were those of class and political-economic status. He focused on how the nature, organization, and opportunities for discourse on politically significant topics might be structured so that class and status inequalities were not an insuperable barrier to political participation.[24] The first issue, of course, was access to the dis-

22. As I shall develop this point minimally, see Jeffrey Goldfarb (1992).

23. I take some heart from Vivien Hart's (1978, xiii) observation that though we inveigh against politicians, we have not lost all faith in government — and especially not in the ideals and constitutional image of American democracy: "The clichés about politicians are an easy way for the inarticulate to express their feelings; deeper probing of these feelings uncovers assessments of the political system as elitist, corrupt, unresponsive, inaccessible, partial to influential groups, and unrepresentative. Yet, curiously, history also suggests that profound doubts about politics have been matched by an equally continuous tradition of the proud affirmation of American democracy." Hart goes on to cite opinion polls indicating that when asked to name "the things about this country" that they are most proud of, some 85 percent of Americans name some feature of the American government or political tradition, compared to 46 percent of Britons, 30 percent of Mexicans, 7 percent of Germans, and 3 percent of Italians. Clearly, we have not altogether ceased to enter into public life, and we have some residual faith on which to build.

24. Habermas's initial focus was on the bourgeois public sphere, one already shaped by class-structured exclusion even while it "bracketed" other economic and status differences among those included. In the later part of his book, Habermas analyzes the transformation of the public sphere — largely, in his eyes, a degeneration — that resulted from the specific forms in which it became more inclusive. Most directly, inclusivity brought a transformation in scale and thereby a reliance on "mass media." At the same time, the larger public sphere was subject to greater manipulation by specialized agents like public relations professionals and in general by a substitution of more instrumental use of language and images for a genuine rational-critical discourse (a concern which continues into Habermas's later work). Habermas's account of this degeneration of the public sphere makes a number of good points but shares many of the problems of mass culture critiques generally. It also tends to foreclose investigation of the conditions under which a serious public exercise of reason might be organized at a scale appropriate to democratic participation in contemporary polities; this must surely involve some level of reliance on the media, which Habermas dismisses

course. This was not so simple as the mere willingness to listen to another's speech, but also involved matters like the distribution of the sorts of education that empowered speakers to present recognizably good arguments. Beyond this, there was the importance of an ideological commitment to setting aside status differences in the nonce egalitarianism of an intellectual argument.

Habermas's approach, however, and that of many working within the frameworks of Marxism and critical theory as well as classical liberalism, has the flaw of treating interpersonal differences primarily as matters of economic interest. This is doubly problematic. In the first place, it leads to neglect of many other kinds of differences. Habermas recognizes the gendered construction of the classical bourgeois public sphere, for example, but passes it by almost without comment. Even when Habermas later acknowledges the importance of gender inclusion/exclusion, he has a hard time seeing the issue as anything other than a matter of the representation or nonrepresentation of one interest group among many; he has difficulty with the notion that the exclusion of women raises more basic categorical issues.[25] He doesn't see, thus, that the eighteenth- and early nineteenth-century European and American public spheres were structured not just by sliding scales of inclusion and exclusion but by a basic incapacity to thematize certain categorical differences among people as appropriate topics for public discourse. The same goes for race; the capacity shown by America's founders and their European Enlightenment forebears and counterparts for ignoring or waffling on the issue is nothing short of astonishing.

The second problem is perhaps even more theoretically basic. Habermas's account of the availability of free actors for participation in the public sphere turns on the development of a private realm that gives individuals the personal identities and the social, economic, and emotional support to constitute such free actors. He accordingly treats identity formation as prior to participation in the idealized public sphere of rational critical discourse. The intimate sphere of the family and the institutions of private life generally created people (men) who were able to enter the public sphere. The economic circumstances that supported individual autonomy were certainly important, but Habermas does not rest content with this kind of support from civil society. The identities of fully formed individuals are not simple, unmediated reflections of their material interests or class positions. The voices of individuals in the public sphere reflect cultural and other differences in orientation, in personal experience, and also, crucially, in the exercise of reason.

This notion, however, locates identity formation entirely

in the realm of private life and therefore outside of politics and public discourse. It is because of this that Habermas cannot see any positive public role for what today are called identity politics. On the contrary, these attempts to affirm or reshape identities through public action appear in his classic work on the public sphere as degenerative intrusions due, first, to growing democratic inclusiveness and, second, to public relations manipulation. Habermas dates this confusion of the public and private spheres especially to the postwar era.

The issue of democratic inclusiveness is not just a quantitative matter of the scale of a public sphere or the proportion of the members of a polity who may speak within it. It is also a matter of how the public sphere incorporates and recognizes the diversity of identities which people bring to it from their manifold involvements in civil society. Where nationalism (or communitarianism) represses difference, it intrinsically undermines the capacity of a public sphere to carry forward a rational-critical democratic discourse.

Identity formation thus needs to be approached as part of the process of public life, not as something that can be fully settled prior to it in a private sphere. The liberal model of the public sphere needs reexamination insofar as it disqualifies discourse about the differences among actors in order to defend the genuinely rational-critical notion that arguments must be decided on their merits rather than on the identities of the arguers. If it is impossible to communicate seriously about basic differences among members of a public sphere, then it will be impossible also to address the difficulties of communication across lines of basic difference. Yet such basic differences cannot feasibly be excluded from the public sphere. Not only is this contrary to the democratic inclusion of women, racial and ethnic minorities, and other groups subject to the same state and part of the same civil society. Not only is the exclusion of difference made enormously more difficult by the continuing movement of people about the globe. In a basic and intrinsic sense, if the public sphere has the capacity to alter civil society and to shape the state, then its own democratic practice must confront the questions of membership and the identity of the political community it represents.

THE PUBLIC IS NOT JUST A SPHERE OF AGREEMENT

Mansbridge has rightly suggested that the phrase "public good" serves us both as a site of contestation and a means of directing approbation.[26] But one of our difficulties in thinking adequately about the public good, as my introductory parable of Indianapolis and the Eastside community suggested, is that the language of the public good appears often as an approbation of how the greater good of the greater number trumps the goods of subsidiary communities. This problem results both from approaching the public good in

---

as almost intrinsically foreign to rational-critical discourse. See Negt and Kluge (1993), Calhoun (1988).

25. See, however, Habermas's discussion of this point—particularly in response to challenges from Nancy Fraser—in the "Concluding Remarks" to Calhoun, ed. (1992).

26. "On the Contested Nature of the Public Good" (this volume).

ways which equate it with a summation of individual goods (following Bentham) and from those that treat it as the good of a singular community (in the way I have criticized). And it undermines the needed contestation.

If we are to produce a dynamic discourse about the conditions of collective life in our large-scale society, we need not just a language of community that celebrates our commonalities but a language of public life that starts with recognition of deep differences among us and builds faith in meaningful communication across lines of difference. It must empower us for discourse about the workings of large-scale social and economic systems, not reduce our large-scale conversations to mass celebrations and mass panics. It must allow us to articulate the different ways in which we are knit into a larger world and not offer us the illusion of sharp boundaries.

An implication of this venture of invigorating and institutionally supporting the public sphere is that we rely on the discourse of this public itself and not assume that we should relegate public matters to bureaucracy and specialized expertise. Noting this will return us more directly from the idea of public to the idea of public good. As Robert Dahl (1989, 337) has written,

> No intellectually defensible claim can be made that public policy elites (actual or putative) possess superior moral knowledge or more specifically superior knowledge of what constitutes the public good. Indeed, we have some reason for thinking that specialization may itself impair their capacity for moral judgment. Likewise, precisely because the knowledge of policy elites is specialized, their expert knowledge ordinarily provides too narrow a base for the instrumental judgments that an intelligent policy would require.

Dahl's criticism is far-reaching, impugning the policy elites' judgment not only of moral issues but of many instrumental matters. If we are not to abandon large-scale societal organization — states, capitalist economies — then these systems will produce and require specialized experts. We must not think we can live without either specialists or expertise. But we do need to recognize that reliance on specialists in system maintenance and expansion is a two-edged sword. If it reassures us in the short run that our systems are in good (because expert) hands, it raises our anxieties in the long run because it further distances us from any sense of participating in the decisions over our fates.

The root of the issue is not the moral incapacities of specialists; it is the fact that the public good is not objectively or externally ascertainable. It is a social and cultural *project* of the public sphere, not an aggregation of the private interests of many individuals. It is created in and through the public process, it does not exist in advance of it. Indeed, to term the voluntary sector private is to impoverish our conception of the public sphere by allowing it to be monopolized by state-organized activity. The same is true of the notion that proper public discourse ought to address objectively ascertainable

or jointly recognized common interests — and not matters of identity or demands for group recognition.

The eighteenth-century public sphere was conceived in part on the model of science, and its task was to discover the public good. Bentham was extreme but not out of line with his age in arguing that this was in principle amenable to a calculus at once altogether rational and fully empirical. Bentham makes us nervous today; even rational choice analysts shrink from his logical consistency and his willingness to address psychology alongside revealed preference. But much of Bentham and his era is still with us, including a belief that the public good is simply found, not forged. This belief paves the way for legislators and revolutionaries who claim to have discovered what the masses need and who offer the public good as an end that justifies its means. It is most properly this point — not all modernity — that is the target of the grand postmodernist rejections of consistency as a theoretical goal and of schemes for making a better world. We can hardly help today but see the seeds of repression in what seemed to the eighteenth century liberating ideas. Adam Smith asserted a natural identity of human interests such that the invisible hand of the market would work without plan to achieve a public good which was at the same time the greatest sum of private goods. Not sure that nature itself offered evidence of this identity of interests, David Hartley argued for the press of social life: "Association tends to make us all ultimately similar; so that if one be happy all must" (cited in Halévy 1952, 17). And if unguided association didn't do the trick, Bentham proposed that the legislator should wield punishments so as to bring people in line with the greatest good for the greatest number. Although he sometimes appealed to natural identity of interests or to Hartley's notion that interests might fuse as a result of association, he also held that where they did not, it was the job of government to achieve an artificial identification of interests. Government could do this in the name of the only definition of the public good that mattered, the principle of utility.[27]

Bentham, unlike many of his heirs in contemporary economics, was arguing against, not for, unbridled egoism. Like David Hume, he was prepared to see men generally as knaves who were ruled by selfish interests, so he had little patience with idealistic moralizing, with appeals to norms that ran counter to interest. If unbridled egoism was a problem for society, then society through its government had better tame and bridle it with laws. The paths to John Stuart Mill and Fabian socialism were not so very distant. Nor was that idealist Jean-Jacques Rousseau altogether in disagreement, as his praise for Rome and Sparta reminds us. While arguing that people were not knaves by nature but made so by inequality and dishonest society, he commended the use of

---

27. See H. L. A. Hart's (1982, esp. 88–89) interesting essay suggesting how J. S. Mill articulated this point and especially the link to the question of what a person may expect of government as a matter of right in a way consistent with but not quite found in the writings of Bentham.

persuasion and even coercion to prevent corruption. Public opinion might have to be molded from above to maintain a cohesive society and to prevent the spread of egoism and consequent deceit (see discussion in Shklar 1969, chap. 3, esp. 100–01).

One thing these founders of our modern ideas of the public good shared, despite their many differences, was the notion that the public good might not be accessible to mere public opinion. Mere public opinion was too flighty, too corruptible, too subject to manipulation. Hence the importance of the public sphere Habermas idealized. In this public sphere, people entered into a discourse carried out under stricter rules than mere opinion formation. Here, by virtue of reliance on reason and rejection of the influence that commonly attended the identities of prestigious individuals, opinion might be forged which truly deserved to instruct the state. Here, democracy might be transformed from mob rule to the highest form of republicanism. And from here, in Habermas's story, the public sphere degenerated as it grew in scale and declined in reasoned argument. Greater democratic inclusivity increased vulnerability to undemocratic manipulations of opinion.

In *The Structural Transformation of the Public Sphere,* Habermas couldn't see his way out of this dilemma. The reason, I think, had to do with a hidden ambivalence in his conception. Did the public sphere decline because it ceased to be an effective tool for *discovering* the public good or did it decline because it ceased to be an effective arena for *constituting* — and *reconstituting* — the public good? Adopting the latter choice helps us cut into the elitist prejudices of Habermas's account. It makes us wonder if the decline has been so precipitous as he thinks, and it reminds us that in the late eighteenth and nineteenth centuries there were multiple publics, each seeking to constitute the public good in somewhat different terms.

Thinking of the public sphere as constituting the public good does not mean that the public sphere is not an arena of decision making or sharing of information. It does mean that it is not only that. It is also an arena of reflexive modification of the people who enter it, of their ideas, and of its own modes of discourse. The public good cannot be fixed in advance because the public itself is always in a process of reconstitution. Our debates about what is good for us are always, in part, debates about whom we want to be. Whether the issue is health care, education, prison reform, or foreign aid, questions of interest are never separable from questions of identity. One of the great faults of the commonplace language of interests is that it obscures this. Of course in some sense we have interests, and of course we can gain greater clarity about our interests through instruction in the consequences of our acts and other more or less externally ascertainable matters. But neither as individuals nor as collectivities are these interests fixed in advance so that the right course of action can simply be deduced from them. Our interests can only be considered when based on understandings of

our identities, and these are at stake in the very public deliberations that weigh our courses of action. Am I both Black and a woman? Then arguments from race and gender each attempt to sway my self-understanding, to persuade me to give one of these aspects of my identity greater salience.[28] It may sound easy to affirm the intersection, to speak of "Black woman" as constituting a single identity, but it is not easy when the predominant discourses of race fail to recognize gender and those of gender fail to recognize race. The identity is not available equally, always, and to all who are Black and female. Its availability is increased, however, at the same time that the identity is given more substance and particularity by such entrants into the public discourse as bell hooks, Alice Walker, Michelle Wallace, and Toni Morrison. Their efforts do not simply identify the interests of some preexisting, fixed group, Black women; they constitute Black woman as a potential self-understanding, not fixed but in the flux of self-making.

But the public sphere — any public sphere — may offer richer or poorer conditions for the project of constituting the public good. In its culture, it may encourage (or discourage) the thematization of difference. It may do so in ways that make differences harder (or easier) to bridge. It may be more (or less) open to associational life. Social movements may more (or less) readily place new issues and identities on their agendas. In each of these ways, the shape of the public sphere, its openness and vitality, affects its capacities to constitute a public such that the members of that public can address together the question of what is good for each or any or all of them.

Instead of building networks of social relationships and mutually engaging public discourse across lines of difference, we tend to identify with categories of people similar to us on one or more dimensions. These include ethnicities and races, both religions and religious orientations — like Evangelical or other coded qualifiers of Christian, and interest affiliations like the National Rifle Association. Unlike political parties, which are in part vehicles for building coalitions among different identities and interests, these categories are frequently represented as though for relevant purposes they are internally homogenous. While they may present images of the public good, therefore, they do not directly facilitate the production of shared ideas of the public good among those with somewhat different initial positions. The extent to which these categories cut across each other is seldom thematized. Rather than interconnections across and among categorical identities, and thus real relationships and discussion with people different from ourselves, we tend to see categorical differences as leaving us the alternatives of conflict or tolerance. To call for tolerance or gain a sense of broader solidarity, we appeal mainly to other more encompassing

28. W. E. B. Du Bois (1903) grasped this issue through his notion of "double consciousness," thinking especially of the duality "negro" and "American." See also Gilroy (1993).

categories of alleged similarity — we are all Americans — rather than to a public discourse that engages us through our conflicts and cross-cutting affiliations.

Tolerance by itself does not ensure engagement across lines of difference. Indeed, we in America seem close to deciding that the only way to tolerate those different from ourselves is to have very little interaction with them, to separate ourselves into enclaves within which everyone is similar. Thus in a sense, we approach communities in a frame of mind similar to that in which people commonly think about nations on the global scene. Even in local residential communities, by a variety of mechanisms from zoning to economically structured planned developments, we produce high levels of economic and social homogeneity. It is as though we presume we can build enjoyable and satisfying social networks only within these categories of similarity. We would save community, on that smaller scale, at the complete expense of public life.

Communities cannot be self-sufficient; they can't even keep up much of an ideological pretense of self-sufficiency anymore. So just as we cannot recover a sense of strong community in mere sameness, we can't find it in isolation. We have to overcome the sense that what happens in New York's South Bronx or in Central Los Angeles is someone else's problem. But to do so requires us to approach such concerns not through false claims to be a single community, as though the interests of those in Beverly Hills and South Central Los Angeles were really the same, but through a recognition of interdependence despite difference and a conception of public discourse that grants participants respect and dignity on bases other than familiarity. The same is true for the various moral issues and movements that set us at each other's throats — for and against abortion, for and against gay rights. We can deal better with these if we are willing to see our task as the development of communication across lines of difference rather than either the discovery of common denominators that make our differences negligible or mere negotiation among people who cannot really communicate about their competing interests.

CONCLUSION

It will now be clear, I hope, why I think communitarian language is problematic for coming to terms with the nature and identity of the public in America today. First, the public must be an institutional arena within which we not only live with but cherish difference. Within our families and our local communities we know we are not all the same — and though we emphasize our commonality, we know also that we are knit together by appreciation of some of our differences. But when those differences appear to us in the larger public realm, they too often appear as enormous categories of people with whom we cannot identify and who inspire mostly fear in us. The language of community is too often used either to evoke a spurious unity of the whole or to describe those categories within which people are "like us." Yet in the country as a whole, as in every family and town, variety is not just the spice of life but one of its essential ingredients. And for the country as a whole, there is no web of directly interpersonal relations to counterbalance purely categorical images or identities.

Second, within the institutional arena of the public sphere we need to nurture modes of discourse that go beyond the forging and affirmation of commonality or identity to the articulation of reasoned arguments. Clearly, abstract, rational reason cannot settle all our debates or solve all our problems. As the exclusive vocabulary of public life, such an idealized notion of reason would neglect soul, spirit, tacit knowledge, practical understanding, prayer, mystery, luck, and a sense of limits. But especially in the public sphere — as distinct from community — it is important to emphasize the giving of reasons. We cannot demand that our discourse be purely rational, but we can demand that those who enter it be prepared to give reasons for their views and to consider those given by others.

Third, the nurturance of this public sphere would require us not simply to identify commonalities with each other but to rebuild civic institutions. One reason we seek unity in visions of an imaginary giant community or in bellicose foreign policy is that we have lost faith in the domestic institutions central to the real, practical unification of American life. Too many of us are not just worried but outright cynical about the legal system, the public schools, the media, and, above all, the government. These are institutions that we depend on to organize our relations — including relations across lines of difference. They are also the institutions that make much of the story of the uniqueness and greatness of American democracy real and not just a chauvinistic claim. Perhaps most important of all, they are institutions that enable us to communicate with each other in a public sphere of civic discussion, to carry on a discourse about what our country means, how we should live together, and what we all need and have to offer. While we must confront cynicism directly as a problem in itself, we must also confront the issue of institutional reform. For both civil society and public sphere are creations of social institutions; discourse is a product not just of minds and mouths but of cafes — and, for that matter, big political barbecues — in which the minds meet and the mouths eat as well as speak. The institutional arenas required include both those that nurture subordinate, subcultural publics — among African Americans, for example, or among those committed to evangelical Christianity — and those that provide for cross-cutting linkages among participants in these subordinate publics.

REFERENCES

Bellah, Robert N., Richard Madsen, William M. Sullivan, Ann Swidler, and Steven M. Tipton. 1985. *Habits of the Heart: Individualism and Commitment in American Life.* New York: Harper and Row.

Berger, Peter, and Richard J. Neuhaus. 1978. *The Naked Public Square.* New York: Basic Books.

Calhoun, Craig. 1980. "Community: Toward a Variable Conceptualization for Comparative Research." *Social History* 5:105–29.

———. 1987. "Class, Place and Industrial Revolution." In *Class and Space: The Making of Urban Society,* ed. P. Williams and N. Thrift, 51–72. London: Routledge and Kegan Paul.

———. 1988. "Populist Politics, Communications Media, and Large Scale Social Integration." *Sociological Theory* 6(2): 219–41.

——— (ed.). 1992. *Habermas and the Public Sphere.* Cambridge: MIT Press.

——— (ed.). 1994. *Social Theory and the Politics of Identity.* Oxford: Blackwell.

———. 1995. *Critical Social Theory: Culture, History, and the Challenge of Difference.* Oxford: Blackwell.

Carter, Stephen. 1993. *The Culture of Disbelief: How American Law and Politics Trivializes Religious Devotion.* New York: Basic Books.

Dahl, Robert. 1989. *Democracy and Its Critics.* New Haven: Yale University Press.

Doyle, Kathleen. 1989. "Madame C. J. Walker: First Black Woman Millionaire." *American History Illustrated* 24:24–25.

Du Bois, W. E. B. *The Souls of Black Folk.* [1903] 1994. New York: Dover.

Ferguson, Earline Rae. 1988. "The Women's Improvement Club of Indianapolis: Black Women Pioneers in Tuberculosis Work, 1903–1938." *Indiana Magazine of History* 84:237–61.

Gilroy, Paul. 1993. *The Black Atlantic: Modernity and Double Consciousness.* Cambridge: Harvard University Press.

Goldfarb, Jeffrey. 1992. *The Cynical Society.* Chicago: University of Chicago Press.

Griffin, William W. 1983. "The Political Realignment of Black Voters in Indianapolis, 1924." *Indiana Magazine of History* 79:133–66.

Habermas, Jürgen. 1984, 1988. *Theory of Communicative Action.* 2 vols. Boston: Beacon Press.

———. 1989. *Structural Transformation of the Public Sphere.* Cambridge: MIT Press.

Halévy, Elie. 1952. *The Growth of Philosophic Radicalism.* London: Faber.

Hamilton, Alexander, James Madison, and John Jay. *The Federalist Papers.* 1961. New York: New American Library.

Haraway, Donna. 1992. "Ecce Homo, Ain't (Aren't) I a Woman, and Inappropriate/d Others: The Human in a Post-Humanist Landscape." In *Feminists Theorize the Political,* ed. Judith Butler and Joan W. Scott, 86–100. New York: Routledge.

Hart, H. L. A. 1982. "Natural Rights: Bentham and John Stuart Mill." In *Essays on Bentham: Jurisprudence and Political Theory,* ed. H. L. A. Hart, 79–104. Oxford: Oxford University Press.

Hart, Vivien. 1978. *Distrust and Democracy: Political Distrust in Britain and America.* Cambridge: Cambridge University Press.

MacIntyre, Alasdair. 1984. *After Virtue.* 2d ed. Notre Dame: University of Notre Dame Press.

———. 1988. *Whose Justice? Which Rationality?* South Bend: Notre Dame University Press.

Nadel, Siegfried. 1954. *Foundations of Social Anthropology.* Oxford: Oxford University Press.

———. 1957. *Theory of Social Structure.* London: Cohen and West.

Negt, O., and A. Kluge. 1993. *The Public Sphere and Experience.* Minneapolis: University of Minnesota Press.

Phillips, Derek. 1993. *A Critical Appraisal of Communitarian Thought.* Princeton: Princeton University Press.

Rawls, John. 1971. *A Theory of Justice.* Cambridge: Belknap Press.

Renan, Ernst. 1990. "What Is a Nation?" In *Nation and Narration,* ed. Homi Bhabha, 8–22. London: Routledge.

Schnorr, Paul. 1993. "Denied a Sense of Community: Problems of Class, Race, and Community Form in a Voluntary Resettlement Effort." Ph.D. dissertation, Northwestern University.

Sen, Amartya. 1979. "Utilitarianism and Welfarism." *Journal of Philosophy* 76:463–89.

Shklar, Judith. 1969. *Men and Citizens: A Study of Rousseau's Social Theory.* Cambridge: Cambridge University Press.

Sorokin, Pitirim. 1957. *Social and Cultural Dynamics.* Boston: Sergeant.

Specht, David. 1989. "A Church and Its Neighborhood." *National Civic Review* 78:456–64.

Taylor, Charles. *Sources of the Self.* 1989. Cambridge: Harvard University Press.

———. 1992. *The Ethics of Authenticity.* Cambridge: Harvard University Press.

———. 1995. "Irreducibly Social Goods." In *Philosophical Arguments,* 127–45. Cambridge: Harvard University Press.

Thompson, E. P. 1992. *Customs in Common.* New York: New Press.

West, Cornel. 1993. *Race Matters.* Boston: Beacon Press.

White, Harrison. 1992. *Identity and Control.* Princeton: Princeton University Press.

3

A L A N   W O L F E

What Is Altruism?

A debate over the relative importance of altruism and egoism is the latest chapter in the long-running story of how social scientists think about human behavior. That story, since at least the nineteenth century, has pitted an economic conception of human beings against a sociological one. The economic conception views the individual as a utilitarian calculator of self-interest, the sociological as an other-regarding member of some larger group or society. This battle has never stopped (Schwartz 1986), and it is not likely to do so in the future. The economistic version has, in recent years, won numerous adherents, often in fields far removed from economics, including sociology (Coleman 1990). But the more popular rational choice theory becomes, the more contested it is; many see rational choice theory as increasingly limited, which raises the possibility of the emergence of a new paradigm that once again pays attention to altruism (Piliavin and Charg 1990; Batson 1990, 1991; Simmons 1991).

In spite of these promising signs, the social scientific study of altruism remains in its very early stages. At a theoretical level, the need for altruism has been demonstrated by those writers who point to the ways in which regard for others can be a rational strategy when it produces benefits for all the players in a game (Axelrod 1984; Frank 1988). Sim-

Special thanks to the editors of this volume for their comments, as well as to Carrie Rothburd, Jane Mansbridge, and Robert Putnam.

ilarly, theorists have demonstrated how otherwise rational individuals find themselves engaged in forms of collective coordination encouraged by group size (Oliver, Marwell, and Teixeira 1985; Oliver and Marwell 1988) or by the density of collective choices (Granovetter 1978; Macy 1991a, 1991b). The success of these efforts at the theoretical level cannot be underestimated, for it is no longer possible to argue, as it was just a decade or two ago, that assumptions of self-regarding behavior are more realistic or predictive than assumptions of other-regarding behavior. To be open to the world around them, social scientists need to go beyond monocausal explanations of human behavior that achieve a certain formal elegance, but do so at the price of prematurely closing off the complexities of human behavior.

If the need for a theoretical appreciation of altruistic behavior is increasingly accepted by social scientists, problems of conceptualization remain formidable. Altruism is a far more tricky concept philosophically than self-interest, for it involves not only defining the motives of an individual actor, but also dealing with the consequences of those actions for a multitude of other actors. It may be that the frustrations of trying to define the term constitute one major reason so many turn to the conceptually clearer notion of self-interest in the first place. Furthermore, efforts to relate theoretical conceptualization of altruism to real world behavior are skimpy compared to assumptions about self-interested behavior;

economic models have been applied to a wide variety of noneconomic behaviors, but altruistic models have been applied infrequently to economic behaviors.

These difficulties suggest the need for some stock-taking with respect to the way social scientists have tried to theorize about and understand altruistic behavior. Such a task could be carried out in two ways. One would be to examine the theoretical and conceptual difficulties facing any attempt to operationalize what altruistic behavior might be. The other is to put such conceptual issues on hold, at least for a while, in an attempt to examine presumptively altruistic behavior in real world or approximate real world conditions. Either approach carries with it certain problems. We cannot learn about a phenomenon in the real world until we have defined precisely the phenomenon itself, for how else will we know whether what we are studying is really what we had planned to study? On the other hand, if we spend all our time engaging in conceptual exercises, we lose the quality of real world applicability that any social science should possess. As a preliminary step, my aim in this chapter is to start with real world or approximate real world efforts to understand altruism, and from them to generalize back to theoretical and conceptual problems rather than the other way around.

Research dealing with the altruistic behavior of real people can be divided into five general types: (1) laboratory situations which do not represent the real world but do attempt to isolate altruistic, helping, or prosocial behavior; (2) studies of altruistic acts such as blood donation, volunteering, recycling, or helping in accidents and disasters; (3) historical accounts of altruistic behavior, such as the rescue of European Jews; (4) ethnographic accounts of altruistic professions, such as nursing or social work; and (5) the examination of institutions that engage in altruistic action, including government in the form of the contemporary welfare state. From these studies, one conclusion can be quickly drawn: social scientists do not agree on the way they define *altruism*. Daniel Bar-Tal (1985/86) has distinguished between behavioral and motivational conceptions of altruism. To these I would add a third: environmental. Each approach to altruism carries both advantages and risks.

BEHAVIORAL ALTRUISM

Behavioral approaches examine what an organism does, irrespective of the state of mind of the organism that does it. (Indeed, some organisms can act altruistically without having any state of mind at all, if by *state of mind* we mean the complex cognition associated with humans and perhaps some other primates). "Altruism," J. Phillipe Rushton writes, "is defined as social behavior carried out to achieve positive outcomes for another rather than for the self" (1980, 8). Animals that sacrifice themselves for the sake of their offspring — a common phenomenon in nature — can, by these terms, engage in altruistic behavior (Trivers 1971).[1] Under-

stood in this naturalistic sense, altruism possesses evolutionary advantages; it exists because it is functional for the efficient reproduction of a particular species (Hamilton 1964). Behavioral definitions of altruism thus have a seemingly great contribution to make; they seem to prove that, despite Hobbesian pessimism, there are solutions to prisoners' dilemma situations that are based on something more solid than temporary agreements or contingent contracts.

It is a short step from a behavioral definition of altruism to the conclusion that human beings are by nature cooperative, social, or even, in some accounts, moral (Wilson 1993). Considering the fact that nineteenth-century intellectual traditions left us with a legacy of claims that self-interest is biologically based, it is refreshing to believe that the opposite may be the case. Refreshing though such a case may be, it is not, however, persuasive. For if we believe that "human beings are disposed to be social before they learn what sociability is about" (Wilson 1993, 125), there would be little need to teach people about their personal responsibility for the fate of others. Nature, in taking care of our morality for us, would allow us little room to be moral agents ourselves.

But is the behavioral understanding of altruism *empirically* adequate; that is, do human beings act altruistically without having altruistic motives? This is an impossible question to answer definitively, given the notorious problems of establishing what motives are, but there are sufficient hints in what we know about altruistic behavior to suggest that the behavioral model has serious empirical flaws.

First, the behavioral approach imagines altruism as a state that is activated by a genetic switch. There are two reasons to question such an approach. One is that altruism possesses clear *developmental* features. One can quibble with Jean Piaget's or Lawrence Kohlberg's account of the stages of moral development, but there is little doubt that as human beings mature, they become more capable of taking the position of an abstract other (Zahn-Waxler 1991). Similarly, we know that altruistic behavior varies from one society to another; the greater the wealth of a society, the more likely it is to distribute some of its wealth to others in the form of the welfare state, a form of social development not dissimilar from individual psychological development (Wilensky and Lebeaux 1959). The question is not so much whether, in any given organism (or society), altruism exists or not, but rather, how much of a disposition to altruism (or, for that matter, egoism) exists?

In addition, it is by no means clear that a precise conceptualization of altruism, one which imagines such behavior as being turned on automatically, corresponds with the way in which individuals pursue activities that have public-regarding intentions or consequences. If people think in different ways about what it means to do good, then the important point for social scientists is not to determine which way of achieving a good is the right and true way; it is rather to recognize, as Jane Mansbridge does (Mansbridge, this volume), that contestation in itself is a goal to which we ought to

---

1. I would argue that only humans have a self.

be committed. Such a point of view imagines altruistic behavior as an emerging reality, whereas behavioral approaches to altruism imagine it as a determined reality. The same point holds organizationally, for even though organizations cannot be understood by treating them as if they were persons, they, too, often have goals that are, in Mark Chaves's words, "inherently ambiguous" (Chaves, this volume).

A second problem with behavioral approaches to altruism is that they ignore the existence of an altruistic personality. Altruism is not a state waiting to be activated but rather something that requires aspects of mind—cognition, self-perception, identity formation, empathy—before it can be said to exist. What differentiated rescuers of Jews from non-rescuers in the study by Samuel and Pearl Oliner was their state of mind: altruistic people tend to believe in the existence of a just world, are more inward looking, and tend to be the children of parents who emphasized similar values. These findings have been replicated in laboratory and everyday life situations by social psychologists (Carlo et al. 1991; Bierhoff, Klein, and Kramp 1991). Mental activity is a dynamic component of altruistic behavior: altruism happens because people use their minds to interpret the world around them and, basing themselves on that information, decide to act in one way rather than another. In other words, an appreciation of altruistic behavior requires a thick psychology, one influenced by a sociological emphasis on how people shape individual cognition and decision making, rather than a psychology that leaves personality out of the picture.

Third, although altruism is learned, it does not take heroic amounts of education or training to instill it. To be sure, there will always be saints whose altruism stands as an unattainable ideal for ordinary people, but most real world altruism is learned through others in the course of everyday life. Altruism, for one thing, usually involves a substantial amount of conformist behavior. For example, people are more likely to give money to the Salvation Army if they see others do it (Hurley and Allen 1974; Krebs 1970). A variety of laboratory studies indicate that when some people act altruistically, others do as well (Reykowski 1980). Even heroic acts of altruism can have a conformist dimension. Rescuers of Jews in Nazi Europe, for example, were more likely to appear in parts of Europe where the moral climate credited their activities. And although rescue was by its very nature secret—and therefore not likely to be conformist—there is evidence that rescuers' neighbors knew of many rescue activities and silently acknowledged them, an indirect form of social approval (Oliner and Oliner 1988, 125).

Altruism, like selfishness, is facilitated by rewards; the reward of selfishness may be increased material benefit, while that of altruism is attachment to group norms. Group solidarity can be as important as individual conscience in contributing to prosocial behavior (Dawes, van de Kragt, and Orbell 1988). Moreover, just as altruism has a conformist dimension, interestingly, so does nonaltruism: the famous bystander effect—that is, people will be more likely not to act

altruistically when they know that others are present—demonstrates the importance of conformity in nonaltruistic responses (Latané and Darley 1970).[2] Learning from others—watching what they do and then deciding to do something similar—is a constitutive feature of altruistic behavior.

Taken together, all these factors are indirect evidence that, at least in human beings, altruism is not a product of preconscious or unconscious drives. We do not, when we act altruistically, respond to hard-wired programs for sacrificial behavior that have been written into our genes through millennia of evolutionary response. To be sure, some aspects of human behavior may have genetic or biological causes: for example, men commit more violent crime than women, parents are more likely to sacrifice for their biological children than for their adopted ones, and so on. But there is a huge gap between such basic, or nonsocialized, drives and the more complex aspects of human altruism. What is most important about altruism is precisely what behaviorism leaves out, namely, the activating factors that transform an instinct into something worth knowing about. When altruism exists, something happens. Behavioral definitions willfully choose to ignore what that something might be.

Whatever the empirical problems facing a naturalistic explanation of altruism, there are normative problems as well. Because hard-wired explanations of human behavior are usually associated with such notions as those of a "selfish gene" (Dawkins 1976), we usually think of biological theories as insufficiently altruistic because they allow little room for imagining people as making complex moral choices. Ironically, such theories are also problematic because they are, in a sense, too altruistic. Altruism in and of itself is not a good. A person who does things for others can do them cruelly as easily as empathically (Holmes 1990); extreme altruism constitutes a form of authoritarianism. Martin Hoffman (1987) identifies role-taking as a crucial feature of altruism, an approach not without its own problems.[3] But role-taking is important in this context for one reason: the kind of cruelty associated with selfless motives—a dictator uninterested in accumulating wealth but willing to sacrifice people to some principle—exemplifies the failure of a person to take the role of his own self and, lacking that capacity, the inability to imagine himself in the role of others. The fact that animals sacrifice themselves for the sake of their offspring does not mean that a human being who did so would be acting in an altruistically appropriate way. Society would face as much trouble reproducing itself if everyone were other-regarding all the time as it would if everyone were self-regarding all the time.

This is not the place for asserting my own normative

2. Similarly, potential kidney donors will hope that a sibling will donate first, when there is a sibling (Simmons 1991).

3. Being cruel to another person is made easier by being able to take the role of the person to whom one wants to be cruel, making the sadist, as Bernard Williams (1985, 91) has pointed out, the supreme role taker.

commitments and judging any particular approach to altruism a failure because it fails to appreciate them. But I do think it appropriate to argue that a minimum normative standard can be developed from empirical grounds. If altruism means an effort to do good for others, then the minimal normative principle that a definition of altruism should meet is respect for pluralism, given that conceptions of the good will be contested (Mansbridge, this volume). A pluralistic perspective on human behavior would be suspicious of any kind of moral perfection or imperfection. People are by nature neither saints nor sinners. We generally know how normatively imperfect a society of sinners is, for most religions have been pointing out those imperfections for centuries. But we also ought to remember, as experiences with totalitarianism in this century remind us, of the problems of moral perfectionism. Behavioral approaches to altruism are insufficiently appreciative of those problems. A society that was perfectly altruistic but that, as a result, lacked a human capacity to err would not necessarily be a good society. We might well prefer a society in which there was some cruelty to others — crime, for example — to one in which such cruelty was completely abolished if the former contained the freedom that makes such things as crime possible.

Assumptions of psychological pluralism, then, raise questions about behavioral approaches to altruism on both empirical and normative grounds. Behavioral definitions of altruism face all the difficulties of behavioral psychology. Two of the most important developments in contemporary psychology are the cognitive and the cultural approaches (Johnson-Laird 1988; Shweder 1991), and behaviorism ignores them both. On the one hand, cognitive issues are not considered especially important because altruistic behavior presumably can take place unthinkingly. (Indeed, from the standpoint of evolutionary efficiency, it is probably better that altruism be reflexive). On the other hand, behavioral approaches ignore the ways in which cognitive and other psychological states differ among cultures and between people. At a time when psychologists themselves have moved well beyond behaviorism, it makes little sense for other social scientists to adopt their discarded models in seeking to understand a phenomenon as complex as human altruism.

MOTIVATIONAL ALTRUISM

Some experimental social psychologists trying to understand prosocial behavior have turned to an examination of the motives people have for taking others into account. The missing ingredient in behavioral accounts, they argue, is *intent;* to be altruistic, an act must be directed specifically toward an altruistic end. The most parsimonious definition of motivational altruism comes from Daniel Batson and Laura Shaw: "Altruism is a motivational state with the ultimate goal of increasing another's welfare" (Batson and Shaw 1991, 108).

Batson makes a distinction between purity of motives and purity of behavior. A motive must be in one state or another;

that is to say, any particular motive must be altruistic or egoistic but not some combination of both. An end, by contrast, can and most often does combine egoism and altruism. If any particular act benefits oneself and another simultaneously, it is because there were two ultimate goals coexisting. If any particular act benefits another unconsciously (that is, without a goal), it is not altruistic. Human beings often find themselves in situations of goal conflict, which means that, in any given situation, they must choose which goal will have salience for them. In a series of ingenious experiments, Batson and his colleagues have tried to show that altruistic goals will be more likely to be chosen when an individual identifies empathically with other people (Batson, Batson, Slingsby, Harrell, et al. 1991; Batson, Oleson, Weeks, Healy, et al. 1989; Batson, Batson, Griffitt, Barrientos, et al. 1989; Batson, Dyck, Brandt, Batson, et al. 1988; Dovidio, Allen, and Schroeder 1990). Such empathy is not the by-product of benefits to the self, such as the relief brought about by minimizing another's distress. There is such a thing as pure motivational altruism, Batson claims. We really are capable of caring for others (Batson 1990).

Batson's work has not been universally accepted by social psychologists. Some are critical of his work because the concept of a motive does not seem to account either for behavior that is without motives or behavior that is guided by motives that cannot be fully articulated. The former situation has been described by Staub (1990); confronted with a person in distress, we do not always think clearly about what we are doing before helping them. A definition of altruism should include the kinds of automatic, unreflective actions that can define heroic action (especially in disasters), but that would not be included under Batson's definition because they would be insufficiently goal-directed. Similarly, Batson's way of thinking about altruism seems to devalue those acts which are a response to another's distress and which are primarily emotional in nature, for emotions are less cognitively dense than the idea of a motivation seems to apply.

Nancy Eisenberg (Eisenberg, Miller, Schaller, Fabes, et al. 1989; Eisenberg 1991, 29) makes an important distinction in this context between empathy, which in her view involves feeling what the other feels, and sympathy, which involves wanting the other person to feel better. To the degree that altruism involves empathy, it involves sentiments which are not quite the same as conscious motivations; generally speaking, we feel what another person feels not after considering the matter and being motivated to do so, but out of a spontaneous emotional reaction. From this point of view, Batson's motivational account of altruism is too demanding; to meet its standard, human beings must not only react empathically to another, but do so by meeting a standard of rationality that is rarely found in real world situations.

Yet from another point of view, Batson's definition does not set a high enough standard of rational conduct. One of the most fully elaborated theoretical accounts of how morality develops is that of Kolhberg, who argues that the most moral acts are those which rise beyond convention and situation to principled reasoning in line with the essentially impersonal Kantian criterion of judgment (Kohlberg 1981). Whatever one thinks of such an account, altruism, in the higher stages of moral development, would not be produced by motives that grow out of empathic identification with the other. It would instead be a reflective response to norms of justice that have been internalized by a particular individual (Eisenberg 1991, 128–29). As every Kantian knows, there are occasions in which the upholding of a norm of justice requires cruelty in specific circumstances; that is, to achieve a higher form of altruism, one must *resist* the desire to act out of empathy in a particular situation. Batson's definition, which tends to exclude emotional identification with a specific other, also tends to exclude rationalized identification with a general principle.

One way of combining these critiques of purely motivational theories of altruism is to point out that motives, like altruism in general, are rarely in one state or another. When we act altruistically, we can be responding at a number of levels and attempting to meet a variety of mixed goals (Mansbridge, this volume). Our inclination to act altruistically could originate in an emotion, as when, confronted with another's pain, we want to do something for that person. At the same time, such a response to another's pain can reflect a principled, cognitive commitment, namely, that it is right that we respond to the pain of another. Not surprisingly, emotions usually accompany altruistic acts: we think of the sacrifices people make for their children, which generally grow out of love, as the most altruistic of acts. Surprising as it may seem, however, altruistic acts are also often motivated by a commitment to principle.

Emotional appeals without any appeal to principle, for one thing, can backfire, exhibiting what has been called psychological reactance (Brehm 1966). When door-to-door solicitors for a charity showed potential contributors pictures of handicapped children, they did find such an effect (Isen and Noonberg 1979). In most cases, showing pictures did not bring about additional contributions; the best that could be said in support of emotional appeals to altruism was that they did not hurt contributions (Thorton, Kirchner, and Jacobs 1991). In addition, much real world altruistic behavior is motivated by commitments to abstract norms of justice. Psychologists have demonstrated that altruistic behavior *is* associated with an orientation toward norms; those who help others usually possess a strong sense that they *ought* to act in ways to help others (Schwartz 1977; Schwartz and Howard 1982). These internalized norms have important real world consequences. We know, for example, that those who have a strong sense of moral obligation are more likely to be blood donors (Zuckerman and Reiss 1978) and that repeat blood donors are more likely to act on the basis of principle than first-time blood donors (Charg, Piliavin, and Callero 1988). Similarly, individuals are more likely to ignore opportunities to act as free riders when they have a strong sense of moral

obligation. For example, individuals are more likely to participate in a recycling program when they believe it is the right thing to do (Hopper and Nielsen 1991).

Because the motives that lie behind altruistic acts are complex, combining, as they do, both emotion and principle, motivational theories of altruism can be faulted, not because they all pay attention to motives, but because they reduce all motives to one thing. Batson is surely correct to stress the importance of motivation; behavior that has altruistic consequences without any altruistic motive is less altruistic than behavior which is intended to help others but which actually harms them. We would be more likely to view the action of someone who tries to save a drowning man but fails as altruistic than the actions of someone whose passing boat acts as a life raft to bring a drowning person to shore. Moreover, there are clear normative advantages to a motivational account; one generally wants to believe that individuals are responsible for their acts and that when they act well it is because they were motivated to achieve the goal of acting well. But Batson runs into problems when he identifies motives with the pursuit of one goal only, for such an account does not give full appreciation to real world, as opposed to laboratory, conditions.

Motivational theories ought to be viewed as establishing necessary but not sufficient conditions for an understanding of altruism. Perhaps because they are usually advocated by psychologists, motivational theories tend to be individualistic, stressing how motives are internally arrived at as people examine the world around them. In this way, motivational theories accept a distinction between a private realm in which motives matter and a public realm in which people act on the basis of their motives. But this distinction, as Calhoun argues, is problematic (Calhoun, this volume). His point applies as much to theories of motivation as it does to other efforts to draw a sharp line between private and public activity. Motives come from somewhere. To the degree that the place from which they come lies outside individuals and their particular cognitive or emotional makeup, to that extent is a motivational account of altruism unsatisfactory.

Some evidence exists that the normative principles associated with altruistic acts *do* come from outside individuals themselves. In her study of blood donations in specific communities, Jane Piliavin found that personal norms did not account fully for variations in altruistic behavior. Any particular individuals' motives for giving blood were reenforced in those communities which were perceived as valuing such acts. In other words, personal norms were connected to social norms and could not be fully understood without an appreciation of the connection (Piliavin and Libby 1985/86). One need not take a Durkheimian position that society stands outside the individual and acts as a conscience for individuals; it is sufficient to recognize that individual motives toward altruism are influenced by the degree to which the society in which the individual lives values altruism. Obviously, as the examples of the rescue of European Jews illustrate, societies that denigrate altruism can still manifest it. Still, real world conditions underscore the point that motivations come from somewhere. We are more likely to see altruism occurring in societies that give social approval to altruism, just as we are more likely to see extreme egoism in cultures that, because they lack the rudiments of self-sufficiency, cannot make care of others a primary goal (Turnbull 1972).

ENVIRONMENTAL ALTRUISM

Relatively few studies by psychologists demonstrate the role played by norms, community standards, historical traditions, religious beliefs, and other social factors in the understanding of altruistic behavior. But the incompleteness of many of the psychological accounts of altruism indicates that the larger social environment may well be an important factor in encouraging or discouraging altruism. (In using the term *environment* in this context, I am not referring to the natural or ecological environment).

One way to illustrate the role that environmental factors play in encouraging or discouraging altruistic behavior is to consider the question of religion because religious beliefs and institutions, since Durkheim, have been understood to be part of the larger social structure—what I am calling the environment—that influences individual conduct. We would generally expect that the more religious people are, the more altruistic their behavior. Although there is some support for this notion, such direct relations do not fully describe the ways in which religious belief and individual altruism affect one another.

For one thing, the relation between religious belief and altruism is a weak one. Somewhat to their surprise, the Oliners discovered that rescuers could not be distinguished from nonrescuers on the basis of religious belief (1988, 156). Similarly, the sociologist Robert Wuthnow wrote, "Participation in religious organizations, it appears, has a genuine, but limited, effect on charitable behavior" (1991, 126). If this were the end of the story, Chaves's argument that religion is a public good which contributes directly and indirectly to philanthropic activity would be hard to explain (Chaves, this volume). But in fact, religion is an important factor in encouraging altruism, even if the relation is indirect.

This indirect relation can be best understood if we think of religious beliefs and institutions as frameworks that enable people to understand the meaning and consequences of altruism. In order to grasp what altruistic behaviors are, Wuthnow argues, we need to look beyond those behaviors themselves to "the languages we use to make sense of such behaviors, the cultural understandings that transform them from physical motions into human action" (1991, 45). One example is the story of the Good Samaritan. Although few Americans possess much factual knowledge about the Bible, 49 percent in one survey said that they could relate the story of the Good Samaritan; among those active in altruistic activity, the percentage was much higher. It seems clear to Wuthnow that

this story is part of the cultural repertoire of a society; it offers language that raises "the possibility of human kindness existing in a society of strangers" (1991, 182).

Chaves's conclusions, published in this volume, can also be interpreted this way. Chaves argues against the notion that religious organizations engage in charitable behavior in order to hold on to or gain members. But he does not go completely in the opposite direction of arguing that religious organizations are directly altruistic. Rather, he suggests, religious organizations generally have "unclear goals, unclear technologies, and fluid participants." The role of religion in encouraging altruism is indirect because organizations, like individuals, have multiple objectives and pursue the good in a variety of ways. This is why it is important to look at the mundane, everyday activities of religious organizations, in which the background frameworks are converted into institutions and patterns that enable individuals to act in altruistic ways.

Environmental accounts of altruism stress that altruism is a variable, not a constant. Because it is not latent in human genes, it has to be activated, and the degree of activation varies across time and space. Some historical periods manifest more altruistic behavior than others, and some countries tend to be more altruistic than others. At a broad level of generalization, such claims appear to be true; the extent to which different societies provide for the unfortunate, not only their own, but those in other countries as well, is a rough indication of its overall altruistic commitments. Clearly there were reasons for a country like Denmark rescuing its Jews when others did not (Jegstrup 1985/86).

Yet one must be careful about relying too much on environmental explanations of altruistic variation. We have already seen that religious belief does not correlate strongly with altruism; neither, in the Oliners' study, did political affiliation or social class (1988, 156–59). Other environmental factors, however, do seem to correlate with altruistic behavior. For all their methodological difficulties, many studies demonstrate that women tend to be more altruistic than men (Russell and Mentzel 1990; Mills, Pedersen, and Grusec 1989). There are stages in the life cycle which suggest that people's level of altruism is correlated with age (Midlarsky and Hannah 1989). Cross-cultural variations in the degree of altruism have frequently been observed (Johnson et al. 1989). Altruism is more frequent in rural areas than in urban ones (Kamal, Mehta, and Jain 1987). Gender may account for the fact that lesbians tend to be much more altruistic than male homosexuals (Weller and Benozio 1987)—and, for that matter, nurses usually more than doctors (Chambliss 1996)—but questions of lifestyle and cultural choice are also involved. Because some things seem to explain altruism better than others, we ought to remind ourselves that environmental explanations of altruism do not offer a foolproof guide to empirical observations; they play a major role, but they always have to be interpreted with some caution.

Environmental approaches to altruism stress the role to be

played, not only by culture, but also by social institutions. Bureaucratic organization can make it possible for altruism to exist in the absence of altruists. Sweden is often viewed as a very altruistic society composed of people who do not want to take any *personal* responsibility for the fate of their neighbors. When altruism is embodied in institutions, as Merton and Gieryn have pointed out, "the institutional arrangements of the professions tend to make it a matter of self-interest for individual practitioners to act altruistically" (1982, 119). From an institutional perspective, motives are the raw materials that are transformed by the institutions into something else, including behavior quite at variance with the original motive. As Selznick has argued, organizations can produce immoral outcomes from the intentions of moral people, but they can also do the opposite, create moral responsibility out of indifferent or even ill-intentioned persons (1992, 265–80). Just as markets can channel a disposition to act for the sake of others into a tendency to act out of self-interest, social institutions can transform selfish intentions into a collectively altruistic result.

There seems little question, then, that a good deal of real world altruistic behavior is related to the strength of social factors like culture and institutions. No empirical account of altruism can be complete without moving from the psychological level to the social. Some social scientists have argued that explanations for altruism, understood as the social capital that makes it possible for societies to avoid civic irresponsibility, have to be traced to historical events occurring as far back as the Middle Ages (Putnam 1993). Yet it would, I believe, be a mistake to move from extreme psychological accounts of altruism that emphasize what individuals do and ignore social and environmental factors to extreme environmental explanations in which individuals' motives are downplayed. Although environmental explanations are polar opposites of genetic ones, both have a tendency to downplay individual acts in favor of determinations at another level: either below the individual in the genes or above the individual in a Durkheimian reification of society. Moreover, it is a hotly contested question — one that cannot be resolved here — whether it would be preferable to live in a nonaltruistic society filled with altruists or in an altruistic society filled with indifference. On both empirical and normative grounds, there is much to say for environmental accounts of altruism, but such accounts should be used judiciously.

CONCLUSION

One of the central themes of this book is the notion that we ought to develop an appreciation of multiplicity. People will always act in a variety of ways; any theory which reduces their behavior to one way of acting is therefore problematic on scientific grounds. But even more, people should act in multiple ways. The best way to avoid the twin extremes of pure value relativism and preaching is to recognize the complexity of human objectives.

Respect for pluralism can be illustrated in two ways from the literature on altruism. In the first place, any theory of human behavior should not posit that egoism always rules over altruism or vice versa. What emerges from the literature in many forms is a sense that altruism and egoism do not constitute mutually exclusive categories. In experimental social psychology, it is recognized that human beings do respond out of empathy for the plight of others, as Batson has shown (for an overview of his work, see Batson and Shaw 1991), but at the same time that empathy often satisfies the relatively selfish function of stress reduction, as Batson's main critic, Cialdini (1991), has argued. (For a compromise position, see Stiff et al. 1988). Likewise, the sociological study of real world altruism, such as blood or kidney donation, indicates that, in the words of Roberta Simmons, "it is very difficult to untangle altruistic and egoistic motives." (1991, 5).

Much the same mixture of motives seems to underlie altruistic professions and institutions. Altruistic professions are caught between many imperatives, not all of them altruistic. On the one hand, those usually helped by such professions increasingly reject altruism as a model that gives meaning to the help provided them; among the deaf, for example, there has been a clear rejection of the notion of giving, replaced by an assertion of rights (Lane 1992). On the other hand, those who entered altruistic professions in order to give end up organizing themselves into unions, engaging in efforts to prevent their exploitation in the name of altruism, and feeling burned out by the demands placed upon them (Chambliss 1996). Similarly, the welfare state, the most extensive altruistic institution of all, has hardly escaped self-interested behavior. Those who work for European welfare states, as well as those who receive benefits from them, can support their altruistic goals perfectly well while receiving egoistic rewards.

Even the most extraordinary altruistic behavior — such as the acts of those who rescued the European Jews — supports the idea that altruism and its opposite exist in a kind of uneasy simultaneity. In their study of rescuers, the Oliners point out that

> they were and are "ordinary" people. They were farmers and teachers, entrepreneurs and factory workers, rich and poor, parents and single people, Protestants and Catholics. Most had done nothing extraordinary before the war nor have they done much that is extraordinary since. Most were marked neither by exceptional leadership qualities nor by unconventional behavior. They were not heroes cast in larger-than-life molds. What most distinguished them were their connections with others in relationships of commitment and care. (259)

So "normal" were the people who rescued Jews, often at great risk to themselves, that, when interviewed many years later, a number of them appeared to be completely conventional, some even vaguely anti-Semitic.

From the laboratory to real life to extraordinary situations, in short, social scientists are moving toward the position that the reduction of all behavior to one motive makes little sense empirically or theoretically. If the models we develop to represent reality are to be as complex as the reality we want to represent, such models should be pluralistic in nature. A pluralistic model would make the following assumptions about human behavior: both egoism and altruism exist; most real world examples of human behavior contain elements of both simultaneously; efforts to attribute to one or the other the determining role in explaining human behavior are inevitably contrived; and as a result, social scientists should use a wide variety of techniques, methods, and approaches to gain insights to how human beings actually act.

Just as we ought to assume a pluralistic position when it comes to identifying egoism and altruism, so we ought to be pluralistic with respect to the approaches to altruism discussed in this chapter. Each approach, as is usually the case in academic literature, thinks of its own conceptions as the most significant, which often leads to a battle of words about which definition is correct and which is inappropriate. Yet it may be that a combination of these approaches best fulfills a commitment to pluralism. Although there are valuable aspects associated with behavioral approaches, they tend to be difficult to incorporate into a pluralistic theory because they tend to reduce all behavior to one thing. We ought, therefore, to think of altruism as containing primarily motivational and environmental components compared to behavioral ones. Most altruistic acts occur in an environment friendly to altruism but require the normative motivation that only individuals can provide.

I think of altruism — or, for that matter, of selfishness — as a template, a preframed response that guides but does not determine individual behavior. We call things altruistic because a long history of social practices, cultural products, religious beliefs, traditions, and ways of thinking — not the least among them a field of inquiry called sociology — label them as such. When we are called upon to make a decision, these bundles of responses called altruism are out there, available to us, helping us frame the complex reality we confront. In most situations, we are fully aware of which reactions are selfish and which are altruistic, and this makes it possible for us to reflect on how we make our decisions as we are in the process of making them.

But it is not culture that determines whether any particular choice we make will be selfish or altruistic. Only our individual attributes — the way we think, the lessons we have internalized, the reactions to past experience — shape how we will respond to the preexisting templates available to us. Only on the rarest possible occasions will we choose either template in its entirety. Most of the time, what we do involves an uneasy combination of motives and intentions, some of them selfish, others altruistic. Indeed, it is precisely because there is nearly always a gap between how we act and the ways that our culture tells us we should act that we have such a thing as

a conscience. We can recognize what altruism is, judge our own behavior as less than perfect in regard to it, and still conclude, rightly, that a little altruism is better than none. The same, of course, applies to selfishness, even if the guilt experienced in not acting the way economists think we should is generally less than the guilt experienced in not acting the way God thinks we should.

Altruism, then, represents that bundle of cultural practices which insist that the decisions we take be made in the light of their consequences for others. In this sense, altruism is primarily an environmental phenomenon; it exists in the stories, traditions, beliefs, and institutional memories of a society, handed down from generation to generation. In one form or another, every society seems to possess such practices, even if they are more fully developed in some places than others. For the behavior of any particular individual to be considered altruistic, it must call upon those beliefs in some way, either by invoking them as a motive for action or (probably more commonly) by rationalizing an act after it has taken place. Account giving, in other words, is a crucial feature of human altruistic behavior, for even if such an account is distorted or simply wrong, the existence of a set of cultural practices enables the society to evaluate the account in the light of what constitutes altruism. The giving of accounts will be influenced by the norms of the society, norms which themselves are derived from the cultural practices that establish standards of altruism. But every individual will have a different relation to those social norms. Some will, because of family upbringing or psychological development, possess strong normative orientations regardless of what others do. Others will respond altruistically when they see those around them responding altruistically. Still others will use social norms as a foil to operate as free riders on the normative obedience of others. There will never be clear markers of who is likely to be more altruistic and who is likely to be less. It is theoretically possible for a particular individual to lack any degree of altruism at all. But for society as a whole, there will always be both altruistic codes and altruistic behavior or else there will be no society.

This is a relatively weak definition of altruism, one that seems to downplay the heroically altruistic — the rescuers of the European Jews, for example. But I think it worth emphasizing that with both self-interest and altruism, we generally find as much as our definitions allow. If social scientists define self-interest broadly and altruism narrowly, they will certainly find more self-interest than altruism. That is certainly one way to protect the notion that, to be scientific, the social sciences need one and only one assumption about human behavior. There is, in response, the temptation to reverse the agenda, to claim that altruism is the norm and self-interest the exception. But this not only maintains the same underlying methodology as self-interest, but is the point of view most compatible with behavioral accounts of altruism, for if altruism is rooted in our genetic structures, it will tend to reign imperially over all other forms of behavior. Strong definitions of altruism run the risk of mimicking strong definitions of egoism.

Furthermore, a weak definition of altruism is more likely to meet the demands of pluralism. There are, I believe, two major threats to a pluralistic understanding of altruism contained in recent social science and social theory. On the one hand, strongly individualistic theories are based on the notion that people already know their preferences, making it unnecessary for them to have strong social institutions and structures that help shape preferences. Individuals under such a construct are singular; we generally know what they want because their preferences are either constant or transitive. On the other hand, certain communitarian tendencies, presumably the opposite of individualistic ones, can, as Calhoun argues in his contribution to this book, emphasize national values in ways that reduce all people to singularity as well; we know what they want because we know the country to which they belong.

Both points of view overtheorize. Both approach individuals as people whose behavior and choices are already shaped. But altruistic acts, as one of the most important things that people do, may not be shaped at all. Altruism requires that an individual make choices in the context of particular situations. Such choices must be a reflection of the way individuals think and develop as they confront contexts within which they must make decisions. Weak definitions of altruism are important because they tend to produce stronger conceptions of individual choice. If we know what altruism is, we need to know little about individuals who act altruistically. If we leave the definition of altruism relatively open, both our understanding of people and our appreciation for their multiple objectives are likely to be enhanced.

REFERENCES

Axelrod, Robert. 1984. *The Evolution of Cooperation.* New York: Basic Books.

Bar-Tal, Daniel. 1985/86. "Altruistic Motivation to Help: Definition, Utility, and Operationalization." *Humboldt Journal of Social Relations* 13:3–14.

Batson, C. Daniel. 1990. "How Social an Animal? The Human Capacity for Caring." *American Psychologist* 45:336–46.

———. 1991. *The Altruism Question: Towards a Social-Psychological Answer.* Hillsdale, N.J.: Erlbaum Associates.

Batson, C. Daniel, Judy G. Batson, Jacqueline K. Slingsby, Kevin Harrell, et al. 1991. "Empathic Joy and the Empathy-Altruism Hypothesis." *Journal of Personality and Social Psychology* 61:413–26.

Batson, C. Daniel, Kathryn C. Oleson, Joy L. Weeks, Sean P. Healy, et al. 1989. "Religious Prosocial Motivation: Is It Altruistic or Egoistic?" *Journal of Personality and Social Psychology* 57:873–84.

Batson, C. Daniel, Judy G. Batson, Cari A. Griffitt, Sergio Barrientos, et al. 1989. "Negative-state Relief and the Empathy-Altruism Hypothesis." *Journal of Personality and Social Psychology* 56:922–33.

Batson, C. Daniel, Janine L. Dyck, Randall J. Brandt, Judy G. Batson, et al. 1988. "Five Studies Testing Two New Egoistic Alternatives to the Empathy-Altruism Hypothesis." *Journal of Personality and Social Psychology* 55:52–77.

Batson, C. Daniel, and Laura L. Shaw. 1991. "Evidence for Altruism: Toward a Pluralism of Prosocial Motives." *Psychological Inquiry* 2:107–22.

Bierhoff, Hans W., Renate Klein, and Peter Kramp. 1991. "Evidence for the Altruistic Personality from Data on Accident Research." *Journal of Personality* 59:263–80.

Brehm, J. W. 1966. *A Theory of Psychological Reactance.* New York: Academic Press.

Carlo, Gustavo, Nancy Eisenberg, Debra Troyer, and Galen Switzer. 1991. "The Altruistic Personality: In What Contexts Is It Apparent?" *Journal of Personality and Social Psychology* 61:450–58.

Chambliss, Dan. 1996. *Beyond Caring: Hospitals, Nurses, and the Social Organization of Ethics.* Chicago: University of Chicago Press.

Charg, H. V., J. A. Piliavin, and P. L. Callero. 1988. "Role Identity and Reasoned Action in the Prediction of Repeated Behavior." *Social Psychology Quarterly* 51:303–17.

Cialdini, Robert B. 1991. "Altruism or Egoism? That Is (Still) the Question." *Psychological Inquiry* 2:124–26.

Coleman, James S. 1990. *Foundations of Social Theory.* Cambridge: Harvard University Press.

Dawes, Robyn M., Alphons J. C. van de Kragt, and John M. Orbell. 1988. "Not Me or Thee but We: The Importance of Group Identity in Eliciting Cooperation in Dilemma Situations: Experimental Manipulations." *Acta Psychologica* 68:83–97.

Dawkins, Richard. 1976. *The Selfish Gene.* New York: Oxford University Press.

Dovidio, John F., Judith L. Allen, and David A. Schroeder. 1990. "Specificity of Empathy-Induced Helping: Evidence for Altruistic Motivation." *Journal of Personality and Social Psychology* 59:249–60.

Eisenberg, Nancy. 1991. "Values, Sympathy, and Individual Differences: Toward a Pluralism of Factors Influencing Altruism and Empathy." *Psychological Inquiry* 2:128–31.

Eisenberg, Nancy, Paul A. Miller, Mark Schaller, Richard Fabes, et al. 1989. "The Role of Sympathy and Altruistic Personality Traits in Helping: A Reexamination." *Journal of Personality* 57:41–67.

Frank, Robert. 1988. *Passions within Reason: The Strategic Role of the Emotions.* New York: Norton.

Granovetter, Mark. 1978. "Threshold Models of Collective Behavior." *American Journal of Sociology* 83:1420–43.

Hamilton, William D. 1964. "The Genetical Evolution of Social Behavior, I and II." *Journal of Theoretical Biology* 7:1–52.

Hoffman, Martin. 1987. "The Contribution of Empathy to Justice and Moral Development." In *Empathy and Its Development,* ed. Nancy Eisenberg and Janet Strayer. New York: Cambridge University Press.

Holmes, Stephen. 1990. "The Secret History of Self-Interest." In *Beyond Self-Interest,* ed. Jane Mansbridge, 267–86. Chicago: University of Chicago Press.

Hopper, Joseph R., and Joyce M. Nielsen. 1991. "Recycling as Altruistic Behavior: Normative and Behavioral Strategies to

Expand Participation in a Community Recycling Program." *Environment and Behavior* 23:195–220.

Hurley, Dennis, and Bern Allen. 1974. "The Effect of the Number of People Present in Nonemergency Situations." *Journal of Social Psychology* 92:27–29.

Isen, A. M., and A. Noonberg. 1979. "The Effect of Photographs of the Handicapped on Donations to Charity: When a Thousand Words May Be too Much." *Journal of Applied Social Psychology* 9:426–31.

Jegstrup, Elsebet. 1985–86. "Spontaneous Action: The Rescue of the Danish Jews from Hannah Arendt's Perspective." *Humboldt Journal of Social Relations* 1985–86:260–84.

Johnson, Ronald C., George P. Danko, Thomas J. Darvill, Stephen Bochner, et al. 1989. "Cross-Cultural Assessment of Altruism and Its Correlates." *Personality and Individual Differences* 10:855–68.

Johnson-Laird, Philip N. 1988. *The Computer and the Mind: An Introduction to Cognitive Science.* Cambridge: Harvard University Press.

Kamal, Preet, Manju Mehta, and Uday Jain. 1987. "Altruism in Urban and Rural Environment." *Indian Psychological Review* 32:35–42.

Kohlberg, Lawrence. 1981. *The Philosophy of Moral Development.* New York: Harper and Row.

Krebs, Dennis L. 1970. "Altruism — An Examination of the Concept and a Review of the Literature." *Psychological Bulletin* 73:258–302.

Lane, Harlan. 1992. *The Mask of Benevolence: Disabling the Deaf Community.* New York: Knopf.

Latané, Bibb, and John Darley. 1970. *The Unresponsive Bystander: Why Doesn't He Help?* Englewood Cliffs: Prentice-Hall.

Macy, Michael W. 1991a. "Chains of Cooperation: Threshold Effects in Collective Action." *American Sociological Review* 56:730–47.

———. 1991b. "Learning to Cooperate: Stochastic and Tacit Collusion in Social Exchange." *American Journal of Sociology* 97:808–43.

Merton Robert K., and Thomas F. Gieryn. 1982. "Institutional Altruism: The Case of the Professions." In Robert K. Merton, *Social Research and the Practicing Professions,* ed. with an introduction by Aaron Rosenblatt and Thomas F. Gieryn, 109–34. Cambridge, Mass.: Apt Books.

Midlarsky, Elizabeth and Mary E. Hannah. 1989. "The Generous Elderly: Naturalistic Studies of Donations across the Life Span." *Psychology and Aging* 4:346–51.

Mills, Rosemary S., Jan Pedersen, and Joan E. Grusec. 1989. "Sex Differences in Reasoning and Emotion about Altruism." *Sex Roles* 20:603–21.

Oliner, Samuel P., and Pearl M. Oliner. 1988. *The Altruistic Personality: Rescuers of Jews in Nazi Europe.* New York: Free Press.

Oliver, Pamela E., Gerald Marwell, and Ruy Teixeira. 1985. "A Theory of Critical Mass I: Interdependence, Group Heterogeneity, and the Production of Collective Action." *American Journal of Sociology* 91:522–56.

Oliver, Pamela E., and Gerald Marwell. 1988. "The Paradox of Group Size in Collective Action: A Theory of Critical Mass II." *American Sociological Review* 53:1–8.

Piliavin, Jane Allyn, and Hong-Wen Charg. 1990. "Altruism: A Review of Recent Theory and Research." *Annual Review of Sociology* 16:27–65.

Piliavin, Jane Allyn, and Donald Libby. 1985/86. "Personal Norms, Perceived Social Norms, and Blood Donation." *Humboldt Journal of Social Relations* 13:159–94.

Putnam, Robert. 1993. *Making Democracy Work: Civic Traditions in Modern Italy.* Princeton: Princeton University Press.

Reykowski, Janusz. 1980. "Origin of Prosocial Motivation: Heterogeneity of Personality Development." *Studia Psychologia* 22:91–106.

Rushton, J. Phillipe. 1980. *Altruism, Socialization, and Society.* Englewood Cliffs, Prentice-Hall.

Russell, Gordon W., and Robert K. Mentzel. 1990. "Sympathy and Altruism in Response to Disasters." *Journal of Social Psychology* 1990:309–16.

Schwartz, Barry. 1986. *The Battle for Human Nature.* New York: Norton.

Schwartz, S. H. 1977. "Normative Influences on Altruism." In *Advances in Experimental Social Psychology,* ed. L. Berkowitz, 221–79. New York: Academic Press.

Schwartz, S. H., and J. A. Howard. 1982. "Helping and Cooperation: A Self-Based Motivational Model." In *Cooperation and Helping Behavior: Theories and Research,* ed. J. Derlega and J. Grzelak, 327–53. New York: Academic Press.

Selznick, Philip. 1992. *The Moral Commonwealth: Social Theory and the Promise of Community.* Berkeley: University of California Press.

Shweder, Richard A. 1991. *Thinking Through Cultures: Explorations in Cultural Psychology.* Cambridge: Harvard University Press.

Simmons, Roberta G. 1991. "Altruism and Sociology." *The Sociological Quarterly* 32:1–22.

Staub, Ervin. 1990. "Moral Exclusion, Personal Goal Theory, and Extreme Destructiveness." *Journal of Social Issues* 46:47–64.

Stiff, J. B., J. P. Dillard, L. Somera, H. Kim, and C. Sleight. 1988. "Empathy, Communication, and Prosocial Behavior." *Communication Monographs* 55:198–213.

Thorton, Bill, Gayle Kirchner, and Jacqueline Jacobs. 1991. "Influence of a Photograph on a Charitable Appeal: A Picture May Be Worth a Thousand Words When It Has to Speak for Itself." *Journal of Applied Social Psychology* 21:433–45.

Trivers, R. L. 1971. "The Evolution of Reciprocal Altruism." *Quarterly Review of Biology* 46:35–57.

Turnbull, Colin M. 1972. *The Mountain People.* New York: Simon and Schuster.

Weller, Leonard, and Motti Benozio. 1987. "Homosexuals' and Lesbians' Philosophies of Human Nature." *Social Behavior and Personality* 15:221–24.

Wilensky, Harold, and Charles N. Lebeaux. 1959. *Industrial Society and Social Welfare: The Impact of Industrialization on the Supply and Organization of Social Welfare Services in the United States.* New York: Russell Sage Foundation.

Williams, Bernard. 1985. *Ethics and the Limits of Philosophy.* Cambridge: Harvard University Press.

Wilson, James Q. 1993. *The Moral Sense.* New York: Free Press.

Wuthnow, Robert. 1991. *Acts of Compassion: Caring for Others and Helping Ourselves*. Princeton: Princeton University Press.

Zadeh, L. A. 1965. "Fuzzy Sets." *Information and Control* 8:338–53.

Zahn-Waxler, Carolyn. 1991. "The Case for Empathy: A Developmental Perspective." *Psychological Inquiry* 2:155–58.

Zuckerman, M., and H. Y. Reiss. 1978. "Comparison of Three Models for Predicting Altruistic Behavior." *Journal of Personality and Social Psychology* 36:468–510.

4

MARK CHAVES

The Religious Ethic and the Spirit of Nonprofit Entrepreneurship

*Not leisure and enjoyment, but only activity serves to
increase the glory of God, according to the definite
manifestations of His will.*

> — Max Weber, *The Protestant Ethic
> and the Spirit of Capitalism*

*From this point of view, an organization is a collection of
choices looking for problems, issues and feelings looking
for decision situations in which they might be aired,
solutions looking for issues to which they might be the
answer, and decision makers looking for work.*

> — Michael Cohen et al., "A Garbage Can
> Model of Organizational Choice"

A significant segment of the nonprofit world contains organizations producing services that have some public benefit.
Educational and health care institutions, for example, provide clear instances of organizations that generate positive
externalities — benefits that accrue even to individuals who
do not directly consume the services of such organizations.

One major concern of those who research and write about
nonprofits has been how to ensure that a society produces
adequate amounts of such publicly beneficial services. This
concern generates a host of specific questions: What activities in fact produce positive externalities or public benefit?
Among those that do, which are most efficiently provided
by government, which by nonprofits, which by private, for-
profit organizations? What government policies best direct
resources toward organizations providing public goods?
What explains historical and cross-national variation in the
extent to which a particular activity, say, primary education,
is carried out by government, nonprofit, or for-profit organizations? What difference do variations in the "market share"
of the three sectors make for a society? What motivates individuals to create nonprofit organizations of various sorts?

The study of religion and religious organizations connects
in complicated ways to these questions about the social production of public goods and nonprofit organization. First,
religion itself is one of the major "products" of the nonprofit

This work was supported by the Program on Governance of Nonprofit Organizations of the Indiana University Center on Philanthropy.
This chapter has benefited enormously from the generous comments of
Victoria Alexander, Richard Chapman, Elisabeth Clemens, Peter Dobkin Hall, William R. Hutchison, Estelle James, Charles Perrow, Walter

Powell, Carrie Rothburd, Mark Schultz, Claire Ullman, Rhys Williams,
and participants in the roundtable discussion that took place at the conference "Private Action and the Public Good," Indianapolis, 1993. Any
logical or empirical flaws in this chapter remain only because I have
paid insufficient attention to the criticisms and suggestions of these
individuals.

sector. Measured by total revenues, religious organizations constitute the third largest subsector of the U.S. nonprofit world, behind health and education. Just over 50 percent of U.S. adults report household contributions to their church or synagogue, representing 60 to 65 percent of total household giving (Independent Sector 1993, xi). In 1995, religious organizations in the United States received more than $60 billion, a figure that represents 44 percent of all charitable donations (Kaplan 1996, 13). The labor donated to religious organizations is a smaller, but still substantial, portion of total volunteer labor in this society: just over 25 percent of adults report volunteering to religious institutions, and the time they contribute represents about 18 percent of total volunteer time (Independent Sector 1993, xi).

Second, religious organizations are instrumental in providing nonreligious public goods. Even though the majority of religious giving goes to maintaining religious congregations themselves, the sheer size of this giving means that church expenditures on charitable activities are substantially more than the charitable giving of either foundations or corporations. In 1986, $8 billion of charity were donated by religious organizations, while in 1985 $4.5 billion were donated by foundations and $4.9 billion by corporations (Doyle 1993, 21). Independent Sector (1993, 1) estimates that, in 1991, $6.6 billion were donated by congregations to other organizations and individuals. Moreover, many activities conducted by congregations themselves are nonreligious. Including the value of volunteer time, Independent Sector (1993, 1) estimates that, in 1991, 40 percent of the $53.3 billion spent by congregations on current activities supported such secular activities as nonreligious education, health care, social services, and the like.

The list of activities supported by religious organizations is impressive in its range: education, human services, health care and hospital services, arts and culture, community development, environmental programs, nutrition assistance, refugee aid, day care, youth camps, advocacy, emergency assistance, disaster relief, clothing, and temporary shelter are among the services provided by religious organizations (Independent Sector 1993, 1; Wood 1990, 256). Religious organizations often shelter and support social movements, both in this country (Morris 1984; Cress 1993) and elsewhere (Anheier 1991; Smith 1991).

This chapter examines religious organizations as sites of both religious and secular activity, and it does so by drawing heavily upon research supported by the Program on Governance at Indiana University's Center on Philanthropy. The first section of the chapter argues that our understanding of the provision of public goods in general can be greatly enhanced by focusing on the social production of religion itself. This section begins by observing an intriguing fact about the complex relationships among religion, nonprofit activity, and scholarly work about nonprofit activity: although religion has historically been considered an important publicly beneficial good, and continues today to be officially and popularly

understood as such, it is almost universally not considered as such by contemporary scholars of the nonprofit sector.

The second section of the chapter focuses on the fascinating and important connections between religious organizations and the provision of nonreligious goods and services. Historical investigations constitute the majority of the work on religion sponsored by the Program on Governance. Consequently, this work is most informative about the central importance of religious organizations to the *founding* of nonprofit organizations of many sorts. Using this and other work, I develop an explanation for the overrepresentation of religious organizations among the founders of nonreligious nonprofits. In particular, I argue that nonprofit organization is often an unintended consequence of restless religious activism. As such, a good dose of Weberian irony is required to account for the nonprofit entrepreneurial activity of those associated with religious organizations.

RELIGION AS PUBLIC GOOD

There is a striking disjuncture between, on the one hand, the historical and official assumption that religion is itself a public good and, on the other hand, the contemporary reluctance of scholars to consider it as such. The easiest way to establish this disjuncture is to compare lists of activities that count as charitable. Such lists are often given as part of both bureaucratic and scholarly definitions of charitable activity because, as James Douglas (1983) has pointed out, the concept of public benefit is vague. Its formal definition almost always requires illustrative lists to flesh it out. While never meant to be exhaustive, such lists offer a glimpse of underlying assumptions about activity that counts as publicly beneficial. Here are four examples of official lists of charitable activities, all from Douglas (1983):

> Repair hospitals, help sick people, mend bad roads, build up bridges that have broken down, help maidens to marry or to make them nuns, find food for prisoners or poor people, put scholars to school or some other craft, *help religious orders* and ameliorate rents and taxes. (Langland, fourteenth-century poem, quoted in Douglas, 165, emphasis added)

> The relief of aged, impotent and poor people; the maintenance of sick and maimed soldiers and mariners, schools of learning, free schools and scholars in universities; the repair of bridges, ports, havens, causeways, *churches,* sea-banks and highways; the education and preferment of orphans; the relief, stock or maintenance of houses of correction; the marriages of poor maids, the supportation, aid and help of young tradesmen, handicraftsmen and persons decayed; the relief or redemption of prisoners or captives; and the aid or ease of any poor inhabitants concerning payment of fifteens, setting out of soldiers and other taxes. (Preamble to the Elizabethan Statute of Charitable Uses of 1601, quoted in Douglas, 57f., emphasis added)

... by bringing their minds and hearts under the influence of education, *religion,* by relieving their bodies from disease, suffering or constraint, by assisting them to establishing themselves in life, or by erecting or maintaining public buildings or works or otherwise lessening the burdens of government. (Justice Gray, 1867, quoted in Douglas, 85, emphasis added)

Relief of the poor and distressed or of the underprivileged; *advancement of religion*; advancement of education or science; erection or maintenance of public buildings, monuments, or works; lessening of the burdens of government; and promotion of social welfare by organizations designed to accomplish any of the above purposes, or (1) to lessen neighborhood tensions; (2) to eliminate prejudice or discrimination; (3) to defend human and civil rights secured by law; or (4) to combat community deterioration and juvenile delinquency. (Reg. 1.501(C)(3)-1(d)(2), U.S. Internal Revenue Service, quoted in Douglas, 57, emphasis added)

These lists differ in many ways, illustrating the changing content of the phrase *charitable activity.* Yet common to all is the inclusion of religion as itself a public good, a charitable purpose in its own right. Compare the following lists offered by contemporary scholars:

There is hardly any public service, apart from national defense, that was not originally pioneered by private philanthropy. Education, hospitals, services for the poor, the elderly, the disabled, the protection of children, the encouragement of the arts, housing for the needy, and scientific and social research were all supported by private philanthropy long before government became involved. (Douglas 1983, 118)

Rather, we have chosen to focus on what we regard as the core functions [of the nonprofit sector] — that is, the activities in which nonprofits play either a preponderant or a particularly vital role[:] . . . popular and high culture . . . health care . . . educational institutions . . . personal social services . . . community-based nonprofits . . . nonprofit social movements. (Powell 1987a, xii)

Moreover, many of the activities that in this country are performed in substantial part by nonprofits are performed in most other developed countries almost exclusively by governmental firms; health care, higher education, and the performing arts are conspicuous examples. (Hansmann 1987, 34)

Such lists, from which religion is conspicuously absent, could be multiplied. The point here is not that analysts are mistakenly excluding religion from their definition of public goods; none of these lists is intended by its author to be exhaustive. Rather, the point is that the absence of religion from such casually constructed lists reveals an interesting

fact about how scholars of the nonprofit sector have tended to think (or not think) about religion. It seems fair to say that, with the exception of some unreconstructed Durkheimians, it simply does not occur to most contemporary scholars of the nonprofit world that religion may be appropriately conceptualized as itself a public good. In this section of the chapter, I want to (a) describe what I take to be the primary reason for the reluctance of scholars to see religion as itself a public good; (b) suggest several ways in which religion might be construed as a public good; and (c) present two examples of scholarly payoff concerning the production of public goods in general that are a direct result of focusing on religion and religious organizations.

Why Neglect Religion?

What explains the apparent reluctance, at least among scholars, to consider religion itself a public good?[1] Peter Dobkin Hall (1992, 116) addressed this question directly:

Why has religion been overlooked in efforts to understand voluntarism and philanthropy? Part of the answer may be that few scholars are likely to possess firsthand knowledge of what churches do and how they do it. The nature of funding for nonprofits research may also play a role, because less than 2 percent of foundation grants are awarded to religious organizations. . . . The organization of nonprofits as an industry may also play a role in diminishing attention to the role of religious nonprofits: of the six hundred members of Independent Sector (IS) in 1985, only twenty-five (4 percent) were identifiable as religious organizations. . . . [Also,] the aloofness of religious organizations [to the mainline nonprofits] complemented secular scholarship's indifference to the role of religion in American philanthropy and voluntarism.

Without denying the relevance of these factors, I believe there is another important cause, of which Fred Beuttler's (1992) work gives a glimpse.

---

1. Beyond, though probably related to, this reluctance to consider religion a public good, research on nonprofit organizations largely neglected religion and religious organizations until the mid-1990s. Hall (1992, 115) reports that (a) only 4.7 percent of the 916 projects in Independent Sector's 1986–87 compendium of research-in-progress dealt specifically with religion; (b) only 1.5 percent of the 130 working papers produced by Yale's Program on Non-Profit Organizations specifically addressed religion or religious institutions; and (c) only 2.1 percent of the 2,195 works listed in Daphne Layton's *Philanthropy and Voluntarism: An Annotated Bibliography* (1987) deal specifically with religion. There are indications, however, that religion has begun to catch the attention of nonprofit scholars. The issue of *Nonprofit and Voluntary Sector Quarterly* for summer 1994, for example, was devoted to articles on religion. Moreover, although 1980s collections of essays on the nonprofit sector tended not to include chapters on religion (see, for example, Powell 1987b and Hodgkinson et al. 1989), more recent collections do tend to have such chapters. See, for example, Van Til et al. 1990 and Clotfelter 1992, not to mention this volume.

Beuttler tells the story of a conflict in 1951 between Chester Barnard and John Foster Dulles over the proper relationship between religion and the "morals project" Barnard was trying to establish at the Rockefeller Foundation, of which he was then president. The conflict arose out of an increasing commitment among foundation trustees to sponsor work in the "field of moral and spiritual values" (Beuttler 1992, 5). One issue with which the foundation staff and trustees had to wrestle was the link between religion and this vaguely specified initiative. As part of this initiative, the Rockefeller Foundation was weighing proposals from both the National Council of Churches (NCC) and from Union Theological Seminary. Although Barnard actively pursued the NCC proposal, Beuttler (1992, 7) reports that he was against the seminary's proposal "on the grounds that it was too 'evangelical and by implication . . . Protestant,' as it bordered on supporting direct mission efforts. Barnard explained . . . that he did not want 'to jeopardize support for activities relating to morals and ethics' that were being considered from the National Council of Churches by tying them too closely with strictly religious efforts." Dulles, a Rockefeller Foundation trustee since 1935, objected to Barnard's willingness to distinguish in this way between moral values in general and religious values in particular. Dulles forcefully questioned why the foundation had "abstained from aid to *religious projects and agencies*" (Beuttler 1992, 7, Beuttler's emphasis).

In a sense, Barnard and Dulles both seem to have won the skirmish: Union Theological Seminary and the NCC both received grants from the Rockefeller Foundation ($525,000 and more than $100,000, respectively). But Barnard's view, which advocated keeping moral concerns distinct from explicitly religious concerns, clearly won the war. Indeed, the grant to Union was only reluctantly approved in 1954 and only because the proposal had been revised to support their "non-denominational, international, and, to some extent, inter-faith" Program of Advanced Religious Studies (Beuttler 1992, 8, quoting Dean Rusk, then foundation president).

The conflict illustrates the general point, developed further in this book by Jane Mansbridge and Craig Calhoun, that what is regarded as a public good in a culture—be it religion, the prevention of cruelty to animals, or something else—is usually contested. As Calhoun (in this volume) puts it, "The public good is not objectively or externally ascertainable. . . . It is created in and through the public process." In addition to Mansbridge's point that such "contested concepts" can be useful precisely because they serve as the site of normative debates over what counts as good and what counts as public, I would point out that there is much to be learned by investigating such clashes. The conflict described above, for example, reveals something interesting about the changing place of religion in an American society becoming increasingly more heterogeneous. The Protestant establishment, represented by the NCC, was, by the early 1950s, no

longer the uncontested arbiter of the moral basis of American society.[2] This story illustrates the fact that religion itself is not an unambiguous public good in a religiously pluralistic society, and I think this is the social reality underlying the striking absence of religion from the lists of public goods offered by contemporary scholars. Our consciousness of religious variation, not to mention religious conflict, changes our evaluation of religion itself as a public good.

A Tocquevillian Approach to Religion as a Public Good
Chester Barnard's reluctance to tie the Rockefeller Foundation too closely to religion was based on the sound conviction that particular religions cannot provide moral consensus in a religiously pluralistic society. Indeed, attempts to use religion in this way seem to promote evil more than they promote good. Especially in settings in which, as James Beckford (1990, 11) put it, "there is a strong alignment of religion with kinship, neighborhood, work, leisure, politics, social standing, and life-chances," we should be extremely wary of claims that religion contributes to the public good. To insist on attributing to religion the Durkheimian function of providing collective solidarity simultaneously commits both a moral and an intellectual error. Such a move promotes religion's least desirable feature—its capacity to reinforce social boundaries—and it misses the ways in which religion is, in fact, publicly beneficial. By analogy to Calhoun's point that community should not be equated with nation, I am arguing that community also ought not be equated with religion.

We should look for religion's public benefit somewhere other than its capacity to promote undesirable collective solidarities. Where religious differences largely cut across other significant social differences, we can, in short, be Tocquevillians rather than Durkheimians in our approach to religion as a public good. This implies that we attend to the concrete activities of diverse religious organizations, activities that may, in fact, generate benefits to those outside the circle of members.

From this perspective, religion can be seen as a public good in at least two ways. First, as already mentioned, religious organizations provide significant amounts of charity and services to individuals other than their own members. Do religious organizations do enough of this, however, to warrant inclusion in the class of publicly beneficial organizations? Given that the concept of public good is both vague and contested, how are we to approach this question?

Burton Weisbrod's (1988) "collectiveness index" allows us to avoid drawing a qualitative distinction between organizations that provide public goods and organizations that do not. Simultaneously, it advances a less vague concept of the publicness of an organization's outputs. Weisbrod's index measures the percentage of an organization's revenue that

2. See Michaelson and Roof (1986) and Hutchison (1989) for deeper discussion of the changing position of this "establishment."

comes from contributions, gifts, and grants (CGG) rather than from either sales or membership dues. The logic here is that an organization is more publicly beneficial to the extent that its products benefit individuals beyond its own customers, members, or constituents, and CGG income is a measure of that propensity.

As applied to religious congregations, the conceptual problem is how to decide the extent to which donations are gifts rather than dues. As a rough indicator, recall that Independent Sector (1993, 1) estimates that, including the value of volunteer time, 40 percent of congregational expenditures are for nonreligious program activities, activities that, in general, are not limited to members. Biddle (1992, 104), using a variety of information sources, including Independent Sector data, estimated that "America's congregations spend 71 percent of their income on mutual benefit activities and 29 percent on philanthropic activities." Hence, to the best of our current knowledge, it seems reasonable to say that sixty to seventy cents of every dollar given to a congregation constitutes membership dues and thirty to forty cents constitutes gifts.[3] A score of thirty to forty on the collectiveness index would place religious congregations in the same general vicinity as organizations primarily engaged in welfare, advocacy, instruction and planning, and housing. These four sectors have CGG scores of forty-three, forty, thirty-seven, and thirty-one, respectively (Weisbrod 1988, 76). Using this index, then, one may straightforwardly include religious organizations on a continuum of publicness, a continuum on which congregations place comparably to other organizations generally thought of as providers of public goods.[4]

Second, religious organizations appear to generate the formation of other nonprofit organizations that serve the public good. The consistent presence of religious elites and religious organizations among the founders of all sorts of nonprofit organizations suggests that religion (or, at least, some

3. Envelopes used by congregations to collect donations often are split into two parts, one labeled "for ourselves" and one labeled "for others." The fact that donations to religious organizations are part dues and part gift is, in such a case, explicit.

4. It seems likely to me that a CGG score of thirty to forty is too generous a collectiveness score for religious organizations. Larger congregations, for example, are overrepresented in the Independent Sector sample, and these congregations may sponsor more social services than smaller congregations. Also, the extent to which a congregation's nonreligious services are available to nonmembers is not completely clear. But even if religious congregations as a group scored only twenty on the collectiveness index, they would be in respectable company. They still would outscore, for example, Meals on Wheels of Greater Steubenville, Ohio (sixteen on the collectiveness index), as well as organizations primarily engaged in "legislative and political action" and "education," both of which score eighteen (Weisbrod 1988, 76, 78). My purpose here is not to demonstrate that religious organizations belong at any particular spot on the continuum of publicness, but rather to show that there is no good reason to exclude religious organizations altogether from this continuum.

forms of religion) is especially adept at generating a certain other-regarding entrepreneurialism.[5] This entrepreneurialism, rooted in religion, is another reason to consider religion as itself a public good.

Scholarly Advantages of Focusing on Religion as a Public Good

My purpose here is not to present a decisive case that religion is, always and everywhere, itself a public good; the essentially contested nature of the public good—not to mention the great variety of religious expression—precludes such a claim. My purpose is rather the more modest one of pointing out that there is no good a priori reason to exclude religion from the category of public goods in settings in which it does not reinforce other social divisions. Excluding religion is particularly unfortunate for the scholarly enterprise because it keeps religious organizations out of the research spotlight, an exclusion that entails major intellectual costs. Below, I present two examples which show how focusing on religion enhances our understanding of the production of public goods in general.

The first example concerns a central public policy issue: To what extent does tax policy affect private giving to nonprofits that deliver desirable public goods? How do policy changes regarding charitable deductions affect voluntary giving to nonprofits?

Maura Doyle's (1993) work demonstrates that it is important to consider religious giving when evaluating the consequences of tax policies for charitable giving in general. She addresses the question of whether or not allowing donations to be tax deductible in fact increases the amounts that individuals give. Previous work on the subject (summarized in Clotfelter 1985 and Steinberg 1990) has produced mixed results. Some find that tax incentives produce higher levels of giving; others find no effect.

Doyle observes that the positive findings often are based on cross-sectional analyses in which the only variation on the independent variable (that is, tax code differences) is state level variation. She further observes that geographical regions within the United States vary in religious composition—Mormons are heavily concentrated in the West; Baptists in the southeast; Lutherans in the upper Midwest; Catholics in the northeast, parts of the southwest, and Louisiana; and so on. Because religious giving accounts for about two-thirds of all giving and because religious groups vary considerably in their giving habits,[6] failing to control for religious

5. Thanks to Lis Clemens for this phrase.

6. A recent study, for example, found that Catholics gave 2.9 percent of their pretax household income to congregations, Lutherans gave 3.7 percent, and Southern Baptists gave 6.9 percent (Hoge et al. 1996, 50). These numbers are from a sample of people strongly committed to their churches, so the percentages are higher than they would be in these denominational populations as a whole. This upward bias notwithstand-

affiliation in cross-sectional analyses could very well produce a spurious effect of tax policy on giving.

Using several data sources to investigate this hypothesis, Doyle reaches compelling results. When religious affiliation is controlled, the relevant tax code effects on religious giving are reduced to trivial, statistically insignificant magnitudes. She concludes that these results "are consistent with the hypothesis that fiscal variables do not affect religious giving and only appeared to because of the omitted cross-sectional variation" (Doyle 1993, 23). Although the results for other types of giving are mixed, Doyle has added to our knowledge of tax policy effects on total giving by focusing on the dynamics of religious giving.

A second way in which concentrating on religion enhances our understanding of the production of public goods in general involves a set of questions about variation in the extent to which particular activities are carried out by governments rather than by nonprofits. What explains variation in the relative market shares of government and nonprofits? What are the consequences for society when government rather than nonprofits deliver a service?

These questions can be pursued quite straightforwardly by focusing on religion. The reason is simple: the extent to which religion is produced by government or by private nonprofits varies markedly both cross-nationally and historically. Today, religion is completely produced in the third sector in the United States, whereas it is almost completely produced in the government sector in Sweden. Many societies (for example, Britain) fall between these two extremes. N. J. Demerath's (1991) descriptions of church-state relations in Pakistan, Indonesia, and Thailand make it clear that variation exists among Islamic and Buddhist countries in the extent to which religion is directly supported by governments. To put this point another way, the classic church-state separation theme in political and social analysis may be reconceptualized as the extent to which government, as opposed to the private sector, is involved in providing religion to the population.

This reconceptualization suggests that government versus nonprofit production of religion may be analyzed much as we already analyze government versus nonprofit production of other services. In particular, Weisbrod's (1977) "theory of the voluntary nonprofit sector" seems a very promising explanation of variation in the extent to which religion is relegated to the third sector. Weisbrod's argument, as it would apply to religion, may be stated like this: Individuals in a given society will want to consume varying amounts of religion and will be willing to pay varying amounts for it. Government will produce religion at the level demanded by the "median voter," the individual who, at a given level of taxation for religion, defines the median quantity of religion demanded by the population. This level of government-

provided religion will therefore leave a portion of citizens undersatisfied — wanting to consume more religion than is paid for from public funds. Thus, a nonprofit sector will arise to supplement the public provision of religion and thereby meet the demand of those who want more religion than government is willing to provide.

Two of the specific hypotheses developed by Weisbrod require some rethinking when we focus directly on the government production of religion. First, Weisbrod's analysis "implies that before a political majority comes to demand governmental provision [of a good], the minority that demands governmental provision of a good will be undersatisfied and will turn to voluntary organizations. Thus, provision by voluntary (nonprofit) organizations is hypothesized to precede governmental provision historically" (Weisbrod 1977, 63). English history supports this idea. In sixteenth-century England, voluntary organizations rather than government supported "schools, hospitals, nontoll roads, fire fighting apparatus, public parks, bridges, dikes and causeways, digging of drainage canals, waterworks, wharves and docks, harbor cleaning, libraries, care of prisoners in jails, and charity to the poor" (Weisbrod 1977, 63). Eventually, however, government came to support these activities.

But, as Douglas (1983, 112) says, this hypothesis is only "partially verified by history." More to the point, the historical trend in the West over the past several centuries in government provision of religion would seem to be in exactly the opposite direction. Increasingly *dis*established religion in the United States is one prominent historical example, but it is by no means the only one. Religion in Ireland, Italy, and France, to name just three additional examples, has been decreasingly supplied by government in recent centuries. At the same time, the Iranian revolution, which of course increased government's share in the provision of religion, shows that there is no universal trend in this direction. Thus, focusing directly on religion complicates Weisbrod's historical hypothesis, but it complicates it in an interesting way. It may still be true, for example, that the underlying variables posited by Weisbrod — the level and heterogeneity of demand for a public good such as religion — are the correct causal variables. The case of religion, however, suggests the important qualification that the historical trend in the levels of those variables is not always upward.

Weisbrod's second hypothesis fares much better with respect to variation in church-state relations: "Since the undersatisfied demanders have been portrayed as the group that gives rise to the voluntary sector, it follows that the relative size of the voluntary sector in an industry can be expected to be a function of the heterogeneity of population demands" (Weisbrod 1977, 61). Because the median voter determines the level of government support for religion (or any other public good), less variation around that median implies less unsatisfied demand and therefore less nonprofit religious activity. More variation will mean more unsatisfied demand for religion and therefore more nonprofit religious activity. As

ing, there is substantial variation in religious giving among religious traditions.

applied to religion, this hypothesis is supported by cross-national evidence. Weisbrod observes,

> The governmental "provision" (that is, support) of, say, church activities — which have a significant public-good component for persons of that faith but not for others[7] — is apparently great in countries where virtually the entire population shares one religion (for example, Spain and Ireland). Similarly, the public provision (financing) is far lower in a country such as the United States, where religious preferences (including atheism) are more diverse. (Weisbrod 1977, 67–68)

One study (Chaves and Cann 1992) found, among eighteen Western developed countries, a correlation of .52 between religious concentration and the extent to which religion is financed and regulated by the state. The more religious homogeneity in a society, the greater the level of direct government support for religion. It appears that Weisbrod's theory offers substantial insight into cross-national variation in the extent to which religion is provided by government.

Other research on this connection, however, introduces a potentially important wrinkle. Inspired by Adam Smith's claim that the clergy's "exertion, their zeal and industry, are likely to be much greater" when they "depend altogether for their subsistence upon the voluntary contributions of their hearers" rather than "from some other fund to which the law of their country may entitle them" (Smith [1776] 1965, 740), Laurence Iannaccone (1991) has developed a supply-side analysis of religious demand and production. He has argued that state support of religion will negatively affect the heterogeneity of demand for religion, mainly by discouraging competition among religious entrepreneurs. Conversely, a more free religious market — one in which no religion receives state subsidies — will encourage religious entrepreneurs and therefore increase religious heterogeneity and, in turn, religious consumption. The central idea is that less government support for religion makes religious entrepreneurship easier, opening the religious market to innovation and segmentation and thereby increasing religious pluralism as well as religious consumption.

This argument implies not only that religious pluralism and religious consumption will be positively correlated, but also that greater state funding of religion will suppress both. At the level of variation among geographical areas within the United States, the empirical evidence for a positive correlation between religious pluralism and religious consumption is mixed (compare Finke and Stark 1988 with Land et al. 1991). At the level of the nation-state, however, this argu-

ment has empirical support (Iannaccone 1991; Chaves and Cann 1992; Finke and Iannaccone 1993; Chaves et al. 1994).

The importance of such findings to Weisbrod's model is their suggestion that the heterogeneity of demand for religion may be endogenous to the extent of government support for religion. That is, they suggest that the demand for religion (and perhaps other public goods?) is itself at least partially *produced* by the activity of government rather than being only an exogenous determinant of the level of government support. If it is true that a more free religious market promotes religious pluralism, then the institutional arrangements between governments and religious organizations are not simply a consequence of the exogenously determined degree of religious pluralism and religious demand. These institutional arrangements may also affect the levels of religious pluralism and demand in a society. Uncovering the true nature and direction of the causal flow(s) between religious heterogeneity, religious demand, and government support for religion probably will require historical rather than cross-sectional investigation. To the extent, however, that the condition of a religious sector affects the vibrancy of the broader, secular nonprofit sector, as Estelle James (1987b) argues, the investigating of these complex relations among churches, states, and religious activity is worth the effort. Indeed, such effort very likely will be a necessary component of any successful attempt to understand what makes for a vigorous nonprofit sector in a society.

RELIGIOUS ORGANIZATIONS AND NONRELIGIOUS PUBLIC GOODS

It is by now well known that religious organizations are deeply involved in the provision of many nonreligious goods and services in the United States. The connection between religion and nonprofit organizations seems even more intimate, however, if we look not at well-developed nonprofit sectors, but at nascent nonprofit organizations. Across a whole range of societies, religious organizations and religious elites appear largely responsible for the creation of nonprofit organizations providing nonreligious services. James has studied this phenomenon extensively, and she does not mince words: "Universally across countries, religious groups are the major founders of nonprofit service institutions" (James 1987a, 6). In a series of articles, James has developed and tested a theory to account for the ubiquity of religious organizations among the founders of secular nonprofits (James 1987a, 1987b, 1989a, 1989b, 1989c, 1993). Historical work supported by the Program on Governance both supports this theory and prompts revision of it. In this section of the chapter, I (a) describe James's theory, (b) describe the ways in which it is supported by the historical work reviewed here, and (c) argue for the revisions that seem necessary in the light of some of this work. The main thrust of the revision I propose involves bringing Michael Cohen's, James March's, and Johan Olsen's "garbage can model" of organi-

---

7. This clause is interesting in that it reveals the standard scholarly assumption concerning the limited public benefits of religion. But, as discussed above, and somewhat ironically, Weisbrod's own "collectiveness index" helps us to see that the public-good component of religious activity often extends beyond the membership of a particular religious group.

zational behavior to bear on the movement of religious elites and religious organizations into secular fields of activity.

James's Theory

James's theory is intended to explain the relative size of the nonprofit sector in a society. She believes three basic variables are important. The first two are the demand variables initially proposed by Weisbrod and developed by James (1987a, b): either *excess* demand or *differentiated* demand will increase the size of a nonprofit sector. Excess demand refers to the existence of individuals who want more of some good, say, education, than the government is providing. Differentiated demand refers to variation in tastes for the kind of service desired (for example, Catholic education as opposed to secular education). James (1987a, 4) identifies four conditions under which differentiated demand will lead to a larger nonprofit sector:

1. Peoples' preferences with respect to product variety are more heterogeneous and more intense, usually owing to deep-seated cultural (religious, linguistic, ethnic) differences;
2. this diversity is geographically dispersed so it cannot be accommodated by local government production;
3. government is constrained to offer a relatively uniform product, the median voter's preferred choice; and
4. the dominant cultural group is not determined to impose its preferences on others; hence private production is a permissible way out.

On the basis of her empirical work on education (for example, 1987a, 1989b), James argues that excess demand drives private production in developing countries while differentiated demand drives private production in advanced industrial societies. It seems reasonable to restate this as two more general hypotheses: (1) excess demand for public goods will produce nonprofit activity in under-supplied sectors of either developing or advanced industrial societies; (2) differentiated demand will be the driving force behind nonprofit activity in well-supplied sectors of either developing or advanced industrial societies. This formulation of James's ideas recognizes that there might be excess demand for certain services (for example, legal aid for the impoverished) even in industrial societies, and such excess demand will lead to nonprofit development in that arena. This reformulation is important because, as we shall see, the connection between nonprofit foundings and religion is qualitatively different in these two types of situation.

James's primary theoretical innovation, however, comes with her third, supply-side variable: High levels of "nonprofit entrepreneurship" in a society will lead to bigger nonprofit sectors (James 1987b, 404). Furthermore, a major determinant of nonprofit entrepreneurship within a society will be the presence of activist religious organizations. The common presence of religious organizations among the founders of nonprofit service institutions strongly suggests that the private sector "will be more important in countries with strong, independent, proselytizing religious organizations competing for clients" (James 1987b, 404).

James finds strong support for her hypothesis by analyzing intrasocietal variation in the relative size of private educational sectors in Japan, Holland, India, and the United States (James 1987a). Under conditions of either excess or differentiated demand, the supply of nonprofit entrepreneurs, measured as the extent of religious activity, positively affects the size of the nonprofit sector.

What explains the propensity for religious organizations to promote nonprofit entrepreneurship? James's answer is that religious elites establish nonprofits "because their object [is] not to maximize profits but to maximize religious faith or adherents" (James 1987b, 405). Similarly, "religious organizations provide education, health, and other social services to maximize their members, socialize them, shape their tastes, and maintain group loyalty" (James 1989a, 35). Missions and missionaries thus are key actors in the creation of nonprofit sectors, especially outside the West.

It is this explanation of the connection between religious organizations and nonprofit entrepreneurship that needs modification. It seems eminently plausible that religious elites would start schools in order to gain or keep adherents; the socialization potential of educational institutions is obvious. But religious organizations seem to be ubiquitous among founders in other arenas as well: in Sweden at least one-third of cultural and recreational nonprofits have religious affiliations (James 1989a, 39). Paul DiMaggio and Helmut Anheier (1990, 141) cite A. Ben-Ner's and T. Van Hoomissen's (1989) finding that the "number of churches strongly predicts intercounty variation in the [nonprofit] share of employment in four New York multiform industries." In Austria, where 17 percent of nursery schools and kindergartens are church-affiliated, 22 percent of senior citizen and nursing homes also have religious connections (Badelt 1989, 166–68). A substantial proportion, perhaps a majority, of private international charities were founded by religious organizations (Smith 1989; Smith, in this volume; also see Pagnucco and McCarthy 1992). Most early nonprofit hospitals in the United States were established and supported by religious organizations (Marmor et al. 1987, 224). Religious organizations have been crucial in the formation of human rights nonprofits in a number of countries, including Chile (Fruhling 1989), El Salvador (Stephen 1994), Brazil (Stephen 1993), and East Germany (Anheier 1991, 89). Many development-oriented organizations in Latin America, Africa, and parts of Asia have their roots in religion (Smith, in this volume). The list could be greatly extended by including other societies and other arenas of activity.

The theoretical significance of religious foundings of nonprofits across a broad spectrum of organizational fields is this: Although it seems much less plausible to suppose that religious leaders create hospitals, refugee programs, international charities, legal aid societies, and the like in order to make converts or to build group loyalty, religious organizations are just as prominent among the founders in these arenas as they are in education. Why? Besides education, James comments only on the religious motivation for hospital foundings: "Hospitals are a service for which people will have an urgent periodic need; hence they constitute an effective way for religious groups to gain entree and goodwill in a society" (James 1987b, 405). Unlike the speculation about the conversion-education connection, the connection between winning souls and building health care organizations seems, on its face, much less compelling. I shall argue that, in fact, the supply-side effect of religion on nonprofit foundings is qualitatively different in situations of excess demand than it is in situations of differentiated demand. Only in situations of differentiated demand does religious nonprofit founding primarily reflect a straightforward desire to form and keep religious adherents. The dynamics are different under conditions of excess demand. Cohen's, March's, and Olsen's garbage can model of organizational behavior, as we shall see, offers a more general theory of the dynamic by which religious organizations establish secular nonprofits. It is a more general account because it does not rely on the presence of an evangelistic motivation to explain religious nonprofit foundings. Rather, it presents a broader picture of organizational process, and instances in which conversion is an explicit goal can be understood as a special case of that more general process.

Differentiated Demand and
Religious Nonprofit Entrepreneurship

The paradigm case of religious nonprofit foundings in a situation of differentiated rather than excess demand is the creation of a Catholic school system in the United States (Dolan 1992, chap. 10). This is straightforwardly a case of a desire to preserve a cultural/religious group identity that seemed threatened by the Protestant-dominated public schools. James (1987a, 10–11) finds that for both elementary and secondary schools the proportion of a state's population that is Catholic is an important predictor of the percent of schools that are private. Indeed, her review of the literature indicates that such a "Catholic effect" is the most stable finding in research on the determinants of the relative size of the private sector in U.S. education. These results strongly support the Weisbrod/James story of nonprofit activity driven by differentiated demand, and it seems unnecessary even to introduce the supply-side notion of religiously motivated entrepreneurship as an additional factor. The Catholic effect, in other words, seems most parsimoniously interpreted as a demand-side effect.

Two projects supported by the Program on Governance provide additional evidence to support the hypothesis that religiously motivated nonprofit formation is sometimes driven by differentiated demand. Interestingly, though perhaps not surprisingly, these studies show that a dynamic similar to the one that operated among American Catholics existed among American Jews. Rose (1994), for example, tells the story of

Neighborhood Centre, a Jewish settlement house in Philadelphia. Founded in 1885 by the largely assimilated German-Jews of the city, the fundamental purpose of the settlement was to Americanize recent Jewish immigrants from Eastern Europe so that their "foreignness" would not reflect badly on the established Philadelphia Jewish community. Though in a way different from the Catholic pattern, the formation of a specifically Jewish settlement house seems a clear case of nonprofit activity in response to differentiated demand. Although there was a broader, secular settlement movement, there was a special demand for a specifically Jewish settlement house: Philadelphia's German-Jews wanted to convert, so to speak, Yiddish-speaking, East European, immigrant Jews into middle-class American Reformed Jews.

The settlement house was not particularly successful in these efforts, however, and Rose describes how the immigrants largely ignored it as they went about the business of creating their own organizations for a variety of purposes. Meanwhile, until 1940, Neighborhood Centre became increasingly tied to the mainstream settlement movement, which meant it became less and less a specifically Jewish settlement house. This trajectory was reversed in 1941. Nazi persecution of Jews persuaded board members of the need for organizations to promote Jewish cultural identity, and they consequently began efforts to "Judaize" the center, "to shift the emphasis from Americanism to Jewish Americanism" (Rose 1994, 17). These efforts were successful. The center was transformed from a neighborhood center to an organization whose primary purpose was "serving the Jewish community," and, in 1965, it "merged with other Jewish community centers to become the Jewish Ys and Centers of Greater Philadelphia" (Rose 1994, 19).

Rose's work describes a nonprofit whose founding and development were driven mainly by demand for a particular type of religious service. Moreover, the nature of the religious activity was just what James's theory would lead us to expect: Jewish elites desired organizations that would promote and protect a religious/cultural group identity.

This conclusion is supported by Richard Mark Chapman's (1993) study of Jewish philanthropy and social service in Minneapolis from 1900 to 1950. Chapman finds the same initial motivation for a specifically Jewish social service as does Rose: new Jewish immigrants threatened the reputation of established Jewish communities in Minneapolis and St. Paul. This special purpose—the differentiated demand—was indicated by the fact that no Jewish relief agencies were among the Minneapolis organizations forming the Associated Charities in 1884. As Chapman (1993, 27) puts it, this "organizational separatism is suggestive of the differences of mission and purpose that set Jewish relief work apart from broader community-wide efforts."

That differentiated rather than excess demand was driving at least some nonprofit formation among Minneapolis Jews is clear from the debate leading up to the founding of a home for Jewish children. Efforts to organize such a home began in

1917 when a Jewish periodical "sounded the alarm that several Jewish children in Minneapolis were being exposed to Christian influences in non-Jewish homes." Interestingly, there was explicit recognition that adequate space for homeless children already existed: "Rabbi Philip Kleinman urged that promoters of the home think twice before quickly establishing a second-rate institution which would be costly. Why not, he implored, continue to send children to the [Jewish] Cleveland Orphan Asylum which was well-equipped and which the community already supported?" But Rabbi Kleinman did not win the day; a Jewish children's home was opened in Minneapolis in 1919. The home's constitution stressed its religious mission: "The Home shall always be conducted by this organization strictly in accordance with the laws and requirements of Orthodox Judaism" (Chapman 1993, 196–98).

These two studies contribute historical richness even as they support James's theory about religious beginnings of nonprofits in situations of differentiated demand, that is, where there is demand for a special type of service rather than for additional quantities of a service. In the same way that Catholics believed that public schools would not preserve Catholic communities, Jews in Minneapolis and Philadelphia believed that mainstream charity and settlement houses would not preserve their communal identities. The religious connections in these cases are thus just as James expects them to be: Religious subgroups form nonprofits for the purpose of maintaining group identity and solidarity.

Both of these studies focus on the contested nature of Jewish identity. Were the communal interests of American Jews best served by assimilating or by maintaining European languages and habits? By practicing a Reformed or an Orthodox faith? These questions were actively debated within the Jewish communities studied by Rose and by Chapman. Furthermore, their accounts make clear that Jewish nonprofit organizations were simultaneously battlefield, weapon, and prize in these contests over what it would mean to be Jewish in the United States. It is perhaps not too much to say that the outcome of such battles over the nature and mission of Jewish nonprofits influenced the nature of Jewish identity in the United States. Not only do nonprofits formed by religious groups emerge from and reflect a demand that is differentiated on religious grounds; such nonprofits — by their constitutions, by their identity-specific services, by the commitments of their boards and staff, and by the effects they have on their clients — also help to construct communal identities. They do not merely maintain preexisting and static communal identities.

From this perspective, nonprofit organizing partakes of a broader process of identity construction that Calhoun (in this volume) sees as fundamental to a functioning public sphere. In such a sphere, according to Calhoun, participation always holds the possibility not just of settling arguments or planning action, but of altering identities. The building of a Catholic school system clearly had this effect, and the work of

Rose and Chapman suggests that a similar claim can be made about the construction of Jewish charitable organizations. If so, then nonprofits that arise to meet differentiated demand are doing exactly what James expects them to do, not to mention what their founders intended them to do, although it is perhaps more accurate to say that distinctive religious identities are constructed, rather than merely maintained, by such activity.[8] Religious foundings in situations of excess demand are a different matter.

Excess Demand and Religious Nonprofit Entrepreneurship

Historical work supported by the Program on Governance is filled with examples of religiously founded nonprofits delivering secular services.[9] In the 1980s, white Protestant congregations in a Midwestern town created a nonprofit for the purpose of resettling and supporting single black mothers and their children within stable middle-class communities (Schnorr 1993). Both black and white religious organizations were instrumental in the founding of black settlement houses in the nineteenth century (Hase 1993). Nondenominational religious associations created the YWCA in 1906 in order "to advance the physical, social, intellectual, moral, and spiritual interests of young women" (*Report of the Second Biennial Convention,* quoted in Robertson 1988, 2). Catholic organizations created and supported social movement nonprofits in El Salvador and Brazil during the 1970s and 1980s (Stephen 1993, 1994). Female Presbyterian missionaries created schools and health care organizations in New Mexico in the latter part of the nineteenth century (Yohn 1995). Day nurseries in nineteenth-century Philadelphia were operated by Catholic, Protestant, and Jewish congregations (Rose 1993). It was an energetic clergyman, W. A. R. Goodwin, who in the 1920s convinced John D. Rockefeller, Jr. to create the Williamsburg Holding Corporation for the purpose of reconstructing colonial Williamsburg and who administered the project in its early years (Greenspan 1992). Even among contemporary women's organizations in New York City, 7 percent were founded by religious groups (Bordt 1993).

Each of these seems an instance of religious organizations

8. Compare this to Anheier (1992), who argues that although Germany's third sector can trace its origins largely to the Catholic Church, it cannot be understood as the result of a differentiated demand on the part of the Catholic minority. Instead, the German third sector "is both the terrain and the result of the conflict between organized religion, political opposition, and the state over the division of labor and spheres of influence" (Anheier 1992, 50).

9. A note on terminology: I shall use the phrase *secular services* or *secular activities* to denote services that are separable from any particular religious tradition (e.g., hospital services, education), and the phrase *religious services* or *religious activities* to refer to activities that are inseparable from the religious tradition in which they are embedded (e.g., preaching, evangelizing, Bible study). I draw this distinction *without regard to the motivations of those individuals providing the services.* This does not imply that individuals providing secular activities lacked religious motivations for that work.

or professionals founding secular nonprofits in a situation of excess demand. Whether that demand was for homes for young female city dwellers, for schools, or for the protection of human rights, religious organizations created nonprofits to meet a demand for services that government was not (yet) providing.

Weisbrod (1977, 64) points out that one clear indication of this dynamic is that those involved in private provision of services also engage in political efforts to expand government responsibility because "those persons having the greatest demands would be expected to wish to share the cost burdens broadly." Susan Yohn and Nancy Robertson describe this phenomenon. Yohn (1995, 11–12) finds that the female Presbyterian missionaries in New Mexico "provided health care, while urging that this become a public concern. Over the years they came to advocate a more expansive role for the state. . . . Missionaries welcomed the Sheppard-Towner Act, which enhanced public health efforts in New Mexico. With the advent of the New Deal, those who remained in New Mexico . . . embraced the Works Progress Administration and federal relief initiatives." Similarly, Robertson (1988, 1) finds that women in the early YWCA believed "in the need to force government to come to grips with the moral problems of their day. If government did not do so, they believed, it was necessary to form voluntary associations to effect that purpose." We seem here to be in the presence of private action in situations of excess demand.[10]

Equally striking as the fact that these instances exemplify private action to meet excess demand is, in most cases, the conspicuous *absence* of explicitly conversionist goals among the religious organizations and people who are delivering the services.[11] Paul Schnorr, for example, studied the Samaritan Project, a "church-centered voluntary effort resettling low-income, urban African Americans to a primarily white, middle-class town" (Schnorr 1993, iii). Although the project "was organized around religion and religious institutions" (71), his account shows that the individuals involved in these efforts had no desire to recruit new families for their religious groups: "While [project participants] did spend a lot of time defining what they understood to be acceptable expenditures,

educational plans, and daily routines for resettled families, the Methodist and Lutheran folks involved were not in the business of proselytizing" (5). In these studies, religious involvement in nonprofit creation is commonly accompanied by the utter absence of the evangelistic goals James leads us to expect.

Michiko Hase's portrait of the beginnings in the 1920s of the Phyllis Wheatley Settlement House, a black settlement house in Minneapolis, is similar. Although the house did not have any official religious affiliation, fund-raising to found it was conducted by the (white) Woman's Christian Association, and black churches and clergy also were involved in initial organizing efforts (Hase 1993, chap. 2, 6–12). Phyllis Wheatley House apparently was not unique in this regard. Although the white settlement movement was avowedly secular, explicitly distinguishing its work from mission work, Black settlement houses were more often affiliated with religious organizations (Hase 1993, Introduction, 6). In Minneapolis, however, professional African American women, not black churches and clergy, led the way in the establishment of the Phyllis Wheatley House.

In spite of the religious connections, Hase's account shows that the motivation for the Phyllis Wheatley House was altogether nonevangelistic. Immediately after World War I, there was a "dire need of housing for black women who had recently migrated to the city" (Hase 1993, chap. 2, 5). This migration, combined with the racial segregation that kept African American women out of white settlement homes, meant that there was a need for suitable housing for single black working women. The religious organizations involved in founding the Phyllis Wheatley House were concerned to meet this need. Hase gives no evidence that specifically evangelistic goals were on the minds of either the black or the white women whose entrepreneurial efforts led to the establishment of this house.

Lynn Stephen's (1994) biography of María Teresa Tula, a Salvadoran human rights organizer, conveys the importance of religious organizations to the Salvadoran human rights movement. Most of the original members of CO-MADRES, for example, an organization of mothers and relatives searching for disappeared, imprisoned, and assassinated family members, "came out of Christian Base Communities" (Stephen 1994, 2). Priests and nuns were central to the organization of these communities, which were in turn important vehicles for creating social and political groups like CO-MADRES. CO-MADRES met at a seminary and was actively and publicly supported by Monseñor Oscar Romero until his assassination in 1980. The following passage, narrated by Tula, is subtly informative about the nature of the connections between the Catholic Church and nonprofit social movement organizations like CO-MADRES:

The mothers had a dinner with Monseñor Romero. When I arrived, I greeted him. I just said hello. But I didn't

10. These examples also illustrate a conceptual problem: It is difficult to clearly distinguish the presence of excess demand for a service from the presence of active suppliers of that service. How would we know that excess demand exists in the absence of suppliers? The possibility that suppliers of any good or service may actively create demand for their products poses a problem for those wishing to differentiate between demand-side effects and supply-side effects. For the purposes of the present argument, however, this issue may be sidestepped. Whatever the relation between demand and supply, it is clear that, in some situations (representing differentiated demand), religious entrepreneurs supply a service that is also available from other sources, while in other situations (representing excess demand) they supply a service available nowhere else.

11. This is not to say that there is an absence of other sorts of religious motivation, a point I shall elaborate further below.

know that when you greet a bishop you are supposed to kiss his hand. When they introduced Monseñor to me, he held out his hand for me to kiss. I didn't know what I was supposed to do. I just reached out and pumped his hand saying, "Good day, Monseñor"....

"Welcome," he said with a smile. He seemed pleased.

After that, he talked with us and read passages from the Bible. He gave us suggestions about how to organize and what to do while looking for our relatives (Stephen 1994, 55–56).

While suggesting the absence of any desire to convert among the religious professionals organizing this nonprofit, this anecdote reveals an absence of religious concern also on the part of at least one beneficiary of the organization. One suspects that this phenomenon—those receiving the services of religiously founded nonprofits displaying little interest in the particular religion involved—is general.

Like the Samaritan Project and the Phyllis Wheatley House, CO-MADRES displays an interesting combination of intimate connection with a religious organization and absence of any hint that the organization's purpose has anything whatsoever to do with winning converts or with maintaining or increasing loyalty to the religious groups involved. Indeed, there is evidence that when religious organizations found and maintain social movement nonprofits, their membership and support from some segments of the population decrease.

Smith (1982, 36–38) reports a negative response to church-sponsored social assistance programs among upper-income, theologically conservative Chileans: "They do not attend services as frequently as before, they have been reluctant to continue monetary support to church programs, and many have withdrawn their children from church-affiliated schools. . . . [Some] have actively promoted challenges to episcopal authority and open schism within churches." This reaction was not limited to Chilean Catholics:

In 1975 a majority of Chilean Lutherans (composed mainly of descendants of German-born immigrants in the South) left their church and formed a new one. The reason was that they strongly disagreed with their bishop, Helmut Frenz, for his participation in the Committee of Cooperation for Peace (as its co-president) and for his urging Lutherans internationally to contribute to human rights projects in Chile as a way of blunting the effects of military brutality.

Smith concludes that "allegiances to socially active Chilean churches are falling off among some of their traditionally staunch supporters, especially in the upper class." Although part of the initial motivation behind "liberation theology" was to reinvigorate Catholic piety among the Latin American poor increasingly drawn to Protestantism (Smith 1991, 14), that evangelistic goal was only one among many.

Something is crucially awry in James's claim that religious organizations launch nonprofits "to maximize religious faith or religious adherents," "to gain entree and goodwill in a society," and "to maximize their members, socialize them, shape their tastes, and maintain group loyalty" (James 1987b, 405; 1989a, 35). Sometimes this is true. But the historical cases reviewed above—and one suspects there are many others—in which maximizing religious faith seems irrelevant to creating nonprofits, suggest that something more is afoot.

Tellingly, if paradoxically, the nature of the causal relationship between conversionist goals and nonprofit activity is ambiguous even when such goals are stated. This is clear, for example, from Robertson's account of the early days of the YWCA. Although the Ladies Christian Union, one of the precursors of the International Board of Women's and Young Women's Christian Associations, formed in 1858 to offer Bible classes for the "spiritual and moral uplift of working women," their goals and activities quickly and decisively became more secular. Seeking to "address the employment needs of young working women," early organizations associated with the international board expanded their services beyond religious activities to include, initially, assistance with employment and housing, and eventually they "came to offer cafeterias, travelers' aid, occupational training, health programs, educational courses, lectures, free libraries, concerts, gymnasiums, recreational activities, and vacation camps" (Robertson 1993, Introduction, 1–2).

If the International Board of Women's and Young Women's Christian Associations, based in northeastern cities, was focused on secular social service, the American Committee of Young Women's Christian Associations, based in midwestern campuses, was focused on saving souls. When these two organizations considered merging, a major bone of contention was whether the new organization would exist primarily to promote salvation or to provide social services. The two organizations merged in 1906, and the official statement of purpose of this new YWCA reflected the dual goals of its predecessor organizations. The new organization would

advance the physical, social, intellectual, moral, and spiritual interests of young women. The ultimate purpose of all its efforts shall be to seek to bring young women to such a knowledge of Jesus Christ as Savior and Lord as shall mean for the individual woman fullness of life and development of character, and shall make the organization as a whole an effective agency in the bringing in of the Kingdom of God among young women (Robertson 1988, 2).

Robertson points out that many in the leadership "did not experience [social service versus saving souls] as an either/or choice" (Robertson 1993, Introduction, 11). This is important because it suggests that, *even when evangelism was a stated goal,* the primary concrete activity in which the YWCA engaged was the delivery of secular social services. Well before the "Kingdom of God" language and the language of religious conversion was dropped from official rhetoric, it was clear to many of those inside the organization that those goals were secondary to social reform and social service: "Women in the YWCA were forced to justify their public activities by the social good they would serve" (Robertson 1993, chap. 1, 11). Robertson's work on the YWCA shows that even an organization explicitly devoted to winning converts, in fact, engaged in a broad array of secular activities, activities that far more effectively placed young women in jobs than in pews.

Eventually, social service became the de jure as well as the de facto organizational priority of the YWCA. Whereas in its early years, the YWCA's statistical reports included numbers of conversions along with data on the size of classes and attendance at gymnasiums, this practice was discontinued by the mid-1910s (Robertson 1993, chap. 1, 8). Not unlike the Young *Men's* Christian Association (cf. Zald and Denton 1963), the YWCA deemphasized evangelism in favor of social service. That a religiously founded organization explicitly intended to make converts should, in short order, be doing everything but that adds more weight to the position I am developing: Perhaps we ought not believe that the desire to maximize converts is the primary causal force leading religious organizations to establish and maintain nonprofits of various sorts.

This suggestion also receives support from Yohn's (1995) work on female Presbyterian missionaries to New Mexico. Female missions to the Southwest began, in part, "as one answer to the failure on the part of male missionaries to convert 'foreigners' successfully." The women were not, however, more successful evangelists than the men: "Once in the field, missionaries were frustrated by their inability to fulfill their spiritual duties, to evangelize and convert. Ultimately they came to realize that most Hispanos were not interested in converting . . . but that they wished to avail themselves of other services such as education that mission women provided" (Yohn 1995, 5). Moreover, just as Robertson finds that the YWCA secularized rather quickly, Yohn describes a similar development in missions: "As mission women met with resistance in the field, as they began to think of themselves as professionals rather than volunteers, and as the organizations grew larger and more bureaucratic, the evangelical content of home mission work diminished to more closely resemble the non-denominational and political work of 'secular' settlement house workers which anticipated the corporate welfare state" (Yohn 1991, 6). Here is yet another example of a vibrant nonprofit enterprise founded by a religious organization — indeed, by missionaries — and espousing conversion as a goal yet directing little activity toward that goal.

Yohn examined the motivations of the Presbyterian women who became missionaries to the Southwest and found a set of concerns different from those James's account would lead us to expect: "The principal actors were Presbyterian women, who, like many other Protestant women in the latter part of the nineteenth century, entered the home mission field for modest personal goals; some wanted to be of greater use to society, to feel closer to God, while others simply desired a change of scenery and some adventure" (Yohn 1995, 1). The women Yohn describes are moved not just by a desire to win converts but also, perhaps primarily, by "a desire, born of their religious convictions, *to do useful work*" (Yohn 1995, 4, emphasis added).

Certain types of religious commitment, it seems, motivate individuals to do useful work. Such motivation may be largely indifferent to the content of that work, so long as it is useful, productive, efficacious, and so forth. Certain types of religion, as Weber emphasized, promote activism, and that activism winds up being channeled (among other avenues) into the creation of organizations to meet excess demand for a variety of publicly beneficial services. That that activism has sometimes been devoted to explicitly evangelistic goals certainly has contributed to the scope of this connection, but in an ironic fashion. The key fact about evangelistic goals is that it is terribly unclear just how to go about gaining converts, and this ambiguity is a crucial mechanism channeling religious activism into nonprofit entrepreneurship. The garbage can model of organizational behavior helps to illuminate how this may be so.

Religious Organizations as Garbage Cans
The account of Cohen, March, and Olsen (1972) goes a long way toward clarifying the connections among religion, religious organizations, and nonprofit foundings. They begin with the insight that, in certain types of situations, it is a mistake to characterize organizational decision making as the rational formulation of solutions to well-understood problems. Decision making will be quite unlike this wherever (a) preferences are problematic or contested rather than given; (b) organizational technology — the relations between organizational ends and means, between organizational goals and available strategies — is poorly understood; and (c) participation by individuals in organizational activities is fluid. Although these three features describe some decision-making situations in all organizations, Cohen et al. (1972, 1) suggest that they are "particularly conspicuous in public, educational, and illegitimate organizations." I would add religious organizations to this list.

Many religious organizations quite clearly fit this description of organizations that have unclear goals, unclear technologies, and fluid participants. The specific ways to properly live out one's faith are rarely obvious. Even when there is agreement on a goal, say, to "evangelize the world in this generation," the technology best suited to reaching that goal is hardly clear. And even committed individuals, be they members of established religions in the United States or missionaries in the field, move fluidly in and out of various activities sponsored by religious organizations. Religious organizations from suburban congregations to missionary societies often are "organized anarchies" in the fundamental sense that their options and the criteria by which choices are to be made are inherently ambiguous.

Even in organized anarchies, however, choices are made, options are pursued, and problems are solved. How does decision making occur under such conditions? Cohen et al. envision such organizations as sites — garbage cans — wherein choices, problems, solutions, and participants mingle. Decisions occur when a choice is made by a particular individual or set of individuals to attach a particular problem to a particular solution. It is common to assume that this process is primarily one of organizational decisionmakers developing solutions to problems that arise. The essence of the garbage can model is to reverse this imagery — under the conditions specified above, we can as aptly describe the decision-making process as solutions finding problems as problems finding solutions. The activity can be one of problem finding rather than problem solving. A crucial emphasis in this metaphor is that individuals inside organizations carry solutions, and they search around for problems to which those solutions may be applied. This is what it means to say that "an organization is a collection of choices looking for problems . . . and decision makers looking for work" (Cohen et al. 1972, 2).

How do decisionmakers select particular problems from the very large, if not infinite, set of possible problems to which their preferred solutions can be applied? Although the matching of problems to solutions sometimes is interpreted as occurring largely by chance (see, for example, Scott 1992, 298), Cohen et al. suggest that certain problems will have a higher chance of being selected than other problems. Two features of problems are relevant. First, they vary in their "energy requirements," which refers to "the energy required to resolve a choice to which the problem is attached" (Cohen et al. 1972, 3). Organizations also possess a certain amount of energy for making choices. That amount is determined by the number of participants and the amount of energy each participant brings to the organization. Decisions — choosing to attach a problem to a solution — are made when the amount of energy participants expend on a choice equals or exceeds the energy requirements of the problems attached to that choice. Thus, at a given organizational energy level, participants will be more likely to pursue choices attached to problems with lower energy requirements. More straightforwardly, decisionmakers looking for work will gravitate toward problems that are more easily addressed than others. The drive to do something will push decisionmakers into choices in which the energy supply of the organization is sufficient to meet the energy demands of the attached problems.

Second, a problem's importance refers to the extent to which it is accessible to more choices. The more choices a problem tends to attach itself to, the greater its importance. In contemporary universities, for example, the problem of achieving cultural diversity appears relevant in many more decision opportunities than does the problem of achieving a winning football record. Participants will tend to pursue problems that are more important in this sense — problems that come up in a larger number of choice situations. Thus, other things being equal, problems that are easy and that come up often will be found more quickly by an organization looking for work.

The essence of the garbage can model is that when goals and/or technologies are ambiguous, pressing problems will tend to be thrown into decision opportunities that arise within the organization, much as we throw yesterday's newspaper into the trash bin or, perhaps more aptly, into the recycling bin. The point is that problems are not simply carried away — disposed of by a solution. They return again and again to the decision opportunities within organized anarchies.

The Religious Ethic and the
Spirit of Nonprofit Entrepreneurship

We now are in a position to see how this model of organizational behavior provides an important corrective to James's theory of religious nonprofit entrepreneurship. I shall develop this argument with specific reference to the case of missionary organizations — religious organizations that profess conversion as an explicit goal. If it is clear that even in these organizations a garbage can process rather than a rational attempt to gain adherents best describes why the organizations so often establish nonprofits, then, a fortiori, that process is very likely operative in religious organizations that lack such an explicit conversionary goal. Five points are important.

First, certain religions motivate individuals to be active. Whether that activity is devoted to generating converts, to gaining one's own salvation, or simply to doing good is of secondary importance to the push toward some this-worldly activism.[12] It also is not necessary to imagine that such an activist urge is felt by all, or even by very many, of a religion's affiliates. All that is necessary is that an activist spirit be promoted among the most committed individuals — the ones who are the decisionmakers in religious organizations. In fact, just such an activist spirit is often observed among the religiously committed. Recall Yohn's finding that missionary women were driven by "a desire, born of their religious convictions, to do useful work" (Yohn 1995, 4). More generally, Hutchison (1987, 7) has portrayed the American missionary movement as driven by an activist spirit. Mission efforts, he writes, "placed a premium on activism and motion, doing and going." The religious ethic to which I am referring is essentially an ethic of restless activism. Religious organizations whose elites are imbued with this spirit are quintessentially organizations whose decisionmakers are looking for work.

The relevant ethic is neither peculiar to Protestantism, nor universal within Protestantism. Hall (1993) has argued, for example, that theological differences among Protestants af-

12. This is why the garbage can model is more general than James's account: The case of explicitly conversionistic goals is a special case of religious activism but, as we have seen, evangelistic goals are by no means necessary to prompt nonprofit entrepreneurship by religious organizations.

fect their proclivity for nonprofit organizing. My argument should not be taken as a denial of the causal importance of theological differences. But it is necessary to specify the relevant theological variable. I am arguing that the relevant variable is not Protestant versus Catholic or Christian versus non-Christian or conversionist versus nonconversionist or Calvinist versus Arminian or any other conventional theological distinction. I am arguing that the key variable is the Weberian notion of a this-worldly activism, one in which the exact purposes of the activism are secondary to the fact of the activism.

Second, this religious ethic rarely specifies the exact direction religious activism ought to take. The goals of religious organizations, in other words, are inherently ambiguous. Hutchison's (1987, 118–19) history of American foreign missions again is relevant. Even during the turn-of-the-century heyday of foreign missions, when there was broad consensus around the goal of "evangelization of the world in this generation," the most salient aspect of this goal was its ambiguity. Did *evangelize* mean to convert or merely to expose the world to the missionaries' message? Did evangelization require missionaries only to preach or did it require them to give priority to the human needs of individuals? All of these issues were contested. Missionaries and mission organizations often had to figure out what to do once they were in the field; actual day-to-day activities rarely were deducible in any obvious way from organizational goals.

Third, a major theme in the literature of Christian missions is the extraordinary difficulty of converting people. Missionaries and missions leaders were well aware of the sometimes uncomfortable juxtaposition of large numbers of mission-run colleges, schools, hospitals, dispensaries, and publishing houses, on the one hand, and paltry numbers of converts on the other (Hutchison 1987, 100). With a few exceptions (for example, Hawaii), until the rise of indigenously led Christian movements, converting individuals to Christianity proved to be exceedingly difficult. In terms of the garbage can model, the problem of direct conversion clearly had exorbitant energy requirements attached to it.

Fourth, it is no wonder, then, that missionaries turned their considerable talents and energies to the creation of a variety of nonprofit organizations. Although some organizations, especially schools, were founded for the instrumental purpose of gaining converts, the pouring of missionary effort into nonprofit creation was largely the result of a more general dynamic by which solutions find problems via a garbage can process. When religious goals are nonconversionist — for example, a religious obligation to do good — then the ambiguity involved in *doing good* creates a garbage can into which participants throw multiple problems and solutions in the process of deciding just how to spend their time. When religious goals are conversionist, the garbage can process enters into play because of ambiguity about the proper technology for achieving such a goal. Either way, the central dynamic is the same.

To approach this point from a slightly different angle, a remarkable feature of religious problems — How do we save souls? How do we gain our own salvation? How do we do good in the world? — is that they can become attached to virtually any concrete solution. One can save souls (or win one's own salvation or live out a commitment to doing good) by preaching on the corner, by opening a school, or by running a soup kitchen. Some of these concrete solutions, of course, also address other problems — lack of adequate education, homelessness, and so forth. When religious organizations form nonprofit organizations devoted to secular services, then, they simultaneously address two problems with one solution. This is why creating decision situations oriented to religious problem solving will tend to produce secular activity: Other problems (for example, feeding the hungry) will be thrown into the decision situation, and the ambiguity of the religious problems makes them easily attachable to solutions more directly geared to social problems. The activities that mission organizations wound up engaging in thus can be seen both as choices gravitating toward social problems like illiteracy and inadequate health care, whose energy requirements were less daunting than evangelizing the world in a single generation, and as religious problems gravitating toward concrete solutions like building a school, which these individuals knew how to do.

Fifth, the garbage can process also helps to explain the rapidity with which many mission organizations, no matter how they begin, wind up providing social services. Robertson (1993) documented how quickly the YWCA shifted from running Bible studies to running typing classes. Zald and Denton (1963) have told a similar story about the YMCA. Yohn (1991) described how the evangelical content of the mission work in New Mexico diminished over time. Indeed, such internal transformation of religious activities and goals in a secular direction long has been a major theme sounded by observers of religious organizations (see, for example, Berger 1969; Luckmann 1967).

Similarly, a major theme in Hutchison's (1987) history of missions is the "Christ-culture dialectic," by which he means the constant debate over whether evangelizing or "civilizing" is the primary purpose of missions. It is clear from his account that mission theorists constantly confronted that issue; it is equally clear that there was very little question about which sort of activities were winning the day in the field: "The dispiriting gap between the generally tiny harvests of converts and the plethora of successful civilizing ventures (a gap that was not emphasized in reports to the home churches, yet was well understood by both missionaries and executives) made the issue of 'civilizing or evangelizing' a personal and often painful one for devoted workers who had been recruited to evangelize the world" (Hutchison 1987, 12).

This tension was more than a difference of priorities between liberal social service providers and conservative evangelists. While Hutchison (1987) documents different modalities in liberal and conservative approaches to missions, he also shows that the evangelizing-civilizing tension cut across the liberal-conservative divide. Even if they resisted more strongly an explicit shift in goals, many conservative as well as liberal mission organizations eventually experienced in practice the transformation from preaching to building schools, running dispensaries, and digging wells. The commonplace nature of this kind of transformation suggests that it is produced by a dynamic other than the instrumental pursuit of converts. The garbage can model helps us to see what that dynamic is: Highly motivated and energetic organizational elites found problems to which they could apply their organizational resources and solutions, and it would have required powerful forces indeed to have prevented them from shifting their efforts to the work that seemed most useful. It is also important, as described above, that this work could be construed simultaneously as solving religious problems.

The last point calls attention to an important but subtle nuance in the foregoing discussion. When we look at a cross section of the nonprofits in a society and observe that some proportion of them have religious origins, it is important to realize that those organizations with religious origins in fact contain two distinct populations. On the one hand, there are organizations like Phyllis Wheatley House that were always devoted to secular social service despite the involvement of religious groups in their foundings. On the other hand, there are organizations like the YWCA that originally had evangelistic purposes but shifted over time to become more secular. A great advantage of the garbage can model is that it can explain both the creation of secular nonprofits by religious organizations and the transformation of evangelizing organizations into secular ones.

So, although there was something "heroic" in the enterprise to make converts, investigators of religion's role in nonprofit foundings should remain squarely focused on "what was most mundanely productive" in mission work, as Hutchison (1987, 13) puts it. The mundane products of mission work are largely nonprofit organizations that met excess demand for a variety of services in a variety of settings around the globe.[13] This connection eventually found explicit recognition in the most liberal theological statements about missions. During the 1960s, the World Council of Churches proposed that "the world and not the church must set the agenda for missions," and the Dutch theologian Johannes Hoekendijk called for missions by "small, flexible, mobile groups of dedicated members who live in commitment and . . . availability" (Hutchison 1987, 184, 186). At

least in some circles, the garbage can quality of missions not only came to be understood, but was even seen as a virtue.

Summary

The work supported by the Program on Governance, along with other scholarship, is replete with examples of religious nonprofit foundings that apparently have little to do with the desire for maximizing adherents. This work prompted a closer look at James's theory about the mechanism underlying the supply-side effect that religion seems to have on the size of the nonprofit sector. The garbage can model of organizational behavior provides a more general account than James's of the "religion effect" in situations of excess demand. It is more general because, while it accounts for the behavior of religious organizations directly driven by the desire to maximize adherents, it also accounts for the behavior of religious organizations whose goal is not conversion and for the common phenomenon by which an evangelizing organization transforms into something else. If the key mechanism is a religious activism that generates a garbage can process, then we can expect religious organizations to be overrepresented among nonprofit founders in many arenas, even in the absence of any evangelistic goals. Such widespread overrepresentation is just what the evidence shows. An explicit desire to evangelize does contribute to the tendency for religious organizations to establish nonprofits, but in an ironic way: Evangelistic motives bring individuals together in highly energetic organizations whose primary purpose—conversion—turns out to be one for which the appropriate technology is difficult to discern, not to mention a goal that is continually and almost universally frustrated. Thus is religious energy—whether oriented to evangelism or not—directed into the creation of nonprofit organizations that meet excess demand for any number of services. In the garbage can, nonprofit organization solves several different types of religious problems.

The garbage can model, more generally, provides an important sociological corrective to an economic theory of organizational behavior. Economists tend to be vexed by the question, "If nonprofit organizations are not seeking to maximize profits, what are they seeking?" (Weisbrod 1988, 101). It is this question that leads James to imagine that it is the desire to maximize converts that, in general, leads religious organizations to found nonprofits. But to the extent that an organization's behavior is governed by a garbage can process, its behavior is not causally produced by attempts to maximize anything, and the attempt to understand its behavior as the straightforward product of maximization will mislead. A garbage can process offers a description of the nonprofit-founding behavior of religious organizations that is more consistent with available evidence than is a maximizing model like James's. Moreover, it takes nothing away from the causal importance of religion to acknowledge that its supply-side effect on nonprofit foundings is often an unintended consequence of the restless activism promoted by

---

13. In 1985, after collecting oral histories from one-time China missionaries, Northeastern University's R. Wayne Anderson was surprised to learn that these individuals "had turned out not to be 'your stereotypic Bible-thumping soul-savers.' Basically, as he told a journalist, 'they were Peace Corps types before the Peace Corps'" (Hutchison 1987, 203). I think this analogy is a helpful one. To contemporary readers it conveys an appropriate image both of the kind of work done by most missionaries and of the typical motivation leading individuals to become missionaries.

some religious traditions rather than an intended product of the desire to make converts or increase loyalty to a religious group.

A normative implication of this way of conceptualizing the relation between religion and nonprofit entrepreneurship is that, as Michael Cohen and James March ([1974] 1986) have noted, ambiguous organizational goals may sometimes be preferable to clear goals. It is, after all, the very ambiguity of religious goals that pushes organizations devoted to reaching those goals into activities that wind up addressing a variety of social problems. From this perspective, religious organizations with ambiguous goals promote what Alan Wolfe, in this volume, refers to as "environmental altruism." That is, they seem to provide settings that generate other-regarding behavior whether or not the individuals involved have altruistic motives. The garbage can theory makes sense of the otherwise paradoxical findings, described by Wolfe, that, among individuals, religious belief does not correlate strongly with altruism while, as described in detail here, religious organizations are continually engaged in altruistic activity. Religious organizations help us see how organizations filled with nonaltruists might wind up generating much altruistic activity. To the extent that such activity depends on an ethic of activism coupled with ambiguous religious goals, it in fact would be undesirable to promote greater clarification and specification of those goals, a point that contemporary theologians and religious officials might ponder.

CONCLUSION

DiMaggio and Anheier (1990, 138–39) point out that there are fundamental sets of questions to be asked about nonprofits. There is the question of *origins*: Why do nonprofits exist? What explains the distribution of societal functions among sectors?; and there is the question of *behavior*: What difference does being a nonprofit make to organizational behavior? This chapter has addressed only the former set of questions — those related to the intersectoral division of labor and the link between religious organizations and the size of a nonprofit sector.

It is fitting to conclude by pointing out that there is considerable need for work that explores religion's relevance to the second basic theme sounded by DiMaggio and Anheier — organizational behavior. Among nonprofits, what difference does religious affiliation make to "performance, structures, service and client mix, strategies, and human-resource policies" (DiMaggio and Anheier 1990, 139)? Initial evidence suggests that religious connections do make a difference: religious nursing homes pay lower wages than either for-profit or secular nonprofit nursing homes (Borjas et al. 1983); directors of religious day care centers in Wisconsin have less previous management experience but more previous experience with children than directors of secular nonprofit day care centers (Mauser 1993; also, this volume); religious nursing homes and facilities for the mentally handicapped are more likely than either for-profits or nonreligious nonprofits to use waiting lists, an indicator of the extent to which a facility refrains from acting like a for-profit organization by raising prices until the market clears (Weisbrod 1988; also, this volume). Furthermore, although church-owned facilities in these two industries do not offer more social activities than other nonprofit facilities, customer satisfaction with those services is significantly greater at the religiously affiliated facilities (Weisbrod, in this volume). These results offer tantalizing hints of what will very likely prove to be myriad ways in which religion affects organizational behavior within a given arena.[14]

As with the other themes explored in this chapter, introducing religion to research on organizational behavior is more than an exercise in expanding our scope. Investigating the effect of "religionness" has broader implications for how we understand the effect of "nonprofitness." As DiMaggio and Anheier (1990, 149) point out, variation *among* nonprofit organizations may very well swamp variation *between* nonprofit organizations and organizations in other sectors. Understanding the variation among nonprofits — and exploiting the possibility that whether nonprofits have a religious affiliation is a likely source of substantial heterogeneity — therefore is a necessary condition for adequately answering the more general, and widely researched, question about the effect of nonprofitness on organizational behavior.

I shall end where I began: Encouraging the provision of publicly beneficial goods is a central concern to those who study nonprofit organizations. Explicit and systematic attention to religion, religious giving, and religious organizations increases in several ways our knowledge of the complex issues surrounding the social production of publicly beneficial services. That it has been possible both to argue and to illustrate this case mainly on the strength of work supported by the Program on Governance is testimony to the substantial contribution represented by this body of work. It also is a sign pointing to the substantial contributions yet to be made to our knowledge about religion, nonprofits, and the production of public goods.

REFERENCES

Anheier, Helmut K. 1991. "West Germany: The Ambiguities of Peak Associations." In *Between States and Markets: The Voluntary Sector in Comparative Perspective,* ed. Robert Wuthnow, 64–93. Princeton: Princeton University Press.

———. 1992. "An Elaborate Network: Profiling the Third Sector in Germany." In *Government and the Third Sector: Emerging Relationships in Welfare States,* ed. Benjamin Gidron et al., 31–56. San Francisco: Jossey-Bass.

Badelt, Christoph. 1989. "Government versus Private Provision of Social Services: The Case of Austria." In *The Nonprofit*

14. See the chapters by Weisbrod and Mauser in this volume for additional ways in which religious nonprofits do and do not differ from secular nonprofits. Mauser and Weisbrod also begin the task of developing theory that explains the complex patterns in the findings.

Sector in International Perspective, ed. Estelle James, 162–76. New York: Oxford University Press.

Beckford, James A. 1990. "The Sociology of Religion and Social Problems." *Sociological Analysis* 51:1–14.

Ben-Ner, A., and T. Van Hoomissen. 1989. "The Relative Size of the Nonprofit Sector in the Mixed Economy: Theory and Estimation." Manuscript. Minneapolis: University of Minnesota.

Berger, Peter L. 1969. *The Sacred Canopy.* Garden City: Anchor Books.

Beuttler, Fred W. 1992. "Morals and Ethics in the Education of a Trustee: Chester I. Barnard at the Rockefeller Foundation." Paper presented at the Fifth Annual Symposium, Indiana University Center on Philanthropy, Indianapolis.

Biddle, Jeff E. 1992. "Religious Organizations." In *Who Benefits from the Nonprofit Sector?* ed. Charles T. Clotfelter, 92–133. Chicago: University of Chicago Press.

Bordt, Rebecca. 1993. Personal correspondence.

Borjas, G. J., H. Frech, and P. B. Ginsburg. 1983. "Property Rights and Wages: The Case of Nursing Homes." *Journal of Human Resources* 17:231–46.

Chapman, Richard Mark. 1993. "To Do These Mitzvahs: Jewish Philanthropy and Social Service in Minneapolis, 1900–1950." Ph.D. dissertation, University of Minnesota.

Chaves, Mark, and David E. Cann. 1992. "Regulation, Pluralism, and Religious Market Structure: Explaining Religion's Vitality." *Rationality and Society* 4:272–90.

Chaves, Mark, Peter J. Schraeder, and Mario Sprindys. 1994. "State Regulation of Religion and Muslim Religious Vitality in the Industrialized West." *Journal of Politics* 56:1087–97.

Clotfelter, Charles T. 1985. *Federal Tax Policy and Charitable Giving.* Chicago: University of Chicago Press.

———, ed. 1992. *Who Benefits from the Nonprofit Sector?* Chicago: University of Chicago Press.

Cohen, Michael D., James G. March, and Johan P. Olsen. 1972. "A Garbage Can Model of Organizational Choice." *Administrative Science Quarterly* 17:1–25.

Cohen, Michael D., and James G. March. [1974] 1986. *Leadership and Ambiguity: The American College President.* 2d ed. Boston: Harvard Business School Press.

Cress, Daniel Miles. 1993. "Mobilization among the Homeless: A Comparative Study of Organization, Action, and Outcomes in Eight U.S. Cities." Ph.D. dissertation, University of Arizona.

Demerath, N. J., III. 1991. "Religious Capital and Capital Religions: Cross-cultural and Non-legal Factors in the Separation of Church and State." *Daedalus* 120:21–40.

DiMaggio, Paul J., and Helmut K. Anheier. 1990. "The Sociology of Nonprofit Organizations and Sectors." *Annual Review of Sociology* 16:137–59.

Dolan, Jay P. 1992. *The American Catholic Experience: A History from Colonial Times to the Present.* Notre Dame: University of Notre Dame Press.

Douglas, James. 1983. *Why Charity? The Case for a Third Sector.* Beverly Hills: Sage.

Doyle, Maura. 1993. "Religious Affiliation, Fiscal Policy and Charitable Giving." Manuscript. Cambridge: Massachusetts Institute of Technology.

Finke, Roger, and Rodney Stark. 1988. "Religious Economies and Sacred Canopies: Religious Mobilization in American Cities, 1906." *American Sociological Review* 53:41–49.

Finke, Roger, and Laurence R. Iannaccone. 1993. "Supply-Side Explanations for Religious Change." *The Annals of The American Academy of Political and Social Science* 527:27–39.

Fruhling, Hugo. 1989. "Nonprofit Organizations as Opposition to Authoritarian Rule: The Case of Human Rights Organizations in Chile." In *The Nonprofit Sector in International Perspective,* ed. Estelle James, 358–76. New York: Oxford University Press.

Greenspan, Anders. 1992. "A Shrine to the American Faith: Americanism and the Restoration of Colonial Williamsburg, 1926–1960." Ph.D. dissertation, Indiana University.

Hall, Peter Dobkin. 1992. *Inventing the Nonprofit Sector.* Baltimore: Johns Hopkins Press.

———. 1993. "Religion and the Organizational Revolution in the United States." Manuscript. New Haven: Yale University.

Hansmann, Henry. 1987. "Economic Theories of Nonprofit Organization." In *The Nonprofit Sector: A Research Handbook,* ed. Walter W. Powell, 27–42. New Haven: Yale University Press.

Hase, Michiko. 1993. "W. Gertrude Brown's Struggle for Racial Justice: Female Leadership and Community in Black Minneapolis, 1920–1940." Ph.D. dissertation, University of Minnesota.

Hodgkinson, Virginia A., Richard W. Lyman, and Associates. 1989. *The Future of the Nonprofit Sector: Challenges, Changes, and Policy Considerations.* San Francisco: Jossey-Bass.

Hoge, Dean R., Charles E. Zech, Patrick H. McNamara, and Michael J. Donahue. 1996. *Money Matters: Personal Giving in American Churches.* Louisville: Westminster John Knox Press.

Hutchison, William R. 1987. *Errand to the World: American Protestant Thought and Foreign Missions.* Chicago: University of Chicago Press.

———, ed. 1989. *Between the Times: The Travail of the Protestant Establishment in America, 1900–1960.* Cambridge: Cambridge University Press.

Iannaccone, Laurence R. 1991. "The Consequences of Religious Market Structure: Adam Smith and the Economics of Religion." *Rationality and Society* 3:156–77.

Independent Sector. 1993. *From Belief to Commitment: The Community Service Activities and Finances of Religious Congregations in the United States,* 1993 edition. Washington, D.C.: Independent Sector.

James, Estelle. 1987a. "The Public/Private Division of Responsibility for Education: An International Comparison." *Economics of Education Review* 6:1–14.

———. 1987b. "The Nonprofit Sector in Comparative Perspective." In *The Nonprofit Sector: A Research Handbook,* ed. Walter W. Powell, 397–415. New Haven: Yale University Press.

———. 1989a. "The Private Provision of Public Services: A Comparison of Sweden and Holland." In *The Nonprofit Sector in International Perspective,* ed. Estelle James, 31–60. New York: Oxford University Press.

———. 1989b. "The Private Nonprofit Provision of Education: A Theoretical Model and Application to Japan." In *The Nonprofit Sector in International Perspective,* ed. Estelle James, 61–83. New York: Oxford University Press.

———. 1989c. "The Nonprofit Sector in Developing Countries: The Case of Sri Lanka." In *The Nonprofit Sector in International Perspective,* ed. Estelle James, 289–318. New York: Oxford University Press.

———. 1993. "Why Do Different Countries Choose a Different Public-Private Mix of Educational Services?" *The Journal of Human Resources* 28:571–92.

Kaplan, Ann E., ed. 1996. *Giving USA: The Annual Report on Philanthropy for the Year 1995.* New York: American Association of Fund-Raising Counsel Trust for Philanthropy.

Land, Kenneth C., Glenn Deane, and Judith R. Blau. 1991. "Religious Pluralism and Church Membership." *American Sociological Review* 56:237–49.

Layton, Daphne Niobe. 1987. *Philanthropy and Voluntarism: An Annotated Bibliography.* New York: Foundation Center.

Luckmann, Thomas. 1967. *The Invisible Religion.* New York: Macmillan.

Marmor, Theodore R., Mark Schlesinger, and Richard W. Smithey. 1987. "Nonprofit Organizations and Health Care." In *The Nonprofit Sector: A Research Handbook,* ed. Walter W. Powell, 221–39. New Haven: Yale University Press.

Mauser, Elizabeth. 1993. "Is Organizational Form Important to Consumers and Managers: An Application to the Day-Care Industry." Ph.D. dissertation, University of Wisconsin-Madison.

Michaelsen, Robert S., and Wade Clark Roof, eds. *Liberal Protestantism: Realities and Possibilities.* New York: Pilgrim Press.

Morris, Aldon. 1984. *The Origins of the Civil Rights Movement.* New York: Free Press.

Pagnucco, Ronald, and John D. McCarthy. 1992. "Advocating Nonviolent Direct Action in Latin America: The Antecedents and Emergence of SERPAJ." In *Religion and Politics in Comparative Perspective,* ed. Bronislaw Misztal and Anson Shupe, 125–47. Westport, Conn.: Praeger.

Powell, Walter W. 1987a. "Preface." In *The Nonprofit Sector: A Research Handbook,* ed. Walter W. Powell, xi–xiii. New Haven: Yale University Press.

———, ed. 1987b. *The Nonprofit Sector: A Research Handbook.* New Haven: Yale University Press.

Robertson, Nancy. 1988. " 'Deeper Even Than Race'?: White Women and the Politics of Sisterhood in the Young Women's Christian Association, 1906–1946." Manuscript. New York: New York University.

———. 1993. " 'Deeper Even Than Race'?: White Women and the Politics of Sisterhood in the Young Women's Christian Association, 1906–1949." Draft of Ph.D. dissertation, New York University.

Rose, Elizabeth. 1993. Personal correspondence.

———. 1994. "From Sponge Cake to *Hamentashen*: Jewish Identity in a Jewish Settlement House, 1885–1952." *Journal of American Ethnic History* 13(3):3–23.

Schnorr, Paul. 1992. "Organizing on the Margins: Race, Class, and Voluntary Association in the Context of Community." Manuscript. Evanston, Northwestern University.

———. 1993. "Denied a Sense of Community: Problems of Class, Race, and Community Form in a Voluntary Resettlement Effort." Ph.D. dissertation, Northwestern University.

Scott, W. Richard. 1992. *Organizations: Rational, Natural, and Open Systems.* 3d ed. Englewood Cliffs: Prentice-Hall.

Smith, Adam. [1776] 1965. *An Inquiry into the Nature and Causes of the Wealth of Nations.* New York: Modern Library.

Smith, Brian H. 1982. "Churches as Development Institutions: The Case of Chile, 1973–1980." No. 50 in the Program on Non-Profit Organizations working paper series, Institution for Social and Policy Studies, Yale University.

———. 1989. "More than Altruism: The Politics of European International Charities." In *The Nonprofit Sector in International Perspective,* ed. Estelle James, 319–38. New York: Oxford University Press.

Smith, Christian. 1991. *The Emergence of Liberation Theology: Radical Religion and Social Movement Theory.* Chicago: University of Chicago Press.

Steinberg, Richard. 1990. "Taxes and Giving: New Findings." *Voluntas* 1(2).

Stephen, Lynn. 1993. "Redefining Gender Relations: A Comparison of Two Rural Women's Organizations in Mexico and Brazil." Manuscript. Boston: Northeastern University.

———, trans. and ed. (1994). *Hear My Testimony: María Teresa Tula, Human Rights Activist of El Salvador.* Boston: South End Press.

Van Til, Jon, and Associates. 1990. *Critical Issues in American Philanthropy: Strengthening Theory and Practice.* San Francisco: Jossey-Bass.

Weber, Max. [1904] 1958. *The Protestant Ethic and the Spirit of Capitalism.* New York: Charles Scribner's Sons.

Weisbrod, Burton A. 1977. "Toward a Theory of the Voluntary Nonprofit Sector in a Three-Sector Economy." In *The Voluntary Nonprofit Sector: An Economic Analysis,* ed. Burton A. Weisbrod, 51–76. Lexington, Mass.: D. C. Heath.

———. 1988. *The Nonprofit Economy.* Cambridge: Harvard University Press.

Wood, James R. 1990. "Alternatives to Religion in the Promotion of Philanthropy." In *Faith and Philanthropy in America: Exploring the Role of Religion in America's Voluntary Sector,* ed. Robert Wuthnow and Virginia A. Hodgkinson, 255–70. San Francisco: Jossey-Bass.

Yohn, Susan. 1991. "Instituting 'Planned Growth': The Rationalization of Women's Philanthropy." Paper presented at the November 1991 meetings of the Project on Governance of Nonprofit Organizations, Indianapolis.

———. 1995. *A Contest of Faiths: Missionary Women and Pluralism in the American Southwest.* Ithaca: Cornell University Press.

Zald, Mayer N., and Patricia Denton. 1963. "From Evangelism to General Service: The Transformation of the YMCA." *Administrative Science Quarterly* 8:214–34.

Part Two

Private Provision of Public Services

5

BURTON A. WEISBROD

Institutional Form and Organizational Behavior

Institutions are the fundamental arrangements through which societies seek to deal with social and economic problems. Thus, it is important to understand the effectiveness of alternative forms of institutions. This chapter focuses on three nongovernmental forms of economic institutions — private firms, church-related nonprofit organizations, and non-church-related nonprofits. The issues and perspectives presented, however, are applicable to the broader array of institutional forms.

I direct attention to two questions: What kinds of differences in behavior should be expected among alternative institutional forms? What evidence is there about comparative institutional behavior, and how should it be interpreted?

Theory and evidence about the virtues and limitations of private enterprise have a centuries-old history, dating back at least to Adam Smith's *Wealth of Nations,* published in 1776. Analysis of the private nonprofit sector, however, is in its infancy. Nonprofit organizations constitute a rapidly growing segment of the U.S. economy, having increased from 309,000 organizations in 1967 to nearly 1 million today, of which some 400,000 can receive tax-deductible contributions (those nonprofits exempt from corporate income taxation under section 501(c)(3) of the Internal Revenue Code), and from 2.3 percent of national income at the close of World War II to approximately 5 percent now.[1] How effective nonprofits are, how their behavior compares with that of private firms, and what society is gaining in return for its many subsidies to nonprofits are increasingly important questions.

Partly in response to the growth of the nonprofit sector, nonprofits are the subject of increased political attention. Tension between nonprofits and private firms has escalated, with charges that nonprofits are guilty of "unfair competition" (U.S. Small Business Administration 1983). Tension is also increasing between nonprofits and governments, as concern over government budget deficits brings closer scrutiny of nonprofits' tax exemptions and deductions (Gaul and Borowski 1993).

At the same time that nonprofits are under growing attack they are being increasingly relied upon to respond to changing economic and social conditions. There is increasing demand for trustworthy institutions as a geographically mobile population and an array of increasingly complex goods pose problems for consumers who seek assurance that they are actually receiving the quality of goods and services they expect. (The chapters by Jane Mansbridge and by Alan Wolfe in this book address the importance of trust, altruism, and

I thank Carolyn Moehling and Kanika Kapur for their research assistance.

1. If the substantial value of volunteer labor — the overwhelming majority of which goes to nonprofits — were counted, the economic importance of nonprofits would be seen to be even greater.

related concepts of public spirit in a world of growing complexity and diversity.)

Still another force increasing attention to nonprofits is an apparent decline in confidence in government and an accelerated search for alternatives. Privatization of social services is a powerful worldwide force today, but there has been little attention paid — by government decisionmakers or by researchers — to the merits and demerits of divestiture to private business firms relative to private nonprofit organizations, let alone to the implications of divesting to a church-related or some other form of nonprofit. The growth of for-profit prisons, for example, has its critics, but the debate has centered on the choice between government and private enterprise (O'Brien 1993; *New York Times* 1994) rather than nonprofits (see, however, Weisbrod 1988).

Two recent events — one in higher education and one in health care — highlight the public policy implications of understanding comparative institutional behavior. First, in 1991 the U.S. Department of Justice brought an antitrust action against the Ivy League universities and the Massachusetts Institute of Technology (MIT) for alleged price fixing in the granting of financial aid to prospective students. The Ivy schools have since agreed to abandon the practice, but MIT has not. It contends that the actions, which it does not deny, promote rather than harm social welfare, in the context of its charitable nonprofit activities. The implicit argument is that although price fixing is undesirable in private, for-profit firms, it should be regarded as desirable when nonprofits (or perhaps only certain nonprofits?) engage in it ("M.I.T. Wins a New Trial in Price-Fixing Case" 1993). The claim is that private firms and nonprofits use price-fixing power in different ways and with different results. The argument, while plausible, has not been subject to careful research, and neither has the implication that some or all antitrust laws ought not apply to all forms of institutions; currently they do.[2]

Second, in 1993 the Clinton administration proposed a health care reform plan that called for hospital mergers to reduce duplication of facilities and reduce costs and prices. Although the prediction that reducing the amount of competition — which hospital mergers within a single community would tend to do — would reduce prices is contrary to basic economic theory, that theory assumes profit-oriented firms. The hospital industry in the United States, however, is heavily dominated by nonprofit organizations. If they achieved greater monopoly power, would they use it to increase prices and profits or to decrease prices and expand socially valuable activities?

In spite of the paucity of theory and of evidence, judgments and assertions about the comparative behavior of pri-

vate firms and nonprofit organizations abound, and these beliefs give rise to conflicting behavioral predictions and public policy prescriptions. One view is that nonprofit sector behavior is socially preferable. The New York State Moreland Commission, for example, responding to charges of improprieties in the nursing home industry in the mid-1970s, proposed to "phase out proprietary nursing facilities in New York and to substitute nonprofit institutions as the mainstay of the industry" (Temporary Commission 1976). The California legislature prohibited for-profit health maintenance organizations from treating Medi-Cal (the California Medicaid) enrollees (Goldberg 1976) in the early 1970s. The debate about the role of for-profit hospitals relative to nonprofits continues even now, with critics of investor-owned hospitals claiming that the high prices they charge relative to nonprofit hospitals means that their "wave has crested" (Freudenheim 1993). Earlier, though at a more abstract level, Kenneth Arrow conjectured that "in the provision of medical services, profit-making . . . arouses suspicion and antagonism on the part of patients and referring physicians, so they do prefer nonprofit institutions" (Arrow 1963). Such a preference would be justified only if nonprofit status connoted behavior that is systematically different and preferable.

The examples just given come from health care. There are similar views and doubts, however, about the limits to profit seeking in day care (Mauser 1988), prisons (O'Brien 1993; Weisbrod 1988) and in certain legal areas (Mansnerus 1993)[3] — all fields in which output quality is difficult to monitor.

In all these areas, policymakers base their decisions on assumptions about similarities and differences in behavior based on institutional form, and they are doing so despite a research base that, while growing (Ben-Ner and Gui 1991), remains weak. Underlying the debates at both the research and policy levels are two fundamental questions: Can nonprofit organizations, church-related or otherwise, be expected to behave in systematically varying ways compared with other forms of organizations, and if so, is their behavior socially preferable? The case for granting special privileges to nonprofit organizations rests on the belief that they do behave differently — that institutional form does matter — and that the nonprofit form of institution is preferable, in some identifiable conditions. Nonprofits that receive public subsidies are assumed to pursue public interest goals even when doing so deviates from ordinary self-interest considerations.

This chapter focuses primarily on the first of these two issues — the positive question of whether different forms of institutions act differently. That is, if nonprofit organizations, private firms, government agencies, and so forth were confronted by the same opportunities, would they make different

2. Another education case involves the attempt by the state of California to close a number of private, for-profit universities regarded as "diploma mills" (*New York Times,* 1994).

3. Most states continue to prohibit for-profit enterprise, but not nonprofit organizations, that refer clients to private law firms (Mansnerus 1993).

choices?[4] The goals of the chapter are to (1) clarify what it means to ask the question, Does institutional form matter?, (2) identify the dimensions in which divergences can be expected, and (3) examine some evidence on comparative institutional behavior. The question whether institutional form matters cannot be answered unless we explore the effects of institutional form on economic behavior, ceteris paribus. Thus, there are three subsidiary questions we must ask: What is meant by an institutional form? What dimensions of economic behavior does society care about? What variables should be included in the ceteris paribus? Each of these will be examined in turn.

The theme of this chapter is that any organization's decisions reflect the interplay of its goals and the constraints on it. Whenever one or both differ among institutions, behavioral differences will result. Economics research that has attempted to predict and to evaluate the decisions made by various forms of institutions has focused on the role of constraints rather than on organization goals. The principal reason is that constraints appear to be more malleable — more easily observed and more subject to legal and regulatory control. One constraint has dominated economics research on the behavior of forms of institutions other than private enterprise: the freedom of the organization and its manager to generate profit and to reward managers and owners accordingly. The lure of profit, economists assume, motivates all entrepreneurs and managers and fosters efficient decision making by private firms. In contrast, nonprofit organizations and government agencies, whose managers face a nondistribution constraint that legally forecloses benefiting from organization profit or surplus, have been assumed to be insulated from competitive pressures and hence prone to inefficiencies.

The structure of this chapter is as follows: after considering the definition of the term *institutional form,* I delve briefly into a theoretic examination of the types of behavior that are relevant in a comparative study of institutional form. Succeeding sections deal with the issue of which variables should be held constant as we seek to identify the independent effects of institutional form and present some recent empirical findings. Finally, policy implications and directions for future research are discussed.

DEFINING *INSTITUTIONAL FORM*

A form or type of institution can be defined usefully by its goals or objective function and the set of constraints it faces for achieving its goals.[5] Thus, a nonprofit organization is a different type of institution from a private firm either because the constraints on it differ or because its objectives differ or

both. A complete typology of institutional forms would consist of the intersection of the full set of potential constraints and goals. The logical possibilities are vast and have not yet been set forth in a comprehensive fashion.

Constraints

Some constraints are imposed technologically — by the state of scientific knowledge — but others result from laws, regulations, and codes of social conduct imposed by society. I assume that technological constraints apply equally to all organizations, while legal constraints may differ. In the United States today the legal constraints on nonprofit (sometimes termed tax-exempt) organizations differ from those on private firms in a number of respects: (1) Nonprofits, which have no owners, are legally prohibited from distributing profit to their management. They are not legally prevented from realizing profit, but they may lawfully use profits only to purchase inputs in subsequent periods.[6] This "nondistribution constraint" (Hansmann 1980) is, in effect, a legal restriction on managerial compensation — in all forms, pecuniary or other; it cuts the link between organization profit and managerial income. (2) Nonprofits also face regulatory constraints on their entry and on their financial interactions with for-profit firms.[7] They also benefit, however, from a variety of explicit subsidies, tax benefits, and exclusions from legal constraints that face private firms, and in these respects nonprofits are less constrained. (3) All nonprofits are exempt from federal corporate profits tax. (4) Some are exempt from state and local taxes on property, sales, and profits. (5) Some are eligible for postal subsidies. (6) Some may receive tax-deductible donations.

Nonprofits may also differ from private firms in (7) factor supply markets, in which labor suppliers, including volunteers, may prefer to work for nonprofit organizations, in which case nonprofits face lower supply prices. The two types of firms may also differ in (8) consumer demand; some consumers may prefer to buy from a nonprofit organization — that is, may be willing to pay a higher price to a nonprofit for the same commodity — either preferring to give a donation to the organization through the price paid or believing that the nonprofit provides a good or service that, while ostensibly the same as the private firm's version, is preferable because it has more of certain attributes that are costly for consumers to observe (for example, "tender loving care" in a nursing home).

Only those nonprofits that are eligible to receive tax-deductible contributions — essentially the organizations granted tax-exempt status under section 501(c)(3) of the Internal Revenue Code — receive the subsidies and exemptions

4. The normative question of whether any such differences, if they exist, justify social encouragement of nonprofit organizations — either in the aggregate or in particular activities — will be dealt with only briefly.

5. An organization's objective function is a statement of each of its (perhaps numerous) goals and the relative weight attached to each.

6. Thus, in a one-period model, the nonprofit organization would be seen as being subject to a zero-profit constraint.

7. One indicator of governmental regulatory constraint is that only 70–75 percent of applications for nonprofit, tax-exempt status are approved by the IRS (Weisbrod 1988, table A.2, p. 170).

noted above.[8] I further distinguish between church-related and other nonprofits. They are currently treated identically under the law — that is, the legal constraints on them are the same — but their economic and social behavior may differ because their goals may differ.

The Nondistribution Constraint. This restriction on the distribution of profit alters incentives in multiple dimensions. The conventional argument is that it reduces the incentive for efficiency because the manager of a nonprofit organization may not lawfully share in any profit or surplus generated by his or her managerial skills (Alchian and Demsetz 1972). What is less recognized is that the nondistribution constraint has additional effects — it also reduces the incentive to engage in activities that, while privately profitable, are socially inefficient. A legally nonprofit organization has little incentive, for example, to pollute the air or water with waste products in the pursuit of organization profit. Similarly, a nonprofit organization has little incentive to skimp on quality of output or otherwise take advantage of poorly informed consumers.

The nondistribution constraint can also affect the manner of distribution of outputs — that is, to whom outputs go. A profit maximizer has the incentive to sell its goods and services to the highest bidders because that is the route to maximum returns to stockholders and managers. A nonprofit organization, by contrast, with no stockholders but with managers facing the nondistribution constraint, has no financial incentive to provide its output to the highest bidders. If the nonprofit pursues public interest goals, behaving in a manner I have characterized elsewhere as "bonoficing" (Weisbrod 1988), it may provide at least some of its output to consumers who are socially "deserving" but who have little or no ability to pay — for example, scholarships to a school, charity care in a hospital, and free admission to a museum. A testable implication of this line of argument is that private firms, church-related nonprofits, and other nonprofits differ in their utilization of price, as opposed to alternative distribution mechanisms such as waiting lists, to determine access to their services.

The nondistribution constraint has been given central attention in the economics literature on nonprofit organization behavior. Although it is unquestionably significant, its importance has been exaggerated. Nonprofit organizations would not exist if they were not given advantages that offset the disadvantage imposed by the nondistribution constraint. Hence, any variations in behavior between nonprofits and

for-profits result not from the nondistribution constraint alone, but from its interactions with all of the aforementioned subsidy and exemption constraints, along with any differences in objective functions.

Enforceability of the Nondistribution Constraint. So far I have assumed implicitly that the nondistribution constraint is fully enforced. Enforcement is costly, however, and hence incomplete. To the extent that a constraint is unenforced it may have little effect on behavior.

Determining whether a manager's compensation is a competitive wage, which is legal, or whether it includes a residual profit component, which would violate the constraint, is complex. The IRS required nearly five years to determine whether the nonprofit PTL Ministry paid its president, Jim Bakker, an excessive salary — that is, one that included a distribution of profit. In 1987 the IRS finally decided that the nondistribution constraint had been violated, and it revoked the PTL tax-exempt status "because a substantial portion of P.T.L.'s net earnings went to benefit . . . Bakker." The IRS claimed that between 1981 and 1983 Bakker was paid "nearly one million dollars more than was reasonable" (Weisbrod 1988, 118–19). Although PTL was a large organization, capable of paying such salaries, Krashinsky (in this volume) notes that the nondistribution constraint is especially difficult to enforce when firms are small, as in day care.

There appears to be a logical internal contradiction involving the nondistribution constraint, which contributes to its enforcement problem. The constraint is generally interpreted as permitting a nonprofit organization to pay a manager a wage equal to what the manager could obtain in a competitive private market; the competitive market wage, however, would be a function of the manager's marginal contribution to the firm's profit, and so that wage is a function of organization profit. Yet the nondistribution constraint typically precludes such a profit-sharing compensation contract. (Occasional exceptions have been made to this proscription, but the general restriction remains.)

Because of enforcement costs, managers seeking to maximize profits (and their own income) might organize as legal nonprofits while operating no differently from private firms. These nonprofits — "for-profit firms in disguise (FPIDs)" — could behave like profit maximizers, distributing their outputs no differently, taking no less advantage of their informational superiorities over consumers, and generating no fewer external costs than private firms (Weisbrod 1988).[9]

---

8. Under current law in the United States, there are twenty-one classes of exempt organizations defined under section 501(c) of the Internal Revenue Code — subsections 501(c)(1)–501(c)(21); these are all exempt from the federal corporate income tax and are subject to the nondistribution constraint. The 501(c)(3) organizations, however, are virtually the only organizations to which one may make a donation that is tax deductible. For data on the numbers of entities that are exempt from federal income taxation under each 501(c) subsection, see U.S.Internal Revenue Service 1991.

9. The question of whether the nondistribution constraint is fully enforced suggests that the constraint is one-dimensional, but it need not be. Indeed, the expense preference or managerial discretion models of nonprofit organization behavior imply that the constraint is two-dimensional. That is, we can think of constraints on the distribution of profit in (a) money form — e.g., as salary, bonus, profit-sharing, etc. — which is fully binding, and in (b) a form such as elaborate office furnishings and lavish expense accounts, which is not binding (Migue and Belanger 1974; Williamson 1964). Legally, there is no such distinction, but en-

Even if the nondistribution constraint were not effective, however, many of the other differences in constraints between legal nonprofit organizations and private firms would remain. The differential subsidies that nonprofits receive would still have effects: Postal subsidies and property tax exemption would still present nonprofits and private firms with different relative input prices, which would cause even the FPIDs to engage in factor substitution; other things being equal, nonprofits, whether they behave like social welfare maximizers or like FPIDs, would utilize the U.S. mail relatively more than would their private firm counterparts and would have input ratios reflecting greater utilization of land and capital, which are subsidized, relative to labor.

Objective Functions

Nonprofits and private firms may also behave differently because their objectives differ. Consider the following three cases: Case I — (a) all managers have identical utility functions of the type U = U(Y,S), where Y = managerial income and S = provision of a socially beneficial good to deserving consumers, and (b) private firms are profit maximizers while nonprofit organizations are subject to the nondistribution constraint and its corollary — having to use all its resources to purchase inputs used for its tax-exempt purpose. In equilibrium, managers of private firms would receive greater compensation in the form of Y, and their counterparts in nonprofit organizations would receive greater utility from S; thus, the observed difference in measured financial rewards, Y, would be a compensating differential that offset the differential in S. Differential financial rewards — nonprofit managers receiving less, other things equal — would be observed across types of institutions even in a world in which managers are homogenous.

Case II — (a) all managers have identical utility functions of the type U′ = U′(Y), with only income mattering, and the conditions under (b), above, also hold here. In equilibrium, there should be no systematic difference in managerial incomes across institutional forms. Nonprofits as well as for-profit firms would have to pay equal rewards, and those rewards could be made only in units of Y.

Case III — This involves heterogeneous managerial utility functions, differing in terms of managers' relative valuations of (or marginal rates of substitution between) Y and S — some persons having utility functions as in case I, others as in case II — and the assumptions in (b) holding. Here we might expect systematic sorting of managers between institutional forms to occur. Managers with greater relative valuation of S will be attracted to the nonprofit sector, where the nondistribution constraint — which restricts compensation in terms of Y but not in the forms of S discussed above — is relatively less restrictive than it is for managers who value S relatively less. Managers with bonoficer-type utility functions will

gravitate to nonprofit organizations, where they can be hired at lower wages because the organization provides more outputs in form S, which serve to compensate wage differentials.

Evidence on systematic differences in managerial preferences is difficult to find, but there is some. First, it appears that the types of people who gravitate to managerial positions in nonprofit organizations are systematically different in their preferences, particularly in their concerns with considerations broader than their own narrow financial self-interest. On psychological tests, managers who choose and are chosen by nonprofits display greater relative concern with being forgiving and helpful than do their proprietary sector counterparts (Rawls, Ulrich, and Nelson 1975). Second, managers of nonprofits appear to be willing to work at lower rates of pay than they could obtain in the private market, which is consistent with the view that such social benefits (for example, helping the poor or the underinformed) — S in the model presented above — serve as compensating differentials. This was found in a study comparing lawyers' earnings in private law firms and in nonprofit, public interest law firms (Weisbrod 1983), although these findings have been questioned (Goddeeris 1988). Similar variations have been found in a recent study of executive compensation in for-profit and nonprofit hospitals (Roomkin and Weisbrod 1997). The bonoficer model appears to fit organizations run by these nonprofit managers better than the profit-maximizing model, but much more research is needed.

Nonprofits, having no owners but subject to IRS regulatory constraints, may come to have objective functions that reflect the utility functions of managers or trustees or both. Trustees, unlike directors of private firms, typically are selected not by an external group analogous to stockholders, but by either the founding entrepreneur or the sitting group of trustees.[10] No economic theoretic model of the role of nonprofit trustees and their relationship to organization management exists. In the balance of this paper I do not distinguish between trustees and management, instead referring to them collectively as managers. The relationship between nonprofit trustees and their management deserves more attention.

Two Models of Organization Behavior

Profit Maximizer. A private firm, which I shall also refer to as a proprietary or a for-profit firm, is an institution that can be regarded as having the objective of profit maximization and facing constraints that include the state of technology, consumer demand, factor prices, and legal rules and governmental regulations. This model assumes that there is no nondistribution constraint and no source of revenue other than sale of output — that is, there is no revenue from gifts or donations or if there is, its amount is determined exogenously.

Bonoficer. An organization might seek to generate less than maximum profit, while engaging in activities that are

forcement costs may be greater with respect to the latter dimension — another matter deserving further study.

10. Some trustees of nonprofit organizations are selected by a voting process analogous to that of private stockholders. For example, some university trustees are elected by alumni.

socially desirable but unprofitable — for example, supplying information to underinformed consumers rather than taking advantage of its informational superiority or helping the poor or avoiding activities that pollute. Thus, a bonoficer might utilize a production process that is more costly but less environmentally degrading than an alternative or distribute output to certain deserving but impecunious consumers.

The bonoficer and profit maximizer models differ in two significant ways: (a) The bonoficer's objective function includes not only profit but also the provision of services that have social value, while the profit maximizer includes only profit; (b) The bonoficer's revenue constraint reflects the greater availability of revenue from donations, which depend, at least in part, on the organization's actions. In this model, donations — which may be in the form of either money or time (volunteer labor) — are determined partly by the organization's decisions about its socially productive but privately unprofitable activities; in effect, donations are receipts from provision of a collective good.[11] Sales revenues, by contrast, are receipts from provision of private goods.

The bonoficer and profit-maximizer models can be seen as special cases of a more general form of objective function:

$$G = \alpha(\pi) + (1 - \alpha)S,$$

where π = organization profit, S = the organization's own provision of services that have social value but are not profitable, and α is a parameter that can range from 0 to 1. For $\alpha = 1$, we have the pure profit maximizer; $\alpha = 0$ is the pure bonoficer; as an organization's preference for S diminishes relative to that for π — that is, as α approaches 1, the bonoficer case collapses to the profit-maximizer case; intermediate cases, in which $\partial f/\partial S > 0$ and $\partial f/\partial \pi > 0$, describe the "weak bonoficer."[12] Later I shall examine the possibility that two classes of nonprofits, church-related and other, differ in their relative positions on this spectrum.

To summarize, if nonprofit organizations are bonoficers, their behavior will reflect the combined effects of (a) the nondistribution constraint, which attenuates property rights and hence reduces incentives for efficiency, (b) other legal constraints and subsidies that apply differentially to nonprofits and private firms, and (c) the bonoficing objective function, which encourages production of goods that are suboptimally provided in private markets. A constraint on profit distribution alters incentives generally — not only to be pri-

vately efficient but also to engage in activities that are privately profitable but socially inefficient. The net effect of these countervailing forces cannot be determined a priori.

Modeling nonprofit behavior is not likely to be a matter of finding a single model. As Wolfe (in this volume) argues, the multiplicity of the bases for behavior leads to a mixture of motives for altruistic institutions. This inevitably confounds the modeling of a single, comprehensive nonprofit objective function. Further, nonprofits are not necessarily homogeneous in their objective functions, some pursuing narrow self-interest goals consistent with profit maximization, while others pursue broader social objectives (bonoficers). Enforcement of the nondistribution constraint may also vary systematically, being less binding on some nonprofits; for example, regulators may assume that church-related nonprofits have bonoficing objective functions and so require less monitoring.[13]

WHAT DIMENSIONS OF INSTITUTIONAL BEHAVIOR SHOULD WE CARE ABOUT?

Efficiency. Do institutional forms differ in the cost at which they convert inputs into outputs? There have been many attempts to compare production costs, but we are still uncertain about how to measure output. Further, it is questionable whether we should assume that the same forms of output are produced regardless of institutional form. The discussion above emphasized the potential of nonprofits to provide outputs precisely in those forms that are most difficult to measure and value — quality in hard-to-monitor forms, external effects, and distribution to persons other than those with the greatest willingness to pay. Unless adequate attention is given to these dimensions of output, it is quite possible that output will come to be measured in ways that capture most or even all of private sector output but less of the output of nonprofits, thus biasing the comparative efficiency data.

Taking Advantage of Consumer Informational Deficiencies. When commodities are complex, so that it is costly for consumers to gauge performance and, hence, for sellers to guarantee the quality of output, organizational form may signal expected behavior because of the interplay of organization objectives and constraints.[14] As noted above, a

11. Nonprofit organizations vary widely in their dependence on donations. Litigation and legal aid organizations received 97 percent of their revenues through donations, while nonprofit sports and athletic organizations received only 4 percent.

12. Note that a legally nonprofit organization that chose to act as a profit-maximizer $(df/dS = 0)$ — which could occur in the light of enforcement costs for the nondistribution constraint — would not behave identically to a private firm even though the objective functions were the same, because the constraints on the two would differ. This is the case in which the nonprofit is a for-profit firm in disguise, taking advantage of subsidies but pursuing profit maximization.

13. The level of monitoring can, however, affect the organization's objective function through the managerial/trustee sorting process. Thus, a lower level of regulatory monitoring could attract more profit-maximizer types of managers, thereby turning the organization into something closer to a for-profit-in-disguise. Although nonprofits are not homogeneous, it is not clear that models should be industry specific (for hospitals, see Newhouse 1970 and Pauly and Redisch 1973). For a discussion of tax policy and the objective function, see Eckel and Steinberg 1993.

14. Zeckhauser and Viscusi (1990) have pointed out that in a world of positive costs of obtaining information, it may be efficient to utilize a proxy for information. Specifically, they note that "mandatory requirements may be preferable to . . . information efforts." Institutional form could perform an analogous informational role.

potentially important consequence of the nondistribution constraint — assuming it is enforced — is its blunting of managerial incentive to maximize profits. This is important because organizations that do not pursue maximum profit do not have an incentive to take advantage of their informational superiority over consumers. Because many goods and services are easily evaluated by consumers, it might be expected that the importance of nonprofit as well as government producers will be greatest in markets in which consumers seek trustworthy sellers who will act as if they are effective agents for consumers — perhaps in health care, schooling, and medical research. Even when such complex commodities are involved, however, the fact that consumers vary in their ability to gauge quality suggests that nonprofit and government providers may be especially useful to those consumers who are least well informed — which has been found in recent work on day care facilities (Mauser 1993).

An example of an informational asymmetry would be the rate of injury of children in day care centers. One of the hard-to-monitor dimensions of organization behavior in this industry is the attentiveness of staff in monitoring the youngsters and thereby preventing accidents. Because attentiveness is difficult to observe and accident rate statistics difficult to obtain and to interpret, it would be useful to determine whether institutional form is a useful proxy for such costly-to-monitor variables as attentiveness to accident prevention.

The possible connection between informational asymmetries and institutional form is exemplified in the following. Every commodity may be seen as a bundle of attributes: a given consumer can determine which attributes are present and at what level, at a cost specific to the attribute and consumer. For simplicity, consider each attribute as being one of two types, for any given consumer — either low cost, type I, or high cost, type II; if a consumer is asymmetrically underinformed, it is, by definition, in type II dimensions.[15]

Type II attributes give the seller — whom I assume to be the better informed — the opportunity to chisel or "shave" quality, given consumers' cost of monitoring. If nonprofit, for-profit, and government organizations do behave differently, it might well be in the extent to which they take advantage of opportunities to capitalize on their (type II) informational superiority, especially in situations in which it is costly for consumers to switch to other sellers when unsatisfactory output is detected — for example, in nursing homes. If nonprofits do take less advantage of their informational advantages, they would provide more type II attributes than private firms, other things equal.

Output Quality. Another relevant dimension of institutional behavior is output quality as reflected by level of resource inputs. It is true that consumers could learn about the level of any seller's input utilization, but this information can be difficult to obtain. Thus, knowledge of the supplier's institutional form might reveal valuable information on quality. To be sure, however, interpretation of divergences is of critical importance. If institutional form *A* utilizes more units of inputs per unit of measured output — for example, a day of service in a hospital, school, nursing home, or day care center — than does institutional form *B,* that could represent (1) lower quality service by *A,* (2) less needy consumers in *A,* or (3) differential output forms, *A* producing more output in unmeasured dimensions.

Output Rationing Methods. Institutional behavior could differ in the means used to distribute output. Two prominent alternatives are price and waiting lists. A profit-maximizing organization would tend to rely on price, increasing it if there is excess demand. This is not to say that private firms never maintain a queue; the key question is whether nonprofits — church-related or not — are more likely to choose to provide their services on a basis other than ability to pay. If nonprofits were better described as bonoficers while private firms placed relatively greater weight on generating profit, then nonprofits would make less use of price to control access and more use of alternative mechanisms such as waiting lists.[16]

As a matter of social policy, we may have a preference, in some industries, for sellers that utilize nonprice distribution techniques rather than providing services to the highest bidders. In the case of human organ transplants, for example, U.S. policy has gone so far as to prohibit the sale of organs; in other industries the optimal solution may be not to prohibit sale altogether but to encourage institutional mechanisms that deploy a variety of distributional mechanisms.

Generation of External Benefits and Costs. Insofar as nonprofits are bonoficers, they tend to engage in more activities that provide more external (uncaptured) social benefits and in fewer activities that impose external costs. Although this is an important dimension of output in terms of which private firms and nonprofits might be expected to differ, I shall not examine it further. There is evidence that nonprofit hospitals are more likely than for-profit hospitals to provide services that are unprofitable but that generate favorable social effects — for example, free or low-priced educational programs on drug abuse (Lee and Weisbrod 1977; Shortell et al. 1986).

15. The dichotomization of attributes into two types is an expositional simplification. Each attribute of any commodity can be arrayed on a spectrum from those that are costless to monitor and evaluate to those that are infinitely costly. Moreover, an attribute can be of type I for some consumers and type II for others; I do not deal with this case here, although it may be quite important in explaining the coexistence of for-profit and nonprofit sellers in the same industry.

16. A waiting list is ordinarily thought of as involving the provision of a commodity of given quality through a mechanism that involves waiting time. A related alternative is to reduce quality. For example, a charitable soup kitchen might plan to serve a bowl of soup to each of the *n* persons expected to appear for lunch, but if 2*n* appeared the kitchen might decide that rather than turn away people it would water down the soup.

WHAT SHOULD BE BOUND UP IN THE "CETERIS PARIBUS"?

Regulatory Constraints?

Whether an organization's institutional form affects its behavior in any specific dimension depends on multiple factors. Institutional form may affect behavior if permitted to do so, but regulatory constraints can preclude that. For example, in the absence of constraints on input utilization—say, a requirement that every nursing home have a registered dietician on the staff—for-profit and nonprofit organizations might choose differently. Similarly, regulatory requirements that all airlines—governmental and private—use particular equipment or serve particular cities (Davies 1971) preclude differential institutional goals from affecting those dimensions of behavior. Still another example involves price regulation; the Medicare Diagnosis Relate Groups (DRG) system of pricing hospital services clearly limits differential pricing policies. In short, if the ceteris paribus includes such exogenous constraints, institutional form may not be permitted to affect certain dimensions of behavior, whereas in the absence of those constraints behavioral differences may be manifest. Mark Schlesinger (in this volume) emphasizes the influence of such external factors as levels of government control in determining the effect of institutional form. The failure to recognize this leads to understating the effects that institutional form would have in the absence of such restrictions and requirements.

Endogenous Variables?

Errors will result in estimating the effects of institutional form if endogenous variables—those that are affected by institutional form itself—are held constant. Doing so precludes finding that a particular form of institution has indirect, as well as direct, effects on some dimensions of organization behavior.[17] Although it is well recognized in econometric work that biased estimates result from failure to control for *exogenous* variables that are correlated with both institutional form and the dependent variable under consideration—the omitted variable problem—it is less well recognized that over-controlling is also a source of biased estimates. If the analyst controls for variables that are affected by institutional form, there can be no finding that institutional forms have different effects influencing these variables which, in turn, affect the variables of interest.

An illustration will be useful. In the nursing home industry, a typical nonprofit facility employs more doctors, nurses, and volunteers per one hundred beds than do proprietary homes. The important question is whether these differences are exogenous to institutional form or are results of, say, differential institutional goals. If the latter is so—as seems likely—then such input differentials should not be held constant in the process of estimating the effect of institutional form on, say, consumer satisfaction.

It is common, however, for econometric estimates of the effects of institutional form to hold constant such endogenous variables, and by so doing they fail to estimate correctly the total effects—direct and indirect—of institutional form, obtaining only partial, direct, effects. For example: (1) In a study of government-owned versus privately-owned packaged liquor stores (Simon 1966), the number of off-premise outlets per capita is held constant in the econometric equation even though that number is arguably a consequence of institutional form. (2) In a study of the relative efficiency of governmental and private refuse collection (Savas 1977), the level of service (for example, curbside versus at the residence) is held constant even though level of service may well be a function of institutional form. (3) In studies comparing nonprofit and for-profit hospitals (Lewin, Derzon, and Marguiles 1981; Herzlinger and Krasker 1987), organization case mix is often held constant even though it is arguably a consequence of differential institutional goals.

The overall point is that *institutional form* is a term encompassing a number of dimensions characterizing an organization; the more of these elements that are controlled for in an econometric estimation process, the smaller the probability that the remaining elements, captured by institutional form, will be found to have sizable behavioral effects.

Another illustration of an endogenous variable that is typically held constant is organization size. Concerned about the possible effects of scale economies on organizational efficiency, analysts have generally included size as an explanatory variable in econometric analyses of comparative institutional behavior. By doing so, they treat size implicitly as exogenous to the choice of institutional form. If, however, for-profit, governmental, church-related nonprofit, and other nonprofit organizations pursue dissimilar goals, which, in turn, causes them to choose systematically different sizes, controlling for size would lead to biased estimation of the effects of institutional form.

In the hospital industry, for example, hospital size does vary across institutional form; in one study, the mean non-profit hospital had 204 beds compared with 155 in the mean for-profit hospitals (Herzlinger and Krasker 1987). The reason for the difference is crucial to the appropriate statistical estimation. If for-profit hospitals are smaller because profit-maximizing behavior causes them to restrict their activities to those that are profitable, and if nonprofits, having access to donations and volunteer labor, can afford to provide unprofitable services, then differential size is a result of institutional form; it should not be controlled for if we are trying to determine the total effect of institutional form, which encompasses effects operating through size—for example, on the variety of services produced.

The issue can be seen as follows. Equation (1) presents a model of the form typically estimated:

---

17. This section builds on my joint research and unpublished paper written with Elizabeth Mauser 1991.

(1) $Y = a W + b X + c Z + u,$

where Y is a dependent behavioral variable, W is a variable (for example, size) that is endogenous to the institutional form of the organization, X is a binary variable for the organization's institutional form, and Z is a vector of exogenous control variables. The question typically asked is: What is the total effect of X on Y, ceteris paribus?

Equations of form (1) have been estimated for a number of industries, and the effect of institutional form, X, on Y has been estimated as b. If, however, size varies because of, and not independently of, institutional form, then equation (2) would hold:

(2) $W = d X + f M + e,$

where M is a vector of variables that affect W but not Y directly. If equation (2) holds—if, for example, size is a consequence of variations in organization objective functions and constraints—then the estimate of b from equation (1) will be only the *partial* effect of X on Y, and, indeed, an incorrect estimate of that, given the mis-specification of equation (1). The *total* effect of X on Y is b* in equation (3), which is the sum of b, from (1), and a, from (1) times d, from (2):

(3) $Y = b^* X + c^* Z + g^* M + u^*.$

If equations (1), (2), and (3) are estimated, we can identify both the direct and indirect effects of institutional form because the total effect, b*, can be derived from (3), and *ad*—the indirect effect of X, operating through W—can be estimated from equations (1) and (2). Note that failure to account for indirect effects does not necessarily lead to underestimating of total effects; the total effects need not exceed the partial effects, for the indirect effects can have any sign.

Equations (1), (2), and (3) have been estimated for a sample of hospitals and are summarized here (Weisbrod and Mauser 1991). Our approach is to estimate b from equation (1) and b* from equation (3) in order to determine whether incorrectly treating variables as exogenous—the equation (1) approach—has produced biased conclusions about the total effect of institutional form on one measure of efficiency, cost per patient day.

With the cooperation of Regina Herzlinger, who generously made available the hospital data she utilized with Krasker in 1987, we reestimated their cost equation. They had concluded that for-profit hospitals average 35 percent lower operating cost-per-patient-day.[18] We believe that their estimate of an equation such as (1) is mis-specified, in part because of the endogenous decisions by for-profit hospitals to avoid providing such unprofitable services as obstetric and emergency services.[19] We postulate that the amount of emer-

gency room care provided by a hospital is endogenous to institutional form and, hence, should not be held constant in an estimate of the effect of institutional form on hospital costs. We assume, further, that availability of emergency room services depends on local hospital market conditions as well as on institutional form. If we proxy market conditions by the local wage index, we can estimate equation (3) in our model, allowing the number of emergency room visits to vary endogenously; thus, the coefficient on institutional form captures the total effect of institutional form—the direct effect plus the indirect effect operating through the number of emergency room visits.

When emergency room care is treated as endogenous, we find that the coefficient on the institutional form binary variable indicates that for-profit hospitals have 30 percent lower cost-per-patient-day, compared with the 35 percent differential originally found in the equation (1) estimate by Herzlinger and Krasker. Because equation (2) can be estimated, with the number of emergency room visits as the dependent variable and institutional form and the local wage index as the independent variables, we can separate the effects of institutional form that are indirect—a times d from equations (1) and (2), which equals +.01—from the direct effect, which is the total effect, b* from equation (3), minus the indirect effect, or −.31. In this illustration, the direct effect of institutional form on cost, operating through size, is relatively small and of opposite sign to the direct effect. Neither of these results, however, is a basis for generalizing. Much more research is needed, in various industries and using various data sets and dependent variables.

All that can be said at present is that more attention needs to be directed, when models are specified and control variables are introduced, to the dangers of over-controlling—holding constant variables that are endogenous to institutional form. Whether one is interested in predicting the behavioral consequences of alternative institutional forms or in making public policy decisions whether to favor one form of institution over another, there is no substitute for careful theorizing about the precise meaning of *institutional form* and for correct specification of the ceteris paribus before proceeding to econometric estimation.

SOME RECENT EMPIRICAL FINDINGS

This section summarizes a number of empirical tests of behavioral differences between proprietary and each of two types of nonprofit organizations, church-related and other, in two institutionally mixed industries, nursing homes and facilities for the mentally handicapped. Special attention is directed to (1) opportunistic behavior by providers who are

18. For a critique of Herzlinger and Krasker, including comments on the possibility of endogeneity bias, see Steinberg 1987.

19. The director of the perinatology center at New York Hospital-Cornell Medical Center reported that the cost of hospitalization and care

for an extremely premature infant—one weighing about 1.5 pounds—was about $90,000 in 1981, a few years preceding the Herzlinger-Krasker data; the state reimbursement covered less than half that cost (French 1981).

more knowledgeable than their consumers about the quality of service being provided; (2) consumer satisfaction with services, especially with those that are difficult to monitor; and (3) the use of waiting lists rather than prices to distribute outputs.[20] The models that are estimated do not force any specific pattern of behavior; they allow differences of any size and direction to be found among the three forms of institutions. If differences are observed, knowledge of a supplier's institutional form would have signal value; they would also have policy relevance once it is decided which behavior is preferred under particular circumstances.

That systematic behavioral differences may not be observed does not imply that institutional form is irrelevant to public policy. It may be that competition drives out all but one form of institution, in which case the industry will not be mixed; or competition may force all surviving forms of institutions to behave in similar ways. It is not necessarily the case that if only one form of institution were permitted in the industry, the choice of form would not matter. In general, competition tends to reduce behavioral differences among organizations having different institutional form; thus, any differences observed tend to understate those that would occur if only one form or another monopolized the industry (Hirth 1993; Wolff and Schlesinger 1992).

Differences among institutional forms in a variety of cost and output dimensions have been examined in a number of mixed industries, but generally not in terms of either type II output dimensions or mechanisms for distributing output. (In the health care sector, see chapter 4 in Gray 1986, and Marmor, Schlesinger, and Smithey 1987; for railroads, Caves and Christensen 1980; for trash collection, Savas 1977; for child care, Krashinsky and Mauser (both in this volume); for airlines, Davies 1971; for international comparisons, Borcherding, Pommerehne, and Schneider 1982; for nursery schools in Austria, Badelt and Weiss 1990; for elementary and secondary schooling, James 1987; Downes 1992; Downes and Greenstein 1993; for worker-owned and corporate plywood cooperatives, Craig and Pencavel 1992. Some of these studies compare private firms with government agencies; others consider private nonprofit providers; the last reference compares types of proprietary firms.)

The rest of this section summarizes some empirical tests of differences in institutional behavior in the dimensions discussed above. Much of the work is ongoing, and this discussion aims merely to offer a flavor of the results obtained.[21]

Test One: Taking Advantage of Informational Disparities — The Use of Sedatives in Nursing Homes

Residents of nursing homes are in complex states of health.[22] Few patients or families of patients are able to assess the medically appropriate medical care or therapy the patient needs.

Thus, any nursing home — for-profit or nonprofit, church-related or other — is typically asymmetrically well informed and hence able to utilize a lower-cost therapy than would be used if the buyer were well informed. The nursing home's actions are observed, but the consumer does not have a sound standard against which to compare the treatment given.

An example of a nursing home's opportunity to capitalize on informational asymmetry to act in its own narrow interest rather than as agent for the patient involves the use of sedative drugs. A nursing home can save money and generate more profit by sedating a troublesome, active patient rather than incurring the greater cost of labor required in caring for such a patient.[23] Consumers have difficulty in determining precisely when the use of such medications is medically justified. The issue is thus whether different goals and constraints faced by proprietary relative to nonprofit nursing homes cause them to make different choices between self-interest in generating profit and consumers' interest in quality care.[24]

Some relevant evidence can be gleaned from a study of the use of sedatives at proprietary and church-owned nonprofit nursing homes (Svarstad, Bond, and Paterson 1984).[25] In 1982–83, a population of 338 newly admitted patients at nine nursing homes was followed for ninety days to determine the extent of variations in the prescribing and utilization of these drugs across homes.

There was, regrettably, no control for medical "need." There is, however, a useful piece of information relative to it: There was no significant difference between the percentages of patients in proprietary and private nonprofit homes who received a sedative prescription from a physician at the time of admission — 36.7 percent versus 33.3 percent, respectively. This suggests that medical need did not vary greatly, although the possibility of degrees of severity of illness cannot be dismissed. These prescriptions permitted nurses to use sedatives on the patients as needed. In sharp contrast, however, with the similarity in percentage of prescriptions, there was a very large and statistically significant difference in the number of dosage units administered to the patients. Proprietary home patients who received sedatives utilized an aver-

20. This section is based heavily on Weisbrod 1996.

21. A thorough discussion of the empirical methodology for most of the following work is in Weisbrod 1996.

22. This discussion is based on Weisbrod 1988, chapter 8.

23. Comments regarding the tradeoff between labor and sedation appeared in the *Wall Street Journal*, which referred to "concerns that such drugs are often prescribed not to treat illness, but simply to sedate troublesome patients" (Winslow 1991), and a *New York Times* editorial, which referred to the view that "the overwhelming majority [of elderly nursing home residents] are restrained or sedated because it makes them easier to handle. . . . State budget officials complained that the new [federal] rules [which restrict the use of drugs and physical restraints] would require more staff." (*New York Times* 1991).

24. I do not assert (or even hypothesize) that there is any significant amount of intentional and medically inappropriate sedating of otherwise active patients. What is involved, at most, are marginal, judgmental decisions.

25. The data in this section were provided to me by Professor Bonnie Svarstad, School of Pharmacy, University of Wisconsin-Madison.

age of 12.5 units of medication per month, compared to 3.0 units in the church-owned nonprofit homes.

Many factors, including differences in the medical needs of patients not captured by the frequency of prescriptions, could explain this disparity in utilization of sedatives. If, however, the explanation is that proprietary homes are more oriented toward increasing profit while the church-owned nonprofits were more bonoficing, then for-profit homes would engage in more substitution of the relatively inexpensive drugs for the more costly labor.

Test Two: Differences in Input Utilization

The Survey of Institutionalized Persons (SIP) (U.S. Bureau of the Census 1978) contains data on the quantities of twenty-one kinds of labor used in each of the sampled facilities in the nursing home and mentally handicapped industries. Insofar as these inputs are proxies for quality of outputs that are difficult for consumers to monitor (type II), they can be examined to determine whether forms of institutions differ in their opportunistic behavior.

Differences in labor utilization could exist for reasons other than organization goals. Utilization would differ if, for example, church-related nonprofits attracted labor at lower wages or attracted more volunteer labor; under these conditions, we would expect these nonprofits to utilize more labor even if their goals were no different than those of for-profit firms — provided, of course, that the differential supplies did not result from beliefs about organization goals. It is likely that if such differential labor supply prices do exist, it is because of such beliefs and the preferences of some persons to work for organizations with bonoficing-type goals. Research on such preferences, however, is very limited.

Thus, if input intensities do vary across institutional forms, it will not be possible to pinpoint the source; still, such a finding would suggest, at the least, that institutional form does connote behavior. Moreover, if consumers eventually learn about the consequences of such input variation, they may become differentially satisfied with the quality of services offered by the various types of providers — and this is a testable implication of behavioral differences in type II dimensions that will be discussed below.

I have examined data on institutional utilization of twenty types of paid labor, including MDs, RNs, LPNs, nurse aides, dieticians, teachers, maintenance workers, and administrators. In addition, volunteers were studied, and they were distinguished between volunteers who perform the same twenty activities and volunteers who perform other activities. Controlling for institutional form as well as for the facility's size, monthly charge, and mix of Medicare and Medicaid beds, the regression estimates indicate that *church-related nonprofit homes, compared with proprietary homes, do differ in their labor input utilization.*[26] (1) In the nursing home industry,

church-related homes employ significantly (at the .10 significance level or better) more full-time (FT) RNs, dieticians, and maintenance workers per one hundred patient beds and significantly more part-time (PT) nurse aides, maintenance workers, and volunteers (performing work in which there are not paid workers). For all other labor inputs, FT and PT, the estimated utilization is not significantly different between church-related and proprietary homes. Thus, without exception among the forty-one labor groups — twenty FT, twenty PT, and volunteers — investigated, either significantly more is used at church-related facilities than at proprietary facilities or there is no difference in utilization.[27] Not a single labor input, FT or PT, is used significantly more by private firms.[28]

(2) In the mentally handicapped facilities industry, again comparing *church-related nonprofits with proprietary facilities,* we find once more that, ceteris paribus, church-related facilities utilize significantly more of some types of labor — FT LPNs and teachers as well as PT MDs, LPNs, and volunteers.

The magnitude of differences is in many cases substantial as well as significant. For example, church-related nonprofit nursing homes have a predicted utilization of 5.0 FT RNs per hundred beds, compared with 2.6 at proprietary homes; 2.4 FT dieticians compared with 0.6; 17.8 FT maintenance workers compared with 12.4; and 40.7 persons who volunteer at least once per month, compared with 24.3.

Turning to differences between *proprietary homes and other (nonchurch-related) nonprofits,* we find a similar pattern. Controlling for the same variables as above, the nursing home industry exhibits the following: this class of nonprofits uses significantly more of some forms of labor — FT RNs (3.7 vs. 2.7 per hundred beds) and PT MDs (1.2 vs. 0.6), LPNs (2.8 vs. 1.5), nurse aides (7.1 vs. 4.5), maintenance workers (9.8 vs. 4.2), and volunteers (50.0 vs. 24.3) — and again, as with the church-related facilities, every significant difference shows a greater intensity for the nonprofits.

For mentally handicapped facilities, the pattern of labor input behavior is broadly consistent with the pattern displayed by nursing homes. These nonprofits, like their church-related counterparts, utilize significantly more labor than do proprietaries, ceteris paribus, in most labor classes: FT program directors, activity directors, teachers and aides, other professional and technical personnel, maintenance workers, and more PT MDs and volunteers not in the paid occupations. They also employ, by contrast, significantly fewer FT administrators and nurse aides than do proprietary facilities.

26. Tobit-form equations were estimated, in light of the truncation of the numbers of workers at zero.

27. Differences in frequency of volunteering for the twenty types of jobs for which there are paid workers were also examined. The numbers were extremely small, however, even though the numbers of volunteers for other kinds of work were quite substantial. Reasons for such variation in the composition of volunteer labor have not been studied rigorously.

28. Evidence from another institutionally mixed industry, day care, also shows that nonprofit and for-profit providers utilize significantly and substantially different production technologies (Mauser 1988).

The overall pattern remains one of predominantly lower utilization of labor in proprietary facilities.

Much prior research has treated the nonprofit sector as essentially homogeneous. My examination of differences between *church-related and other nonprofits* suggests that understanding the role and behavior of the nonprofit sector requires disaggregation.

Do church-related and other nonprofits behave differently from each other—even though both face the same legal nondistribution constraint? They would if their goals differed or if private market constraints—for example, labor supply or consumer demand—on them differed. (The latter point deserves more attention, for insofar as church-related facilities provide services that are judged by some consumers to be distinct, such facilities enjoy a degree of monopolistic power.) The labor input analyses discussed above provide some evidence, though weak, that the two types of nonprofits do differ in important dimensions. Labor input intensities in church-related nonprofits and proprietary firms tend to differ more than do the input intensities between other nonprofits and proprietary firms. Three differences between the two types of nonprofits are significant—FT LPNs, dieticians, and maintenance workers—and all three show larger intensities at church-related nursing homes. The expected number of FT dieticians, for example, is 2.5 per hundred beds at church-related nursing homes compared with 1.1 at other nonprofit homes, and 0.6 at private facilities, other things being equal. Once more we find a consistent pattern of institutional behavior: every difference between the two classes of nonprofits is either not significant or shows a greater intensity for church-related facilities.

Comparing the two types of nonprofits in the mentally handicapped facilities industry, however, we find little difference. Only one labor input, PT LPNs, has a significantly different estimated utilization rate, with church-related facility utilization being greater (1.5 vs. 0.4). The other factor-intensity differences, both FT and PT, are not significant.[29] Utilization of volunteers is significantly greater at both types of nonprofit nursing homes than at proprietary homes but is not significantly different at the two types of nonprofits.

Test Three: Differences in Consumer Satisfaction

Input utilization conveys indirect information about outputs in the proprietary and in each nonprofit sector. Consumer satisfaction with various elements of service is another indicator of output quality. Does satisfaction differ systemati-

cally across types of institutions, ceteris paribus? Does the generally higher level of labor inputs in nonprofit facilities, and particularly in those that are church-related, translate into higher levels of consumer satisfaction?[30]

If proprietary and nonprofit providers do take differential advantage of their informational superiority, this could be manifested in systematically different levels of consumer satisfaction across forms of institutions. Elizabeth Mauser (in this volume) addresses a similar question in the day care industry by comparing consumer perceptions of institutional differences in quality to actual differences in quality. Interestingly, even though the average quality provided by nonprofits—as measured by experts—was higher than at proprietary institutions, only a quarter of consumers perceived a difference in quality.

The SIP asked family members questions relating to general satisfaction and, separately, satisfaction with buildings and grounds, rooms and furnishing, staff, social activities, and treatment.[31] These measures are likely to capture unobservable, type II attributes of output because type I attributes,

29. Similarly, when data are examined for volunteers in each of the paid labor categories, we find, as we did for nursing homes, that there are few facilities of any institutional form that have such volunteers. The sharply contrasting findings for volunteers performing work for which there are paid workers and other volunteers shed a bit of light on the question of whether volunteers and paid labor are substitutes, complements, or neither. It appears that they are essentially independent inputs, at least where professional (paid) skills are involved.

30. It is beyond the goals of this chapter to examine alternative models of satisfaction, coming to like a complex service, or complaining to a government agency or anyone else (Hirschman 1970). It would be useful, however, to learn more about such processes, given the wide availability of data on satisfaction with and complaints about all sorts of services and conditions such as jobs, public services, social institutions, etc. There would appear to be valuable information in such data, but their interpretation remains unclear (Rubin et al 1993).

One model of complaints (the exercise of "voice") would have them registered whenever a consumer's expectations exceeded realizations. (How expectations are formed is yet another matter.) In this case differential complaint frequencies between for-profit and either church-related or other nonprofit organizations would represent differential disappointment with quality of service. In another model a person would complain whenever he or she judged that doing so would lead to beneficial action and not reprisal. If such a benefit-cost model described the complaint-generating process, interpretation of how complaints (or statements of dissatisfaction) relate to consumers' actual utility levels would be more complex; one form of institution could generate more complaints than another simply because it was more responsive, even if the level of consumer satisfaction with its services was actually higher. In that case, a higher level of complaints would indicate more confidence in an organization, not less gratification from its services.

31. Family members were also asked whether they like or don't like the services provided to their relative. The overall question was, "Do you feel this facility has provided the kind of services and care [the patient] needs?" Only yes and no responses were permitted. Other questions involved specific aspects of the overall service package: "Do you like or dislike the following facilities and services offered by [name of facility]? (1) Building(s) and grounds? (2) Condition of the rooms and furnishings? (3) Treatment services—such as medical, nursing, rehabilitation? (4) Relations with staff? (5) Social activities, things to do? For this set of five services, three responses were possible: "Like it," "Don't like it," and "Don't know/no opinion." The context of these questions, following immediately the one on overall satisfaction, was such that it seems reasonable to interpret them as asking about satisfaction with each of the types of facilities and services.

being observable prior to admission (or purchase), are less likely to be a source of dissatisfaction.

The results from this empirical analysis are strong; every measure of satisfaction is greater for church-related nonprofits than for proprietary facilities. This is so in both industries, and most of the differences are significant.[32] By contrast, levels of satisfaction with other nonprofits and proprietary facilities are essentially indistinguishable. This is further evidence of the lack of homogeneity of the nonprofit sector and the importance of disaggregation.

Differences in satisfaction levels across institutional form, even when significant, however, are not quantitatively enormous. The estimated percentage of respondents satisfied overall with nursing homes is 97 at church-related facilities, 92 at other nonprofits, and 91 at proprietary facilities. Although these differences are relatively modest and not significant, satisfaction with the various service components differs somewhat more, and differences are generally significant statistically. With respect to treatment facilities, for example, estimated satisfaction, controlling for the variables noted earlier, ranges from 92 percent at church-related nursing homes to 87 percent at other nonprofit homes and 80 percent at proprietary homes. At mentally handicapped facilities, satisfaction levels are also generally in the 80 percent or higher range; for buildings and grounds, however, there is a 30-percentage-point difference between the satisfaction level at church-related and for-profit facilities.[33]

Tests Four and Five: Differences in Distribution of Output

To the extent that nonprofits, church-related or other, are bonoficers or to the extent that they lack the incentive to maximize profit, they would distribute outputs differently from proprietary sellers. Hence, another dimension in terms of which private firms and each form of nonprofit organization might diverge is the mechanism through which output is allocated. A private firm would, presumably, sell its services to the highest bidders and, more generally, to everyone who is willing and able to pay a price exceeding marginal cost. A nonprofit organization, church-related or not, might behave similarly or it might choose to provide outputs to some who

are unable or even unwilling to pay, offsetting costs through reduced profit and donated revenues.[34]

Do proprietary firms, church-related nonprofits, and other nonprofits use different mechanisms for determining access to their services? One test is whether they have different price-cost margins. A second way is to find out whether they make differential use of waiting lists. If either church-related or other nonprofits are bonoficers, more motivated than for-profit firms to provide access to some group of deserving consumers, they might sell below full cost or make greater use of such nonprice-rationing mechanisms as waiting lists. On the other hand, if nonprofits of either type are FPIDs, there would, presumptively, be no difference across institutional form in their use of nonprice-distributional mechanisms.[35]

Test Four: Price-Cost Margins. SIP data permit estimation of the differences between price and average cost for each facility in the three institutional forms and in both industries. Controlling for facility size[36] and the proportion of its beds that are certified for Medicare and for Medicaid (skilled and intermediate) patients, we find that among nursing homes, the two types of nonprofit facilities have price-cost differences that are a statistically significant \$120–\$125 lower (in absolute value) than in for-profit homes, ceteris paribus, while among mentally handicapped facilities the differences, also significant, are \$55–\$105 lower. These differences constitute approximately 19 and 15 percent, respectively, of the mean reported average cost in the two industries. Nonprofit and for-profit facilities do have distinguishable pricing policies. (Differences in the margins between the two types of nonprofits, however, are not significant in either industry.)

Test Five: Waiting Lists. The SIP data allow analysis of differential utilization of nonprice-rationing mechanisms among institutional forms. Other variables held constant, are there systematic differences in the use of waiting lists between private firms and nonprofits, and do the two types of nonprofits differ?

In both industries, church-related facilities are significantly and substantially more likely than proprietary facilities to have a waiting list—92 percent and 65 percent, respectively, among nursing homes, and 92 percent and 60 percent, respectively, among facilities for the mentally handicapped, evaluated at the mean values of the explanatory vari-

32. The nursing home equation for rooms and furnishings could not be estimated because the estimated variance matrix is singular.

33. A priori, we might expect differences in satisfaction between nonprofit and proprietary institutions to be greatest for services having the relatively largest type II elements, about which consumers are least well informed at time of admission. Distinguishing between type I and type II attributes of care is complex. Relations with staff and the quality of treatment services might seem to have the largest type II components, being the most difficult to observe prior to admission or to embody in a service contract. However, although some elements of other services such as building and grounds are easy to observe prior to admission (location, for example), others are costly to observe (for example, how suitable the layout of the building is for the uncertain and changing needs of a specific patient).

34. The claim that for-profit firms skim the profitable patients and leave the unprofitable ones for the public and private nonprofit sectors has often been made, particularly in the hospital industry (Ermann and Gabel 1983; Wohl 1984).

35. Even a profit maximizer might find it useful to utilize a waiting list under some circumstances; thus, the key question is not whether there is any utilization of waiting lists but whether there are systematic differences across institutional forms, other things being equal.

36. Earlier I raised a question about the assumption that size was an exogenous variable that should be held constant in the econometric analysis. The matter is complex and as yet unresolved, but I have followed convention in controlling for size, thereby facilitating comparability of these findings with those of prior studies.

ables. A comparison of other nonprofits with proprietary facilities discloses smaller differences; among nursing homes, other nonprofits have an estimated 73 percent frequency of maintaining a waiting list, which is not significantly different from the 65 percent private firm level. At mentally handicapped facilities the corresponding figure for other nonprofits is 69 percent, a difference that is significant though smaller than that between church-related and proprietary facilities. Overall, in both industries, the rankings are identical; church-owned facilities are most likely to have a waiting list, proprietary facilities are least likely, and other nonprofits are intermediate, with most differences significant.

Turning to the length of waiting lists — the number of names listed — my estimates indicate that, after controlling for facility size as well as for the other variables mentioned above, church-related nursing homes have the longest waiting lists and proprietary homes have the shortest. Moreover, church-related facilities' lists are significantly longer than the lists of both proprietary homes and other nonprofits; at the mean values of the regressors, a church-related nursing home is estimated to have forty-eight names on its waiting list, compared with twenty-eight at an other nonprofit and nineteen at a proprietary facility. At facilities for the mentally handicapped, proprietary facilities also have the shortest waiting lists, but none of the differences is significant.

POLICY IMPLICATIONS AND DIRECTIONS FOR FUTURE RESEARCH

This line of analysis has highlighted a number of potentially critical matters which deserve research attention before public policy action is considered. One is the effect of the nondistribution constraint, especially its separability from the effects of other differences in constraints that accompany it. In particular, I have noted that as long as the private enterprise option with its unrestricted profits and profit disposition is available, no entrepreneur or organizer would ever form a nonprofit organization if doing so meant nothing more than the imposition of a nondistribution constraint. In fact, however, what we actually observe is that along with that constraint comes a variety of offsetting benefits and subsidies; thus, any observed behavior of nonprofit organizations cannot be attributed to the effects of the nondistribution constraint alone. The need for research to separate the various effects and their interactions has barely been recognized.

A second matter involves analysis of the enforceability of the nondistribution constraint. It is difficult, indeed, to determine when a nonprofit organization manager is receiving excessive compensation that is, in effect, an illegal distribution of profit. In addition, although the nondistribution constraint legally applies to compensation in any form, enforcement problems are especially severe with respect to nonpecuniary rewards such as expense accounts and other perquisites.

Another issue deserving research attention is the process of organization goal formation in the nonprofit sector. To

some analysts, the behavior of nonprofits is seen as reflecting attempts to surmount the nondistribution constraint for private gain — behavior I have termed that of for-profits in disguise. To others, however, the key element in explaining nonprofit organization behavior and in distinguishing it from private enterprise is its public-serving, charitable, altruistic, or bonoficing goals. What determines the supply of nonprofit sector entrepreneurs with various goals is a largely unanswered question.

Research reported above highlights another issue deserving more attention and involving important public policy implications: Are there differences within the nonprofit sector such that differential enforcement of the nondistribution constraint and differential access to subsidies are warranted? We have found, for example, substantial distinctions between two types of nonprofit organizations — church-related and other — but similar studies would be useful for other institutionally mixed industries and perhaps for other divisions within the nonprofit sector.

Nonprofit organization goals, including their heterogeneity, need to be better understood in order to judge the degree to which assumptions about private sector behavior extend to nonprofits. For example, antitrust laws do not distinguish between private firms and nonprofits — church-related or other; yet a case for such a distinction could be made if, for example, nonprofits use monopoly power in more socially productive ways than do private firms.

An illustration of the relevance of differential institutional goals is the recent governmental proposal to finance the Clinton administration health care plan partly through a federal tax on hospitals (Pear 1993). If for-profit and, say, church-related nonprofit hospitals have differing goals, a change in costs — in the form of a new tax — would tend to have different effects on their behavior, although much would depend on the form of the tax.[37]

Many nonprofit organizations engage in activities that compete with government agencies as well as with private firms. The comparative institutional behavior evidence cited above is limited to the private sector, but it is also important, for public policy purposes, to understand better the comparative behavior of government and private nonprofit providers. Both are subject to the nondistribution constraint, but government organizations have access to tax revenue and are part of a political system, whereas private nonprofits have greater access to private donations but not to tax revenue and are not subject to the same political constraints.

In all these areas there is entwining of interests between

37. This would be true, ceteris paribus. If other constraints differed, however, there could be interaction effects. Thus, a progressive tax on a hospital's gross revenue would have a greater impact on nonprofit hospitals, which are generally larger; and even a proportional tax on a hospital's wage bill would have different effects across types of institutions if labor-capital ratios differed, perhaps as a result of capital subsidies to nonprofits.

policymakers and researchers. What society needs to know is not simply whether institutional form matters, not merely whether private firms, nonprofit organizations, and government agencies act differently, but if they do, in what ways this matters, under what conditions, and for whom.

REFERENCES

Alchian, Armen, and Harold Demsetz. 1972. "Production, Information Costs and Economic Organization." *American Economic Review* 62:777–95.

Arrow, Kenneth. 1963. "Uncertainty and the Welfare Economics of Medical Care." *American Economic Review* 53:941–73, at 950.

Badelt, Christoph, and Peter Weiss. 1990. "Specialization, Product Differentiation and Ownership Structures in Personal Social Services: The Case of Nursery Schools." *Kyklos*, Fasc. 1:61–81.

Ben-Ner, Avner, and Benedetto Gui. 1991. "Forward." *Annals of Public and Cooperative Economics* 62, no. 4:469.

Borcherding, Thomas, Werner W. Pommerehne, and Friedrich Schneider. 1982. "Comparing the Efficiency of Private and Public Production: Evidence from Five Countries." *Zeitschrift für Nationalökonomie*, Supplement 2:127–56.

"California Trying to Close Worthless-Diploma Schools." 1994. *New York Times*, August 31, 38.

Caves, Richard, and Laurits R. Christensen. 1980. "The Relative Efficiency of Public and Private Firms in a Competitive Environment: The Case of Canadian Railroads." *Journal of Political Economy* 88:958–76.

Craig, Ben, and John Pencavel. 1992. "The Behavior of Worker Cooperatives: The Plywood Companies of the Pacific Northwest." *American Economic Review* 82:1083–1105.

Davies, David. 1971. "The Efficiency of Public versus Private Firms, the Case of Australia's Two Airlines." *Journal of Law and Economics* 14:149–65.

Downes, Thomas A. 1992. "Evaluating the Impact of School Finance Reform on the Provision of Public Education: The California Case." *National Tax Journal* 45:405–19.

Downes, Thomas A., and Shane M. Greenstein. 1993. "Understanding the Supply Decisions of Nonprofits: Modeling the Location of Private Schools." Working paper, Center for Urban Affairs and Policy Research, Northwestern University.

Eckel, Catherine, and Richard Steinberg. 1993. "Tax Policy and the Objectives of Nonprofit Organizations." Working paper, Department of Economics, Indiana University/Purdue University at Indianapolis.

Freudenheim, Milt. 1993. "The Hospital World's Hard-Driving Money Man." *New York Times,* October 5, C1.

Gaul, Gilbert M., and Neill A. Borowski. 1993. "Warehouses of Wealth: The Tax-Free Economy." Seven-part series, *Philadelphia Inquirer,* April 18–24.

Goddeeris, John. 1988. "Compensating Differentials and Self-Selection: An Application to Lawyers." *Journal of Political Economy* 96:411–28.

Goldberg, Victor. 1976. "Some Emerging Problems of Prepaid Health Plans in the Medi-Cal System." *Policy Analysis* 55.

Gray, Bradford, ed. 1986. *For-Profit Enterprise in Health Care.* Committee on Implications of For-Profit Enterprise in Health Care, Division of Health Care Services, Institute of Medicine. Washington, D.C.: National Academy of Sciences Press.

Hansmann, Henry. 1980. "The Role of Nonprofit Enterprise." *Yale Law Review* 89:835–99.

Herzlinger, Regina E., and William S. Krasker. 1987. "Who Profits from Nonprofits?" *Harvard Business Review* 65:93–106.

Hirth, Richard A. 1993. "Information and Ownership in the Nursing Home Industry." Ph.D. dissertation, Department of Economics, University of Pennsylvania.

James, Estelle. 1987. "The Public/Private Division of Responsibility for Education: An International Comparison." *Economics of Education Review* 6:1–14.

Lee, A. James, and Burton A. Weisbrod. 1977. "Collective Goods and the Voluntary Sector: The Case of the Hospital Industry." In *The Voluntary Nonprofit Sector*, ed. Burton A. Weisbrod, 77–100. Lexington, Mass.: D. C. Heath.

Lewin, Lawrence S., Robert A. Derzon, and Rhea Marguiles. 1981. "Investor-Owned and Nonprofits Differ in Economic Performance." *Hospitals* 55:52–55.

Mansnerus, Laura. 1993. "Bar Groups are Happy to Find You a Lawyer." *New York Times,* February 27, A30.

Marmor, Theodore, Mark Schlesinger, and Richard Smithey. 1987. "Nonprofit Organizations and Health Care." In *The Nonprofit Sector: A Research Handbook,* ed. Walter W. Powell, 221–39. New Haven: Yale University Press.

Mauser, Elizabeth. 1988. "The Supply of Center-Based Day Care in Massachusetts: Nonprofits versus For-Profits." Department of Economics, Wellesley College.

"M.I.T. Wins a New Trial in Price-Fixing Case." 1993. *New York Times,* September 18, 6.

Newhouse, Joseph. 1970. "Toward a Theory of Nonprofit Institutions: An Economic Model of a Hospital." *American Economic Review* 60:64–73.

O'Brien, Timothy L. 1993. "Private Prison Market Attracts More and More Firms." *Wall Street Journal,* June 10, B2.

Pear, Robert. 1993. "Clinton Scrambles to Find Financing for Health Plan." *New York Times,* September 12, 1:18.

Rawls, James R., Robert A. Ullrich, and Oscar T. Nelson, Jr. 1975. "A Comparison of Managers Entering or Reentering the Profit and Nonprofit Sectors." *Academy of Management Journal* 18:616–23.

Roomkin, Myron, and Burton A. Weisbrod. 1997. "Executive Compensation in For-Profit and Nonprofit Hospitals." Working paper, Department of Economics, Northwestern University.

Savas, E. S. 1977. "Policy Analysis for Local Government: Public Versus Private Refuse Collection." *Policy Analysis* 3:49–74.

Shortell, Stephen, Ellen Morrison, Susan Hughes, Bernard Friedman, James Coverdill, and Lee Berg. 1986. "Hospital Ownership and Nontraditional Services." *Health Affairs* 5(4):97–111.

Simon, Julian L. 1966. "The Effects of State Monopoly on Packaged-Liquor Retailing." *Journal of Political Economy* 74:188–94.

Temporary Commission on Living Costs and the Economy. 1976. *Report on Nursing Homes and Health Related Facilities.* Albany: State of New York.

U.S. Bureau of the Census. 1978. *1976 Survey of Institutionalized Persons*. Current Population Reports, Special Studies, Series P-23, no. 69. Washington, D.C.: Government Printing Office.

U.S. Small Business Administration. 1983. "Unfair Competition by Nonprofit Organizations with Small Business: An Issue for the 1980s." Washington, D.C.

Weisbrod, Burton A. 1983. "Nonprofit and Proprietary Sector Behavior: Wage Differentials among Lawyers." *Journal of Labor Economics* 246–63.

———. 1988. *The Nonprofit Economy*. Cambridge: Harvard University Press.

———. 1996. "Does Institutional Form Matter? Comparing Behavior of Private Firms, Church-Related Nonprofits, and Other Nonprofits." Northwestern University, Center for Urban Affairs and Policy Research.

Weisbrod, Burton A., and Elizabeth Mauser. 1991. "Partial versus Total Effects of Institutional Form: Disentangling Endogenous from Exogenous Variables." Department of Economics, Northwestern University.

Wolff, Nancy, and Mark Schlesinger. 1992. "Changes in Ownership-Related Differences in Hospital Performance in Response to Intersectoral Competition." Institute for Health, Health Care Policy, and Aging Research, Rutgers University.

Young, Dennis. 1983. *If Not for Profit, for What?* Lexington, Mass.: D. C. Heath.

6

MARK SCHLESINGER

Mismeasuring the Consequences of Ownership: External Influences and the Comparative Performance of Public, For-Profit, and Private Nonprofit Organizations

Our understanding of the relationship between an organization's legal form of ownership and its behavior has grown increasingly imbalanced. The past fifteen years have seen significant refinements and elaborations of conceptual models of this relationship. Empirical research, however, has lagged behind in at least two important ways.

First, the theoretical insights developed since 1980 suggest that ownership-related differences in organizational performance depend on the environment in which the organization operates. More specifically, influences from outside the organization are both the source of ownership-related dif-

This chapter draws on data collected under a research grant from the National Institute of Mental Health. Robert Dorwart, Sherrie Epstein, and Harriet Davidson worked with me to design and field the survey with the advice of Paul Cleary and a board of advisors. Preliminary work on this paper was supported by a fellowship from the Center on Philanthropy at Indiana University. These preliminary analyses were improved by the comments from a number of participants at the seminars that were a part of this fellowship program. In roughly its current form, this chapter was first presented at the conference "Private Action and the Public Good," Indianapolis, November 4–6, 1993. A revised version was presented at Program on Non-Profit Organizations, Yale University, New Haven, Connecticut, April 12, 1994. It was further improved by comments at both the seminars, as well as by editorial suggestions from Woody Powell and Elisabeth Clemens. Burt Weisbrod provided a final review, offering additional insights and catching several flawed arguments.

ferences and mediate the extent of those differences. Researchers conducting empirical studies, however, continue to search for generic ownership-related differences that persist whatever the external conditions (DiMaggio and Anheier 1990). Although empirical models control statistically for the influence of various environmental factors — the intensity of competition, the sociodemographic characteristics of the community — they do so in a manner that implicitly assumes that these external conditions have the same effects on organizations of different ownership. But this assumption is exactly what one would *not* expect, given our understanding of why ownership-related differences in behavior emerge in the first place. Put in somewhat more technical language, past empirical research *controls* for various external factors but fails to allow for the *interaction* of ownership with these external influences.

Second, in spite of the large number of predicted differences in ownership-related behavior that emerge from the theoretical literature, researchers have difficulty documenting any consistent empirical differences. Reviews of this research by economists (Patel et al. 1993; West 1989; Sloan 1988; Pauly 1987) and sociologists (DiMaggio and Anheier 1990; Ferris and Grady 1989) reach similar conclusions. The sociologists report that "the research literature is vast and inconclusive" (DiMaggio and Anheier 1990, 149), while the economists conclude that "the empirical literature reveals little or no difference" with respect to ownership (Sloan 1988, 138). The intellectual predispositions and ideological leanings of the two disciplines lead to different interpretations. Economists typically conclude that "ownership differences turn out to be much less important than they might seem" (Pauly 1987, 262). Sociologists are more inclined to argue that ownership-related differences are substantial but obscured by a variety of unmeasured factors that also shape organizational behavior. Efforts to actually identify these omitted factors, however, ordinarily reveal only trivial effects (Clarke and Estes 1992). Even the researchers who report more substantial differences in the performance of for-profit and nonprofit organizations find that these distinctions appear inconsistently, varying in seemingly inexplicable ways across types of service, periods of time, and geographic areas (Weisbrod 1993; Patel et al. 1993; Gray 1991; Weisbrod 1988; Marmor et al. 1987).

A central thesis of this chapter is that the apparent inconsistency in empirical findings related to ownership form can be explained in large part by flawed specifications in the statistical models. By failing to model the interaction of ownership and external conditions (for example, market conditions or the regulatory environment), this research arguably misses the most important and consistent features of ownership-related differences. Because virtually all previous research on ownership suffers from this shortcoming, it is little wonder that the findings of these studies are inconsistent. External influences vary significantly from one industry to the next, across geographic regions, and over time, and existing specifications do not adequately take this variation into account. Later in the chapter, I describe and illustrate an alternative approach for modeling ownership-related differences in performance that should provide more reliable and consistent results.

The shortcomings of past empirical studies of ownership are not simply the result of researchers failing to correctly translate theoretical insights into empirical specifications. Some of the problems in the empirical research reflect shortcomings in our theoretical models of how ownership influences organizational performance.

First, contemporary theories of ownership are useful for predicting the conditions under which nonprofit and for-profit organizations will differ in their behavior but offer little guidance about the form that these differences will take. For example, the nondistribution constraint can be expected to induce nonprofits to offer their managers and employees compensation that emphasizes nonpecuniary rewards to a greater extent than do comparable proprietary organizations (Weisbrod 1988; Preston 1988). But this tells us little about what form these nonproprietary rewards might take (James 1992). Plausible forms include more pleasant working conditions (for example, nicer offices or more support staff), prestigious organizational involvements (for example, research and innovation), and various forms of community service (for example, providing free services to indigent clients).

Most of the empirical literature comparing nonprofit and for-profit performance measures only one of these forms of nonpecuniary activity in each study, with different studies focusing on different outcomes. Theory does *not* predict that there will be significant ownership-related differences in any one of these outcomes; it predicts that differences will emerge in at least one of these outcomes. Lacking a more complete theory of when particular forms of nonpecuniary rewards will be used, empirical research generates inconsistent findings. By focusing to a greater extent on the influence of various actors outside the organization, we can bring greater specificity to our predictions about how nonprofit and for-profit behavior will differ.

A second shortcoming in the theoretical literature involves the portrayal of *how* external factors mediate ownership-related performance. Most discussions presume that the more substantial are the external constraints—for example, the more intense the competition, the more pervasive government regulation, the more extensive professionalization of the services provided by the organization—the smaller will be the differences between nonprofit and for-profit behavior (Campbell and Ahern 1993; Clarke and Estes 1992). This prediction seems intuitively plausible: As external factors move all organizations toward a common set of behaviors, there will be less discretion or leeway that can be influenced by ownership-related incentives. Although plausible, however, under some circumstances this prediction is clearly wrong. External actors may have different expectations for nonprofit than for-profit agencies. The influence of external actors also may be greater on some forms of ownership than others—for example, nonprofit firms may be less responsive to competitive forces than are for-profit firms but more responsive to regulatory pressure. Increasing external influences under these circumstances can increase rather than reduce ownership-related differences in behavior.

In three subsequent sections I explore more carefully the influence of external factors on ownership-related behaviors. The first section examines the relationship between external influences and the impact of ownership on organizational behavior. I also review the methods and findings of empirical studies of ownership. The next section of the chapter applies some of the insights from this review to an industry with a mix of for-profit, private nonprofit, and public providers—hospitals providing inpatient psychiatric care. Data from a national survey conducted in 1988 allow us to examine certain external influences (for example, regulatory pressures and community oversight) that are largely ignored in previous work. They also afford an opportunity to study factors that have been examined in past research (for example, the role of competition), but to do so in a manner that more appropriately captures the interaction of that factor with ownership. The results reveal that ownership, at least in this one industry, has dramatically different implications depending on the nature and extent of external influences. I conclude with a discussion of the empirical findings and their implications for our understanding of institutional forms and its relationship with public policy.

A REVIEW AND REINTERPRETATION OF THE LITERATURE ON OWNERSHIP FORM AND ORGANIZATIONAL BEHAVIOR

I divide my review of the literature into three parts. The first examines the mechanisms through which ownership is thought to induce behavioral differences, mechanisms that in large part depend on actors outside the organization. Second, I consider various other external factors that mediate the influence of ownership by constraining the discretion that administrators have in managing an agency. Third, I explore how particular external factors shape the specific form that ownership-related differences can be expected to take.

Why Is Behavior in Nonprofit and For-Profit Organizations Expected to Differ?

The Origins of Ownership-Related Differences. Theory suggests three broad processes through which ownership influences organizational behavior. The first is associated with the incentives for administrators and employees (Steinberg 1987; Hansmann 1987; Yoder 1986; Newhouse 1970). The second involves how organizations are perceived by those who purchase services from them (Chillerni and Gui 1991; Weisbrod 1988; Easley and O'Hara 1988; Hansmann 1980). The third is associated with differences in regulatory treatment (Patel et al. 1993; DiMaggio and Anheier 1990; West 1989; Hansmann 1987).[1]

Those who work in nonprofit settings, administrators and service providers, cannot be compensated through profit-sharing. This situation is typically referred to as the non-distribution constraint. Other financial incentives, although not strictly illegal, may be discouraged as potentially incompatible with the image of the nonprofit organization (Young 1987). Pecuniary benefits being somewhat restricted, compensation to those who work in nonprofit organizations is shifted toward various nonpecuniary rewards. Because some of these involve characteristics of the organization or the services it produces, changing patterns of compensation are reflected in differences in organizational performance (Steinberg 1987; Newhouse 1970).

Perceptions by purchasers can lead to ownership-related differences in several ways. The earliest versions of this analysis focused on organizations, primarily charities, financed through philanthropy (Hansmann 1980). Because philanthropists rarely observe the delivery of the services they finance, there are significant asymmetries of information between the buyer and seller of services. Under these circumstances, providers may exploit information asymmetries to their advantage, in extreme cases taking donations but providing no services in return. Donors who are concerned about exploitation will seek providers who they believe are trustworthy. Nonprofit ownership may serve as a signal of trustworthiness under two conditions: first, because the nondistribution constraint limits the monetary rewards that result from exploiting information asymmetries, the level of exploitation in nonprofit settings may be lower; second, if the nonpecuniary rewards that are emphasized in nonprofit organizations are themselves incompatible with exploitation, nonprofit agencies may appear more trustworthy as a consequence of pursuing other organizational goals.[2]

A comparable situation exists when buyers cannot fully assess the characteristics of the product they are purchasing. A variety of services, including day care, health care, and financial intermediation, involve aspects of product quality that are difficult for the average consumer to measure. Service providers have incentives to promise high quality (at correspondingly high prices) but shirk their obligation to deliver those aspects of quality that are hard to observe (Hansmann 1980). Buyers who are most concerned about exploitation or who value most those aspects of services which they cannot directly measure will seek out providers who they believe are least likely to exploit these information asymmetries. Under a variety of conditions, ownership may prove a reliable signal of trustworthiness (Chillerni and Gui 1991; Easley and O'Hara 1988; Weisbrod 1988; Weisbrod and Schlesinger 1986; Schlesinger 1984).

The more an organization is perceived as trustworthy, the fewer resources (for example, marketing efforts) it must devote to convincing potential donors or clients that it is trust-

1. A fourth source of ownership-related differences is sometimes attributed to processes of selection, through which managers or employees with particular preferences gravitate toward particular forms of ownership (Preston 1988; Young 1983). This is not, however, a logically distinct source of ownership-related differences. Selection is assumed to occur *because* the opportunities and constraints are different in nonprofit and for-profit settings. In the absence of these differences, sorting would not take place. Thus, self-selection processes may exacerbate ownership-related differences but cannot in themselves be a cause of differences.

2. Consider the following example: Two international relief organizations solicit donations for famine relief in Third World countries. One is organized under nonprofit auspices, the other for-profit. Donors cannot directly observe whether either organization actually delivers the aid. They may view the nonprofit organization as more trustworthy because its staff cannot garner the profits if they supply less famine relief or because those who work in nonprofit settings are thought to obtain more personal satisfaction from assuring that the hungry are fed, so that it is in their self-interest to ensure that the donations are well spent. If some forms of nonpecuniary reward make it *more* likely that donors will be misled about the use of their philanthropy, and if these rewards are a more important part of compensation in nonprofit settings, then nonprofit firms will actually be *less* trustworthy than their proprietary counterparts. Consider, for example, two hospitals, one for-profit, the other nonprofit. Donations are made to each in the expectation that the money will be used to finance care for the indigent. But suppose hospital administrators derive more nonpecuniary benefits from using the money to support the purchase of some prestigious new technology. A nonprofit hospital that places stronger emphasis on technology acquisition might actually be more likely to mislead donors about the use of their funds.

worthy. This frees additional resources for other purposes. Thus trustworthiness can become a self-fulfilling expectation: Organizations that are trusted to provide high quality services need not spend resources convincing clients that they provide such services and can devote more resources to actually improving quality.

A third source of ownership-related differences is sometimes referred to as asymmetric advantage — differential treatment by regulators based on an organization's ownership. Regulatory advantages are typically argued to favor nonprofit organizations, which are clearly the beneficiaries of preferential tax treatment (West 1989; Hansmann 1987) and may also receive preferential treatment under other forms of regulation (Gray 1986).

The full consequences of preferential treatment, however, depend on the quid pro quo expected by the regulators or the implicit incentives created by the preferential treatment. For example, tax officials have increasingly sought quantifiable measures of community service from nonprofit organizations (Potter and Longest 1994; Gray 1993; Campbell and Ahern 1993), which results in an emphasis on these measurable aspects of organizational performance in nonprofit settings. Dependence on donations should shift the behavior of nonprofit organizations toward those activities favored by philanthropists (Vladeck 1976). As the number of external constituencies grows, it may also slow the response of nonprofit firms to changing external conditions (Powell and Friedkin 1987). In the words of one study, "The varying standards of clients, donors and others . . . make it difficult for them [nonprofit firms] to innovate or change. . . . the larger number of groups claiming to define values for a nonprofit organization, the more difficult measurement and making needed adjustments become" (Kanter and Summer 1987, 163).

External Influences as Sources of Ownership-Related Differences in Behavior. In the literature, the outcomes of any of these three processes are referred to as ownership-related differences in organizational performance. This phrasing suggests that they result from some intrinsic quality of the organization, more precisely, its legal form. Yet virtually everything that we refer to as ownership-related depends in a critical manner on the actions of some party outside the organization. This is most obvious in the differences that emerge from asymmetric advantages. The consequences of tax exemption depend in part on how tax officials define notions of community service and the criteria they establish for behavior that is sufficient to justify exempt status (Potter and Longest 1994; General Accounting Office 1990). The impact of tax deductibility depends in part on the preferences of philanthropists, in part on their efforts to exert control over the organizations to which they have made donations.

The other sources of ownership-related differences also depend, although somewhat less obviously, on factors outside of the organization. For incentives to be different in nonprofit settings, the nondistribution constraint not only must exist, but must be enforced. In the absence of enforce-

ment, there is no guarantee that those within the organization will abide by the constraint. Indeed, there is a long history of ostensibly nonprofit firms that operated as for-profits in disguise, surreptitiously channeling profits to subsidiaries, suppliers, or other venues where they might be legally garnered (Gray 1993; Gray 1991; Weisbrod 1988; Etzioni and Doty 1981). Enforcement need not be limited to actions taken by legal or tax authorities. Social norms also may play a role, especially if the organization depends on the goodwill of the local community for philanthropy or other support. For example, Dennis Young concluded that nonprofit firms made less use of financial incentives (even those not strictly prohibited by the nondistribution constraint) because

> any public perception that these organizations are being used as means of personal enrichment can be damaging. This is one reason that nonprofit organizational policies tend to be biased against the use of bonuses or other practices that might be interpreted as profiteering at the expense of the needy. Nonprofit workers must be seen to pursue service objectives of their own volition, uncorrupted by selfish financial objectives. (1987, 175)

Ownership-related differences that emerge from asymmetric information also depend on external factors. If the nondistribution constraint is not enforced, there is little reason to expect nonprofit firms to be on average more trustworthy. Even if nonprofits were initially more trustworthy, in the absence of enforceable constraints profiteering entrepreneurs would simply style themselves as nonprofits and exploit the ignorance of their trusting customers. Even if the nondistribution constraint is enforced, ownership-related differences will emerge only if clients *believe* that nonprofits are more trustworthy and therefore deal with them differently (Weisbrod and Schlesinger 1986).[3]

The extent and nature of ownership-related differences thus depend on factors and actors outside the organization. This represents my first hypothesis about external influences:

H1: External factors have different effects on the behavior of nonprofit and for-profit organizations. More specifically, regulators and community-based interests will have a larger influence on nonprofit than for-profit behavior.

Past analyses of ownership have acknowledged the important role of these external factors, particularly the enforcement of the nondistribution constraint (Weisbrod 1988; Sloan

---

3. There are actually two ways in which an organization may be trustworthy: fidelity (doing fully what was agreed upon between the customers and the provider) and agency (doing what the customers would have wanted had they been fully informed). These two forms of trustworthiness are not only different, in some cases they may be in direct conflict with one another (e.g., when a client, out of ignorance, requests services that are potentially harmful or otherwise problematic). Strictly speaking, only the first of these forms of trustworthiness depends on customer beliefs that the provider is trustworthy.

1988). This recognition is most evident in discussions of the "stakeholders" or "constituencies" whose interests are associated with nonprofit enterprise (Ben-Ner and Van Hoomissen 1993; Gui 1993; Kanter and Summers 1987). The empirical literature, however, has all but ignored the issue.[4] There have been no tests of the role of regulatory factors in shaping ownership-related differences.[5] Recently, several studies have included measures intended to capture some aspects of local community norms for the provision of public goods and hence the external pressures that these norms create for nonprofit and for-profit organizations (Patel et al. 1993; Frank et al. 1990).[6] The way in which these factors were included in the models, however, presumes that all organizations respond in similar ways and to a similar extent to local norms. Yet the theoretical arguments presented above suggest that nonprofit organizations are likely to be *more* responsive to these norms than are their proprietary counterparts. No tests of these differential effects have been attempted.

How Do External Influences Mediate the Effects of Ownership?

External influences can mediate the extent to which ownership influences organizational behavior by limiting the amount of discretion allowed to administrators of the organization. It is in this sense that most past discussions of ownership acknowledge the role of external influences. Both economists and sociologists have explored mediating influences, the first focusing on competition, the second on various forms of "institutional isomorphism" (DiMaggio and Powell

1983).[7] Although different in analytic style, the two approaches have a common limitation at the conceptual level: They presume that external factors invariably act to *constrain* ownership-related differences. Under some circumstances the very factors that are predicted to limit the differences between nonprofit and for-profit behavior may actually exacerbate those differences.

Institutional Isomorphism. Paul DiMaggio and Walter Powell (1983) identified three external characteristics that they argued have substantial influence on contemporary organizational behavior: (a) the growth of large purchasers who obtain services from many organizations, (b) uncertainty about the appropriate way to deliver services and thus about the appropriate goals for the organization, and (c) professional norms for delivering services. Because the objective of their article was to explain similarities of behavior across apparently diverse organizations, each of these factors was portrayed as producing convergence in behavior. For this reason, the three sets of influences were labeled "coercive isomorphism," "mimetic isomorphism," and "normative isomorphism."[8] Subsequent literature has adopted this framework, along with the presumption (not apparently intended by DiMaggio and Powell) that these factors necessarily made organizations act more alike (Clarke and Estes 1992; Ginsberg and Buchholtz 1990). However, two of these factors can, under equally plausible circumstances, exacerbate differences in performance. The third produces a form of convergence that may be quite different for nonprofit firms than for other organizations.

Normative isomorphism is argued to result whenever professionals play an important role in determining clients' needs and in overseeing how services are delivered. Common training and interactions through professional networks homogenize the behavior of professionals; this in turn leads to convergence in performance of the organizations in which they work. DiMaggio and Powell write, "Such mechanisms create a pool of almost interchangeable individuals who occupy similar positions across a range of organizations and possess a similarity of orientation and disposition that may override variation in tradition and control that might otherwise shape organizational behavior" (1983, 152).

Under certain circumstances, professional norms will

---

4. One exception involved a study of nonprofit organizations converting to for-profit status in response to changing environmental conditions (Ginsberg and Buchholtz 1990). This article provided a rich analysis of the external conditions that fostered or inhibited conversion but obviously offered little insight into the comparative performance of organizations operating under different forms of ownership.

5. One study (Patel et al. 1993) did incorporate an indirect measure of regulatory expectations, claiming that regulators might expect larger hospitals to provide more community services than smaller hospitals. Because studies have found that the amount of community service does increase with the size of the hospital, this may indicate a role of regulatory factors. The logic linking hospital size to regulatory attitudes, however, is strained at best. Size differences may just as well capture scale effects in the provision of services or reflect the visibility of the hospital in the local community.

6. Both studies examined whether local norms influenced the willingness of hospitals to treat indigent patients. Norms were measured indirectly, by average level of indigent care at hospitals with the same ownership operating in the same community. Results were inconsistent: one study found no influence of local norms (Frank et al. 1990). A second found some positive influence, but only for some states and time periods, not for others (Patel et al. 1993). Apart from the inconsistent results, this seems a questionable way to measure the influence of community groups. The implicit claim is that when the average hospital in a community provides more indigent care, this reflects community norms. It could, however, just as readily reflect market conditions or other forms of interorganizational comparisons that are discussed later in the text.

7. Sociologists occasionally write about competitive pressures as well (Hannan and Freeman 1977). In fact, the conception of competition in these sociological models is often far richer and more complex than that assumed in most treatments by economists. Yet the way in which economists have portrayed competition has had a larger impact on empirical studies of ownership, so I shall focus primarily on this portrayal in the body of the chapter.

8. Clark and Estes (1992) refer to a fourth set of influences, which they refer to as "accommodative isomorphism." Although the use is a bit vague, the term appears to refer to common organizational arrangements that lead different organizations to pursue similar approaches to service delivery. Because it is unclear that this process can be empirically differentiated from mimetic isomorphism, it is not discussed here.

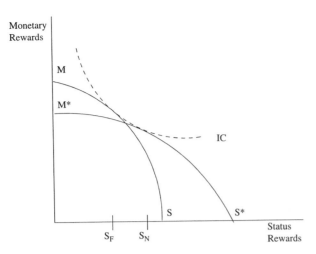

Figure 6.1. Ownership and Preferred Rewards

undoubtedly make organizations behave more similarly. Professional norms clearly have an influence on organizational performance, whatever the form of ownership, but this influence is likely to be most pronounced in those industries in which nonprofit and for-profit agencies coexist. Professionalization is most pronounced for these services, having developed in response to the same informational asymmetries that create a rationale for nonprofit service delivery (Salamon 1992; DiMaggio and Anheier 1990; Majone 1984). In health care, for example, it has been suggested that proprietary organizations be considered "not-only-for-profit" firms because their reliance on physicians and other health care professionals entails that they pursue some of the nonpecuniary goals that professionals favor (Evans 1984).

Examining the mechanisms through which this process is thought to occur suggests several circumstances under which increased professional influence in an industry may actually lead to a divergence of behavior between nonprofit and for-profit agencies. As an illustration of this, consider the following simple model.

Assume that firm behavior can be characterized by the proportion of resources devoted to a nonpecuniary aspect of performance, which we'll refer to as status, and a set of monetary rewards (for example, salary, profit-sharing, bonuses of various sorts). These can be traded off along a production possibilities curve (which for proprietary firms takes the form of *MS* in figure 6.1). The preferences of those who manage the organization can be characterized by a set of indifference curves, like IC_1, along which individuals are equally satisfied with different combinations of monetary and nonmonetary rewards (Wolff and Schlesinger 1995). Managers are best off at the tangency of the indifference curves and the production possibilities curve, which leads to status S_F.

In nonprofit settings, the nondistribution constraint makes it more difficult to use monetary rewards, so that the production possibilities curve for rewarding those who work in the firm become flatter. Unless nonprofit firms are subsidized

through preferential taxes or regulation, people are willing to work for less in nonprofit settings, or markets for nonprofits are less competitive so that the firm has a larger surplus, no one would work in nonprofit settings. Because there appears to be both preferential treatment and differential competition (Patel et al. 1993; Hansmann 1987), the reward opportunities in nonprofits become more generous. Entry or exit by nonprofit firms occurs until their extra surplus is sufficient to provide rewards for working in nonprofit settings that are equivalent in value to those available in for-profit organizations in the same industry.[9] For-profit firms operate with status S_F, nonprofit firms with the larger status S_N but less generous financial rewards.[10]

The influence of professionalization can be incorporated into this simple model in two ways. If professionals are employees (or otherwise contractually affiliated with the organization) as opposed to administrators, then they will have goals that are distinct from those who control the agency. To operate, administrators at the agency must negotiate with professionals who will actually deliver the services. Professionals will value certain status-producing attributes of the organization or its services. Organizational behavior thus depends on the negotiation between administrators and professionals. Alternatively, the administrators themselves may be professionals. In this case, professionalization changes their own preferences and hence their willingness to trade off various forms of nonpecuniary rewards for monetary benefits.

Assume initially that professionals are not managers and that professionalization leads all service providers to favor the same level of nonpecuniary outcomes.[11] In terms of our simplified model, let this professional norm be represented by S_P. The behavior of a firm is determined by its negotiations with professional employees, with the resulting performance falling somewhere (depending on the relative strengths of negotiators) between the norms favored by the profession and the objectives of the firm's management.

9. That is, the two reward possibilities curves are both tangent to the same indifference curve. In figure 6.1, the reward possibilities in nonprofit settings are captured by the curve *M*S**.

10. Recent work by Roomkin and Weisbrod on the hospital industry suggests that managers working for public and nonprofit hospitals do receive lower incomes, controlling for job complexity, than do their counterparts in for-profit hospitals (Roomkin and Weisbrod 1994). These differences, however, were generally found only in the highest echelons in management, suggesting that middle managers are less motivated by status rewards in this industry. A greater share of managerial income in for-profit hospitals took the form of bonuses, indicating that there may also be differences in risk aversion between managers operating under different forms of ownership.

11. This is obviously a heroic assumption—but useful for making the basic points in the text. Past studies of the professional training and values suggest that various forms of status rewards are important (Abbott 1988; Kultgen 1988), so that shared training ought to increase the salience of these aspects of organizational behavior for the professionals associated with the organization.

Under some circumstances, this process will unambiguously lead to convergence across ownership forms. In our example, if the level of status favored by professionals falls between S_F and S_N, then however much professionals influence organizational behavior, they cause proprietary firms to favor higher status activities, nonprofit firms to deemphasize status. Nonprofit and for-profit performance becomes more similar when there are professional service providers than when there are not. For this case, professional norms are isomorphic.

Consider instead the case in which the status favored by professionals exceeds that favored by managers in both for-profit and nonprofit organizations (that is, $S_P > S_N > S_F$). Negotiating with professionals increases status-producing activities in both settings. Whether there is convergence or divergence depends on whether the behavior of nonprofits or for-profits responds more substantially to the pressure exerted by professional interests. If for-profits are more responsive, then convergence again occurs. It is typically argued, however, that professionals have greater affinity for nonprofit settings because nonprofit agencies are more responsive to professional interests than are for-profit firms (DiMaggio and Anheier 1990; Young 1987; Majone 1984). Under these circumstances, one would predict that professionalization creates divergence between nonprofit and for-profit performance.

Consider now the case in which the administrators themselves are professionalized. Under this scenario, professionalization leads managers to place a greater value on status than they otherwise would have. In our graphical schema, the indifference curves become steeper (for example, shift from IC_1 to IC_2 in figure 6.2) because managers must be compensated by a larger increase in monetary benefits for a given loss of status. Professionalization shifts both nonprofit and for-profit organizations to provide more status-oriented activities. But without knowing the shape of the indifference or production possibility curves, it is impossible to determine

whether the gap between nonprofit and for-profit behavior grows smaller or larger.

Thus, although professional norms may produce institutional isomorphism, there is no reason to presume that they do so. Professionalization can plausibly lead to greater differences between nonprofit and for-profit behavior. Under our first form of professionalization, we can be somewhat more precise about our predictions about when convergence will occur. For nonpecuniary rewards that are not emphasized by professionals (that is, $S_P < S_N$), professionalization will produce convergence. By contrast, in dimensions emphasized by professional norms ($S_P > S_N$) professionalization will expand ownership-related differences if nonprofit organizations are more responsive to professional influence. This is my second hypothesis:

H2: When professionals work for an organization, professionalization will produce convergence between for-profit and nonprofit behavior for those nonpecuniary aspects of organizational behavior that are not favored by professional norms. In those aspects most favored by professionals, professionalization will more often lead to greater ownership-related differences.

Coercive isomorphism is conceptually similar to normative isomorphism, although in this case the influence comes from some external agency or authority that organizations depend upon for resources or legitimacy.[12] To the extent that these outside agencies have common expectations for the nonprofit and for-profit organizations with which they deal, the behavior of these organizations can be expected to become more similar than it otherwise would have been. One would anticipate that this sort of isomorphism would be particularly important in mixed industries, such as health care, because government programs have over the past thirty years become significantly more important as purchasers of services (Marmor et al. 1987; Hollingsworth and Hollingsworth 1987).

As with normative influence, however, convergence follows only if the funding agency has (a) common expectations for and (b) equal influence over organizations operating under different ownership forms. Historically, neither of these conditions appears to have been true for health care. Government purchasing programs treated nonprofit and for-profit health care providers in distinct ways. For example, the federal Medicare program (insuring the elderly and disabled) paid for-profit hospitals in a slightly different manner (involving reimbursement of capital expenses) than it did nonprofit hospitals. Various state Medicaid programs set different prices for nursing home care provided by nonprofit homes than for services from otherwise comparable for-profit agencies (Schlesinger 1984).

12. DiMaggio and Powell include both purchasers and regulators in this category of external influence. Because I have previously discussed the role of regulators, the discussion here focuses on the influence of large public purchasers.

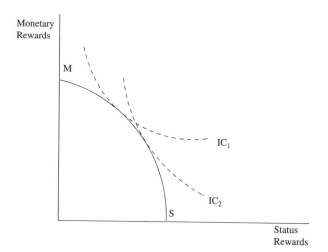

Figure 6.2. Professionalization and Rewards

The actions of government purchasing programs may also have had a different impact on the opportunities available to nonprofit and for-profit agencies. It has been hypothesized that private philanthropists will react to an expanded role for government by reducing their charitable donations, since they see government intervention as reducing the size of the needy population (Steinberg 1993; Schiff 1985). If this prediction is accurate, greater government involvement would decrease donations to nonprofits and reduce their surplus. Under these conditions, nonprofits have less capacity to subsidize various activities that generate nonpecuniary rewards to those who affiliate with them. This should produce a convergence between nonprofit and for-profit behavior. It has also been suggested, however, that a larger government role might increase philanthropy, if government purchasers encouraged nonprofit providers to act in ways that were more compatible with the goals of philanthropists (Rose-Ackerman 1986). Under these conditions, a greater role for government increases philanthropy. Because tax subsidies favor donations to nonprofit settings, this has a larger impact on nonprofit agencies than on their for-profit counterparts. Larger differences in ownership-related behavior result.

The impact of large purchasers thus depends on assumptions about their goals and their influence. Historically the growth of large public purchasers may have encouraged diverging behavior between nonprofit and for-profit firms. More recently, conditions appear to favor convergence. This is again most readily observed in health care. Over the past thirty years, philanthropy has become a less important source of revenue for health care providers (Sloan 1988). It is therefore unlikely that government involvement would stimulate a significant influx of donations. Beginning in the early 1980s, federal and state governments began to abandon many of the distinctions that they had previously made between nonprofit and for-profit health care providers (Dorwart and Schlesinger 1988). Programs that treat the two types of organizations on similar terms are more likely to engender similar types of behavior. Consequently, studies of contemporary organizational behavior should observe the following:

H3: In industries with minimal philanthropy, where there is a larger role for government purchasing of services, there will be smaller differences in performance between nonprofit and for-profit firms.

A third isomorphic process, *mimetic behavior,* is predicted to operate in a different fashion. Faced with technological or other uncertainties, organizations are thought to model themselves on other organizations viewed as "more legitimate or successful" (DiMaggio and Powell 1983, 152). Because nonprofit and for-profit organizations commonly compete to provide services for which there is little agreement over the appropriate goals or standards (for example, day care, nursing home care) or considerable technological change (for example, hospital treatment), one might expect mimetic processes to reduce ownership-related differences in

performance. Experience suggests that nonprofit and for-profit organizations do emulate one another, but in a more complex manner than prevailing theory would predict. Legitimacy becomes an unexpectedly volatile aspect of comparisons across ownership forms.

These complications can be clearly observed in the health care arena. Between the 1930s and mid-1970s, general hospitals in the United States were predominantly nonprofit enterprises (Bays 1983; Steinwald and Neuhauser 1970). The institutions with national reputations, the academic medical centers that were the leaders in the industry, were exclusively nonprofit. During the latter part of the 1970s and early 1980s, investors grew more interested in the health field, and a substantial number of proprietary hospitals were constructed. Following the hypothesis of mimetic isomorphism, one would have predicted that these new hospitals would emulate their better-established nonprofit counterparts.

What one observed was quite the opposite. By the mid-1980s, administrators in nonprofit hospitals were reporting that they felt compelled to emulate practices found in for-profit facilities (Seay and Vladeck 1987). As one former administrator wrote, "Any hospital CEO who doesn't do all he can to fend off as many general assistance patients as he can . . . just isn't being 'business-like' and will be so judged by his board of trustees" (Kinzer 1984, 9–10). Empirical research reinforces these anecdotal reports. By the mid-1980s, in geographic areas with more for-profit competitors, the behavior of nonprofit health care providers became more like that of their proprietary counterparts (Frank et al. 1990; Ginsberg and Buchholtz 1990; Schlesinger et al. 1987). One team of academic researchers concluded that "throughout the country voluntary hospitals are attempting to model themselves after for-profit hospitals" (Hollingsworth and Hollingsworth 1987, 129).

This unexpected outcome reflects the peculiar nature of mimetic processes when they involve differences in ownership form. Although nonprofit ownership dominates certain industries, these are enclaves in a much larger profit-oriented economy. As a result, the legitimacy of nonprofit enterprise is fragile. It must always be justified through an argument of exception, an explanation about why particular services are different from those common to the economy as a whole (Weisbrod 1988). Substantial entry by for-profit organizations into an industry undermines this rationale. The experience of the hospital industry suggests that even relatively modest shifts in the mix of ownership in an industry—the market share of proprietary hospitals grew by only a few percentage points between 1975 and 1985—can reverse the orientation that provides legitimacy to hospitals. This sensitivity to small changes—sometimes referred to as tipping behavior—can lead to substantial shifts in organizational performance.

Mimetic processes continue, whatever the standards of institutional legitimacy. They reduce the magnitude of ownership-related differences. If the standards of legitimacy can quickly shift from nonprofit to for-profit in origin, however, this mediates the consequences of mimicry. In geographic areas or service lines in which nonprofits retain their legitimacy, mimicry leads proprietary firms to emulate nonprofit behavior. In areas where legitimacy has shifted to a for-profit orientation, it is the nonprofits who must adapt their behavior. Under these conditions, comparisons over time or across different geographic areas will yield seemingly inconsistent findings because the implicit standards toward which organizational behavior is converging are different.

H4: In markets in which proprietary behavior is the norm (for example, there has been substantial for-profit entry), nonprofit behavior will become more like their for-profit counterparts. In markets in which nonprofit behavior remains the norm, the reverse will be true.

Although mimicry reduces differences of behavior in each area, it does not necessarily reduce the range of behaviors across areas. Return to the example in figure 6.1. Assume that in one part of the country, for-profit entry is limited, so that nonprofit organizations retain their legitimacy. For-profit firms emulate them, so that status-generating behaviors in for-profit settings exceed S_F and approach S_N. (Nonprofits continue to operate at S_N.) In a second region, for-profit entry has delegitimized the nonprofit role. Nonprofit firms thus try to emulate for-profits, reducing their level of status-producing behavior. (For-profits continue to operate at S_F.) Comparing nonprofit and for-profit performance within common geographic areas reveals smaller differences than comparing performance across areas, given that the norms toward which organizations are converging differ from one area to the next and do not themselves change over time.

Competitive Market Pressures. Nonprofit organizations that generate all their revenue by selling goods or services ("commercial nonprofits" in Hansmann's [1980] schema) can behave differently from their for-profit counterparts only to the extent that they have resources to fund these activities. In the absence of philanthropy, any unprofitable activities must be subsidized out of retained earnings. As with all commercial enterprises, the less intense the competition that nonprofits face, the higher the price they can charge for their services and the larger their surplus. In markets in which philanthropy is limited, profits made from selling services become the primary funding for the various nonpecuniary activities that are purported to distinguish nonprofit from for-profit behavior.

Recent studies suggest that there is a complex interaction between competition and ownership-related behaviors (Salkever and Frank 1990, 1988; Patel et al. 1993; Wolff and Schlesinger 1995; Schlesinger et al. 1995). Most of these studies have focused on the impact of competition on services for indigent clients in nonprofit settings. To simplify this discussion, consider the following case. Assume that nonprofit and for-profit firms compete to provide a service in a given community. Two types of clients seek the service: private clients, who pay full market price, and public clients, who pay less than market price (either because they have limited personal resources or are relying on government subsidies that do not fully pay for the service. Costs of the service depend both on the individual characteristics of the client (more complex cases cost more to serve) and the number of clients the firm is serving, with marginal costs increasing as the number of clients becomes greater. All private clients must be served at the same price. Revenues from public clients are lower than the private price, but for clients with sufficiently simple cases will cover their costs.

Profit-maximizing service providers serve all private clients for whom marginal revenue equals marginal costs. They may also treat some public clients, so long as they can provide sufficient revenues to cover the costs of their services. Nonprofit providers serve some unprofitable public clients as a form of community service.[13] They pay for this out of the organization's surplus. Assume further that selling of services is the only source of funds — there is no philanthropy and no other sources of unrelated business income.

Consider a local market that historically has had limited entry, so that all firms make some monopoly profits. Competition intensifies when a new organization enters the market.[14] In the face of increased competition, profit-maximizing providers increase their number of public clients to substitute for private clients who are drawn off by the newly entering firm.[15] Intensity of competition is thus positively related to treatment of public clients in for-profit providers.

This same process of substituting public for private patients occurs in nonprofit settings that face increased competition. But an additional factor comes into play for nonprofit firms. They were previously treating some public clients by cross-subsidizing their services from the surplus made from private clients. As competition intensifies, this surplus falls. Consequently, the nonprofit is able to pay for less community service than in the past. If this reduction is larger than the substitution effect that occurs in both nonprofit and for-profit settings, then intensity of competition can be negatively related to treatment of public clients in nonprofit settings (Frank and Salkever 1990).

This negative effect may be reinforced by a second factor.

13. They might also treat more expensive private patients who are unprofitable to treat (Wolff and Schlesinger 1995). To simplify the discussion in the text, I assume that this does not occur.

14. Competition might also intensify because purchasers develop new technologies that enable them to more effectively choose among competing providers. In health care markets — a major role for nonprofit organizations — this is exactly what occurred in the early 1980s (Zwanziger and Melnick 1988). This form of increased competition somewhat complicates the analysis presented in the text but leads to largely similar predictions (Frank and Salkever 1990).

15. Because the firm has increasing marginal costs, when it has fewer private patients it can accept some public patients that formerly would have been unprofitable to serve.

The value that the nonprofit assigns to community service may depend on the extent of unmet need that it observes in the community or it may simply be a function of the extent to which the organization itself acts to meet that need. In the first case, if the new competitor is another nonprofit organization, then existing nonprofits may conclude that they can cut back on their own community service because the new organization can be expected to serve some unprofitable public clients (Salkever and Frank 1990). This is sometimes referred to as the crowding out of community service in nonprofit settings.

Although highly simplified, this portrayal of competition reveals one key conclusion: competitive effects are potentially different (indeed opposite in direction) for organizations under different forms of ownership. This conclusion generalizes to all aspects of an organization's performance that must be subsidized out of surplus — as competition reduces the surplus, it will reduce the magnitude of ownership-related differences in performance.

H5: Nonprofit and for-profit providers will respond in different ways to competition and may change their behavior in opposite directions. For activities that are subsidized out of the organization's surplus, competition will reduce ownership-related differences in behavior.

Past Empirical Studies of Competition and Ownership. Economists have documented that (a) competition affects the behavior of both nonprofit and for-profit organizations (Steinberg 1987) and (b) for-profit and nonprofit organizations are often situated in different local markets, so that they operate in somewhat different competitive environments (Patel et al. 1993; Marmor et al. 1987). Studies of nonprofit hospitals revealed that as competition increased, they reduced their treatment of indigent clients (Thorpe and Brecher 1988). This decline appears to be more closely associated with the amount of surplus in the facility than with the number of competitors suggesting that crowding out was less a factor than was the organization's ability to finance community services (Ahern and Campbell 1993; Frank et al. 1990).

Most studies intended to compare the behavior of nonprofit and for-profit organizations have wrongly specified measures of competition. The investigators control for the intensity of competition (typically with measures of market structure) simply by including these measures as independent variables in the regression equation. But this approach measures the *average* response to competition among the organizations in the sample. Unless nonprofit and for-profit organizations respond to competitive pressures to comparable degrees and in similar ways, a measure of this sort does not adequately control for the combined effects of competition and ownership on organizational performance. As discussed above, theory suggests that their responses will in fact be quite different. And the empirical research that has distinguished the competitive response of nonprofit and for-profit organizations supports this prediction.

These studies indicate that, as competitive pressures increase, (a) nonprofit general hospitals are less likely to discontinue unprofitable services than are for-profit providers (Schlesinger et al. 1994; Shortell et al. 1987; Marmor et al. 1987); (b) nonprofit psychiatric hospitals shift their nonpecuniary outputs toward more readily observable aspects of community service (Wolff and Schlesinger 1995); (c) differences in efficiency (for example, cost of services) between nonprofit and for-profit nursing homes grow larger (Arling et al. 1987); and (d) the provision of services to indigent clients by general hospitals becomes more sensitive to the size of the organization's surplus in nonprofit compared to for-profit settings (Campbell and Ahern 1993).[16] These results suggest that as competition increases, ownership-related differences converge in some dimensions (services for the indigent) while diverging in others (scope of services). This conclusion provides only limited support for our hypothesis. However, the differing response of service mix to competitive pressures in nonprofit settings may reflect the mediating influence of professionals, a factor which I now consider at greater length.

The Interaction of Professional Norms and Competitive Pressures. The impact of competition may interact with each

16. Campbell and Ahern report a quite different interpretation of the results of their study. They conclude that "the view that a more competitive and cost conscious environment will force hospitals under different ownership control to become more similar . . . is not supported by this study" (1993, 288). Their interpretation draws on a mistaken assessment of their own findings. Their study predicts determinants of the provision of indigent care by hospitals. The regressions that they estimate include two measures of competition and two measures of ownership. As in most studies, the regressions include the usual dummy variables for ownership form and measures of market concentration to capture the intensity of local competition. But they also include separate measures of the organization's surplus, interacted with ownership form. Because competition directly affects surplus, this is a second measure of the impact of competition (one that is potentially more accurate than market concentration). The authors estimate regressions using data from two points in time, arguing that the second period represents a more competitive marketplace.

Campbell and Ahern find that as hospital markets became more competitive over time, the gap in indigent care provided by (nonreligious) nonprofit and for-profit hospitals increased (that is, the dummy variables in the second time period showed larger differences than in the first). But this ignores the effect of surplus on the provision of indigent care. The regressions also showed that (a) the provision of indigent care was positively related to the hospital surplus for nonprofit (nonreligious) hospitals, but not for proprietary hospitals, (b) the amount of indigent care in nonprofit settings was growing more sensitive to surplus over time, and (c) as hospital markets became more competitive, hospital surplus was declining. This suggests that competition was *reducing* ownership-related differences. The full impact of competition on ownership-related differences is captured by the combination of the dummy variable measures of ownership and the coefficients on the variables measuring the effects of surplus. (Religiously affiliated hospitals provide more indigent care than do other nonprofit hospitals, and such provision appears to be unrelated to the hospital's surplus.)

of the other external mediating factors that I have identified. But the interaction of competition and professional norms is likely to have the most substantial consequences. There is little reason to expect that the influence of large purchasers over ownership-related differences will be altered by competition. Purchasers will have more negotiating power the more competitive are markets for service providers. If purchasers treat nonprofit and for-profit providers similarly, however, this should not change the relative performance of the two types of organizations. Competition may affect patterns of mimetic behavior because more competitive markets appear to add to the perceived legitimacy of profit-oriented behavior (Schlesinger et al. 1987; Seay and Vladeck 1987). But this simply reinforces the prediction that competition leads to convergence between nonprofit and for-profit behavior.

The interaction of competition and professionalism is more complex. It can take two different forms. The first mediates the effects of competition, the second alters the very nature of the competition. Professional norms may affect the response of both nonprofit and for-profit firms to competitive pressures. For example, as competitive forces reduce market prices, organizations will find it no longer profitable to supply some services that they had previously provided (Dranove et al. 1992). Professional norms, however, may favor full-service organizations that offer a complete array of options for clients (Eisenberg 1986). To the extent that nonprofit organizations are more influenced by professional norms, they will be less likely to discontinue services. Because competition reduces the organization's surplus, however, and unprofitable services must be subsidized from that surplus, the same professional norms that buffer changes in services will exacerbate changes in other aspects of organizational behavior that must be subsidized from the surplus.

H6: As competition reduces the magnitude of ownership-related differences, the declines will be smallest in those dimensions of performance most favored by professionals and largest in the other dimensions.

The presence of professionals may also change the nature of competition. In most markets, the organization providing services markets itself directly to clients. In markets for professional services, however, the professional often serves as an independent agent who directs clients to the organization which provides them with services. Most physicians, for example, are not employed by hospitals but are affiliated as part of its staff.[17] The sustained bond or contract in this market is

between patient and physician. Until recently, hospitals attracted patients almost exclusively by attracting physicians.[18]

Under these circumstances, competition is more likely to focus on factors that attract professional affiliations. In terms of our earlier analyses, competitive markets increase the negotiating power of professionals. Depending on how professional goals relate to those favored by managers of nonprofit or for-profit agencies (see Hypothesis 2), this may encourage either greater convergence or divergence in ownership-related behaviors.

H7: If professionals are a primary source for attracting clients, competition will increase ownership-related differences in dimensions that are most favored by professionals but decrease them in dimensions that have less professional support.

In What Ways Are Nonprofit and For-Profit Organizations Expected to Differ?

External influences thus affect the magnitude of ownership-related differences in organizational behavior. Measuring these effects, as well as discerning their normative implications, depends on the specific forms that these differences take. For example, under the nondistribution constraint, compensation to those who work in nonprofit organizations is shifted toward various nonpecuniary rewards. Six sorts of nonpecuniary benefits are commonly identified in the literature: (a) organizational characteristics, such as size, that expand the power and decision-making scope of administrators (Rose-Ackerman 1986), (b) organizational amenities, such as plush offices, abundant support staff, or extended job tenure (Clarkson 1980), (c) enriched benefits for employees, beyond the compensation they could expect through normal labor markets (e.g., Feldstein's [1971] "philanthropic wage"), (d) ideological beliefs about the appropriate ways to deliver services,[19] (e) prestigious organizational outputs, such as high quality services, innovative technologies, or other advances in knowledge that create status for those associated with the organization (Newhouse 1970), and (f) community service, providing those services or dealing with clients who are unprofitable but who represent a well-defined local need (Steinberg 1987).

From the standpoint of societal welfare, it matters which of these forms of nonpecuniary rewards is most common. Those inclined toward favorable views of the nonprofit sector generally emphasize the fifth and sixth dimensions (Gray

17. This process may play an important role even in those industries in which professionals are employees of the organizations for which they provide services. For example, when lawyers change law firms, they are likely to take with them a set of clients whose loyalty is to the lawyer rather than to the firm. Consequently, the same competition for professionals occurs as in medical markets, though in a somewhat less obvious manner.

18. This is beginning to change as hospitals directly market themselves to patients. In spite of initial enthusiasm for marketing during the 1980s, however, it appears that most consumers continue to rely on their physician to determine the hospital at which they will receive medical services.

19. For example, the administrator of a nursing home might favor a warm and caring environment even if there was limited demand for these conditions (e.g., residents were so debilitated as to be insensate and their relatives so distant as to exert no influence over the home). See Weisbrod (1993) or Weisbrod and Schlesinger (1986).

1993; DiMaggio and Anheier 1990). Skeptics place particular importance on the first two dimensions (West 1989; Clark 1980). But the theory that predicts that there will be ownership-related differences in compensation offers no hints about what form the nonpecuniary benefits will take (James 1992).

External Influences and the Form of Ownership-Related Differences. Identifying external influences can lead to more specific predictions. I single out four sets of actors who are thought to affect ownership-related behavior: (1) government regulators, (2) community-based philanthropists, (3) professional service providers, and (4) large government purchasing programs. To the extent that one can identify distinct goals for each of these actors, one can predict the dimensions of behavior in which ownership differences are likely to emerge or be magnified.

To fully specify the ways in which these four outside parties are likely to influence ownership-related behavior, one would need a complete theory of behavior for each of them as well as a more complete model of the ways in which they interact with the organizations providing services. Because analysis in this detail is lacking, this last set of hypotheses is necessarily more speculative than those developed in previous sections. It seems important, however, to begin to push our thinking to more concrete predictions about the forms of ownership-related differences. This speculation serves as an initial step in that direction.

Government Regulation and Accountability. Because regulators are monitored by politicians who claim to spend the public's money wisely, they have a primary concern with accountability, with being able to determine whether the preferential treatment accorded nonprofit organizations is actually benefiting the community (Potter and Longest 1994; Gray 1993). This concern leads them to be oriented primarily to those aspects of performance that are quantifiable (General Accounting Office 1990; Weisbrod and Schlesinger 1986). Consequently, when ownership-related differences emerge primarily from differences in regulatory oversight, one would expect countable forms of nonpecuniary benefits (for example, number of indigent clients served) to be emphasized over other nonpecuniary attributes of the organization (for example, educational mission, cutting-edge technologies).

H8: Because government regulators will be most concerned with issues of accountability, they will favor quantifiable measures of performance. In markets with more regulatory influence, ownership-related differences will therefore be more closely associated with measurable sorts of nonpecuniary aspects of organizational behavior (*for example*, the number of indigent clients the organization serves).

Philanthropy and Concrete Forms of Activity. Donors are motivated at least in part by the status that accrues when their name is associated with the organization's activities. This attitude leads them to favor subsidizing more concrete aspects of organizations because these afford an obvious embodiment of their generosity that can be observed by others in the community. At its most literal, this inclination takes the form of buildings with the donor's name prominently displayed. Consequently, ownership-related differences that emerge from differential access to philanthropy should be reflected in more tangible aspects of the organization, what Bruce Vladeck (1976) once referred to as the "edifice complex" in nonprofit agencies.

H9: Because philanthropists are motivated in part by self-aggrandizement, they will favor more concrete forms of organizational performance. For this reason, in markets with more pronounced influence of community-based interests, the differences between nonprofit and for-profit behavior will emphasize readily observed features, such as new services, buildings, and the like.

Professionals and Prestigious Innovation. Professional training emphasizes various aspects of behavior, including an emphasis on technical knowledge, effective agency on behalf of clients, and concerns for broader forms of societal well-being (Eisenberg 1986). These factors coincide in encouraging professionals to favor innovative aspects of services. Being on the cutting edge — for example, using prestigious new technologies, applying services in original ways — reflects mastery of the specialized knowledge that is the sine qua non of professionalism. Professionals, wanting their clients to get the best, will seek out for them the most innovative settings. Professionals concerned with meeting community needs will emphasize rapid diffusion of new technologies. One therefore would expect that:

H10: Where professional influence is greater, ownership-related differences will be most pronounced in the provision of innovative, technically advanced services.

Government Purchasers and Access. I suggested above that when nonprofit and for-profit agencies serve a common group purchaser, their behavior will become more similar. This convergence should be most pronounced in those dimensions of behavior in which the purchaser has some interest. For example, nonprofit and for-profit providers will have a more similar mix of services when selling to a large government agency if the services are going to be used by beneficiaries of that agency. If, on the other hand, the services are used only by other clients, they are largely irrelevant to the group purchaser. One would expect to see convergence in ownership-related differences for the first set of services, but not necessarily for the second. For these reasons,

H11: Because government purchasing agents will be most concerned with assuring access for government-funded clients, the larger the influence that the purchasing agent has, the more similar will be the behavior of nonprofit and for-profit providers (see Hypothesis 3) in providing services used particularly by the clients of that agency.

Empirical Research on Dimensions of Ownership-Related Behavior. Past empirical research makes little effort to control for these external conditions that may mediate the behavioral effects of ownership. Consequently, it is not surprising to find that the results relating ownership to different organizational outcomes are extremely inconsistent. Some studies suggest that nonprofit and for-profit firms are different; others find their behavior to be roughly equivalent.

Empirical research has proceeded piecemeal, each study generally focusing on a single outcome for a single industry.[20] (Hospitals and nursing homes have been the favorites, though there is a growing literature on day care and other types of health care organizations.) This leads to two types of problems. The first involves the construction of the statistical models used to identify ownership-related differences. Researchers specify with great care the factors that are thought to influence the particular outcome they are studying. They completely ignore all the other outcomes that might vary with ownership. Because all nonpecuniary outcomes are financed from the same budget they are by definition related (the surplus that a nonprofit agency spends developing an innovative new program cannot be devoted to serving the poor). Statistical models that ignore this relationship are misspecified and are likely to produce biased measures of the impact of ownership.

A second problem emerges when researchers inadvertently use other forms of nonpecuniary outcomes as variables explaining the primary outcome on which they are focused. For example, virtually all studies comparing nonprofit and for-profit behavior include as an independent variable the size of the organization in regression models, along with ownership form and other explanatory variables. Studies of charity care in hospitals often conclude that large teaching hospitals treat more indigent clients, that most large teaching hospitals are nonprofit, but that, controlling for whether a hospital is large with a teaching affiliation, ownership has a modest influence on the provision of indigent care (Sloan et al. 1986). Larger size and teaching status may be forms of nonpecuniary rewards favored in nonprofit settings. Controlling for them inappropriately nets out some of the consequences of ownership for treatment of indigents or whatever other outcome is of interest to the researcher.[21]

More accurate assessments of the relationship between ownership and outcomes thus require studies that consider simultaneously each of the ways in which ownership might affect organizational performance. Such studies must measure the ways in which these different aspects interact with one another to provide an unbiased measure of ownership-related effects. The next section presents some tests of these hypotheses. These draw on data from a particular industry in which nonprofit and for-profit organizations actively compete, professional norms have an important (albeit inconsistent) influence on service delivery, and both regulators and community groups influence organizational performance.

AN EMPIRICAL APPLICATION: HOSPITALS PROVIDING INPATIENT PSYCHIATRIC SERVICES

In this section of the chapter, I draw on data collected from psychiatric hospitals to explore some of the hypothesized relationships among external influences, ownership, and organizational performance. Although psychiatric hospitals are not necessarily representative of other mixed industries, a case study of this sort can demonstrate the extent to which measures of ownership-related performance are sensitive to the specification of the model, particularly the modeling of external influences.

Psychiatric Hospitalization as a Case Study
Inpatient mental health services afford a useful test case for the hypotheses developed above. The industry includes a mix of for-profit, nonprofit, and government providers, substantial differences in the intensity of competition among local markets, significant interstate variation in regulation, and extensive, albeit somewhat inconsistent, professional involvement in treatment.

Historically in the United States, inpatient mental health care was almost exclusively the responsibility of government. As late as 1970, 93 percent of all hospital beds devoted to psychiatric care were in government-operated facilities. The remainder were in primarily private nonprofit settings, proprietary institutions providing only about 1 percent of all inpatient care (Dorwart and Schlesinger 1988). The industry has undergone rapid change in the past quarter century. By the late 1980s, the aggregate share of beds under government auspices had fallen to 65 percent. The market share of for-profit facilities had risen to about 15 percent (Dorwart and Schlesinger 1988). This rapid shift in the auspices under which services are being provided occasioned considerable concern from policymakers and a growing body of research on the role of ownership in the industry (McCue et al. 1993; McCue and Clement 1992; Wolff and Schlesinger 1995; Frank and Salkever 1992; Dorwart et al. 1991; Wolff 1989; Schlesinger and Dorwart 1984).

The growth of inpatient mental health care under private auspices was encouraged by changing conditions in the market for health care services. Large proprietary corporations, which had purchased general hospitals and nursing homes during the 1970s, began to seek other investments in the 1980s. During the 1970s, states had begun to require that insurers cover mental illness (Frank 1989). This significantly increased demand for hospital care by the privately insured (Marmor et al. 1987). By the mid-1980s, investor-owned hospital chains had begun to respond, building new hospitals and in some cases creating intense local competition (Dorwart and Schlesinger 1988).

---

20. For exceptions, see Weisbrod (1988) and in this volume.

21. See Weisbrod and Mauser (1993) for a more extended discussion of this problem of "overcontrolling" for the influences of ownership.

The growing private provision of inpatient psychiatric care was also the result of deliberate efforts by government to privatize mental health services. Privatization of mental health care was often accompanied by efforts to increase the intensity of competition among private providers, though states have varied in their efforts in this regard as well as their success in achieving this goal (Brotman 1992; Schlesinger et al. 1986). States have also used different strategies for regulating the emerging market for mental health services (Davidson et al. 1991).

In addition to a changing and varied external environment, the technology of inpatient mental health care underwent considerable change during this period. In part this reflected increased attention to particular disorders or groups of mentally ill, including the elderly, children, and adolescents, those with eating disorders and substance abuse problems. This led to the development and diffusion of services targeted to these groups. It also encouraged the creation of contracts and referral agreements with other service providers who specialized in these populations.

A second major source of innovation came from changes in the ways that mental health services were purchased. Historically, hospitals had attracted patients by competing for the physicians who treated them. But increasingly over the past decade, hospitals have directly marketed themselves to potential individual clients, to employers who operate worksite-based mental health care programs (referred to as employee assistance plans, or EAPs) and to insurance plans that have preenrolled populations (Dorwart and Schlesinger 1988). At the same time, purchasers of services have grown more cost conscious, adopting payment systems that encouraged treatment of shorter duration and the creation of case management programs to limit unnecessary care (Lazarus 1994).

Contemporary inpatient mental health care thus is a useful venue for studying the effects of a number of external influences identified earlier. The uncertainties associated with changing treatment practices and the hospital's environment may make mimetic processes an important influence on organizational behavior. Because for-profit entry has been pronounced in some geographic areas but not in others, one can compare the relative performance of nonprofit and for-profit hospitals in each of these settings. Some local markets are highly competitive, while others that remain more heavily regulated are not. This allows one to compare the differential effects of competition on ownership-related behavior using cross-sectional data. Variation in state regulation also makes it possible to assess the differential effects of regulatory influences.

Professionals play a somewhat different role in psychiatric hospital care than in other forms of hospital treatment. Mental health care is provided under the auspices of three competing professions: social workers, psychologists, and psychiatrists (Smith and Lipsky 1992). Each profession has different and in some cases conflicting norms of appropriate treatment. Such diversity has undermined the authority of medical professionals, especially in the case of chronic conditions, an aspect of care in which professionals have shown relatively little interest (Caplan 1987). Consequently, the influence of professionals is likely to vary from one hospital to another, depending on the client mix and the strength of other countervailing interests.

As government has begun to purchase more services from private hospitals, the potential for purchasing authorities to influence hospital practices has grown. In a typical nonprofit hospital, slightly less than half of all revenues come from government programs (Dorwart and Epstein 1993). The role of public purchasing programs is smaller in for-profit hospitals but still represents about 30 percent of all revenues. Most revenues come from three sources: the Medicare program, the Medicaid program, and direct state contracts with hospitals. Because the first program is the most uniformly administered nationwide, it is likely to produce the greatest isomorphic pressures on hospital practices.

The one set of external influences that cannot be readily captured in this industry is the role of philanthropists. Although philanthropy was historically an important source of funding for nonprofit psychiatric hospitals, its role has waned in recent years. In contrast, the influence of other community groups has grown. Consumer and family groups, most notably the so-called alliances for the mentally ill, have gained influence over the past fifteen years. Representing the interests of clients, these groups appear to be principally concerned with the array of services provided at the hospital (Flynn 1994).

In light of these features of inpatient psychiatric services, it seems sensible to revise several of our hypotheses linking particular external interests to specific dimensions of organizational performance. Because philanthropy is virtually absent, other community interests are likely to have the greatest influence over locally defined concerns. Because these groups are most linked to families of the mentally ill, one would expect them to be most concerned with ensuring that the array of services in the hospital was adequate. These concerns will be most influential in nonprofit settings if administrators are worried about the ability of local groups to undermine the legitimacy of the nonprofit's mission of community service.

H9A: Community interests will encourage a broader array of services in the hospital. Because the legitimacy of the nonprofit's mission depends in part on support from these groups, where community interests are stronger, there will be larger ownership-related differences in service mix.

As in other fields, professionals should favor the provision of prestigious services. Their lack of enthusiasm for treatment of chronic conditions may lead them to discourage the use of organizational resources to subsidize these activities. Because privately insured clients are more likely to use innovative services, while government-financed patients are more likely to need chronic support services, one might also expect professionals in this industry to favor privately insured clients over those supported by government. To the extent that professionals exert greater influence in nonprofit settings, one would expect to observe that

H10A: Where professional influence is greater, ownership-related differences will be more pronounced in the provision of innovative, technically advanced services and in efforts to attract privately insured patients. Greater professional influence will produce greater convergence in services for the chronically ill and in the treatment of publicly sponsored patients.

Methods of Analysis

The Data for the Analysis. Data for this study are drawn from a national survey of hospitals providing inpatient mental health care. The survey was fielded in late 1987 and data collected through the beginning of 1988. The sample frame included psychiatric specialty hospitals and general hospitals with psychiatric inpatient units. The survey was sent to approximately 1,500 facilities and had an overall response rate of just over 60 percent, yielding 915 observations. The survey collected (through a mailed questionnaire with telephone follow-up) data on a variety of characteristics of the hospital and the patients that it treated. These included the services that the hospital offered, referral arrangements and contracts with outside agencies, quality assurance and patient monitoring practices, composition and compensation of the staff, the diagnostic and payer mix of patients, as well as the hospital administrator's assessment of the competitiveness of the local market, the mission of the facility, and the amount of influence that various groups had in hospital decisions (Dorwart et al. 1991).

As part of the survey, hospital administrators were asked to define the service area of their hospital. Information on sociodemographic characteristics and health care resources was then aggregated to describe the hospital's potential patient population, using this self-defined service area. The bulk of this data was drawn from the Area Resource File, maintained by the National Technical Information Service. Variables characterizing the array of other mental health care providers in the area were calculated from the Inventory of Mental Health Care Organizations collected by the National Institute of Mental Health.

Dependent Variables for Measuring Organizational Performance. Theory suggests that to the extent that nonprofit and for-profit organizations differ, they will do so along several different dimensions, characterized here as (1) organizational attributes, (2) prestigious attributes of output, such as quality of services, and (3) community service. Cast in terms of the previous analysis, the organizational attributes represent nonpecuniary rewards that are most likely to be attractive to hospital administrators, prestigious output to medical professionals, and community service to external community

groups or regulators. Data from the survey can be used to construct five measures, each of which captures these three dimensions to varying degrees.

The first three variables are constructed from data on the services and managerial practices at the responding hospitals. Following the advice of an expert advisory panel, the survey was designed to collect information on aspects of hospital performance that would measure each of the three forms of nonpecuniary benefits described above. The first variable is an index (NEWMNDX1) combining four management practices oriented toward increasing admissions of privately insured clients: direct marketing to patients, encouraging of short-term treatment, contracting with insurance plans, and contracting with EAPs. These managerial practices have become basic strategies of administrators of psychiatric hospitals to protect or expand their client base, particularly in competitive markets (Jellinek and Nurcombe 1993). Although one would expect both nonprofit and for-profit hospitals to adopt these practices, nonprofit administrators who are maximizing the size of their organization are likely to pursue them more aggressively than will their counterparts in proprietary hospitals.

A second variable is intended to capture more prestigious aspects of mental health care treatment. This index (INDEX) combined four innovative services: treatment units for children/adolescents, geriatric psychiatry, eating disorders, and substance abuse. These are the aspects of mental health care in which there is the greatest professional interest in innovation and thus a potential sources of nonpecuniary rewards for professionals. Because services of this sort may also attract more patients, they may support a larger scale facility, generating nonpecuniary benefits of this sort as well. The managerial practices measured in NEWMNDX1, however, are unlikely to generate any prestige as a cutting-edge technology and thus are less likely to appeal to professionals or administrators who are more prestige-oriented.

The third variable is an index (NEWMNDX2) of management practices oriented primarily to the chronic mentally ill, who typically are publicly financed patients. This includes case management services as well as contracts with nursing homes and home health agencies. These are services that are appropriate primarily for people with chronic conditions. By attracting patients, these practices could also generate nonpecuniary benefits in the first dimension. But these services are not particularly prestigious and thus are less appealing to professionals than the innovative services in INDEX. The nonpecuniary benefits associated with them primarily involve serving a need that is normally unmet in most communities (Office of Technology Assessment 1990).

The fourth and fifth variables measure more directly quantifiable forms of community service: (a) the treatment of indigent patients (measured by the proportion of uncompensated care to all revenues) (INCOLL) and (b) the proportion of revenues from state contracts for care of the chronic mentally ill (GOVT). Care of the indigent is a conventional measure of community service. Treating patients under contracts with the state is less obviously a form of community service. These patients are often the most complex and difficult to treat, however, so that hospitals may lose money on them even if the state is ostensibly paying for their care. One might therefore see hospitals subsidizing the treatment of state contract patients out of motives similar to those for treating patients with no payment source at all (Wolff and Schlesinger 1995; Schlesinger and Dorwart 1984).

Independent Variables for Testing Hypotheses. For purposes of this chapter, the variable of greatest interest is facility ownership. This is measured by the self-reported legal form under which the facility is incorporated. Conventionally, studies comparing the performance of different forms of ownership simply enter ownership as a dummy variable. Variables of this sort are included here, reflecting nonprofit (NPROF) and for-profit (FPROF) ownership. (Public ownership is the omitted comparison group.)

I have suggested that the magnitude and nature of ownership-related differences will be related to a set of external influences on organizational behavior. One must therefore measure the prevalence of each of these external factors: market pressures, regulatory oversight, influence by community groups, purchase of services by large government programs, and provision of services by professionals.

The competitiveness of the local market for inpatient psychiatric services is measured here by the administrator's report of the intensity of competition, COMPIN (scored on a 1 to 5 scale in order of increasing competition). Though embodying the limitations of any subjective measure, reported competition seems preferable to the usual measures of market concentration (Herfindahl index or concentration ratios).[22] The service areas for hospitals providing mental health care are quite broad geographically because individuals often prefer hospitalization far from their home to reduce the risk of stigmatizing disclosures about mental illness. Hence, psychiatric hospitals tend to have market areas that are less localized than those of other hospitals and more difficult to define in geographic terms.

Following the logic developed above, competition was entered as an interactive term with ownership. COMPPROF and COMPNPRF measure the respective differential re-

sponse of for-profit and nonprofit hospitals to reported intensity of competition, relative to the response of government facilities.

The influence of community groups, state regulators, and the medical profession on hospital policies and practices was based on assessments reported by the hospital administrator. Administrators were asked to rate the influence of different groups on decisions about budgeting, clinical practices, and service mix at the hospital.[23] These were combined to form a single rating for the medical staff (MDINF), state regulators (STAINF) and local community groups (COMMINF).

Again, the appropriate empirical approach involves assessing the interaction of each of these influences with ownership, given that facilities under some forms of ownership are predicted to be more sensitive to these external pressures than are others. The measures of influence for regulators and community groups were therefore interacted with ownership, yielding two measures for nonprofit hospitals (STATNPRF and COMMNPRF, respectively) and two for proprietary hospitals (STATFPRF and COMMFPRF).

The influence of professional norms must be addressed in a somewhat different fashion. I suggested above that professional norms can interact with other external influences, particularly competitive pressures. The appropriate regression model must therefore do more than interact the influence of professionals with ownership alone. Details of this approach are discussed below.

The final external factor involves the influence of larger purchasers. Unfortunately, the survey did not collect data from hospital administrators on the influence that purchasers had over practices within the facility. As a substitute, I shall simply measure the proportion of the hospital's revenues that come from government programs. As suggested above, the program likely to produce the greatest isomorphism is Medicare, so the proportion of a hospital's revenues that came from Medicare (MCARE) served as the measure of what DiMaggio and Powell termed "coercive isomorphism."[24] Medicare payments ranged from a low of zero to a high of

---

22. Administrators' assessments of competition were inversely correlated with the Herfindahl index, as one would expect, but the simple correlation coefficient was a modest 0.08. Given the difficulties in using measures of market concentration in the health care field (White and Chirikos 1988) the subjective measures appear to be more reliable. In a complementary survey of administrators in community mental health centers (CMHCs), respondents were asked to rate the intensity of competition among hospitals in their service area. These assessments from CMHCs strongly correlated (a correlation coefficient of 0.35) with the reports from the hospital administrators and were more correlated with the subjective ratings by hospital administrators than with the Herfindahl index of market concentration.

23. Each of these was measured on a three-point scale, so that the cumulative index for the three aspects combined ranged from 3 to 9.

24. Because decisions by hospital administrators affect who is admitted to the facility, involvement with Medicare could be viewed as an endogenous variable, violating the assumptions that assure that the coefficients in ordinary-least-squares regressions will be unbiased. There is certainly evidence that hospital management attempts to alter physicians' admitting practices to achieve a more profitable payer mix (Schlesinger et al. 1987). Evidence from other sources, however, suggests that during the late 1980s, relatively few psychiatric hospitals attempted to influence the admission of Medicare beneficiaries. A survey conducted by the American Psychiatric Association found that a substantial number of hospitals attempted to discourage the admission of uninsured patients as well as patients covered by Medicaid. Fewer than 5 percent of psychiatrists with hospital affiliations reported that their hospital attempted to discourage the admission of Medicare patients.

80 percent of all hospital revenues. To capture differential effects, this variable is also interacted with for-profit (MCRFPROF) and nonprofit (MCRNPROF) ownership.

Measuring the impact of mimetic isomorphism is the most challenging empirical task. As discussed above, the norms that define the behavior to be emulated will themselves vary based on the extent of for-profit entry into an industry. To the extent that norms of legitimacy have been recast for psychiatric hospitals nationwide, it will be impossible to measure through a cross-sectional survey. To the extent that the norms are more local, it is possible to measure geographic variation in the convergence process by comparing areas with high entry by for-profits to those which have experienced limited entry. If my revised theory of mimetic behavior is accurate, one should observe nonprofit hospitals behaving more like for-profits in the first areas, proprietary facilities acting more like nonprofits in the second.

To test this hypothesis, one would need longitudinal data to measure the response of nonprofit hospitals to entry by for-profit competitors, compared to the prevailing practices in nonprofit facilities in areas in which there was no proprietary presence, controlling for the greater intensity of competition caused by the newly entering for-profit firms. In a one-time survey, the best one can do is to compare the magnitude of ownership-related differences in areas with minimal for-profit entry to areas in which entry has been more substantial. So long as the proprietary role in the first set of areas was sufficiently limited to have not shifted norms of legitimacy, one can test for impact of norms by comparing the performance in the two types of areas, again controlling for the intensity of competition. Unfortunately, we have no clear standard for when there has been sufficient entry to erode the legitimacy of nonproprietary goals in a local community. Consequently, any such categorization of areas will be somewhat arbitrary.

In the analyses presented below, several different measures were used. Some used the state in which the hospital was located as the relevant geographic area, others the county in which it was located. Various thresholds were used to define areas in which there was a large for-profit presence. The results reported below are based on one such definition: hospitals located in states in which more than 30 percent of the hospitals were operated for-profit were defined as being in high proprietary states (the results remained the same for different thresholds). Hospitals in states in which fewer than 10 percent of the hospitals were for-profit were defined as being in low proprietary states. Of all responding hospitals in the survey, 29 percent met the first criteria, 28 percent the second. Just over a quarter of all for-profit hospitals were located in low proprietary states, identified by a dichotomous variable (ISOPRFLO). A quarter of nonprofits were located in high proprietary states, also identified by a dichotomous variable (ISOPRFHI).

Other Independent Variables to Control for Exogenous

Influences on Hospital Performance. Other variables were included in the regression to capture the demand for different services or managerial practices in the facility. These included the level of income (PCI84), education (MSCH25), and extent of urbanization (URBNPOP) in the hospitals' service area. The first two variables are thought to increase both demand and awareness of service options. Higher population density should also make it easier to compare facilities located close to one another, increasing the demand for innovation. The regressions also included several facility characteristics that could influence the diffusion of innovations: the length of time under current ownership (OWNYR) and whether the hospital was a community general hospital (SPECHOSP) as opposed to one that specialized in psychiatric care. Because some hospitals were recently purchased by for-profit corporations, the incentives associated with the new ownership may not yet have influenced organizational practices. (Conversely, hospitals long under the same ownership may have closer ties to the local community and thus be more oriented toward community service.) General hospitals may be less sensitive to market pressures involving psychiatric care because they provide other services as well. Because they are not specialists in this field, general hospitals are less likely to have a full array of innovative services. The means and standard deviations for these variables, categorized by ownership, are presented in table 6.1.

Several variables were deliberately not included as statistical controls, although they are typically included in most studies of ownership in health care. This includes the size of the institution as well as whether the hospital was affiliated with a teaching program. Both of these variables differ significantly by ownership, and each is plausibly related to the dependent variables—large hospitals and teaching-affiliated hospitals are more likely to adopt services than are otherwise comparable facilities (Cromwell and Kanak 1982; Russell 1978), and teaching hospitals provide a disproportionate amount of uncompensated care (Sloan et al. 1986). These variables are excluded because they are themselves influenced by ownership. Controlling for them would thus obscure some of the implications of ownership.

Specification of Regression Models. Although some of the dependent variables are indices with a limited number of values, all five are treated here as continuous and the regressions estimated using ordinary least squares. Partially for heuristic reasons, partially because of the limited number of observations in the survey, four different sets of regressions were estimated using somewhat different approaches.

The first, simplest set—referred to here as the baseline regressions—is modeled on the conventional approach used in empirical studies of ownership. The effects of ownership are measured solely using the dummy variables. (These include both the standard dummy variables measuring the legal form of ownership and the two dummy variables calculated to measure mimetic isomorphism.) The influence of external

Table 6.1. Means and Standard Deviations of Variables Used in the Analyses

	Government-Run		Private Nonprofit		For-Profit	
	Mean	*S.D.*	*Mean*	*S.D.*	*Mean*	*S.D.*
Dependent Variables						
Private-Sector Contracting (NEWMNDX1)	1.31	0.99	2.09	1.15	2.34	1.27
Innovative Services (INDEX)	0.99	1.02	0.70	1.02	1.52	1.02
Public-Sector Contracting (NEWMNDX2)	0.63	0.77	0.75	0.79	0.26	0.52
Uncompensated Care (INCOLL)	33.58	29.62	11.69	12.53	8.52	8.76
State-Financed Patients (GOVT)	25.11	35.9	4.2	11.6	2.9	8.2
Independent Variables						
Intensity of Competition	1.99	1.37	3.49	1.18	4.04	1.03
Medical Influence	6.82	1.53	6.68	0.69	6.78	1.56
Community Influence	3.96	1.17	3.51	0.91	3.39	0.75
Influence by State Regulators	5.95	2.19	4.56	1.58	4.08	1.36
Percent Revenue from Medicare	18.7	16.3	24.1	13.3	15.1	14.4
Per Capita Income	12,703	2379	13,188	2418	13,302	2418
Median Years of Education	11.8	0.37	12.6	0.34	12.3	0.44
Percent Urban	73.1	21.4	76.31	21.29	79.69	18.62
Specialty Hospital	0.40	—	0.86	—	0.25	—
Years Under Current Ownership	57.26	42.86	55.84	40.94	8.90	10.03
Sample Size	296		477		142	

factors (competition, professional norms, regulators, community interest groups, and Medicare) is measured using the continuous variables described above, without allowing for interaction effects between the external influence and ownership. The results from this model emulate the measures of ownership that one finds in the literature, though they control for a more complete set of external influences than has any past study. To simulate the effects that would typically be estimated for ownership in most studies, the regressions were also estimated excluding all external factors except competition (the one environmental influence that is typically a part of past studies).

The second set of regressions introduces interactive effects — that is, allows each of the external factors to influence the behavior of nonprofit and for-profit facilities in different ways or degrees. I shall refer to these as the interaction regressions. As noted above, however, the influence of professional service providers is predicted to be more complicated than can be measured by these simple interactive terms — professional norms are predicted to mediate a variety of other external influences, particularly competition. To capture these effects, it is necessary to split the sample into facilities that report high and low levels of professional influence and estimate two separate sets of regression models.

The distribution of the measure of professional influence (MDINF) is roughly similar across the three forms of owner-

ship, with some modest differences in the tails (a chi-squared test determined there to be ownership-related differences in the distributions at a 5 percent confidence level). It therefore seems sensible to adopt a consistent measure of high medical influence that applies across all three forms of ownership, though the specific cutoff point is somewhat arbitrary. Consequently, the analysis of professional influence was based on several different definitions for *high medical influence*. The results from only one of these definitions is reported here.[25] (Changing the dividing criteria did not substantially alter the results.)

Because we have a limited number of observations, estimates that rely on a split sample and the full set of ownership-related interactive terms are likely to be unreliable (that is, the standard errors on the regression coefficients will be large). The limitations of the data make it impossible to address this problem in a completely satisfactory manner. The interaction regressions were estimated in two different ways. The first version uses the full sample. It includes interactive

25. Defining *high influence* as a score for MDINF greater than six places 61 percent of the hospitals in this category. Setting of the cutoff at scores greater than seven identified 37 percent of the hospitals in the high influence group. To identify those facilities that have the highest levels of professional influence, the results reported in the test use the high threshold.

terms for all the external factors other than professional norms (for example, competition, regulation, community interests, Medicare, and mimetic processes). A simple measure of professional influence is included as a control variable in these regressions.

The second set of interaction regressions divides the sample into high and low levels of professional influence. These will be labeled the split sample regressions. These regressions include measures of the other external effects, but *not* interacted with ownership. The sole exception involves competitive effects, which were predicted to be mediated by professional norms. The full set of ownership-related interactive measures for competition are included in these regressions.

As I noted in the critique of past empirical research, it is implausible to treat each aspect of the organization or its practices as independent of other aspects. Each organization has a limited surplus, so that devoting more of it to one activity that yields nonpecuniary rewards means devoting less to some other potentially rewarding practice. Other relationships between the dependent variables may exist as well. For example, the hospital that offers a more innovative array of services may find it easier to establish contracts for private clients.

These predicted interactions among the dependent variables have implications for the specification of the regression models. In principle, one ought to estimate all five regressions as part of a simultaneous system, incorporating in each regression the other four dependent variables, to measure how each dependent variable effects the others. To do this, however, one must be able to identify the regressions — that is, each regression must include some independent variables that affect the provision of the dependent variable in that regression, but none of the other dependent variables from the other equations. Unfortunately, this survey lacked a sufficiently rich set of variables to adequately identify all five regressions. In particular, there are no variables that could plausibly be argued to affect treatment of clients covered under government contracts, but not indigent patients. Similarly, there are no plausible measures that affect contracts for chronic care services (NEWMNDX2), but not willingness to treat government-funded clients, who mostly have chronic mental illness.

Because we cannot fully identify our equations, the primary results presented in this section are not based on estimating a simultaneous system. It is important, however, to consider whether these interactions among dependent variables are in fact occurring, both for interpreting the findings here and as an illustration of more general principles that should be addressed in future empirical work in this area. For this reason, a fourth set of regressions are estimated using four of the dependent variables — the number of clients supported by government contracts is dropped from the analysis. This smaller set of equations can be sensibly identified, using variables which are described below.

Regression Results

I consider first the results from the baseline regressions, then the relevant findings for each of the eleven hypotheses drawn from the interaction regressions. To simplify comparisons of results across the five regressions, the tables in this section will present the findings in a standardized format: Each estimated effect will be presented as a percentage change relative to the mean of the dependent variable for all hospitals in the sample.[26] I conclude by discussing the results from the simultaneous equation system.

The Baseline Regressions. Theory suggests that one should find significant ownership-related differences in all of our five dependent variables. The results from the baseline regressions indicate that, if one does not control for the influence of external factors (other than competition), there are substantial ownership-related differences in each of these five areas. In only four of these dimensions, however, are nonprofit hospitals ranked higher — it is for-profit hospitals that offer a broader array of innovative services. The differences range in magnitude from over 80 percent of the mean to just under 10 percent of the mean (see table 6.2). All are statistically significant at conventional levels. Controlling for the more complete set of external influences only slightly changes these results.

Although the various external controls do not, in this specification, greatly affect the estimates of ownership-related differences, they do influence the five aspects of organizational performance measured in this study. Market competition and Medicare have the most consistent effects, being significant in three and four regressions, respectively. Both community groups and state regulators appear to influence some aspects of organizational behavior, but not others. We had hypothesized that each of these actors would favor particular dimensions of organizational behavior. As predicted, hospitals which reported higher levels of influence by regulators treated more indigent clients and more patients under state contracts (though only the latter of these two relationships was statistically significant). Also as hypothesized, hospitals that reported more influence by community groups offered more innovative services and had more contracts to provide for chronic care. (Only the first of these relationships was statistically significant.)

In this set of regressions, the medical staff at the hospital did not consistently influence hospital practices. As we shall see, however, this apparent lack of influence is an artifact of the manner in which professional influence was modeled in these regressions.

The dual measure of mimetic isomorphism also did not

---

26. Space limitations prevent publication of the complete regression results for the various specifications of these models. The complete results can be obtained from the Program on Non-Profit Organizations at Yale University, under a working paper bearing the same title as this chapter.

Table 6.2. Magnitude of Ownership Related Differences, as a Percent of Mean Dependent Variable Baseline Regressions with and without Controls for External Influences

Terms of Comparison (Regression Specification)	Measures of Organizational Behavior				
	NEWMNDX1	INDEX	NEWMNDX2	INCOLL	GOVT
	NPRF vs. FPRF	NPRF vs. FPRF	NPRF vs. FPRF	NPRF vs. FPRF	NPRF vs. FPRF
Baseline Regressions[1]	8.2%#	−26.8%*	62.2%*	18.1%#	82.7%*
Including Other External Influences	12.1%*	−14.1%	46.0%*	13.6%	86.7%*

\# Stat. significant at 10% confidence level

* Stat. significant at 5% level

[1] These regressions control only for competition

reveal any influence on ownership-related behavior.[27] This lack of positive findings may indicate that mimicry does not in fact depend on the prevailing mix of ownership in a locality. On the other hand, it may simply reflect our inability to specify clearly the point at which this shift in legitimacy takes place. In any case, given this failure to document any effects, these variables were omitted from subsequent regressions.

The Interaction Regressions. In general, these regressions suggest that some, though not all, external factors appear to influence nonprofit and for-profit organizations in different ways or in differing degrees. To provide a more detailed assessment, it is useful to consider each of the specific hypotheses in the order that they were presented above.

State Regulators and Community Interests. The first hypothesis predicted that regulators and community interest groups would exert greater influence over the behavior of nonprofit than for-profit firms. There are several ways in which this influence might be measured. The first involves the direct reports from administrators. As can be seen in table 6.1, administrators in nonprofit hospitals report substantially larger influence by state regulators than do their counterparts in for-profit facilities. The influence of community groups is only slightly larger in nonprofit settings, and this difference is not statistically significant.

A second way of assessing external factors is through their influence on organizational performance. This can be derived from the regression coefficients on the influence variables. Averaging across the five dependent variables, a given increase in either community or regulatory influence is associated with a change in organizational behavior that is

27. For dimensions in which nonprofit hospitals typically are more involved than their for-profit counterparts, if there is ownership-related mimicry one ought to observe a negative sign on ISOPRFHI and a positive sign on ISOPRFLO. In only one of the dimensions was this the case (NEWMNDX1), and even here the differences were not statistically significant.

two-thirds larger in nonprofit than for-profit settings (table 6.3). These differences in magnitude are mirrored in the statistical significance of the relationships between community and regulatory influences and the five dependent variables. In only one case are these relationships statistically significant in for-profit hospitals. They are significant half the time in nonprofit hospitals.

Measured in any of these terms, the results support the first hypothesis — that pressures from regulators and community interests are significantly more important in shaping the behavior of nonprofit organizations than of otherwise similar for-profit organizations. These external influences are more pronounced in nonprofit settings and have greater consequences in changing practices. The interactive effects appear to be greatest for government regulation, perhaps because community-based philanthropy does not play a major role in this industry.

One goal of specifying the external influences that mediate ownership is to predict with greater accuracy the particular form that ownership-related differences will take under variations in circumstances. I suggested that in those dimensions most favored by outside actors, an increase in outside influences could increase ownership-related differences if those actors had a greater influence on nonprofit organizations than on for-profit facilities. The baseline regressions suggest that regulators are most interested in quantifiable measures of hospital behavior, while community interest groups are most concerned about the availability of services through the hospital. Each of these groups appears to have greater influence over nonprofit hospitals. One should therefore expect to find that greater external influences exacerbate ownership-related differences in these dimensions.

The results from the interaction regressions provide some support for these hypotheses. For example, compare hospitals operating under little state regulation (the first two rows of table 6.4). (In table 6.4 and those that follow, each entry represents the magnitude of ownership-related differences

Table 6.3. Differential Impact of External Influences, by Ownership of Organization

Types of External Influence	Ownership of Responding Organization	
	Private Nonprofit Hospitals	For-Profit Hospitals
Average Impact (Absolute Value)[1]		
Community Interests	20.2%	12.3%
State Regulators	14.9%	8.6%
Percent Statistically Significant		
Community Interests	40 Percent	20 Percent
State Regulators	60 Percent	None

[1]Predicted change in the dependent variable for a 30% change in the dependent variables.

for a given aspect of hospital behavior and the specified change in external influence.) Among hospitals reporting high levels of influence by community groups (row 2), the ownership-differential for innovative services (INDEX) was 86 percent of the mean value for this variable; for contracts involving long-term care (NEWMNDX2) the difference was 70 percent. Among hospitals in which community influence was small (row 1), ownership differences in these two dimensions were also small. Higher levels of regulatory influence are associated with larger differences in the availability of treatment for indigent patients by nonprofit hospitals, compared to the standards of their for-profit counterparts. Compare hospitals with small influence by community groups (the first and third rows in the table). When regulatory influence is low (row 1) the difference in the provision of uncompensated care (INCOLL) is less than 10 percent of the mean. When regulatory influence is high (row 3), the difference in uncompensated care is predicted to be 40 percent of the mean.[28]

Assessing the influence of regulators and community groups did yield some unexpected results, particularly associated with the impact of regulation on ownership-related behavior. Where regulators had more influence, nonprofits did not appear distinctly more open to treating patients under state contract. Regulation was associated, however, with a larger differential in contracting for chronic care services (the difference for NEWMNDX2 grows from −6 percent in row 1 to 51 percent in row 3). Because patients under state contracts are more likely to need these services, it appears that regulators are using their greater authority in nonprofit settings to leverage changes in service mix, rather than access to the hospital. Also surprising, regulatory influence appears to distinctly discourage the adoption of innovative services by nonprofit hospitals.[29] Taken together, these find-

ings may reflect efforts by regulators to shift nonprofit hospitals away from the market for the privately insured toward other community needs.

Professional Influences. Assessing the impact of professionalization is complicated because professionals may mediate the influence of other factors and have a particularly complex role in terms of competitive pressures on hospital behavior. As a result, there is no simple measure of the influence of professionals — because that influence depends on the intensity of competition in local markets. The estimated effects are summarized in table 6.4, which reports the predicted size of ownership-related differences in the five dependent variables under high and low levels of professional influence as well as high and low levels of competition.[30] Although one can use these results to examine the effects of both professionalism and competition, I consider only the first of these at this point.

The results from these split sample regressions suggest that the apparent lack of influence of professions over hospital behavior in the baseline regressions was deceptive. Varying levels of professional influence are associated with substantial shifts in the magnitude of ownership-related differences in behavior.

Conventional analyses of professionalization and ownership predict that professional norms will reduce ownership-related differences in behavior. The analysis presented above, however, predicts that in dimensions that professionals most favor, their influence may actually increase ownership-related differences. I suggested that psychiatrists will be most in favor of innovative treatments and privately insured clientele. One would therefore predict that the greater the professional influence, the larger the ownership-related differences in these dimensions, but the smaller for the other three variables.

28. These particular values depend on the level of other external influences, such as competition and purchasing by Medicare. However, the *relative* magnitude of ownership-related differences as one moves from high to low regulation, or high to low influence by community groups, is unrelated to these other factors.

29. This is not simply relative to for-profit hospitals. Nonprofits that were more influenced by regulators were less likely to adopt innovative

treatments in an absolute sense, as well as relative to hospitals operating under other forms of ownership.

30. Because these split-sample regressions did not interact ownership with the other external influences, these simply act as controls in the regressions.

Table 6.4. The Influence of State Regulation and Community Interest Groups on Ownership-Related Differences in Hospital Performance

	Measures of Organizational Behavior				
	NEWMNDX1	INDEX	NEWMNDX2	INCOLL	GOVT
Terms of Comparison (Type of External Influence)[1]	NPRF vs. FPRF	NPRF vs. FPRF	NPRF vs. FPRF	NPRF vs. FPRF	NPRF vs. FPRF
Low State/Low Community#	49.5%	15.1%	−6.3%	8.5%	51.8%
Low State/High Community	−20.0%	86.0%	69.8%	0.1%	146.9%
High State/Low Community	52.6%	−75.3%	50.8%	40.3%	30.5%
High State/High Community	−16.8%	−0.1%	127.0%	36.6%	125.5%

\# Influence of state regulators is self-reported by hospital administrators, with multiple responses combined into a seven-point scale. Low influence represents a scale score of one, high influence a scale score of seven. The influence of community groups is coded and scored in a similar manner.
[1] Regression results assume the competitive pressures and influence of government purchasers are at intermediate levels.

For hospitals located in less competitive markets, this is exactly what one observes (see the first two rows of table 6.5). Higher levels of professional influence are associated with larger ownership-related differences for innovative services and private-sector contracting, but smaller differences for services for the chronically ill, treatment of indigent patients, and treatment of patients paid for through state government contracts. The pattern is quite different in highly competitive markets, a complication to which I shall return below.

Purchasing by Large Government Agencies. Following the logic of coercive isomorphism, it was argued that the greater the dependence of the hospital on a nationwide program such as Medicare, the more standardized would be its operation and the smaller the ownership-related differences in organizational practices. The baseline regressions suggest that Medicare involvement is associated with significant differences in hospital behavior. The interaction regressions suggest that this influence does in fact produce significant convergence of behavior, though only for some dimensions of organizational performance (table 6.6). Convergence is most pronounced in the innovative services offered at the facility and the extent of treatment of patients under state contracts. Substantial involvement with Medicare is associated with the tendency for nonprofit hospitals to offer more innovative services; but in high-Medicare hospitals, nonprofits' greater involvement with state-financed patients is half as large as in hospitals with few Medicare patients.

Competitive Pressures. Theory suggests that competitive pressures should produce a convergence in the behavior of nonprofit and for-profit organizations. The interaction regressions suggest that this is generally the case (table 6.7). If one compares areas under limited competitive pressures (the first row) to those in which competition is more intense (the second and third rows), the magnitude of ownership-related differences tends to be larger in the first set of markets. The sole exception to this pattern involves contracting for long-term care services, but in this case the estimated relationship between competition and organizational performance was not statistically significant.

It was hypothesized that competition might interact with professional influence in either of two ways. In the first, professionals act as buffers to protect certain aspects of organizational behavior from cuts when competition has reduced the organization's surplus (hypothesis 6). To test this hypothesis, we return to the results from the split sample regressions (see table 6.5). If the hypothesis is correct, then when professionals exert a strong influence over hospital practices and competition grows more intense (compare the second and fourth rows in the table) there should be smaller declines in ownership-related differences in more private-sector innovations (the first two columns) than in treatment of indigent or state-financed patients (the last two columns). This does not appear to be the case.

I had also hypothesized that competition among hospitals might increase the bargaining power of professionals and thus increase ownership-related differences in those dimensions they most favor. If this were the case, one would expect that moving from low to high MD influence would exert a larger influence on organizational behavior in high competition areas than in low competition areas (that is, the change in the ownership-related differential would be larger comparing rows 3 and 4 than rows 1 and 2). This is in fact true for innovative treatments but not for contracts to attract privately insured patients.

Although these results offer little support for the hypothesized interactions of professional norms and competitive mar-

Table 6.5. Professional Influences and Ownership-Related Differences in Organizational Behavior

Terms of Comparison (Type of External Influence)	Measures of Organizational Behavior				
	NEWMNDX1 NPRF vs. FPRF	INDEX NPRF vs. FPRF	NEWMNDX2 NPRF vs. FPRF	INCOLL NPRF vs. FPRF	GOVT NPRF vs. FPRF
Low MD#/Low Competition*	31.5%	24.8%	66.7%	61.4%	191.8%
High MD/Low Competition	59.1%	33.9%	27.2%	29.2%	34.7%
Low MD/High Competition	−7.6%	−64.6%	60.2%	11.8%	79.2%
High MD/High Competition	4.5%	−1.8%	77.8%	16.5%	110.5%

\# Levels of professional influence calculated as reported in the text.

* Competition is measured on a five-point scale. "Low competition" represents the lowest score on the sacle, "high competition" the highest score.

kets, they do reveal a curious pattern between these two external influences. In areas with limited competition, hospitals in which the medical staff is most influential have substantially smaller ownership-related differentials in treating indigent clients or patients covered by state contracts or providing chronic care services. This seems compatible with professional preferences. In areas with high competition, however, the opposite pattern occurs. Greater professional influence is associated with larger ownership-related differences.

One possible explanation would emerge if competition had so reduced the ability of nonprofit hospitals to differentiate themselves that professionals grew uncomfortable and demanded that resources be shifted to these areas. The findings involving care of indigent patients fit this story. The difference between nonprofit and for-profit hospitals in terms of uncompensated care in areas with high competition and limited professional influence is smaller than the difference in areas with little competition and substantial professional influence. Professionals may expect certain differences from nonprofit organizations and act to preserve those differences in the face of competition. Yet this rationale cannot explain the findings for state contract patients or chronic care services. In these dimensions, hospitals that face high competition and have limited influence from their medical staff have larger ownership-related differences than hospitals in which the medical staff has significant influence and there are few competitive pressures. But increased professional influence is still associated with larger ownership-related differences for these variables.

Interactions among the Dependent Variables. The hypothesis-testing in this chapter drew on a number of different specifications for the regressions relating ownership and external influences to organizational performance. As noted earlier, though, in at least one sense these specifications are inappropriate: they fail to directly model the interaction of the five dimensions of organizational behavior. These are almost certainly related, in part by budgetary considerations, in part because the various external actors will have preferences that combine several of these dimensions. Ignoring of these effects introduces an unknown bias into the findings.

Because I was unable to fully identify the five equations as a simultaneous system, I have to this point ignored this interaction. By restricting the analysis to four variables (INDEX, NEWMNDX1, NEWMNDX2 and INCOLL), however, the system can be estimated. Each equation was identified by introducing explanatory variables thought to be uniquely related to that dependent variable.[31] The system was estimated by a three-stage least squares technique.

Because the system was not very well identified and because it omitted some dimensions of organizational perfor-

31. Identifying equations is something of an exercise in ad hoc rationalization. I will not present at length the rationale for the use of particular variables but simply list them here. The variables included in the regression for innovative services (INDEX) were (1) whether the state had a certificate-of-need program that regulates hospitals adding new services, (2) the supply of psychiatrists in the local community (county), and (3) whether the hospital had a teaching affiliation. The variables included in the regression on private sector contracting (NEWMNDX1) were (1) the number of HMOs operating in the county, (2) whether the state had passed legislation enabling the development of preferred provider insurance plans (these selectively contract with providers), and (3) the generosity of the state's requirements for private insurance coverage of inpatient psychiatric treatment. Variables included in the regression on chronic care services (NEWMNDX2) were (1) whether the state Medicaid program covered psychiatric hospitalization for the elderly and (2) whether the Medicaid program paid for intermediate care facilities for the mentally ill. Variables associated with the level of uncompensated care at the hospital (INCOLL) included (1) the state's mandated levels of insurance coverage for both inpatient and outpatient treatment and (2) the generosity of state spending on public mental health care services.

Table 6.6. The Influence of Medicare on Ownership-Related Differences in Hospital Behavior

Terms of Comparison (Type of External Influence)[1]	Measures of Organizational Behavior				
	NEWMNDX I	INDEX	NEWMNDX2	INCOLL	GOVT
	NPRF vs. FPRF	NPRF vs. FPRF	NPRF vs. FPRF	NPRF vs. FPRF	NPRF vs. FPRF
Low Medicare #	50.0%	45.1%	−5.1%	11.9%	67.7%
Moderate Medicare	48.9%	14.0%	−7.0%	8.9%	51.9%
High Medicare	47.9%	−17.2%	−8.9%	6.3%	32.1%

\# Low involvement = 10% of revenues from Medicare, moderate involvement = 20%, high involvement = 30%.

[1] Regression results assume that competitive pressures are at intermediate levels, state and community influences are low.

mance (for example, GOVT), one should not place great credence in the estimated relationships. They do suggest that there are, as expected, significant interactions among the four dimensions. A hospital's orientation toward innovative treatment was positively correlated with the extent of uncompensated care at the facility but negatively correlated with the extent of contracting for chronic care services. There was also a positive correlation between contracts for chronic care services and contracts with the private sector, presumably reflecting a common orientation toward attracting more patients to the facility. These findings suggest that future research related to ownership should recognize the interaction among different dimensions of organizational performance.

DISCUSSION AND CONCLUSION

Having reviewed an extensive literature, developed a number of hypotheses, and tested them using a variety of empirical specifications, I think it is probably useful to step back to a somewhat more general level of discussion, returning to the basic questions with which I began this chapter. I can now shed some additional light on these issues and also explore in organizational terms some of the issues that were identified at the individual level in the accompanying chapters by Alan Wolfe and Jane Mansbridge.

This inquiry is motivated by two basic claims. The first is that empirical studies of ownership are fundamentally flawed by their failure to accurately model the ways in which external factors mediate the relative performance of nonprofit and for-profit organizations. The second claim is that the theoretical literature has been misinterpreted as it is applied to the role of these external influences. Past discussions presume that external factors invariably induce convergence in organizational behavior. They overlook equally plausible and potentially important ways in which those external factors may encourage — in some cases are a necessary condition for — persisting differences between nonprofit and for-profit behavior.

The foregoing empirical analysis of inpatient psychiatric

hospitals offers some support for each of these claims. Greater influence by community groups, state regulators, and medical professionals was associated with *larger* differences between nonprofit and for-profit behavior. The findings suggest that community groups and regulatory agencies do exert greater influence in nonprofit settings than in otherwise comparable proprietary organizations. Larger purchasers and competitive pressures narrow ownership-related differences, though competitive pressures in some cases appear to be offset by the influence of professional service providers.

The nature and magnitude of ownership-related differences consequently depend to a considerable extent on the organization's external environment. From the standpoint of organizational theory, this proposition ought to seem virtually self-evident. Yet those who study the role of legal ownership persist in trying to answer the question, Does ownership matter? or its close cousin, How does ownership matter? In light of the important role of external factors in creating and sustaining ownership-related differences, the more appropriate question should be, Under what conditions does ownership matter?[32]

Because appropriate framing of this question is so important, it merits a return to our findings for purposes of illustration. Attempts to answer the question, Does ownership matter? for psychiatric hospitals yield results such as those presented in table 6.2. The sophistication of the researcher (as evidenced by the number of external factors included in the regression as control variables) has some influence on the

32. Even in this revised form, the accurate measuring of the relationship between ownership and organizational performance is not a simple matter. It is complicated by the fact that external conditions that influence ownership-related differences may also affect the mix of ownership in an industry by encouraging either nonprofit or for-profit firms to disproportionately exit. As Weisbrod has observed, one is measuring performance only among the survivors. Consequently, the influence of any external factor involves both its direct effect on organizations that provide services and the indirect effect from altering the mix of ownership and thus the norms that legitimate particular standards of organizational behavior.

Table 6.7. The Influence of Competition on Ownership-Related Hospital Performance

Terms of Comparison *(Type of External Influence)*[1]	Measures of Organizational Behavior				
	NEWMNDX1 NPRF vs. FPRF	INDEX NPRF vs. FPRF	NEWMNDX2 NPRF vs. FPRF	INCOLL NPRF vs. FPRF	GOVT NPRF vs. FPRF
Low Competition*	73.2%	76.3%	−14.7%	27.1%	77.0%
Moderate Competition	50.0%	45.1%	−5.1%	11.9%	67.7%
High Competition	26.8%	11.8%	4.4%	−4.7%	58.3%

* Competition measured on a five-point scale reported by hospital administrators. Low competition = 1, moderate = 3, high = 5.
[1]Regression results assume that influence of Medicare, state regulations, and community groups are all low.

results, but basically they seem quite stable. Nonprofit hospitals are more inclined to treat government-sponsored patients and to provide services oriented to chronic care. Other than that, differences are quite modest, with some evidence that nonprofit hospitals offer a less innovative set of services.

Contrast these findings with several scenarios captured in our subsequent analyses. Consider the relative performance of nonprofit and for-profit hospitals in what could be termed monitored industries, that is, industries in which the influence of both community groups and state regulators is high (see the fourth row in table 6.4). Under these circumstances, nonprofit hospitals are even more pronounced in their differential treatment of state-financed patients and those with chronic conditions. But they are also distinctly more likely to treat patients with no insurance at all. And there are no discernable differences in the degree of innovation between nonprofit and for-profit hospitals. Contrast this with hospital behavior in unmonitored environments (see the first row in table 6.4). Here, nonprofit organizations seem to shift their attention to the private sector and are no more inclined to address chronic illness or indigent care than are their for-profit counterparts. Compare this with hospital behavior in which there is low competition and limited influence by medical professionals (see the first row in table 6.5). In these settings nonprofit hospitals differentiate themselves even more substantially by their treatment of the poor. But they are also distinctly *more* innovative than their for-profit counterparts and also more likely to establish contracts with the private sector.

In short, the picture of how ownership matters appears to depend greatly on the setting in which the organization operates. In each setting, some ownership-related differences exist, but the prevailing combination is different in each setting. For each of the five dependent variables, the differences are substantial under at least some set of external conditions. But only one of these measures (serving state-financed patients) demonstrates differences that persist under all the combinations of external conditions studied here.

By ignoring these interactions or by measuring the effects of ownership through dichotomous measures of legal status, analysts of organizational behavior are essentially replicating the error that Wolfe accuses psychologists of making when they cast altruism solely in terms of individual motivation. Both approaches set behavior apart from its social context, which makes it impossible to accurately predict behavior. Equally important, it makes it impossible to understand the meaning of the behavior being studied. For example, a hospital that uses 5 percent of its revenues to care for the uninsured in a highly competitive market may be more deeply motivated by altruism than its counterpart that has 7 percent of its patients uninsured in a community in which it is the sole provider. The first institution may be devoting its entire surplus to uncompensated care. The second hospital likely has a much larger surplus and may be using much of it for purposes that simply further the self-interest of its administrators.

Focusing more carefully on the extent and nature of external constraints is not simply a way to remedy past methodological errors. It also offers the opportunity to increase the predictive capacity of existing models of ownership. At least for psychiatric hospitals, knowing which external factors exert the strongest influence allows one to predict, in a somewhat reliable manner, the dimensions in which nonprofit and for-profit organizations will behave most distinctly. Using this approach, one can go beyond the overly general prediction that the nondistribution constraint encourages greater use of *some* form of nonpecuniary reward. Once there has been more complete analysis of the role of external factors, researchers should be better able to predict the consequences of ownership for various socially valued outcomes.

This chapter should be viewed as an exploratory inquiry into this broad set of issues. Because it draws on data from a single industry, there is little reason to expect that the specific findings will generalize to other types of services, particularly to those in which professional norms are significantly stronger or philanthropy a more important source of revenue than it is for psychiatric hospitals. The analysis is further limited by some flawed empirical measures. Many of the external factors were measured through reports by hospital administrators; such subjective measures may contain biases. The measure of competition can be somewhat validated using other data (Schlesinger et al. 1995). No comparable validation was available for influences by the community, state regulators, or physicians.[33] And we lacked an adequate array of variables to identify the sort of simultaneous system that ought to be used to understand the interactions among different hospital practices.

These limitations can be addressed in subsequent empirical research. But it seems unlikely that any methodological refinements will overturn the basic conclusions presented here: that the consequences of differences in legal ownership depend on the environment in which an organization operates. Findings of this sort shed some light on Mansbridge's proposal to "nest" altruistic motives in an appropriately supportive social context. If one takes treatment of the uninsured as a marker for altruism in the psychiatric hospital industry, it is apparent that some external factors (for example, competitive markets, influence by large collective purchasers) weaken the distinctive nonprofit commitment to altruistic endeavors, while others (for example state regulatory influence) strengthen those ownership-related differences.

The two factors that undercut the nonprofit role in serving the indigent stem from distinctly different ideologies, one resting on market principles, the other on government's efforts to secure a right to health care for a specific population. Yet both factors change the broad criteria under which nonprofit organizations are assessed by society, criteria which had previously, in Mansbridge's terms, "publicly acknowledged and praised the public-spirited motivation." In so doing, both these changes in the financing of health care undermined social recognition for altruistic endeavors by nonprofit medical providers. By emphasizing businesslike practices, a market orientation may not only reduce the approbation for altruistic activities, but portray them as essentially unprofessional (Kinzer 1984). By expanding the notion of a government-financed right to health care, public insurance programs like Medicare create the (false) impression that there is little need for health care providers to be concerned with indigent patients, particularly when Medicare covers the groups that are viewed as the most deserving by society (Gray 1993; Marmor et al. 1987).

But if these findings reinforce one point that Mansbridge makes, they cast doubt on a second. She suggests that government authorities allow nonprofit organizations more discretion to reward their more altruistic orientation. Yet data from psychiatric hospitals suggest that when the influence of

state regulators is low, ownership-related differences in the treatment of the uninsured virtually disappear (see table 6.4). Regulatory oversight appears to be a prerequisite for altruistic behavior, at least in this industry and the forms measured by this study.[34] When this oversight is absent, other ownership-related differences emerge, including a greater emphasis on innovative services in nonprofit settings. But these have very different implications for societal welfare than do services that benefit the indigent.

These findings also raise some deeper conceptual questions. Is ownership more appropriately conceived as a set of institutional restrictions or a set of social relations? To the extent that outside actors hold certain expectations based on their perceptions of ownership, and those perceptions are self-reinforcing (for example, they lead the organization to behave in a manner compatible with the expectation), are these perceptions any less inherent in what we view as ownership than are legal requirements?

These are not questions that are simply answered. They must, however, be addressed because they hold important implications for both public policy and our understanding of the role of nonprofit organizations in modern societies. Many policymakers see nonprofit organizations as low-cost means of achieving socially desirable goals because their nonprofit nature assures that they will behave in a responsible manner in the absence of external monitoring (Smith and Lipsky 1993). Our analyses suggest that while some ownership-related differences exist when there is little external oversight, they may not reflect the goals most favored by policymakers.

Ownership-related differences that emerge only when there is regulatory oversight are no less a product of ownership. But in this case ownership creates the potential for differences, which are realized only under the appropriate conditions. If the distinction between potential and real effects is understood, the former can be just as valuable to society. But until policymakers comprehend the importance of external factors in mediating the effects of ownership, this form of institutional design will never yield the benefits that would otherwise be achievable.

REFERENCES

Abbot, Andrew. 1988. *The System of Professions: An Essay on the Division of Expert Labor.* Chicago: University of Chicago Press.

33. An indirect form of validation was possible by examining correlations between the variables used here and others that should be plausibly associated with them. For example, hospitals that reported more influence from the community were also the ones with the most active connections to community-based institutions (CMHCs). Hospitals that reported more physician influence were also more likely to be affiliated with a medical school. Such correlations are reassuring but offer no true validation.

34. On this point, it merits reemphasizing the dangers of generalizing from the experience with a particular service or industry. The psychiatric hospital industry is extremely competitive, professionalized, and commercialized. In some other industry, one in which donations provided more substantial funding for nonprofit firms, in which volunteers played a larger role, and in which community-based philanthropists had more influence on an organization's policies, regulatory influences might suppress rather than enhance ownership-related differences in serving the indigent.

Allen, Robin. 1992. "Policy Implications of Recent Hospital Competition Studies." *Journal of Health Economics* 11:347–51.

Arling, Greg, Richard Nordquist, and John Captiman. 1987. "Nursing Home Cost and Ownership Type: Evidence of Interaction Effects." *Health Services Research* 22(2):255–69.

Bays, Carson. 1983. "Why Most Private Hospitals Are Nonprofit." *Journal of Policy Analysis and Management* 2:366–85.

Ben-Ner, Avner, and Theresa Van Hoomissen. 1993. "Nonprofit Organizations in the Mixed Economy: A Demand and Supply Analysis." In *The Nonprofit Sector in the Mixed Economy,* ed. Avner Ben-Ner and Benedetto Gui, 27–58. Ann Arbor: University of Michigan Press.

Brotman, Andrew. 1992. "Report from the Field—Privatization of Mental Health Services: The Massachusetts Experience." *Journal of Health Politics, Policy and Law* 17:541–51.

Campbell, Ellen, and Melissa Ahern. 1993. "Have Procompetitive Changes Altered Hospital Provision of Indigent Care?" *Health Economics* 2:281–89.

Caplan, Arthur. 1988. "Is Medical Care the Right Prescription for Chronic Illness?" In *The Economics and Ethics of Long-Term Care and Disability,* ed. S. Sullivan and M. Lewin. Washington, D.C.: American Enterprise Institute.

Chillerni, Ottorino, and Benedetto Gui. 1991. "Uninformed Customers and Nonprofit Organization." *Economics Letters* 35(1):5–8.

Clarke, Lee, and Carroll Estes. 1992. "Sociological and Economic Theories of Markets and Nonprofits: Evidence from Home Health Organizations." *American Journal of Sociology* 97(4):945–69.

Clarkson, Kenneth. 1972. "Some Implications of Property Rights in Hospital Management." *Journal of Law and Economics* 8:363–84.

Cromwell, J., and J. Kanak. 1982. "The Effects of Prospective Reimbursement Programs on Hospital Adoption and Service Setting." *Health Care Financing Review* 4(2):67–88.

Davidson, Harriet, Mark Schlesinger, Robert Dorwart, and Elizabeth Schnell. 1991. "States' Purchase of Mental Health Care: Models and Motivations for Maintaining Accountability." *International Journal of Law and Psychiatry* 14:387–403.

DiMaggio, Paul, and Helmut Anheier. 1990. "The Sociology of Nonprofit Organizations and Sectors." *Annual Review of Sociology* 16:137–59.

DiMaggio, Paul, and Walter Powell. 1983. "The Iron Cage Revisited: Institutional Isomorphism and Collective Rationality in Organizational Fields." *American Sociological Review* 48:147–60.

Dorwart, Robert, and Sherrie Epstein. 1993. *Privatization and Mental Health Care: A Fragile Balance.* Westport, Conn.: Auburn House.

Dorwart Robert, Mark Schlesinger, Harriet Davidson, Sherrie Epstein, and Claudia Hoover. 1991. "A National Study of Psychiatric Hospital Care." *American Journal of Psychiatry* 148(2):204–10.

Dorwart, Robert, and Mark Schlesinger. 1988. "Privatization of Psychiatric Services." *American Journal of Psychiatry* 145:543–53.

Dranove, David, Mark Shanley, and Carol Simon. 1992. "Is Hospital Competition Wasteful?" *Rand Journal of Economics* 23(2):247–62.

Easley, D., and M. O'Hara. 1988. "Contracts and Asymmetric Information in the Theory of the Firm." *Journal of Economic Behavior and Organization* 9:229–46.

Eisenberg, John. 1986. *Doctors' Decisions and the Cost of Medical Care.* Ann Arbor: Health Administration Press.

Etzioni, A., and P. Doty. 1981. "Profit in Not-for-Profit Corporations: The Example of Health Care." *Political Science Quarterly* 91:431–53.

Evans, Robert. 1984. *Strained Mercy.* Toronto: Butterworths.

Feldstein, Martin. 1971. "Hospital Price Inflation: A Study of Nonprofit Price Dynamics." *American Economic Review* 61:853–72.

Ferris, James, and Elizabeth Grady. 1989. "Fading Distinctions among the Nonprofit, Government and For-Profit Sectors." In *The Future of the Nonprofit Sector,* ed. Virginia Hodgkinson and Richard Lyman, 123–41. New York: Jossey-Bass.

Fisher, Caroline, and Claire Anderson. 1990. "Hospital Advertising: Does It Influence Consumers?" *Journal of Health Care Marketing* 10(4):44–46.

Flynn, L. 1994. "Managed Care and Mental Illness." In *Allies and Adversaries: The Impact of Managed Care on Mental Health Services,* ed. R. Schreter, S. Sharfstein, and C. Schreter, 203–12. Washington, D.C.: American Psychiatric Press.

Frank, Richard, David Salkever, and Jan Mitchell. 1990. "Market Forces and the Public Good: Competition among Hospitals and Provision of Indigent Care." In *Advances in Health Economics and Health Services Research,* ed. L. Rossiter and R. Scheffler. Greenwich, Conn.: JAI Press.

Frank, Richard, and David Salkever. 1991. "The Supply of Charity Services by Nonprofit Hospitals: Motives and Market Structure." *Rand Journal of Economics* 22(3):430–45.

Frank, Richard. 1989. "Regulatory Policy and Information Deficiencies in the Market for Mental Health Services." *Journal of Health Politics, Policy and Law* 14(3):477–502.

General Accounting Office, U.S. Congress. 1990. *Nonprofit Hospitals: Better Standards Needed for Tax Exemption,* GAO HRD-90-84. Washington D.C.: General Accounting Office.

Ginsberg, Ari, and Ann Buchholtz. 1990. "Converting to For-Profit Status: Corporate Responsiveness to Radical Change." *Academy of Management Journal* 33(3):445–77.

Gray, Bradford. 1991. *The Profit Motive and Patient Care.* Cambridge: Harvard University Press.

———. 1993. "Ownership Matters: Reform and the Future of Nonprofit Health Care." *Inquiry* 30(4):352–61.

———, ed. 1986. *For-Profit Enterprise in Health Care.* Washington D.C.: National Academy Press.

Grob, Gerald. 1992. "Mental Health Policy in America: Myths and Realities." *Health Affairs* 11(3):7–22.

Gui, Benedetto. 1993. "The Economic Rationale for the 'Third Sector': Nonprofit and other Noncapitalist Organizations." In *The Nonprofit Sector in the Mixed Economy,* ed. Avner Ben-Ner and Benedetto Gui, 59–80. Ann Arbor: University of Michigan Press.

Hannan, M., and J. Freeman. 1977. "The Population Ecology of Organizations." *American Journal of Sociology* 83:929–64.

Hansmann, Henry. 1980. "The Role of Nonprofit Enterprise." *Yale Law Journal* 89:835–901.

——. 1987. "Economic Theory of Nonprofit Organizations." In *The Nonprofit Sector: A Research Handbook,* ed. Walter W. Powell, 27–42. New Haven: Yale University Press.

Hollingsworth, Rogers, and M. Hollingsworth. 1987. *Controversy about American Hospitals: Funding, Ownership and Performance.* Washington D.C.: American Enterprise Institute.

James, Estelle. 1992. "Commentary." In *Who Benefits from the Nonprofit Sector?* ed. Charles Clotfelter, 244–55. Chicago: University of Chicago Press.

Jellinek, Michael, and Barry Nurcombe. 1993. "Two Wrongs Don't Make a Right: Managed Care, Mental Health and the Marketplace." *Journal of the American Medical Association* 270(14):1737–39.

Kanter, Rosabeth, and David Summers. 1987. "Doing Well While Doing Good: Dilemmas of Performance Measurement in Nonprofit Organizations and the Need for a Multiple Constituency Approach." In *The Nonprofit Sector: A Research Handbook,* ed. Walter W. Powell, 154–66. New Haven: Yale University Press.

Kinzer, David. 1984. "Care of the Poor Revisited." *Inquiry* 21:5–16.

Kultgen, John. 1988. *Ethics and Professionalism.* Philadelphia: University of Pennsylvania Press.

Lazarus, Arthur. 1994. "Disputes over Payment for Hospitalization under Mental Health 'Carve-Out' Programs." *Hospital and Community Psychiatry* 45(2):115–16.

McCue, Michael, and Jan Clement. 1992. "Relative Performance of For-Profit Psychiatric Hospitals in Investor-Owned Systems and Nonprofit Psychiatric Hospitals." *American Journal of Psychiatry* 150:77–82.

McCue, Michael, Jan Clement, and Thomas Hoerger. 1993. "The Association of Ownership and System Affiliation with the Financial Performance of Inpatient Psychiatric Hospitals." *Inquiry* 30:306–17.

Majone, G. 1984. "Professionalism and Nonprofit Organizations." *Journal of Health Politics, Policy and Law* 8:639–59.

Marmor, Theodore, Mark Schlesinger, and Richard Smithey. 1987. "Nonprofit Organizations and Health Care." In *The Nonprofit Sector: A Research Handbook,* ed. Walter W. Powell, 221–39. New Haven: Yale University Press.

Newhouse, Joseph. 1970. "Toward Theory of Nonprofit Institutions: An Economic Model of a Hospital." *American Economic Review* 60:64–74.

Noether, Monica. 1988. "Competition among Hospitals." *Journal of Health Economics* 7:259–84.

Office of Technology Assessment, U.S. Congress. 1990. *Confused Minds, Burdened Families: Finding Help for People with Alzheimer's and Other Dementias,* OTA-BA-403. Washington, D.C.: Government Printing Office.

Patel, Jayendu, Jack Needleman, and Richard Zeckhauser. 1993. "Who Cares? Hospital Ownership and Uncompensated Care." Working paper, John F. Kennedy School of Government, Harvard University.

Pauly, Mark. 1987. "Nonprofit Firms in Medical Markets." *American Economic Review* 77(2):257–62.

Potter, Margaret, and Beaufort Longest. 1994. "The Divergence of Federal and State Policies on the Charitable Tax Exemption of Nonprofit Hospitals." *Journal of Health Politics, Policy and Law* 19(2):392–419.

Powell, Walter, and Rebecca Friedkin. 1987. "Organizational Change in Nonprofit Organizations." In *The Nonprofit Sector: A Research Handbook,* ed. Walter W. Powell, 180–94. New Haven, Yale University Press.

Preston, Ann. 1988. "The Nonprofit Firm: A Potential Solution to Inherent Market Failures." *Economic Inquiry* 26(3):493–506.

Robinson, James, and Harold Luft. 1986. "Competition, Regulation and Hospital Costs, 1982 to 1986." *Journal of the American Medical Association* 260:2676–81.

Roomkin, Myron, and Burton Weisbrod. 1994. "Managerial Compensation in For-Profit and Nonprofit Hospitals: Is There a Difference?" Draft manuscript, Center for Urban Affairs and Policy Research, Northwestern University.

Rose-Ackerman, Susan. 1987. "Ideals versus Dollars: Donors, Charity Managers and Government Grants." *Journal of Political Economy* 95:810–23.

Russell, Louise. 1979. *Technology in Hospitals: Medical Advances and Their Diffusion.* Washington, D.C.: Brookings.

Salamon, Lester. 1992. "Social Services." In *Who Benefits from the Nonprofit Sector?* ed. Charles Clotfelter, 134–73. Chicago: University of Chicago Press.

Schiff, Jerry. 1985. "Does Government Spending Crowd Out Charitable Contributions?" *National Tax Journal* 38(4):535–46.

Schlesinger, Mark. 1984. "Public, For-Profit and Private Nonprofit Enterprises: A Study of Mixed Industries." Ph.D. dissertation, University of Wisconsin.

Schlesinger, Mark, Robert Dorwart, Claudia Hoover, and Sherrie Epstein. 1997. "Competition and Access to Hospital Services: Evidence from Psychiatric Hospitals." *Medical Care* 35(7): Forthcoming.

Schlesinger Mark, Judith Bentkover, David Blumenthal, Robert Musacchio, and Jan Willer. 1987. "The Privatization of Health Care and Physicians' Perceptions of Access to Hospital Services." *Milbank Quarterly* 65:25–58.

Schlesinger, Mark, Robert Dorwart, and Richard Pulice. 1986. "Competitive Bidding and States' Purchase of Services in Mental Health Care." *Journal of Policy Analysis and Management* 5:245–63.

Schlesinger, Mark, and Robert Dorwart. 1984. "Ownership and Mental Health Services: A Reappraisal." *New England Journal of Medicine* 311:959–65.

Seay J., and Bruce Vladeck, eds. 1988. *In Sickness and In Health: The Mission of Voluntary Health Care Facilities.* New York: United Hospital Fund.

Shortell Stephen, Ellen Morrison, James Hughes, Bernard Friedman, James Coverdill, and Linda Berg. 1986. "The Effects of Hospital Ownership on Nontraditional Services." *Health Affairs* 5(4):97–111.

Sloan, Frank. 1988. "Property Rights in the Hospital Industry." In *Health Care in America,* ed. H. E. Frech, 103–41. San Francisco: Pacific Research Institute for Public Policy.

Sloan, Frank, Joseph Valvona, and Ross Mullner. 1986. "Identifying the Issues: A Statistical Profile." In *Uncompensated Hospital Care: Rights and Responsibilities,* ed. F. Sloan, J. Blumstein, and J. Perrin. Baltimore: Johns Hopkins University Press.

Smith, Steven, and Michael Lipsky. 1993. *Nonprofits for Hire: The Welfare State in the Age of Contracting.* Cambridge: Harvard University Press.

Steinberg, Richard. 1993. "Does Government Spending Crowd Out Donations: Interpreting the Evidence." In *The Nonprofit Sector in the Mixed Economy,* ed. Avner Ben-Ner and Benedetto Gui, 99–125. Ann Arbor: University of Michigan Press.

Steinberg, Richard. 1987. "Nonprofit Organizations and the Market." In *The Nonprofit Sector: A Research Handbook,* ed. Walter W. Powell, 118–38. New Haven: Yale University Press.

Steinwald, Bruce, and Duncan Neuhauser. 1970. "The Role of the Proprietary Hospital." *Journal of Law and Contemporary Problems* 35:817–38.

Thorpe, Kenneth, and Charles Brecher. 1988. "The Social Role of Nonprofit Organizations: Hospital Provision of Charity Care." *Economic Inquiry* 29:472–84.

Vladeck, Bruce. 1976. "Why Nonprofits Go Broke." *The Public Interest* 42:86–101.

Weisbrod, Burton. 1988. *The Nonprofit Economy.* Cambridge: Harvard University Press.

Weisbrod, Burton, and Elizabeth Mauser. 1993. "Partial versus Total Effects of Institutional Form: Disentangling Endogenous from Exogenous Variables." Working paper, Northwestern University, Center for Urban Affairs and Policy Research.

Weisbrod, Burton, and Mark Schlesinger. 1986. "Ownership and Regulation in Markets With Asymmetric Information: Theory and Empirical Applications to the Nursing Home Industry." In *The Economics of Nonprofit Institutions,* ed. Estelle James and Susan Rose-Ackerman, 133–51. New York: Oxford University Press.

Weithorn, Linda. 1988. "Mental Hospitalization of Troublesome Youth: An Analysis of Skyrocketing Admission Rates." *Stanford Law Review* 40:773–838.

West, Edwin. 1989. "Nonprofit Organizations: Revised Theory and New Evidence." *Public Choice* 63:165–74.

White, Stephen, and Thomas Chirikos. 1988. "Measuring Hospital Competition." *Medical Care* 26(3):256–62.

Wolff, Nancy. 1989. "Professional Uncertainty and Physician Medical Decision-Making in a Multiple Treatment Framework." *Social Sciences and Medicine* 28(2):99–107.

Wolff, Nancy, and Mark Schlesinger. 1995. "Changes in Ownership-Related Differences in Hospital Performance in Response to Intersectoral Competition." Working paper, Institute for Health, Health Care Policy and Aging Research, Rutgers University.

Yoder, Sunny. 1986. "Economic Theories of For-Profit and Not-For-Profit Organizations." In *For-Profit Enterprise in Health Care,* ed. Bradford Gray. Washington, D.C.: National Academy Press.

Young, Dennis. 1987. "Executive Leadership in Nonprofit Organizations." In *The Nonprofit Sector: A Research Handbook,* ed. Walter W. Powell, 167–80. New Haven: Yale University Press.

Young, Dennis. 1983. *If Not For Profit, For What?* Lexington, Mass.: Lexington Books.

Zwanziger, Jack, and Glenn Melnick. 1988. "The Effects of Hospital Competition and the Medicare PPS Program on Hospital Cost Behavior in California." *Journal of Health Economics* 7:301–20.

7

MICHAEL KRASHINSKY

Does Auspice Matter? The Case of Day Care for Children in Canada

In spite of some early research on nonprofit institutions (see Newhouse 1970; Nelson and Krashinsky 1973), it is only in the past fifteen years or so that economists have focused their attention on nonprofit activity. Most of that recent work has grown out of an important article by Henry Hansmann (1980) which argued that nonprofits develop when "contract failure" makes market production unattractive. By this Hansmann meant that a variety of problems might make it difficult for the consumers of a particular commodity to police the conduct of producers by normal contractual or market mechanisms. In a later piece, Hansmann (1987, 29) restates this thesis:

> Nonprofits of all types typically arise in situations in which . . . consumers feel unable to evaluate accurately the quantity or quality of a service a firm produces for them. In such circumstances, a for-profit firm has both the incentive and the opportunity to take advantage of customers by providing less service to them than was promised and paid for. A nonprofit firm, in contrast, offers consumers the advantage that, owing to the non-distribution constraint, those who control the organiza-

tion are constrained in their ability to benefit personally from providing low-quality services and thus have less incentive to take advantage of customers than do managers of a for-profit firm.

Hansmann's approach has required some extension. For example, government activity is clearly an alternative to nonprofits when there is contract failure (Weisbrod 1988). And Hansmann's focus on individual consumers ignores the role of the government in choosing to contract out some of its activities to nonprofits (Krashinsky 1990). Furthermore, some of the motivation for nonprofit activity lies on the supply side. Entrepreneurs who are less motivated by profits than by other considerations may find nonprofits attractive (Young 1981). In some cases, the religious motivations of those running the organization have generated nonprofit activity (James 1987).

These modifications notwithstanding, Hansmann's vision has stood the test of time.[1] Consumers, whether individual or collective, seem to feel that nonprofit organizations are more trustworthy than for-profit firms — that is, less likely to exploit the consumer's inability to monitor and enforce contracts. Yet if nonprofit institutions are really different from other types of organizations — that is, if auspice matters —

This chapter draws on work done earlier with Ted Harvey of SPR Associates for the Canadian Parliamentary Committee on Day Care. The author would also like to thank Gord Cleveland for his input and assistance.

1. See Steinberg and Gray (1992) for a discussion of Hansmann's contribution and the ensuing literature.

the question remains, How much can consumers or donors or governments rely on these differences?

Clearly, in Hansmann's vision, the advantage offered by the nonprofit firm depends critically on the effectiveness of the nondistribution constraint. By agreeing not to appropriate any profits for themselves, owners and managers are agreeing to eliminate, at least in part, the incentive to cut quality and to exploit consumers. But all this presumes that such an agreement is enforced by someone. If enforcement is lax, then the advantages of the nonprofit firm disappear.

The problem is that managers of nonprofits will be more likely to violate the nondistribution constraint — that is, to behave as "for-profits-in-disguise" (Steinberg and Gray 1992, 6) — when the chances of detection are relatively low and when the rewards for cheating are relatively large. The second point means that it is precisely when nonprofits are most valuable (because for-profit firms are in a position to make significant profits by exploiting the trust of consumers) that enforcement of the nonprofit constraint will be most problematic (because for-profit firms will have the largest incentive to obscure their behavior by masquerading as nonprofits). Thus, the more that consumers find it useful to distinguish between nonprofit and for-profit forms of production, the more entrepreneurs will have an incentive to make that distinction more obscure.

This issue has come to the fore in recent years in Canada, where the various levels of government subsidize day care in a variety of ways. Day care advocates and policymakers have debated extensively the extent to which subsidies should be limited to nonprofit providers. One of the ideological positions taken by those opposed to funding for-profits has been that the providers of this kind of service ought not to earn profits. Buried in this position is the belief that for-profit providers cannot be trusted to place the interests of children ahead of profitability. This is the specific issue raised by Hansmann.

This chapter examines the role of auspice in determining performance within the context of the Canadian policy debate. I shall begin by discussing briefly the evolution of day care policy in Canada regarding auspice. To provide some information on the quality issue, I shall then consider two data sets which look at how quality varies by auspice across Canada. I conclude by developing a brief theory of auspice and the enforcement of the nondistribution constraint and suggesting that the use of auspice in public policy should be somewhat limited.

THE POLICY DEBATE OVER AUSPICE IN CANADA

Most day care centers in Canada are owned privately (a limited number in Toronto and Edmonton are owned by the government) and operate either as for-profit or nonprofit enterprises.[2] Recently, the number of nonprofit centers has grown.

For example, in 1984, there were approximately 130,000 places provided by private operators, slightly more than half (56 percent) being provided by nonprofit operators.[3] The role of nonprofit enterprise, however, varied significantly across the country: in general, nonprofit centers dominated the landscape in Quebec, Manitoba, and Saskatchewan, while for-profit centers were preeminent in Alberta and, to a lesser extent, Newfoundland and British Columbia. The picture changed somewhat in 1988, when nonprofit centers became relatively more important in British Columbia, Ontario, and Quebec, while for-profit became relatively more important in Prince Edward Island and Newfoundland. The distribution of centers by auspice across the country is shown in table 7.1.

Variations among the provinces occur in large part because of very different provincial policies regarding day care. Day care policy in Canada is made simultaneously at the different levels of government. Although the Canadian constitution gives the provinces exclusive responsibility for social programs, the federal government is heavily involved in funding day care.

Under the Canada Assistance Plan (CAP), the federal government shares half the cost of provincial day care subsidies to those in need. To be eligible for these funds, however, provinces must determine need by using either an income test or a needs test.[4] For provinces which choose the income test, CAP provides federal cost sharing only for children in nonprofit centers. On the other hand, if the province uses a needs test to determine eligibility, federal cost sharing is provided for subsidized children in both nonprofit and for-profit centers. Only Ontario uses a needs test.

Beyond this cost sharing, the federal government provides subsidies directly to parents through a federal income tax deduction for child care expenses.[5] This deduction is independent of the auspice of the center and also applies to informal child-care arrangements.[6] Thus while CAP funding would seem to favor nonprofit care, the deduction treats all day care arrangements equally.

The provinces themselves have different policies concerning auspice and subsidies. In general, day care centers receive money from the provincial government in two ways. First, as discussed above, the provinces provide subsidies to low-income families.[7] Second, the provinces may provide grants to centers independent of the income or needs of the

---

2. A significant number of after-school places are also provided by the Ministry of Education in Quebec.

3. The data in this paper are from the late 1980s, so the discussion of policy will focus on that period.

4. An income test considers only family income and family size in determining eligibility for subsidy, whereas a needs test also looks at the specific costs (rent, medical expenses, etc.) borne by the individual family.

5. In two-parent families, the deduction is claimed by the parent with the lower annual income.

6. The deduction can be claimed for babysitting expenses, so long as receipts are provided.

7. Assistance is also provided to children who might otherwise be at risk.

Table 7.1. For-Profit vs. Nonprofit Day Care by Province, 1988

Province and Age Group		For-Profit Slots	Nonprofit Slots	Nonprofit % of all Private
British Columbia	— all ages	9472[1]	16958	64
	— 3 to 5 yrs	3486	5014	59
Alberta	— 3 to 5 yrs	16322	5154	24
Saskatchewan	— all ages	84	3638	98
	— 3 to 5 yrs	69	3037	98
Manitoba	— all ages	1665	12668	88
	— up to 5 yrs	1187	5946	83
Ontario	— all ages	32813	49936	60
	— 3 to 5 yrs	25641	33395	57
Quebec	— up to 5 yrs	9552	29442	76
Prince Edward Island	— up to 5 yrs	783	470	38
Nova Scotia	— all ages	2161	3395	61
Newfoundland	— 2 to 5 yrs	1404	333	19

[1] All data from Pence (1992, 53, 151, 233, 302, and 393; and 1992a, 49, 214, 291, and 366). No data were provided in the two Pence volumes for New Brunswick, and outside data were not used to ensure comparability. Nonprofit slots for ages three to five in Ontario were extrapolated from the data provided, which included government centers.

parents or children using the center. In each case, the province may choose to discriminate in favor of (or, conceivably, against) nonprofit centers. For example, some provinces choose to negotiate subsidy arrangements only with nonprofit centers and may write grant legislation so that nonprofits qualify for larger grants.

In Canada in the later 1980s (Pence 1992, 1992a), five provinces—British Columbia, Alberta, New Brunswick, Prince Edward Island, and Newfoundland—treated nonprofit and for-profit day care centers essentially the same with respect to both licensing and funding.[8] The remaining five provinces favored nonprofits in quite different ways. Saskatchewan did not licence for-profit centers at all.[9] Manitoba awarded significant across-the-board grants only to nonprofits, but subsidized low-income families using both types of care. Ontario introduced significant across-the-board provincial grants to nonprofit day care in late 1987. The subsidy situation in Ontario is cloudier because local authorities administer subsidies (paying 20 percent of the cost) and are free to choose the types of centers with which they negotiate subsidy arrangements. Discrimination by auspice can go either way, so there is no easy way to tell if, in general, nonprofit centers in Ontario are favored through subsidies.[10] Quebec provided significant grants to nonprofit

centers and also had a policy in the 1980s of directing subsidies only to nonprofits (however, since April of 1990, some subsidies, especially for infant care, are being directed to for-profit centers). Finally, Nova Scotia provided subsidies only through nonprofit centers.

The provinces differ in their definition of what constitutes a nonprofit center. While most provinces accept the corporate definition (the principal restriction of which is the nondistribution constraint), Saskatchewan requires all nonprofit centers to have a parent-dominated board, while Quebec distinguishes between nonprofit centers with and without parent boards and provides subsidies only to those with such boards.

This mix of funding arrangements across the provinces reflects the complex debate on auspice in Canada. The rapid increase in labor force participation by mothers with young children has made day care a significant political issue. While most of the pressure on government has been for increases in funding, there has also been serious discussion about auspice. For example, just prior to its defeat in 1984, the federal Liberal government set up a government Task Force on Child Care. In its report in 1986, this body proposed a radical expansion of public funding for day care, to be made available only through nonprofit centers. In contrast, the new Conservative government set up another body—the Parliamentary Committee—which argued for a smaller expansion of funding aimed directly at parents through the tax system.[11] These funds would be available for use in both for-

8. Some of the five provinces had very small grants (usually startup grants of one sort or another) that might discriminate in favor of nonprofit centers, but these will be ignored. The large grants that matter are usually ongoing grants of money each month for each child in the center, termed operating grants.

9. The small number of spaces in for-profit care (see table 7.1) occur because the legislation "grandfathered" for-profit centers, allowing those that existed when the legislation was passed to keep operating.

10. Because some local decisionmakers might prefer the supposed reliability of nonprofit operators, while others might have an ideological

preference for the free competitive (and hence for-profit) market, it is not clear which way any discrimination might go.

11. The Parliamentary Committee was set up prior to the report by the task force. It might be argued that the Conservative government set up that committee so as to have a counterweight to the task force in place. The existence of the Parliamentary Committee would partially

profit and nonprofit day care centers as well as in other forms of child care. Furthermore, the committee suggested that the CAP be changed to allow cost sharing for subsidies to both nonprofit and for-profit day care.

The debate over auspice remains unresolved. The basic argument against for-profit day care is that entrepreneurs are fundamentally untrustworthy. Faced with parents who may find it difficult to measure the quality of the care received by their children, centers will reduce quality in order to increase profits, and children will end up being hurt.[12] This concern echoes Hansmann's notion of market failure. The argument in this case, however, is not based upon any hard data on the quality of care provided by the different types of centers. The task force's strong recommendation in 1986 that for-profit day care be eliminated was not based on any explicit studies of the quality of care (although the task force did have some information on wages that might have reflected quality indirectly).[13]

One explanation for the absence of hard evidence is that the debate over auspice is only part of a fundamental debate over the future of day care in Canada. Many day care advocates look forward to a time when day care will be fully funded for all children, much like public education, and when quality standards will be higher than they are today. Because for-profit centers have not generally been strong advocates of higher regulatory standards for quality[14] and because Canadian governments have generally not directed funds for various social services (including health and education) through the for-profit sector, day care advocates see little role for for-profit centers in a world of fully funded universal day care. In that sense, a strong, expanding for-profit sector is seen as a natural impediment to full funding and higher quality.

Notwithstanding this subtext, serious discussion of the auspice issue clearly requires more thinking and some data. That is the concern of the rest of this chapter.

AUSPICE AND QUALITY ACCORDING TO DAY CARE CONSULTANTS

In 1986, I carried out a study of the quality of day care, differentiated by auspice, for the Canadian House of Commons Special Committee on Child Care (SPR 1986).[15] The study evaluated quality by surveying the consultants employed by the provinces to inspect day care centers in order to ensure their compliance with regulatory standards. The day care director in each province was asked to select one consultant within each area of the province.[16] Consultants were asked to prepare a list of all centers which they inspected, to identify each center by type (public, nonprofit, independent for-profit, and for-profit associated with a chain), and to rate each center on overall quality relative to provincial regulatory standards.[17] To ensure confidentiality, the ratings deleted any information that would have identified individual centers.[18] The process generated ratings for 927 centers, and 47 of the 49 consultants contacted responded to the survey.

The results of this survey are reported in table 7.2. They do not provide a perfect evaluation of quality because directors may have been biased in choosing which consultant in each area was questioned and because the consultants had been deeply involved in day care over the years and would be expected to have strong feelings and opinions, especially about auspice. On the other hand, the consultants know as much about measuring quality in day care as anyone in the country, so this process generated a significant data set with which to analyze quality.

The results on quality of auspice are striking. Ignoring the government centers, which are generally very well funded, the nonprofit centers provide on average a higher standard of care than the for-profit centers. Half the nonprofits are rated as better than adequate, compared with about one-third of the for-profits. In contrast, one-tenth of the nonprofits fall below regulatory standards, compared with one-quarter of the independent for-profits (and 15 percent of those for-profit centers that are part of chains).

The spread of quality within each category of auspice is considerable, however, so that variation in quality within each auspice is more important than the differences in average quality of care among the auspices. For example, the standard deviation of the quality rating within the sample of nonprofit centers is 0.94, which is more than twice the difference between the average value for nonprofit centers and for-profit centers. Clearly, the nonprofit nature of a center does not in itself guarantee high quality.

---

diffuse the task force report, which the Conservatives suspected (correctly) would not be consistent with the Conservative political agenda.

12. A less sophisticated version of this argument is that because for-profit centers must earn a return on their capital, while nonprofit centers do not, it follows that nonprofit centers can afford to pay more to increase quality (holding the price constant). This argument is incorrect because, unless the nonprofit is given the money to buy its capital equipment, it will have to pay interest on the loans used to buy that capital that are roughly equivalent to the returns on investment earned by the for-profit entrepreneur.

13. For example, Schom-Moffat (1984) found that day care workers were paid less in for-profit centers that in nonprofit centers. If this attracts workers with more training, increases motivation, and reduces turnover, then it would contribute to higher quality.

14. In the 1970s, when Ontario was considering lowering day care standards to stretch its day care dollars over more spaces, the for-profit centers were somewhat supportive of that move. Standards were not in fact changed, but since that time, the nonprofit centers and day care advocates in general have not viewed the for-profit centers as allies.

15. I was the principal investigator on a study through SPR, a Toronto social policy consulting firm.

16. The director is the senior civil servant in charge of day care.

17. A chain was defined as more than one center owned by the same individual or corporation.

18. The consultants were more likely to be honest if they were assured that it was impossible for anyone to identify how they had rated specific centers.

Table 7.2. Consultants' Quality Ratings of Day Care

Quality[1]	Auspice			
	Government	Nonprofit	Profit (Independent)[2]	Profit (Chain)
Very poor[3]	0[4]	2	6	0
Poor	2	9	19	15
Adequate	18	40	43	56
Good	46	33	22	29
Excellent	34	17	10	0
"Average"[5]	4.12	3.53	3.11	3.14

[1] One consultant was chosen in each area of each province. Because larger provinces generally have more consultants per area than small provinces, small provinces were overrepresented in the sample.

[2] Independent for-profits are those which are not jointly owned with any other centers. Chain for-profits are those centers operated for-profit by an owner (an individual or corporation) who also owns at least one other center.

[3] Consultants provided an overall rating of each center, relative to regulatory standards in their provinces, according to the following five point scale:

  1 — *Very Poor* — extremely deficient, violates important standards

  2 — *Poor* — falls short of some provincial standards

  3 — *Adequate* — meets standards and reasonable quality criteria

  4 — *Good* — somewhat better than required by provincial standards

  5 — *Excellent* — much better than required by provincial standards

[4] Ratings are reported as column percentages.

[5] "Average" is obtained by averaging scores on 5-point scale for each type of center.

Two other approaches can be used to illustrate this last point. First, I ran a simple regression to predict the overall quality rating of a center using auspice as the explanatory variable:

$$(1) \quad QUALITY_i = \beta_0 + \beta_1 GOVT_i + \beta_2 NONPROFIT_i + \mu_i$$

where $GOVT_i$ and $NONPROFIT_i$ are dummy variables, equal to 1 when the ith center belongs to that particular auspice and to 0 otherwise. The coefficients on GOVT and NONPROFIT were, as might be expected, 1.03 and 0.44 (reflecting the differences between the averages in table 7.2). But the corrected R-squared statistic was only 0.085, suggesting the natural interpretation that auspice can explain only 8.5 percent of the variation in quality.

Second, I considered how a randomly selected nonprofit center would compare with a randomly selected for-profit center. The nonprofit center would be superior (have a higher overall quality rating) less than half the time (48 percent of the time if the for-profit is independent, 46 percent if it is part of a chain), and the for-profit center would be superior just under a quarter of the time (24 percent of the time if the for-profit is independent, 21 percent if it is part of a chain). Again, nonprofit auspice is not a guarantee of higher quality.

Some of the higher quality attributed to nonprofit centers may be due to the explicit subsidies available to those centers in some provinces. It would be useful to look at the quality ratings by province to examine the role of provincial policies which favor nonprofit centers, but these data cannot be reported because one condition of cooperation by the day care directors was a commitment not to release any province-specific data. To get a flavor of the impact of province and subsidization, however, the following equation was estimated for a limited subsample of the centers:[19]

$$(2) \quad QUALITY_i = \beta_0 + \beta_1 GOVT_i + \beta_2 NONPROFIT_i + \beta_3 SUBSIDY_i + \Sigma\gamma_j PROV_{ji} + \mu_i (2)$$

where $SUBSIDY_i$ is a dummy variable equal to 1 when the center has subsidized children and to 0 otherwise, and $PROV_{ji}$ are eight dummies representing the provinces.[20] When equation (2) was run without the subsidy and provincial dummies, the coefficients on GOVT and NONPROFIT were .789 and .326, respectively, and both were significant at the 5 percent level.[21] The adjusted R-squared statistic was .117. When the complete version of equation (2) was estimated, the coefficients on GOVT and NONPROV fell to .541 and .261, respectively (the second was now barely insignificant), and the adjusted R-squared statistic rose to .299. Although the provincial coefficients cannot be reported (because of confidentiality), this result does suggest that provincial policy is very important in determining quality (perhaps more important than auspice) and that some of the higher quality in nonprofit centers may reflect government policy in some provinces in providing differential subsidies to nonprofit centers.

19. The consultants were asked to provide more detailed information about the typical center within each category of auspice. It is these centers for which there is information on subsidies.

20. One of the ten provinces was omitted because of data limitations, and a second was omitted to avoid overspecification.

21. The results are somewhat different from those reported for equation (1) because the sample is different, including only the "typical" centers.

AUSPICE AND QUALITY ACCORDING TO DAY CARE PARENTS

An alternative and somewhat different evaluation of day care centers can be obtained by asking parents what they think of their child-care arrangements. In the fall of 1988, the Canadian National Child Care Survey was carried out, in which more than twenty-four thousand families with more than forty-two thousand children under the age of thirteen were interviewed. My interest is only in the relatively small subset of families that used day care. They were asked if their center operated on a for-profit or nonprofit basis, and how they felt overall about their care arrangement. Elimination of those families that did not answer both questions left the 1,181 responses which are summarized in table 7.3. Although parents were slightly more positive about nonprofit child care, the results are hardly suggestive of enormous differences in evaluation based on auspice.

Unlike the earlier survey, this one had no confidentiality issue, so the results can be broken down by province. To examine the effect of provincial differences systematically, two variations of the quality variable reported in table 7.3 were defined.[22] First, the dummy variable $HAPPY_i$ was set equal to 1 when parents had no reservations about their day care arrangement and equal to 0 when parents had any reservations at all. Second, the dummy variable $UNHAPPY_i$ was set equal to 1 when parents had some important or major reservations about their day care and to 0 when parents had no reservations or minor ones only. Then the probability that each variable was equal to 1 was estimated for four different specifications of the model using PROBIT analysis. The results are reported in tables 7.4 and 7.5.

The PROBIT models used the following variables:

1. nine provincial dummy variables (NFLD, NB, NS, PEI, QUE, MAN, SASK, ALB, and BC) equal to 1 when the day care center is in that particular province and to 0 otherwise (Ontario is omitted to avoid overspecification);
2. a general nonprofit dummy variable (NONP) equal to 1 when the day care center has been identified by the parent as being nonprofit and to 0 otherwise;
3. ten province-specific nonprofit dummy variables, indicated by the province abbreviation (see number 1) followed by NONP (NFLDNONP, NBNONP, NSNONP, PEINONP, QUENONP, ONTNONP, MANNONP, SASKNONP, ALBNONP, and BCNONP) equal to 1 when the day care center is both nonprofit and within that particular province to and 0 otherwise;
4. a categorical variable measuring the total income of the parents in the household (DASPINCR); and
5. a continuous variable measuring the amount paid for day care by the family (AMTPAID).

22. Parents were asked to state whether they had no reservations, only minor reservations, some reservations, or major reservations about the kind of care their children were receiving.

Table 7.3. Parents' Quality Ratings of Day Care

| Quality | Auspice[1] | | | |
	Nonprofit		Profit	
No reservations	395	(73.7)[2]	464	(71.0)
Minor reservations	118	(22.0)	130	(20.2)
Some important reservations	18	(3.4)	35	(5.4)
Major reservations	5	(0.9)	16	(2.5)

[1] The question on auspice was "Does the centre operate on a profit or nonprofit basis?" There were 1,264 responses, plus 538 responses of "don't know." The question on quality was "Overall, how do you feel about this care arrangement?" There were 1,331 responses, plus 32 nonresponses.

[2] Ratings are given both as number of responses and as column percentages.

Tables 7.4 and 7.5 are consistent with the simple cross-tabulation provided in table 7.3. Although having a nonprofit center seems to have no effect on parents' being happy with their arrangements (having no reservations about care), it does seem to make them slightly less unhappy (having some important or major reservations about care). The coefficient −.265 on NONP in table 7.5 must be interpreted with care because the PROBIT technique estimates a transformation of the dependent variable. In this case, evaluated at the mean of the dependent variable, this coefficient translates to a decrease in the probability of being unhappy of about 3.2 percent.

When province-specific nonprofit dummies are used, both equations suggest that in Alberta alone nonprofit care clearly dominates. Independent of whether family income and the cost of care are included in the equations (2, 3, and 4), the coefficient on ALBNONP is about .57 in table 7.4, which translates to an increase in the probability of being happy (at the mean of the dependent variable) of about 19 percent when the center is nonprofit. The coefficient is about −.79 in table 7.5, which translates to a decrease in the probability of being unhappy of about 21 percent. Both results are significant at the 5 percent level. The positive impact on happiness is matched by a decrease in happiness in nonprofit centers in Ontario.

The Alberta result seems consistent with what we know about government policy in that province. In Alberta, there is no discrimination against for-profit centers, and they are encouraged by an across-the-board grant (the only one in Canada paid to for-profit centers). Relatively generous funding, especially in the 1980s (when my data were collected), was combined with relatively lax regulatory standards (see Friesen 1992, 143–51). Ineffective regulation would attract entrepreneurs whose first commitment is not to quality.

The Ontario result is somewhat unusual. Interestingly, the lower level of happiness reported by parents about day care is not matched by a higher level of unhappiness, suggesting that parents using nonprofit centers are more prone to find small faults with their centers (to have minor reservations). The explanation for this finding may be that parents have higher expectations of nonprofit centers and hence are more

Table 7.4. Estimating the Probability that Parents are Happy with Their Day Care Arrangements

Variable[1]	Equation 1 coefficients		Equation 2 coefficients		Equation 3 coefficients		Equation 4 coefficients	
CONSTANT	**.638**	**(5.64)**[2]	**.904**	**(5.61)**	**1.271**	**(6.49)**	**1.354**	**(6.72)**
NFLD	.227	(0.81)	−.087	(0.28)	−.098	(0.31)	−.129	(0.41)
NB	.069	(0.30)	−.388	(1.39)	−.428	(1.52)	−.461	(1.63)
NS	.099	(0.44)	−.474	(1.46)	−.452	(1.38)	−.475	(1.44)
PEI	**.581**	**(1.96)**	.358	(1.01)	.295	(0.83)	.255	(0.71)
QUE	.105	(0.80)	−.048	(0.24)	−.038	(0.19)	−.092	(0.45)
MAN	−.044	(0.27)	−.338	(1.22)	−.398	(1.43)	−.437	(1.56)
SASK	.213	(1.21)	.122	(0.44)	.086	(0.31)	.022	(0.08)
ALB	**−.443**	**(3.25)**	**−.879**	**(4.60)**	**−.909**	**(4.73)**	**−.961**	**(4.94)**
BC	−.105	(0.64)	−.344	(1.54)	−.376	(1.67)	−.418	(1.84)
NONP	.008	(0.10)	—		—		—	
NFLDNONP	—		4.297	(0.01)	4.427	(0.01)	4.367	(0.01)
PEINONP	—		−.195	(0.29)	−.245	(0.36)	−.265	(0.39)
NBNONP	—		.910	(1.62)	.921	(1.64)	.908	(1.60)
NSNONP	—		.614	(1.50)	.514	(1.25)	.459	(1.11)
QUENONP	—		−.208	(1.29)	−.232	(1.43)	−.219	(1.35)
ONTNONP	—		**−.474**	**(2.23)**	**−.475**	**(2.22)**	**−.512**	**(2.38)**
MANNONP	—		.048	(0.18)	.074	(0.28)	.055	(0.21)
SASKNONP	—		−.295	(1.01)	−.371	(1.27)	−.368	(1.26)
ALBNONP	—		**.571**	**(2.99)**	**.570**	**(2.98)**	**.569**	**(2.98)**
BCNONP	—		−.076	(0.28)	−.085	(0.31)	−.118	(0.44)
DASPINCR	—		—		**−.081**	**(3.37)**	**−.063**	**(2.42)**
AMTPAID[3]	—		—		—		−.270	(1.94)

[1] The mean of the dependent variable (untransformed) is .727; the number of observations is 1,181.

[2] The number in parentheses to the right of the coefficient is the absolute value of the t-ratio. Coefficients that are significant at the 5% level are shown in bold.

[3] AMTPAID is the amount paid per week in hundreds of dollars.

easily disappointed in them. This same phenomenon does not take place in other provinces, however. Furthermore, Ontario is one of the provinces that favors nonprofit centers, although the legislation took effect only several months before this survey and so may not yet have had an impact on quality.

The Ontario result points out the major weakness in evaluating quality through parents' reactions. Parents are not professionals and do not evaluate day care against some objective standard. Thus any judgment involving reservations may say as much about parents' expectations as it does about center quality. Furthermore, given the importance of children, it is difficult for parents using a day care center to admit that they are unhappy with the center they have chosen.

It is not at all clear, moreover, that most parents can judge quality accurately. If they could, of course, then, following Hansmann, there would hardly be a strong argument for the existence of nonprofit centers in this sector. It should also be pointed out that parents often do not know whether or not their center is nonprofit or for-profit, making it even more difficult to draw hard conclusions from these results.

CAN AUSPICE BE USED TO INCREASE QUALITY?

The empirical results discussed above are somewhat mixed. The day care consultants found that nonprofit centers are superior to for-profit centers, although differences in quality among nonprofit centers or among for-profit centers (that is, among centers within each auspice) are more important than differences in quality between the average nonprofit center and the average for-profit center. On the other hand, if we ignore Alberta, parents in the rest of Canada found no differences between for-profit and nonprofit centers, except in Ontario, where, perversely, for-profit centers seemed superior. And this occurred even though a number of provinces (for example, Manitoba and Quebec) clearly favor nonprofit centers and provide them with the resources to improve quality.

If we accept the argument that the consultants are more likely to provide accurate evaluations, then the conclusion would be that nonprofit day care offers some advantages, but that only in Alberta are these differences large enough to be noticed by a significant numbers of parents. In the other provinces, regulation appears to enforce a standard of care that minimizes differences in quality between for-profit and nonprofit centers, at least to the extent that parents might perceive these differences.

The argument made by a number of day care advocates in Canada has been that the advantages to using nonprofit centers are significant and that governments ought to exploit those advantages by consciously encouraging the development of the nonprofit sector. In fact, the advocates usually go

Table 7.5. Estimating the Probability that Parents Are Unhappy with Their Day Care Arrangements

Variable[1]	Equation 1 coefficients		Equation 2 coefficients		Equation 3 coefficients		Equation 4 coefficients	
CONSTANT	**−1.299**	**(8.45)**[2]	**−1.370**	**(6.93)**	**−1.286**	**(5.19)**	**−1.320**	**(5.18)**
NFLD	.181	(0.56)	.280	(0.80)	.280	(0.80)	.295	(0.84)
NB	−.157	(0.48)	.035	(0.10)	.027	(0.08)	.041	(0.11)
NS	−.117	(0.36)	.302	(0.77)	.310	(0.79)	.316	(0.80)
PEI	−.541	(1.22)	−4.359	(0.01)	−4.377	(0.01)	−4.359	(0.10)
QUE	**−.514**	**(2.47)**	−.458	(1.64)	−.456	(1.63)	−.433	(1.53)
MAN	−.034	(0.15)	−.209	(0.53)	−.223	(0.56)	−.206	(0.52)
SASK	.327	(0.27)	−.342	(0.90)	−.355	(0.93)	−.332	(0.86)
ALB	.091	(0.49)	.263	(1.12)	.259	(1.10)	.281	(1.18)
BC	−.065	(0.28)	−.117	(0.39)	−.119	(0.40)	−.104	(0.35)
NONP	**−.265**	**(2.06)**	—		—		—	
NFLDNONP	—		−4.639	(0.00)	−4.607	(0.00)	−4.580	(0.00)
PEINONP	—		4.661	(0.01)	4.654	(0.01)	4.660	(0.01)
NBNONP	—		−4.393	(0.01)	−4.396	(0.01)	−4.388	(0.01)
NSNONP	—		−4.661	(0.01)	−4.687	(0.01)	−4.663	(0.01)
QUENONP	—		−.229	(0.74)	−.236	(0.76)	−.244	(0.79)
ONTNONP	—		−.114	(0.40)	−.114	(0.40)	−.103	(0.36)
MANNONP	—		.084	(0.21)	.093	(0.23)	.101	(0.25)
SASKNONP	—		−.091	(0.20)	−.103	(0.23)	−.102	(0.22)
ALBNONP	—		**−.789**	**(2.38)**	**−.790**	**(2.38)**	**−.792**	**(2.39)**
BCNONP	—		.119	(0.32)	.115	(0.31)	.134	(0.36)
DASPINCR	—		—		−.019	(0.56)	−.028	(0.74)
AMTPAID[3]	—		—		—		.121	(0.60)

[1] The mean of the dependent variable (untransformed) is .063; the number of observations is 1,181.

[2] The number in parentheses to the right of the coefficient is the absolute value of the t-ratio. Coefficients that are significant at the 5% level are shown in bold.

[3] AMTPAID is the amount paid per week in hundreds of dollars.

further, suggesting, as in Saskatchewan, that for-profit day care ought to be actively discouraged.

This argument is suspect. First, the differences in quality that I have reported are hardly overwhelming, and, as I mentioned earlier, there is no good study that finds large differences. Nonprofit operators may be motivated to provide high quality, but the consultants suggest (as reported in table 7.2) that sometimes those operators miss the mark rather badly. For-profit operators may be interested in maximizing profits, but public regulation may well prevent significant exploitation of parents and their children, and some centers provide care of quite high quality.

Second, even if the differences in quality between for-profit and nonprofit centers were large, it is not clear how government policy could exploit them so easily. The problem is that the quality differences that we now see occur in an environment in which there is no particular penalty in choosing auspice. That is, for-profit centers may have a lower average level of quality, but if governments do not discriminate to a large extent and if consumers are not even aware in many cases of auspice and are unaware of the differences in quality, then there is no reason for an entrepreneur running a low-quality center to worry about the fact that governments and consumers can identify the center as being for-profit.

If, on the other hand, governments do actively discourage for-profits, then the for-profit-in-disguise problem discussed at the beginning of the chapter can emerge. Young (1981) suggests that entrepreneurs have divergent motivations and that they sort themselves into various fields and sectors of business accordingly. In choosing an industry, these entrepreneurs depend upon a variety of structural characteristics of the industry and within the industry and will sort themselves by auspice (for-profit and nonprofit, in the day care case) according to their goals — to make money, to be creative, to provide service, to achieve autonomy, and so on.

Faced with government action to restrict for-profits, for-profit entrepreneurs can either leave the industry or incorporate as nonprofit centers. Young suggests that the motivation to choose industry is stronger than the motivation to choose auspice. Thus, government restriction on auspice may well lead many for-profit entrepreneurs to switch their centers to the nonprofit sector. This will lead to a more heterogeneous entrepreneurial mix (that is, the motivations among "nonprofit" operators will be less distinctive).

The government policy of favoring nonprofit day care centers will thus be ineffective unless the government can detect profit making among nonprofits and punish it. The problem is that such mechanisms are, at present, lacking in Canada. There is little problem incorporating as a nonprofit either federally or provincially.[23] In Ontario, for example, applicants submit an outline of their objectives and receive informal help from the government in completing the paperwork satisfactorily. Few applications are rejected, and I know of no case of rejection of a nonprofit day care center.

Once incorporated, nonprofit institutions are expected to obey the nondistribution constraint, but there is no effective monitoring of this at the provincial level. I consulted with several lawyers in Toronto who worked with nonprofits, and they indicated that they knew of no case in which a nonprofit corporation in Ontario had been disincorporated for earning and distributing profits. Revenue Canada, the federal income tax department, also monitors nonprofit institutions, paying some attention to their use of any surplus in a manner consistent with the long-run goals of the institution. But they do not monitor the paying out of salaries, fees, or honorariums, so long as they are reasonable and in line with what is paid out in normal arm's-length transactions. Thus there would be no difficulty were the former owner of a for-profit center to incorporate as a nonprofit and arrange to be paid for services as a director and teacher, for managing and consulting, or for use of facilities and capital belonging to that former owner. The profits that had been earned when the center was for-profit would now accrue to the former owner as payments for various services. Because the profits in day care centers are not extraordinarily high (given the significant competition on fees among centers and implicit competition from babysitters), it is hard to believe that even the most unscrupulous operator could have any difficulty falling within the Revenue Canada guidelines.

Of course, the government could increase its monitoring of the nondistribution constraint. But this would not be either trivial or costless. And we do not have much experience with how this might be done effectively and cheaply. There has been little research on this type of monitoring, but certain general principles might be deduced. Detection is more likely when institutions are large and formal (although even the largest nonprofit organizations might still require monitoring). In small, informal institutions like day care centers, the line between profits and expenses is hard to draw, and the issue of self-dealing (that is, disguising profits by paying them to the entrepreneur for a variety of services) is much more significant.

This idea — that the nondistribution constraint can be applied most effectively to large, formal organizations — has been implicit in much of the existing literature on the nonprofit sector. For example, although most analysts accept Hansmann's argument that nonprofit firms will arise when consumers have great difficulty in judging quality, no one suggests that nonprofit used car lots or nonprofit auto body shops or repair shops would solve the problem of consumer uncertainty in those sectors. The reason for this is obvious.

Small operations are difficult to monitor, and consumers would not believe any claims by a used car dealer that he is a genuine nonprofit organization, concerned only for the welfare of his clients.

On the other hand, large organizations are difficult to direct for personal gain. Universities, functioning as nonprofit corporations controlled by large boards of directors, involve relatively limited amounts of self-dealing. Although there has been some recent concern about uses of research overhead by universities, this concern has focused on the diversion of this money for other legitimate activities of the university (cross-subsidization) rather than for private enrichment.

The same issues apply to charities. We would have little faith in a charity operated by an individual or a small group of individuals.[24] Charities run by large groups are more trustworthy, although donors still must be alert.

This is consistent with our real world experience. When producers are small firms, governments usually choose to regulate quality directly, sensing that this approach will be more effective than any reliance on the nondistribution constraint. In the case of day care, what prevents low quality in Canada is direct regulation of certain aspects of quality, including staff-child ratios, training for staff, and so on. When regulation is less stringent, as in Alberta, quality tends to fall. Reliance on the nondistribution constraint as an alternative to regulation may well be problematic.

Another way to address enforcement of the nondistribution constraint is to restrict the form of the nonprofit organization. In Saskatchewan, nonprofit day care centers are required to have parent boards; in Quebec, only nonprofits with community boards are eligible for special grants. In each case, the assumption is that the boards will serve as effective limits on self-dealing and the for-profit-in-disguise problem.

An alternative approach is to use large nonprofits to regulate the nondistribution constraint within small organizations. Thus day care centers run by religious organizations might be less likely to exploit consumers financially (at least in order to divert funds to private entrepreneurs for personal gain). As another example, when the government in Canada wishes to support family day care (that is, day care run within the home of the provider), it makes little sense to direct money to those organizations directly because they are the ultimate in small firms. Instead, funds are directed through large charitable organizations which closely monitor the behavior of the small day care providers. In a similar way, individual donors rely on the United Way to oversee the activities of small charities, including some small day care centers. Governments might extend this approach by funding individual nonprofit centers only through large nonprofit institutions.

23. Of course, obtaining a tax number to issue charitable receipts is more difficult.

24. We do, however, trust individuals, operating for profit, to handle money intended for others. These individuals are usually lawyers, bound by fiduciary obligations. Lawyers face significant penalties for exploiting their position for personal gain.

CONCLUDING COMMENTS

I began this chapter with the question of whether auspice matters. In the case of day care, the short answer is that it does but that using that fact in the formation of public policy is somewhat problematic. Nonprofit day care centers do appear to offer somewhat higher quality than for-profit centers. But nonprofit centers can be low quality, and for-profit centers can be high quality. Furthermore, when governments attempt to lean on the distinction — that is, by directing large grants to nonprofit centers or by eliminating for-profit centers — there is a significant risk that for-profit entrepreneurs will incorporate as nonprofits and continue to earn profits through self-dealing. There is reason to believe that the non-distribution constraint may be particularly difficult to enforce when firms are small, and this is a problem in day care.

REFERENCES

Friesen, B. F. 1992. "A Sociological Examination of the Effects of Auspice on Day Care Quality." Ph.D. dissertation, University of Calgary.

Hansmann, H. 1980. "The Role of Nonprofit Enterprise." *Yale Law Journal* 89:835–98.

———. 1987. "Economic Theories of Nonprofit Organization." In *The Nonprofit Sector: A Research Handbook,* ed. Walter W. Powell, 27–42. Yale University Press, New Haven.

James, E. 1987. "The Nonprofit Sector In Comparative Perspective." In *The Nonprofit Sector: A Research Handbook,* ed. Walter W. Powell, 397–415. Yale University Press, New Haven.

Krashinsky, M. 1990. "Management Implications of Government Funding of Nonprofit Organizations: Views from the United States and Canada." *Nonprofit Management and Leadership* 1(1):39–53.

Nelson, R. R., and M. Krashinsky. 1974. "Public Control and Organization of Day Care for Young Children." *Public Policy* 22(1):53–75.

Newhouse, J. P. 1987. "Towards a Theory of Nonprofit Institutions: An Economic Model of a Hospital." *American Economic Review* 60:64–74.

Pence, A. R., ed. 1992. *Canadian Child Care in Context: Perspectives from the Provinces and Territories.* Volume 1 (British Columbia, Alberta, Saskatchewan, Manitoba, Ontario, Yukon). Ottawa: Statistics Canada, Health and Welfare.

———. 1992a. *Canadian Child Care in Context: Perspectives from the Provinces and Territories.* Volume 2 (Quebec, New Brunswick, Prince Edward Island, Nova Scotia, Newfoundland, Northwest Territories). Ottawa: Statistics Canada, Health and Welfare.

SPR Associates, Inc. 1986. "An Exploratory Review of Selected Issues in For-Profit versus Not-For-Profit Child Care." Report prepared for the House of Commons Special Committee on Child Care.

Steinberg, R., and B. H. Gray. 1992. "The Role of Nonprofit Enterprise in 1992: Hansmann Revisited." Paper presented at the Annual Conference of the Association for Research on Nonprofit Organizations and Voluntary Action.

Weisbrod, B. A. 1988. *The Nonprofit Economy.* Cambridge: Harvard University Press.

Young, D. R. 1981. "Entrepreneurship and the Behavior of Nonprofit Organizations: Elements of a Theory." In *Nonprofit Firms in a Three-Sector Economy,* ed. M. White. Washington, D.C.: Urban Institute.

8

ELIZABETH MAUSER

The Importance of Organizational Form: Parent Perceptions versus Reality in the Day Care Industry

Recent demographic changes in the United States have increased the demand for child care in centers, preschools, and nursery schools. The labor force participation rate of women has increased dramatically from 43.3 percent in 1970 to 57.3 percent in 1991. At the same time, the number of children under eighteen living in single-parent families has risen to 22 percent in 1991. In 1988, roughly 26 percent of children younger than five were cared for in an organized child-care facility (United States Bureau of the Census 1992).

These demographic changes have led to a national debate over the accessibility of affordable, high-quality child care. The coexistence of nonprofit and for-profit centers in the day care industry is one of the distinctive features of this industry. Although close to 50 percent of day care centers in the United States are nonprofit, the percentage of nonprofit centers varies considerably by region and state. Because there is very little information available to explain why nonprofit and for-profit firms coexist within an industry and whether organizational behavior differs across nonprofit and for-profit firms in the business sector, it is difficult to formulate policies that make quality care more accessible to parents.

Nonprofit and for-profit firms generally coexist in industries in which the consumer has poor information relative to the provider about the quality[1] of the service (that is, the health care, nursing home, and day care industries). Even though, as Burton Weisbrod notes in an earlier chapter, there is no conclusive evidence about whether nonprofit and for-profit organizations behave differently in industries in which they coexist, nonprofit providers are generally thought to have more altruistic goals, while for-profit providers are thought to be more self-interested. Susan Rose-Ackerman (1986) argues that we find both nonprofit and for-profit providers in the day care industry because there are not enough "altruistic managers" to meet the demand of consumers, and parents are forced to use for-profit providers. Weisbrod (1994) suggests that when consumers cannot evaluate quality because of the complexity of the service produced, the organizational form of a firm may be a signal to the consumer about the expected behavior of a provider. Unlike previous research on nonprofit organizations, mine focuses on consumer perceptions about whether behavioral differences exist across private nonprofit, religious nonprofit, and for-profit

---

1. Certain characteristics representative of the quality of care in a day care center are harder for a parent to observe than others. For example, it is easy for a parent to observe the equipment in a day care center, but the parent may have difficulty knowing whether the day care center is providing tender, loving care to her child during the day.

organizations. My goal is to shed some light on the theoretical debates in the literature over whether nonprofit organizations are less likely to take advantage of informationally underinformed consumers and more likely to provide higher quality care.

Whether nonprofit providers behave differently from for-profit providers may depend not only on the incentives created by an organization's internal environment and structure, but also on the organization's external environment. As Alan Wolfe notes in another chapter in this book, how exactly social and environmental factors impact altruistic behavior is still an area for further inquiry. We do know that for an organization to survive, it must respond to competitive pressures. A nonprofit (or for-profit) firm located in a geographic area with a high level of competition perhaps behaves differently from one located in an area with very few providers. In this book, Craig Calhoun argues that we must acknowledge the interdependence of communities in spite of their differences; similarly, we must recognize the interdependence of organizations competing with each other. For instance, nonprofit and for-profit firms competing in the same market area either may try to differentiate their services in order to form their own market niches or try to offer similar services.

Consumers who live in highly competitive geographic areas may find it difficult to obtain information about individual providers. When there are very few providers in a community, each provider develops a well-defined reputation in the community through word of mouth. As the number of providers increases and the probability of a consumer knowing someone who has used a particular provider falls, it may become more difficult to gather information about the quality of a particular provider. If the reputation of a provider is less defined in a highly competitive area, a parent who finds it costly to evaluate the quality of care in a center may rely more on a center's organizational form as a signal of expected behavior. This assumes, of course, that parents believe organizational form conveys some information about behavior.

The goal of my research is to examine the importance of organizational form to parents in choosing a day care center. I investigate whether parents perceive that there are differences in the quality and attributes of care across organizational forms. By comparing parental perceptions about quality differentials to actual differentials in the day care industry, I can evaluate how closely parental perceptions match reality. Finally, I explore whether organizational form is more (or less) important to parents in geographic areas that differ by the level of competition among providers, and how the competition among providers affects a parent's choice of organizational form.

DESCRIPTION OF DATA

The data in this paper come from two different sources. National data on centers in the United States are from "A Profile of Child Care Settings" (PCCS), a study conducted for the United States Department of Education, while data from Wisconsin are from surveys I conducted in January 1992 among parents who use center-based day care and among the directors of those centers. Some of the information collected from the PCCS is similar to the data that I collected in Wisconsin; however, the Wisconsin surveys focus on questions that gather information about the importance of organizational form to both parents and directors.

The data from PCCS provide national information about both family and center-based child-care programs. These data contain information about (1) the attributes of care, (2) admission policies, (3) types of children served, (4) subsidies, (5) activities, and (6) revenue sources. Interviews with 589 regulated family day care providers and 2,089 center-based early education and child-care programs occurred between October 1989 and February 1990. For the center-based programs, 88.7 percent of those sampled participated in the study. In this chapter, I include only the for-profit, private nonprofit, and religious nonprofit centers surveyed. The distribution of centers across organizational forms is as follows: 559 centers are for-profit, 586 are private nonprofit, and 235 are religious nonprofit.

In January 1992, I conducted mail surveys of parents who use center-based day care in Wisconsin and directors of day care centers. The parent survey contained questions regarding (1) parental characteristics, including the market wage of both the mother and father, (2) the importance of organizational form to a parent's choice of a center, (3) the relative importance of the characteristics of a center to a parent, (4) parental perceptions about difference in care across organizational forms, (5) the extent of parental effort put into finding a provider, and (6) parental perceptions of the difficulty of recognizing high-quality programs. The director survey included questions about (1) the characteristics of the director and the center, (2) the importance of organizational form in choosing a center as a workplace, and (3) ways in which the service and work environment differ across organizational forms.

To form the sampling frame for the Wisconsin surveys, I randomly selected 150 centers from licensing lists obtained from the Department of Health and Social Services in Wisconsin. I sent letters to directors of these centers to ask if they were willing to hand out surveys to parents and/or fill out the director survey. Roughly a third of the directors agreed to hand out surveys to parents. In the empirical analyses, I adjusted for the choice-based sample of parents. The centers where directors agreed to participate in the parent portion of the study do not differ from those centers where directors were unwilling to participate in terms of organizational form, size, ages of children served, region of Wisconsin where the center is located, and hours of operation. The response rate to the parent survey was 42 percent and yielded a sample of 417 parents. Roughly 25 percent of the parents in the sample purchase care from for-profit programs, 32 percent use private nonprofit programs, while the remaining 43 percent send their children to religious nonprofit programs. Approximately 75 percent of the directors who agreed to fill out the director survey completed it, generating a sample size of 50.[2] Of the 50 directors, 12 run for-profit centers, 23 run private nonprofit centers, and 15 run religious nonprofit centers.

PARENT PERCEPTIONS ABOUT THE
NONPROFIT SECTOR IN THE DAY CARE INDUSTRY

When there is no well-defined output in an industry that is easy to observe, some consumers may find it costly to evaluate product quality. A consumer's information costs — the costs of evaluating a service — consist of the cost of observing how the service is provided and of understanding how a high-quality service is produced. A consumer with limited knowledge or experience may find it difficult to evaluate a complex, nonstandardized service such as day care. A further complicating factor in the day care industry is that the payer or the parent differs from the one directly receiving the service, the child. Consumers who have higher information costs and consumers who find it more costly to observe the less visible characteristics of a service will be more likely to choose the type of firm that they perceive to be less likely to take advantage of any informational asymmetries.

Contract-failure theory suggests that nonprofit firms arise in industries in which informational asymmetries exist between the consumer and the supplier, making it difficult to enforce the contract between the two (Nelson and Krashinsky 1973; Nelson 1977; Hansmann 1980; 1986; Easley and O'Hara 1983; 1986). This theory argues that providers have less of an incentive to take advantage of informationally underinformed consumers when they cannot personally benefit monetarily from increasing the profits of the firm. Thus, it is thought that nonprofit providers will be more trustworthy or less likely to take advantage of consumers by cutting costs through reductions in quality. Although contract-failure theory is central to the theoretical work on nonprofit organizations, most of the empirical work in this area has focused on whether nonprofit and for-profit firms differ in terms of efficiency or other observable dimensions. Previous studies have not explored whether organizational form is, in fact, an important consideration in a consumer's decision to purchase services from a particular firm.

When consumers find it costly or difficult to observe the attributes of a service, they may prefer nonprofit firms if they feel that they provide a high-quality service. Data from the survey of parents who use center-based day care in Wisconsin reveal that approximately 56 percent of parents can correctly identify how their day care center is organized (Mauser 1993). Only 14 percent, however, cite organizational

2. Such observable characteristics as organizational form do not differ across the centers from which directors responded and did not respond to the director survey.

form as an important determinant in their choice of a program. Almost all of the parents who said that organizational form was important to them use nonprofit centers. When asked whether they thought the care differs across nonprofit and for-profit providers, only 25 percent of parents said they feel that nonprofit and for-profit centers provide a different type of service to consumers. Additionally, roughly 29 percent of the parents said that they believe that the care differs across private nonprofit and religious nonprofit centers. Among parents who feel that the care differs across nonprofit and for-profit providers, the consensus is that nonprofit providers offer higher quality care. The majority of parents said that the care differs across nonprofit and for-profit programs because the number-one priority in for-profit centers is making a profit rather than serving children, while nonprofit centers focus more on quality by attracting better qualified staff, having higher staff-child ratios, and putting less emphasis on the quantity of care provided.

Although the parent survey suggests that there is a group of parents who believe that the care differs between nonprofit and for-profit centers, most parents do not think that it does and do not cite organizational form as being important in their choice of a program. Even though parents may not cite organizational form as important, they may unknowingly prefer one form of organization over another for the set of attributes that the organizational form represents. Roughly 51 percent of parents who use religious nonprofit centers said that having a provider with values similar to their own was important to them in choosing a program, while 37 percent and 25 percent of parents using private nonprofit and for-profit centers, respectively, said that this was important. Of parents who chose for-profit centers, 74 percent said the turnover of staff was important to them when choosing among centers, whereas 81 percent and 91 percent of parents who use private nonprofit and religious nonprofit centers, respectively, said they cared about the turnover of staff. In the following sections, I explore how quality actually differs across nonprofit and for-profit programs and whether organizational form is more important to parents in geographical areas where the competition among providers is higher.

QUALITY DIFFERENTIALS IN THE NONPROFIT
AND FOR-PROFIT SECTORS

A number of measures are used to evaluate the quality of care in a day care center. Child-care experts suggest that the quality of care in a center depends on the staff turnover rate, the staff-child ratio, the sizes of the groups, and the experience and training of the staff. As the turnover rate in a center increases, there is more disruption in the center, and the children need to adjust frequently to new caregivers. In centers that have high staff-child ratios, the children are more likely to receive individual attention. Similarly, it is easier to pay attention to the needs of each child if the children are put into small groups.

Table 8.1. Coefficients of Variation for the Different Quality Measures Across Organizational Forms Using the PCCS Data

	For-Profit Centers	Private-Nonprofit Centers	Religious-Nonprofit Centers
Turnover of staff	2.879	1.649	1.633
Staff-child ratio	0.943	2.193	0.890
Group size	0.595	0.720	0.892

Source: Profile of Child Care Settings (Kisker and Piper 1992)

Table 8.2. Coefficients of Variation for the Different Quality Measures Across Organizational Forms Using the Wisconsin Data

	For-Profit Centers	Private-Nonprofit Centers	Religious-Nonprofit Centers
Turnover of staff	0.797	1.148	0.727
Staff-child ratio	0.389	0.307	0.459

Source: Director Survey (Mauser 1993)

There is evidence that, on average, nonprofit centers—both private and religious—provide higher quality care than for-profits. Data from PCCS indicate that the turnover of staff is 21 percent and 33 percent in nonprofit and for-profit centers, respectively (Kisker and Piper 1992). Similarly, data from Wisconsin suggest that the average turnover of staff in private nonprofit and religious nonprofit centers is 18 percent, whereas it increases to 35 percent in for-profit centers. The staff-child ratio also indicates that the quality of care is higher in nonprofit centers. According to the PCCS, for three-year-olds, there is one staff person for every 10 children in for-profit centers, while there is one staff person for roughly 9 children in private nonprofit and religious nonprofit centers. In Wisconsin, there is, on average, one person for 7.5 children in the nonprofit centers and one staff person for 8 children in the for-profit centers. However, data from the PCCS suggest that for-profit centers have smaller groups relative to nonprofit centers, but the differences in the group sizes are small, with the average for-profit center having 15 children in each group and the average nonprofit center having 16.

Another measure of the quality of a day care program is the experience and training of the staff. The PCCS data suggest that teachers in nonprofit centers have more education than those in for-profits. Roughly 52 percent of the nonprofit teachers had completed college, whereas 36 percent of the for-profit teachers had done so. Although the PCCS did not ask questions about the experience and training of each staff member, it did so of one randomly selected teacher per center. The experience and training of the randomly selected teachers did not differ significantly across organizational forms. More than 90 percent of the teachers in for-profit, private nonprofit and religious nonprofit centers had some form of special child-care training. In nonprofit centers—both religious and private—the teachers had less than a year more experience in child care relative to for-profit teachers.

Even if the average quality of care was the same across nonprofit and for-profit centers, the dispersion of quality around the mean level might differ. The quality of care may be distributed widely around the average in one type of day care arrangement, while the quality of care may fall within a relatively narrow range of the average in another day care arrangement. Consumers who are risk averse will prefer to choose the type of center that has a low variability in quality. On the other hand, parents who are risk seekers may prefer the type of day care with high variability in quality as a consequence of the chance of getting an exceptionally high-quality day care arrangement.

To explore how the relative dispersion of quality differs across organizational forms, I compare the coefficient of variation[3] for the different measures of quality for for-profit, private nonprofit, and religious nonprofit centers. Table 8.1 contains the coefficients of variation for the various measures of quality using the PCCS data, while table 8.2 includes the coefficients of variation calculated from the Wisconsin data. There is not a consistent pattern across organizational forms in terms of whether the quality of care is less varied in nonprofit relative to for-profit centers. The national data from the PCCS suggest the turnover of staff is less varied in nonprofit centers—both religious and nonreligious. The staff-child ratio is more varied, however, in private nonprofit centers compared to for-profit and religious nonprofit centers. The data from the PCCS and Wisconsin indicate that in for-profit and religious nonprofit centers the turnover of staff is more varied than the staff-child ratio. Both data sets suggest that, overall, the quality of care is the least variable in religious nonprofit centers. Because the quality of care is higher on average in religious nonprofit centers relative to for-profit centers and tends to be less variable than the quality of care in both for-profit and private nonprofit centers, parents who are risk averse should prefer religious nonprofit centers, all other things being equal. In his work on nursing homes and facilities for the mentally handicapped, Weisbrod (1994) finds the satisfaction with services of family members significantly greater for church-owned nonprofits relative to proprietaries but not significantly different between other nonprofits and proprietaries.

THE EFFECT OF COMPETITION ON PARENTAL CHOICE OF ORGANIZATIONAL FORM

Day care services can be seen as reputational goods—differentiated goods that consumers find through talking to friends,

3. The coefficient of variation is simply the standard deviation divided by the mean.

Table 8.3. Percentage of Nonprofit and For-Profit Centers Located in Each Region of Wisconsin

Region	% of Nonprofits	% of For-Profits
Northern	33	67
Western	46	54
Eastern	52	48
Southeastern	80	20
Milwaukee	79	21
Southern	65	35
Total	62	38

Source: Licensing lists from the Department of Health and Social Services in Wisconsin (September 1991).

relatives, and neighbors. Data from Wisconsin reveal that 53 percent of parents who use for-profit centers learned about their day care provider from friends and family, while 67 percent and 72 percent of parents using private nonprofit and religious nonprofit centers, respectively, found their provider through word of mouth. When there are very few providers in an area, each provider develops a reputation that is spread by friends and relatives in the community. If there are many providers in a community and information about providers is spread through word of mouth, it may be harder for a particular provider to develop a reputation in the community. Where there are many providers, it is more costly for a consumer to search for one because the range of choice is wide and the reputation of a particular provider is less defined than in a community in which there are few options. Mark Pauly and Mark Satterthwaite (1981) argue that as the number of physicians in an area increases, the quality of consumer information about providers falls because it is more difficult to obtain and process information about each provider.

More for-profit centers are located in the rural areas of Wisconsin, which include the northern, western, and eastern regions of the state. Table 8.3 contains the percentage of nonprofit and for-profit centers in the different regions of Wisconsin. As can be seen in the table, there is a marked difference in the percentage of for-profit centers located in the urban and rural areas. Because day care is a reputational good, information about day care providers may be less costly to obtain in rural areas, with the result that the nonprofit/for-profit distinction makes little difference to consumers living in these areas. Also, in rural areas, there may be more small, for-profit, Mom and Pop centers that function like nonprofit centers. Because there tends to be less competition among providers in rural areas, there may be less differentiation across types of providers. According to data from the PCCS study, the average staff-child ratio in for-profit and nonprofit centers is the same for centers located in less populated areas — areas where the population is less than the average population for the counties of the centers surveyed in the PCCS study. In the less populated areas, both for-profit and nonprofit centers have on average one staff person for every ten children, while in the more populated areas there is a

significant difference in the staff-child ratio between for-profit and nonprofit — private and religious — centers. There is on average one staff person for twelve children in for-profit centers, whereas there is one staff person for every eight children in the nonprofit ones. The coefficient of variation on the variable measuring the staff-child ratio for for-profit centers is 0.57 in the less populated areas, while it is 2.08 in the more populated areas.

If organizational form is a signal to consumers about expected behavior of providers, it may be more important in geographic areas where the competition among providers is high. The contract-failure theory suggests that nonprofit providers will be less likely to take advantage of any informational asymmetries; thus, we would expect consumers who have higher information costs to choose nonprofit providers, all other things being equal. Although the contract-failure theory assumes that consumers view nonprofit firms as more trustworthy, one of the purposes of this research is to test this assumption. Using data collected from parents in Wisconsin, I estimate through a multinomial logit model how a parent's preferences, characteristics, and information costs — the costs of evaluating and gathering information about the quality of care — affect her choice of organizational form. (For a description of the multinomial logit model, see Maddala 1983.) I specifically explore how a parent's choice differs between more and less competitive geographical areas in Wisconsin. More or less competitive areas were determined by calculating the Herfindahl index for day care centers for each county of Wisconsin.[4] If a parent chooses a center in a county in which the Herfindahl index is lower than the overall Herfindahl index for Wisconsin, the parent is assigned to the more competitive sample. I assume that the county is the market area in which parents search.

Description of Estimation

The dependent variable in the multinomial logit estimation — organizational form (ORG) — is the organizational form of the center that a parent has chosen. The organizational forms include for-profit, private nonprofit, and religious nonprofit centers. The independent variables in the estimation measure a consumer's information costs, her preferences, and how difficult she finds observing the less visible characteristics of a service that measure quality.[5] Table 8.4 contains a description of the variables included in the estimations.

The information costs of a consumer consist of several different components: (1) a parent's opportunity cost of time spent searching and observing; (2) a parent's experience with children; and (3) a parent's knowledge about day care. As a

4. The Herfindahl index measures the level of competition in an industry by summing the squares of the market shares of each firm. The index ranges from zero to one, and smaller values imply that the market is more competitive.

5. The fees charged to parents are not statistically different across for-profit and nonprofit centers in Wisconsin; thus, I have not controlled for the fees in this analysis.

Table 8.4. Variables Included in MNL Model for Parental Choice of Organizational Form

WAGE	Market wage of the mother.
FRIEND	Binary variable; it equals 1 if parent found provider through a friend or relative and equals 0 otherwise.
STOPIMP	Ranges from 1 to 4; it equals 1 if it was not important at all to the parent whether a program allowed her to stop by during the day and equals 4 if this policy was very important in choosing a program.
PRIOREXP	Ranges from 1 to 4; it equals 1 if the mother had no experience with children prior to having her own and equals 4 if the mother had a great deal.
OLDEST	Age of oldest child in family.
EARLYEDU	Binary variable; it equals 1 if the mother and/or father has had training in early childhood education and equals 0 otherwise.
OBSERVE	This variable combines through factor analysis three questions from the parent survey to measure how difficult it is for a parent to observe the less visible characteristics of day care which include whether a center provides tender loving care, individual attention, and activities that promote the educational and emotional development of the child.
RECOG	Ranges from 1 to 4; it equals 1 if the parent thought it would not be difficult at all to identify a high-quality program when she began to look for day care and equals 4 if she thought it would be very difficult.
MARRIED	Binary variable; it equals 1 if the mother is married and equals 0 otherwise.
IMPTYPE	Binary variable; it equals 1 if the organizational form was important in a parent's choice of a center and equals 0 otherwise.
SIMVALUE	Ranges from 1 to 4; it equals 1 if it was not important at all to a parent that a provider had similar beliefs and values when choosing a program and equals 4 if this was very important.
EQUIP	Ranges from 1 to 4; it equals 1 if the parent said that the equipment and facilities were not important at all when looking for a program and equals 4 if these were very important.
TURNOVER	Ranges from 1 to 4; it equals 1 if the turnover of staff was not important at all to a parent when looking for a program and equals 4 if this was very important.
HOME	Binary variable; it equals 1 if the mother stays home and equals 0 otherwise.

parent's opportunity cost of time, as measured by the parent's market wage (WAGE), increases, it is more costly for the parent to search for day care and to stop by a center to monitor the quality of care. The wage may also reflect an individual's education and preferences. An educated person may be more efficient at observing the care provided and may also be more aware of the potential differences that exist between for-profit and nonprofit providers. As a parent's experience and knowledge about children and early childhood education increase, it becomes easier for a parent to recognize a high-quality center and process the information needed to evaluate the quality of care. The experience and knowledge of a parent are measured through the following variables: (1) how much experience a mother has had with children prior to having her own (PRIOREXP); (2) the age of the oldest child in the family (OLDEST); and (3) whether the mother or father or both have had any training in early childhood education (EARLYEDU).

Preferences about day care centers vary among parents. A number of variables are included in the estimation to measure the preferences of parents across organizational forms. On the parent survey, parents evaluated the importance of various characteristics of day care when choosing a provider. The following characteristics are included in the estimations: (1) the importance of the equipment and facilities at the center (EQUIP); (2) the importance of staff turnover (TURN-OVER); and (3) the importance of a provider having similar values and beliefs (SIMVALUE). The organizational form of a program may be important to a parent in choosing a pro-

vider. Thus, a variable is included to measure the overall importance of organizational form in a parent's choice of a program (IMPTYPE). Because a mother who works within the home may send a child to day care for different reasons than a mother who works outside the home, I include a variable to control for whether a mother stays home (HOME). The marital status of a mother is expected to affect both her decision to seek care as well as the time constraint faced by the mother (MARRIED). A single mother may have less time to monitor a center and thus may be more likely, assuming risk aversion, to choose a nonprofit if its quality is perceived to be either higher or less variable, all other things being equal.

How hard a parent feels it is to observe the quality of care in a center is reflected through a series of variables. The first combines three questions from the parent survey that ask a parent how difficult she thinks it is to observe whether a center provides: (a) tender, loving care; (b) individual attention; and (c) activities that promote the educational and emotional development of her child. These three questions are combined through factor analysis into one variable capturing the perception of observability (OBSERVE) of the less visible characteristics of day care. If OBSERVE is greater than zero, it is harder for this parent to observe the quality of care relative to the average parent, while if OBSERVE is less than zero, it is easier for this parent to observe the quality of care relative to the average parent. The second variable measures how difficult a parent thought it would be to identify a high-quality program when she began to look for day care (RECOG).

A parent who is risk averse or concerned about evaluating

the quality of care in a center may prefer a recommendation from someone she knows or trusts because this will reduce her anxiety about evaluating the quality of a program. A binary variable is included that equals one if the parent found the provider through a relative, friend, or neighbor and equals zero otherwise (FRIEND). Since a parent who is very concerned about the quality of care may feel that it is very important to be able to stop by a program during the day, the estimation contains a variable that measures how important it is for a parent to stop by unannounced to see her child (STOPIMP).

Empirical Results

Some differences are apparent in the characteristics and preferences of parents choosing different organizational forms. The hourly market wage for mothers who use for-profit and private nonprofit programs is approximately $8.40 and $9.10, respectively, whereas the hourly wage for mothers using religious nonprofit programs is roughly $10.70. The organizational form of a program is the most important to parents who use religious nonprofit programs, while it is the least important to parents using for-profit providers. Parents who use for-profit programs are less likely to have found the provider through a friend or relative. Table 8.5 summarizes selected characteristics of the parents using different organizational forms.

Because the sample of parents is a choice-based sample, I weight the likelihood function for the multinomial logit model by the ratio of the frequency that a particular alternative is chosen in the population to the frequency of this alternative in the sample. This ensures consistency and asymptotic efficiency of the estimated coefficients (Manski and Lerman 1977; Manski and McFadden 1981; Amemiya 1985). The estimated coefficients with the weights do not differ significantly from the coefficients without any weights. In this chapter, I report only the estimations without any weights.

In the estimation, I use the mother's market wage rather than the father's to measure the opportunity cost of time of a parent because 19 percent of the sample are single mothers (12 percent are divorced, separated, or widowed, while 7 percent have never been married). Roughly 28 percent of the mothers in the sample, however, are not employed in the labor force. I estimate the multinomial logit two ways: (1) I assign mothers not in the labor force a wage by estimating what someone with similar characteristics would earn using data from the Current Population Survey (1990); and (2) I estimate the model including only employed mothers using a selection correction term (see Heckman 1974, 1976 for an explanation of the sample selection correction). In the first type of estimation, I underestimate the reservation wage[6] of a mother who is unemployed. Results from the second type of estimation suggest that there is not significant selectivity bias

6. The reservation wage is the amount of money an individual would have to be given to be induced to work the first hour.

Table 8.5. Selected Characteristics of Parents Across Organizational Forms

	For-Profit (n = 103)	Private Nonprofit (n = 130)	Religious Nonprofit (n = 179)
Wage of mother	8.32	9.10	10.66
	(3.85)	(4.84)	(6.40)
Percentage of parents who cited the following program characteristics as important in choosing a program			
Provider having similar values	25	37	51
Equipment	99	95	95
Turnover of staff	74	81	91
Organizational form	4	13	23
Being able to stop by unannounced	78	81	79
Percentage of parents who think it is difficult to identify a high-quality program			
	53	53	62
Percentage of parents who found provider through friends or family			
	53	67	72
Percentage of parents who think it is difficult to observe these characteristics of care			
Tender loving care	33	36	42
Individual attention to each child	56	52	58
Activities that promote development of child	17	19	29
Percentage of mothers with a great deal or some experience with young children prior to becoming a parent			
	80	83	69

in using the subset of mothers in the workforce.[7] The overall findings do not differ significantly for the two types of estimations. Here I report the first estimation that includes all mothers in the sample. Table 8.6 contains the parameter estimates for the two samples. The first sample contains parents who use centers in low-competition areas, while the second includes parents who send their children to centers in high-competition areas.

In both the more and less competitive samples, the probability of a mother choosing a for-profit provider decreases as a mother's wage rises. As a mother's wage rises by one standard deviation — $5.46 — the probability of choosing a

7. The selection correction term may not be very accurate because I use only the education of the mother, her marital status, and the number of children under six in the household to predict the probability of a mother working.

for-profit program relative to a private nonprofit program decreases by 43 percent in the more competitive sample, whereas it decreases by 10 percent in the less competitive sample.

Whether a parent finds a provider through a friend or relative does not affect choice in the more competitive sample. Parents in the less competitive sample, however, are less likely to use a for-profit provider if they found the provider through word of mouth. If it is more difficult for parents living in more competitive geographical areas to gather information about providers through word of mouth, parents must depend on their own monitoring and knowledge to evaluate the quality of care. In the more competitive sample, parents who find it hard to observe the less visible characteristics of care are less likely to choose for-profit providers. In contrast, the variable measuring the difficulty a parent perceives observing the less visible characteristics of care does not affect choice in the less competitive sample. When the variable OBSERVE increases by one standard deviation, making it even harder for a parent to observe the less visible characteristics of day care, the probability of a parent choosing a for-profit relative to a religious nonprofit provider decreases by 67 percent, whereas the probability of choosing a for-profit center relative to a private nonprofit center decreases by 40 percent in the more competitive sample.

Parents in more and less competitive geographical areas who are more knowledgeable about early childhood education and have had more experience with children are less likely to choose religious nonprofit providers, all other things being equal. Parents with more experience with children can more easily interpret the relevant information required to evaluate the quality of care in a program, lowering their information costs.

In both the high-competition and low-competition samples, there is a similar pattern in terms of how a parent's preferences affect choice. If a parent is concerned about the equipment of the facility, the parent is more likely to choose a for-profit, while a parent who is concerned about the turnover of staff or about whether the program has providers who share similar values is more apt to choose a religious nonprofit provider, all other things being equal.

If organizational form is important to a parent, the parent tends to choose either a private nonprofit or religious nonprofit program. Organizational form seems to be more important to consumers in high-competition areas. In the more competitive areas in the Wisconsin sample, 23 percent of the parents cited organizational form as important in their choice of a center, whereas only 9 percent of the parents in the less competitive sample stated organizational form as important. Furthermore, 21 and 39 percent of the parents think that the care differs across nonprofit and for-profit providers in the less and more competitive areas, respectively. It appears that the organizational form may be used more as a signal about the type of care provided in the more competitive areas or

that there may be more differentiation of services in the highly competitive areas.

SUMMARY AND CONCLUSION

Even though only 14 percent of parents cite organizational form as important in their choice of a program, and only 25 percent of parents feel that the care differs across nonprofit and for-profit providers, differences do exist across organizational forms in terms of the quality of care. The quality of care is higher, on average, in private nonprofit and religious nonprofit programs relative to for-profit programs, but the quality of care is not less variable in private nonprofit programs compared to for-profit ones. The quality of care in religious nonprofit programs, however, is generally less variable than that found in both for-profit and private nonprofit programs.

There is some consumer sorting in all geographic areas, but there seems to be more consumer sorting in areas where the competition among providers is high. Consumers in high-competition areas who find it hard to observe the less visible characteristics of day care are more likely to choose religious nonprofit centers. The difficulty a parent finds in observing the less visible characteristics of day care does not affect parental choice in low-competition areas.

Although organizations are often divided into three groups consisting of for-profit, nonprofit, and government firms, there seems to be an important distinction between religious and nonreligious organizations. Religious nonprofit day care providers offer higher quality care, and parents appear to have more trust in them. The chapter by Mark Chaves in this book focuses on why religious organizations exist as providers of secular public goods. Chaves sets forth what he calls a "garbage can model of organizational behavior":

> An explicit desire to evangelize does contribute to the tendency for religious organizations to establish nonprofits, but in an ironic way: Evangelistic motives bring individuals together in highly energetic organizations whose primary purpose — conversion — turns out to be . . . a goal that is continually and almost universally frustrated. Thus is religious energy . . . directed into the creation of nonprofit organizations that meet excess demand for any number of services. (Chaves, p. 62 in this volume)

Not only excess demand for day care but also excess demand for a certain type of day care may explain the existence of religious nonprofit centers in the day care industry.

This chapter raises a number of questions that should be explored further in future work. Although I suggest here that there may be differences in terms of quality and the attributes of care in more and less competitive areas, it would be worthwhile to examine more closely how the competition among providers affects the type of service provided across nonprofit and for-profit providers. With regard to competition, it

Table 8.6. Parameter Estimates for Low and High Competition Samples

	Low-Competition Sample		High-Competition Sample	
	Parameter Estimate	*Std Error*	*Parameter Estimate*	*Std Error*
CONSTANT				
1 vs 2:[1]	2.706	2.012	−4.698	4.391
1 vs 3:	6.535	2.305	−4.190	4.277
2 vs 3:	3.829	2.431	0.509	2.282
WAGE				
1 vs 2:	−0.027	0.052	−0.084	0.090
1 vs 3:	−0.158	0.063	−0.111	0.088
2 vs 3:	−0.131	0.061	−0.028	0.032
FRIEND				
1 vs 2:	−1.228	0.420	0.108	0.853
1 vs 3:	−1.843	0.562	−0.352	0.820
2 vs 3:	−0.615	0.581	−0.460	0.455
STOPIMP				
1 vs 2:	0.025	0.231	−0.095	0.415
1 vs 3:	−0.286	0.267	−0.369	0.389
1 vs 3:	−0.311	0.281	−0.274	0.231
OBSERVE				
1 vs 2:	0.052	0.196	−0.505	0.429
1 vs 3:	0.032	0.249	−1.107	0.421
2 vs 3:	−0.020	0.249	−0.603	0.243
RECOG				
1 vs 2:	−0.244	0.278	0.209	0.599
1 vs 3:	−0.478	0.346	0.297	0.575
2 vs 3:	−0.234	0.350	0.088	0.313
EARLYEDU				
1 vs 2:	0.716	0.434	0.050	0.798
1 vs 3:	0.352	0.530	−0.146	0.765
2 vs 3:	−0.364	0.544	−0.196	0.471
PRIOREXP				
1 vs 2:	−0.660	0.496	0.001	1.050
1 vs 3:	0.162	0.555	0.840	0.980
2 vs 3:	0.822	0.583	0.084	0.547
OLDEST				
1 vs 2:	−0.104	0.046	0.038	0.100
1 vs 3:	0.051	0.066	0.073	0.099
2 vs 3:	0.154	0.065	0.035	0.051
MARRIED				
1 vs 2:	−1.889	0.850	1.751	1.254
1 vs 3:	1.239	0.745	1.069	1.266
2 vs 3:	3.128	1.009	−0.682	0.511
HOME				
1 vs 2:	0.221	0.624	0.257	1.091
1 vs 3:	−0.322	0.686	−0.746	0.997
2 vs 3:	−0.543	0.713	−1.003	0.673
SIMVALUE				
1 vs 2:	0.130	0.204	−0.515	0.386
1 vs 3:	−0.702	0.265	−0.667	0.373
2 vs 3:	−0.832	0.264	−0.152	0.206
EQUIP				
1 vs 2:	0.761	0.360	1.189	0.823
1 vs 3:	1.093	0.444	1.456	0.796
2 vs 3:	0.332	0.416	0.267	0.410
TURNOVER				
1 vs 2:	−0.352	0.265	−0.394	0.528
1 vs 3:	−1.544	0.402	−0.757	0.508
2 vs 3:	−1.192	0.400	−0.363	0.302

Table 8.6. *Continued*

	Low-Competition Sample		High-Competition Sample	
	Parameter Estimate	*Std Error*	*Parameter Estimate*	*Std Error*
IMPTYPE				
1 vs 2:	−1.601	0.690	−0.185	1.244
1 vs 3:	−0.989	0.980	−1.578	1.153
2 vs 3:	0.612	0.901	−1.393	0.626
−2 Log Likelihood for Full Model	301.97		−2 Log Likelihood for Full Model	206.36
Percent Correctly Predicted	61.75		Percent Correctly Predicted	73.29

[1] Categories are designated as follows: 1 — profit; 2 — private nonprofit; 3 — religious nonprofit

would also be useful to compare how the quality and attributes of care differ across nonprofit providers located in more and less competitive areas. A similar analysis should be conducted for for-profit providers.

I have divided the types of programs into three categories — for-profit, private nonprofit, and religious nonprofit. The nonprofit/for-profit distinction is a crude one. Among for-profit providers, there are small and large centers, chains, and investor-owned programs. Similarly, the size and organization of nonprofit programs also differ across firms. In the future, it would be useful to explore some of these distinctions within organizational types to see how they affect organizational behavior.

REFERENCES

Amemiya, Takeshi. 1981. "Qualitative Response Models: A Survey." *Journal of Economic Literature* 19:1483–1536.

Current Population Survey. 1990. Washington: Bureau of Labor Statistics, Bureau of the Census.

Easley, David, and Maureen O'Hara. 1983. "The Economic Role of the Nonprofit Firm." *Bell Journal of Economics* 14:531–38.

———. 1986. "Optimal Nonprofit Firms." In *The Economics of Nonprofit Institutions,* ed. Susan Rose-Ackerman. New York: Oxford University Press.

Hansmann, Henry B. 1980. "The Role of the Nonprofit Enterprise." *Yale Law Journal* 89:835–99.

———. 1986. "The Rationale for Exempting Nonprofit Organizations from Corporate Income Taxation." In *The Economics of Nonprofit Institutions,* ed. Susan Rose-Ackerman. New York: Oxford University Press.

Heckman, James J. 1974. "Shadow Prices, Market Wages, and Labor Supply." *Econometrica* 42:679–94.

———. 1976. "The Common Structure of Statistical Models of Truncation, Sample Selection and Limited Dependent Variables and A Simple Estimator for Such Models." *Annals of Economic and Social Measurement* 5:475–92.

Kisker, Ellen E., and Valarie Piper. *A Profile of Child Care Settings: Center-Based Programs* 1992. Los Altos: Sociometrics Corporation, American Family Data Archive.

Maddala, G. S. 1983. *Limited-Dependent and Qualitative Variables in Econometrics.* Cambridge: Cambridge University Press.

Mauser, Elizabeth. 1993. "Is Organizational Form Important to Consumers and Managers?: An Application to the Day-Care Industry." Ph.D. dissertation, Department of Economics, University of Wisconsin-Madison.

Manski, Charles F., and Steven R. Lerman. 1977. "The Estimation of Choice Probabilities from Choice Based Samples." *Econometrica* 45:1977–88.

Manski, Charles F., and Daniel McFadden. 1981. "Alternative Estimators and Sample Designs for Discrete Choice." In *Structural Analysis of Discrete Data,* ed. Charles F. Manski and Daniel McFadden. Cambridge, MIT Press.

Nelson, Richard. 1977. *The Moon and the Ghetto: An Essay on Public Policy Analysis.* New York: W. W. Norton.

Nelson, Richard, and Michael C. Krashinsky. 1973. "Two Major Issues of Public Policy: Public Subsidy and the Organization of Supply." In *Public Policy for Day Care for Young Children,* ed. Dennis Young and Richard Nelson. Lexington: Lexington Books, Lexington.

Pauly, Mark A., and Mark A. Satterthwaite. 1981. "The Pricing of Primary Care Physicians' Services: A Test of the Role of Consumer Information." *Bell Journal of Economics* 12:488–506.

Rose-Ackerman, Susan. 1990. "Competition between Non-Profits and For-Profits: Entry and Growth." *Voluntas* 1:13–25.

U.S. Bureau of the Census. 1992. *Statistical Abstracts of the United States: 1992.* 112th ed. Washington, D.C.

Watt, J. Michael, Steven C. Renn, James S. Hahn, Robert A. Derzon, and Carl J. Schramm. 1986. "The Effects of Ownership and Multihospital System Membership on Hospital Functional Strategies and Economic Performance." In *For-Profit Enterprise in Health Care,* ed. Bradford H. Gray. Washington, D.C.: National Academy Press.

Part Three

Nonprofits and Modern States: Allies or Alternatives?

9

Markets, Politics, and Charity: Nonprofits in the Political Economy

State and market organizations exercise significant control over nonprofit financial resources in the United States and shape other aspects of the organizational environment in which nonprofits operate. The political economy of the United States creates enduring institutional patterns which determine the structural opportunities for relations among the three sectors in a particular industry. Nonprofits, however, have both strategic and dynamic relations to the public and for-profit sectors and do not play a passive role in compensating for general shortcomings in the political or market systems, as most observers implicitly assume. Nonprofit, public, and market actors can and do advance their own interests, creating an iterative process of strategic action and response. As a result, relations among the three sectors are constantly developing.

In terms of nonprofit-market relations, nonprofits serve specialized economic functions by compensating for imperfections in the market economy associated with inadequate demands or hidden producer exploitation. By doing so, nonprofits change market structures and reduce their own com-

The analysis presented in this paper draws heavily on findings and interpretations from my recent book *Understanding Nonprofit Funding* (Grønbjerg 1993). I want to thank Gerry Suttles, Woody Powell, Lis Clemens, and Carrie Rothburd for very helpful comments and suggestions on earlier drafts.

petitive advantages. Nonprofit and market organizations also manipulate one another for strategic advantages in resource relations, as a result of which nonprofits come to serve as an arena in which economic elites consolidate their power.

In terms of nonprofit-government relations, nonprofits have vested interests in the scope and structure of public sector activities. As nonprofits act to protect those interests, they engage in interest group politics. Where they come to share in the delivery of public goods, their political interests become especially well focused and their relations with the public sector institutionalized and difficult to restructure.

The character of these strategic structures and dynamic processes is most clearly evident from a comparison of industries that differ in the relative dominance of market and public sectors. Where the market sector is relatively weak, nonprofits have few incentives or occasions to pursue market activities themselves. In such fields, nonprofits are likely to be of less strategic relevance to market sector actors and present few opportunities for the exercise of elite power. Such nonprofits will therefore face difficulties in establishing resource relations with private firms.

Where the public sector is relatively undeveloped, nonprofits have legitimate occasions for pursuing political actions that focus on the scope and general structure of public sector mandates. They also, however, have few opportunities to become an integral part of the delivery of public goods and to benefit from the legitimacy, financial resources, and entry to negotiations about crucial administrative details that flow from such participation.

Here I focus on the fields of social services and community development to illustrate these processes. By social services I mean such direct client services as counseling, foster care, youth development, senior services, drug rehabilitation, and case management. By community development I mean activities that target and promote a specific geographic area, such as community economic development, community safety, community organizing, commercial or residential projects, and so forth.

The two fields differ in the strength and direct involvement of market sector organizations and therefore in how relevant nonprofits are to market sector organizations. The latter present a low profile in social services and a relatively high one in community development. The fields also differ in how well developed the public sector is and therefore in the amount, reliability, and concentration of financial and political resources available to nonprofits: social services are fairly well developed with extensive public resources while community development is much less so.

In this chapter, I first characterize the political economy of the United States with specific reference to social services and community development and argue that this economy differentially shapes the role of nonprofits vis-à-vis public and market sector organizations in their respective fields. I use findings from case studies of six social service and seven community development organizations[1] in the Chicago area to illustrate variations in the structure and dynamics of sectoral relations that result from these differences. Finally, I extend this approach and point to systematic variations in manifestations of the United States political economy across other industries and argue that there are corresponding differences in how nonprofits relate to market and state organizations in these fields.

THE ROLE OF SOCIAL SERVICE AND COMMUNITY DEVELOPMENT NONPROFITS IN THE U.S. POLITICAL ECONOMY

The political economy of the United States is shaped by the joint operation of two driving forces. The first of these is the

---

1. All were medium-sized organizations with revenues between $250,000 and $1.5 million in 1987 and located in the Chicago area. They were selected to allow for systematic comparisons by field and by major type (commercial, public, donations) and stability of funding (stable, turbulent). The social service agencies include Minority Search (fee-stable), Christian Therapists (fee-turbulent), Alcohol Treatment (public-stable), Hispanic Youth Services (public-turbulent), Youth Outreach (donation/mix-stable), and Immigrant Welfare League (donation/mix-turbulent). The community development organizations include Preservation Council (event-stable), Hispanic Neighbors and New Town Sponsors (event-turbulent), Economic Development Commission (public-stable), African-American Neighbors (public-turbulent), Community Renewal (donation-stable), and United Residents (donation/mix-turbulent).

ideological dominance of a classical economic model which defines free markets and competing market organizations as the fundamental institutions of society, leaving government and nonprofits to play secondary and supportive roles. The second and closely related force is deeply ingrained suspicion of virtually all public programs and authorities, which are viewed as inefficient, subject to favoritism, and antagonistic to the much-preferred system of private initiative, unless carefully controlled and monitored.

The result is a persistent preoccupation with and celebration of market forces, a relative absence of strong restraints on private initiatives, and a system of public policy mandates that have developed late and remain narrow, contentious, and incomplete, especially in the area of social policy.[2] The combination of these outcomes may have produced the world's most powerful economy as measured by gross national product or similar monetary standards, but it has been at the expense of addressing fundamental social issues.

Nonprofits play a critical role in the U.S. political economy. As voluntary associations, they suit the American preference for private auspices. As institutions established for charitable or common purposes, they alleviate the need for such action under public auspices. Yet nonprofit organizations do not have the economic and political clout of private and public sector organizations. The latter therefore influence major aspects of the organizational environment in which nonprofits operate. For example, state and/or market actions determine the payment levels of public assistance grants, the quality of public schools, the state of the economy, and investment and location decisions by business corporations. In turn, these actions affect the types and magnitude of problems that nonprofit social service agencies encounter among their clients and that community development organizations experience in their communities.

RELATIONSHIPS WITH THE PRIVATE SECTOR

The prominence of private market activities in the United States (and their protection in law and public policy) means that private sector organizations dominate the economy and condition the economic and social needs that nonprofits seek to address. As I show below, however, nonprofits also have specialized economic functions in the market economy and may serve as an arena in which economic elites exercise power. Both of these features differ among social service and community development organizations.

Nonprofit Functions in the Market Economy

Economic theories of nonprofit organizations (Hansmann 1980, 1987; Rose-Ackerman 1986; Weisbrod 1975, 1977, 1988) usually imply that nonprofits fulfill narrow but important functions in compensating for imperfections in standard market relationships, in which informed customers shop for

---

2. The United States remains one of the few developed nations to not have universal health insurance or family allowance program.

the best bargain and producers seek the largest profit. Nonprofits solve two kinds of problems in these relations: market failure and contract failure. Market failure occurs when demands for a product or service are so low or thin that private firms cannot generate sufficiently high profits to stay in business by meeting the demand. Because nonprofits have access to private donations and are exempt from certain taxes and fees, they can subsidize service activities or products and still meet operating costs in spite of low demand.

Contract failure occurs when the customer does not have sufficient information to evaluate the quality or competitive value of goods and services available in the marketplace. This may occur if the quality of the service is difficult to determine (for example, counseling) or the customer possesses only limited ability to exercise judgment (for example, because of age or impairment or ignorance). In these cases, market transactions occur under conditions of asymmetric information that impede the free operation of market forces. That is, if customers do not know what they are buying, providers can exploit their ignorance to maximize profit without affecting demand. Nonprofits avoid these inefficient tendencies because they are legally restricted from distributing any economic gains to private individuals. Because nonprofits have no incentives to exploit customer ignorance, they are more likely to deliver high-quality services and warrant the consumer trust made necessary by asymmetric information under conditions of contract failure.

Case studies show nonprofit social service agencies serving the specialized functions of overcoming both market and contract failure. One nonprofit social service agency, Minority Search, which defined itself as a nonprofit business, exemplifies the ability of nonprofits to overcome market failure. It charged major corporations a flat annual fee for providing long-term training to minority college students who worked in internship positions with the corporations during the summer. The agency pointed to the amount and length of training involved (four years) and the difficulty of recruiting suitable raw material (minority students with minimal risk of failure) as reasons for proprietary firms' inability or unwillingness to provide the service.[3]

Another social service agency, Christian Therapists, provided therapy to born-again Christians. This service is a classic example of a thin market operating under conditions of asymmetric information. The market is thin because born-again Christians are reluctant to seek help from secular organizations for fear that their Christian faith will be ignored or subverted in the process. The information is asymmetric because the quality of therapy is notoriously difficult for clients to evaluate.

As at many other social service organizations and among

professional therapists generally, the agency required clients to pay a fee for services received. It argued that the willingness to pay a fee is evidence of commitment to therapy. Only clients who are committed to therapy are likely to obtain full benefit from the treatment received. Payment of a fee, even just a token amount, is taken to demonstrate a minimum level of commitment to treatment.

Clients who are willing to pay fees, of course, also serve another important function for the agency: They confirm that they find the agency's services of value. The result is a self-reinforcing process by which counselors or other staff members of an agency, by serving fee-paying clients, find personal and professional rewards and the agency obtains revenues (Hasenfeld 1978).

Commercial actions of community development organizations fit mainly the market failure model of thin or inadequate demand. Inner-city neighborhoods experienced major, prolonged decline as middle-class families, businesses, and manufacturing firms moved to the suburbs after World War II. The more recent economic decline of the Northeast and the Midwest has accelerated that process for these regions. The absence of commercial investments has forced increasing numbers of community organizations in cities like Chicago to devote sustained attention to housing and economic development in their communities to counteract these trends.

Several of the community organizations I studied have participated in construction projects (for example, of housing developments and strip malls) in partnership with local businesses, real estate developers, and manufacturing firms, at times also involving governmental units as active or passive partners. In some cases, they have created formally incorporated joint ventures with proprietary firms, receiving a share of the profit.

Federal regulatory developments such as community reinvestment requirements for financial institutions and efforts to eliminate redlining have opened up new market niches and sources of earnings for nonprofit community development organizations. Thus, several of the case study organizations discussed here have worked closely with financial institutions to help local commercial establishments negotiate the borrowing process in return for loan-packaging fees.

Special events constitute another market niche created by nonprofit organizations of all types, catering to increasingly sophisticated demands for recreation and entertainment while at the same time affording new sources of revenues to many nonprofits. Three of the community development organizations, Hispanic Neighbors, New Town Sponsors, and Community Preservation Council, obtained the bulk of their revenues from major neighborhood festivals, attracting tens of thousands of visitors and clearing hundreds of thousands of dollars. This market niche has expanded greatly in recent years to the point where some commercial enterprises now specialize in organizing and catering events like the leasing of luxury boats for casino excursions.

These commercial explorations by nonprofits are part of a

---

3. To subsidize its services, the agency benefited from its tax-exempt status as a nonprofit organization. It also requested its corporate customers to make a flat annual donation for purposes of expanding the recruitment pool of minority talent, in effect a voluntary fee.

dynamic, iterative process so that over time, the availability of commercial services and products from nonprofits helps change consumer tastes and stimulate demand.[4] At some point, the demand increases sufficiently to entice entrepreneurs or profit-making organizations into the newly created market niche. The process by which nonprofits pave the way for proprietary incursions into a given market niche is most clearly evident in the case of Christian Therapists. Therapists employed by the agency eventually demanded that it adopt a group practice model and pay them in proportion to the business they generated. When the agency's board refused, eleven of thirteen staff members and the executive director resigned. Most set themselves up as individual practitioners in direct competition with the agency.

Community organizations face increasing competition from for-profit providers in their efforts to generate fee income. On the one hand, those that seek to support and provide services to private sector firms benefit from the expectations of local businesses to pay for services received. They encounter few, if any, protests by community residents, board members, or clients if they charge for their services. By the same token, however, once the loan-packaging market is established, local lending institutions or enterprising consultants easily enter the market.

By creating new markets in this way, nonprofits attract private firms into the fray. By establishing standards for organizational behavior that reassure uneasy customers about the quality of services they receive, as in the case of Christian Therapy, nonprofits allow private sector firms to overcome customer fears of exploitation. These dynamics are likely to intensify as the private economy continues to restructure and shift away from manufacturing toward a service economy.

At the same time, both social service and community organizations are increasingly turning to fees and other commercial receipts to supplement their revenues. The combi-

4. Such commercial activities may also subvert the charitable mission of nonprofits and endanger other resources. Both Minority Search and Christian Therapists pursued fee strategies to the point of disengaging themselves from low-income individuals with complex problems (Cloward and Epstein 1965; Grønbjerg 1990). Minority Search found itself recruiting an increasingly middle-class population of minority students in order to maintain the quality of trainees and sustain corporate interest. These students already had many opportunities available to them, however, and Minority Search found it difficult to force them to accept the full demands of the program, thus potentially endangering its capacity to deliver a quality product to its corporate clients. At Christian Therapists, individual therapists came to define the work of providing therapy to residents of public housing projects as inappropriate or too difficult. The agency relegated the increasingly unsuccessful solicitation of donations to maintain the program to the most marginal staff person who also provided the services (the lone, black female social worker among the remaining white, male, clergy-therapists). Not only did this virtually assure the program's failure, but it also threatened to alienate board members affiliated with the agency's parent organization, a non-denominational church, which served as a source of referral for clients and critical bridge loans to the agency.

nation of these developments — the intrusions by for-profit organizations into nonprofit market niches and the cultivation by nonprofits of for-profit revenue streams — suggests that the boundary between the two sectors may become increasingly blurred and contentious. So far, representatives from the for-profit sector have been most vocal in defending their territory. They claim that nonprofit organizations compete unfairly with small businesses (Bennett and DiLorenzo 1989) because their access to donations and avoidance of tax payments allow them to operate at lower costs.

Nonprofits as Arenas for Economic Elites
In addition to performing these specific economic functions, nonprofit social service and community development organizations serve other strategic purposes for market organizations as they seek to use such firms for their benefit. Given the dominance of private firms in American society and the financial resources they control, it is not surprising that nonprofits have sought to establish explicit linkages with the for-profit sector. Nonprofits pursue such relations when they solicit corporate donations or sponsorship of special events, and they formalize the linkages when they appoint corporate leaders to serve on their boards of directors. Of course, by cultivating the corporate community in this manner, nonprofits themselves come to constitute an arena within which economic elites are able to exercise and consolidate power.

The ability of nonprofits to attract sizable corporate support and top corporate leadership to their boards in part reflects the extent to which these linkages present status opportunities or claims to legitimacy for both parties (Galaskiewicz 1985, 1986). The nonprofit organization's size and prestige and the opportunities it provides for networking or exercise of leadership will influence the degree of interest corporate leaders have in joining the board. Such large, well-established nonprofit organizations as United Ways, foundations, universities, hospitals, and major cultural institutions have been quite successful in attracting corporate support and corporate leaders (or their spouses) to board memberships (Ostrander 1984; Odendahl 1990; Schiller 1989; Useem 1984; Brilliant 1990).

Most social service organizations, by contrast, find it difficult to be equally successful. They are too small and numerous to stand out in the pack of major nonprofits seeking corporate contacts at the highest level of the firm. More important, in contrast to the services offered by institutions of higher education and major cultural organizations, theirs are rarely of key interest to major corporations. In fact, only one of the social service agencies included in my case studies (Minority Search) had succeeded in attracting a large number of top corporate leaders to its governing board. It was also the only social service agency to provide services of *direct* interest to corporate leaders: helping them recruit talented minority managers. The agency's horizontal integration with major corporations explains why all board members were actual or potential customers of the agency. In fact, the agency was so successful in generating corporate interests in its activities that it established an advisory board to accommodate an even larger number of corporate representatives.

None of the other social service agencies offered services of similar strategic importance to major corporations, although two, Youth Outreach and Immigrant Welfare League, were able to generate some corporate interest. Youth Outreach, which provided counseling and preventive services to low-income students on-site in public schools, benefited from its early affiliation with Episcopal Charities and the elite membership of this denomination and at one point recruited board members from Chicago area churches. The agency also profited from recent corporate attention to problems of inner-city public schools, the location of all the agency's services, and had attracted some fairly high level corporate executives to its very large fifty-member board.

Immigrant Welfare League, which provided immigration services, job training, and a range of other services to a large white ethnic group, also had some attraction to corporate leaders because of its affiliation with the Catholic Church and the powerful political position of the ethnic group it served. It therefore served as a specialized arena for business organizations targeting this sizable ethnic population. Perhaps more important, both agencies were the oldest in the study, having been established in the early 1920s, and had been able to build corporate connections over a long period of time.

The mechanism by which these two agencies recruited corporate board members shows both the recruitment process in action and the tenuousness of the agencies' relationships with the corporate sector. Youth Outreach looked for candidates with high-level positions in specific corporations who would be able to ensure a stream of donations from their firm. It was able to land several such candidates because a few existing board members had the necessary personal contacts and because its executive director played an active role in key civic organizations. Some of these strategic board members never attended board meetings, made no personal donations to the agency, and afforded no access to corporate donations but were kept on the board because their names attracted other board members and because their resignation might signal the agency's inability to provide the appropriate arena for contacts.

Immigrant Welfare League was less sophisticated. It routinely offered a position on its board to any individual or organization that donated ten thousand dollars or more. My review of the agency's correspondence shows that several donors declined the invitation to serve on the board with sufficient vigor to suggest its inappropriateness.[5] Perhaps for this reason, the agency had not been able to extend its corporate board membership much beyond its own ethnic group and businesses targeting this ethnic group.

The situation for community organizations is more mixed but illustrates better how nonprofits serve as an arena for market action. Although disadvantaged by their smallness, community organizations present specific strategic advantages to firms and institutions located in a given community. Although few of the community organizations attracted any top corporate executives to their board, most were successful in involving the local managers of major firms with operations in their community or executives of such important local institutions as banks, real estate firms, hospitals, universities, and churches.

There are good reasons for their success. Three of the case study organizations, New Town Sponsors, Economic Development Commission, and United Residents, had access to local banks, large businesses, major employers, and institutions of higher education in their communities; they had cultivated relationships with the cast of community institutions.[6] The three had also developed special mechanisms to institutionalize the financial support involved, for example, by varying the membership dues of commercial property owners according to the assessed evaluation of the real estate involved.

Major community institutions are important actors in community development organizations. The former have vested, legitimate interests in the community, and community organizations cannot oppose or ignore them without incurring potential costs. The relationship is reciprocal in that each sees the other as providing an opportunity to influence development without having to take full responsibility for direct and aggressive community action.

Because of the variety of strong local institutions in the communities, these three community development organizations defined their role as one of providing opportunities to air and resolve diverse community interests. They sought to supply a forum in which local community actors could interact and kept their direct political involvement focused on issues of direct local impact around which negotiated positions could be developed. Had they attempted to play a more forceful role, they would have risked offending portions of their constituency and losing donations or dues. This happened to United Residents when it attempted to use revenues from a special service area taxing district to push a particular redevelopment project. Opposition from a handful of local businesses who saw themselves as benefiting only marginally from the project killed the taxing district after three years.

Another case study organization, Community Renewal, illustrates a more extreme version of the process by which community organizations serve the interest of local institutions. This group obtained the bulk of its funding from a single institution with major investments in the community and approached a condition of co-optation. The institution had devoted significant resources to expanding and protecting its

---

5. E.g., "We cannot possibly accept board memberships for each of the many organizations we fund."

6. Some communities are so impoverished that organizations obtain little business support locally. This was the case for Hispanic Neighbors and African-American Neighbors.

interests in the community. Rather than undertaking these activities internally, however, it delegated much of its visible activities to Community Renewal. The decoupled structural arrangement ensured that the efforts received full-time management attention, while protecting the institution from controversy and risk of failure; the institution remained separate from such controversial, forceful efforts as lawsuits against local property owners that might have entailed substantial financial or symbolic costs.

Only a narrow range of community institutions are likely to want to influence or control a community development organization to the point of co-optation. Factories, hospitals, universities, major commercial establishments, leading banks, and large corporate headquarters all exercise direct control over sizable portions of local real estate holdings if they are located in a small community. They cannot avoid having a major impact on local communities in managing these holdings. They also have vested interests in many of the arenas in which community development organizations are active: decisions on land use patterns, enforcement of building codes, and crime control. These types of community institutions therefore have major incentives to define their interests in the community broadly and to pursue them actively by collaborating with or co-opting community development organizations.

As these examples show, corporate participation in nonprofit boards serves the direct economic interests of both parties. Well-connected boards of directors afford nonprofits personalized access to such important resources as corporate and foundation grants, in-kind support for special events and marketing efforts, and financial and legal advice. For corporate leaders, financial support of nonprofit organizations and membership on nonprofit boards of directors are indirect opportunities to promote corporate interests and extend their sphere of influence.[7]

These opportunities develop as corporate leaders interact with one another in the neutral settings offered by nonprofits and through specific actions by individual firms. The latter include efforts to create goodwill and market recognition (that is, cause-related marketing), shape policy agendas and definitions of problems, and, more generally, ensure that corporate positions and interests are known and incorporated into nonprofit activities as well as in the corporate world (Useem 1984; Schiller 1987).

Such attempts at mutual exploitation may take on a life of their own and become difficult for either party to control. For nonprofits, the risk is one of dependence on fickle corporate goodwill, if not actual co-optation. For corporate actors, participation in nonprofit social service and community development activities may risk involvement in controversies that antagonize potential customers or complicate already thorny

business relations.[8] Such risks, coupled with the smallness of nonprofit social service agencies, explain why these types of agencies may find it difficult to attract corporate leadership to their boards. In the case of community development organizations, the benefits to corporate actors may outweigh the risks because of the strategic role that development organizations play in the local business community.

RELATIONS WITH THE PUBLIC SECTOR

Nonprofit social service and community development organizations also maintain distinctive relationships with the public sector. The peculiar nature of the American welfare state is especially important to social service agencies and relevant to community development organizations as well.

National social welfare policies developed late in the United States and continue to be beset—for ideological and other reasons that run counter to the celebration of private initiative and free markets noted earlier—by a general reluctance to expand public mandates. These features help explain the emergence of a welfare system in which non–public service providers play an important role in executing public mandates (Grønbjerg, Street, and Suttles 1978; Sosin 1990; Wilensky and Lebeaux 1965). Indeed, nonprofits are the main providers of nonpublic services in the social service field but have more complex relations with the public sector in the community development field.

Nonprofits and Indirect Demand Structures

The public sector uses a combination of fiscal and monetary policies to guide the nation's economic and social development and to meet the needs for specific public services. Fiscal policies refer to public spending and revenue policies, monetary policies to efforts to guide private investments, as, for example, by changing Federal Reserve Bank discount rates. Some of these policies affect nonprofits indirectly by influencing demand for their services. Others have a direct impact on nonprofits, depending on the scope and payment structure of public spending.

The nature of monetary policies (for example, Federal Reserve Bank discount rates) and the structure and size of tax systems indirectly modify demands for services by both social service and community development nonprofits. In the case of social services, monetary policies influence the general state of the economy and therefore overall employment and wage levels. The widening inequality of wages in the United States (Phillips 1990) is unchecked by central planning or effective wage policies, leaving increasing portions of the population in low-wage jobs, including many jobs in the nonprofit sector, and increasing the need for social services.

The structure of tax systems affects the volume of discre-

7. In Granovetter's terms (1973), nonprofit boards provide the opportunities for corporate leaders to develop and maintain weak ties with one another.

8. This is most evident in the insistence by corporate board members that United Way organizations, which they dominate, stay out of controversies (e.g., abortion services, affirmative action on behalf of gays and lesbians) as much as possible.

tionary income and financial security available to different income groups. The relatively regressive tax system in the United States disproportionately targets low-income groups (Reynolds and Smolensky 1977; Edsall 1984), further reducing their economic well-being and increasing their need for free or heavily subsidized compensatory services. At the same time, middle- and upper-income groups receive extensive asset-building support in the form of tax deductibility of mortgage interest payments, real estate taxes, and employment-related retirement savings (Sherraden 1991). These income groups therefore have a greater capacity than low-income earners to make donations to nonprofits and to pay near-market fees for nonprofit services, thereby encouraging nonprofits to provide services of particular interest to these groups.

Monetary and tax policies also affect the demand for community development efforts. The United States still does not effectively distinguish between productive investments and leveraged buyouts and has only recently begun to use monetary and tax policies to encourage reinvestment in existing structures as opposed to new infrastructures. Widespread celebration of growth and newness tends to favor the latter, leaving older communities with deteriorating infrastructures and cumulative disinvestment, thus increasing the need for community development organizations to take action to counteract or overcome these trends.

Nonprofits and Direct Public Spending

The amounts and purposes of public spending directly shape the community needs and service demands that nonprofits encounter, whether or not they have any public funding themselves. The United States has a fairly limited definition of public goods. It lags behind most other industrial nations in the proportion of gross national product allocated to public welfare spending, especially outside the area of health care, and still lacks universal health insurance or family allowance programs (Palmer, Smeeding, and Torrey 1988).

Almost two-thirds of total public spending for welfare purposes in the United States goes to income insurance programs (38 percent, for example, to social security) or medical benefits (24 percent). These expenditures have grown ninefold over the period 1950–88, even adjusting for inflation and population growth, to the benefit primarily of the elderly, those who have experienced long-term employment, and the medical establishment.

By contrast, means-tested income-assistance programs (for example, Aid to Families with Dependent Children) and other services for the poor have increased only modestly, barely doubling in constant per capita dollars, and jointly account for only about one-tenth of total public welfare spending. Low levels of spending for traditional welfare purposes mean that nonprofits are faced with meeting a wide range of basic needs which are not directly addressed by public spending.

All other welfare services targeted at low-income groups accounted for only about 3 percent of total public welfare expenditures in 1984, although that percentage represented more than a tripling of real spending per capita in 1950. Nonprofit social service and community development organizations obtain most of their public funding from this latter, smallest, and slow-growing component of public welfare spending.

In local communities like Chicago, state and local government spending may deviate from these national trends. Illinois consistently trails other industrial states in many public policy efforts, although its per capita income ranked it among the top six from 1929 through the late 1970s, when it dropped to eighth place. The state has faced continuous fiscal problems since 1982. It has made few, if any, attempts to compensate for the reduced value of federal funding or to implement any extension of human services, except in the child welfare field. The city of Chicago also has not established strong commitments to human services from its own funding sources but relies extensively on state and federal grants for many of its human service efforts.

Public spending for community development activities and support for community organizations has seen much more drastic change. Beginning with public housing projects and urban renewal efforts in the 1950s, the Community Action Programs of the 1960s, and a variety of anticrime and employment and training programs since then, federal funding increasingly targeted inner-city communities. Richard Nixon's revenue sharing program and Jimmy Carter's Community Development Block Grants sought to provide local government with the financial resources to address key problems of housing, development, and community organizing, while reducing direct federal involvement. Almost all of these programs have been eliminated or severely curtailed in recent years.

The structure of public policy and priorities means that the United States has major service needs and service gaps. Nonprofit social service and community development organizations benefit from these patterns in monetary, tax, and fiscal policies because they leave them with an important role to play in addressing major societal problems.

Direct Nonprofit-Public Linkages

Although the volume of public spending is clearly important, assessing the form that spending takes is even more critical for understanding how nonprofit and public sectors interact. Some public spending takes the form of direct payments to individuals (for example, public aid and social security payments) or vouchers that individuals exchange for specified services (for example, food stamps, student loans, Medicare, Medicaid, Section 8 Housing vouchers). These payment systems are of interest to nonprofits because they give individuals discretion over where to obtain services. Consequently, nonprofits must compete with free public services (in the case of direct public provision) and with each other and for-profit organizations for fee-paying or credit-bearing clients.

Nonprofits therefore have a vested interest in limiting the scope and quality of these payment systems because lack of competition makes their own program activities more attractive and needed.

A third payment structure, public subsidies to private providers, usually in the form of grants or contracts, is of greater direct interest to nonprofits because they tend to be the preferred recipients of such support. Nonprofits can couch their self-interest in this system in ways that appeal to broader ideological preferences for private initiatives in the United States. The contract system thus not only supports market goals of efficiency by forcing the public sector to exploit available (nonpublic) infrastructures, but also obviates the need for expansion or creation of public infrastructures at taxpayer expense, activities presumed to be mismanaged or operated inefficiently.

The contract system lends hidden support to persistent suspicions about the deservingness of low-income clients in the United States—beliefs that they are at fault for their predicament and should not be entitled to free services at taxpayer expense. By channeling public spending targeted at such clients through nonprofit subcontractors, the system avoids leaving service decisions in the hands of clients assumed to be ill-informed or unworthy or both. Instead, nonprofits come to act as gatekeepers, able to provide the most appropriate service and to weed out those with questionable claims to legitimacy.

The contract system not only provides nonprofits with revenues and gives them a culturally approved role to play, but also simplifies some management tasks. It reduces the need of nonprofits to compete for and satisfy, in the case of social agencies, a large number of individual clients with fickle interests or, in the case of community organizations, apathetic or warring community residents and institutions. Instead, nonprofits with public contracts must satisfy only a limited number of funders, over whom they can exercise some degree of control, and they obtain substantial levels of funding, secure for the duration of the contract and often beyond.

Cooperation in Social Services. The nonprofit-public relationships differ for social service and community development organizations because the volume and structure of public spending vary. Federal and state governments share responsibility for social services in Illinois. For the Chicago/Cook County area, the federal government was the major source (59 percent) of the $377.5 million in public spending for social services in 1984, yet it dispensed only 3 percent directly.[9] The rest was transferred to state agencies or units of local government.

While the state paid for one-third (35 percent) of public social services in Cook County, it dispensed two-thirds (64 percent), including most indirect federal funds, and controlled three quarters (76 percent), including funds passed on to local government and dispensed there. Local governments contributed only 3 percent to the total cost of social services but dispensed and controlled almost one-third (32 percent).

Opportunities for nonprofits to provide services under contract with public agencies were extensive in the social service field, accounting for almost half (47 percent) of all public spending. Current patterns are likely to be similar.[10] Although the level of spending has increased more in some fields than others, there have been no major changes in policy that would fundamentally shift the overall structure of these patterns.

The dependence is mutual: public agencies depend on nonprofits to deliver their social services, and public funding is a major source of revenue for social service nonprofits. The majority of residential (60 percent) and other social service nonprofits (62 percent) in Illinois reported some public funding in 1991 (Grønbjerg et al. 1992). For about one-third (31 and 38 percent, respectively, for residential and other social service nonprofits), it was the major source of funding, accounting for more than half of each organization's revenue.

The spending structure is strengthened by the dynamics under which public-nonprofit resource relationships play themselves out in the social policy arena. Once the public-nonprofit grants or contract funding system is established, public agencies purchase more than service capacities and access to infrastructures, and nonprofits obtain more than revenues. The relationship comes to involve also the exchange of legitimacy, knowledge, and influence (Saidel 1991). The result is a self-reinforcing process in which nonprofit social service agencies develop complex interorganizational relations with public sector agencies.

The linkage is evident from tendencies toward isomorphism between the two sectors and the types of operational practices that public funding encourages in or imposes on the nonprofit partners. The receipt of public funding by nonprofit social service agencies means that they must track the fallout from budget negotiations and shifting priorities up and down

9. It is difficult to document the structure of intergovernmental relations at the level of local communities, the scale at which most nonprofits operate. Federal support for programs become incorporated in public budgets at each level of government involved, the geographic allocation of funds by higher levels of government rarely coincide with

local jurisdictions, and fiscal periods may differ considerably among governmental units (Grønbjerg et al. 1984).

10. The child welfare field, dominated by the Illinois Department of Children and Family Services (DCFS), is a case in point. In 1984, DCFS by itself accounted for roughly one-third of public spending for social services in Cook County and was a major source of funding for nonprofits. That pattern has continued. Over the 1985–89 period, the department awarded roughly $1 billion (1989 dollars) in contracts for client services, roughly two-thirds of the department's total appropriations. Residential and other social agencies received almost two-thirds of this amount ($620 million) and were also the primary beneficiaries of the 34 percent increase in DCFS contract funding (in constant dollars) over the period, getting more than three-fourths (77 percent) of the increase (Chen, Grønbjerg, and Stagner 1992).

the paths of intergovernmental transfers. They must adhere to rules and regulations that limit internal management discretion, meet work-intensive reporting requirements, and survive cost control and cost sharing. They must also overcome their built-in proclivities toward fragmentation and the ad hoc planning associated with managing multiple contracts with idiosyncratic requirements and timetables. Finally, they must weigh opportunity costs associated with pursuing alternative sources of funding.

In return for accepting these contingencies, nonprofit social service agencies obtain sizable, dependable funding. The four Chicago-area social service agencies with public funding that I studied—Youth Outreach, Hispanic Youth Services, Immigrant Welfare League, and Alcohol Treatment— rarely lost an existing public grant or contract.[11] Indeed, the evidence shows that it is difficult for public agencies to terminate funding relations. For example, in late 1987, the Illinois Department of Children and Family Services (DCFS) decided to allow new agencies to bid for certain counseling contracts in competition with existing subcontractors. When DCFS awarded contracts to several new agencies (including Youth Outreach) with higher proposal review scores than existing providers, the latter took their case to the governor and forced DCFS to cancel the contracts the day before services were supposed to start.

On the other hand, nonprofit social service agencies do obtain access to new opportunities for public contracts as the information network alerts them to leftover funding or newly created funding streams and as public agency administrators come to accept them as reliable subcontractors. In fact, one public agency not only alerted Immigrant Welfare League of a new source of funding in another public agency, but advised it on how to write the application.

There is other evidence that important state agencies have come to depend on access to a reliable, cooperative infrastructure of nonprofit organizations in order to carry out their mandates, especially in child welfare, community mental health, and substance abuse treatment and prevention. For example, membership in key nonprofit coalitions is the best single predictor of the amount of funding that nonprofits received from the Illinois DCFS in 1989 (Grønbjerg, Chen, and Stagner 1992).

Indeed, nonprofit statewide coalitions and major child welfare agencies remain among the organizations most called upon to help formulate or comment upon social policies. They view themselves as the indispensable partners of public agencies, providing high-quality, professional social services, and believe they are entitled to adequate public (that is, state) reimbursements for those services. The state has accepted these claims, at least in the child welfare field,

and established a formal structure for negotiating rate setting with nonprofit child welfare agencies.

The nonprofit-public relationship in social services thus approximates a pattern of cooperation because the public sector depends on nonprofit service providers to execute public mandates. This dependence derives from and bolsters shared goals. The absence of strong for-profit competitors in the field supports the assumption of good faith in contractual relations. Yet the process is a self-reinforcing one. Funding relations become increasingly institutionalized as either party becomes reluctant or unable to undertake major modifications. At the same time, the relationships become increasingly complex and costly to the participants because both parties seek to exploit available opportunities to exercise control over the relationship. Neither party appears to be fully successful in doing so.

Symbiosis in Community Development. The relationship of nonprofit community development organizations with the public sector differs notably from that of the social services. In 1984, total public spending for community development in Cook County was $234.4 million,[12] about two-thirds the amount spent for social services. In contrast to public spending for social services, this was almost entirely (97 percent) financed by the federal government with little participation by state agencies in funding (2 percent), administering (3 percent), or controlling (9 percent) the programs. Instead, activities were administered almost entirely (96 percent) by several units of local government.

Equally important, almost all the funding (94 percent) was used by the public sector itself, only 4 percent being available to nonprofit agencies in the field ($9.4 million). From a fiscal point of view, nonprofits are much less important to public sector activities in community development than they are in delivering publicly financed social and mental health services.

In spite of low reliance by the public sector on nonprofits in community development, these nonprofits still depend on public funding for a significant portion of their revenues. Almost half (45 percent) of them had public funding in 1991, and for one quarter, this was their primary source of funding. The dependence is therefore not symmetric: Nonprofits in the field depend much more on government for their resources than government depends on them for program activities.[13]

This helps explain why in the community development

11. For Hispanic Youth Services and Immigrant Welfare League, terminated or one-time contracts amounted to only 5 to 6 percent of total public funding received over a five-year period. Neither Alcohol Treatment nor Youth Outreach had any such awards.

12. This includes $74.5 million in operating support for public housing authorities but not Section 8 housing vouchers.

13. That pattern is possible because community development organizations are relatively few in number and small in size. A statewide survey of Illinois human service organizations conducted in 1991 found that community development organizations accounted for 11 percent of the organizations, but for only 2 percent of revenues. In contrast, residential and other social service agencies accounted for 46 percent of the organizations, but 67 percent of aggregate revenues (Grønbjerg et al. 1992).

field, the pattern of relationship to the public sector approximates symbiosis. Rather than functioning as a critical part of the publicly funded service infrastructure, nonprofits in the community development field play an intervening or mediating role in the overwhelmingly political interactions between public and market organizations. These two each attempt to enlist community organizations on their side, just as community organizations may negotiate alliances with either.

In contrast to social service agencies, community development organizations rarely have the capacity or resources to carry out relevant activities themselves, for example, build or repair housing and create new jobs. Only recently have new sources of public support become available to them for such purposes, and not in large amounts. Instead, the role of community development organizations has centered on identifying needs or gaps in public services and on closely related efforts to promote or resist public or private sector developments. Some engage in limited partnerships with the public or private sectors, especially in the planning phases of housing and community development projects (for example, commercial strip development and incubator ventures) but also as managers or coordinators of ongoing efforts.

Such brick and mortar projects highlight land use and geographic considerations and therefore local politics. That makes involvement in party politics a highly salient and legitimate activity for community development organizations. Their claim to represent the interest of a geographic community further propels them into political involvement. They often find themselves mediating or directly involved in politics as partisans in inter- or intra-community conflicts. Many such conflicts mobilize local politicians who may use their control over public spending for community development to reward supporters and punish opponents.

In fact, among the case study organizations, each community development organization with public funding had been caught in the political process. African-American Neighbors, for example, dropped from $612,000 in city grants and contracts to $19,000 two years later because the organization took a lead role in the boycott of a favored event sponsored by then-mayor Jane Byrne. When the mayor retaliated and pulled the organization's public contracts, African-American Neighbors protested in vain, and other community development organizations were reluctant to enter the fracas.

This is a drastic example, but community development organizations do encounter greater uncertainty in securing access to stable public funding than social service agencies and must expect to encounter terminated public contracts.[14] Funding uncertainty is aggravated by ongoing federal efforts

to reduce spending in the Community Development Block Grant, the primary source of public funding for community development activities in many communities.

To overcome these uncertainties, some community development organizations have sought to obtain direct control over tax dollars through the use of Special Service Area Taxing Districts. Two of the organizations, United Residents and Economic Development Corporation, helped establish such districts: they researched the topic, wrote the ordinance, organized the campaign to place the necessary referendum on the local ballot and secure its passage, nominated commissioners for the taxing district, and had themselves appointed as managers of the district's activities. But this may not be a long-term solution either. United Residents saw its district disbanded in a political battle over the higher property taxes involved, and the Economic Development Corporation has faced concerted efforts by the city to assume control over the tax district and its activities.

Even so, public funding for community development organizations is more certain than most other sources of funding available to nonprofits.[15] And, although some public grants and contracts are fairly small, few revenue sources offer a similar scale of funding to these types of organizations. The three community development organizations with public funding received twenty-seven grants and contracts during one fiscal year, totaling almost $1 million and averaging almost $36,000 per award. Few other sources of funding can deliver similar amounts on a more or less continuing basis.

As in the case of social service agencies, there are major costs to community development organizations associated with the receipt of public funding. The costs are quite similar because the grants and contract system operates under comparable principles. However, community development organizations have less certain access to continued funding, greater need for paying careful attention to party politics, and less severe problems of coordination because of their smaller scale of operation. Of thirty-eight characteristics on which I have systematic information for individual proposals or active grants and contracts, sixteen (42 percent) differ significantly among social service and community development organizations.[16] Most of these differences reflect operational

14. Although none of the four social service agencies with public grants or contracts had more than 6 percent of such funding in the form of terminated or one-time awards over a five-year period, the corresponding proportions ranged between 24 and 45 percent for three community development organizations.

15. The thirteen case study organizations provided year-by-year data on twenty-nine aggregated streams of private donations (e.g., all individual gifts). More than half (sixteen) of these streams have annual fluctuations of more than 50 percent, including one-third (nine) with annual fluctuations of 100 percent or more. Only those donation streams that involve highly institutionalized relationships with particular donors (e.g., the United Way, affiliated churches, co-opting institutions) tend to provide stable funding.

16. For example, compared to social service agencies, community development organizations are less likely to have contracts preapproved (9 vs. 43 percent), get what they requested (11 vs. 46 percent), and have short deadlines for performance reports (82 vs. 46 percent), although they submit less complex contracts (9 vs. 59 percent) or detailed reports

requirements associated with particular funding streams or administrative traditions of different units of government.

In short, there are important divergences in how nonprofit social service and community development organizations relate to market and public sector actors. Social service agencies have less direct utility to private firms than community development organizations and have fewer opportunities to develop institutionalized linkages or ongoing support from such firms. There are, however, many more and somewhat larger social service agencies than community development organizations, and they are more likely to rely on public funding and to have institutionalized relationships with public agencies as well as other nonprofit organizations.

More important, social service agencies are of greater significance to public agencies and have greater control and leverage over public funding. This is shown by their better access to stable, continued funding than community development organizations and by their acceptance as legitimate, expert participants in the technical debate on how to administer public human service programs. Community development organizations, by contrast, are more likely to be viewed as organized, local constituency groups, among the many with which local politicians have to contend, albeit ones with potentially powerful allies in the local business community.

INDUSTRY VARIATIONS IN THE
U.S. POLITICAL ECONOMY

The differences in how nonprofit social service agencies and community development organizations relate to state and market organizations have broad applicability and are useful for understanding interactions among the three sectors in other industries as well. Indeed, nonprofits are active in a variety of fields, as the National Taxonomy of Exempt Entities illustrates: health care, civil rights, public affairs, religion, education, environmental protection, employment and training, social services, youth development, housing, arts and culture, community organizing, philanthropy, research, and so forth (Hodgkinson et al. 1992). These industries are also influenced by the two major driving forces in American society: the dominance of market models and the scope and structure of public sector activities, although the political economy manifests itself differently across industries.[17]

Nonprofit Relations to the Market Sector

The relationships between nonprofits and private sector organizations differ from industry to industry. In some industries, nonprofits compete directly with market organizations, while corporate support for nonprofits in some fields offers strategic advantages to private firms. There are costs to the firms associated with such support: valuable executive time, direct outlays in the form of corporate grants or sponsorships, and inability to escape the fallout when nonprofit partners undertake controversial activities.

In some fields, nonprofits do not compete directly with private firms and afford access mainly to expertise and technology (for example, higher education and medical research) or enhance the quality of life for corporate staff and leadership (for example, through arts and cultural institutions and some health organizations). Not surprisingly, these fields tend to receive the bulk of corporate donations and to have strong corporate linkages on their boards.[18]

In fields such as social services, for-profit organizations are relatively few and unimportant, with the exception of day care and homemaker services, and public and nonprofits dominate the service fields. Market organizations may supply funding for nonprofits in the form of smaller donations and other subsidies because they view themselves as benefiting at least marginally from the array of services that they provide. Market organizations rarely have immediate interests in these services, however: they neither compete directly with nonprofits, nor clearly depend on having access to nonprofit services or products in order to carry out their activities. Their funding for any specific nonprofit organization is therefore likely to be episodic, uncertain, and difficult for the nonprofit organization to influence or control.

In service fields like health and job training, nonprofits compete directly with market organizations or are vertically integrated with them. Thus for-profit health clinics refer patients to nonprofit hospitals, or nonprofit job training agencies seek private sector placements for their trainees. In health care, individual providers like doctors and pharmacists, group practices, and major corporations such as insurance companies and pharmaceutical industries traditionally have dominated the field, while for-profit hospitals and long-term care facilities have gained prominence in recent years.

The active participation of the for-profit sector imposes marketlike transactions on nonprofits as well, blurs the line between the two sectors, and imposes greater complexity on their interactions. Even public subsidies take marketlike forms. For example, the Medicare and Medicaid systems both incorporate critical elements of consumer choice, while

---

(11 vs. 40 percent). Community organizations are less likely to have fixed payment schedules (11 vs. 54 percent) and frequently experience payment delays of four weeks or more (62 vs. 49 percent).

17. There are other important differences among nonprofit industry fields that I do not discuss here. For example, they differ in terms of the nature of activities involved, the size and composition of organizations active in the fields, and the extent to which the industry itself is highly institutionalized. These differences both reflect and influence how attractive the field is or might be to public, nonprofit, or market organizations respectively.

18. Since the early 1980s, education has accounted for roughly 40 percent of corporate donations, with health about one-quarter to one-third. Arts and culture have received a stable 10 percent of corporate funding.

the Job Training Partnership Act uses a performance-based payment system.

In still other fields, including housing and community development, environmental control, and civil rights, the for-profit sector also has a vested interest in nonprofit activities. The basis for nonprofit-market interactions, however, is not direct competition between the two sectors or corporate desire for nonprofit services, but the likelihood that nonprofit actions will impose external control over the market sector's own productive capacity, discretion, and access to critical opportunities. That is the case when nonprofit community organizations oppose (or support) private sector development projects, when environmental groups seek restrictions on industrial pollution, and when civil rights organizations press for affirmative action in private sector employment.

Under these circumstances, relationships between nonprofit and for-profit organizations become highly complex, with either party viewing the other as a potential opponent, constituent, or customer (that is, a purchaser of technical expertise in the field). To the extent that for-profit organizations become constituents or customers of nonprofits, they are likely to be stable and fairly controllable sources of market transactions or subsidies for nonprofits. Even so, the relationships are rarely static but subject to continuing negotiations and strategic action by either party. Relationships are likely to become particularly contentious in fields in which nonprofits are changing the market structure by creating new markets or standardizing products, as appears to be the case in health and social services.

Nonprofit Relations to Public Sector

Although deep suspicion surrounds virtually all government action in the United States, the size and structure of public sector activities differ significantly across policy arenas. There are also local variations within specific service fields, reflecting timings, patterns of settlement, and other special circumstances. Nevertheless, for historical and ideological reasons, the public sector has been involved earlier, more extensively, and more directly in the provision of some services than others. For example, the public sector took early and full responsibility for elementary education and directly operated schools and closely related institutions like libraries. Over time, these direct responsibilities have expanded to include higher education, previously controlled almost entirely by nonprofits.[19]

The United States has been much more reluctant in assuming responsibility for health and social services and for job training. In these fields, early public efforts were limited to special activities such as public health and in-patient care for the mentally ill and are still restricted to groups who meet particular eligibility requirements. The United States assumed these responsibilities at a later stage in its development, and did so less extensively than with education and with considerable reliance on non–public service infrastructures that were already in place at the time.

In social services, the infrastructure has been largely controlled by the nonprofit sector, and in health, by a combination of nonprofit and for-profit entities (hospitals, pharmaceutical firms, medical practitioners). In job training, the infrastructure has been located mainly in for-profit organizations that train their own workers, although the capacity for job training of most direct relevance to low-income or other specialized groups is located in public schools and nonprofit social service agencies.

In still other fields, such as environmental control, arts and culture, civil rights, housing, and community development, public sector responsibilities are even more recent and limited in scope. As a result, they have not been fully institutionalized and are still subject to considerable debate, focusing mainly on the proper role of government vis-à-vis that of the private sector, with only minimal attention to the nonprofit sector. Nonprofits are nevertheless very important because they are actively involved in shaping the debate through advocacy and related activities. But they do not otherwise play a major role in providing the public sector with access to significant portions of the service infrastructure. (Arts and culture may be an exception to this pattern, perhaps because public sector involvement is extremely limited and relatively unimportant.) Finally, public sector activities are more or less completely absent from such fields as philanthropy and religion.

Partly for these reasons, the mechanisms by which public-nonprofit funding relationships operate also differ greatly among service fields, and these variations in the scope and structure of public sector activities exert marked control over the organizational environment in which different types of nonprofit organizations operate. In education and health, the payment structure gives extensive control to market forces and to the mutual selection process at work between service recipients and providers. The amount of public funds received by nonprofits in these fields depends on the degree to which they attract and accept clients who carry cash or credit

19. It is an intriguing question why the development of a public mandate in higher education took the form of establishing public institutions, rather than a system of operating subsidy or grants and contracts to nonpublic organizations, as was the case in social services. I don't know the answer to this question but speculate that at least two factors operated. First, the well-established tradition of direct and extensive public responsibility for elementary and secondary education (justified on the basis of creating an educated citizenry capable of democratic decision making) created an important precedent for public involvement in

higher education. Second, higher education is clearly aimed at a deserving population — those who have proven themselves capable of performance — while social services traditionally have been tainted by the image of serving losers or those of questionable character. Given the suspicions that generally surround public mandates in the United States, it should be not surprising to find the public sector better able or willing to take direct responsibility for activities that will be associated with promotion of individual success than those likely to be associated with individual failures.

from public sources, that is, tuition grants, student loans, and eligibility for Medicare or Medicaid reimbursements.[20]

Public-nonprofit payment structures in most other fields (social service, employment and training, housing and community development, arts and culture) are organized more along the lines of formal grants and contracts that link provider agencies directly to their respective public funders. In this case, clients have little to say about the size of the public-nonprofit exchange, and market forces are correspondingly attenuated.

Public sector dependence on nonprofit infrastructures varies along parallel lines, and the type and degree of dependence determine not only whether and how much public sector funding is available to nonprofits but also the leverage that nonprofits are likely to have over public sector agencies. Thus, the dependence may be low and nonprofit leverage minimal because the public sector maintains its own infrastructure (education). In this case, nonprofits are likely to focus mainly on keeping public sector outlays sufficiently low and narrow in focus to protect their own competitiveness. At the other extreme, public sector dependence may be direct and fairly high (social service). Nonprofit leverage is then extensive because the public sector needs access to nonprofit infrastructures to meet its own mandates.

Alternatively, public sector dependence on nonprofits may be direct and mixed with dependence on for-profit infrastructures (that is, health, job training). Nonprofit leverage is important here but lower than if dependence was extensive and limited to nonprofits because the public sector does not rely exclusively on nonprofit infrastructures. Finally, the public sector's dependence may be low, indirect, and limited to setting and shaping agendas (civil rights, community development, environmental issues). As a result, nonprofit leverage is also indirect and highly politicized because the public sector seeks to induce actions in the private sector and does not require direct access to nonprofit service infrastructures of any kind, although nonprofit advocacy and other political efforts are highly relevant.

CONCLUSION

I have argued that nonprofits have distinctive relations with market and public sector organizations and documented dif-

20. This pattern is fully understandable for the health field, given the prominence of market institutions noted earlier. The pattern is more interesting for higher education, given the dominance of nonprofit institutions. Why has the public funding that benefits nonprofit colleges and universities not been channeled into grants and contracts as it was for social service agencies? I speculate that several factors are important. First, nonprofit colleges and universities have traditionally relied extensively on well-established market resources (e.g., tuition fees), while social service agencies traditionally relied on donations. Hence, the public funding structures were adapted to existing resource patterns. In addition, colleges and universities have always competed with one another for students and are large and well established. Most likely, they could successfully resist special subsidies to their competitors.

ferences in these relationships for social service and community development organizations. These patterns have broad applicability and are useful for understanding interactions among the nonprofit, market, and public sectors in other industries as well. There are major differences in how nonprofits relate to market organizations. In some industries, nonprofits compete with private firms (health), are vertically integrated with them (job training), or otherwise provide important services to them (education, arts/culture), have potential consequences for their internal decision making (civil rights, environmental issues), or are mainly neutral arenas for elite interaction (social services).

There are also major industry variations in how nonprofits relate to the public sector. They either compete with public sector organizations (for example, education), operate in partnerships with them through subsidy relations (for example, social service, health), define them as forces to be mobilized (for example, civil rights, environmental issues, community development), or view them as alien to the primary purpose of the organization (for example, philanthropy, religion).[21]

Equally important, these economic and political interactions are dynamic and ongoing. They reflect the configuration of strategic opportunities that the sectors present to one another. Individual organizations active in a given field make use of these opportunities to actively promote their own interests and secure stable resources, expanding markets, and increased power. There are several implications that should be highlighted. First, nonprofits are not passive targets for market or public sector interests but take active roles in shaping their environment and resource opportunities. Second, over time, the division of labor among the three sectors will shift as some strategies are more effective than others. Third, in the process of pursuing organizational self-interests, a good deal of public goods are delivered, although not necessarily in the most efficient manner or in ways that assure effective attention to major social issues.

REFERENCES

Bennett, James T., and Thomas J. DiLorenzo. 1989. *Unfair Competition: The Profits of Nonprofits.* Lanham: Hamilton Press.

Brilliant, Eleanor L. 1990. *The United Way: Dilemmas of Organized Charity.* New York: Columbia University Press.

Chen, Ted H., Kirsten A. Grønbjerg, and Matthew W. Stagner. 1992. *An Analysis of Financial Payments to Service Providers of the Illinois Department of Children and Family Services.* Report prepared for the Children's Policy Project. Chicago: Chapin Hall Center for Children.

Cloward, Richard A., and Irwin Epstein. 1965. "Private Social Welfare's Disengagement from the Poor: The Case of Family

21. These generalizations are, of course, simplistic. For example, nonprofits are involved in advocacy efforts across all industries. However, I believe these descriptions capture the dominant character of how the respective industries interact with the public sector.

Adjustment Agencies." In *Proceedings of the Annual Social Work Day Institute*. Buffalo: State University of New York at Buffalo, School of Social Welfare.

Edsall, Thomas Byrne. 1984. *The New Politics of Inequality*. New York: W. W. Norton.

Galaskiewicz, Joseph. 1985. *Social Organization of a Corporate Grants Economy: A Study of Business Philanthropy and Nonprofit Organizations*. Orlando: Academic Press.

———. 1986. *Gifts, Givers, and Getters: Business Philanthropy in an Urban Setting*. New York: Academic Press.

Granovetter, Mark. 1973. "The Strength of Weak Ties." *American Journal of Sociology* 78:1360–80.

Grønbjerg, Kirsten A. 1990. "Poverty and Nonprofit Organizational Behavior, Contingencies, and Linkages." *Social Service Review* 64:208–43.

———. 1993. *Understanding Nonprofit Funding: Managing Revenues in Social Service and Community Development Organizations*. San Francisco: Jossey-Bass.

Grønbjerg, Kirsten A., Ted Chen, and Matthew Stagner. 1992. "Market Forces and Leverage: Contracting Relations in a Child Welfare System." Paper presented at the American Political Science Association meetings, Chicago, September 4, 1992.

Grønbjerg, Kirsten A., James Musselwhite, Jr., and Lester M. Salamon. 1984. *Government Spending and the Nonprofit Sector in Cook County/Chicago*. Washington, D.C.: Urban Institute Press.

Grønbjerg, Kirsten A., Ami Nagle, Lauree Garvin, and Lori Wingate. 1992. *Nonprofit Human Service Facilities in Illinois: Structure, Adequacy, and Management*. Report prepared for the Illinois Facilities Fund.

Grønbjerg, Kirsten A., David P. Street, and Gerald Suttles. 1978. *Poverty and Social Change*. Chicago: University of Chicago Press.

Hansmann, Henry. 1980. "The Role of Nonprofit Enterprise." *Yale Law Journal* 89:835–901.

———. 1987. "Economic Theories of Nonprofit Organization." In *The Nonprofit Sector: A Research Handbook*, ed. W. W. Powell, 27–42. New Haven: Yale University Press.

Hasenfeld, Yeheskel. 1978. "Client-Organization Relations: A System Perspective." In *The Management of Human Services*, ed. Rosemary C. Sarri and Yeheskel Hasenfeld, 184–206. New York: Columbia University Press.

Hodgkinson, Virginia A., Murray S. Weitzman, Christopher M. Toppe, and Stephen M. Noga. 1992. *Nonprofit Almanac, 1992–1993: Dimensions of the Independent Sector*. San Francisco: Jossey-Bass.

Odendahl, Teresa. 1990. *Charity Begins at Home: Generosity and Self-Interest among the Philanthropic Elite*. New York: Basic Books.

Ostrander, Susan A. 1984. *Women of the Upper Class*. Philadelphia: Temple University Press.

Palmer, John L., Timothy Smeeding, and Barbara Boyle Torrey, eds. 1988. *The Vulnerable*. Washington, D.C.: Urban Institute Press.

Phillips, Kevin. 1990. *The Politics of Rich and Poor: Wealth and the American Electorate in the Reagan Aftermath*. New York: Random House.

Reynolds, Morgan O., and Eugene Smolensky. 1977. *Public Expenditures, Taxes, and the Distribution of Income: The U.S., 1950, 1960, and 1970*. New York: Academic Press.

Rose-Ackerman, Susan. 1986. *The Economics of Nonprofit Institutions: Studies in Structure and Polity*. New York: Oxford University Press.

Saidel, Judith. 1991. "Resource Interdependence: The Relationship between State Agencies and Nonprofit Organizations." *Public Administration Review* 51:543–53.

Schiller, Herbert I. 1989. *Culture, Inc. The Corporate Takeover of Public Expression*. New York: Oxford University Press.

Sherraden, Michael. 1991. *Assets and the Poor: A New American Welfare Policy*. Armonk, N.Y.: M. E. Sharpe.

Sosin, Michael R. 1990. "Decentralizing the Social Service System: A Reassessment. *Social Service Review* 64:617–36.

Useem, Michael. 1984. *The Inner Circle: Large Corporations and the Rise of Business Political Activity in the U.S. and U.K.* New York: Oxford University Press.

Weisbrod, Burton. 1985. "Toward a Theory of the Voluntary Non-Profit Sector in a Three-Sector Economy." In *Altruism, Morality, and Economic Theory*, ed. E. S. Phelps, 171–95. New York: Russell Sage.

———. 1977. *The Voluntary Nonprofit Sector*. Lexington, Mass.: Lexington Books.

———. 1988. *The Nonprofit Economy*. Cambridge: Harvard University Press.

Wilensky, Harold L., and Charles N. Lebeaux. 1965. *Industrial Society and Social Welfare: The Impact of Industrialization on the Supply and Organization of Social Welfare Services in the U.S..* New York: Free Press.

10

LESTER M. SALAMON AND HELMUT K. ANHEIER

The Third Route: Government-Nonprofit Collaboration

in Germany and the United States

Much of the recent debate on the future of the modern welfare state has tended to focus on a choice between two major routes for the provision of social welfare services: reliance on the state or reliance on the private sector. It is the argument of this chapter, by contrast, that a third route exists for the provision of human services in a market system, a route that involves neither sole reliance on the state nor sole reliance on the private sector, but rather a partnership between the two. What is more, we suggest that this third route offers certain advantages over the other two in that it captures the benefits of the two respective sectors while minimizing their respective drawbacks.

To illustrate these points, this chapter examines two important examples of the operation of this third route to social welfare provision: the United States and Germany. In spite of some important differences in origins and operations, both of these countries utilize an essentially collaborative model in their social welfare systems. In the pages that follow we first describe the social welfare systems that exist in the two countries, then investigate the bases on which the two systems operate, and finally assess the advantages and disadvantages of the approach they embody. To set the discussion in context, however, we begin with a framework for thinking about the alternative models of social welfare provision that are available.

MODELS OF SERVICE PROVISION

The idea that only two basic models of social welfare provision can exist in a market system rests on three basic assumptions: first, that only two major sectors exist in a typical market society, the state and private businesses; second, that these two sectors differ fundamentally in purpose and outlook; and third, that each of these sectors operates, or should operate, autonomously within its appropriate sphere.

In fact, however, these assumptions are questionable at best. In the first place, a significant third sector made up of private, nonprofit organizations also exists in many modern welfare states, though its scope and role have generally been discounted or ignored by scholars in the field (see Flora 1986; Flora and Heidenheimer 1981; Offe 1985; Heidenheimer, Heclo, and Adams 1983, as cases in point). This sector combines elements of the other two, sharing with government the mission of serving public purposes while sharing with the business sector an independent status outside the state. In the second place, it is quite possible to think of government human service programs as embracing several distinct functions that, at least in theory, can be carried out by a variety of institutions. In particular, it is possible to separate the *authorization and financing* of human services from their *actual delivery* and to leave the former in government hands while vesting responsibility for the latter in any of a variety of other institutions, both nonprofit and for-profit (Salamon 1981). Finally, in view of this, there is a wide area of potential collaboration between the state and the private sector and particularly between the state and the nonprofit portion of the private sector. Nonprofits can deliver not only services they finance themselves, but also services financed by the state (Salamon and Abramson 1982; Salamon 1987).

Based on these considerations, Gidron, Kramer, and Salamon (1992, 18) identify four models of social welfare systems, each reflecting a particular relationship between government and the nonprofit sector in financing and delivering human services. First is the *government-dominant model,* which prevails where government is both the principal funder and deliverer of human services. The Scandinavian social democratic states and Japan, all based on a high level of governmentally provided social welfare, are exemplars of this government-dominant form, and the Swiss model of a highly decentralized public sector with limited nonprofit input is also a feasible variant (Wagner 1992). At the opposite extreme is the *third sector–dominant model,* where the primary responsibility for both financing and delivering human services is left to the nonprofit sector. The United States prior to the New Deal of the 1930s constitutes an example of this type of model. In between these two extremes lie mixed cases: the *dual model* and the *collaborative model.* In both, nonprofits and government have major roles. In the former, however, they operate in distinct spheres, with little interaction. This notion of "mutually exclusive spheres" characterized much of British social welfare policy prior to about 1950 (Kramer 1981). In the latter, by contrast, the two sectors operate with a high level of overlap, though with government tending to concentrate on the financing of services and nonprofits on their delivery.

Gidron, Kramer, and Salamon (1992) further differentiate the collaborative model in terms of the degree of discretion left to the nonprofit organizations that collaborate with government in the provision of services. In the *vendor* variant, nonprofits function merely as agents of the state, with fairly routine responsibilities. By contrast, the *partnership* variant obtains where nonprofit organizations enjoy a significant degree of discretion, whether intentionally or not, in the operation of public programs. As a general rule, the degree of discretion is affected both by the nature of the activity and the form of the relationship between the state and its partners (Salamon 1989). The more complicated the activity, the more autonomy that ultimately ends up in the hands of the delivery agent. Delivering family counseling services to needy families thus inevitably entails more discretion than producing No. 2 pencils, even though both may be done on contract to the government. At the same time, however, some types of relationships create more opportunities for the exercise of discretion than others. Specific purchase-of-service contracts, for example, leave the least room for discretion whereas general support grants typically leave the most. In

between are various voucher and reimbursement systems (Kramer 1981; Salamon 1981).

The factors identified here are not the only bases on which social welfare systems can be differentiated, of course. An alternative, and far more common, basis for differentiation focuses on the *scope* or *extent* of collective welfare provision. To some extent, this alternative basis overlaps the four models identified here. As a general rule, it is probably the case that the third sector–dominant model is most likely to be present where the scope of collective welfare provision is the smallest, and the government-dominant model where the scope of collective welfare provision is the greatest. But this correspondence is far from complete, and it is quite possible to have a high level of social welfare provision using either a government-dominant model, a collaborative model, or any of the other two. In other words, the four models identified here do indeed offer a significantly independent basis for grouping social welfare systems.

THE U.S. AND GERMAN SOCIAL WELFARE SYSTEMS

The cases of the United States and Germany illustrate these points well. These two countries differ markedly in the scale of their social welfare provision, with Germany devoting proportionately 50 percent more of its gross national product to this purpose than the United States (OECD 1994, table 1). Perhaps because of this, the conventional wisdom tends to assign Germany and the United States to quite different models. Thus, the United States is generally viewed as a rather pure case of a third sector–dominant model, with limited government involvement in social and economic life and primary reliance on private philanthropy and the nonprofit sector to cope with human needs. Germany, by contrast, is conventionally viewed as a classic government-dominant welfare state, indeed, the country in which the concept of the welfare state was born and in which government plays the dominant role in the provision of welfare services.

In fact, the United States and Germany have far more in common than conventional wisdom suggests, at least with respect to the structure, if not the scale, of their social welfare systems. In practice, both societies are striking examples of what Gidron, Kramer, and Salamon (1992) call the collaborative model, and of the partnership variant of the model at that.

America's Mixed System of Welfare
The conventional image of the American social welfare system as a third sector–dominant model is certainly correct in pointing to the existence of a sizable private, nonprofit sector, extensive private charitable giving, and relatively limited government activity as the most salient features of the system in comparison with other developed countries.[1] Long after most other developed industrial countries had

1. The discussion here draws heavily on material presented more fully in Salamon 1992, 33–89.

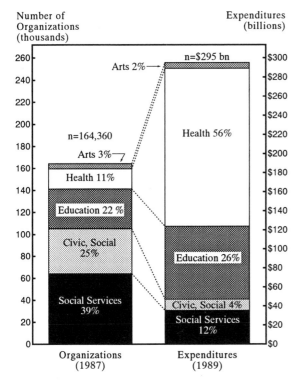

Number of Organizations (thousands) | Expenditures (billions)

Figure 10.1. Scope of U.S. Nonprofit Public-Benefit Service Sector

adopted state-financed old-age pension and unemployment systems, America adopted such innovations haltingly and in piecemeal fashion (see Skocpol 1992). Not until 1935, therefore, was a basic social insurance plan enacted at the national level, and even then its coverage was limited. Basic income protections for the poor and unemployed were unavailable to much of the population until well into the post–World War II period, and universal health insurance is still not available. Although many state governments have expanded social welfare protections for their residents, national involvement has been more limited, and significant variations consequently exist from state to state, even in programs that are partly financed from federal sources.

Given this patchy character of public social welfare protections, considerable room has been left for the operation of private philanthropy and private nonprofit organizations. Indeed, American culture places a high value on this form of voluntary approach to coping with human needs and resists the concept of a universal right to public welfare support. Reflecting this, in 1990 alone, Americans contributed $122.6 billion to charitable causes. This represented slightly more than 2 percent of total personal income (AAFRC 1991, 89). More than 80 percent of this total came from individuals, but some $8 billion came from grant-making charitable foundations, of which there are more than 30,000 in the United States with assets totaling $138 billion in 1989 (Renz 1991, 2). Partly as a consequence of this private support, well over a million private, nonprofit organizations exist in the United

States, of which approximately 740,000 are public-serving, as opposed to member-serving, organizations, and close to 400,000 are nonreligious organizations providing services in pursuit of broad public purposes. As of 1989, these latter organizations had expenditures of $295 billion, or almost 6 percent of the gross national product (Salamon 1992, 25). The most numerous of these organizations, as reflected in figure 10.1, are providers of social services—day care, family counseling, adoption assistance, substance abuse treatment, and the like. By far the largest share of the expenditures, however, are accounted for by health and education institutions—hospitals, clinics, universities, nursing homes—which together comprise 33 percent of the nonprofit service agencies, but 82 percent of the expenditures.

Although the relatively limited governmental protections and the sizable nonprofit sector make the American case look very much like the third sector–dominant model, three other features of the U.S. social welfare system suggest that something quite different is going on. The first is the presence in most social welfare fields not only of nonprofit institutions but of for-profit and governmental ones as well, often in varied and confusing relationships to one another. What exists in practice, in other words, is not an exclusively private nonprofit system, but a mixed system (Salamon 1992, 55–89). In some spheres nonprofit organizations play the dominant role, in others for-profit organizations, and in still others government. Thus, as shown in table 10.1, nonprofit organizations play the dominant role in the *hospital sector*. Just over half of all hospitals are private, nonprofit organizations, and these institutions account for 56 percent of the hospital beds. By comparison, governments—usually at the state and local level—operate 32 percent of the hospitals and private businesses 17 percent. A similar pattern exists in the *social services field*, in which nonprofits account for 59 percent of

Table 10.1. America's Mixed Economy of Welfare

Field	% Accounted for by		
Indicator	Nonprofits	For-profits	Government
Hospital care			
Institutions	51	17	32
Beds	56	11	33
Social services			
Establishments	59	41	N.A.
Employees	58	19	23
Clinic care			
Establishments	32	68	N.A.
Employees	45	55	N.A.
Nursing home care			
Institutions	20	75	5
Beds	22	71	7
Higher education			
Institutions	49	7	45
Students	20	2	78

Source: Salamon 1992, 60, 63, 65, 73, 84.

Table 10.2. Sources of Social Welfare Spending in the United States, 1989

Field	Share of Spending Accounted for by		
	% Government	% Private Philanthropy	% Private Purchase
Hospital care	54	5	41
Nursing home care	48	2	49
Clinic care	60	9	31
Education	72	3	25
Social services	44	28	29

Source: Salamon 1992, 59, 71.

the establishments and a comparable share of the employment. By contrast, in the fields of *clinic and outpatient care* as well as *nursing home care,* for-profit businesses are the dominant providers, accounting for 68 percent and 75 percent of the establishments, respectively. Different still is the picture in the field of *higher education.* In terms of numbers of institutions, nonprofit organizations have a clear edge. But the vast majority of students are enrolled in public institutions, which tend to be much larger.

If the prevalence of a mixed system is one feature overlooked in the conventional image of the American social welfare system, the sizable presence of government is a second. In spite of the attention lavished on the role of private philanthropy in the operation of the American welfare system, the fact is that government plays a much larger role in almost every sphere. Thus, as shown in table 10.2 above, government accounts for 54 percent of all hospital spending, 48 percent of all nursing home spending, 60 percent of all clinic spending, 72 percent of all education spending, and 44 percent of all social service spending (Salamon 1992, 59, 71, 82). By contrast, in only one of these spheres does the share represented by private philanthropy exceed 25 percent, and in most it is well below 10 percent. Although the state may not play as active a role in the American version of the modern welfare state as it does in many European countries, it nevertheless outdistances private philanthropy by several orders of magnitude.

This, in turn, suggests a third critical feature of the American social welfare system that tends to be overlooked in the conventional image: the role that government plays in the financing of nonprofit activity. As it turns out, government is not only a major source of overall social welfare spending, but its funding flows in significant part to private, nonprofit providers in these fields. In fact, government support to these organizations outdistances the support they receive from private philanthropy by a substantial margin. Thus, as shown in figure 10.2 below, for the nonreligious, nonprofit service sector as a whole, government accounted for 31 percent of all revenues as of 1989, compared to only 18 percent from private charity (Salamon 1992, 27). In some spheres, such as social services, moreover, the government share is substantially higher than this.

In short, behind the rhetoric of privatism, the United States has built a mixed economy of welfare that features extensive involvement of both public and private agencies and heavy governmental subsidization of the nonprofit sector. In the terms introduced earlier, what exists in fact is not the third sector–dominant model but the collaborative model.

Germany's Corporatist System

If the U.S. system of social welfare is far more governmental than the conventional wisdom acknowledges, the German system is far more private. To be sure, government is a larger presence in the German welfare state than in the American, as the conventional wisdom would lead us to expect. Thus, government spending on social welfare services accounts for 31 percent of gross national product in Germany, as compared with less than 20 percent in the United States (OECD 1991; Salamon 1992, 36). What is more, an elaborate system of public social protection is available, guaranteeing universal pensions for the elderly, children's allowances, basic income support, and guaranteed health insurance.

To conclude from the significant level and range of government social welfare spending that Germany is a case of the government-dominant model, however, is to misread significantly the character of the German welfare state. To the contrary, side by side with government is a massive network of private, nonprofit organizations that share important social welfare functions. At the center of this network are six large conglomerates, the so-called free welfare associations (*freie Wohlfahrtsverbände*). Included here are the Catholic and Protestant social welfare agencies — Caritas and Diakonisches Werk, respectively. These are massive federations of local welfare agencies spread throughout the country. Caritas is rooted in Catholic social ethics and is integrated into the religious hierarchy. Diakonisches Werk began in 1848/9 as a welfare-oriented evangelical movement, often in conflict with the secular political world. These two religiously oriented social welfare networks have in turn helped inspire the creation of three others. The Arbeiterwohlfahrt (workers' welfare association) was founded in 1919 and has historically been linked to the Social Democratic Party. For the Social Democrats, who advocated public rather than private welfare provision, the creation of the Arbeiterwohlfahrt was the result of a "reconciliation of workers and the capitalist state" (Bauer 1978). The Zentralwohlfahrtsstelle der Juden

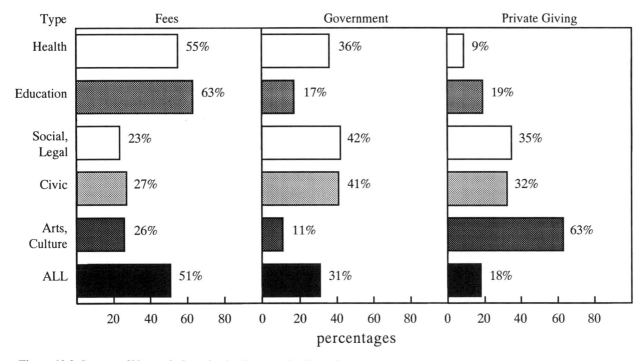

Figure 10.2. Sources of Nonprofit Organization Revenue, by Type of Agency, 1989

in Deutschland (The central welfare association for Jews in Germany) was created in 1917 to coordinate the numerous Jewish local welfare committees and activities. Dissolved by the Nazis, it was reestablished after World War II to assist concentration camp victims. In recent years, it has become increasingly involved in assisting Jews from Eastern Europe and the Soviet Union. The Deutscher Paritätischer Wohlfahrtsverband, founded in 1920, is a consortium of nondenominational, nonpartisan private welfare organizations. It began as a federation of independent hospitals called the Fifth Welfare Association and has grown in significance during the last two decades. Finally, the Deutsches Rotes Kreuz (German red cross) is both a relief organization (disaster aid, emergency assistance) and a social service organization.

These free welfare associations represent a major presence in the German social welfare scene, with an estimated 650,000 full-time equivalent employees and 1.5 million volunteers (Spiegelhalter 1990). Taken together, they run 68,466 institutions in the areas of health care and youth and family services as well as services for the handicapped, elderly, and the poor (Bundesarbeitsgemeinschaft 1990).

Reflecting the presence of the free welfare associations, the nonprofit sector plays a major role in key areas of the German social welfare system. At the same time, however, this role is more segmented than is the case in the United States. Thus, as table 10.3 below shows, nonprofit organizations account for more than 60 percent of the employment in such fields as family services, services for the elderly, services for the handicapped, nursing home care, and child day care. By contrast, nonprofits are much less prominent in such fields as vocational training, clinic and hospital care, educa-

tion, libraries, and culture and the arts. In these areas, it is the public sector which dominates. In the case of universities, for example, the only fully nonprofit institution is related to the Catholic Church, although various initiatives to found nonprofit universities have been under way in recent years; other nonprofit establishments in the field of higher learning tend to be seminaries and similar church-related institutions sometimes affiliated with public universities.

Although the structure of the social welfare system seems more segmented in Germany than in the United States, it would be wrong to conclude that something resembling the dual model exists here. Rather, extensive collaboration prevails. Instead of separate government and nonprofit spheres, each financing and delivering its own range of services, what exists in practice is extensive government financing of services delivered by nonprofit organizations—a pattern that is much closer to the collaborative model identified above. Arbeiterwohlfahrt, the workers' welfare federation, reports, for example, that it spends approximately 40 percent of its operating budget on "participation in public tasks of the Federal Government," and that about 45 percent of its revenues comes from direct public subsidies. Additional public funding comes, moreover, from third-party payments that government makes on behalf of purchasers of other services from these same organizations. In the case of Diakonisches Hilfswerk and Caritas, direct public subsidies comprise between 25 and 40 percent of revenues, exclusive of third-party payments. Taken together, therefore, it seems reasonable to conclude that the level of government subsidization of the nonprofit sector in Germany is in excess of 40 percent, or slightly higher than in the United States, and this is without

Table 10.3. Nonprofit, For-profit, and Public Shares of Social Service Employment in Germany, by Field

Industries	For-Profit Sector %	Nonprofit Sector %	Public Sector %	Total Employment in Industry
Family services	9	73	18	28,566
Services for the elderly	18	68	15	67,140
Services for the handicapped	10	84	7	96,518
Nursing homes	20	63	17	128,510
Child day care	1	62	37	155,874
Vocational training	18	22	61	202,898
Clinics and hospitals	14	34	51	722,734
Other health institutions	48	36	16	91,586

Source: Anheier 1991.

including the "church tax" which the government collects on behalf of the Catholic and Protestant churches and which is used in part to support social welfare activity through the free welfare associations.

In short, contrary to conventional wisdom, both the United States and Germany have complex mixed systems of social welfare characterized by active involvement on the part of both the state and the private nonprofit sector. Far from withering away with the growth of government, the private, nonprofit sector seems to have prospered instead. What is more, government and the nonprofit sector appear to operate in many of the same spheres, with extensive public funding flowing to nonprofit organizations to help them carry out their activities. To be sure, the mixture of public and private roles seems more amorphous in the American setting than in the German one, where nonprofit organizations seem more heavily focused on a more narrow range of fields. In addition, the scope of collective welfare provision is considerably higher in Germany than in the United States. Despite these differences, however, what is most striking is the similarity between the two systems. In the terms introduced earlier, instead of the competing third sector–dominant and government-dominant models often portrayed in the conventional wisdom, the two countries are good examples of the operation of something much closer to the collaborative model.

UNRAVELING THE PARADOX: THE THIRD ROUTE TO SOCIAL WELFARE PROVISION

How can we explain this strikingly similar pattern of welfare state development in the United States and Germany? Given that, historically, these countries have taken radically different paths to modernization, what explains the simultaneous growth of both public and private welfare in the two settings? The answer, it seems, lies in the form that welfare state growth has taken. In particular, both the United States and Germany pursued a middle, or third, route in the development of their social welfare systems, eschewing *both* principal reliance on the state and principal reliance on the voluntary sector and choosing a collaborative pattern in-

stead. How they arrived at this route, however, differed considerably in the two countries. In particular, welfare state development in the United States proceeded through an ad hoc practice of "third-party government," whereas in Germany it flowed from the application of an explicit policy called subsidiarity.

"Third-Party Government": The American Pattern

The emergence of an extensive pattern of cooperation between the voluntary sector and the state in the United States is part of a broader structure of government activity in this country that Salamon has termed "third-party government" (Salamon 1981, 1989).[2] The central feature of third-party government is the sharing of significant discretionary authority over the operation of government programs between government agencies and a host of third-party implementers that help to deliver publicly financed goods and services. This form of government action reflects the antimonarchical and antigovernment sentiments that have dominated American thinking since the Revolution and the fragmented political system the country adopted as a consequence. Both of these have given advantages to opponents of government action, particularly in the social welfare field. It is for this reason that government action in this field lagged behind that in most other urban-industrial societies, as noted above. When the pressures for some form of government response to poverty and economic distress mounted in the 1930s and again in the 1960s, therefore, third-party government provided a convenient response. In a sense, this form of government action allows government to expand its activities without expanding the government bureaucracy in the process. This is done by dividing the authorizing and financing of government programs from the delivery of the resulting services and assigning delivery to some type of third party — a hospital, a university, a social service agency, an industrial company, a bank, or any of a host of other institutions. In a sense, third-party government allows Americans to "have their cake and

2. The discussion here draws heavily on Salamon 1981. See also Salamon 1989, Kettl 1988.

Table 10.4. Share of Government-Funded Human Services Delivered by Nonprofit, For-profit, and Government Agencies in Sixteen U.S. Communities,[1] 1982 (Weighted Average)[2]

| | *Proportion of Government-Funded Services Delivered by* | | | |
| | Nonprofits | For-Profits | Government | Total |
Fields	%	%	%	%
Social services	56	4	40	100
Employment/training	48	8	43	100
Housing/community development	5	7	88	100
Health	44	23	33	100
Arts/culture	51	—[3]	49	100
Total	42%	19%	39%	100%

Source: Salamon, Musselwhite, and DeVita 1986.

[1] The sixteen communities were New York, Providence, Pittsburgh, the Twin Cities, Chicago, Flint, Boise, San Francisco, Phoenix, Dallas, Atlanta, Jackson (MS), plus four rural counties (one each in Pennsylvania, Michigan, Arizona, and Mississippi).

[2] Figures are weighted by the scale of government spending in the sites. Percentages shown represent the share of all spending in all sites taken together that fall in the respective categories.

[3] Less than 0.5 percent

eat it too," to expand the range of governmental protections without expanding the size of the governmental bureaucracy. It has also afforded a vehicle through which private interests with a stake in a field can be cut in to a "piece of the action" in the operation of public programs.

Thanks to the practice of third-party government, government—certainly the federal government—does very little itself in the United States, at least in the domestic sphere. What it does, it does through other institutions—other levels of government, private businesses, and nonprofit groups. Beneficiaries of the federal government's higher education student loan program, for example, do not go to the U.S. Department of Education for their assistance. Rather, they go to a private, commercial bank, which extends the loan and then receives insurance for the loan from the federal government. The private bank is consequently a third party assisting the national government in delivering financial assistance to college students. Because programs inevitably leave a considerable degree of discretion to the administrative officials charged with their operation, however, this system involves the extensive sharing of public authority with a host of other public and private institutions.

Because of their fundamentally public purposes and because the patchy character of government protections left substantial room for their operation, nonprofit organizations have been in an excellent position to benefit from the third-party system. The upshot is an elaborate network of ties between government and the nonprofit sector in virtually every policy field. These ties take at least three different forms, moreover (Salamon and Abramson 1982). In the first place, the federal government often provides grants directly to nonprofit organizations to allow them to carry out specific activities considered to be in the public interest. This is the case, for example, with research grants to private, nonprofit

universities. In the second place, the federal government also provides grants to state and local governments, which in turn often contract with nonprofit agencies on a fee-for-service basis to carry out specific public functions. This is the pattern that holds in the Social Service Block Grant Program, under which the federal government finances a wide array of social services, from day care to meals-on-wheels for the shut-in elderly. Finally, some government support takes the form of voucher payments made to a service provider on behalf of a citizen entitled to a certain kind of public benefit. Under the federal government's health program for the elderly (Medicare), elderly residents in need of hospital care can go to the hospital of their choice, and the hospital is then reimbursed for the cost of their care from the federal government. Not only has the federal government financed existing nonprofit organizations, moreover, it has also helped to create new ones. This was a major thrust of the antipoverty program created in the mid-1960s, for example. Concerned that existing public and private institutions gave insufficient attention to the very poor, the federal government created a program to stimulate the creation of a whole network of nonprofit Community Action Agencies featuring extensive participation by the poor.

Through these and other routes, an elaborate pattern of government-nonprofit partnership has emerged in a wide variety of fields. Reflecting this, as of the early 1980s nonprofit organizations were delivering a larger share of government-funded human services than were government agencies themselves, as shown in table 10.4 above (Salamon, Musselwhite, and DeVita 1986). In some fields, such as social services, in fact, the nonprofit share of government-funded social services exceeded 50 percent as of the early 1980s.

Even though the practice of third-party government is very extensive in the United States, it did not emerge from any coherent principle or reflect an explicit policy. Rather, as is common in American political life, it represents a pragmatic, piecemeal adaptation to prevailing realities that emerged in ad hoc fashion in different fields. The relative roles of public and private agencies are therefore not spelled out in any coherent form. What is more, the roles vary from field to field, reflecting the strength of the nonprofit and government actors, the nature of the field, and a variety of other historical circumstances. Perhaps because of this ad hoc pattern of development, many Americans, including many policymakers and scholars, are not even aware that this pattern obtains.

The Principle of Subsidiarity: The German Case

Whereas in the United States collaboration between the state and the nonprofit sector results from a pragmatic series of political compromises that differ markedly from field to field, in Germany it grows out of a much more coherent governmental policy.[3] Indeed, the policy is formalized in a series of legal provisions and in a doctrine called subsidiarity (Anheier 1991; 1992).

The doctrine of subsidiarity essentially holds that the responsibility for caring for individuals' needs should always be vested in the units of social life closest to the individual — the family, the parish, the community, the voluntary association — and that larger, or higher level, units should be enlisted only when a problem clearly exceeds the capabilities of these primary units. Thus individuals should turn first to their families, then to their local community, then to their unit of local government, and only if no relief is forthcoming from these should the national government be involved. What is more, the doctrine holds that the higher units have an obligation not only to avoid usurping the position of the lower units, but to help the lower units perform their role.

This doctrine originated in nineteenth-century Jesuit thinking and Catholic moral philosophy. It came to real prominence, however, in Pope Pius XI's encyclical *Quadragesimo anno* of 1931. In its original formulation, the principle of subsidiarity advocated a corporatist, static society with fixed, hierarchical relations among individual, family, local groups, occupational groupings, and the state. In this system, the larger social unit (for example, the state) was forbidden from assuming responsibilities that could be achieved by the smaller unit (for example, the church).

The rise of subsidiarity from a political ideology in opposition to the centralizing and secularizing tendencies of the modern state to a blueprint policy governing large parts of Germany's welfare system is a product of several different forces. The first was the widespread loss of faith in the legitimacy of the state as provider and guarantor of social welfare that resulted from the failures of the Prussian-dominated monarchy, the Weimar Republic, and particularly Nazi totali-

---

3. This section draws on a fuller discussion of subsidiarity and related issues presented in Anheier 1991, 1992 and Anheier and Seibel 1993.

tarianism. The Nazi regime had taken over and centralized all previously independent welfare associations, which left a social and political vacuum after the German defeat in 1945. In the aftermath of World War II, the religious organizations, the Red Cross, and similar institutions were therefore met with less suspicion than what remained of the public welfare services. Heavy reliance on the free welfare associations was endorsed as well by the victorious Allies, who sought to prevent the reemergence of a highly centralized German state and therefore pushed for an arrangement that kept as many matters as possible in local, private hands.

Finally, the adoption of subsidiarity as the foundation of German social policy resulted from the great strength of the church in postwar Germany and the link between the church and the Christian Democratic Party, which governed from 1949 to 1969, either alone or as the senior partner of coalition governments. In a sense, subsidiarity defined a working compromise between the state and the church under which the church agreed to endorse state action in the social welfare field, but only if the state agreed to let the church and its affiliated social welfare agencies deliver the services thus created. Moreover, rather than take any chances, the advocates of subsidiarity in the German context pushed to enshrine the principle in formal law. Between 1950 and 1975, therefore, three separate laws were passed implementing the concept of subsidiarity as the basis of the German social welfare system.

This basic framework was first fully established in the Social Assistance Act of 1961, a comprehensive piece of legislation on the public and private provision of welfare and social services. The Social Assistance Act first obliges the "public bodies responsible for social assistance" to "collaborate with the public law churches and religious communities and with the free welfare associations" and to do so in a way that acknowledges "their independence in the targeting and execution of their functions." What is more, in section 3 the act requires the public bodies to "support the Free Welfare Associations appropriately in the field of social assistance." Finally, the act virtually guarantees a local monopoly to the nonprofit providers by forbidding public agencies from establishing their own offices at the local level "if suitable establishments of the free welfare associations . . . are available, or can be extended or provided."

Social legislation in particular policy fields spells out the implications of these basic relationships. Thus, the Youth Welfare Act stipulates particular nonprofit roles in the provision of youth services, and other acts assign additional responsibilities in such fields as health finance and employment and training. Finally, the Social Code, enacted in 1976 to codify and systematize the various bodies of social legislation that were enacted between the late nineteenth century and the 1970s, restates in article 2 the primacy of individual help and care over any form of private or public social assistance and then establishes in article 3 the obligation for the public sector and the nonprofit sector to work together to "effectively complement one another for the benefit of those receiving assistance" (Deutscher Verein 1986). In a sense, this code thus formalizes the basic framework for government-nonprofit interaction in the operation of the German welfare state.

The consequence of these various enactments is a dense network of legal and financial relationships between the state and the nonprofit sector. Broadly speaking, the relationships take four different forms. In the first place, the state provides *direct subsidies and block allocations* to support the basic operations of nonprofit service providers in certain key fields. These direct subsidies can originate from either the national or the state governments and show up as specific budget line items indicating "subsidy to [nonprofit organization] in accordance with the [Social Assistance Act or Youth Welfare Act, and so on]." Such subsidies are also provided for capital expenditures associated with the construction of schools, day care centers, and hospitals.

In the second place, federal, state, and local governments provide additional support to nonprofit organizations in the form of *grants* for particular projects that fall within the public interest as stipulated in relevant sections of the Budget Structure Act. These flows support activities other than the basic operations and investments supported by the statutory funds. For example, a special program aimed at the transition of handicapped youth to work would be supported with a public grant rather than a statutory subsidy.

A third form of government support to the nonprofit sector in Germany results from statutory transfers of particular responsibilities to voluntary organizations. In such cases public budgets *reimburse* nonprofit organizations for services provided to individuals or families on behalf of the state. A slightly different situation exists when nonprofit organizations carry out fee-for-service functions on behalf of public or private insurance schemes or the social security system. These tend to be "civil law" transactions in the German system, that is, private contracts for the delivery of certain services.

Beyond these financial transactions, public authorities in Germany are required by law to consult the free welfare associations in matters of social policy, and an elaborate consultative apparatus has been established to implement this requirement. In addition, as noted above, government must secure the endorsement of the associations for the establishment of public sector organizations in the social welfare field. In a sense, therefore, nonprofit organizations are guaranteed a share not only of public resources, but also of the authority for making public policy.

Summary

The United States and Germany have thus developed essentially collaborative models for the provision of basic welfare services, but they have pursued this approach along rather different paths. In the United States, a widespread pattern of third-party government is, in effect, linking government and nonprofit providers in particular policy spheres. However, the relationships between government and the nonprofit providers in this system reflect the pragmatic compromises reached between the supporters and opponents of government action in each policy area and for each separate program, rather than any single, overarching principle. The system is consequently loose and unstructured, so much so that few observers even recognize it exists.

In Germany, by contrast, a legitimacy crisis on the part of the state in the context of extensive church influence helped to fasten an explicit doctrine of subsidiarity on the relationships between the state and the nonprofit sector, and this doctrine has been firmly enshrined in law. Under it, the state owes the nonprofit sector certain privileges, and a clear legal premise in favor of nonprofit involvement has been established in the social welfare field. What is more, the law obligates the state to help guarantee the viability of nonprofit organizations and also to consult with the nonprofit sector in the development of state policy. The German model has thus taken the implicit American practice of third-party government and institutionalized it in both legal and political terms.

EVALUATION

How has this collaborative model worked in practice? What lessons does it hold for other countries contemplating new approaches to social welfare policy and practice? And what are the relative advantages and disadvantages of the respective German and American variants of this model? Unfortunately, clear answers to these questions are not easy to find. Evaluations of entire systems are difficult to undertake because of the great number of extraneous factors that can confound the results, and comparative analysis is still in its infancy. Nevertheless, it is possible to offer at least some tentative indications.

In the first place, the collaborative model of human service delivery seems to have a number of clear advantages. At its best, it combines the respective strengths of government and the nonprofit sector while avoiding their respective weaknesses. And as it turns out, these respective strengths and weaknesses complement each other quite well. Thus, government, at least democratic government, is especially well equipped to define societal priorities and generate resources for them, but it is not generally adept at delivering human services in a flexible fashion and on a human scale. Because of their smaller scale and greater flexibility, nonprofit organizations are much better able to deliver services to those in need, but they historically have difficulties generating the resources needed to support such services. By combining the strengths of the two systems, the collaborative model increases the likelihood that social policy will succeed.

The collaborative model also has the advantage of flexibility, which makes it possible to design programs that work by combining financing and delivery systems tailored to specific needs and populations rather than having the delivery system dictate the structure of the program. This feature also enables the government to experiment more freely, to try out new approaches without having to make the long-term personnel and administrative commitments that might otherwise be required. By relying on other institutions to help implement government programs, the state can more easily terminate an experiment if it does not work. In addition, this approach makes it possible to expand public protections without unduly expanding the size of the governmental workforce. Indeed, it helps ensure the survival of a substantial private, nongovernmental sector, which can be important in promoting pluralism and protecting liberty.

Although it has some critical advantages, however, this approach poses some important challenges. Most important, it significantly complicates the management of public programs, making it necessary for government agencies to mobilize and supervise the activities of a host of largely independent outside agents. In a sense, the third-party government approach, in either its American or German variant, turns the running of government programs, and with it a significant share of the public authority, over to a host of third-party agents over which government has at best imperfect control (Salamon 1981; Kettl 1988). In the process, moreover, it complicates accountability, making it difficult to determine who is responsible for program performance (Salamon 1987). In addition, it creates potential inequities because of the lack of uniform coverage and access to services in every locale.

From the point of view of the nonprofit implementers, the arrangement poses other challenges. For one thing, dependence on government financial support can undermine the independence of the nonprofit sector, making nonprofit organizations reluctant to criticize government and therefore limiting the advocacy role of this sector. In the second place, government funding can distort the missions of nonprofit organizations, inducing them to take on functions that are not central to their purpose. Finally, involvement in government programs can destroy some of the informality that gives nonprofit agencies their special character. Almost inevitably, government funding brings with it requirements for record keeping, for professionalization of management, and even for professionalization of staffing that can change the character of organizations in important ways (Smith and Lipsky 1993).

For the most part, experience with the operation of the collaborative model has shown most of these challenges to be manageable. There is little evidence in the United States, for example, that nonprofit organizations have suffered a serious loss of independence as a consequence of government funding. To be sure, there is some indication that the availability of government funding has forced (or allowed) nonprofits to focus their activities more heavily on the poor (Salamon 1993a, 156, 169). For the most part, however, such funding has enabled these organizations to pursue more extensively goals to which they were already committed (Salamon 1987, 114–15; Kramer 1981, 160; Hartogs 1978, 8–9). Indeed, there is some evidence that government agencies in the human service field become more beholden to the non-

profit providers than vice versa (deHoog 1985). This is so because government is frequently required to distribute funds quickly to get a program up and running but is prevented from hiring its own staff to do so. It is therefore often in the position of having to accept the services that the existing array of agencies is capable of providing rather than the ones it would ideally like to offer. What is more, government agencies rarely have the resources to conduct effective evaluation and follow-up. The nonprofit providers therefore often find themselves in the enviable position of enjoying government support with only limited government supervision and control. The one major countervailing factor is the looseness of the system—the fact that nonprofits are not guaranteed a role in public programs but must fight for it each time, that government program managers are given considerable latitude in deciding whether to contract with nonprofit providers to deliver services, that government support is for particular services only and little general support is provided, and that individual agencies face real or potential competition from other nonprofits and from for-profit providers for the government "business" that is available. While they keep the system from becoming overly rigidified, however, these features also expose nonprofit organizations to a considerable level of anxiety and uncertainty, which can be counterproductive in terms of designing long-term approaches to complex problems. The recent dramatic increase of for-profit involvement in the American welfare "market" makes it clear, moreover, that such anxiety may be well deserved (Salamon 1993b).

In Germany, nonprofit organizations face far less uncertainty because these elements of looseness are not present. The results, however, are not wholly benign. As we have seen, the role of the nonprofit sector in the operation of the German social welfare system is much more firmly enshrined in law than it is in the American case. The legal stipulations implementing the principle of subsidiarity have created a virtual protected market for the free welfare associations. Protection here has a dual meaning: nonprofits are protected from funding uncertainties that might affect their operations and even threaten their survival thanks to a system of general support grants, and they occupy a privileged position vis-à-vis potential for-profit and public competitors, who face serious barriers to entering the nonprofit sector's fields. The principle of subsidiarity thus creates a kind of quasi-monopolistic market for the free welfare associations. The presence of the church tax accentuates this situation by affording those parts of the nonprofit sector linked to the churches a stable source of income that is not dependent even on government policy. Taken together, these features create a powerful incentive for German nonprofits to favor the status quo and to avoid lurches in policy. They also limit the need for agencies to be client-sensitive or market-driven. In a sense, the major client of the free welfare associations is the government, not the recipients of their services. Although the result can be viewed as an efficient, responsive, and decentralized system in which the advantages of private and public involvement are realized to everybody's benefit (Spiegelhalter 1990), it also has the marks of a corporatist arrangement whereby the churches and other conservative political forces extend their control into the vital area of social welfare by creating quasi-monopolies (Heinze and Olk 1981; Thränhardt 1983).

Whatever the political and programmatic consequences, it seems clear that the highly structured collaboration characteristic of the German case has accentuated the impact that the collaborative model has on the internal structure of nonprofit agencies. In a sense, the free welfare associations have come to be seen by government officials and the public alike as an extension of the government. Increasingly, public sector administrative rules, reimbursement procedures, and salary scales are simply extended to include the free welfare associations. Although the situation in the American setting is far less formalized, similar impulses are at work there as well. Recipients of government grants and contracts are required to maintain sophisticated accounting records and thus to formalize their management structures. In addition, involvement in government contracting exposes organizations to a variety of other government requirements — for equal opportunity hiring practices, nondiscrimination, adherence to human subject protections in testing and research, limitations on certain overhead expenses, and the like. In addition, professional groups often use government regulations to impose certain professional requirements on agency staffing. Nevertheless, the formalization is still greater in the German setting. The upshot is to rigidify the system and reduce its responsiveness to those in need of services.

CONCLUSION

There is thus a third route to the provision of welfare services beyond primary reliance on the state or primary reliance on private philanthropy. This third route involves the active collaboration of the state and the nonprofit sector in the provision of welfare services, with the state specializing principally in the authorizing and financing of services and the nonprofit sector in their delivery. This arrangement combines the respective strengths of government and of the nonprofit sector while avoiding, or at least minimizing, their respective weaknesses. Most important, it offers a way to cope with the social welfare problems of an advanced, industrial society without having to create a massive, centralized state bureaucracy.

The United States and Germany both exemplify this third route, though they have approached it along different paths and with somewhat different results. Thus, the American system, the by-product of a long-standing hostility to state-provided welfare services, is highly fragmented, loose, and ambiguous, with considerable uncertainty about the exact role of nonprofit providers in particular programs and no overall direction about the form that the collaboration should take. In Germany, by contrast, a formal compact between an

influential church and a discredited state led to a situation in which nonprofits are guaranteed a role not only in the delivery of services but in their development as well. What is more, these organizations receive grants for their general operations and control the entry of other suppliers into their fields. Neither municipalities nor other potential suppliers may establish child care or youth institutions in local areas if the free welfare associations are planning to do so.

These differences reflect variations in the patterns of social and political life in the two countries and in the overall level of collective social welfare provision that exists. Having a higher level of centrally funded social welfare, a long-standing tradition of centralization, and a public law legal system that places more authority in the state, Germany understandably has a more formalized and structured form of collaboration.

Whether one or the other of these variants is preferable is difficult to say with any precision. In part, it depends on one's preferences between flexibility and uncertainty on the one hand and certain coverage for those in need on the other. What does seem clear, however, is that the third route described here has much to recommend it as a model for organizing the social welfare functions of a modern society, and that this route is available not only to historically decentralized, democratic countries like the United States, but also to continental countries like Germany that have far less experience with democracy and decentralization.

REFERENCES

AAFRC. *Giving USA*. 1991. New York: American Association of Fund Raising Counsel.

Anheier, Helmut K. 1991. "Employment and Earnings in the German Nonprofit Sector: Structure and Trends." *Annals of Public and Cooperative Economics* 62(4):673–94.

———. 1992. "An Elaborate Network: Profiling the Third Sector in Germany." In *Government and the Third Sector: Emerging Relationships in Welfare States,* ed. Benjamin Gidron, Ralph Kramer, and Lester M. Salamon. San Francisco: Jossey-Bass.

Anheier, Helmut K., and Wolfgang Seibel. 1993. "Defining the Nonprofit Sector: Germany." *Working Papers of the Johns Hopkins Comparative Nonprofit Sector Project,* no. 6. Baltimore: Johns Hopkins Institute for Policy Studies.

Bauer, Rudolph. 1978. *Wohlfahrtsverbände in der Bundesrepublik, Materialien und Analysen zu Organisation, Programmatik und Praxis, Ein Handbuch.* Weinheim: Basel.

Bundesarbeitsgemeinschaft der Freien Wohlfahrtspflege. 1990. *Gesamtstatistik 1990.* Bonn.

deHoog, Ruth Hoagland. 1985. "Human Services Contracting: Environmental, Behavioral and Organizational Conditions." *Administration and Society* 16:427–54.

Deutscher Verein für öffentliche und private Fürsorge. 1986. *Voluntary Welfare Services.* Frankfurt: Deutscher Verein.

Gidron, Benjamin, Ralph M. Kramer, and Lester M. Salamon. 1992. "Government and the Third Sector in Comparative Perspective: Allies or Adversaries?" In *Government and the*

Third Sector: Emerging Relationships in Welfare States, ed. Benjamin Gidron, Ralph Kramer, and Lester M. Salamon. San Francisco: Jossey-Bass.

Flora, Peter. 1986. *Growth to Limits: The Western European Welfare States since World War II.* Berlin: De Gruyter.

Flora, Peter, and Arnold J. Heidenheimer, eds. 1981. *The Development of Welfare States in Europe and America.* New Brunswick, N.J.: Transaction Books.

Hartogs, Nelly, and Joseph Weber. 1978. *Impact of Government Funding on the Management of Voluntary Agencies.* New York: Greater New York Fund.

Heidenheimer, Arnold J., Hugh Heclo, and Carolyn T. Adams. 1983. *Comparative Public Policy: The Politics of Social Choice in Europe and America.* New York: St. Martin's Press.

Heinze, Rolf G., and Thomas Olk. 1981. "Die Wohlfahrtsverbände im System sozialer Dienstleistungsproduktion: Zur Entstehung und Struktur der bundesrepublikanischen Verbändewohlfahrt." *Kölner Zeitschrift für Soziologie und Sozialpsychologie* 1:94–114.

Kettl, Donald F. 1988. *Government by Proxy: (Mis?) Managing Federal Programs.* Washington, D.C.: Congressional Quarterly Press.

Kramer, Ralph. 1981. *Voluntary Agencies in the Welfare State.* Berkeley: University of California Press.

OECD. 1991. *National Accounts, Detailed Tables, Volume II 1977–1989.* Paris: Organization for Economic Cooperation and Development.

———. 1994. "New Orientations for Social Policy." *OECD Social Policy Studies,* no. 12. Paris: Organization for Economic Cooperation and Development.

Offe, Klaus. 1985. *Disorganized Capitalism.* Cambridge: MIT Press.

Renz, Loren. 1991. *Foundation Giving: Yearbook of Facts and Figures on Private, Corporate, and Community Foundations.* New York: Foundation Center.

Salamon, Lester M. 1981. "Rethinking Public Management: Third-Party Government and the Changing Tools of Government Action." *Public Policy* 29:255–75.

———. 1987. "Partners in Public Service: The Scope and Theory of Government-Nonprofit Relations." In *The Nonprofit Sector: A Research Handbook,* ed. Walter W. Powell. New Haven: Yale University Press.

———. 1989. *Beyond Privatization: The Tools of Government Action.* Washington, D.C.: Urban Institute Press.

———. 1992. *America's Nonprofit Sector: A Primer.* New York: Foundation Center.

———. 1993a. "Social Services." In *Who Benefits from the Nonprofit Sector?* ed. Charles T. Clotfelter. Chicago: University of Chicago Press.

———. 1993b. "The Marketization of Welfare: Changing Nonprofit and For-Profit Roles in the American Welfare State." *Social Service Review* 67:16–39.

Salamon, Lester M., and Alan J. Abramson. 1982. *The Federal Budget and the Nonprofit Sector.* Washington, D.C.: Urban Institute Press.

Salamon, Lester M., James C. Musselwhite, Jr., and Carol J. DeVita. 1986. "Partners in Public Service: Government and the Nonprofit Sector in the American Welfare State." Paper delivered at the Independent Sector Spring Research Forum, 13–14 March 1986, New York.

Skocpol, Theda. 1992. *Protecting Soldiers and Mothers: The Political Origins of Social Policy in the United States.* Cambridge: Belknap Press of Harvard University Press.

Smith, Stephen Rathgeb, and Michael Lipsky. 1993. *Nonprofits for Hire: The Welfare State in the Age of Contracting.* Cambridge: Harvard University Press.

Spiegelhalter, Franz. 1990. *Der Dritte Sozialpartner.* Bonn: Lambertus.

Thränhardt, Dietrich. 1983. "Ausländer im Dickicht der Verbände: Ein Beispiel verbandsgerechter Klientelselektion und korporatistischer Politkformulierung." 1983. In *Sozialarbeit und Ausländerpolitik,* ed. F. Hamburger et al. Neuwied, Darmstadt: Luchterhand.

Wagner, Antonin. 1992. "The Interrelationship between the Public and Voluntary Sectors in Switzerland: Unmixing the Mixed-Up Economy." In *Government and the Third Sector: Emerging Relationships in Welfare States,* ed. Benjamin Gidron, Ralph Kramer, and Lester M. Salamon. San Francisco: Jossey-Bass.

11

C L A I R E   F.   U L L M A N

Partners in Reform: Nonprofit Organizations and the Welfare State in France

One of the striking features of the evolution of the welfare states of the West in the past few decades is the growing role played by nonprofit organizations in the provision of social services, a phenomenon often referred to as the privatization of the welfare state. Nevertheless, existing explanations of this phenomenon are unsatisfying. They attribute the trend to "the crisis of the welfare state" but falter in their attempts to define that crisis. They associate the trend with neoconservative politics, although new roles for nonprofits have often been created by governments of the Left. And they criticize the growing role of nonprofits as an attempt to roll back the welfare state, in spite of evidence that the role of nonprofits has grown most in policy areas in which the welfare state is expanding.[1]

Some of the problems with existing explanations for the growth of nonprofits' role in social service provision stem

I gratefully acknowledge the support provided for this research by a Chateaubriand Fellowship from the government of France, a fellowship from the Governance of Nonprofit Organizations Program of the Indiana University Center on Philanthropy, and a grant from the Nonprofit Sector Research Fund of the Aspen Institute.

1. Studies documenting and offering explanations for the trend include Kramer et al. 1993; Smith and Lipsky 1993; Salamon 1993; Gidron, Kramer and Salamon 1992b; Kamerman and Kahn 1989; Lipsky and Smith 1989; Johnson 1989; Brown 1988; Hood and Schuppert 1988; Ostrander and Langton 1987.

from confusion. In spite of the efforts of many scholars to distinguish among the various forms of privatization (Gidron, Kramer, and Salamon 1992a; Starr 1990), most analysts of the international trend have failed to distinguish between dumping responsibility on nonprofit organizations and delegating responsibility to them. Dumping responsibility on nonprofit organizations is the goal of Reagan/Thatcher-style neoconservatism. Government, according to this policy paradigm, should retreat and leave the provision of many social services to private initiatives, returning responsibility for the well-being of individuals to the private sector — the family, congregations, and nonprofit organizations. By contrast, in delegating responsibility to nonprofit organizations, public agencies contract out the provision of social services to nonprofit organizations while maintaining ultimate responsibility for the funding and oversight of the programs involved. Public spending in a given issue area is not necessarily diminished as a result of delegation to nonprofits; it may even increase. The rhetoric of the 1980s notwithstanding, dumping responsibility on nonprofits has actually been much less common, even in the United States, than delegation of responsibility.[2] In most of the West, indeed, delegation has become increasingly common, and the trend in that direction shows no signs of abating.

2. On the United States, see Smith and Lipsky 1993.

Based on an examination of France, this chapter will offer an explanation for the trend in industrial societies on both sides of the Atlantic toward increased delegation to nonprofit organizations of responsibility for social service provision. Like other observers, I link the trend to a crisis of the welfare state. While others tend to define the crisis of the welfare state as a fiscal crisis, however, I argue that there is another side to the welfare state's problems. Welfare states are afflicted with a crisis of methods, of competence, and of definition which is at least as important as the failure of tax revenues to meet ever-growing expenses. This crisis has its origins in the years of prosperity which preceded the oil shocks of the 1970s, not in the recession which followed them.

There have in fact been two crises of the welfare state. One of these crises could be called a crisis of welfare, in that faltering economies and the inability of tax revenues to keep up with mounting needs have threatened our ability to continue to provide the expensive social insurance programs which ensure our welfare. The other is a crisis of the state, characterized by a crisis of confidence in the state's ability to accomplish the tasks which it has taken on in modern societies. Based on my analysis of the political processes by which delegation to nonprofits became important as a public policy in France, I argue that rather than being prompted by the first crisis, delegation to nonprofits has primarily been tied to the second crisis, which I call a crisis of state capacity.

THE CRISIS OF STATE CAPACITY

State capacity is the term used to describe a state's ability to accomplish its goals, an ability which is influenced by the state's institutions and its relationships with relevant groups in society.[3] A crisis of state capacity, as I define it, occurs when the state is unable to accomplish its goals for reasons related not to a lack of funds but to a lack of competence. A crisis of state capacity cannot be solved by pouring additional funding into existing government programs, but instead must be addressed by finding new ways to accomplish public goals.

In France, political elites began their analysis of the problem of state capacity as early as the 1960s. Three separate groups of political reformers developed critiques of the functioning of the French state during the years between the founding of the Fifth Republic in 1958 and the election of François Mitterrand as president in 1981. Each group recommended a larger role for nonprofit organizations in public life as part of the solution to the varying problems of state capacity which it identified. These reformers, all of them with a strong stake in the power of the state and many of them socialists, sought to recruit nonprofit organizations as partners of the state, not in order to roll back the state but to bolster and extend its power by appropriating the skills and flexibility of nonprofit organizations for use by the state.

They sought this increase in state capacity in order to achieve two goals: to strengthen democratic institutions of governance, and to reform and extend welfare programs to reach more of the disadvantaged and to respond more effectively to the changing needs of society.

The efforts of the three groups converged after the elections of 1981, when the Socialist administration of President Mitterrand and Prime Minister Pierre Mauroy enacted many of the recommendations of these groups and gave nonprofits a new role in French public life. In the course of the 1980s, the relationship between nonprofit social service providers and the French welfare state changed dramatically. The Socialist government offered nonprofits unprecedented roles in the administration of welfare state programs, delegating to them significant new responsibility for the implementation of public programs and providing them with substantial public funding. Indeed, every major poverty policy initiative of the 1980s in France relied on nonprofits for its implementation, including a campaign against hunger and homelessness, a law implementing a national right to housing, and, most important, major legislation creating a guaranteed minimum income. Nonprofits were also granted formal roles in both national and local political bodies. By the end of the decade, nonprofit organizations had used their new access to money and power to form a social policy lobby which played an important role in extending both the scope of the welfare state in France and the role of nonprofit organizations within it. Nonprofit organizations had achieved a new status as partners of the welfare state. In the process, the French state underwent important changes in its stance toward civil society and in the architecture of the institutions which administer significant components of the welfare state.

The process by which a policy of delegating roles in social service provision to nonprofits became common in France flatly contradicts common expectations that such delegation will be motivated by conservative plans to decrease the scale of state intervention in society and diminish the generosity of the welfare state.[4] It also illuminates the factors at work in other nations in which delegation to nonprofits has been a newly prominent strategy of the welfare state. France's state-centered political style and history of centuries of mistrust and repression of intermediate organizations make it one of the least likely candidates among Western democracies to enlarge the role of nonprofit organizations. As a result, France plays the role of the "hard case" in my analysis, the case in which a given change is so unlikely that the factors causing it are exposed in stark relief. The factors which have been important in driving the evolution in nonprofits' roles in other countries are exaggerated in France, making them easier to observe and analyze. Strong cultural and institutional barriers had to be overcome for nonprofits to gain important roles in French public life. Consequently, reformers seeking to enlarge the role of nonprofits in France have focused their

3. See, for example, Evans, Rueschemeyer, and Skocpol 1985, and Skocpol and Finegold 1982.

4. See, for example, Starr 1990, Mishra 1990, and Johnson 1990.

efforts explicitly on transforming the state and have developed careful analyses of the nature of the relationship between state capacity and the strength of civil society.

DELEGATION TO NONPROFITS IN FRANCE

The election of the Socialist government of President Mitterrand and Prime Minister Mauroy in 1981 ushered in a new era for the French nonprofit sector. For the first time, national leaders brought nonprofit organizations into the circle of "social partners" in their discourse, thus including them among the principal interest groups with which the state must negotiate in making policy. Previously, they had ignored nonprofits or scorned them as special interests.[5] During the first years of the new government, nonprofit organizations[6] were granted representation on their own national council and on the consultative national Economic and Social Council, which exists alongside the bicameral legislature as the third representative body of the French state. Nonprofit organizations were recruited to provide social services as part of new initiatives against poverty, and in the late 1980s, they were included in the analysis, formulation, and implementation of a major social policy initiative, a national minimum income program (the *revenu minimum d'insertion,* or RMI). By 1990, nonprofit organizations had developed such a powerful public role that they were able to score a major lobbying victory in the enactment of a law to implement a national right to housing.

To understand the magnitude of the change which occurred in the relationship between the nonprofit sector and public authorities in France in the 1980s, it is necessary to abandon American preconceptions about the value of citizen activism and the relative undesirability of public bureaucracies. In the United States, both the culture and many political theorists celebrate the contribution which citizen activism makes to the public good; in France, on the other hand, groups of citizens acting independently of the state have not only generally been mistrusted but often outlawed.

5. The groups encompassed by the term *social partners* vary according to the type of policy under discussion but generally include business, labor, and agriculture. For an interesting discussion of the use of the term *social partners* and its opposite, "special interests," see Jobert and Muller (1987, 173) and Jobert (1991, 243).

6. In fact, the universe of organizations represented in these bodies was larger: it was the whole population of *associations.* The word *association* in French refers to any sort of noncommercial association of individuals acting in concert, including such diverse entities as neighbors organized to demand a streetlight, a bicycling club, the national group which works to combat racism, a volunteer-staffed food bank, a social service agency managing huge budgets and facilities, and the teachers' federations. I will most often use the terms *nonprofit organization* and *nonprofit sector* as translations for the French *association* and *vie, monde, mouvement* and *secteur associatif(ve).* These translations, while not exact, are the best available and are the most appropriate for the set of *associations* I will usually be discussing, i.e., relatively institutionalized social service providers.

Freedom to form private associations was not granted in France until 1901. Before that time, associations were variously banned altogether or else came under heavy restrictions. From the time of Jean-Jacques Rousseau to the very recent past, French political theorists, with a few notable exceptions such as Alexis de Tocqueville, have argued that only the public sector could serve the general interest; all private activity, even when charitable in nature, was regarded with suspicion (Hall 1990; Chevallier 1991). Although nonprofits have existed in France since before the French Revolution, until recently they were relatively few in number and mostly affiliated with the Catholic Church.

At present, France's nonprofit organizations can essentially be divided into two groups: those entirely dependent on the state and those which before the 1980s had no relationship with the state but now function as the state's partners. The first kind tend to be large institutions such as orphanages, nursing homes, and long-term emergency shelters. Often affiliated with the church, these organizations were already in existence when the welfare state was created and were incorporated into the new structure of service provision. They have generally received 100 percent of their funding from the national agency responsible for the population they serve, and their funding is automatically renewed from year to year (Inspection générale des Affaires sociales 1984). Indeed, they function essentially as extensions of the state, and advocates for the nonprofit sector do not consider them to be genuine nonprofits.

By contrast, the other group of nonprofits had little or no relationship with the state before the 1980s; they operated entirely on private funds and often met with considerable antagonism from state officials mistrustful of their independent activity. Their workers were sometimes threatened by public officials because of their activities on behalf of the poor, and social workers at public agencies were forbidden to work with these nonprofit organizations or appeal to them for help with clients (Fauqueux 1989, 20). The role of these nonprofits changed significantly during the 1980s, when many of them were welcomed into a new partnership with the welfare state. Now, these organizations receive public funding for some of their activities, operating programs under contract with the state. Unlike the wholly dependent organizations, these nonprofits maintain considerable autonomy even as they accept public funds.

The number of nonprofit organizations in France has increased dramatically in the past twenty-five or thirty years (Archambault 1985, 1992). Two sets of factors have contributed to this growth in numbers. Demographic changes, including increased levels of education and mobility, drove some of the growth. These changes were partly responsible for the formation, beginning in the 1960s, of citizen associations advocating such causes as the protection of the environment, women's rights, and community development (Bruneau 1986). Additionally, some of the growth in the population of nonprofits was driven by public policy. Before the

1980s, this public policy mostly involved changes in the law which created incentives for the formation of sporting clubs and the like.

In spite of the growth in their numbers, nonprofits still lacked legitimacy in French public life until the dramatic changes of the 1980s. With the exception of some environmental and urban community groups, their lobbying efforts were considered illegitimate, and a public/private partnership would have been considered an abdication of responsibility on the part of the public agencies involved (Chevallier 1981).

Although it is clear that there has been a significant change in the role of nonprofit organizations in politics and in their importance in social service provision in France, documentation of the precise extent of nonprofit provision of publicly funded services does not exist. At the national level, studies have not yet traced the changing levels of public funding received by nonprofit organizations over the years, either in the aggregate or within specific categories such as social services. Indeed, information as to the proportion of public spending currently going to nonprofit organizations is not now being collected.[7] Nonetheless, the policy initiatives of the 1980s and, most notably, the creation in 1988 of the RMI, which is administered in large part by nonprofit organizations and involves extensive job training and other rehabilitative programs run by nonprofits, have surely brought about an increase in such funding (Commission nationale d'évaluation du Revenu minimum d'insertion 1992, 333–402). This conclusion is supported by a study which demonstrates that *local* government funding of nonprofits grew significantly during the 1980s (Mizrahi-Tchernonog 1991, 25). Thus, although data documenting the precise extent of the change in the financial relationship between the state and the nonprofit sector do not exist, one can safely say that a significant change has occurred.

LAYING THE GROUNDWORK FOR DELEGATION: THREE PROGRAMS FOR REFORM

The explanation for this evolution in the relationship between the welfare state and the nonprofit sector in France does not lie in efforts to reduce the scope of the welfare state. Delegation of responsibility for social service provision was initiated in France in arenas in which the welfare state was expanding — for example, in the administration of the new

national guaranteed minimum income program — and it occurred under the leadership of Socialist governments. Furthermore, in France, unlike in some other countries, delegation to nonprofit organizations does not in fact save the state much money.[8] Nonprofits providing services under contract with the state are reimbursed for the full amount of their costs,[9] and differentials in pay scales between the nonprofit and public sectors do not always work to hold nonprofits' costs down.[10]

As noted above, the explanation lies instead in the deliberate efforts of three separate groups of reformers to reconstruct the relationship between the French state and French society. In each case, the reformers' efforts began well before the fiscal crisis which afflicted France beginning in the mid-1970s and were oriented toward reform of the French state.

Modernizing Elites and the New Importance of Civil Society

The prominent civil servants and intellectuals who composed the first of the three groups of reformers advocated an increased role for nonprofit organizations in French life as a way of invigorating French democracy. Active from the late 1950s through the 1980s, this group had an evolving membership. Yet it was always led by a core of committed individuals, including, most notably, François Bloch-Lainé, a very prominent government official and former leader in the French Resistance.

This group had two principal incarnations. It first took shape as a political reflection club, the Club Jean Moulin, founded in 1958 during the transition from the Fourth to the Fifth Republic to figure out ways to bolster democratic stability in France (Mossuz 1970; Lindseth 1992).[11] It was in

7. Typically, the most comprehensive government study of the nonprofit sector addresses the question of levels of public funds going to the nonprofit sector only in passing, despite its exhaustive detail in other regards (Cheroutre 1993). Ministry budgets are not configured so as to make the collection of this sort of data possible for the academics who are now investigating the nonprofit sector in France (Mizrahi-Tchernonog 1992). Although data are particularly scarce for France, however, problems with collecting data on the nonprofit sector appear to be international. In recent studies a team of authors has pointed out serious flaws in existing data on the nonprofit sector in the United States (Bowen 1994; Turner 1993).

8. Policymakers report that they do not regard delegation to nonprofits as a cost-saving measure (Fragonard 1992; Worms 1992).

9. Indeed, private donations make up a very small portion of the income of nonprofits in France by comparison with the United States. A smaller percentage of the population makes donations, and they make much smaller donations. One reason is that their donations are tax-deductible to only a minuscule extent. For a fuller discussion, see Cheroutre 1993.

10. Delegation can save the state money when nonprofits hire low-skilled workers at lower wages than are offered by the public sector. However, although public pay scales are higher than private for low-skilled workers, for higher-skilled workers the public sector pays less. In addition, once a nonprofit agency has started to receive government contracts for service provision, pay for the lower-skilled workers tends to rise to approach levels in the public sector. See Mizrahi-Tchernonog 1991. Interestingly, Susan Rose-Ackerman (1990, 158) observes the same phenomenon of nonprofit sector wages rising to match public sector wages in the United States.

11. Political reflection clubs have flourished at several junctures in French history. In the 1960s, they served as an important outlet for criticism of the new Gaullist regime. Their style of functioning is comparable to that of the United States' Council on Foreign Relations, in that they promote discussion among their members and publish analyses intended to influence policy.

this club that Bloch-Lainé and others first developed the idea that nonprofit organizations might play a crucial role in creating the social conditions for democracy, an idea they advocated in 1968 in a book entitled *Pour nationaliser l'État* (To Nationalize the State) (Alphandéry et al. 1968).[12]

For the authors and for French society, this book represented a major conceptual innovation. The Club Jean Moulin had spent ten years analyzing how best to invigorate French democracy, but it was not until 1968 that the members of the group, mostly civil servants, overcame their mistrust of intermediate organizations sufficiently to advocate that citizen groups be regarded as a positive contribution to democracy (Bloch-Lainé 1980, 7). One of the main reasons for their change of heart was their perception that the state was failing to meet its obligations on its own.

The authors of *Pour nationaliser l'État* criticized the French state for its overextension, its excessive centralization, and its lack of flexibility and responsiveness (Alphandéry et al. 1968, 8–9). They argued that, in contradiction to the prevailing French belief that the state is the sole guarantor of the public interest, direct state intervention is not warranted in all aspects of public life and urged that the state delegate roles to intermediate organizations, whether local governments, nonprofit organizations, or other structures (24–25). Offering a clear indication that, in 1968, the crisis of state capacity was already apparent to these reformers, the authors of *Pour nationaliser l'État* listed the many areas in which the definition of the public interest was expanding to include vast new areas of responsibility, areas in which public sector programs might be neither effective nor appropriate. They argued,

> Even if it wanted to and if it had all the material means necessary, the public sector would not be able itself to take responsibility for all of these activities. The issue is that, by their nature, they cannot be "administered."
> They require forms of management which are not those of a public bureaucracy: pluralism and liberty; suppleness and rapidity; aptitude for calling into play human strengths such as generosity, devotion, enthusiasm, even such human strengths as the genius of creation, that of leadership or that of organization; the possibility of changing, renouncing, failing as well as persevering or succeeding. (220)[13]

In the 1970s, this group of reformist civil servants and intellectuals took a new form as the leadership of an association of nonprofit organizations working to achieve some of the policy goals advocated by the Club Jean Moulin. Many members of the group also participated in another political reflection club, called Échange et Projets (Exchange and Projects).

Bloch-Lainé, who had been a founding member of the

12. A translation of the title which is less literal but which expresses the authors' intention better is "For a State that Belongs to the Nation."

13. Unless otherwise indicated, all translations are my own.

Club Jean Moulin, became the president of the new Association pour le développement des associations de progrès (Association for the Development of Progressive Associations), known as the DAP. This organization, founded in 1975, held three major conferences—in 1976, 1979, and 1981—to bring members of the nonprofit sector together to define its goals with regard to public policy and to work to achieve them (Association pour le Développement des associations de progrès 1977, 1979; Fondation pour la vie associative 1981). The creation of the DAP represented the first time nonprofit organizations in France had mobilized as a sector to address issues of concern to the sector as a whole (Viannay 1988, 376). Indeed, as Bloch-Lainé observed to the members in 1979, one of the organization's purposes was to "contribute to a certain structuring of the nonprofit sector" (Bloch-Lainé 1979, 7).

The DAP had considerable success in building support for the nonprofit sector among public officials. It developed a detailed platform of policy changes intended to reform relations between the state and the nonprofit sector and united a wide variety of nonprofit organizations in support of that platform. By the time a receptive government came to power in 1981, the DAP had built support among legislators, bureaucrats, and leaders of the nonprofit community for a clearly delineated program of reform.

**The Second Left and *Autogestion*:
A New Vision of State-Society Relations**
The second group of reformers, whose ideas heavily influenced the Socialist Party after the mid-1970s, was the socialist faction called the Second Left. Its theories, which rejected traditional socialist prescriptions for a dominant, centralized state in favor of new power for civil society, opened the Socialist Party to partnerships with groups in society. During the 1980s, these theories had a powerful influence on social policy even during the periods when more traditional socialists within the party were controlling economic policy.

At a time when French socialism was in crisis, suffering from disillusionment with the Soviet model and searching for new paths, the leaders of the Second Left borrowed a new concept from the student protests of May 1968 and made it a centerpiece of their theorizing (Brown 1982; Hall 1986, 214–19). *Autogestion,* which literally means self-management, has been understood in a variety of ways, but it has generally involved a rejection of the idea that the state should have full control of the economy, advocating instead greater power for workers and, more generally, for citizens. The concept was used to advocate the devolution of authority from plant managers to workers' councils, from the central state to local government authorities, and from public bureaucracies to private citizens. The Socialist Party advocated *autogestion* in nationalized industries as a way to reconcile its planned nationalization of industry and banks with its commitment to individual freedom (Brown 1982, 52–54). The party's leaders also used the term in advocating increased autonomy for civil society, calling for the "*autogestion* of everyday life" (Commissariat général au Plan 1982, 257).

Decentralization of government and increased delegation to nonprofit organizations became important elements of the Socialist Party's platform by the late 1970s, owing largely to the influence of the Second Left.[14] Ties forged between party leaders and the DAP, the nonprofits' lobby, also strengthened the party's commitment to the nonprofit sector. For example, in 1979 the DAP recruited Pierre Mauroy to be the keynote speaker at its second conference, which was held in Lille. Mauroy was mayor of Lille and an important figure in the Socialist Party — two years later he would be prime minister. He had also been involved in the nonprofit sector for many years as one of the leaders of a national organization that provided continuing education and cultural and other activities to workers and their families. DAP leaders chose Lille as the site for their conference and Mauroy as the keynote speaker in a calculated attempt to win his support for their cause (Raffi 1992).

In his speech, Mauroy analyzed the problems of the French state and the role which he saw for nonprofit organizations in solving them. Mauroy echoed the analysis of the Second Left when he told the assembled DAP members, "The current situation is characterized by an overgrown and centralized state, a political society which is quite weak and is dependent on the state, and a civil society whose structures are fragmented and too often marginalized." He described the nonprofit sector as a critical factor in reinforcing democracy and redressing the imbalance between state and society (Mauroy 1979, 4).

When Mauroy became prime minister two years later, his government announced its commitment to a program of reform aimed at revitalizing civil society, in part by offering new roles for nonprofit organizations. In doing so, it reflected the profound changes which the Second Left had wrought in the Socialist Party's conception of socialism and of the appropriate role of the state in society.

Les Exclus and the Crisis of the Welfare State: Opening a Door to Nonprofits

The third group of reformers was composed of policy analysts who developed a critique of the welfare state in a series of studies beginning in the mid-1970s. The civil servants and political figures involved in this effort played an important role in paving the way for significant changes in the way in which the welfare state approached social problems. In the process of drafting their studies, these individuals built ties to

nonprofit social service organizations and developed a foundation for those organizations' later inclusion in the implementation of social programs.

The impetus for these studies of the welfare state was the publication of *Les Exclus* (The Excluded) by René Lenoir in 1974 (Lenoir 1989). Lenoir documented the presence in France of pockets of stubborn poverty — an underclass of individuals without a history of regular employment and hence no access to many of the social insurance programs of the state.[15] Even those welfare programs for which they were eligible were failing to reach these individuals, who were often afraid of public authorities, ill-equipped to benefit from public education and job training programs, and mired in a multigenerational legacy of poverty. Lenoir's analysis caused considerable alarm in France and put pressure on the government to respond to the problems he outlined.

The government responded by commissioning a series of studies, beginning in 1976, to identify the gaps in France's social safety net and recommend measures to fix them. From the beginning, the civil servants in charge of the studies asked for the help and advice of representatives of the nonprofit sector (Pequignot 1979; Oheix 1981; Wresinski 1987). Over time, these studies opened the way to increased delegation to nonprofits in several ways. First, they brought representatives of various nonprofits into contact with senior civil servants, giving those organizations new access to the state. Second, the studies convinced political actors that poverty was a serious problem and that nonprofits were already involved in dealing with its effects. And third, the studies advocated increased roles for nonprofits in the administration of public programs. In doing so, these studies laid the groundwork for the nonprofit sector's involvement in the development and implementation of poverty policy in the 1980s. Their advocacy of an enhanced role for nonprofit organizations in the delivery of social services was heeded when their recommendations with regard to the reform of poverty policy were eventually enacted.

THE SOCIALISTS IN POWER: RECOGNIZING NEW SOCIAL PARTNERS

When Mitterrand and Mauroy came to power in 1981, the pieces were in place for a major change in the role of nonprofit organizations in public life.[16] Owing to the influence of the Second Left, the newly elected government was dedicated to revitalizing civil society, and many of the top officials, including, most notably, Mauroy, were deeply committed to the

14. Decentralization was, in fact, enacted in 1983 and was one of the major accomplishments of the Socialist government. Social policy was the domain most affected by decentralization, and as a result decentralization had a significant impact of its own on the evolution of the French welfare state and on relations between local governments and nonprofit organizations. For a discussion of decentralization and the nonprofit sector, see Ullman 1995; Schmidt 1990; Brovelli 1989; Guillois 1988; Grémion 1987.

15. Although some of *les exclus* are immigrants, most are native French. In public policy terms, problems of immigration and problems of exclusion are regarded as separate issues in France.

16. There were some preliminary moves to grant nonprofits access to the policy-making process during the 1970s, primarily involving the inclusion of environmental and urban development advocacy groups in local planning. Widespread change in nonprofits' roles followed the Socialist victory, however. See Bruneau 1986.

nonprofit sector. Equally important, a blueprint for the new relations between state and society had been drawn up and was available to the leadership. The DAP and the various commissions which had studied poverty had brought top civil servants and the leaders of nonprofits together to devise detailed policy recommendations to improve nonprofits' access to private contributions, establish them on a more equal footing with public sector funders, and increase their participation in all aspects of public policy. Once in power, the new government institutionalized formal roles for nonprofits in policy analysis, formulation, and implementation.[17]

The New Vision Implemented

The government of Prime Minister Mauroy worked rapidly to implement its vision of a more democratic polity, responding to the critiques of the French state developed by Second Left theorists and by others, including the Club Jean Moulin.[18] Although Mauroy himself was not a member of the Second Left group, he was sympathetic to many of its goals for civil society (Hamon and Rotman 1982, 273). In addition, as a long-time member and leader of a large nonprofit organization, he was personally committed to the nonprofit sector (Bloch-Lainé 1994). Even as his government was carrying out a social-democratic program of nationalizing major industries and banks, it was taking steps to invigorate civil society. For example, Mauroy created a new ministry, the Ministry of Free Time, intended to encourage all types of social participation not related to employment, including participation in citizens' groups and volunteer work. At the same time, the pointed inclusion of nonprofit organizations in the roster of the social partners in the statements of the new government marked an important change in French political discourse.[19]

In 1983, the government created the first official body to represent the nonprofit sector, the Conseil national de la vie associative (National Council of the Nonprofit Sector), which was attached to the prime minister's office. Then, in 1984, nonprofit organizations were included among the sectors of society represented in the Economic and Social Council, marking the nonprofit sector's most significant institu-

---

17. This pattern of the creation of organized interests through subsidies and access to consultative bodies was not confined to the nonprofit sector; it was a characteristic feature of the general evolution of French politics in the 1980s. See Hall (1990, 82).

18. Readers will note that the discussion which follows does not address the famous U-turn in which the Mitterrand administration abandoned its projects for a greatly more generous welfare state in favor of a policy of *rigueur,* that is, austerity. The reason for this omission is that *rigueur* had relatively little impact on the developments discussed in this chapter, although it had a significant impact on the core social insurance programs of the welfare state. Furthermore, to the extent it did have an impact on the nonprofit sector, it was primarily at the level of local politics. On *rigueur* and the French welfare state, see Freeman 1990; Ross 1988; Ross 1987; and Freeman 1985.

19. For example, Commissariat général du Plan 1982, iii–xxxi.

tional gain of the 1980s. The Economic and Social Council is one of the three national representative bodies created by the constitution, although it is the least powerful of the three. The Economic and Social Council is composed of representatives of the principal interest groups in France, as well as prominent intellectuals. It serves a purely consultative or advisory role, being empowered to issue reports on matters of policy interest either at the request of the government or on its own initiative. Although not binding, these reports sometimes have a great deal of influence. Thus the inclusion of nonprofit organizations on the council is significant both because it expresses recognition of the important role played by the nonprofit sector in public life and because it increases the influence of nonprofits in the making of public policy.

Nonetheless, sectoral groups within the Economic and Social Council have only a limited impact compared with their organized lobbies in society. Although the government's inclusion of the nonprofit sector on the council certainly increased the sector's influence on public policy, the government probably did more to help nonprofits gain power—particularly in the arena of social policy—when it provided them with significant new funding as part of a campaign against poverty.

The "Poverty Plans" and the Creation of a Social Policy Lobby

Soon after coming to power in 1981, the new government was faced with a crisis of dramatically increasing levels of poverty in France. In addition to *les exclus,* whose existence had started to cause alarm in the 1970s and continued to do so to an increasing degree, France was experiencing what was called new poverty, the poverty of people who had once been employable but, under changing economic conditions, were no longer. Homelessness and hunger rose to alarming levels (Barthe 1987; Houillon 1987).

In 1983, the government announced an initiative to combat extreme poverty through measures to improve access to certain types of social programs and to offer new funding to charitable organizations and public agencies which were providing emergency services. This initiative became an annual winter program officially called *Lutte contre la pauvreté et la précarité* (Fight against Poverty and Economic Vulnerability), but usually referred to as the "poverty plans" (Mariller and Janvier 1988, 27–28).

From the beginning, nonprofit organizations were at the center of the poverty plans. Before announcing the measures, President Mitterrand met with representatives of eight of the major charitable organizations to win their support (Petitpas 1983). Most of the funding distributed by the plans went to nonprofit organizations, passed either directly by the state to national organizations or through prefects to local groups (Janvier 1987, 16–19). For the nonprofit sector, the poverty plans offered somewhat increased funding, access to public officials, and a new role in social policy implementation. At the same time, organizations were forced to professionalize their style of operation as they negotiated operating contracts with public authorities, often for the first time (Sassier-Robert 1992). Most important, the poverty plans also provided the impetus for nonprofit organizations to form a social policy lobby, joining forces across the traditionally divisive left/right and religious/secular cleavages.

Once nonprofits became involved in implementing the government-funded poverty plans, they were politicized. They began to question the government's definition of the problems of the new poor and *les exclus* and to develop their own policy demands. At least partly on the initiative of Bloch-Lainé, the former president of the DAP who had recently become president of the national federation of nonprofit organizations in the health and social sectors, UNIOPSS, many of the organizations involved in the poverty plans began to meet as a poverty task force in 1984 under the federation's auspices (Groués 1993). The purpose of the task force was to develop a common stance among its members on policy issues related to poverty and to mobilize its members to pressure legislators for change.

As a newly formed social policy lobby, the nonprofits were a critically important factor in the enactment of two new social entitlements in France, the guaranteed minimum income, which was enacted in 1988, and a set of measures designed to implement a national right to housing, enacted in 1990. Through their lobbying, nonprofits extended their involvement in the welfare state from the social service programs at its periphery to the social insurance role at its core. In doing so, they played a role in bringing about increased welfare state expenditures.[20]

WELFARE STATES UNDER PRESSURE

The victories of the nonprofit sector in lobbying for the enactment of these new social programs demonstrate the political legitimacy and power which the French nonprofit sector had achieved in the realm of social policy in the course of the 1980s.[21] That legitimacy and power, in turn, testify to the emerging conviction in France that groups in civil society can make a positive contribution to society as a whole. Such tolerance for pluralism overcomes centuries of arguments that the state alone can serve the general interest and signals

the arrival in France of a new conception of the process by which the public good may be achieved.[22]

This new conception of the relationship between the state and civil society was the product of the efforts of the reform movements I have described. In essence, they undertook what Paul Starr has called an institution-building program, that is, an "attempt to create an enabling framework for civil society" (1990, 30). Starr assumes such a program will be found only in the former Eastern bloc and some developing countries. In France as well, however, elements of both law and political culture had to be changed for nonprofits to achieve a larger role in public life. For this to happen, leading figures in French political life had to articulate an alternative vision to that which had dominated French political culture and to use their personal authority to give legitimacy to the newly formed nonprofit movement.

The goal of these reformers was to bring nonprofit organizations into new roles in public life in order to revitalize French democracy and to diversify and personalize the French welfare state's services. Mostly affiliated with the Left and all dedicated to the idea that the nation has responsibility for the well-being of its inhabitants, these reformers saw a partnership between the state and nonprofits as both a boon to French politics and a benefit to the clients of the welfare state. In their eyes, delegation to nonprofits would not in any way reduce the responsibility of the state; it would merely change its mode of operation to make it more beneficial to society. Responding to a crisis of state capacity, they sought a partnership with nonprofit organizations in order to appropriate for public use qualities which public agencies lack.

The analyses of the French reformers demonstrate clearly the role which a crisis of state capacity played in prompting policymakers to delegate responsibilities to nonprofits in France. The similarities between the problems they observed in France and those experienced by other welfare states throughout the West in the past few decades suggest that this crisis has played an important role in other nations as well. Based on the French case and building on the work of other scholars,[23] I identify two broad social trends which have pushed welfare states to the point of a crisis of state capacity:

1. pressure on the welfare state for the *democratization* of its functioning, in the form of demands that the barriers between citizens and the state be lowered in

20. The similarity of these events to the effect which Title XX of the Social Security Act had in creating nonprofit social policy lobbies at the local level in the United States is striking. See Smith and Stone 1988.

21. It does not, however, necessarily contradict those authors who argue that interest groups in France have real power only when it is granted by the state. The nonprofit lobby was fighting on the same side as the government against a recalcitrant parliament, rather than against the government, and its importance in political life was to some extent the result of the government's engineering. Nevertheless, it is significant both that the state had granted power to the nonprofit sector and that the sector had learned to put it to very good use. On interest groups in France, see, for example, Hall 1990; Hayward 1990; Jobert and Muller 1987; Keeler 1987; and Schmidt 1992.

22. The struggle over the conception of the potential contribution of nonprofits to the public good waged by the modernizing elites of the DAP and by the Second Left offers an example of the sort of contestation often provoked by the notion of the public good. The change brought about subtly changes the definition of the word *public* in the phrase, by delinking the good of the public (defined as the citizenry at large) and the good of the state. On notions of the public good, see the chapters by Mansbridge and Calhoun, this volume.

23. In particular: Alber 1988; Rosanvallon 1988, 1993; Smith and Lipsky 1993; Glazer 1981, 1988; and Hood and Schuppert 1988.

ways which increase ordinary people's participation and sense of investment in public programs; and

2. pressure on the welfare state for greater *responsiveness,* in the form of demands for state action to address a widening array of increasingly complex social problems.

Pressure for democratization has come both from reformist political elites and from new social movements. In many nations, reformers active in the 1960s and 1970s pressed states to democratize their interaction with citizens in ways which would allow greater citizen participation in the management of public life. In some instances, such reform movements were driven by the actual failures of democratic institutions. In France, for example, the collapse of the Third and Fourth Republics drove the efforts of reformers, and in the United States, the political and social disenfranchisement of part of the population drove the efforts of the civil rights movement. In these and other nations, however, democratizing movements also arose from the frustrations of increasingly educated and assertive populations. A variety of groups called for the lowering of barriers between citizens and the state through increased citizen participation in policy formulation and implementation and through the decentralization, debureaucratization, and deinstitutionalization of state programs.

Efforts to democratize public programs often precipitate a crisis of state capacity of the sort which leads to expanded roles for nonprofit organizations. For example, when the state is pressed to provide culturally sensitive programs to various ethnic groups, it may find that it cannot do so without violating the code of standardized treatment to which public agencies are held. Caught between competing commitments, policymakers are unable to adapt existing public agencies to meet new program goals. As a result, they may choose to contract out programs to the nonprofit sector. Similarly, when the state devolves responsibilities to local governments in response to demands for decentralization, overburdened local governments may delegate their new responsibilities to nonprofit organizations because they lack the capacity to undertake them directly.

At the same time that welfare states are being asked to do things more democratically, they are being pressed to do more and to do it in ways that are more responsive to individual needs. The mandate of the welfare state has been extended from the protection of workers and their families against the vicissitudes of the market to intervention in a whole range of situations. The new roles of the welfare state often center on people targeted for their pathologies rather than their relationship to the labor market. Examples include programs for the victims and perpetrators of domestic violence, teen pregnancy prevention programs, homeless shelters, substance abuse programs, and the like. The welfare state has been called on to respond to ever more nuanced and personal situations.

It has also been called on to improve its efforts to prevent poverty, efforts which were once believed to be one of the great modern success stories. Some populations, it turns out, have remained untouched by the social insurance programs which are the welfare state's core. They have not benefited from these programs because of their lack of connection to the labor market and because of their personal and political marginalization. These people are identified by a variety of terms — in France, they are called *les exclus,* in the United States, the underclass — but everywhere their existence has forced welfare states to develop new programs to address problems of long-term poverty and marginalization.

As welfare states have expanded into these new arenas, they have delegated more and more responsibility to nonprofit organizations. Convinced that public agencies are unable to offer effective programs to meet the new demands on the welfare state, policymakers have looked for alternative methods of delivering services. They have sought to compensate for the lack of state capacity by recruiting nonprofit organizations as partners. To policymakers, nonprofits seem better equipped than government bureaucracies to reach marginalized populations, to provide culturally sensitive services, to run small-scale and personalized programs, and to offer clients avenues for participation in the management of their care. Nonprofits' structure allows them much greater flexibility than government regulations allow public programs. In addition, they have often developed experience and skills acting in the domains newly defined as public responsibility, where the state has no prior experience.

Thus policymakers throughout the West have confronted real limits to what welfare state structures can accomplish alone and have initiated partnerships with nonprofit organizations to enlarge or reinforce the capabilities of the welfare state. In the process, they have transformed part of the architecture of the state as bureaucracies providing public services have given way to contractual relationships between supervisory agencies and service-providing private entities. They have also changed the constellation of interest groups which influence the development of the welfare state: nonprofit organizations, once empowered with public funding and given a stake in the programs of the welfare state, have in many countries become an effective lobby in the public policy arena.

Delegation to nonprofits is, of course, not the only possible response to a crisis of state capacity, whether in France or elsewhere. Individuals can independently furnish for themselves or others what the state has failed to provide or the state can develop new capacity through innovation and reform. Throughout the West, however, the trend has been for policymakers concerned with social policy to look to nonprofit organizations for help in overcoming problems with state capacity, making reliance on nonprofit organizations a characteristic feature of the newest phase in the evolution of Western welfare states.

The choice of delegation to nonprofits in this situation is

tied to a larger trend in the structuring of organizations. Organizations of all sorts, from states to firms, have been forced to reconsider their modes of operation in recent years. Large bureaucratic structures, once regarded as necessary for economies of scale and efficiency, are increasingly seen as rigid and unresponsive. They are being replaced with flattened and decentralized structures in the public and private sectors alike. In the private sector, just-in-time inventory practices have been developed to make firms more responsive to consumer demand, and there has been a rapid growth in the practice of outsourcing, which is a firm's equivalent of delegation (Zukin and DiMaggio 1990; Piore and Sabel 1984). In the public sector, shifting responsibilities have not been limited to the welfare state. There is a general trend toward privatization, wherein public industries are sold to private ownership and potentially lucrative functions (such as garbage collection) are contracted out to private firms (Suleiman and Waterbury 1990; Osborne and Gaebler 1992).

CONCLUSION: DELEGATION TO NONPROFITS AND THE PUBLIC GOOD

Welfare states' new inclination to delegate responsibilities to nonprofit organizations has many implications for both politics and society. One of the implications for politics is the development of a new balance of power among interest groups. In France, new constellations of interests have already been formed by the practice of delegation. Nonprofit social service providers mobilized politically once they were offered public funds to implement government programs and were successful in influencing two major pieces of legislation which extended the welfare state. The nonprofit sector has developed an interest in the shape of French social policy and has mobilized successfully to represent itself in the policy process. The addition of a new interest group has changed the political dynamic surrounding the formulation of social policy.

The nonprofit sector is an unusual interest group in that the interests it represents are not exclusively its own; instead, nonprofits generally enter the policy process claiming to represent the interests of the clients they serve. This further influences the dynamics of social policy making by introducing a new voice that speaks for the most marginalized and disenfranchised populations.

Of course, while nonprofit organizations and their clients gain political power, other interests inevitably lose ground. For example, delegation to nonprofits can have the effect of undermining the numbers and importance of organized labor. The employees of nonprofit organizations, unlike those of public welfare agencies, are seldom unionized, so state preferences for service delivery by nonprofit organizations shift jobs away from union members. In addition, the increased importance of nonprofit organizations as advocates for the poor diminishes labor's importance as the voice of opposition to business interests.

Delegation to nonprofits may also, as Bloch-Lainé and his group of reformers certainly hoped, have implications for the functioning of democracy. Robert Putnam's (1993) recent study of regional governments in Italy argues convincingly that the functioning of democratic institutions is linked to the nature of the society in which they operate, specifically, to the existence of a "civic community." One of the principal identifying features of a civic community, for Putnam, is the extent to which citizens participate in associations of all sorts, ranging from sports clubs to charitable organizations. Putnam and his two collaborators show that, in Italy, the degree to which a civic community exists in each region depends on the impact of hundreds of years of history. He is pessimistic, therefore, about the potential of reformers to create a civic community in order to ensure the success of democratic institutions. France's experience, however, may show that in fact, to a limited extent, building a civic community is possible.

The members of the Club Jean Moulin, like Putnam, saw a vibrant civil society as a necessary foundation for democracy. Through the subsequent efforts of the DAP, the development of such a civil society was promoted through the mobilization of grassroots networks of associations. It was also encouraged through the introduction of legislation easing the financial obstacles to citizen organization and offering new sources of public funding for the efforts of nonprofits. The number of associations in France has soared in the past few decades, and their importance in public life has grown enormously. At the same time, whether as a consequence or coincidentally, French democracy has been normalized. The "immobilism" of the Third and Fourth Republics has been vanquished, the semiauthoritarian grip of the Gaullist party on power ended with the election of a Socialist administration in 1981, and voters have moved from the fringes toward the political center, particularly on the Left.[24] Only an intensive study of the type which Putnam and his collaborators undertook could show whether in fact there has been an appreciable change in the extent to which France is a civic community, and whether this change can be plausibly linked to the consolidation of French democracy. Yet the coincidences are suggestive.

On the other hand, it should not be overlooked that delegation to nonprofits may also have injurious effects on society and on democracy itself. Certainly, while bringing many benefits to citizens it also brings risks. Delegation may substantially improve the services that clients of the welfare state receive because they will be dealing with small, flexible organizations rather than with government bureaucracies. Recipients may not know, however, that the services they receive are publicly funded and may therefore imagine themselves to be the beneficiaries of private charity. Understanding and implementing aid as an entitlement of citizenship

---

24. See, for example, Kesselman 1989; Hoffmann 1991; Schain 1991; and Jenson 1991.

rather than as charity is one of the great achievements of modern welfare states. Unless the connection between the services provided by nonprofits and government programs is made clear both to clients of the programs and to the general public, that progress will be reversed.

The use of nonprofit organizations to deliver services also offers welfare state clients advantages in that it allows them to seek out the services of agencies run or staffed by people similar to them in some way — for example, in terms of ethnic group, religion, or sexual orientation. There is a risk, however, that the clients' affiliation with that group rather than with a larger universe of citizens may be reinforced.[25] The full implications of such an effect are not clear, but in an era in which ethnic, racial, and religious tensions are growing both within Western nations and among their neighbors, the reinforcement of subgroup identities as a basis for aid should be examined carefully. Both the reinforcement of ascriptive identities and the undermining of a sense of entitlement have long-term implications — and potential costs — for welfare state clients' experience of citizenship, for the politics of social policy, and for democracy.

Another problem posed by delegation to nonprofits is that it can be inefficient. Because it relies on the availability of nonprofit organizations and their willingness to undertake certain types of tasks, it can result in a level of services which is uneven both geographically and among client groups. The practice of funding programs in response to private initiatives may prevent the state from achieving a rational distribution of resources. Better organized and financed groups are more likely to have the technical skills and other resources necessary to propose programs than are groups which, while less organized, are more needy. Similarly, organizations propose the sorts of programs that they wish to engage in, which are not necessarily the ones that the community most needs. For example, a study in France found that one departmental administration received numerous requests for funding for programs to help women in difficulty, a population for which three centers already existed, while there was at the time no center for drug addicts in the department (Severino et al. 1987).

Additionally, delegation to nonprofits may be financially inefficient. Rather than rewarding efficiency, public funding occasionally has the opposite effect: funding may be channeled to the programs in most difficulty rather than being used to extend the efforts of programs operating more efficiently. It is also difficult for a funding authority to hold nonprofits fully accountable for their use of funds, the nature of the work performed, and program quality.

Most of these difficulties can be minimized by improving the process of delegation. This would involve, for example, employing better contracts and oversight procedures and exercising diligence in making sure that government, not the availability of nonprofit partners, dictates what types and

amounts of services will be provided.[26] One problem is potentially very serious for the future health of the welfare states, however. That is the way in which delegation obscures the relationship between taxes collected and programs delivered. Taxpayers may not understand that the programs provided by nonprofits are supported by public funds. As a result, they may think that their taxes, once collected, disappear without doing any good. Such a perception can contribute to tax revolts and attacks on the welfare state as ineffective. Unless the relationship between taxes and the programs offered by nonprofit organizations under contract with the state is made clear, the welfare state may suffer a critical loss of voter support.

Delegation to nonprofits offers a countervailing benefit for welfare states, however. As we have seen, nonprofit organizations to which responsibility for the provision of publicly funded social services is delegated may be empowered to mobilize themselves, forming a potentially powerful lobby in the social policy arena. In France and in the United States such lobbies have played important roles in extending welfare state spending and programs. The future health of the welfare states may owe a lot to this new constituency.

The practice of delegation to nonprofits in France and elsewhere continues to grow in importance, responding to the widespread crisis of state capacity. It is transforming the very architecture of the welfare state and changing the configuration of interests and identities in society. Yet studies of what Lester Salamon (1993) has called "the global associational revolution" have to date mostly concentrated on the changing structure of the nonprofit sector itself or on the relationship of nonprofit organizations with government agencies. The impact of delegation on the welfare state itself, on democracy, and on the politics of social policy has been largely ignored. Future scholarship must contribute explicitly political and comparative studies of the changing architecture and politics of welfare states in the new delegationist era.

REFERENCES

Alber, Jens. 1988. "Continuities and Changes in the Idea of the Welfare State." *Politics and Society* 16(4):451–68.

Alphandéry, C., Y. Bernard, F. Bloch-Lainé, et al. 1968. *Pour nationaliser l'État.* Paris: Éditions du Seuil.

Archambault, Édith. 1985. "Démographie des associations." *Revue de l'économie sociale*, no. 4 (April-June): 99–112.

———. 1992. "L'Économie sociale en France." In *Les Associations, l'éthique et la transparence,* ed. La Fondation de France, 24–30. Paris: La Fondation de France.

25. I am grateful to Ira Katznelson for this observation.

26. Steven Rathgeb Smith and Michael Lipsky (1993) argue forcefully that in order for the practice of contracting out service provision to nonprofit organizations to achieve effective and just results, government must undertake to step in and provide services directly in areas where there are few nonprofit organizations or where the ones which exist are unwilling to take on the new roles desired by policymakers. See especially pages 221–23.

Association pour le Développement des associations de progrès. 1977. *Travaux du colloque de Reims: 26/27 novembre 1976.* Paris: DAP.

———. 1979. *Colloque de Lille: Actes du colloque 19/20 janvier 1979.* Paris: DAP.

Barthe, Marie-Annick. 1987. "Les Formes de la pauvreté dans la société française." *Revue française des affaires sociales* 41(2):113–25.

Bloch-Lainé, François. 1994. Interview with the author. Paris, June 22.

———. 1979. "Exposé introductif." In *Colloque de Lille: Actes du colloque 19/20 janvier 1979,* ed. Association pour le Développement des associations de progrès, 7–16. Paris: DAP.

———. 1980. "Pour le progrès des associations." *Pour* 74:7–71.

Bowen, William G., Thomas I. Nygren, Sarah E. Turner, and Elizabeth A. Duffy. 1994. *The Charitable Nonprofits: An Analysis of Institutional Dynamics and Characteristics.* San Francisco: Jossey-Bass.

Brovelli, Gérard. 1989. "Les Incidences de la décentralisation sur les associations: L'Exemple du domaine sanitaire et social." *Revue française des affaires sociales* 43(2):23–72.

Brown, Bernard. 1982. *Socialism of a Different Kind: Reshaping the Left in France.* Westport, Conn.: Greenwood Press.

Brown, Michael K., ed. 1988. *Remaking the Welfare State: Retrenchment and Social Policy in America and Europe.* Philadelphia: Temple University Press.

Bruneau, Chantal. 1986. "Associations et pouvoirs publics: Vingt années d'évolution." *Les Cahiers de l'animation* 1(55):5–19.

Cheroutre, Marie-Thérèse. 1993. *Exercice et développement de la vie associative dans le cadre de la loi du 1er juillet 1901.* Paris: Conseil économique et social.

Chevallier, Jacques. 1981. "L'Association entre public et privé." *Revue du droit public et de la science politique en France et à l'étranger,* no. 4 (July-August): 887–918.

Commissariat général au Plan. 1982. *Plan intérimaire: Stratégie pour deux ans 1982–1983.* Paris: Flammarion.

Commission nationale d'évaluation du Revenu minimum d'insertion. 1992. *RMI: Le Pari de l'insertion,* Volume 1. Paris: La Documentation française.

Evans, Peter B., Dietrich Rueschemeyer, and Theda Skocpol, eds. 1985. *Bringing the State Back In.* Cambridge: Cambridge University Press.

Fauqueux, Michel. 1989. "Les Associations caritatives entre sécularisation et prophétisme en France." In *Charité et pouvoirs publics: Ve colloque organisé par la Fondation Jean Rodhain, Lourdes, 10–13 novembre 1988,* 19–29. Paris: Éditions S.O.S.

Fondation pour la vie associative. 1981. *Pour une nouvelle règle du jeu social: le rôle des associations. Actes du Colloque de la DAP, Grenoble, janvier 1981.* Paris: FONDA.

Fragonard, Bertrand. 1992. Délégué interministériel au RMI. Interview with the author. Paris, May 7.

Freeman, Gary. 1985. "Socialism and Social Security." In *The French Socialist Experiment,* ed. John S. Ambler, 93–115. Philadelphia: Institute for the Study of Human Issues.

———. 1990. "Financial Crisis and Policy Continuity." In *Developments in French Politics,* ed. Peter A. Hall, Jack Hayward, and Howard Machin, 188–200. New York: St. Martin's Press.

Gidron, Benjamin, Ralph M. Kramer, and Lester M. Salamon. 1992a. "Government and the Third Sector in Comparative Perspective: Allies or Adversaries?" In *Government and the Third Sector: Emerging Relationships in Welfare States,* ed. Benjamin Gidron, Ralph M. Kramer, and Lester M. Salamon, 1–30. San Francisco: Jossey-Bass.

Gidron, Benjamin, Ralph M. Kramer, and Lester M. Salamon, eds. 1992b. *Government and the Third Sector: Emerging Relationships in Welfare States.* San Francisco: Jossey-Bass.

Glazer, Nathan. 1981. "Roles and Responsibilities in Social Policy." In *The Welfare State in Crisis: An Account of the Conference on Social Policies in the 1980s,* ed. Organization for Economic Cooperation and Development, 240–55. Paris: OECD.

———. 1988. *The Limits of Social Policy.* Cambridge: Harvard University Press.

Grémion, Catherine. 1987. "Decentralization in France: A Historical Perspective." In *The Mitterrand Experiment: Continuity and Change in Modern France,* ed. George Ross, Stanley Hoffmann, and Sylvia Malzacher, 237–47. New York: Oxford University Press.

Grouès, Bruno. 1993. UNIOPSS. Personal communication with the author. June 28.

Guillois, Thierry. 1988. "Associations et subventions." *Revue française de finances publiques,* no. 23:47–65.

Hall, Peter A. 1990. "Pluralism and Pressure Politics." In *Developments in French Politics,* ed. Peter A. Hall, Jack Hayward, and Howard Machin, 77–92. New York: St. Martin's Press.

———. 1986. *Governing the Economy: The Politics of State Intervention in Britain and France.* New York: Oxford University Press.

Hamon, Hervé, and Patrick Rotman. 1982. *La Deuxième Gauche: Histoire intellectuelle et politique de la CFDT.* Paris: Éditions Ramsay.

Hoffmann, Stanley. 1991. "The Institutions of the Fifth Republic." In *Searching for the New France,* ed. James F. Hollifield and George Ross, 43–56. New York: Routledge.

Hood, Christopher, and Gunnar Folke Schuppert, eds. 1988. *Delivering Public Services in Western Europe: Sharing Western European Experience of Paragovernment Organization.* London: Sage.

Houillon, Michel. 1987. "Le Retour des misérables: La Société duale en question." *Futuribles* (February): 33–40.

Inspection générale des Affaires sociales. 1984. *La Politique sociale et les associations.* Paris: Ministère des Affaires sociales et de la Solidarité nationale, Inspection générale des Affaires sociales.

Janvier, Guy. 1987. "Les Interventions spécifiques de l'État en faveur des personnes en situation de pauvreté et de précarité." *Solidarité Santé – Études statistiques,* no. 2 (March-April): 15–25.

Jenson, Jane. 1991. "The French Left: A Tale of Three Beginnings." In *Searching for the New France,* ed. James F. Hollifield and George Ross, 85–112. New York: Routledge.

Jobert, Bruno, and Pierre Muller. 1987. *L'Etat en action: Politiques publiques et corporatismes.* Paris: Presses universitaires de France.

Jobert, Bruno. 1991. "Democracy and Social Policies: The Example of France." In *The French Welfare State: Surviving*

Social and Ideological Change, ed. John S. Ambler, 232–58. New York: New York University Press.

Johnson, Norman. 1989. "The Privatization of Welfare." *Social Policy and Administration* (May): 17–30.

———. 1990. *Reconstructing the Welfare State: A Decade of Change.* New York: Harvester.

Kamerman, Sheila B., and Alfred J. Kahn, eds. 1989. *Privatization and the Welfare State.* Princeton: Princeton University Press.

Keeler, John T. S. 1987. *The Politics of Neocorporatism in France: Farmers, the State, and Agricultural Policy-making in the Fifth Republic.* New York: Oxford University Press.

Kesselman, Mark. 1989. "La Nouvelle Cuisine en politique: La Fin de l'exceptionnalité française." In *Idéologies, partis politiques et groupes sociaux,* ed. Yves Mény, 159–73. Paris: Presses de la Fondation nationale des sciences politiques.

Kramer, Ralph M., Hakon Lorentzen, Willem B. Melief, and Sergio Pasquinelli. 1993. *Privatization in Four European Countries: Comparative Studies in Government-Third Sector Relationships.* Armonk, N.Y.: M. E. Sharpe.

Lenoir, René. 1989. *Les Exclus: Un Français sur dix.* 4th ed. Paris: Éditions du Seuil.

Levy, Jonah D. 1994. "Tocqueville's Revenge: Dilemmas of Institution Building in Post-Dirigiste France." Ph.D. dissertation, Massachusetts Institute of Technology.

Lindseth, Peter Lincoln. 1992. "Left Leanings and Liberal Flirtations: The Club Jean Moulin and the Idea of Modern Democracy. An Essay on the Evolving Political Culture of the French Left in the Late 1950s and 1960s." Master's thesis, Columbia University.

Lipsky, Michael, and Steven Rathgeb Smith. 1989. "Nonprofit Organizations, Government, and the Welfare State." *Political Science Quarterly* 90:625–48.

Mariller, Noelle, and Guy Janvier. 1988. "Les Programmes gouvernementaux de lutte contre la pauvreté et la précarité." *Revue française des affaires sociales* 42(2):23–33.

Mauroy, Pierre. 1979. "Ouverture du Colloque." In *Colloque de Lille: Actes de Colloque, 19/20 janvier 1979,* ed. Association pour le développement des associations de progrès, 3–6. Paris: DAP.

Mishra, Ramesh. 1990. *The Welfare State in Capitalist Society: Policies of Retrenchment and Maintenance in Europe, North America and Australia.* New York: Harvester Wheatsheaf.

Mizrahi-Tchernonog, Viviane. 1991. "Gestion des politiques sociales locales: Analyse du recours communal aux associations." Paris: Laboratoire d'économie sociale, Université de Paris I Panthéon-Sorbonne (December).

———. 1992. Laboratoire d'économie sociale, Université de Paris I. Interview with the author. Paris, October 21.

Mossuz, Janine. 1970. *Les Clubs et la politique en France.* Paris: Librairie Armand Colin.

Oheix, Gabriel. 1981. *Contre la précarité et la pauvreté: 60 propositions.* Paris: La Documentation française.

Osborne, David, and Ted Gaebler. 1992. *Reinventing Government: How the Entrepreneurial Spirit is Transforming the Public Sector.* Reading, Mass.: Addison-Wesley.

Ostrander, Susan A., and Stuart Langton, eds. 1987. *Shifting the Debate: Public/Private Sector Relations in the Modern Welfare State.* New Brunswick, N.J.: Transaction Books.

Pequignot, Henri. 1979. *La Lutte contre la pauvreté.* Report of the Conseil économique et social. Reproduced in *Journal officiel de la république française, Avis et rapports de Conseil économique et social,* no. 9 (6 mars).

Petitpas, Jocelyn. 1983. "Les Nouveaux Pauvres." *Le Figaro,* January 25.

Piore, Michael, and Charles Sabel. 1984. *The Second Industrial Divide: Possibilities for Prosperity.* New York: Basic Books.

Putnam, Robert D. 1993. *Making Democracy Work: Civic Traditions in Modern Italy.* Princeton: Princeton University Press.

Raffi, Guy. 1992. Former Secretary General of the DAP and former Deputy (PS). Interview with the author. Paris, October 19.

Rosanvallon, Pierre. 1988. "Beyond the Welfare State." *Politics and Society* 16(4):533–43.

———. 1993. "La Nouvelle Crise de l'État-providence." *Notes de la Fondation Saint-Simon* (September).

Rose-Ackerman, Susan. 1990. "Efficiency, Funding and Autonomy in the Third Sector." In *The Third Sector: Comparative Studies of Nonprofit Organizations,* ed. Helmut K. Anheier and Wolfgang Seibel, 157–63. New York: Walter de Gruyter.

Ross, George. 1987. "From One Left to Another: Le Social in Mitterrand's France." In *The Mitterrand Experiment: Continuity and Change in Modern France,* ed. George Ross, Stanley Hoffmann, and Sylvia Malzacher, 199–216. New York: Oxford University Press.

———. 1988. "The Mitterrand Experiment and the French Welfare State: An Interesting Uninteresting Story." In *Remaking the Welfare State: Retrenchment and Social Policy in America and Europe,* ed. Michael K. Brown, 119–38. Philadelphia: Temple University Press, 1988.

Salamon, Lester M. 1993. "The Global Associational Revolution: The Rise of the Third Sector on the World Scene." Occasional Paper #15 of the Institute for Policy Studies, Johns Hopkins University.

Sassier-Robert, Monique. 1992. Reporter for the Commission nationale d'évaluation du Revenu minimum d'insertion. Interview with the author. Paris, May 5.

Schain, Martin A. 1991. "Toward a Centrist Democracy? The Fate of the French Right." In *Searching for the New France,* ed. James F. Hollifield and George Ross, 57–84. New York: Routledge.

Schmidt, Vivien. 1990. *Democratizing France: The Political and Administrative History of Decentralization.* Cambridge: Cambridge University Press.

———. 1992. "The Statist Pattern of Policy-Making: The Case of France." Paper presented at the Annual Meeting of the American Political Science Association, Chicago, September 4.

Severino, J. M., F. Villeroy de Galhau, N. Huchet-Coppinger, and P. Fleuriot. 1987. "Un Essai d'évaluation d'éfficacité : Le Cas des centres d'hébergement et de réadaptation sociale." *Revue française des affaires sociales* 41(1):143–57.

Skocpol, Theda, and Kenneth Finegold. 1982. "State Capacity and Economic Intervention in the Early New Deal." *Political Science Quarterly* 97(2):255–78.

Smith, Steven Rathgeb, and Michael Lipsky. 1993. *Nonprofits for Hire: The Welfare State in the Age of Contracting.* Cambridge: Harvard University Press.

Smith, Steven Rathgeb, and Deborah Stone. 1988. "The Unexpected Consequences of Privatization." In *Remaking the*

Welfare State: Retrenchment and Social Policy in America and Europe, ed. Michael K. Brown, 232–52. Philadelphia: Temple University Press.

Starr, Paul. 1990. "The New Life of the Liberal State: Privatization and the Restructuring of State-Society Relations." In *The Political Economy of Public Sector Reform and Privatization,* ed. Ezra N. Suleiman and John Waterbury, 22–54. Boulder: Westview Press.

Suleiman, Ezra N., and John Waterbury, eds. 1990. *The Political Economy of Public Sector Reform and Privatization.* Boulder: Westview Press.

Tocqueville, Alexis de. 1969. *Democracy in America.* Trans. George Lawrence and ed. J. P. Mayer. Garden City, N.Y.: Anchor Books, Doubleday.

Turner, Sarah E., Thomas I. Nygren, and William G. Bowen. 1993. "The NTEE Classification System: Tests of Reliability/Validity in the Field of Higher Education." *Voluntas* 4(1):73–94.

Ullman, Claire F. 1995. "The Welfare State's Other Crisis: Explaining the New Partnership between Nonprofit Organizations and the State in France." Ph.D. dissertation, Columbia University.

Viannay, Philippe. 1988. *Du Bon Usage de la France: Résistance, Journalisme, Glénans.* Paris: Éditions Ramsay.

Worms, Jean-Pierre. 1992. Député (PS). Interview with the author. Paris, June 17.

Wresinski, Joseph. 1987. *Grande Pauvreté et précarité économique et sociale.* Report of the Conseil économique et social. Paris: Journal Officiel de la république française.

Zukin, Sharon, and Paul DiMaggio, eds. 1990. *Structures of Capital: The Social Organization of the Economy.* Cambridge: Cambridge University Press.

12

HELMUT K. ANHEIER AND WOLFGANG SEIBEL

The Nonprofit Sector and the Transformation of Societies: A Comparative Analysis of East Germany, Poland, and Hungary

Research on nonprofit organizations has gathered considerable momentum in the last decade (see Powell 1987; DiMaggio and Anheier 1990; Anheier and Seibel 1990, for overviews). Researchers have offered several competing and complementary approaches to explain the rationale, existence, and general features of third sectors and their organizations (Powell 1987; Rose-Ackerman 1986; James 1989; Anheier and Seibel 1990). Economists have highlighted the competitive advantage of nonprofit organizations over market firms and public agencies in the case of information asymmetries (Hansmann 1980) or demand heterogeneity (Weisbrod 1988). Sociologists have emphasized the integrative effect of voluntary associations in modern society (Coser 1956) and their role in status competition (Collins and Hickman 1991) and elite control (Middleton 1987; DiMaggio 1987). Political scientists describe nonprofit organizations in terms of pluralism, participation, and grassroots democracy (Douglas 1987).

When we apply current theoretical thinking about nonprofit organizations to the study of societal transformations, it is easy to see that most approaches are based on implicit assumptions about the stability and the contours of a given social order. Microeconomic approaches assume competition between and among different forms, explaining differences in competitiveness and performance related to outcomes and organizational survival (see Seibel 1992a). This

may be the case in part for the United States in the area of child care and segments of the health care industry, but such microeconomic thinking may be much less applicable to European corporatist regimes, in which organizational environments for nonprofits tend to be highly structured and designed to curb rather than to encourage competition. Thus in virtually all European countries, the organizational environment is based not on competitive substitutability but on noncompetitive concertation of tasks and responsibilities between the public and the third sector. The German system of subsidiarity (Anheier and Seibel 1992; Seibel 1990) and the Dutch *verzuiling*, or pillarization (Kramer et al. 1993, 70–72), are prominent examples of how much the political economy of the third sector in Western Europe differs from the assumptions of conventional economic models, which see the state as a secondary, passive actor at best, not as a primary force behind the formation of the nonprofit sector. In both the Dutch and the German cases, it is the corporatist arrangement with the state, deeply embedded in social welfare and other legislation, that accounts for the major contours of the nonprofit sector, and not competition and efficiency considerations.

Social and political theories make assumptions, too. For example, the integrating effect of membership in voluntary associations requires a relatively stable social order, at least in the sense of an identifiable organizational infrastructure.

177

The effects on elite cohesiveness of overlapping memberships on executive boards and committees, for example, demand some minimum level of stability among elites to materialize. Thus for the incentives and routines of voluntary cooperation to take effect, the consolidation of civil society qua nonprofit organizations must rest on relatively stable patterns of social stratification and elites. Moreover, the political benefits of nonprofit organizations as additional expressions of pluralism outside the political party system can materialize only if diversity in political or cultural terms is imprinted in values widely shared in society. Among the population, lack of legitimacy of the state and the institutions of civil society may result in a loss of perceived efficacy in dealing with social and economic problems (Linz and Stepan 1978; Marody 1993). Thus, it seems that some form of trust between government and society is required for the constitution of a viable third sector.

Several observers (DiPalma 1991; Mueller 1991; Offe 1991; Schöpflin 1991; Srubar 1991; Sztompka 1991) suggest that Central East European countries underwent a process of *relative social and political demodernization* under state socialism. Within the context of the relative underdevelopment of most Central East European countries prior to state socialism (Gerschenkron 1962; Schöpflin 1991), social and political demodernization interacted with the massive, large-scale economic modernization efforts of the Stalinist era. By the 1980s, the dual processes of modernization and demodernization resulted in societies that can be described as complex combinations of modernized and demodernized niches and segments. Examples of this pattern are East Germany with its large and highly rationalized *Kombinate* of related industries that exist next to the "niche society" of its citizens, and Hungary with its second economy, a network of quasi-market transactions, reciprocity, and barter relations that is parallel to the formal socialist economy.

The Third Sector as a Contingent Phenomenon. McCarthy et al. (1991, chap. 1) and Douglas (1983) suggest that the emergence and development of a third sector are dependent on several prerequisites such as freedom of association, individualization, a nonautocratic state, relative degrees of decentralization, social stability, and economic development. In somewhat simplified form, such reasoning assumes that major obstacles must be removed and other factors added for third sectors to develop. In such a conceptualization, third sectors develop in a certain manner and in more or less discrete stages after the groundwork for them has been laid. This framework would lead us ultimately to expect much similarity and few differences among third sectors cross-nationally.

In contrast to such reasoning, we see the development of the third sector as a more contingent phenomenon. In the following comparative analysis, we suggest an institutional model of the emerging nonprofit sector in Central Eastern Europe, in which the institutions of civil society, class, religion, and the political system interact to shape the basic contours of the nonprofit sector. Some of the factors in the complex institutional chemistry of the nonprofit sector reflect deep historical continuities, such as the role of the Catholic Church in Poland, while others are more recent in origin and the product of state socialism and the transformation period itself. Three statements summarize the conditional character of the institutional development of nonprofit sectors:

- Prior to transformation, societies may develop institutional forms and mechanisms that partially compensate for the absence or lack of prerequisites for third sector development. For example, the Hungarian second economy or society developed many quasi-associations and other hybrid forms while freedom of association remained prohibited in the official society.

- The starting position in which a society finds itself on the eve of transformation will affect the initial transformation, the subsequent phases, and consolidation periods as well as the outcome of third sector development. For example, the fragile alliance between intellectuals, the labor union Solidarity, and the Catholic Church in Poland, while able to overcome the regime, is at the same time unable to give clear direction to future political and economic development. As a result, the emergent third sector replicates some of the factionalism of Poland's political system.

- Dependent on starting positions and phases, societies develop distinct patterns of transformation that involve different sets of institutional actors. For example, the process of unification led to a far-reaching replacement of East German organizations by West German nonprofit organizations. This friendly colonialism in the reconstruction of the East German third sector was made possible by the disintegration of the German Democratic Republic and the collapse of its discredited political system.

Echoing Alexander Gerschenkron's argument about the industrialization process in Europe (1962, 7), we propose that processes of third sector development in relatively underdeveloped countries are considerably different from those of more advanced countries, with regard to not only the speed of development (the rate of third sector growth) but also the patterns and organizational structures of the emerging third sector. In his essay "Prerequisites of Modern Industrialization," Gerschenkron (1962) points to the great elasticity and variability of industrialization processes. He rejects the notion of uniform economic development and argues that such countries as France, Germany, Bulgaria, Denmark, Italy, and Russia were able to compensate for their lack of such preconditions as capital availability, labor supply, and entrepreneurial capacities. Examples are the prominent role of investment banks in France and Germany in compensating for insufficient capital and management skills in private industry and the significant role of the state in German and Italian economic development—factors that made up for general deficiencies in the countries prior to industrialization, deficiencies that the most advanced country at that time, England, did not experience in its economic development.

Following Gerschenkron's comparative-historical approach (1962), we argue that transformation processes have differing starting points, pass through differing phases, develop varying patterns, and reach divergent end points in terms of institutional effects and orientations. Applied to the role of the third sector in the societal transformation of Central Eastern Europe, Gerschenkron's method of examining contingent processes leads us to examine three crucial areas: the patterns of state-society relationship prior to the initial transformation (that is, before 1989), the patterns of transformation, and the patterns of institution building (table 12.1):

- *The patterns of state-society relationship prior to the initial transformation*, in our scheme, describe significant aspects of the starting position or status quo ante as they relate to the third sector—for example, the ways and means by which socialist societies deal with political opposition, increasing apathy and escapism among the population, and the persistent scarcity of goods and services. Nonprofit organizations typically fulfill two functions: aggregating interests and providing services. Thus, we are primarily interested in analyzing the political economy of socialist countries at two crucial junctures: the relationship between the state and civil society to examine the interest function, and the state of the socialist economy to explore the service functions of nonprofit organizations.
- *The patterns of the transformation process* itself are examined, first, through the *pattern of dissent* that evolved in the initial phase leading to the shift from state socialism. What was the strategy of the political opposition? Did counterelites form? How did they organize? What influence did they have? Following this, we examine the *patterns of conflict settlement* and look at the relationships among the various conflicting parties and at the *institutional base and form* of the third sector in this process.
- *The patterns of institution building* refers to the initial outcome of the transformation process. Both state-society relationships and the role and orientation of the third sector can be assessed by asking, What characterizes the political economy in which nonprofit organizations find themselves? What is the general orientation of the third sector in terms of state versus market direction? What are typical organizations, and how are the two major functions of nonprofit organizations — advocacy and service provision — combined?

COMPARATIVE ANALYSIS

The former German Democratic Republic (East Germany), Poland, and Hungary share both the initial impetus and ultimate pressure toward political and economic reform. In contrast to the Soviet Union, Bulgaria, and Romania, where modernizing groups and counterelites among the ruling strata of society introduced changes from above, East Germany, Poland, and Hungary were changed by nonelite groups. In other aspects, however, the three countries differ sharply in their status quo ante, their transition period, and their outcome. In what follows, we probe these differences and focus on the third sector as part of the overall political economy of societal transformation in these countries.

Throughout our analysis, we emphasize the variability of the conditions and processes of third sector development. Even the most cursory look across the social and economic landscape of Eastern and Central Europe in the fall of 1989 reveals significant differences in state-society relationships, ranging from overt political oppression and economic decline in Romania to the fragile truce in the struggle for political power in Poland to the relative prosperity and strict political control of East Germany. Having set out from these different starting positions, the countries of the region are passing through differing transformation phases, generating divergent patterns of institution building, and developing nonprofit sectors that vary in size, structure, and orientation.

East Germany

Pre-1989 Patterns of State-Society Relationship. The former German Democratic Republic (GDR) was erroneously considered to be the most stable country in the former Soviet bloc. This misconception rested on several factors: the relatively high level of economic development, the absence of organized opposition movements with any significant mobilization potential, and the absence of any counterelite. In fact, East Germany had not witnessed any mass protest or popular uprising since 1953. According to an often-quoted description by West Germany's former envoy to East Germany, Günther Gauss (1983), East Germany had developed into a niche-society: People had apparently come to terms with the communist regime by withdrawing from official politics and ideology to the reclusive world of modest consumerism and private *Gemütlichkeit* (comfort). This withdrawal was encouraged in no small part by the subtle force and intimidation of the state security service, or Stasi (from *Staatssicherheitsdienst*). The triple combination of relative economic prosperity, social withdrawal, and subtle oppression hand in hand with extensive surveillance led to East Germany's having become a tranquilized society.

Patterns of Transformation. The GDR is obviously a unique case because it disappeared as a sovereign country in the transformation from state socialism. The sharp contrast, however, between the country's disintegration in 1990 and the tranquility of the state-society relationship before 1989 is most remarkable and can be explained by the situation in which East Germany found itself—a situation which shaped both the pattern of dissent and conflict settlement. Unlike

Table 12.1. Societal Transformation and Third-Sector Characteristics

Country	Pre-1989 Pattern of State/Society Relationship	Pattern of Transformation				Pattern of Institution Building		Third Sector	
		Pattern of Dissent	Pattern of Conflict Settlement	Institutional Form and Bases of Third Sector	Importance of Third Sector	State/Society Relation	Characteristics	General Orientation	Prototype Organization
East Germany	tranquilized society	"exit" unorganized confrontational	disintegration friendly takeover confrontational	church citizen committees	− −	benevolent colonialism	vacuous top-down prefabricated	state-centered centralized	free welfare association
Poland	preventive stalling	"voice" organized confrontational	gradual erosion takeover by elite	workers' movement church	+ +	arduous muddling-through	fragile bifurcating	patron-centered decentralized	small organizations resource-poor
Hungary	cooperative segmentation	"voice" organized consensual	accelerated erosion negotiation	intellectual circles	+	controlled muddling-through	entrepreneurial opaque formation	market-oriented decentralized	operating foundation

other citizens of Central East European countries, the East Germans had a concrete alternative — the West. The almost exclusive pattern of dissent in East Germany was what Albert Hirschman (1993) would describe as the "exit option." About 2.7 million of the 18 to 19 million East Germans left the state when the Berlin Wall was erected on August 13, 1961 (Ammer 1989, 1207, quoted in Hirschman 1993). Even after 1961, when exit was no longer a realistic option, West Germany remained the almost mythical land of escape for East German society. This is, presumably, the main reason that neither influential counterelites nor organized opposition movements emerged in East Germany. As Hirschman put it, "The presence of the exit alternative can . . . atrophy the development of the art of voice" (Hirschman 1970, 43).

Ironically, it was this state of atrophy which made the communist regime collapse so rapidly and drastically when finally challenged. The crisis of 1989 was triggered when thousands of vacationing East Germans sought refuge in the West German embassies in Budapest and Prague. Spurred by the dramatic coverage of West German television, which reached most of East Germany, the unorganized movement gained momentum from continuous mass rallies; the communist government was forced to promise free elections. At the mass rallies, the previous exit option was transformed into an immediate demand for unification with West Germany. The disintegration of East Germany, which implied a friendly takeover by the West German Federal Republic, remained the only viable option in conflict settlement.

Societal Bases and Institutional Forms of Transformation. In East Germany, the Protestant Church and independent citizen committees, although the basis of a weak opposition, did not play a substantial role in the peaceful revolution of 1989.[1] The patterns of dissent and conflict settlement were clearly dominated by mass rallies and the early infiltration of West German institutional patterns, especially in the form of political parties and politicians (Lehmbruch 1990). The emerging social and political vacuum was a direct consequence of the prevailing exit option, which in turn had shaped the pattern of dissent. Yet it was also a consequence of the contradictory role of the church under state socialism. The churches were able to maintain some autonomy in financial and personnel matters, but they were severely restricted in their advocacy and service-providing role. The price the churches had to pay for relative autonomy was absolute restraint from any open conflict with the regime (Daehn 1982).[2]

The citizen committees formed only in the fall of 1989,

and, when compared to Poland and Hungary, organized opposition under state socialism had a brief and peculiar history. The committees were initiated largely by intellectuals in search of a "third way" between capitalism and communism (Knabe 1992) and seemed somewhat detached from the popular demands for reunification. They occurred typically in the form of round tables and, because they rejected the option of a swift reunification, which they realistically perceived as an absorption of East Germany into the West German Federal Republic, ultimately played a marginal role in the transformation of East Germany.

Patterns of Institution Building: Benevolent Colonialism. In the GDR, as in all the other soviet-type regimes, including Hungary and Poland, so-called societal organizations existed beside the immediate realm of the communist party and the party-controlled state.[3] These included unions, youth organizations, the Red Cross, and many other organizations with cultural or recreational purposes, such as an Association for German-Soviet Friendship and the Association of Writers. Another feature common to all Central and East European countries was the role of the church, not as a shelter for political opposition but as provider of social services, especially hospitals and care for the elderly and handicapped (cf. Anheier and Priller 1991). Regardless of their formal independence, however, the societal organizations were more or less strictly controlled by the communist Sozialistische Einheitspartei Deutschlands (Unified socialist party). Most such organizations went into rapid decline after 1989, and the period from 1989 to 1991 is characterized by the rise of a new third sector according to the West German model.[4]

West German welfare associations have been acting as benevolent colonialists in East Germany since early 1990, and they have implemented an organizational structure covering the entire East German territory. Welfare associations enjoy legal privileges in Germany on the principle of subsidiarity, which stipulates the priority of private charities over government agencies in the provision of social services. Accordingly, mobilization of monetary resources was not a serious problem for West German welfare associations be-

1. These committees were formed only when the collapse of the communist regime was imminent.

2. Even when the church became the only institutional shelter for political opposition groups and mistrust between the state and the churches continued to prevail, some church leaders cooperated with the state and even with the Stasi (State security service). The East German churches had neither a Cardinal Mindszenty nor a Karol Wojtyla within their leadership.

3. In what follows, we have to cope with an imbalance in available data: East Germany is much better covered than Hungary and, especially, Poland. Moreover, one might argue that East Germany no longer presents an authentic case because the main feature of transformation is the institutional transfer of West German institutions to the eastern parts of the country. Nonetheless, the East German case turns out to be instructive owing to the legacies of a centrally planned economy and an authoritarian regime — two factors it continues to share with Hungary and Poland.

4. The two church-related welfare associations Diakonisches Werk (Protestant) and Caritas (Catholic) were more independent. Despite forced cooperation with the communist regime, the churches were the most stable and self-assured independent organizations. Ironically, this has made their integration more difficult than for the few societal organizations which survived the process of reunification and democratization.

cause of their embeddedness in a corporatist network of associations, political parties, and state agencies (Seibel 1990).

Scarcity of public funds is currently not a serious problem for the welfare associations in East Germany either, owing to the fact that the West German funding system, which relies primarily on regional and local sources, is not yet fully implemented in East Germany. Therefore, the rebuilding of welfare associations in East Germany is generously sponsored through federal subsidies, as are the services they provide locally. This system is based on agreements between the welfare associations and the West German government reached early in the course of unification.

The peculiarity of the West German third sector is its corporatist structure at a federal, regional, and local administrative level. This system of macro-, meso-, and microcorporatism is not transferable because the structural prerequisite, a stable center-periphery relationship in terms of funding and service provision, does not exist in East Germany. The funding of nonprofit activities in East Germany may be negotiated at the federal level, but programs have to be implemented locally. What is missing is the local embeddedness which would require a sufficient degree of volunteer input, a local network among elites, and a reservoir of skilled nonprofit managers. This missing link makes the building of organizational structures at the local level, the implementation of enduring social programs, and even spending money remarkably difficult: Nonprofit organization boards of directors are difficult to recruit, voluntary inputs are hard to mobilize, and networks of local elites as a prerequisite of stable government-nonprofit relationship are absent.

The absence of volunteers, local elites, and managers is a characteristic legacy of fifty-six years of totalitarianism and state socialism combined. Volunteers are simply hard to mobilize in a society that experienced state control over all kinds of individual and collective initiative since 1933. Moreover, social strata were leveled according to the egalitarian requirements of Marxist-Leninism. Finally, until 1961, West Germany absorbed the bulk of the East German intellectuals and entrepreneurs, which accounts for the relative absence of local middle classes in East Germany and the narrow base for recruiting members for the governing boards of nonprofit institutions.

These structural weaknesses are difficult to overcome because they are rooted in the macrosociological characteristics of East German society. The effect is, presumably, a much more centralized and "artificial" third sector with a higher degree of state dependency than that in West Germany.

Poland

Pre-1989 Patterns of State-Society Relationship. In most respects, communist Poland presents a counterimage to East Germany. Poland witnessed continual political unrest from 1956 to the intense mass protests of the 1970s and 1980s.

Gradually, an alliance formed between the workers' movement, the Catholic Church, and the well-organized intellectual counterelite. No other country in the Eastern Bloc was able to develop the same potential for political opposition against the communist regime. When the labor union Solidarity was founded in 1979, political conflict intensified and brought with it the imminent risk of military intervention by the Soviet Union. While the declaration of martial law in December 1981 may have preempted military intervention conflict through oppression (Staniszkis 1984, 319–38), it also preserved the political tensions that prevailed at that time.

Patterns of Transformation. The citizens of Poland and Hungary had much less of an "exit" option; they had to raise their "voices" in order to overcome state socialism. Poland displayed an impressive pattern of dissent and conflict settlement, both in terms of conflict duration and the strength of the opposition movement. Polish society had already experienced a long period of continuous conflict with the incumbent regime. This prolonged conflict forced the opposition to seek a broader socio-political basis than in any other communist country. The pattern of dissent was the fight of "civil society against the state" (Kennedy 1992, 38). By the late 1970s, the most important social groups and ideological currents — workers, intelligentsia, and the Catholic Church — had formed a coalition, Solidarity, with the communist state as the focal adversary. The state and the communist party itself remained more or less monolithic and maintained a confrontational style of action.

Accordingly, the pattern of conflict settlement in Poland was one of gradual erosion of the communist regime. The process lasted from 1979, when Solidarity was founded, to 1989, when the first elections in which noncommunist parties participated took place. Change came in the form of a gradual takeover by a cohesive alliance of counterelites. The organizational strength of the conflicting parties — state and opposition — made the process of transformation confrontational and controlled at the same time. In spite of its general development in terms of democratic values and the political success of the opposition, Poland was among the last countries in Central East Europe to organize free elections: full multiparty elections were not held until 1991.

Societal Bases and Institutional Forms of Transformation. In contrast to the leaders of East Germany, who in 1989 were soon to be replaced by West German politicians, those who initiated and realized the transformation in Poland became the representatives of the new democratic order. But the organizational strength of the opposition prior to 1989 did not survive its own success. Once the coalition of the workers' movement, intellectuals, and the church had achieved power, it began to disintegrate. Characterized by an extreme form of proportional representation in parliament, the politics remained highly diverse (Lijphart 1992), and constitutional conflicts about presidential and parliamentary forms of democracy remained unsettled until the elections of September 1993, when, under reformed election procedures, the Socialist Party became the strongest political force.

What happened in Poland after 1989 is a moderate example of the "thawing effect" in Central Eastern Europe. As soon as the common opponent disappeared, hidden tensions and conflicts within the opposition began to emerge, and the three pillars of the Solidarity movement—workers, intellectuals, and the clergy—developed quite different interests. The workers' commitment to Solidarity had been based on a promise of economic prosperity and the charismatic politics of Lech Walesa (cf. Marody 1990, 260–61). Psychologically, the support of democracy as a political value remained mingled with "learned helplessness" (Marody 1988, 101) or an inclination to blame whichever authority was in power for the political and economic status quo (Kolarska-Bobinska 1990; Marody 1988).

With Solidarity no longer the center of civic and political coordination, the Polish intelligentsia became increasingly fragmented along party lines. The culture of political clubs and civic committees, which predated the formation of Solidarity, experienced a revival. It remains, however, unclear if the clubs will contribute to civil society or increase political segmentation (Fehr 1991).

Poland, like most previously state socialist countries, lacks a strong entrepreneurial middle class (Kennedy 1992; Schöpflin 1991) but has a relative surplus of professionals trained to fulfill administrative and technical functions in the state bureaucracies. This makes it difficult to achieve political balance between the dominating intellectual element, the relatively passive group of professionals, and the smaller entrepreneurial segments of a still-weak middle class. As Kennedy (1992, 30) points out, the intellectual elites may well undermine their own political influence by fostering the development of a market economy.[5]

The church, finally, has partially withdrawn as a general political actor. While focusing on political and moral issues closer to Catholic doctrine like abortion, some church initiatives have proven highly controversial and can be seen as ill-disguised attempts to establish a confessional state. This change, again, is likely to undermine further what remains of the coalition against the previous communist regime because the liberal faction of the former alliance resents what it sees as the church's conservative political bias.

In contrast to the pre-1989 era, Poland is currently suffering from a "weak state-weak society syndrome," to paraphrase Nordlinger (1981). The precarious economic situation, demands for populism and charismatic leadership, a feeble democratic tradition, and, until 1993, an ill-suited par-

liamentarian system are factors unfavorable for stabilizing democracy (Goldfarb 1991).

Patterns of Institution Building: Arduous Muddling-Through. As in East Germany, some societal organizations in Poland continue to operate but suffer from serious financial shortage. Moreover, newly founded nonprofit organizations remain relatively small and resource-poor (Wunker 1991, 105; Kietlinska 1993). The third sector apparently suffers from the disintegration of the antiregime coalition. The new nonprofit organizations are loosely linked to or ideologically grouped around the Catholic Church or Solidarity as patron.

The creation of foundations was legalized in Poland in 1984 (Wunker 1991, 93), apparently to make delivery of public goods and services more flexible by contracting out to private but state-controlled institutions. In addition, communist authorities might have hoped to attract money from abroad in order to improve strained foreign currency reserves by legalizing foundations. Associations were legalized only in 1988.

Compared to East Germany, the overall situation in Poland is characterized by a scarcity of monetary resources. The Polish government cannot subsidize nonprofit institutions to an extent similar to that maintained by its German or even its Hungarian counterpart. It is, however, questionable whether this lack of resources sufficiently explains the precarious situation of the emerging third sector in Poland. What we described above as the disintegration process of the former Solidarity coalition also seems to play a crucial role.

First, as in the case of East Germany, learned helplessness among the working class and scapegoating, that is, the tendency to blame public authorities for social and economic difficulties (Kolarska-Bobinska 1990; Marody 1988), impede social participation and activism. As Wunker (1991, 93) points out, a potential basis for volunteerism may remain only in rural areas in the form of self-help and mutual support.

Second, the Catholic Church, as one of the potentially important pillars of the future third sector in Poland, seems reluctant to take on the task of long-term institution building. One reason may be that active involvement in social service provision beyond its current scope of utility would entail incalculable financial commitments. A more substantive reason is the conservative ideological stance of the church in post-1989 Poland, with corresponding shifts in spending patterns from social to religious purposes.[6] The role of the church indicates that the nonprofit landscape in Poland is apparently less pragmatic and more ideological than in East Germany or Hungary, where the nonprofit sector is both more secular and less politicized.

The intellectual middle class, too, has been, in a sense, overpoliticized (cf. Schöpflin 1991, 243). In contrast to Hun-

---

5. This political vacuum can easily be exploited by political "hazardeurs" like Stanislaw Tyminski, the presidential candidate who surpassed Tadeusz Mazowiecki at the ballots in 1991.

6. One also has to bear in mind that Poland has recently witnessed several grassroots religious movements with small but active groups, primarily among younger cohorts (Tatur 1990).

gary, where the second economy had always afforded the opportunity not only to escape from politics but also to experience the challenges of quasi-entrepreneurship, in Poland intellectuals had hardly any alternative to politics. This is why the newly emerging "Clubs" (Fehr 1991) are likely to remain an intellectual affair and are unlikely to become the basis for a service-providing institutional segment of the nonprofit type.

Hungary

Pre-1989 Patterns of State-Society Relationship. Like East Germany, Hungary has been at first glance a politically stable country since the uprising of 1956, which was suppressed through Soviet military intervention. Under the reform communist Janos Kadar the country witnessed relative economic prosperity. Unlike East Germany, Hungary experienced the emergence of an intellectual counterelite (Bruszt and Stark 1991, 218–22); however, in contrast to their Polish counterparts, the Hungarian dissidents remained ideologically closer to Marxism (Kennedy 1992, 43). The communist elite itself was fragmented and split mainly into hard-liners and compromise-oriented reformists (Bruszt and Stark 1991, 209–18; Simai 1992, 54–58). Large parts of the workforce, including the working class, participated in a second economy, with informal social networks as the basic tissue (Hankiss 1990) linking nearly all parts of Hungary's social structure. The encompassing effect of the second economy formed the basis for usually tacit, sometimes open, *cooperation* between the formal and the informal, the official and the unofficial sphere. This quasi-*segmentation* of social, economic, and political spheres mitigated political tensions.

Patterns of Transformation. In Hungary, two factors influenced the pattern of dissent: first, an organized opposition of marxist and nonmarxist intellectuals,[7] and, second, the reform-oriented policy of the communist regime itself (Bruszt and Stark 1991). The communist party was less monolithic in Hungary than in Poland or East Germany. The Hungarian Democratic Forum (MDF), in particular, was in fact a forum for both reform communists and anticommunists. The alliance between factions of the old regime and the intellectual leaders of the opposition led to an accelerated erosion of the communist order in 1989, when it became clear that the Soviet Union would not intervene if the regime toppled. The result was a "negotiated revolution" (Bruszt 1990) in which reform communist officials remained in office and maintained key positions, while opposition leaders successively gained access to power.

At the same time, however, large parts of the population, workers in particular, remained relatively passive. The social distance between intelligentsia and working class remained.

7. The Hungarian Democratic Forum, founded in 1987, the Federation of Young Democrats (FIDESZ), created in 1988, and an umbrella organization for all opposition groups, the Opposition Round Table (EKA).

The legacy of the second society persisted, and people continued to seek and maintain niches in local community life and entrepreneurial opportunities (Kennedy 1992, 50, 66).

Societal Bases and Institutional Forms of Transformation. Of those countries we studied, Hungary displays the highest degree of continuity in state-society relations in the process of transformation. The compromise between reform communists and the opposition, and the legacy of the second economy, continue to influence postsocialist Hungary. The absence of a powerful organizational center for the opposition movement increased the importance of networks among intellectuals and officials. What is more, the compromise between opposition and old regime temporarily strengthened rather than weakened the position of the latter. Former communist officials and even members of the *nomenklatura* were not as radically replaced as their East German or Polish counterparts had been. Rather, they found niches for individual survival, some in hastily founded nonprofit institutions.

The continued importance of the second economy is an important feature of postsocialist Hungary. Weak and informal as it may be, the second economy provides quasi-market experiences to many Hungarians. In this respect, it may favor the emergence of a new entrepreneurial middle class (Schöpflin 1991, 243, 249; Stark 1992, 244). By the same token, however, the persistence of the second society may turn out to be a serious obstacle to the reconstruction of a modern market economy. Not only may it foster a subtle black market mentality; it also diverts talent, goods, and services from the "first society" (Kennedy 1992, 66).

Patterns of Institution Building: Controlled Muddling-Through. Hungary displays the same pattern as East Germany and Poland when it comes to the general dissolution of societal organizations (Marschall 1990), though more seem to have survived the transition period compared with East Germany. As Eva Kuti (1992, 1–2) points out, most of these quasi-nonprofits "de-politicized" in order to adjust to the new political and regulatory environment. Some, however, were transformed into "bellicose advocacy organizations" (Kuti 1992, 2) for representatives of the old regime—a unique situation among the three countries examined.

Compared to Poland, Hungary displays a more active pattern of institution building. On the one hand, government plays a vital part in regulating, funding, and controlling the third sector, and it even uses the nonprofit form, though reluctantly (Kuti 1992, 9), as a tool for denationalizing the previously state-owned industry. On the other hand, operating foundations are a frequent type of nonprofit institution in postcommunist Hungary. Because large endowments are unlikely in the resource-poor environment of postsocialism, most foundations rely on fund-raising and fee income. This situation seems to indicate a considerable entrepreneurial presence in Hungary's third sector.

Foundations were legalized under the communist regime

in Hungary in 1987. As in Poland, the hope of attracting foreign money for the sake of mitigating the country's difficult budget situation might have been an important incentive in this context. Associations were legalized in 1989. From the beginning, the regulation of foundations and associations was very liberal in terms of auditing and oversight. Tax terms were highly favorable for foundations. Until December 31, 1991, any donation to foundations was tax-exempt, whereas donations to associations were not (Kuti 1992, 3). According to official sources (quoted in Kuti 1992, 4), the number of registered foundations grew from four hundred in December 1989 to six thousand in October 1991. In the same period, the number of registered associations grew from eighty-five hundred (including the societal organizations) to eleven thousand. Thus, the birthrate of foundations was at 1,400 percent, well above that of associations at 30 percent only.

Foundations apparently have become a sort of catchall for nonprofit activities in Hungary. Public hospitals, schools, and universities set up foundations for fund-raising and other types of business activities not necessarily related to the official purpose of their respective institutions (Kuti 1993, 12). The revenue of Hungarian foundations, however, comes primarily from government. According to a survey carried out by Kuti (1993), the government's share of all donations to foundations was 61.5 percent in 1990. Undoubtedly, government plays an active role in fostering and regulating the emerging third sector in Hungary. Currently, a "comprehensive system of rules and regulations for the whole third sector" (Kuti 1993, 14) is being drafted on the basis of models taken from the German regulatory framework.

Apparently, the government intends to use the third sector as one vehicle of privatization. On the one hand, the government's interest in the third sector brings with it political control.[8] On the other hand, the relative dominance of operating foundations implies a more entrepreneurial style of organizational behavior which, in the long run, may make the third sector more independent of governmental interference.

Owing to the importance of monetary as opposed to voluntary labor inputs, foundations may represent for-profit enterprises in disguise (Kuti 1992, 11; 1993, 12). In this respect, the pragmatic, opportunistic legacy of the second society becomes salient. Scandals, fraud, and mismanagement have already affected the third sector's reputation (Kuti 1992, 11), leading the government, in turn, to introduce more rigid regulations for tax exemption in December 1991. Thus, contradictory currents run through Hungary's third sector, currents which presumably reflect the competing cultural patterns of the first and second economies.

In the early 1990s, Hungary was the only country in Central Eastern Europe in which U.S. capital held the major share (60 percent) of all foreign investment. This situation mirrored political and cultural linkages which were obvious

in the third sector, too. The entrepreneurial approach to nonprofit activity is certainly closer to the American than to European models. The American-style nonprofit activity, however, seems mingled with a very second society mentality (Hankiss 1988; 1991) in its preference for small-scale social and economic activity of the muddling-through type instead of rational action in larger-scale settings that involves trust in impersonal rules and public institutions.

CONCLUSION

The notion of the relative demodernization of Central and East European societies is a prominent way of interpreting the situation in this part of Europe today (DiPalma 1991; Mueller 1992; Offe 1991; Schöpflin 1991; Srubar 1991; Sztompka 1991). Indeed, our preliminary findings on the situation of the third sector in Germany, Poland, and Hungary support such reasoning.

For East Germany, we detected an absence of elites and a continued lack of citizen participation in the new social and economic order as the most significant shortcomings of its nonprofit sector. These domestic deficits interact with the friendly colonialism of West German organizations to produce a ready-made third sector that seems vacuous and without the local embeddedness necessary for indigenous development. We expect that the third sector in East Germany will be more centralized and state-centered than the West German one.

In Poland, we found an emergent third sector potentially trapped in a double impasse in terms of resource mobilization. On the one hand, neither the state nor the churches are able or willing to provide sufficient funds. On the other hand, neither volunteering nor nonprofit entrepreneurship are common elements of Polish civil society. The third sector in Poland, presumably, will have to go through the painful experience of organizational muddling-through. Most independent nonprofit organizations (Wunker 1991, 105) will be fragile and oriented toward obtaining monetary and nonmonetary support from two prevailing ideological patrons, the remainder of what was Solidarity and the Catholic Church. The withdrawal and conservative backlash of the church are indicative of the potential secular-religious conflict in Poland. What the French Revolution solved in France in the eighteenth century and various concordats managed to achieve in other European countries in the nineteenth and twentieth centuries remains to be accomplished with respect to the relationship among church, state, and society in Poland.

In Hungary, we assume that the quasi-American entrepreneurial style of nonprofit activity leads to a hybridization of institution building. The Hungarian third sector is characterized by what we call controlled muddling-through. Where entrepreneurship mingles with the mentality of the second society, it will probably be subject to more rigid legal control. It is, therefore, not surprising that Kuti (1993, 14, 18) states that the Hungarian third sector is subject to American

---

8. Kuti (1992, 9) reports that the board of a major youth service foundation was dissolved by government following a political dispute.

Table 12.2. Approaches to Service Provision

Approach	Function		
	Provision	Finance	Regulation
State-oriented	government	government	government
Traditional pluralism	government and nonprofit sector	government and private sources	government and self-governing nonprofit bodies
Contemporary pluralism	government, nonprofit sector, and for-profit sector	government and private sources	government, self-governance, and market
Market-oriented	for-profit sector and nonprofit sector	private sources	market

Source: Based on initial formulation by Taylor 1992, 150.

influence in terms of organizational behavior and to German influence in terms of the legal tradition and a comprehensive regulatory framework.

The traditional cleavages of third sector development in Europe run between autocratic state and citizen, secular state and organized religion, and labor and capital. In Central Eastern Europe, they reappear in a modified, slightly backward form. The state versus citizen cleavage is replayed between West Germany as benevolent colonizer and East Germany as the passive colony; the state-church split reflects the situation of the third sector in Poland; and the characteristic conflict of the nineteenth and early twentieth centuries between labor and capital is replicated in the seemingly precapitalist frictions between the first and second economies in Hungary.

Likely Trajectories. What models or approaches are realistic for postsocialist countries? A definitive answer to this question is beyond the scope of this paper, yet we can nonetheless suggest a range of options for the different trajectories of these three countries. Rather than trying to predict the future of the nonprofit sector as a whole, we briefly look at possible approaches to service provision because this field is of special relevance given the disengagement of the public sector. In most Western market economies, there seems to be a general trend to separate the *financing function* from the *provision function.* Government assumes the responsibility for directly and indirectly financing substantial portions of nonprofit sector activities in the areas of health, education, and welfare as well as in research, culture, and recreation. In some countries, such as the United States, the Netherlands, and Germany, the separation rests on some principle such as third party government or subsidiarity.

The separation between financing and provision leads to a third task: *regulation and governance* (table 12.2) (Taylor 1992, 150; Kramer et al. 1993, 192–93). This function allows for different arrangements among public sector, nonprofit organizations, and business firms. In the *state-oriented ap-*

proach, perhaps best exemplified by the socialist state, all functions are concentrated in the public sector. The second approach, here labeled *traditional pluralism,* involves an often corporatist division of labor between the public sector and the nonprofit sector, usually combined with shared roles in regulatory activities. This type of approach is characteristic of countries in which the principle of subsidiarity governs the relationship between the two sectors, as it does in the Netherlands and Germany. The contemporary variant of traditional pluralism forms the third approach, and it differs in the sense that market firms emerge alongside public sector and nonprofit organizations. Relations among providers are competitive rather than corporative, and unlike the traditional model, this one does not assign role and responsibilities explicitly. Social service delivery and health care in the United States have moved closer to this approach. Finally, the market-oriented approach is characterized by the relative absence of a governmental role in provision, financing, and regulating.

In reality, of course, the various approaches presented in table 12.2 form a continuum, ranging from government- to market-dominated systems. As suggested by the two pluralist models, various combinations among function and organizational form and governance are possible. What is important with respect to current policy debates is that very few Central East European countries would regard either the government or the market-oriented approach as the only feasible option both in practical as well as in political terms, although the free market ideology and the promise of socialist stability are attractive to different segments of their populations. The extremes delineate the possible range of policy options that countries have in working out new arrangements in such fields as social services, health, education, and culture. Thus there are different ways and modes of privatization and different modes of government engagement and disengagement alike. Which role combination among functions and forms seems the most feasible depends at least to some degree on the consensus that exists about the general trajectory of social policy in each country. In light of our comparative institutional analysis, we would expect that the patterns of transformation and institution building themselves exert significant influence on which approach a country follows.

For East Germany, we hypothesize a trajectory that brings the third sector close to traditional pluralism, with strong public sector involvement in nonprofit sector affairs as part of a corporatist arrangement dependent on public funds. Although the current recession will bring with it calls for a greater market orientation on behalf of the East German third sector, the structural inertia exerted by the West German third sector, particularly in the field of social services, will most likely reduce the impact of marketization. In conclusion, we expect the East German nonprofit sector to become relatively state-centered and centralized.

For Poland, we expect an uneasy combination characterized by fluctuation between predominantly state-oriented approaches and traditional pluralism. The fluctuation is the result of two political forces: the Catholic Church, which tries to reduce secular state involvement, and the government, which won the election in 1993 on the strength of its emphasis on social security and stability over market reform. Thus, state-oriented and traditional pluralist models are the likely product, in which the notion of subsidiarity will be the ideological battlefield between state, church, and an increasingly secular society. On balance, however, we predict a patron-centered, segmented, and relatively decentralized nonprofit sector with predominantly resource-poor organizations.

In Hungary, we hypothesize a third sector that comes closest to the model of contemporary pluralism in which government, nonprofit institutions, and for-profit firms play significant roles in social service provision. Over time, the tradition of a second society may well grow out of its present form and combine with a reformed public sector, based on the German administrative legal system, to produce a sector that is largely free of secular-religious frictions. In this sense, the future Hungarian third sector, relatively unrestrained by religious and ideological inertia, will operate most closely to notions of comparative efficiency.

Our initial analysis of the development of the third sector in three postsocialist countries will certainly not be the last word on the role of nonprofit organizations in the process of societal transformations. What seems to emerge from the analysis, however, is the fact that the development of the third sector is a more contingent phenomenon than conventional economic theories of the sector suggest. The nature and strength of civil society and such political factors as the overall posture of the state toward the third sector shape the contours of this set of institutions, in terms of its role in both interest mediation and service provision.

REFERENCES

Ammer, Thomas. 1989. "Stichwort: Flucht aus der DDR." *Deutschland Archiv* 22.

Anheier, Helmut K., and Wolfgang Seibel. 1990. *The Third Sec-* tor: *Comparative Studies of Nonprofit Organizations.* Berlin: DeGruyter Publications.

———. 1992. "Defining the Nonprofit Sector: Germany." *The Johns Hopkins Comparative Nonprofit Sector Project Working Papers,* no. 5. Baltimore: Johns Hopkins University Institute for Policy Studies.

Anheier, Helmut K., and Eckhard Priller. 1991. "The Non-Profit Sector in East Germany." *Voluntas* 2:78–94.

Bauer, Rudolph. 1990. "Voluntary Welfare Associations in Germany and the United States: Theses on the Historical Development of Intermediary Systems." *Voluntas* 1(1):97–111.

Bruszt, Laszlo. 1990. "1989: The Negotiated Revolution in Hungary." *Social Research* 57:365–87.

Bruszt, Laszlo, and David Stark. 1991. "Remaking the Political Field in Hungary: From the Politics of Confrontation to the Politics of Competition." *Journal of International Affairs* 45:201–45.

Collins, Randall, and Neil Hickman. 1991. "Altruism and Culture as Social Products." *Voluntas* 2(2):1–15.

Coser, Lewis. 1956. *The Functions of Social Conflict.* New York: Free Press.

Daehn, Horst. 1982. *Konfrontation oder Kooperation? Das Verhaeltnis von Staat und Kirche in der SBZ/DDR 1945–1980.* Opladen: Westdeutscher Verlag.

DiMaggio, Paul. 1987. "Nonprofit Organizations in the Production and Distribution of Culture." In *The Nonprofit Sector: A Research Handbook,* ed. Walter W. Powell. New Haven: Yale University Press.

DiMaggio, Paul, and Helmut K. Anheier. 1990. "The Sociology of Nonprofit Organizations." *Annual Review of Sociology* 16:137–59.

DiPalma, Giuseppe. 1991. "Legitimation from the Top to Civil Society: Politico-Cultural Change in Eastern Europe." *World Politics* 44:49–80.

Douglas, James. 1983. *Why Charity? The Case for a Third Sector.* London: Sage.

———. 1987. "Political Theories of Nonprofit Organization." In *The Nonprofit Sector: A Research Handbook,* ed. Walter W. Powell. New Haven: Yale University Press.

Fehr, Helmut. 1991. "Eine Untersuchung des Beitrags politischer Clubs zur Entwicklung einer demokratischen Infrastruktur in Polen." WZB-Berichte. *Berichte des Wissenschaftszentrums Berlin fuer Sozialforschung,* mimeo.

Gauss, Guenther. 1983. *Wo Deutschland liegt.* Hamburg: Hanser.

Gerschenkron, Alexander. 1962. *Economic Backwardness in Historical Perspective.* Cambridge: The Belknap Press of the Harvard University Press.

Gidron, Benjamin, Ralph Kramer, and Lester M. Salamon, eds. 1992. *Government and the Third Sector: Emerging Relationships in Welfare States.* San Francisco: Jossey-Bass.

Goldfarb, Jeffrey. 1991. *After the Fall: The Pursuit of Democracy in Central Europe.* New York: Basic Books.

Habermas, Jürgen. 1962. *Strukturwandel der Öffentlichkeit.* Frankfurt: Suhrkamp.

Hankiss, Elmer. 1988. "The 'Second Society': Is There an Alternative Social Model Emerging in Contemporary Hungary?" *Social Research* 55:13–42.

———. 1990. *East European Alternatives.* New York: Oxford University Press.

Hansmann, Henry. 1980. "The Role of Nonprofit Enterprise." *Yale Law Journal* 89:835–901.

Havel, Václav. 1992. "A Dream for Czechoslovakia." *New York Review of Books* 39(12):8–12.

Hirschman, Albert O. 1970. *Exit, Voice, and Loyalty: Responses to Decline in Firms, Organizations, and States.* Cambridge: Harvard University Press.

——. 1993. "Exit, Voice, and the Fate of the German Democratic Republic." *World Politics* 45(2):173–203.

James, Estelle, ed. 1989. *The Nonprofit Sector in Comparative Perspective.* Oxford: Oxford University Press.

Kennedy, Michael. 1992. "The Intelligentsia in the Constitution of Civil Societies and Post-Communist Regimes in Hungary and Poland." *Theory and Society* 21:29–76.

Kietlinska, Krystyna. 1992. "Comment on 'The Promise of Nonprofits in Poland and Hungary: An Analysis of Third Sector Renaissance.' " *Voluntas* 3(3):365–74.

Knabe, Hubertus. 1992. "Opposition in einem halben Land." *Forschungsjournal Neue Soziale Bewegungen* 9–15.

Knoke, David, and James R. Wood. 1981. *Organized for Action: Commitment in Voluntary Associations.* New Brunswick: Rutgers University Press.

Kolarska-Bobinska, Lena. 1990. "Civil Society and Social Anomy in Poland." *Acta Sociologica* 33:277–88.

Kramer, Ralph, Lorentzen Hakon, Willem B. Melief, and Sergio Pasquinelli. 1993. *Privatization in Four European Countries: Comparative Studies in Government-Third Sector Relationships.* Armonk: Sharpe.

Kuti, Eva. 1990. "The Possible Role of the Nonprofit Sector in Hungary." *Voluntas* 1(1):6–41.

——. 1992. "Social, Political and Economic Roles of the Nonprofit Sector in Hungary in the Period of Transition." Paper presented at the Third International Conference on Voluntary and Nonprofit Organizations, Indianapolis, March 11–13, 1992.

——. 1993. "Definition Problems in a Newly Emerging Nonprofit Sector: The Case of Hungary." *The Johns Hopkins Comparative Nonprofit Sector Project Working Papers,* no. 13. Baltimore: Johns Hopkins University Institute for Policy Studies.

Lehmbruch, Gerhard. 1990. "Die improvisierte Vereinigung: Die Dritte Deutsche Republik." *Leviathan* 18:462–86.

Lijphart, Arend. 1992. "Democratization and Constitutional Choices in Czecho-Slovakia, Hungary and Poland 1989–91." *Journal of Theoretical Politics* 4:207–23.

Linz, Juan, and Alfred Stepan, eds. 1978. *The Breakdown of Democratic Regimes.* Baltimore: Johns Hopkins University Press.

Marody, Mira. 1988. "Antinomies of Collective Subconsciousness." *Social Research* 55:97–110.

——. 1990. "Perceptions of Politics in Polish Society." *Social Research* 57:257–74.

——. 1993. "Polish Democracy." Paper presented at the *88th Meeting of the American Sociological Association.* Miami Beach. August 1993.

Marschall, Miklos. 1990. "The Nonprofit Sector in a Centrally Planned Economy." In *The Third Sector: Comparative Studies of Nonprofit Organizations,* ed. Helmut K. Anheier and Wolfgang Seibel, 277–92. Berlin and New York: De Gruyter.

McCarthy, Kathleen, et al. 1991. *The Nonprofit Sector in the Global Community.* San Francisco: Jossey-Bass.

Middleton, Melissa. 1987. "Nonprofits Boards of Directors: Beyond the Governance Function." In *The Nonprofit Sector: A Research Handbook,* ed. Walter Powell. New Haven: Yale University Press.

Mueller, Klaus. 1991. " 'Modernising' Eastern Europe: Theoretical Problems and Political Dilemmas." *Archive Européenne Sociologique* 33:109–50.

Nordlinger, Eric. 1981. *On the Autonomy of the Democratic State.* Cambridge: Harvard University Press.

O'Donnell, Guillermo, and Philippe Schmitter. 1986. *Transitions from Authoritarian Rule: Prospects for Democracy.* Baltimore: Johns Hopkins University Press.

Offe, Claus. 1991. "Das Dilemma der Gleichzeitigkeit: Demokratisierung und Marktwirtschaft in Osteuropa." *Merkur* 45:279–92.

O'Neill, Michael. 1989. *The Third America: The Emergence of the Nonprofit Sector in the United States.* San Francisco: Jossey-Bass.

Powell, Walter, ed. 1987. *The Nonprofit Sector: A Research Handbook.* New Haven: Yale University Press.

Rose-Ackerman, Susan. 1986. *The Economics of Nonprofit Institutions.* Oxford: Oxford University Press.

Salamon, Lester M. 1992. *America's Nonprofit Sector: A Primer.* New York: Foundation Center.

Salamon, Lester M., and Helmut K. Anheier. 1992. "In Search of the Nonprofit Sector I: The Question of Definitions." *Voluntas* 3(2):125–53.

Schöpflin, George. 1991. "Post-Communism: Constructing New Democracies in Central Europe." *International Affairs* 67:235–50.

Seibel, Wolfgang. 1990. "Government Third Sector Relationship in a Comparative Perspective: The Cases of France and West Germany." *Voluntas* 1:42–60.

——. 1992a. *Funktionaler Dilettantismus: Erfolgreich scheiternde Organisationen im Dritten Sektor zwischen Markt und Staat.* Baden-Baden: Nomos.

——. 1992b. "Necessary Illusions: The Transformation of Governance Structures in the New Germany." *Tocqueville Review* 13(1):177–97.

Simai, Mihaly. 1992. "Hungarian Problems." *Government and Opposition* 27:52–65.

Srubar, Ilja. 1991. "War der reale Sozialismus modern? Versuch einer strukturellen Bestimmung." *Kölner Zeitschrift für Soziologie und Sozialpsychologie* 43:415–32.

Staniszkis, Jadwiga. 1984. *Poland's Self-Limiting Revolution.* Princeton: Princeton University Press.

Stark, David. 1992. "From System Identity to Organizational Diversity: Analyzing Social Change in Eastern Europe." *Contemporary Sociology* 21:299–304.

Sztompka, Piotr. 1991. "The Intangibles and Imponderables of the Transition to Democracy." *Studies in Comparative Communism* 24:295–311.

Tatur, Melanie. 1990. "Von der Volkskirche zur sozialen Bewegung? Die 'religioese Erneuerung' in Polen." *Osteuropa* 40:441–52.

Taylor, Marilyn. 1992. "The Changing Role of the Nonprofit Sector in Britain: Moving toward the Market." In *Govern-*

ment and the Nonprofit Sector: Emerging Relationships in Welfare States, ed. Benjamin Gidron, Ralph Kramer and Lester M. Salamon, 147–75. San Francisco: Jossey-Bass.

Weisbrod, Burton. 1988. *The Nonprofit Economy.* Cambridge: Harvard University Press.

Wunker, Stephen. 1991. "The Promise of Non-Profits in Poland and Hungary: An Analysis of Third Sector Renaissance." *Voluntas* 2:89–107.

Wuthnow, Robert, ed. 1991. *Between States and Markets: The Voluntary Sector in Comparative Perspective.* Princeton: Princeton University Press.

Part Four

To Contribute or Control: The Politics of Sponsorship

13

NANCY MARIE ROBERTSON

Kindness or Justice?: Women's Associations and the Politics of Race and History

Making the world is undeniably a political act. Writing histories that imply alternative ways in which the world might have been made are also political acts.

— Thomas Holt, "Introduction,"
The State of Afro-American History

A growing number of scholars have set about to analyze the connections between the activism of women's groups and government policy in the late nineteenth and early twentieth centuries (Baker 1984; Clemens 1993; Gordon 1991, 1992; Kessler-Harris 1993; Koven and Michel 1990; Lemons 1973; McCarthy 1982, 1990; Muncy 1991; Scott 1991; Sklar 1985; Skocpol 1992; Ware 1981, 1987). They have stressed the relationship between women's voluntary associations and the creation of social services and political programs that in the United States culminated in the New Deal and the welfare state. Many political analysts previously ignored these efforts as frivolous because they were conducted by women or because they entailed such seemingly noncontroversial items as promoting sanitary conditions in a town (Scott 1991, 157–

This chapter benefited from comments on earlier versions by Debra C. Minkoff, Elisabeth S. Clemens, Carrie Rothburd, and Walter W. Powell and from discussions at the conference "Private Action and the Public Good" (November 1993). I also appreciate the careful readings and thoughtful comments of Ilana Abramovitch, Ellen Gruber Garvey, Jane Holzka, Ellen Kellman, and Nina Warnke.

58). Yet, at a time when women were limited, if not barred, by law or tradition from engaging in conventional public arenas, including politics, business, and churches, they utilized education campaigns and lobbying to develop their own political style and to gain legislative and judicial victories. Women's efforts to establish playgrounds, libraries, and public health programs and their activism in state and local government contributed to the development of federal programs like Social Security and Aid to Dependent Children (the precursor to Aid to Families with Dependent Children). Their voluntary associations constituted a link between grassroots women's groups and those women who gained national power and recognition, for example, Frances Perkins, the first female cabinet member. These women were able to build on small, local issues to lay the groundwork for the campaigns for social justice that ultimately shaped national policy. Their broad notion of what constituted politics challenges traditional notions of what is private and what is public. The transition from private efforts to public programs has been central to discussions of the welfare state. The recent literature on women and the state prompts us to ask why women's efforts (for programs like kindergartens and milk inspection) have been conceptualized as private and frivolous while the campaigns that men engaged in (regulation of trusts and creation of New Deal programs, for example) were (and are) defined as part of a political struggle over the public good.

As a body, this work is an important corrective to views of women and the state that either ignore women altogether or see them as the victims of (patriarchal) state programs.

The history of women that these scholars recount is one in which the members of a politically disadvantaged group — women — empowered themselves through voluntary associations and thereby sometimes gained a position in the larger political arena. They urge us to look at the interlocking ties in the twentieth century between private voluntary associations and public governmental agencies (Muncy 1991, xvi, 159). There are profound disagreements among these scholars, including their assessments of the unity found among women's groups, the relative importance of individual reformers and groups of reformers (New York versus Chicago, national leaders versus local groups), and the role that class (and labor groups) or race played.[1] These historical actors usually spoke of their efforts as being intended to benefit all women, if not society as a whole. Yet not all women benefited equally in the process of moving into politics. Many of the groups restricted membership to women of similar class, racial, or religious background.

In looking at how different women (or different groups of women) fared in the programs and policies advocated by women's groups, one must question how to categorize white, middle-class women's efforts on behalf of "other" women. Did they empower other women or co-opt them? Do we see their motives as altruistic or self-interested? Were they concerned with social justice or social control? Such either/or dichotomies, however, are problematic, and it is useful to redefine the question: What happens when cooperation involves people with different goals and with different amounts of power? The point of such questions is not simply to provide a corrective to the historical debates, but to suggest that there are important lessons for public policy discussions today to be learned from an analysis of the activities of these reformers. Many of these women sought to influence and promote the government programs of the Progressive Era and the New Deal through voluntary associations; the limitations of their understanding of racial issues continue to be evident in present-day policy debates.

The Young Women's Christian Association (YWCA) provides a vantage point from which to explore these questions. The YWCA was part of the network of women's organizations that sought to improve the greater society. Yet unlike most other women's groups, the YWCA had both white and black women active at the local and national levels. As such, debates within it shaped and reflected a larger societal discussion about, in Gunnar Myrdal's words, the "American Dilemma" — the contradiction between the "American Creed" of democracy and "Christian precepts" versus the treatment of African Americans in the United States (Myrdal 1944, xlvii). The differing experiences white and black women brought to bear on the question of how to improve society meant that while both groups shared concern over "the race problem," they defined it and its solution differently. Even when they used a similar vocabulary, they had different and sometimes conflicting goals. Their struggles frequently included differences over definitions of the public good as well as over whose interests were seen as public and whose as private. We need to ask whose point of view we should adopt in assessing these women's goals, accomplishments, and limitations. There are, in fact, multiple stories to tell about the YWCA's racial policies. Although focusing on the stories told by white women, this chapter includes the voices of African-American women in order to reveal the unstated assumptions underlying white women's view of the world.[2]

ONE STORY ABOUT THE YWCA

White YWCA women's strong sense of history and their belief in the importance of their association in the United States and the world is reflected in their accounts of the YWCA and its efforts to achieve social justice (Boyd 1986; Calkins 1960; Sims 1936, 1950, 1969; Wilson 1933). In examining the YWCA's reform efforts, women associated with it emphasized the YWCA's origins in both evangelical Protestantism and a nineteenth-century notion of the "bond of a common womanhood" (Hammond 1917, 18). Although the YWCA movement dated back to the religious revivals of the 1850s, the organization as currently structured was launched in 1906 "to advance the physical, social, intellectual, moral and spiritual interests of young women . . . [and to] make the organization as a whole an effective agency in the bringing in of the Kingdom of God among young women" (YWCA 1909, 107–08). It was, as its participants called it, "a woman's movement" (they would not have used the term *feminist*),[3] and its purpose was deeply infused with the social gospel, a form of Christian socialism found in mainstream Protestantism at the time. Assumptions about the meaning of womanhood and religion produced an ideology of "Christian sisterhood." Women in the YWCA — both white and black, middle class and working class, old and young — spoke of the need for

2. For a highly developed effort to capture a variety of possible stories in another situation, see James Goodman's (1994) discussion of the Scottsboro case.

3. The word *feminist* was generally applied to those women who focused on passage of the Equal Rights Amendment (for example, the National Woman's Party) rather than to the women who advocated a wide range of social reforms. The latter, including members of the YWCA, opposed the ERA because they feared it would eliminate protective legislation for working women, one of their primary goals. There is a long-standing debate among historians of women on the use of the term *feminism* (Cott 1989; Gordon 1993, 156), but I prefer to use these women's self-description.

1. See the interchange between Gordon and Skocpol as well as Skocpol's delineation of the different schools of thought about women and the state (Gordon 1993; Skocpol 1993).

women as sisters to work *with* each other, not simply *for* each other.[4]

Although the association initially focused on the needs of white, native-born women, especially young working women, members expanded their social agenda to address the needs of white immigrant women and girls. The YWCA joined many of the campaigns by women's groups to work for economic and social justice for the economically disadvantaged, initially by providing services like housing and recreation but ultimately by supporting union efforts and labor legislation. By the 1920s, members of the YWCA began to address some of the racial issues evident in both the North and South. In contrast to other white-dominated, middle-class organizations, including such secular women's groups as the General Federation of Women's Clubs and such religiously based male-dominated ones as the Young Men's Christian Association (YMCA), members of the YWCA took a combination of steps to respond to the needs and demands of African Americans.[5]

The YWCA not only offered programs and activities in African-American communities but expanded them dramatically during the World War I; it had African-American women on its national staff and, by 1924, on its National Board. In 1922, the association mandated interracial seating at its national conventions, a practice that meant conventions were not held again in the South until after World War II. In the 1920s and 1930s, the YWCA sponsored interracial conferences and meetings on college campuses, even in the South. In the 1930s, members shifted their strategies for racial justice to include support of federal legislation, joining in efforts to lobby Congress for federal anti-lynching laws and fair employment practices and against the poll tax.[6] In

the 1930s and 1940s (and, in some cases, even into the 1960s), the YWCA was one of the only places in southern towns and cities where interracial meetings could and did take place. And although the YWCA initially permitted segregated local associations in both the North and South, members mandated integration in 1946 (Bell and Wilkins 1944; Haynes 1946).[7]

As one of the largest women's organizations in the United States, the YWCA was highly visible, and its actions carried weight.[8] There was a price to be paid for this activism, however, and it was paid by both local associations and the national body. They lost funds and members and were both race-baited and red-baited. Their support for federal legislation — especially for civil rights — prompted critics to ask whether the *C* in YWCA stood for *Christian* or *Communist* (Dilling 1936, 250). They were named before the House Committee on Un-American Activities.[9]

In their accounts of the organization's history, white women emphasized that they addressed racial problems in order to meet the needs of all young women and to make the association truly Christian and democratic. The fact that the YWCA, like other religiously oriented white-dominated women's groups, was more likely than secular, white-dominated women's organizations to address racial issues reinforces Craig Calhoun's point on the significance of religious language to political as well as moral discourse (Calhoun, in this volume). Mark Chaves's suggestion that the goals of religious organizations are not only the winning of converts but also "to do useful work" (what he calls "restless activism") bears repeating as well (Chaves, in this volume). As ambiguous as "bringing in the Kingdom of God" might have been as an institutional rationale, the fact that religiously based white-dominated women's groups took more liberal stands on racial issues differentiated them from secular white-dominated women's groups (Gordon 1991; Hartmann 1979, 1982; Lasch-Quinn 1993; Scott 1991).[10] Women of the YWCA

4. The formulation of *with* not *for* captures part of the distinction laid out by Craig Jenkins of the difference between participation and representation and between a political or a charity-oriented perspective (Jenkins, in this volume).

5. The YWCA also included Native-American, Asian-American, and Latina members, but African Americans represented the largest minority group in the association and also shared, according to the authors of a YWCA study on race relations, "a common culture and a common religious background with the white people of this country" (Bell and Wilkins 1944, 12). Almost all discussions in the YWCA on race in the first half of the twentieth century focused on white and black race relations. One must note that the YWCA's Protestant roots suggest that the "common religious background" referred to Protestantism, thereby making Jews and Catholics invisible among "the white people of this country."

6. Federal anti-lynching laws were intended to punish people who had engaged in lynchings when local governments refused to respond adequately or at all, much in the way federal civil rights legislation is used today. The proposed laws also included provisions to punish local law enforcement officers who failed in their duty to prevent lynchings and levied fines against counties in which lynchings took place (Sitkoff 1978, 281–82). During World War II, African Americans pressured the government for the creation of the Fair Employment Practices Commis-

sion; Franklin D. Roosevelt established the commission, but it lasted only until the end of the war. Poll taxes that required people to pay a tax in order to vote were found in eight southern states and served to disenfranchise both black and white poor people.

7. The existence of segregated branches in northern cities dating back to the nineteenth century forcefully reminds us that the race problem and segregation were not only southern problems in these years.

8. Membership figures are often hard to determine, but it would appear that, in 1920, the YWCA was the third largest autonomous women's group after the General Federation of Women's Clubs and the Women's Christian Temperance Union; by the late 1940s, only the former was larger.

9. The efforts against them, nonetheless, pale in comparison to those groups and individuals destroyed in anticommunist purges (Caute 1978).

10. "Bringing in the Kingdom of God" remained part of the YWCA's purpose until 1949. Although it qualifies in Chaves's argument as an ambiguous concept as far as explaining the origins of the YWCA, it

were decidedly more progressive on race than the men of the YMCA, which suggests that their ideology of Christian *sisterhood* (women as sisters working with each other in fellowship) contributed to their policies. Even while men in the YMCA spoke of the "brotherhood of men," they were more likely to stress recreation programs and avoid controversial issues, including race (Atwood 1946; Hopkins 1951; Mjagkij 1994; Zald 1970).

In many of their histories, white women acknowledged the existence of racial problems in their associations — segregated locals, for example — and admitted that the efforts of African-American women to challenge the policies were essential to change. But they often smoothed over profound differences in the ways white and black women looked at the same situations. By examining the history as told by African-American women, we gain a fuller picture of the YWCA and, specifically, of the unstated assumptions in the white women's accounts.

It is not that the story told by black women is the true story of the YWCA. Rather, the often competing histories of white and black women compose another arena for the political struggles that took place within the organization. Learning of the contributions of white women's associations to the welfare state requires rethinking political development but not ignoring those efforts in which white men dominated. Likewise, contrasting the story of white women with the accounts focused on African Americans' experiences reveals racial assumptions underlying the white women's narratives. The differences between accounts tell us much about race. White women's statements about black women frequently reveal more information about whites than about the African-American women of whom they purportedly spoke and, in doing so, expose underlying white assumptions.

What is telling about these white women's accounts is often not their overt racism (although that can be found), but their silence about their own racial identity. White women's stories reveal that white, middle-class women frequently saw themselves as women first and foremost and defined their concerns as *women's* concerns; they did not identify themselves as white, middle-class women or see their concerns as arising from their class and racial identities as well as their gender. Unlike African-American women, who could never forget (or were never allowed to forget) their race, white women described themselves as women, without modifiers, while women of other classes and races were referred to (in the language of the day) as industrial women, colored women, and so forth. That the General Federation of Women's Clubs was in actuality the General Federation of White

Women's Clubs, for example, is not readily apparent unless one knows about the National Association of Colored Women's Clubs. In the YWCA, the white association in a city was the central association, while the African-American association was the branch or, usually, the "colored branch."[11] In this scenario, the white association is not only the primary one, but the one that requires no racial modifier.

RACE AND THE EMBODIMENT OF THE NORMAL

Scholars examining the political activism of African-American women have often perpetuated the "women without modifiers" vision held by white YWCA women. They have frequently structured their analysis around the issue of whether black women saw their concerns as race- *or* gender-based. The question of the connection between race and gender interests is not usually asked of white women. Such an approach fails to analyze how white women's race shaped their goals and activism.[12] As with other privileged groups, these women are allowed to be silent about their racial identity. Richard Dyer has observed that power can pass itself off not only as that which is superior, but as that which is "embodied in the normal" (Dyer 1988, 45). He and other writers have been uncovering the social construction of whiteness (Dyer 1988; Frankenberg 1993; hooks 1992; Roediger 1991; Spelman 1988; Ware 1992). Arguing both that whites have a racial identity and that whites' and blacks' understandings of their identities are shaped in relation to each other through both cooperation and conflict, they call for an analysis of the consequences of whites' greater social and political power in this interaction.[13]

In the late nineteenth and early twentieth centuries, white and black women alike appealed to the values of a common womanhood and motherhood to justify their public activism and to make alliances with women of other races and classes. Both spoke of the important role women could play for the betterment of the race (a word that could mean humans in general or a specific race or both). In the YWCA, each group emphasized the shared values found in Christian sisterhood

11. Even though white southerners were more explicit than other whites about their racial identity, they too frequently used *woman* and especially *lady* to mean only white females.

12. There are arguments parallel to the one I am making about race that can be made for class and other categories of social analysis. While I will raise some issues of class, I am focusing this chapter on questions raised by race and gender.

13. My understanding of race as a social relation is shaped by those who have analyzed the social relations of class and gender (Kelly-Gadol 1976; Scott 1986; Thompson [1963] 1966). In examining black-white race relations in this chapter, it is not my intention to overlook the problems inherent in presenting that relation as paradigmatic for all other race relations. Even as early as the 1940s, women in the YWCA acknowledged this limitation but emphasized that African-American women and girls were the largest minority group both in the United States and in the YWCA's constituency (Bell and Wilkins 1944, 12).

certainly seemed to sanction qualitatively different policies and practices than those found in secular organizations. These differences suggest that the distinction Chaves attempts to draw between secular services and religious ones and between services and motivations may not be as clear-cut as he argues (Chaves, this volume).

that bound women together not only in the United States but around the world.[14]

But as ensuing struggles revealed, the common rhetoric often masked important differences in the lived experiences of black and white women. White women, in particular, often overlooked the significance of their social power in setting the agenda for what were called common projects. By looking at the hidden racial underpinnings of womanhood in U.S. history, one can better analyze how some white people understood and took for granted their racial identities even when they did not explicitly identify themselves as having a race. Although they were frequently silent about their own race, they were not silent about other women and implicitly defined themselves by defining whom they were not.

When white and black women came together in the YWCA to address race problems, they faced a widespread debate about the nature of black womanhood that was related to beliefs about the character of the entire race. Many whites shared the sentiments of one white journalist who claimed that the "negroes in this country are wholly devoid of morality. . . . The women are prostitutes and all are natural liars and thieves" (Jacks 1895). More invidious, however, was the late nineteenth- and early twentieth-century effort throughout the country to commemorate the "mammy." In the words of one white critic, there was a "cult of the Old Black Mammy" (Hammond 1917, 32). One of the more notable examples of this trend was the campaign by the United Daughters of the Confederacy in the early 1920s asking Congress to set aside land for a monument in Washington, D.C., "in memory of the faithful colored mammies of the South" (*Congressional Record* 1923b, 4839; Johnson 1923; Jones 1990b; Neverdon-Morton 1989; Parkhurst 1938; Thurber 1992; Work 1925, 74–75). The statue was to display a mammy holding a white baby while, in the words of its designer, "pickaninnies [were] trying to have their mother pay attention to them instead of devoting all her time to the white children" ("Rival's 'Mammy' Statue" 1923).

A congressman from North Carolina advocated this plan as a monument to those women who had "desired no change in their condition of life . . . . The very few who are left look back to those days as the happy and golden hours of their lives" (*Congressional Record* 1923a, 1509). He implied that those who had criticized slavery or the current treatment of African Americans were mistaken. White southerners in his account cared deeply for the African Americans, who, in return, cared deeply for them. Implicit in this outlook were assertions that southern whites knew what was best for African Americans and that racial problems were caused by agitators who stirred up African Americans who would otherwise have remained content.

14. To pick up on Craig Calhoun's notion of the difference between community and the public, these women created a national, even international, conception of community (Calhoun, in this volume).

The belief that there was mutual caring between whites and African Americans was not limited to white southerners. Many, if not most, of the mammy songs popular in the early twentieth century were of northern composition (Thurber 1992). Abby Aldrich (Mrs. John D. Jr.) Rockefeller was a white northern woman on the National Board of Directors of the YWCA who was active in the administration of programs for African Americans in the association. In 1924, she cautioned against using the term *mammy* when referring to the service workers in the YWCA's segregated hotel in Washington, D.C., writing, "As you know, at the present moment the colored people are feeling very touchy and are watching everything that we say and do. They are particularly feeling that their dignity is constantly being undermined by the white people speaking of them as 'Mammies' and 'Darkies' etc., even tho [*sic*] these are terms of affection" (Rockefeller 1924). Even as Rockefeller acknowledged African Americans' resentment for the appellations used to describe them, she trivialized their feelings and the disrespect implicit in these terms. She defended, without question, the belief that white people's affection for black people was what should determine how African Americans regarded the use of the terms.

Not surprisingly, the African-American community, including women active in the YWCA at both the local and national levels, had a very different view of what the mammy represented, and they mounted a campaign against the monument. Eva Bowles, the senior national African-American staff member, spoke out against it "as an 'insult both to the "mammy" and to the Negro race,' which would be repudiated by no one more quickly than by the old mammies" ("Miss Bowles" 1923). In the words of one writer, the appeal of the mammy was the desire to substitute "kindness" for "justice" (Kerlin 1920, 29). If white people were concerned about the plight of real mammies and their descendants, they argued, a more fitting monument would be to end lynching, deal with discrimination in education and public accommodations, and address political disenfranchisement. Although the Senate passed a bill supporting the request to allocate a site for the statue, the ensuing controversy killed the legislation in the House.[15]

15. It was the United Daughters of the Confederacy that sought, in 1993, the renewal of the patent for its logo, which included a Confederate flag. Carol Moseley-Braun (D-IL), the first African-American female senator, led the battle to defeat the effort. John Kerry (D-MA) supported her, observing, in part, "We are 98 White men and women standing up and debating whether we ought to be sensitive to the feelings of one African-American woman and one native American man [Ben Nighthorse Campbell (then D-CO)]" ("Carol Moseley-Braun" 1993). Although Kerry's sentiments may have been in the right place, his characterization of the racial composition of the Senate was off: there were, in fact, two other "nonwhite" members, Daniel K. Akaka (D-HI) and Daniel K. Inouye (D-HI).

Jesse Helms (R-NC), who introduced the bill, stated that "race

UPLIFTING THE RACE

White and African-American women in the YWCA believed it was important to challenge the image of the mammy in order to improve race relations. As Lily Hardy Hammond, a white woman of a former slave-owning family, put it, the "status of the Negro women and the Negro home in the minds of the privileged white women will determine the status of the [Negro] race" (Hammond 1917, 29). This formulation — that what white women thought about African-American women was important to the whole race — shaped the strategy developed by women interested in race relations in the YWCA as well as in other white-dominated groups, such as the Southern Methodist Church's women's division and the Commission on Interracial Cooperation (Hall 1979; McDowell 1982), and in African-American organizations like the National Baptists' Women's Convention (Higginbotham 1993). In contrast, many whites, even white liberals, denied any responsibility for the position of African Americans, emphasizing that African Americans bore the burden alone for their own "uplift" (Lasch-Quinn 1993). At a time of growing white concern over intensifying "racial friction" (increases in lynching and race riots, migration to the North by African Americans, and a resurgence of the Ku Klux Klan), women active in the YWCA sought to expose white women to educated African-American women — the New Negro woman, to use the language of the day — through lectures, meetings, and publications so that white women would come to a better appreciation of the black woman. By seeing the conditions that these middle-class black women experienced, white women were supposed to change their attitudes toward African Americans and thereby promote racial harmony.

But while white women emphasized a *goal* of racial harmony and ending race friction, African-American women challenged their motivations. Some black women voiced concern that white women wanted to improve the racial situation in order to stem migration to northern cities. They argued that southern white women wanted black women to stay in the South where they could continue as domestic servants and that northern whites feared the growing political power base of African Americans in cities like Chicago (Hall 1979, 88; Higginbotham 1993).

African-American women advocated racial harmony as a means to advance the race and eventually end segregation. Through such books as *A New Negro for a New Century,* they forged an image of the educated and refined African Ameri-

can aimed at both African Americans and whites (Gates 1988; MacBrady 1900). They intended the New Negro to inspire the majority of poor African Americans with a sense of race pride and encourage respectable behavior. As part of this effort, some African-American women policed the appearance and behavior of others. Individual women were held accountable for the position of the race as a whole. In the words of one group of black churchwomen in 1913, the "woman who keeps a dirty home and tolerates trifling shiftless inmates [is] . . . as great an enemy to the race as the man who devotes his life to persecuting and maligning the race" (Higginbotham 1993, 202–03; White 1993).

African-American women also sought to foster a sense of race pride through noting the accomplishments of African Americans, and they led one of the earliest national efforts against lynching. Through associations like the National Association of Colored Women's Clubs, founded in 1896, African-American women launched a campaign for improving the situation of African Americans that preceded the formation of groups that have traditionally been viewed as the backbone of the early civil rights movement: the National Association for the Advancement of Colored People (NAACP) and the National Urban League. They were instrumental in creating a network of social welfare programs at a time when African Americans were denied access to publicly sponsored services.[16]

African-American women also hoped the image of the New Negro would persuade white people to recognize the rights of African Americans. Much of the impetus for and the strategy of the black clubwoman's movement was to improve the image of African-American women both as a means of racial uplift and to gain support from white women for their race (Davis 1933; Higginbotham 1993; Lerner 1973; Neverdon-Morton 1989; Salem 1990; White 1993).[17] Whatever their concerns about the motivations of white women, black women utilized the perception of shared interests and goals to win allies in efforts to gain resources for their community and to promote interracial events.

White women in the YWCA believed that what they thought about African Americans would "determine the status of the [Negro] race" at a time when other white Americans ignored the plight of African Americans or blamed them for their status. But in assuming this obligation, white women could also deny African-American women agency in improving their own position and in defining the key issues affecting their community. African-American women voiced their concern over this tendency by demanding that white women live up to their goal of working with black women, not merely for

---

should never have been introduced" as an issue in the debate (McGrory 1993). Helms's comment reflects the belief (or desire) of some white southerners that the Confederacy be seen as separate from the issue of race, a belief not shared by most African Americans and many other whites.

Interestingly, the figure of the mammy resurfaced in this incident when an editorialist for the *New Pittsburgh Courier,* a conservative African-American newspaper, declared that the senators supporting Moseley-Braun had been "mammy-whipped" (Williams 1993).

16. An examination of the role of black women suggests that accounts of the struggle for civil rights in the twentieth century that rely on a model of politics based solely on men's (black or white) public activism should be rethought; see White (1993).

17. The National Association of Colored Women's Clubs' motto was, "Lifting As We Climb" (Davis 1933).

them. They struggled for African-American control over programs for African-American women and girls, asking not just for kindness or noblesse oblige but for self-determination (Giddings 1984; Hall 1979; Jones 1990a; Rouse 1989).

Compared to white women who thought of all African-American women as mammies at best, white women who argued that (some) African-American women were like middle-class white women were more likely to support the YWCA's expanded programs for African Americans. Some listened to African-American women who promoted interracial efforts in the 1920s in the YWCA, activities that permitted white and black women to work together. Through a program of interracial meetings and lectures by African-American staff members, white women and girls met educated African-American women (Taylor 1984). These interchanges led some white women to become active in struggles for racial justice both inside and outside the YWCA.

But a focus on African-American women who were like white women set the white, middle-class experience as the norm; all others were human and Christian only insofar as they approximated that norm. Furthermore, the focus on how white women regarded African Americans promoted a response that focused on what *individuals* thought or felt and was inadequate to address the more structural expressions of racism. Even when white women in the YWCA shifted to a legislative attack on institutional racism, eventually urging desegregation in the association and the nation as a whole, they remained influenced by the assumption that their experience was (and ought to be) the norm.

"SUCH A FINE WOMAN"

An important African-American woman involved in the project to expose white women to educated black women was Juliette Aline Derricotte. Born in 1897, Derricotte grew up in Athens, Georgia, and attended Talladega College, an African-American school run by the American Missionary Association. While there, she was active with the campus YWCA. Following graduation in 1918, she joined the YWCA's national staff to work with "colored students." In that capacity, she visited every African-American college that had a YWCA and many white schools as well. Derricotte represented the YWCA at international Christian student meetings in England and India. Following her time in India, she conducted a lecture tour in countries like China and Japan, focusing on the role of students in race relations around the world. Derricotte had an international stature far above that of most YWCA women of any race. Her articles in the YWCA's *Womans Press* introduced her to an unknown number of YWCA members, while a smaller number knew her personally from these conferences, interracial discussions on college campuses, and working with her (Leffall 1982; Wygal 1932b).

More than fifty years later, Fern Babcock Grant, a white woman, would describe the importance of having met Derricotte when she, Grant, was a college student:

The only black person I really knew was Aunt Josie, who came to our house once a week to wash the clothes, leaving her own children at home uncared for. As I heard Miss Derricotte describe how difficult it was to be a black person in America, never knowing even in the north what hotel or restaurant or bookstore would refuse to serve her or him, I realized that she was describing a situation I had known all my life, without ever really thinking about it. When I shook hands with her at the end of the meeting, it was the first time I had ever looked straight across at a black person as an equal. As I rode home on the streetcar the battle in my mind continued. How could my perfect America treat such a fine woman so abominably? What could I do to change the situation? (Rossman 1983, 373)

Grant's words highlighted the emotional impact that meeting an educated, middle-class black woman could have on whites. Seeing Derricotte as an equal forced Grant to question how her country treated "such a fine woman." Her subsequent involvement in struggles for racial justice in and out of the YWCA seemed to confirm that there could be a resulting political transformation. Yet, Grant left unexamined whether an "Aunt Josie" merited that treatment. With her children at home uncared for and being responsible for the domestic chores of a white home, Aunt Josie bore a striking resemblance to the mammy—down to her title of Aunt rather than her full name.

The strategy that focused on the image of middle-class black women could imply that African Americans deserved rights only insofar as they resembled white middle-class women. It could serve to make invisible the conditions faced by the majority of African American women who were working class (Higginbotham 1993; Morton 1991; Palmer 1989). Concentrated in occupations like domestic and laundry work, they did the very work, as one African-American woman observed, that made possible the leisure time that allowed other women—white and black—to engage in reform work (McDougald 1925, 691). The YWCA's strategy of exposing white women to the "colored woman of exceptionally fine type" (Hammond 1917, 25) reflected class divisions found in both the African-American and white communities.

Derricotte left the YWCA in 1929 to become dean of women at Fisk University, an African-American college in Nashville. In 1930, YWCA members elected her to the YWCA's National Board. In late 1931, Juliette Derricotte died after an automobile accident (DuBois 1932; Wygal 1932a; Wygal 1932b). She had been traveling by car to avoid Jim Crow laws that forced African Americans to travel in segregated, unequal compartments aboard public transportation. Outside a small Georgia town, her car was struck by another vehicle, and she was injured. There were no medical facilities in town that were open to her because of her race, so she was driven more than fifty miles on back roads to the "colored hospital" in Chattanooga, where she ended up in an institution that did not have a full nursing staff and lacked such essentials as an x-ray machine. She died the following night.

White YWCA women had to respond not only to the loss of a colleague but also to the questions her death posed to a strategy for racial justice that emphasized the attitudes of individual whites toward African Americans. Most accounts of the accident by both African Americans and whites agreed that Derricotte had been treated with kindness by all. Her death, however, laid bare the conditions under which African Americans were forced to live, including those women whom these white women knew and referred to as colleagues. Segregation and the discrimination facing African Americans, they discovered, were the result of a "social pattern," not only of the attitudes of individual people (Wygal 1932a, 58). Her death indicated to them that the race problem clearly necessitated a social analysis or, in the words of the writer quoted above, justice, not only kindness, was required.

It would vastly overstate the significance of Derricotte's death to say that it caused all white YWCA women to convert to a prointegrationist stance. It did not. But for a group of white women involved in the leadership of the YWCA's national programs, it was one factor that encouraged them to turn toward political action in the 1930s. At the meeting of the YWCA's National Student Council in December 1931, some felt they could publicize the incident as "the reason we wish to work on the segregation problem" (YWCA/NSC 1931, 7). Juliette Derricotte's death made visible to white women what African-American women already knew: segregation was not merely an arrangement humiliating the spirit of black women (something that as Christian women they might be expected to endure and overcome), but a social condition that could have fatal consequences.

WOMEN'S WORK

Starting in the mid-1930s, white women in the YWCA began to support the legislative efforts for racial justice favored by groups like the NAACP and the National Council of Negro Women, including federal efforts to outlaw lynchings and the poll tax and to establish a permanent Fair Employment Practices Commission. This agenda was not actively supported by the secular, white-dominated women's groups like the General Federation of Women's Clubs, the American Association of University Women, and the National Woman's Party (Hartmann 1979, 1982; Rupp and Taylor 1990).

Many of these women's groups had focused their efforts on programs seen as more universal, such as Social Security and Aid to Dependent Children. Yet like much of the New Deal, many of the programs ignored the work that most African-American women actually did. Occupations like domestic and agricultural work were excluded from Social Security coverage and labor regulations. An African-American woman researching black women workers for the YWCA and the United States Women's Bureau observed that "about 9 in every 10 Negro women still were engaged in farm work or in domestic and personal service" (Brown 1941, 18). Representatives from the YWCA did, in fact, testify before Congress urging that Social Security coverage be extended to cover these occupations. Their efforts failed, yet programs that did not cover all people were still defined as universal. The distinction between what was seen as a race-specific agenda and what was defined as a general program marked the creation of the welfare state and continues in discussions of today's social policies.

The differing experiences that white and black women had with public agencies and programs prompted a different analysis of the relation between voluntary efforts and government to promote the public good. Examining the network of white women active in the Children's Bureau, one historian has observed that they favored public agencies over private voluntary groups to address social problems in part because these women got jobs in the agencies, but also because they perceived public agencies as being more reliable than private associations in delivering services (Muncy 1991, 99–100, 107–08). But the dependability of public programs for African Americans is challenged by the observation that exclusion of African Americans from governmental programs meant that African-American female social welfare reformers usually concentrated on "building private institutions" (Gordon 1991, 560–61). Clearly, white and black women could weigh the comparative merits of governmental and private efforts differently. The interracial composition of the YWCA and its members' increasing interest in racial issues may have been a factor that encouraged the organization to support both private and governmental means to social reform. In addition, as a membership organization, the YWCA supported political strategies that gave a role to a wide range of women (members could lobby their representatives and conduct surveys for the Women's Bureau as well as educate their communities) rather than focusing on the activism of a small group of white women in Washington.[18]

Historical analysis of the notions of gender that underlay most reformers' political and social efforts has demonstrated that white men and women alike promoted a family wage to

18. The limitations of public programs, however, should not be read as a case in favor of replacing governmental efforts with those of voluntary associations. White and black women in the YWCA argued for both private and political efforts to address the issue of social justice. YWCA members endorsed legislative and judicial action and worked with governmental agencies like the Women's Bureau to conduct studies of conditions for women. But they also continued to support the role of voluntary associations in educational efforts to address social and racial issues. For instance, in the 1950s, they developed materials to inform people about the implications of *Brown v. Board of Education* (Lynn 1992). A continued commitment to private as well as governmental efforts reflected a broad notion of what constituted politics but also gave the YWCA a reason to continue to be a political player rather than to assume that the government could or should take over all of its functions. See also Elisabeth Clemens's discussion of the relation between women's politics and their educational strategies (Clemens 1993, 783–84).

allow men to support their families and encouraged married women to stay home with their children (Gordon 1992, 48–49; Skocpol 1992, 408). Scholars are quick to acknowledge the racism implicit in programs that did not cover African Americans.[19] But as work on settlement houses suggests, many social programs were deliberately designed to keep black women, including married ones, in white homes as domestics in order to expose them to a proper home and help them to develop the values that would uplift their race (Crocker 1992, 77, 149). The disparity between the universal rhetoric and its race- and class-based implementation may have been a cynical ploy by white women to hold onto black labor. But there is a more profound analytical point here: in a nexus of race and gender, reformers and historians see some women (black women) as less womanly than others. Many supposedly universal descriptions and prescriptions for women — for example, women should stay home, supported by their husbands, and take care of children — turn out to be true for only some women. If the image of the mammy had kept many whites from seeing the New Negro woman, the belief that womanhood and motherhood were universal prevented acknowledgment of the profoundly variable social positions among women.

Although the supposed universal values of home and motherhood helped white women to recognize their duty to other women, they also served to mask the realities of many women's lives. When a white woman like Lily Hardy Hammond wrote of the "bond of a common womanhood," she meant the connection between "the privileged white women" and the "colored woman of exceptionally fine type" (Hammond 1917, 18, 25, 29). Most African-American women were not like the college-educated Juliette Derricotte, but rather were working-class or poor women. Those women, the mammy and the Aunt Josie, were supposed to ignore their own children in order to care for white children. The tension continues today in discussions that assume that day care is a women's issue without examining the competing interests between women who want day care to be affordable and those women who support themselves and their own children on what they earn from the work.[20] Both then and now, middle-class white women fail to see how their ability to be women engaging in meaningful work depends on the labor of other women. What white women do or want is seen as the goal for normal women, whereas African-American women's concerns are defined as racially specific.

19. Gordon, in particular, develops the contrast between white female reformers who advocated for needs-based programs and African-American women who created a rights-oriented vision of welfare (Gordon 1991).

20. Describing child care as a women's issue — whichever women — also relegates it to the private realm or, at best, to the world of special interests, rather than defining it as a political issue and part of the public good. Such a description also does not question the fact that men's ability to work is dependent on the availability of women, paid or unpaid, to provide child care.

"INCLUSION IN THE MAIN STREAM"

Even when white women in the YWCA came to accept the goal of integration, they — like most whites — imbued it with the assumption that their experiences were the norm.[21] The members passed the YWCA's Interracial Charter, which recommended the "inclusion of Negro women and girls in the main stream of Association life" at their convention in 1946 (YWCA 1946, 70). They did so under the assumption that black women and girls would integrate into their associations, that their world was the mainstream, that others could participate in it insofar as they, blacks, were like them, whites. As an anonymous white college student quoted in a study of YWCA interracial activities put it, "Some members of the Association itself will have to really accept the Negro girl as just another girl like herself — with nothing different but a darker complexion" (Wilkerson 1948, 111). The members referred to are clearly white members, and it is they who are the standard (that is, they are not described as just like the Negro girls only with a lighter skin). In this view, equality is possible only if there is sameness and sameness means being like the dominant group.

Even at the time, black YWCA women faulted the tendency of whites to treat minorities "as merely a 'plus' to a white group" (Lowry 1946, 2). There was little or no appreciation on the part of whites that African Americans had a culture and history of their own. Now, more than forty years after the Supreme Court made its ruling in *Brown v. Board of Education,* the continuing inability of white people in the United States to address the meaning of integration is connected to a legacy that views their racial identity as the norm.[22] As Craig Calhoun points out, we have little sense of how to unite except around sameness (Calhoun, in this volume), regardless of whether this sameness is illusory.

CONCLUSION

The competing stories about the YWCA point to its importance, at times its uniqueness, as a space for women's interracial struggle and cooperation. Placing accounts by white and African-American women together reveals the complexities of cooperation between different social groups. Each group

21. By the late 1940s, the consensus among whites — or at least white liberals — that segregation was legitimate was breaking down. Both the YMCA and the Federal Council of Churches challenged segregation shortly after the YWCA did in 1946 (Haynes 1946; Mjagkij 1994). Jackie Robinson joined major league baseball in 1947. The Association of University Women desegregated in 1949 (Leone 1989). The Armed Forces of the United States began to desegregate in 1948–49 (Berry and Blassingame 1982).

22. At least one observer of the Clarence Thomas hearings has observed that some conservative African Americans held it "a media triumph for the race" because the audience was exposed to "a succession of articulate, well-dressed blacks rather than the crack-dealing, violent criminals or homeless derelicts common to the six o'clock news!" (Thelwell 1992, 117).

cooperated for different reasons and had access to varying amounts of power, making cooperation an arena for struggle over its meaning and desired outcome. Examining the racial underpinnings of white women's views of womanhood and black women reminds us that white women belong to a race.

At a time when most white-dominated women's groups neither encouraged African-American women to participate nor addressed racial problems, the YWCA represented an alternative social space for women of different backgrounds and racial identities to work and struggle to advance their visions of a better society. White YWCA members as well as black women joined the civil rights movement beginning in the 1950s and, later, the women's movement. The bridge between the woman's movement of the first part of the twentieth century and the women's liberation movement of the last part can be found not in explicitly political groups like the League of Women Voters or the women's divisions of political parties but rather in voluntary associations (Chafe 1980; Evans 1980; Lynn 1992). A restricted conceptualization of voluntary associations as private and sharply delineated from the public (or from government) limits our understanding of the political struggles necessary to promote the public good.

Asking whether black women were empowered or co-opted in the YWCA can place one between the Scylla of romanticization and the Charybdis of victimization. At both the local and national levels, white women from the YWCA addressed the racial issues of their day, whether discussing the need for a black community center in a small city or testifying before Congress in behalf of expanded Social Security legislation or anti-lynching laws. Some white women's involvement in racial issues in and out of the YWCA in the 1930s and 1940s suggests that they *were* transformed by their exposure to African-American women. We need not, however, romanticize their commitment to interracial work and racial reform. The power differential between white and black women ultimately meant that kindness or altruism was not sufficient to implement the requirements of justice.[23] White women may have been motivated by opportunism; after all, they could expect to be in control in a white-dominated group, and speaking on behalf of an interracial group gave

them legitimacy in the larger political arena, particularly at a time when race was becoming a more important political issue.[24] But they needed African-American women's continuing presence in their association to have this authority.

Black women obtained some leverage by insisting that white women in the YWCA consider or take on various projects and issues related to race. The willingness of some African-American women to remain in the YWCA suggests that they found something of value in its interracial programs.[25] To cast the story only as one of co-optation and social control renders invisible what African-American women accomplished. They along with their white allies struggled to make the association more responsive to racial issues even while most white women overlooked their concerns.[26] In Brian Smith's phrasing, they empowered themselves (Smith, in this volume).

Racial privilege allowed white women in the YWCA to remain silent about their race. Their ability not to explicitly identify themselves in racial terms was rooted in their political and social power: the power to be seen as normal. Contemporary scholars have sometimes treated white women's silence about race as meaning that white women articulated a gender identity unaffected by race (a pure feminism as opposed to a black feminism, and so forth). But the goals and motivations of white women were as racially based as those of African-American women. When they described what women did or should do, they frequently meant white women. To regard white women's silence about their race as meaning that it was insignificant in their lives is to replicate a political relationship that defined them as normal and other women as somehow different. And ultimately, they were not so silent; they articulated assumptions about their own racial identity in their discussions of other people's identities. They regarded Juliette Derricotte as "such a fine woman" because her education and refinement mirrored what they expected of themselves.

As I suggested at the beginning of this chapter, we need to ask ourselves, Whose story are we hearing or telling? Whose interests are seen as universal and part of the public good?

23. The distinction between altruism and justice was powerfully conveyed by the social gospel theologian Washington Gladden in his autobiographical *Recollections*, written at the end of his life. In his history of the social gospel, Ronald C. White, Jr., summed up Gladden's analysis: "Dominant in the *Recollections* was Gladden's understanding of the universe as based on morality and the kingdom of God as based on justice. Relationships between people, Gladden argued, are to be placed within this context and cannot be based on altruism, which makes justice something to be dispensed by a beneficent individual or society rather then rooted in the moral fabric of society itself. This kind of analysis was the basis for Gladden's contention that the Social Gospel must move beyond charity to justice. Charity, which is too beholden to the good offices of the giver, does not address the root problems in modern urban and industrial society" (White 1990, 146).

24. Both Robyn Muncy and Deborah Gray White remind us, however, that when women were forced to base their claim for respect or power on the backs of other women, this problem reflected the discrimination they encountered from the larger society (Muncy 1991, xv; White 1993, 264).

25. African-American women mentioned the leadership skills they had gained in the YWCA; many subsequently prominent black women had some experience with the YWCA. Crystal Bird Fauset, the first black female state legislator, and Elizabeth Ross Haynes, social researcher and political appointee, were just two of the African-American women who had worked for the YWCA early in their careers. Their ability to use their political positions on behalf of their race meant that their personal gain was not necessarily distinct from the good of their race.

26. The middle-class black women active in the YWCA also had some power as the representatives of the needs of working-class black women; for a discussion of this issue in a larger context, see White 1993.

Whose are seen as particularistic or special or private? As Jane Mansbridge advises, these are contested terms (Mansbridge, in this volume). But it is not only that there are several stories and competing definitions at play in every historical retelling. Some groups have more power than others, and their history is the one told more often. And beyond that, it is frequently history without modifiers. We learn about American history in classes and textbooks but have to go to specific places to learn women's history or African-American history. Just as introducing the activities of women's associations into the analysis of the welfare state requires challenging the periodization and characterization of conventional politics and government, so, too, examining the activities and visions of African Americans forces rethinking assessments of the style of women's activism and the goals, accomplishments, and limitations of women's voluntary associations.

REFERENCES

Atwood, J. Howell. 1946. *The Racial Factor in YMCA's: A Report on Negro-White Relationships in Twenty-four Cities.* New York: Association Press.

Baker, Paula. 1984. "The Domestication of Politics: Women and American Political Society, 1780–1920." *American Historical Review* 89(3):620–47.

Bell, Juliet O., and Helen J. Wilkins. 1944. *Interracial Practices in Community Y.W.C.A.'s.* New York: Woman's Press.

Berry, Mary Frances, and John W. Blassingame. 1982. *Long Memory: The Black Experience in America.* New York: Oxford University Press.

Boyd, Nancy. 1986. *Emissaries: The Overseas Work of the American YWCA, 1895–1970.* New York: Woman's Press.

Brown, Jean Collier. 1941. "The Negro Woman Worker." *Aframerican Woman's Journal* 2(2 & 3):18–25.

Calkins, Gladys Gilkey. 1960. "The Negro in the Young Women's Christian Association: A Study of the Development of the YWCA Interracial Policies and Practices in Their Historical Setting." M.A. thesis, George Washington University.

"Carol Moseley-Braun Makes Victorious Stand in Senate Against Confederate Flag." 1993. *Jet* 84 (August 9, 1993): 4–6.

Caute, David. 1978. *The Great Fear: The Anti-Communist Purge under Truman and Eisenhower.* New York: Simon and Schuster.

Chafe, William H. 1980. *Civilities and Civil Rights: Greensboro, North Carolina, and the Black Struggle for Freedom.* New York: Oxford University Press.

Clemens, Elisabeth S. 1993. "Organizational Repertoires and Institutional Change: Women's Groups and the Transformation of U.S. Politics, 1890–1920." *American Journal of Sociology* 98(4):755–98.

Congressional Record. 1923a. 67th Congress. 4th session. v.64, pt.2 (January 9, 1923).

Congressional Record. 1923b. 67th Congress. 4th session. v.64, pt.5 (February 28, 1923).

Cott, Nancy F. 1989. "What's in a Name? The Limits of 'Social Feminism'; or, Expanding the Vocabulary of Women's History." *Journal of American History* 76(3):809–29.

Crocker, Ruth Hutchinson. 1992. *Social Work and Social Order: The Settlement Movement in Two Industrial Cities, 1889–1930.* Urbana: University of Illinois Press.

Davis, Elizabeth Lindsay, comp. 1933. *Lifting as They Climb: The National Association of Colored Women.* [Washington: NACW].

Dilling, Elizabeth Kirkpatrick. 1936. *The Roosevelt Red Record and Its Background.* Self-published.

DuBois, W. E. B. 1932. "Dalton, Georgia." *Crisis* 39(3):85–87.

Dyer, Richard. 1988. "White." *Screen* 29(4):44–64.

Evans, Sara. 1980. *Personal Politics: The Roots of Women's Liberation in the Civil Rights Movement and the New Left.* New York: Vintage Books.

Frankenberg, Ruth. 1993. *White Women, Race Matters: The Social Construction of Whiteness.* Minneapolis: University of Minnesota Press.

Gates, Henry Louis, Jr. 1988. "The Trope of a New Negro and the Reconstruction of the Image of the Black." *Representations* 24:129–55.

Giddings, Paula. 1984. *When and Where I Enter: The Impact of Black Women on Race and Sex in America.* New York: William Morrow.

Goodman, James. 1994. *Stories of Scottsboro.* New York: Pantheon Books.

Gordon, Linda. 1991. "Black and White Visions of Welfare: Women's Welfare Activism, 1890–1945." *Journal of American History* 78(2):559–90.

———. 1992. "Social Insurance and Public Assistance: The Influence of Gender in Welfare Thought in the United States, 1890–1935." *American Historical Review* 97(1):19–54.

———. 1993. "Gender, State, and Society: A Debate with Theda Skocpol" and "Response to Theda Skocpol." *Contention* 2(3):139–56, 185–89.

Hall, Jacquelyn Dowd. 1979. *Revolt against Chivalry: Jessie Daniel Ames and the Women's Campaign against Lynching.* New York: Columbia University Press.

Hammond, [Lily Hardy]. 1917. *Southern Women and Racial Adjustment.* [Lynchburg, Vir.: J. P. Bell/John Slater Fund].

Hartmann, Susan M. 1979. "Women's Organizations during World War II: The Interaction of Class, Race, and Feminism." In *Woman's Being, Woman's Place: Female Identity and Vocation in American History,* ed. Mary Kelley, 313–28. Boston: G. K. Hall.

———. 1982. *The Home Front and Beyond: American Women in the 1940s.* Boston: Twayne Publishers.

Haynes, George Edmund. 1946. "Along the Interracial Front." *New York Age* (April 6, 1946): 6.

Higginbotham, Evelyn Brooks. 1993. *Righteous Discontent: The Woman's Movement in the Black Baptist Church.* Cambridge: Harvard University Press.

Holt, Thomas C. 1986. "Introduction: Whither Now and Why?" In *The State of Afro-American History: Past, Present and Future,* ed. Darlene Clark Hine, 1–10. Baton Rouge: Louisiana State University Press.

hooks, bell. 1992. *Black Looks: Race and Representation.* Boston: South End Press.

Hopkins, [Charles] Howard. 1951. *History of the Y.M.C.A. in North America.* New York: Association Press.

Jacks, Jno. W. 1895. Letter to Florence Balgarnie. March 19, 1895. (reprinted) [Mary Church Terrell Papers. Box 102–2.

Folder 46. Manuscript Division, Moorland-Spingarn Research Center, Howard University].

Johnson, James Weldon. 1923. "Views and Review: The 'Black Mammy' Monument." *New York Age* (January 6, 1923): 4.

Jones, Adrienne Lash. 1990a. *Jane Edna Hunter: A Case Study of Black Leadership, 1910–1950.* Brooklyn: Carlson Publishing.

Jones, Beverly Washington. 1990b. *Quest for Equality: The Life and Writings of Mary Eliza Church Terrell, 1863–1954.* Brooklyn: Carlson Publishing.

Kelly-Gadol, Joan. 1976. "The Social Relation of the Sexes: Methodological Implications of Women's History." *Signs* 1(4):809–23.

Kerlin, Robert T. 1920. "Good-by, Black Mammy." In his *The Voice of the Negro, 1919,* 29. New York: Dutton.

Kessler-Harris, Alice. 1993. "Women and Welfare: Public Interventions in Private Lives." *Radical History Review* 56:127–36.

Koven, Seth, and Sonya Michel. 1990. "Womanly Duties: Maternalist Politics and the Origins of Welfare States in France, Germany, Great Britain, and the United States, 1880–1920." *American Historical Review* 95(4):1076–1108.

Lasch-Quinn, Elisabeth. 1993. *Black Neighbors: Race and the Limits of Reform in the American Settlement House Movement, 1890–1945.* Chapel Hill: University of North Carolina Press.

Leffall, Dolores. 1982. "Juliette [Aline] Derricotte." In *Dictionary of American Negro Biography,* ed. Rayford W. Logan and Michael R. Winston, 174. New York: Norton.

Lemons, J. Stanley. 1973. *The Woman Citizen: Social Feminism in the 1920s.* Urbana: University of Illinois Press.

Leone, Janice. 1989. "Integrating the American Association of University Women, 1946–1949." *Historian* 51(3):423–45.

Lerner, Gerda, ed. 1973. *Black Women in White America: A Documentary History.* New York: Vintage.

Lowry, Genevieve. 1946. Memorandum to Mrs. J. Ross Tuttle. May 24, 1946. YWCA papers. Sophia Smith Collection, Smith College.

Lynn, Susan. 1992. *Progressive Women in Conservative Times: Racial Justice, Peace, and Feminism, 1945 to the 1960s.* New Brunswick, N.J.: Rutgers University Press.

[MacBrady, John E.], ed. 1900. *A New Negro for a New Century.* Chicago: American Publishing House.

McCarthy, Kathleen D. 1982. *Noblesse Oblige: Charity and Cultural Philanthropy in Chicago, 1849–1929.* Chicago: University of Chicago Press.

———. 1990. "Parallel Power Structures: Women and the Voluntary Sphere." In *Lady Bountiful Revisited: Women, Philanthropy, and Power,* ed. Kathleen D. McCarthy, 1–31. New Brunswick, N.J.: Rutgers University Press.

McDougald, Elise Johnson. 1925. "The Double Task: The Struggle of Negro Women for Sex and Race Emancipation." *Survey Graphic* 53(11):689–91.

McDowell, John Patrick. 1982. *The Social Gospel in the South: The Woman's Home Mission Movement in the Methodist Episcopal Church, South, 1886–1939.* Baton Rouge: Louisiana State University Press.

McGrory, Mary. 1993. "Freshman Turns Senate Scarlet." *Washington Post* (July 27, 1993): A2.

"Miss Bowles, Y Secretary, Made Survey of Association Work on the Pacific Coast." 1923. *New York Age* (August 4, 1923): 2.

Mjagkij, Nina. 1994. *Light in the Darkness: African Americans and the YMCA, 1852–1946.* Lexington: University of Kentucky Press.

Morton, Patricia. 1991. *Disfigured Images: The Historical Assault on Afro-American Women.* New York: Praeger.

Muncy, Robyn. 1991. *Creating a Female Dominion in American Reform, 1890–1935.* New York: Oxford University Press.

Myrdal, Gunnar. 1944. *An American Dilemma: The Negro Problem and Modern Democracy.* New York: Harper and Bros.

Neverdon-Morton, Cynthia. 1989. *Afro-American Women of the South and the Advancement of the Race, 1895–1925.* Knoxville: University of Tennessee Press.

Palmer, Phyllis. 1989. *Domesticity and Dirt: Housewives and Domestic Servants in the United States, 1920–1945.* Philadelphia: Temple University Press.

Parkhurst, Jessie W. 1938. "The Role of the Black Mammy in the Plantation Household." *Journal of Negro History* 23(3): 349–69.

"Rival's 'Mammy' Statue Arouses Artist's Wrath." 1923. *Washington Post* (June 28, 1923): 2.

Rockefeller, Abby A. 1924. Letter to Mary A. Lindsley. November 11, 1924. Rockefeller Family archives. R.G. 2. Abby Aldrich Rockefeller series. Box 28. Dodge Hotel folder. Rockefeller Archive Center.

Roediger, David R. 1991. *The Wages of Whiteness: Race and the Making of the American Working Class.* New York: Verso.

Rossman, Parker. 1983. "Seeking a Dynamic Student Christian Movement: A Conversation with Fern Babcock Grant." *Christian Century* 100(12):373–75.

Rouse, Jacqueline Anne. 1989. *Lugenia Burns Hope: Black Southern Reformer.* Athens: University of Georgia Press.

Rupp, Leila J., and Verta Taylor. 1990. *Survival in the Doldrums: The American Women's Rights Movement, 1945 to the 1960s.* Columbus: Ohio State University Press.

Salem, Dorothy. 1990. *To Better Our World: Black Women in Organized Reform, 1890–1920.* Brooklyn: Carlson Publishing.

Scott, Anne Firor. 1991. *Natural Allies: Women's Associations in American History.* Urbana: University of Illinois Press.

Scott, Joan W. 1986. "Gender: A Useful Category of Historical Analysis." *American Historical Review* 91(5):1053–75.

Sims, Mary S. 1936. *The Natural History of a Social Institution—The Young Women's Christian Association.* New York: Woman's Press.

———. 1950. *The YWCA—An Unfolding Purpose.* New York: Woman's Press.

———. 1969. *The Purpose Widens, 1947–1967.* New York: National Board of the Young Women's Christian Association of the U.S.A.

Sitkoff, Harvard. 1978. *A New Deal for Blacks: The Emergence of Civil Rights as a National Issue,* vol. 1, *The Depression Decade.* New York: Oxford University Press.

Sklar, Kathryn Kish. 1985. "Hull House in the 1890s: A Community of Women Reformers." *Signs* 10(4):658–77.

Skocpol, Theda. 1992. *Protecting Soldiers and Mothers: The Political Origins of Social Policy in the United States.* Cambridge: Harvard University Press.

———. 1993. "Soldiers, Workers, and Mothers: Gendered Identities in Early U.S. Social Policy." *Contention* 2(3):157–83.

Spelman, Elizabeth V. 1988. *Inessential Woman: Problems of Exclusion in Feminist Thought.* Boston: Beacon Press.

Taylor, Frances Sanders. 1984. " 'On the Edge of Tomorrow': Southern Women, the Student YWCA, and Race, 1920–1944." Ph.D. dissertation, Stanford University.

Thelwell, Michael. 1992. "False, Fleeting, Perjured Clarence: Yale's Brightest and Blackest Go to Washington." In *Racing Justice, En-gendering Power: Essays on Anita Hill, Clarence Thomas, and the Construction of Social Reality,* ed. Toni Morrison, 86–126. New York: Pantheon Books.

Thompson, E. P. [1963] 1966. *The Making of the English Working Class.* New York: Vintage.

Thurber, Cheryl. 1992. "The Development of the Mammy Image and Mythology." In *Southern Women: Histories and Identities,* ed. Virginia Bernhard, Betty Brandon, Elizabeth Fox-Genovese, and Theda Perdue, 87–108. Columbia: University of Missouri Press.

Ware, Susan. 1981. *Beyond Suffrage: Women in the New Deal.* Cambridge: Harvard University Press.

———. 1987. *Partner and I: Molly Dewson, Feminism, and New Deal Politics.* New Haven: Yale University Press.

Ware, Vron. 1992. *Beyond the Pale: White Women, Racism and History.* New York: Verso.

White, Deborah Gray. 1993. "The Cost of Club Work, the Price of Black Feminism." In *Visible Women: New Essays in American Activism,* ed. Nancy A. Hewitt and Suzanne Lebsock, 247–69. Urbana: University of Illinois Press.

White, Ronald C., Jr. 1990. *Liberty and Justice for All: Racial Reform and the Social Gospel (1877–1925).* New York: Harper and Row.

Wilkerson, Yolanda B. 1948. *Interracial Programs of Student YWCA's.* New York: Woman's Press.

Williams, Walter E. 1993. "A Minority View: Social Parasites vs. Us." *New Pittsburgh Courier* (November 27, 1993): A6.

Wilson, Grace H. 1933. *The Religious and Educational Philosophy of the Young Women's Christian Association: A Historical Study of the Changing Religious and Social Emphases of the Association as They Relate to Changes in its Educational Philosophy and to Observable Trends in Current Religious Thought, Educational Philosophy, and Social Situations.* New York: Teachers College.

Work, Monroe N. 1925. *Negro Year Book: An Annual Encyclopedia of the Negro, 1925–1926.* Tuskegee: Tuskegee Institute.

Wygal, Winnifred. 1932a. "The Death of Miss Derricotte." *Christian Century* 49(2):58–59.

———. 1932b. "Juliette Derricotte: An Interpretation." *Crisis* 39(3):84–85.

Young Women's Christian Association. 1909. [cited as YWCA 1909]. *Report of the Proceedings of the Second Biennial Convention of the Young Women's Christian Associations of the United States of America, St. Paul, Minnesota, April 22–26, 1909.* New York: National Board of the YWCA.

———. 1946. [cited as YWCA 1946]. *Report of the Proceedings of the Seventeenth National Convention of the Young Women's Christian Associations of the United States of America, Atlantic City, New Jersey, March 2–8, 1946.* New York: National Board of the YWCA.

Young Women's Christian Association's National Student Council. 1931. [cited as YWCA/NSC 1931]. Report of Meeting of Headquarters Committee. December 9, 1931. YWCA papers. Sophia Smith Collection, Smith College.

Zald, Mayer N. 1970. *Organizational Change: The Political Economy of the YMCA.* Chicago: University of Chicago Press.

14

J. CRAIG JENKINS

Channeling Social Protest: Foundation Patronage of Contemporary Social Movements

Foundation patronage of social movements has long been a lightning rod of political controversy in the United States. Conservative critics have argued that allowing foundations to contribute to social causes constitutes a tax subsidy of private political expression and stirs up baseless grievances, thereby weakening respect for public authority (Brownfield 1969; Hart 1973; Metzger 1979; McLlaney 1980; Bennett and DiLorenzo 1985). Leftist critics have also been skeptical, questioning the altruism of funders and the effectiveness of foundation patronage. According to these critics, social movement philanthropy is a type of "gilted guilt" that allows the wealthy to retain private control while "cooling out" social movements that might otherwise bring about major social changes (Arnove 1980; Wilson 1983; Roelofs 1983, 1987; *New Republic* December 8, 1986). Even moderate sympathizers have questioned foundations' methods of se-

This paper benefited from the comments of Lis Clemens, Woody Powell, Debra Minkoff, Robert Bothwell, Susan Ostrander, David Brown, and the participants in the conference "Private Action and the Public Good." The research on social movement funding and movement actions was assisted by Craig Eckert and Abbey Halcli. Doug McAdam provided the social movement action counts that Craig Eckert and I extended to capture movement development. Financial help was provided by the National Endowment for the Humanities, the Russell Sage Foundation, the Program on Non-Profit Organizations at Yale University, and the National Committee for Responsive Philanthropy.

lecting projects, arguing that foundations need to ensure that there is significant support before funding social change projects (Moynihan 1969; Simon 1973).

At the center of these controversies is the nature of the public interest in a democratic polity. Is upper-class patronage of social movements compatible with Americans' conception of democratic government and politics? Defenders of social movement philanthropy contend that patronage strengthens democratic institutions by providing voice for underrepresented interests and excluded groups. By giving resources to social movement organizations that represent the underrepresented and promote broader citizen participation, these foundations are seen as creating a more open and democratic political and social system. The critics contend instead that it allows a self-designated wealthy elite to promote their own definitions of desirable social change while remaining unaccountable to either the general public or the constituencies they claim to be helping.

The starting point for this discussion, then, is the meaning of democracy and its relationship to conceptions of the public good. Theories of democracy fall into three general camps: (1) a *representation model*, which focuses on the accountability of political leaders; (2) a *participation model*, which emphasizes direct involvement in decision making by those affected by the decisions; and (3) a *descriptive model*, which targets parity between the social makeup of the com-

206

munity and the characteristics of decisionmakers (Pitkin 1967; MacFarland 1984, 93–107).

The representation model is also known as pluralism, polyarchy, or democratic elitism. Its central tenet is that competition among elites, and the organization of significant social interests, constrains elites' actions and thereby ensures public accountability. The public good, then, is a procedural question of ensuring voice for the various private interests in society and restraining the self-interested behavior of political elites. Foundation patronage of social movements is justified insofar as it provides voice for unorganized interests and ensures that elite behavior is constrained by that voice.

The participatory model, also known as grassroots or participatory democracy, similarly takes a procedural approach but emphasizes direct, face-to-face discussion among equal citizens in the resolving of political issues. The public good is served by maximizing direct participation in collective decision making. Foundation patronage, then, is warranted insofar as it furthers such grassroots participation and reduces social inequalities that impede such participation. Grassroots participation by members of the social movements in philanthropic decision making is a direct extension of this model of democracy.

The descriptive model focuses on the match (or mismatch) between the social groups in the community and the social characteristics of decision makers. If these are significantly out of balance, then elites are unrepresentative, that is, undemocratic. Measures to ensure demographic representation on philanthropic boards and to incorporate excluded groups into decision making are central to this perspective. Because descriptive democracy is often seen as a device for ensuring voice and grassroots participation, it is often combined with the other two models.

This chapter raises two questions about social movement philanthropy. First, why are foundations involved in funding social movements at all? Are these wealthy patrons responding to their private definitions of the public good or are they altruistic citizens providing voice and participatory access to the disadvantaged? Second, what is the impact of this philanthropy on social movements? Does it create and strengthen them, especially those representing new voices and mobilizing grassroots participation? Or does it respond to such grassroots challenges in ways that co-opt and "defang" them? Is social movement philanthropy compatible with Americans' ideas about democratic government and politics? In addressing these questions, I focus on foundation funding of progressive social movements in recent American politics.

THE NATURE OF
SOCIAL MOVEMENT PHILANTHROPY

A first step in addressing these questions is simply to gauge the nature and scope of social movement philanthropy. Past discussions have relied on anecdotal accounts with little systematic information about the scope or the types of projects

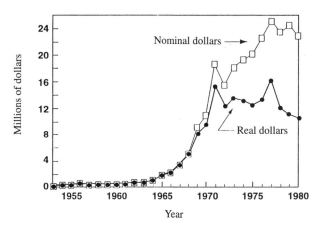

Figure 14.1. Trends in Social Movement Philanthropy

being funded. This has allowed critics to draw elaborate portraits of social movement philanthropy without the discipline of systematic evidence. To capture the nature of social movement philanthropy, I examined the giving programs of all foundations that I could identify as having awarded a grant to a social movement organization between 1953 and 1980.[1] This generated a list of 130 foundations, including 102 private foundations, 16 public charities, 6 corporate foundations, 5 community foundations, and 1 operating foundation.

By a *social movement,* I mean any planned attempt to bring about institutional change by organizing or representing the collective interests of some disadvantaged or underrepresented group. This excluded service projects that assist individuals and efforts that are not focused on institutional change. It also excluded institutionalized organizations like churches and universities that have become involved in social movement projects. Over the period examined, foundation giving to movement projects grew steadily from $85,700 in 1953 to a peak of $25.2 million in 1977 (fig. 14.1). After that it remained essentially stable through 1980. Adjusted for

1. This list began with the members of the National Network of Grantmakers, an association of progressive funders which encourages social movement funding along with nontraditional philanthropy (Shellow 1981). Additions were made from Richard Parker's (1983) list of progressive funders and suggestions by movement leaders and foundation directors. In a recent restudy of social movement philanthropy in 1990, I found 146 foundations active in the area. This restudy listing consisted of combining the earlier list with the foundations in the third edition of *The Grant-Seekers Guide* (Shellow 1987). This slightly enlarged pool of funders contributed $88,070,000 toward social movement projects. When compared with the $22,863,000 contributed in 1980, this indicates a remarkable growth in social movement philanthropy during the 1980s. If we convert these into constant (i.e., deflated) dollars, there was a 200 percent increase over the 1980s in total social movement giving. Still, this constitutes overall but a small percent of total foundation giving. In 1990, social movement philanthropy constituted only 1.1 percent of total foundation giving, and, in 1980, constituted 0.8 percent. For earlier attempts to estimate the scale of social movement philanthropy, see Carey (1977) and Tully (1977).

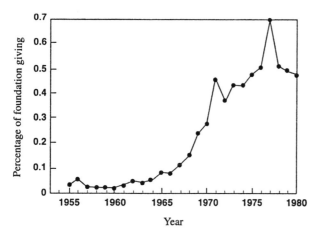

Figure 14.2. Movement Grants as a Percent of Total Foundation Giving

inflation, the high point in giving came in 1977, when it constituted a mere 0.69 percent of total foundation giving (fig. 14.2).

If foundation giving to social movements is so small a part of total donations, then why has it been so controversial? The average social movement grant during the period studied was $24,534, roughly enough to support one full-time organizer for a year. More than a third of the grants were less than $10,000, meaning that movements had to either secure multiple grants or have alternative sources of support to operate. In addition to being criticized for its populist image as the strong arm of arrogant, unaccountable elites, social movement philanthropy has come under fire because of its political potential. Even small amounts of money can make a major difference to a social movement by providing such technical resources as facilities for national conferences or professional staff. Such resources are the coin of established political institutions and, as such, are critical to movements in their efforts to mobilize and gain political voice.

Foundation support is also generally a source of special project money which cannot be easily replaced by other sources and frequently carries few restrictions on program operation. Foundations typically give money with the simple restriction that it be spent legally; they rarely become involved in operational details. Some movement organizations are financially dependent on foundation patronage. The National Association for the Advancement of Colored People (NAACP), for example, relies on foundation grants to make up more than half of its national budget, chiefly through its Special Contribution Fund. Local movement groups like women's rape crisis centers and neighborhood organizations often depend on foundations for a third or more of their funding. Without this funding, these organizations would be considerably weakened, and some would cease to exist.

What has been the focus of social movement grants? We need to distinguish between *empowerment movements,*

which attempt to alter the distribution of power by organizing previously unorganized and underrepresented groups such as racial minorities and women, and *public interest movements,* which pursue broad collective goods, such as peace, a clean environment, or consumer rights. Table 14.1 provides a general breakdown of the issues raised by these movements. Racial minorities were the largest single recipient of foundation support, receiving 30 percent of all grants and a little more than 40 percent of the total amount of money. Economic justice projects, which focused on the interests of the poor and the working class, received about 16 percent of the grants and roughly 19 percent of the funding. Other disadvantaged groups, such as women, children, and the handicapped, received another 15 percent of the grants. Public interest movements received about 35 percent of the grants and 25 percent of the money. In general, the largest grants went to such unorganizable constituencies as children and the handicapped, which averaged $48,794 and $35,371, respectively. Controversial movements like antinuclear activism, homosexual rights, and the peace movement received fewer and smaller grants. The antinuclear activists, for example, received less than 2 percent of the grants, which averaged around $5,714; homosexual activists got about 0.5 percent of the grants, for an average of $3,121; and peace activists got less than 5 percent of the grants, averaging $9,532.

The foundations have also favored a specific style of movement organizing. Borrowing from John McCarthy and Mayer Zald's (1987) discussion of professional social movements, I distinguish between *indigenous movement organizations,* which are involved in face-to-face organizing and which derive their resources primarily from their proclaimed beneficiaries, and *professional movement organizations,* which are staff-driven, derive their resources from institutions and isolated constituencies, and "speak for" rather than organize their official beneficiaries. Among the latter, I distinguish between *advocacy organizations,* which emphasize legal and political advocacy, and *technical support organizations,* which provide such services as research and publicity or training for community organizers. Because the technical support organizations often service local indigenous groups, they often function as "movement halfway houses" to organizers involved with indigenous movement organizations (Morris 1984). The empowerment movements are typically centered around indigenous organizations, while the public interest movements are organized around professional organizations. Of the movement grants studied here, 23 percent of the money went to indigenous organizations while 32.1 and 37.4 percent went to advocacy and technical support organizations, respectively.[2] Another 7.5 percent of the money

2. In terms of grant dollars, the professional emphasis was slightly greater, with 16.5 percent going to indigenous movement organizations, 42.6 percent to advocacy groups, and 32.9 to technical support organizations. Another 8 percent went to institutionalized groups.

Table 14.1. The Distribution of Social Movement Grants

Social Movement Projects	Number of Grants	Percent	Grant Amount	Percent	Mean Grant
Racial Minorities					
African Americans	1,819	18.02	$ 56,895,243	22.97	$31,278
Mexican Americans	271	2.68	15,833,677	6.39	58,427
Native Americans	310	3.07	9,095,165	3.67	29,339
Puerto Ricans	101	1.00	3,358,537	1.36	33,252
Asian Americans	91	.90	593,626	.24	6,523
Minorities in general	458	4.54	15,021,604	6.06	32,798
Total	3,050	30.21	100,797,852	40.69	33,048
Ethnic Groups					
Appalachians	147	1.46	2,309,105	.93	15,708
White ethnics	4	.04	14,250	.01	3,563
Total	151	1.50	2,323,355	.94	15,386
Economic Justice					
Poor people's advocacy	192	1.90	3,361,750	1.36	17,509
Working-class advocacy	1,461	14.47	43,863,775	17.71	30,023
Total	1,653	16.37	47,225,525	19.07	28,570
Other Groups					
Women's rights	949	9.40	16,602,912	6.70	17,495
Children's advocacy	250	2.48	12,198,503	4.92	48,794
Prisoners' rights	172	1.70	5,009,091	2.02	20,036
Handicapped rights	103	1.02	3,643,163	1.47	35,371
Aged advocacy	61	.60	668,819	.27	10,964
Homosexual rights	58	.57	181,005	.07	3,121
Total	1,593	15.77	38,303,493	15.45	24,045
Peace and World Order					
Student movement	53	.52	865,423	.35	16,329
Peace movement	502	4.97	4,785,003	1.93	9,532
Third world advocacy	101	1.00	250,610	.10	2,481
Veterans' rights	9	.09	18,200	.01	2,022
Total	665	6.58	5,919,236	2.39	8,901
Public Interest Movement					
Environmentalism	920	9.11	25,206,367	10.18	27,398
Antinuclear movement	192	1.90	1,097,078	.44	5,714
Consumer rights	675	6.69	12,779,896	5.16	18,933
Other public interest	1,147	11.36	13,836,904	5.59	12,064
Total	2,934	29.06	52,920,245	21.37	18,037
Unclassified	51	.51	231,400	.09	4,537
All grants	10,097	100.00	$247,489,706	100.00	24,511

went to established institutions, such as churches and universities, which served in turn as sponsors or close allies of movement projects.

Foundations' preference for these professional movement organizations stems from several considerations. First, these projects are relatively expensive and, for certain issues, essential. Children and consumers of auto insurance, for example, are unlikely to organize to represent their interests. So professional organization appears to be essential if these interests are to have voice. Indigenous organizations are able to organize their own support and are therefore viewed as less deserving. Many indigenous groups are not incorporated or are not legally tax-exempt public charities. They are therefore not legally eligible for foundation grants. Perhaps most important, this giving pattern reflects the political caution of social movement funders. Professional projects are typically organized hierarchically and directed by experienced, full-time managers who are likely to share the professional and social values of foundation executives and trustees. These organizations are sufficiently isomorphic with the hierarchical and professionalized organizations of the business and nonprofit world from which come foundation trustees and managers that these donors readily see them as being legitimate. Indigenous organizations, by contrast, often lack a track record and are more decentralized, relying on the voluntary contributions of local activists and part-time staff. They are less accountable to a central board or professional manager and more likely to become involved in protests and other actions that might stir criticism.

THREE STYLES OF
SOCIAL MOVEMENT PHILANTHROPY

The sources and impact of social movement philanthropy depend on the locus of foundation control. There are three types of foundation governance among movement funders: *family foundations, institutionalized foundations,* and *alternative foundations*. Each has a distinct style of giving with its own promise and pitfalls.

The traditional and overwhelmingly dominant form of movement philanthropy has been the family foundation in which an individual or family group rationalizes its tax-deductible giving by establishing a private foundation. Control remains in the family, which selects the causes or issues to which the foundation contributes. Many lack full-time or permanent staff, which ensures family control over the giving program.

In institutionalized foundations, the board of trustees has drifted out of family hands into those of a set of institutional elites who are chosen because of their special expertise, business success, notoriety, and prominence in national civic organizations and politics (see Nielsen 1972, 1985). Most of these foundations have professional staff, who assume a central role in identifying worthy projects and developing giving programs. This gives greater continuity and an emphasis on professional expertise to the giving program.

The alternative foundations, by contrast, are generally incorporated as public charities and are based on the philanthropy of a large number of donors. Their most distinctive trait is the incorporation of representatives of the movement community onto their giving board. Although donors sometimes remain on the board, these alternative foundations are experimenting with descriptive and participatory ideas about democracy, giving activists from the donee community a decisive say in actual grantmaking (see Ostrander 1993, 1995).

Of the 130 foundations considered here, 103, or 79.2 percent, were family foundations, 13 were institutional foundations, and 14 were alternative foundations.[3] The family foundations handed out the bulk of the grants: 72.4 percent of them. The institutional foundations made 8.5 percent of the grants, and the alternative funders made 19.1 percent. Because of major differences in endowments, however, the institutional foundations were much more significant when grant dollars are considered. The institutional foundations gave 39.1 percent of the total money, 58.9 percent came from the family foundations and a meagre 2 percent from the alternative funders. The mean institutional foundation grant was $112,708, while that for family foundations was only $19,969 and that for alternative funders only $2,592.

The major criticisms of movement philanthropy have been directed at the motives of the family and institutional foundations. Are they genuinely altruistic or are they really self-interested givers? As the chapters in this volume by Alan Wolfe and Jane Mansbridge point out, however, altruism and self-interest are not mutually exclusive. Altruism is ultimately rooted in self-interest, which means that self-interest inevitably shapes decisions about philanthropic "worthiness." Critics have played on confusions about the relationship between altruism and self-interest to argue that the family members and elites who dominate foundation boards are socially advantaged and therefore unable to act on the interests of disadvantaged groups. This has given rise to conflicts between the foundations and their donees, especially the empowerment movements. Foundation boards are inclined to emphasize charity in their view of social problems, identifying with the plight of disadvantaged groups or threatened populations. The social movements, by contrast, have taken a political perspective on these problems, advocating the empowerment of disadvantaged groups and the representation of underrepresented interests. Because the empowerment movements focus primarily on increasing the autonomy and power of disadvantaged groups, they have been the most likely to confront a tension between financial dependence

3. Family control was determined by the presence of a donor or family member on the board of directors of a private foundation in 1980. Institutional control depended on the absence of such representation. Grassroots funders are a select group of public charities which have banded together and identified themselves as an alternative to traditional philanthropy. Their most prominent statement is George Pillsbury's *Robin Hood Was Right* (1982), which articulates the rationale for this type of movement-controlled philanthropy. I also found 6 corporate foundations involved in movement philanthropy. They have been treated here as family foundations because they were associated with family-controlled corporations. Corporate philanthropy brings in the complication of public relations and advertising for name brand products, thus making inference about motive more complex. Nonetheless, they operate more akin to family foundations than institutional ones. I also found 5 community foundations which were treated as family foundations because their primary donors remained on the boards and directed funding priorities. In these cases, they were chartered as public charities but primary donors continued to determine grant priorities.

Table 14.2. The Funding Priorities of Social Movement Foundations

| | Percent of Movement Grant Dollars | | | |
	Indigenous Groups	Professional Advocacy Organizations	Technical Support Centers	Institutional Groups
Family foundations	21.1	34.2	37.0	7.7
Institutional foundations	17.1	40.6	29.7	12.6
Alternative foundations	32.8	20.5	42.7	4.0

and their aspirations. Hence, even when foundation boards and staff accept a political view of solutions, there is a strong possibility of resentment among the grant recipients, leading to charges of paternalism and insensitivity.

One of the most notable of these clashes was that between civil rights activists and the so-called white angels who early in the movement funded bail costs and legal support. The students in the Student Non-Violent Coordinating Committee (SNCC) were especially vocal about the contradiction between their black power ideology, which called for a "black-staffed, black-controlled and black-financed" empowerment movement, and their financial dependence on white, middle-class donors and foundations (Carson 1981, 197–98; Wofford 1980, 165). Similarly, the Congress for Racial Equality (CORE), which had been at the forefront of the freedom rides and voter registration efforts, experienced a major internal clash over the role of white funders and white staff, a conflict that eventually destroyed the organization (Meier and Rudwick 1973, 376–408). In this book, Nancy Robertson tells a similar story of the clash in worldviews between the upper- and middle-class white women in the YWCA who promoted "racial uplift" and the African-American women who had a broader empowerment agenda, including racial desegregation, as a major objective. The alternative foundations represent an as-yet small-scale attempt to eliminate this tension by giving movement activists direct control over the giving program.

A second, related criticism of these foundations has focused on the priorities of these supposedly unaccountable boards. Charging that their upper-class backgrounds make them unable to identify with the interests of the disadvantaged, the critics have argued that such insularity leads to a strong preference for professionalized projects and an avoidance of grassroots movement groups. In terms of grant-giving priorities, this should mean that family and institutional foundations have a set of priorities different from that of alternative foundations.

My grant data partially support this idea. The differences, however, are not as overwhelming as one might suspect. As shown in table 14.2, professional advocacy organizations were the leading recipients of grant money from the family and institutional foundations. They received 34.2 percent of the family foundation money and 40 percent of the institu-

tional grant money while getting only 21 percent of the alternative foundation funding. The difference in terms of funding of indigenous groups, however, was small. Family and institutional funders put about one-fifth of their money in grassroots groups whereas alternative foundations invested a third. There was not a vast difference in terms of funding of institutional recipients. Nor was there a large difference in the funding of technical support centers. The alternative foundations invested 40 percent of their money in support centers, while the other foundations invested between 30 and 37 percent of their money this way. One explanation is that the alternative foundations viewed technical support centers as having extensive grassroots ties. Because many of these centers provide technical services to local grassroots groups, they favor this type of funding because it reaches the broadest constituency. At the same time, however, the family and institutional foundations also saw these centers as major targets for funding. Overall, then, the differences are not as stark as one might expect.[4]

A third criticism of movement philanthropy has emphasized the financial limits of foundation support. Movement groups have frequently complained that foundations are unpredictable and unwilling to make sustained commitments. Movement grants are typically project grants rather than unrestricted operating grants. In response, the foundations have extolled the virtues of project grants, arguing that they minimize financial dependence and maximize the impact by complementing what movement groups can do on their own. In an early defense of social movement philanthropy, John Simon (1973) argued that foundations should impose a constituency test for movement grants, requiring evidence of a supportive

4. The pattern is slightly weaker if one looks at the number of movement grants. The family and institutional foundations invested 21.1 and 17.1 percent of their grants, respectively, in indigenous groups, while the alternative foundations put in 32.8 percent. Similarly, family and institutional foundations invested 34.2 and 40.6 percent of their grants, respectively, in professional advocacy organizations, while alternative foundations put in only 20 percent. In terms of technical support centers, family and institutional foundations invested 37 and 29.7 percent of their grants, respectively, while alternative foundations invested 42.7 percent. Finally, family and institutional foundations invested 7.8 and 12.6 percent of their grants, respectively, in institutional recipients, while alternative funders put in only 4 percent.

body of people before funding a controversial project. This would ensure the significance of the social need and the likelihood of follow-through on the project. Although the notion was framed as a principle to guide social movement philanthropy, its underlying assumption is that grants to indigenous groups will have the greatest social impact. Some also praise these groups because they are thought to minimize the likelihood of financial dependency. Even professional movement organizations have confronted this constituency test: the Natural Resources Defense Council, for example, was pressured by the Ford Foundation to launch a direct mail fund campaign to demonstrate broader public support for its efforts. This not only mobilizes more resources but also lends legitimacy to the claim that the professional movements speak for significant constituencies.

THE IMPACT OF SOCIAL MOVEMENT PHILANTHROPY: CO-OPTATION OR CHANNELING?

The most persistent charge against foundations has been that they co-opt the social movements, diverting activists into less militant, moderate projects. Some critics have claimed that such co-optation is intentional, while others have argued that it is simply an inadvertent by-product of social movement philanthropy. In the heat of the early civil rights movement, the journalist Louis Lomax claimed that the "white angels" who funded the initial voter education projects were "out to defang the civil rights movement" (1962, 284). By diverting the sit-in protestors into voter registration, he argued, the foundations were attempting to quell the protests and blunt the desegregation struggle. Other critics have contended that by funding professionalized advocacy, the foundations have created a corporatist system of political representation which allows elites to control who represents the unrepresented while simultaneously making the system appear responsive, thereby blunting dissent (Wilson 1983; Arnove 1980; Roelofs 1983, 1986). Even sympathizers of social movement philanthropy have pointed to the limits of professional movement organizations, arguing that public interest advocates lack the grassroots support and political leverage to ensure that their legal victories are effectively enforced (Handler 1978; McCann 1986; Rosenberg 1991).

At its core, the co-optation thesis is an argument about social movement professionalization. By *co-optation,* I mean the incorporation of movement personnel into elite-sponsored positions and the subsequent goal displacement and reduced militancy (Ash 1977, 14). By *social movement professionalization,* I mean the formation of professional movement organizations as well as the creation of permanent staff positions in indigenous organizations. In its strong form, the co-optation thesis entails three major claims. First, that the aim of the foundations is social control, which accounts for their funding of professionalized projects that are not militant and have moderate goals. Second (and related), that there is a positive *radical flank effect* (Haines 1988), meaning that

the timing of the funding is spurred by increases in the militancy and radicalism of the movements. The social movement funders respond to the political threat of increased militancy and radicalism by funding the moderate alternative. Third and most important, that the resulting professionalization siphons movement activists from grassroots organizing, thereby diverting them from their original goals and demobilizing the movements. In some formulations, this is an inadvertent by-product of foundation funding (Piven and Cloward 1977; McAdam 1982), while in others it is the primary intent of the funders (Roelofs 1983, 1987).

The co-optation thesis grossly oversimplifies the intent of social movement funders, which varies widely and combines genuine support for the movement groups with social control. It also seriously distorts the impact of movement funding, which has often been central to the realization of movement goals. It is most relevant in highlighting the importance of indigenous organizing as a spur to movement philanthropy and in pointing to the professionalizing impact of this funding.

A *channeling* thesis offers a better overall interpretation of social movement philanthropy. This thesis argues, first, that foundation goals are complex, ranging from genuine support of movement goals to social control. Because altruism is always embedded within a self-interest framework, movement support is inevitably constrained by political interests. Second, the thesis argues that the main impact of movement philanthropy has been professionalization, evident both in the growth of professional movement organizations and in the increasing professionalization of indigenous movement groups. Third, it argues that professionalization has frequently created greater mobilization and social movement success. Foundation support for the public interest movements has allowed movement entrepreneurs to advocate broad, diffuse interests that would otherwise go unrepresented. For the empowerment movements, the foundations have provided technical resources that have often helped consolidate social movement gains.

To begin with the question of foundation intent, an excellent test case is the foundation funding of voter education in the early civil rights movement. In response to the initial sit-in victories, the Kennedy administration convinced a group of private foundations with long-standing programs in race relations to fund the Voter Education Project (VEP). The Taconic, Norman, Field, and New York foundations initiated the effort, soon to be joined by several others. The Kennedy administration was concerned about the political backlash from the sit-ins and was interested in mobilizing African-American voters, who had provided the margin of victory in the presidential election of 1960 (Navasky 1971, 118–19). The foundations saw the new militancy as evidence of the deep-seatedness of the race problem and voter registration as a new device for addressing it. Funding for the VEP followed the radical flank pattern: rising militancy spurred funding of the moderate groups, especially the NAACP and a separate

VEP organization, while little funding went to the militants in SNCC and CORE (Haines 1988, esp. 82–99). There were also clear limits to the foundations' willingness to fund insurgency. When the militants adopted a black power position, the foundations cut off their support and boosted their investments in the moderates and a set of new professional advocacy organizations.

Voter education funding did not, however, blunt the movement's militancy. In spite of Robert Kennedy's foolish assessment that it would be less politically controversial ("How can anybody really get very mad because you're making an effort to make sure that everybody votes," quoted in Haines, 1988, 156), the voting campaign provoked massive white resistance, including terrorist attacks and a campaign of harassment against movement activists. Civil rights activists then organized mass protests and launched the Mississippi Freedom Democratic Party, which challenged the segregated regular delegation to the Democratic National Convention in 1964 (Carson 1981, 70–82, 96–110). Eventually this protest campaign, which included the March on Washington and major voter registration protests throughout the South, pressured the White House and Congress to attack the Jim Crow voting laws. In sum, voter education funding fueled the protest movement. Although the Kennedy administration and the foundations did not initially expect to fund mass protest or the resulting violent conflicts, they were committed to attacking racial discrimination and helping the civil rights protestors who made this their goal.

Professionalization has been the most direct impact of movement philanthropy. There has been a major growth in the number of professional movement organizations, including both professional advocacy and technical support centers. One consequence has been a major growth in the public interest movement, which has grown in terms of its visibility and organizational clout in national politics (Berry 1984; Schlozman and Tierney 1983). A second has been the increasing professionalization of indigenous social movements, which have hired permanent staff and turned to relying on institutional tactics like direct mail fund-raising and lobbying to influence public policy.

Professionalization has also led to significant movement successes. For the most part, it has worked to consolidate gains that were initiated by indigenous organizing and protests. In the civil rights movement, mass protests created pressure on the White House and Congress for federal intervention to protect African-American voting rights. Early voter education funding helped fuel this effort and, with the passage of the Civil Rights Acts of 1964 and 1965, the foundations perceived the field as clear for attacking the Jim Crow system and poured money into the Voter Education Project. By the early 1970s, the VEP had mobilized sufficient black voters in the Deep South to force significant improvements in urban services, employment opportunities, and the removal of formal racial barriers (Button 1989). Although considerable racial economic inequality and housing seg-

regation persist today and are growing outside the South (Jaynes and Williams 1989), there is evidence that professionalized legal advocacy has helped narrow the racial earnings gap (Burstein and Edwards 1994). Indigenous organizing and mass protests were the major source of the pressure that initiated these changes, but professionalization was also vital in providing the legal and organizational resources to ensure that the new civil rights laws were enforced and that movement gains did not erode.

What, then, explains the link between the growth of foundation funding in the late 1960s and the decline of mass protest in the early 1970s? This association has been viewed as causally central by proponents of the co-optation thesis. In an earlier study, I argued that this was largely due to movement successes and to the movement shift to intractable targets, such as school segregation and poverty, which were less amenable to protest tactics (Jenkins and Eckert 1986). Such blatant racial discrimination as the Jim Crow laws could readily be targeted by protest tactics, but more deep-seated problems, such as poverty and housing segregation, could not be as easily attacked by these measures. Activists gradually shifted to other tactics, including legal advocacy and community organizing, which required professionalization and relatively few mass protests. Protests did not entirely disappear, however, but rather shifted to a community level and thereby became less central to national politics during the later 1970s.

Foundation support and professionalization have been even more critical to the public interest movements. Because these movements pursue broad, "collective" goods which will accrue regardless of individual contributions — clean air, safe products, and accountable government, for example — there are few incentives for individuals to contribute. As a result, the movements confront major problems with free riders, that is, people who do not contribute, hoping to ride on the efforts of others. In such cases, professionalized advocacy, often supported by foundations and other institutional donors, is critical. The foundations have provided startup funding as well as project support for a wide range of these types of professionalized advocacy projects (Berry 1984; Walker 1991). The Natural Resources Defense Council, for example, was launched by several law professors at New York University and the editor of the *New York Times,* who were opposed to the proposed construction of the Storm King Power Plant on the Hudson River. The Ford Foundation linked them up with a group of Yale law students who were trying to set up an environmental law firm to litigate environmental law violations. Ford then provided the startup funding, which was later supplemented by direct mail fund-raising and other foundation grants (Adams 1974). Another group, the Environmental Defense Fund, started with a small, direct mail effort called the Rachel Carson Fund created by the Audubon Society. With concerted direct mail fund-raising and foundation grants, it grew into a major, science-directed environmental law firm. By the early 1980s, the environmental law movement had grown to more than a dozen firms and become a major actor in environmental policy, working to monitor and enforce environmental laws as well as to lobby for statutory and administrative changes.

If the co-optation thesis were valid, professional organizations would compete with indigenous organizations and displace them over time without contributing to lasting movement successes. This would indicate that they were driving the indigenous groups out of their niche and siphoning off the movement activists. The professional movement organizations, however, have largely been concentrated in the public interest movements, and there is little evidence of displacement. Instead, they have typically played a complementary support role in the empowerment movements, supplying legal defense and technical services to indigenous groups. In the public interest movements, they have constituted the core of movement action.

Drawing on content analysis of news stories abstracted in the *New York Times Annual Index,* I traced the types of movement actors for five major social movements between 1953 and 1980.[5] For the African-American civil rights and black power movements, professional organizations represented only 13.9 percent of the actions. Although foundation funding helped these professionals to grow to the point where they were responsible for almost a third of movement actions, indigenous groups still constituted more than two-thirds of movement activity. At the end of the 1970s, mass protests and indigenous activity were actually growing with the spread of school desegregation conflicts and disputes over city government. In the women's movement, only 7.5 percent of the activity was by professional organizations and, despite an overall decline in reported movement actions in the late 1970s, more than 90 percent remained indigenously based. In the peace and student movements, professional organizations did not even surface. These movements also received little foundation support, which made them an infertile area for professional organizations (see table 14.1). By contrast, 21.3 percent of environmental actions and 59.6 percent of consumer rights activities were carried out by professional movement organizations. In the environmental movement, grassroots activism was dominant beginning with the air pollution protests in the early 1960s and constituted 60 to 80 percent of movement activity in the late 1970s. Professional activism reached a peak in the early 1970s with the boost in foundation support and then gradually subsided as the movement moved into localized efforts against hazardous wastes, industrial pollution, and nuclear power plants. The most professionalized movement has been the consumer movement, which has been 60 to 80 percent professional since its emergence in the late 1960s. It has also been the

5. For coding procedures on the African-American movement actions, see Jenkins and Eckert (1986). The same procedures were applied to the other movements.

smallest movement in terms of total activity, averaging ten to twelve actions per year as opposed to sixty to a hundred for the other movements.

A complementary picture is given by looking at foundation funding. In two of the empowerment movements, indigenous organizations were the largest recipients. Indigenous groups received 31 percent of the money going to the African-American movement and 37 percent of the women's movement. By contrast, professional organizations and institutional actors received 85 percent of the environmental funding and 93 percent of the consumer funding. The most cautious foundation strategy has been in the peace movement where 46 percent of the grant dollars has gone to institutionalized organizations, primarily churches, and another 38 percent to professional organizations with only 16 percent going to indigenous groups. Yet even here there is no evidence of organizational displacement, indigenous groups generating all of the peace movement activity.

A more sophisticated criticism of social movement philanthropy is that foundation patronage has reduced the incentives for movement leaders to pursue indigenous organizing and thus indirectly weakened the movements. There is some evidence to support this idea. Costain (1992) has argued that the women's movement benefited initially from institutional patrons, including large grants from the Ford Foundation and other leading foundations. Although this led to several initial policy victories, it also discouraged indigenous organizing, and it was not until the late 1970s, when the movement confronted a major challenge by the anti-ERA forces, that the movement launched a significant grassroots campaign. Many think this failure to launch grassroots organizing was key to the ERA defeat and the victories of the political conservatives in the early 1980s.

A final criticism of movement philanthropy is the corporatism thesis that professionalization has allowed the foundations and other institutional elites to create a monopoly on political representation. Our evidence on movement activity, however, suggests that the American political system is too pluralistic for this type of monopoly to be successful. An intriguing example is the Ford Foundation creation of the National Council of La Raza and the Mexican-American Legal Defense Fund (or MALDEF). Ford originally launched these organizations in the late 1960s to provide an "NAACP for Mexican-Americans." The National Council quickly became involved in community organizing projects and, after funding several "brown power" groups that launched an electoral campaign against Representative Henry Gonzales (D.-Texas) and raised congressional ire at foundation meddling. Ford reorganized the council and transferred its headquarters from San Antonio to Washington, D.C. Fearing a similar problem, Ford reorganized MALDEF, appointing a new director and board of trustees and moved the headquarters to San Francisco. Indigenous organizing proved too controversial for the Ford Foundation. These moves also weakened the ability of these organizations to develop a grassroots constituency (Sierra 1983). At the same time, however, they have had to compete against numerous indigenous movement groups, which has prevented anything remotely akin to a representational monopoly among Mexican-Americans.

Yet there are significant limits to foundation patronage. As proponents of participatory democracy have argued, professionalization typically contributes little to grassroots participation. The foundations have also avoided funding movement groups in certain highly controversial areas, such as peace and problems of poverty. As shown in table 14.1, the peace movement has never received more than token support from foundations, and most of this has gone to institutional groups, like churches. Similarly, although foundations have been greatly concerned about the problems connected to poverty, they have focused on ameliorative efforts, typically service projects and "bricks and mortar" community development efforts, and avoided controversial efforts to organize the poor or advocate their interests. Economic justice projects with poor people as the primary constituency made up less than 2 percent of social movement philanthropy (see table 14.1). The disastrous experience of several foundations with the Movement for Economic Justice stands as a strong reminder to many foundations that poverty is a complex issue and, given strong cultural definitions that poverty is due to personal failures, social movement efforts are likely to prove counterproductive (Kotz and Kotz 1977; West 1981). Instead they have focused on community development efforts and more moderate welfare reform policies emphasizing such disadvantaged individuals as children, the aged, and the handicapped.

A GRASSROOTED POLITICAL SYSTEM?

Social movement philanthropy has helped open up the political system by creating new advocates for the public interest and providing technical resources to indigenous movements working to empower disadvantaged groups. Its strongest role has been in the public interest area, where foundations have provided the start-up money and project support for these movements. Environmentalism and consumer rights have relied heavily on foundation patronage. Although direct mail and other fund-raising devices have created new sources of support for movement projects, some of these public interest organizations are financially dependent on the foundations. They have sustained their efforts, using lobbying, litigation, and governmental monitoring to protect citizens against environmental problems, predatory business practices, and governmental secrecy.

In the empowerment movements, indigenous organizing has provided the major impetus for social change. The foundations have helped professionalize these movements which, instead of co-opting them, has provided technical resources for consolidating movement victories and ensuring that these gains remain in place. Although funding movements have been at the cost of some acrimony about the authenticity of

foundation intent, it is not a simple co-optation process. There are, of course, clear political limits to foundation patronage. The foundations have veered away from radical campaigns and typically responded to increasing militancy by funding the moderate alternatives. But the process is more complex than simple co-optation. Increased militancy has convinced foundations that certain problems are major and that there is an active, concerned constituency pressing to bring about changes. Overall, the foundations have been moderate reformers, funneling most of their support to the moderate wing of the movements and the professionalized groups. But, rather than co-opting these movements, they have channeled them into professionalized structures. In many respects, this has been a benefit to the movements, allowing them to consolidate their gains and protect themselves against attack.

There are, however, significant limits to social movement philanthropy. Participatory democracy has not been the central goal of the foundations. They have instead taken an indirect approach, funding professional organizations which have removed legal and institutional barriers to minority political participation or operated as advocates for unrepresented groups. But the professional movement organizations are controlled by their staffs and have little grassroots participation. The foundations have also shunned movements that operate in contentious areas, such as international peace and poverty. If we take instead a representation model of democracy, the foundation record is considerably better. They have contributed heavily to the public interest movement and funded several empowerment movements oriented toward opening up the political system. Indirectly, these efforts have built new institutions and launched significant political changes, such as the dramatic increase in minority and women's political representation.

A final assessment depends on one's conception of democracy and the public good. If one deems removing barriers to participation and ensuring the formal representation of social interests to be the central test, then social movement philanthropy has been a remarkable success. If direct participation or descriptive and substantive equality are your touchstones, then it has been a very limited victory. It has been in response to descriptive and participatory ideas about democracy that the alternative foundations brought social movement activists onto their giving boards. While this represents but a tiny portion of social movement giving, it is a suggestive trend. In her classic *The Concept of Political Representation,* Hannah Pitkin (1967) argued that there are multiple models of democratic representation that are mutually reinforcing and appropriate in various circumstances. Instead of arguing for a single abstract model, she urged that we examine common practices which combine participatory, representative, and descriptive representation. By this criterion, social movement philanthropy has been a qualified success, and its persistence into the 1990s suggests that it may continue to shape reforms in American politics.

REFERENCES

Adams, John H. 1974. "Responsible Militancy: The Anatomy of a Public Interest Law Firm." *Record of the Bar Association of the City of New York* 29:631–45.

Arnove, Robert. 1980. *Philanthropy as Cultural Imperialism.* Boston: G. K. Hall.

Ash, Roberta. 1977. *Social Movements.* Chicago: Rand McNally.

Bennett, James T., and Thomas J. DiLorenzo. 1985. *Destroying Democracy.* Washington, D.C.: Cato Institute.

Berry, Jeffrey. 1984. *The Interest Group Society.* Boston: Little, Brown.

Brownfield, Edward. 1969. *Financing Revolution.* Washington, D.C.: American Conservative Union.

Burstein, Paul, and Mark Evan Edwards. 1994. "The Impact of Employment Discrimination Litigation on Racial Disparity in Earnings." *Law & Society Review* 28:79–111.

Button, James W. 1989. *Blacks and Social Change.* Princeton, N.J.: Princeton University Press.

Carey, Sara. 1977. "Philanthropy and the Powerless." In Commission on Private Philanthropy and Public Need (Filer Commission). *Research Papers.* 109–64. Washington, D.C.: GPO.

Carson, Clayborne. 1981. *SNCC and the Black Awakening.* Cambridge: Harvard University Press.

Costain, Anne. 1993. *Inviting Women's Rebellion.* Baltimore: Johns Hopkins University Press.

Haines, Herbert. 1988. *Black Radicals and the Civil Rights Mainstream, 1954–1970.* Knoxville: University of Kentucky Press.

Hart, Jeffrey. 1973. "Foundation and Public Controversy: A Negative View." In *The Future of Foundations,* ed. Fritz Heimann, 99–116. Englewood Cliffs, N.J.: Prentice-Hall.

Jaynes, Gerald D., and Robin M. Williams, Jr. 1989. *A Common Destiny: Blacks and American Society.* Washington, D.C.: National Academy Press.

Jenkins, J. Craig. 1987. "Nonprofit Organizations and Policy Advocacy." In *The Nonprofit Sector,* ed. Walter W. Powell, 296–318. New Haven: Yale University Press.

Jenkins, J. Craig, and Craig M. Eckert. 1986. "Channeling Black Insurgency." *American Sociological Review* 51:812–29.

Kotz, Nick, and Mary Kotz. 1977. *A Passion for Equality.* New York: Norton.

Lomax, Louis. 1962. *The Negro Revolt.* New York: Harper and Row.

MacFarland, Andrew. 1984. *Common Cause.* Chatham, N.J.: Chatham House.

McAdam, Doug. 1982. *Political Process and the Development of Black Insurgency.* Chicago: University of Chicago Press.

McCann, Michael W. 1984. *Taking Reform Seriously.* Ithaca: Cornell University Press.

McCarthy, John, and Mayer Zald. 1987. *Social Movements in an Organizational Society.* New Brunswick, N.J.: Transaction Books.

McLlaney, William H. 1980. *The Tax-Exempt Foundations.* Westport, Ct.: Arlington House.

Meier, August, and Elliott Rudwick. 1973. *CORE.* New York: Columbia University Press.

Metzger, Ralph. 1979. *The Coercive Utopians: Their Hidden Agenda.* Denver: Public Service Corporation of Colorado.

Morris, Aldon. 1984. *The Origins of the Civil Rights Movement.* New York: Free Press.

Moynihan, Daniel P. 1969. *Maximum Feasible Misunderstanding.* New York: Free Press.

Navasky, Victor. 1971. *Kennedy Justice.* New York: Atheneum.

Nielsen, Waldemar. 1972. *The Big Foundations.* New York: Oxford University Press.

Ostrander, Susan A. 1993. "Diversity and Democracy in Philanthropic Organizations: The Case of Haymarket Peoples' Fund." In *Governing, Leading and Managing Nonprofit Organizations,* ed. Dennis Young, Robert M. Hollister, and Virginia A. Hodgkinson, 193–213. San Francisco: Jossey-Bass.

———. 1995. "Charitable Foundations, Social Movements and Social Justice Funding." In *The Nonprofit Sector and Social Justice,* ed. John H. Stanfield II. Bloomington: Indiana University Press.

Parker, Richard. 1983. *An Index of Progressive Funders.* San Francisco: Public Media Center.

Pillsbury, George. 1982. *Robin Hood Was Right.* Boston: Haymarket People's Fund.

Pitkin, Hannah. 1967. *The Concept of Representation.* Berkeley: University of California Press.

Piven, Frances, and Richard Cloward. 1977. *Poor People's Movements.* New York: Pantheon.

Roelofs, Joan. 1983. "Foundation Influence on Supreme Court Decision-Making." *Telos* 62:59–67.

———. 1987. "Foundations and the Left." *Insurgent Sociologist* 14:31–72.

Rosenberg, Gerald N. 1991. *The Hollow Hope: Can Courts Bring About Social Change?* Chicago: University of Chicago Press.

Shellow, Jill, ed. 1981. *The Grant-Seekers Guide.* Chicago: National Network of Grantmakers.

———. 1987. *The Grant-Seekers Guide,* 3d ed. Mt. Kisco, N.Y.: Moyer-Bell.

Simon, John. 1973. "Foundations and Public Controversy: An Affirmative View." In *The Future of Foundations,* ed. Fritz Heimann, 68–98. Englewood Cliffs, N.J.: Prentice-Hall.

Sierra, Christine Marie. 1983. "The Political Transformation of a Minority Organization: The Council of La Raza, 1965–1980." Ph.D. dissertation, Stanford University. Ann Arbor, Mich.: University Microfilms.

Schlozman, Kay L., and John T. Tierney. 1983 "More of the Same: Washington Pressure Group Activity in a Decade of Change." *Journal of Politics* 45:351–77.

Tully, Mary Jean. 1977. "Who's Funding the Women's Movement?" Commission on Private Philanthropy and Public Needs (Filer Commission). *Research Papers* 2:1383–84. Washington, D.C.: GPO.

Walker, Jack. 1991. *Mobilizing Interest Groups in America: Patrons, Professions and Social Movements.* Ann Arbor: University of Michigan Press.

West, Guida. 1981. *The National Welfare Rights Movement.* New York: Praeger.

Wilson, John. 1983. "Corporatism and the Professionalization of Reform." *Journal of Political and Military Sociology* 11:53–68.

Wofford, Harris. 1980. *Of Kennedys and Kings.* New York: Farrar, Straus and Giroux.

15

BRIAN H. SMITH

Nonprofit Organizations in International Development: Agents of Empowerment or Preservers of Stability?

In the past two decades nonprofit organizations (NPOs) have significantly expanded their involvement in international development. In 1970 American, Canadian, and European NPOs transferred $2.7 billion to developing countries, and by 1990 the amount totaled $7.2 billion (in constant 1986 dollars). The Organization for Economic Cooperation and Development (OECD) listed 1,600 North Atlantic NPOs involved in foreign assistance in 1980, 2,500 in 1989, and more than 4,000 in 1996. Their aid now reaches approximately 250 million people, or about one in five of the 1.3 billion people living in absolute poverty in developing countries (Clark 1990, 40; OECD 1981, 1988, 1989, 1996; UNDP 1993, 88; Smilie 1993, 3).

Funds for NPO development work originate primarily from two sources: individual private donations and grants from the foreign assistance ministries of North Atlantic governments. Over the past two decades not only has the total amount from these two sources dramatically increased (as indicated above), but the proportion contributed by each has changed significantly. In 1970, of the $2.7 billion given to NPOs, only 1.5 percent ($40 million) originated from governments, but by 1988 public subsidies accounted for 34.6 percent of the total ($1.8 billion of $5.2 billion) (Clark 1990, 40).

This chapter draws on some of the material in my book (Smith 1990). In its present form, it has greatly benefited from the constructive criticisms of Elisabeth Clemens, Woody Powell, and Debra Minkoff.

Thus, although (in constant terms) private donations increased 25.9 percent (from $2.7 billion to $3.4 billion), government support grew 4,400 percent (from $40 million to $1.8 billion) during this eighteen-year period. The major factor, therefore, in the expansion of NPOs' international commitments since the 1970s has been increases in public, not private, aid.

Indigenous nonprofit organizations in developing countries at the national and regional levels act as intermediaries in channeling this international assistance to the poor in their own societies. They have also grown in number significantly over the past two decades. It is estimated that there are now at least 30,000 to 35,000 intermediary nonprofit development organizations at the national and regional levels in Asia, Africa, and Latin America.

These intermediary NPOs sometimes carry out projects but more frequently act as brokers between local groups at the grassroots level who have formed their own smaller NPOs. The intermediary NPOs offer these smaller grassroots NPOs both technical assistance in drawing up project proposals for foreign NPO funding and advice in the implementation and evaluation of the actual projects that receive funding from abroad. The smaller grassroots NPOs presently number in the hundreds of thousands (Fisher 1993, 5, 23; Durning 1989, 55).

Thus, there is a clear hierarchy in the transnational nonprofit aid network: NPOs in the North Atlantic countries raise private and public funds for development projects overseas. National and regional NPOs in developing countries receive these funds from abroad and disperse them on a project-by-project basis. Finally, local NPOs in these same societies run the actual projects at the grassroots level among the poor.

The indigenous NPOs in developing countries — national, regional, and local — have been able to function under different types of governmental regimes. Democracies and authoritarian governments alike have allowed them to support projects in their territories even though NPO foreign assistance is not dispersed through their own public agencies.

In this chapter I discuss why this cooperation among governments and NPOs has grown so significantly in recent decades. I also compare the intentions of the North Atlantic donors with the actual projects funded in developing societies and assess if empowerment is occurring for the grassroots poor abroad as a result of this assistance. Finally, some challenges facing the transnational NPO network in the future will be identified.

NPO-GOVERNMENT COOPERATION

The American Experience

Many large NPOs currently engaged in foreign assistance originated as relief agencies to alleviate the effects of wars and other disasters. During both world wars many American humanitarian organizations were formed to assist refugees, orphans, and other victims of conflicts in Europe. All received strong encouragement from the U.S. government to undertake relief work, and some were given public subsidies even during the early years of the respective world wars when the United States was technically neutral (Curti 1963; Ringland 1954).

During the early 1950s, with the reconstruction of Europe winding down, American relief NPOs, rather than disband their sizable institutional networks, searched for a new mission and turned their attention to Asia, Africa, and Latin America — an illustration of the "garbage can" theory of organizational goal expansion (see Chaves, in this volume). In the mid-1950s, the U.S. government expanded its purchase of surplus wheat and dairy products from American farmers and began employing American relief NPOs to dispose of such commodities abroad so as not to depress American food prices at home.

As the Cold War continued, the U.S. government and private citizens alike shared an interest in keeping newly emerging nations from opting for alliances with the Soviet Union. Accordingly, the creation of private institutions to alleviate poverty and stimulate popular participation in the civic life of these societies became a major objective of U.S. foreign policy.

In 1966, Congress mandated that some U.S. foreign aid be channeled through American credit unions, cooperatives, and savings and loans associations to help create similar institutions in developing societies abroad. The new focus on private institution building in American foreign aid in turn stimulated the creation of new American NPOs to carry out such tasks. It also encouraged older NPOs engaged in relief and food distribution to begin to include a technical focus in their work abroad. This role expansion by NPOs is another illustration of the garbage can theory of organizational growth.

The growing alliance between NPOs and the American government advanced to another plateau in the early 1970s. Congress was becoming increasingly dissatisfied with the inability of U.S. economic aid to alleviate poverty abroad. A series of studies at the time criticized American assistance for not reaching the poorest sectors abroad, claiming much of it was being siphoned off by corrupt or inept government bureaucracies or spent on projects benefiting the minority of middle- and upper-income groups (Goulet and Hudson 1971; Adelman and Taft Morris 1973; Paddock and Paddock 1973). The failed war in Vietnam was winding down, and various attempts by the Central Intelligence Agency to undermine legitimate governments abroad were coming to light. Americans were becoming increasingly cynical about American foreign policy and unenthusiastic about foreign aid.

Reacting to these criticisms, Congress in 1973 mandated "new directions" for U.S. foreign aid that were to give it a more humanitarian focus by concentrating on basic needs of the poor abroad — food production, nutrition, health, education, and rural development. Representatives of some of the large American NPOs like CARE, Catholic Relief Services, and Church World Service testified on behalf of this legislation at congressional hearings. They argued that the focus of American nonprofits abroad now included just such an emphasis and that NPOs should be given increasing amounts of government assistance to expand their new development projects overseas among the poor.

In its final form, the Foreign Assistance Act of 1973 praised NPOs for "embodying the American spirit of self-help" and for "mobilizing private American financial and human resources to benefit poor people in developing countries." The new law stipulated that NPOs receive additional public funds to accomplish these goals abroad more effectively (U.S. Congress 1973).

In succeeding years, a steady increase in U.S. government subsidies to American NPOs leveled off by the late 1980s at about the 25 percent level of overall NPO budgets. The U.S. government continued to rely on American NPOs as a means to dispose of surplus food commodities abroad, and as of 1992, food and food-related aid constituted nearly one-third (32 percent) of all public subsidies to NPOs (USAID 1992, 82).

American NPOs engaged in foreign assistance have proven to be strong domestic advocates of economic assistance to developing countries in an era when foreign aid has continued to remain unpopular among most Americans. NPOs regularly testify in support of increased foreign assistance at congressional hearings and are among the most reliable lobby groups the State Department has to support foreign aid. Many also have begun development education programs at home since the mid-1980s (some with government grants) to make their donors and other citizens more aware of the needs of developing countries, thus hopefully enlarging the constituency for American aid to such societies.

The European and Canadian Experiences

In Europe, similar factors have accounted for the emergence of close working relationships between governments and NPOS in foreign assistance. Many European NPOS were founded earlier in this century to alleviate the destruction caused by major wars in their societies. After World War II, they, like their American counterparts, moved abroad to find new tasks rather than dismantle their operations.

NPOS proved useful to such governments as Britain, France, Belgium, and the Netherlands as alternate means of maintaining cultural influence in territories in which home-country colonial offices were being phased out during the era of political independence. In Sweden and Canada, where no colonial heritage existed, and in the Federal Republic of Germany, where such a heritage had not existed for more than a generation, NPOS pioneered in setting up new ties between the home country and newly emerging societies that set the stage for later commercial and investment relations.

Newer NPOS were also formed during the 1960s, when pressures were building on a by-then economically recovered Europe to do more for developing countries. Often European governments found that channeling of public aid through NPOS rather than government agencies was more cost-effective because the overhead expenses in these smaller private agencies were lower.

The use of NPOS became increasingly attractive by the mid-1970s. During those years, left-of-center coalitions were in power in Canada and most of Western Europe, and they sympathized with the New International Economic Order (NIEO) endorsed by the United Nations General Assembly, which called for very substantial increases of economic aid to developing countries targeted at the basic needs of the poorest sectors. Given the impact of two major oil price rises in the 1970s, however, these governments were not able to take on significant new commitments in foreign aid. But they did begin to increase their grants to NPOS. Such subsidies were small compared to the massive new commitments called for by the NIEO, but Canadian and European governments could claim that they were meeting some NIEO objectives because the small-scale development projects of NPOS almost all reached the grassroots poor in developing countries.[1]

Thus, between 1973 and 1983 public subsidies to NPOS in Europe and Canada more than quadrupled (in constant 1986 dollars). They jumped from $160 million to $680 million in this ten-year period as governments channeled increasing amounts of their own foreign assistance through NPOS that sponsored projects abroad among some of the poorest sectors of the populations. Government subsidies to NPOS in Europe and Canada, in fact, grew much faster than private contributions during these years; the percentage of overall NPO revenues that such subsidies comprised increased from 16 percent in 1973 ($160 million of $998 million) to 36 percent in 1983 ($680 million of $1.9 billion).

Some important differences exist between American NPOS and those in other North Atlantic countries. One is the smaller amount of food aid channeled through NPOS by the European and Canadian as compared to the American governments. The discrepancy is attributable to the types of farm subsidy programs that exist in each area. The European and Canadian governments do not buy and store excess food from farmers and thus do not rely on NPOS as conduits for disposing of it abroad. Almost all government aid to European and Canadian NPOS is in the form of cash grants for development projects, not of commodities to alleviate hunger.

In addition, many of the Canadian and European NPOS created in the post–World War II era were formed by groups who had close ties to labor organizations, professional associations, and leftist political parties. These ties have continued, and many large Canadian and European NPOS continue to attract executives and staff with similar ties. Unlike the American NPOS, which have no close links to domestic political movements and tend to avoid partisan issues, European and Canadian NPOS include in their fund-raising and development education programs criticisms of home-country policies they feel harm developing countries in the areas of tariffs, immigration quotas, investment priorities, and weapons transfers. They are thus far more political in their style than their American counterparts (see Ullman, in this volume). They thus view development not merely as an economic issue but one requiring a redress of power imbalances between rich and poor nations and between elites and masses in developing countries (a perspective shared by proponents of the NIEO agenda).

Experiences of Developing Countries

NPOS in developing countries date back to charitable organizations started by Christian missions in the sixteenth century in Latin America and in the following three centuries in Asia and Africa. In the post–World War II era, and especially

---

1. Claire Ullman (in this volume) argues that limitations in state bureaucracies led policymakers in North Atlantic countries to reach out to NPOS as conduits for public service delivery. A similar phenomenon of government limits (particularly incapacities of developing country bu-

reaucracies to administer foreign aid efficiently) made NPOS attractive conduits of foreign economic assistance for European governments by the 1970s. An added attraction was that overhead costs of transnational NPOS were also considerably cheaper than those of home-government foreign aid ministries.

in the 1960s, these missionary groups shifted their focus from relief to development as they began to emphasize as part of their work long-term strategies to attack poverty — literacy and job training, formation of production and consumer, cooperatives, primary health care, water development, and support for small-scale farming (Smith 1990, 232–33; Landim 1987, 31).[2]

By the 1970s, however, two major factors in developing countries stimulated the expansion of church-related service organizations and the creation of a series of new secular NPOS focusing on similar small-scale development projects among the grassroots poor. One was the cutback in public services by governments in the 1970s and 1980s, and the other was the disenchantment of middle-class professionals with the public sector as a means to help the poor.

Governments in the non–oil producing countries of Asia, Africa, and Latin America began to cut back educational and health services to the poor after rises in petroleum prices in 1973 and 1978. Many governments borrowed from private international banks that were glutted with investments from the oil-producing countries of the Middle East, and this led to ever-increasing debts. By the early 1980s, they had difficulty meeting even interest payments on such loans, and a new round of cuts in central government spending on social services occurred. This left the bottom 40 percent of their populations in even more dire straits than before (George 1990).

The austerity measures adopted by many third world governments precipitated a search among middle-class professionals in these countries for alternate strategies to assist the poor. Government corruption and policies geared to the preservation of elite interests had begun to sour idealistic professionals in many developing countries as early as the 1960s. Once substantial numbers had lost their jobs in governments or national universities owing to cutbacks in public expenditures, they began looking for new employment opportunities that would also realize their ideals for service. This combination of factors gave rise to the creation of a series of new NPOS staffed by these professionals to assist urban and rural poor in their countries (Fisher 1993, 77; Bratton 1989, 570–71; Garilao 1987, 114).

Many new NPOS were also created in Africa and Latin America in the late 1960s and early 1970s, when authoritarian regimes replaced elected democracies. This change of regimes (especially in Latin America) created new cadres of unemployed professionals or former party activists who had lost their jobs for political reasons under newly established military governments. These NPOS often took the form of research organizations aimed at keeping alive alternate perspectives

2. Mark Chaves (in this volume) sees this as part of a wider trend emerging among Christian organizations in Western societies over the past generation. He believes these are increasingly shifting from religious to secular functions as a means to maintain a service ideal in the face of the declining attraction of their religious ministries.

on development, and some became technical assistance organizations for self-help projects among the grassroots poor. A series of new private organizations was also created, many under the auspices or protection of the churches, to assist victims of human rights violations and to provide needed social services no longer available from governments (Smith 1990, 236–37; Landim 1987, 31–32; Smith, 1980).

A final factor which made intermediary NPOS attractive to those seeking alternate means of helping the poor and oppressed in Africa, Asia, and Latin America was the availability of new funds from international NPOS. From the mid-1970s on (as described earlier), American, Canadian, and European NPOS received increasing amounts of home-government subsidies, and they found ready recipients in newly created intermediary NPOS in developing countries — many of which could neither have begun nor continued without foreign NPO assistance (Fisher 1993, 174).

Some of these intermediary NPOS brokered resources from northern NPOS to local development projects carried out by grassroots groups in their own societies. Others acted as support institutions offering their technical expertise to these local groups in such areas as primary health care, small-scale agricultural development, prefabricated housing, credit management, production and marketing cooperatives, and environmental preservation. Still others focused on policy research and dissemination of information on alternate strategies for attacking poverty, and some of these also provided training in community development to rural and urban grassroots leaders.

Hence, crises in public sector service institutions in developing countries that came to a head in the 1970s stimulated the proliferation of nonprofit organizations. It was not so much that governments reached out to embrace NPOS, as they did in the North Atlantic countries. It was rather an opportunity seized by NPOS when state budgets shrank (as has been the case recently in Eastern Europe — see Anheier and Seibel, in this volume) or when state repression increased. This new opening for NPOS in Asia, Africa, and Latin America occurred at the very time that North Atlantic NPOS were coming into a windfall of new resources from their governments and were looking for private clients abroad to disperse the funds and materials. Thus, the transnational NPO network for development was forged.

INTENTIONS OF DONORS VS. CHARACTER OF THE PROJECTS

In spite of this convergence of factors that stimulated the growth of NPOS both north and south of the equator in the 1970s and 1980s, questions arise as to why governments, private donors, and NPOS would continue to collaborate even though they had differing interests. Some northern NPOS are staffed by persons who articulate strong criticisms of home-country foreign policies, and who advocate changes that will

Table 15.1. Weighted Priorities of American, Canadian, and European NPOs (1982–1983)

Priorities	U.S. (N = 13) Rank (Score)	Canadian (N = 5) Rank (Score)	European (N = 19) Rank (Score)
Immediate relief of suffering (hunger, sickness, etc.)	4 (48)	6 (5)	5 (37)
Increasing income and employment	2 (53)	5 (12)	6 (28)
Improving skills, capacities to solve problems	1 (57)	3 (20)	4 (71)
Building institutions and networks of participation operated by the poor	3 (49)	1 (26)	1 (99)
Enhancing bargaining power of poor with merchants, landlords, governments	5 (41)	4 (18)	3 (76)
Empowerment of poor to challenge and change dominant political and economic structures in their environment	6 (22)	2 (24)	2 (80)

cost private citizens in increased taxes or higher prices for imported goods. Abroad, those staffing intermediary NPOs often criticize their government's policies toward the poor. Some are former activists in political movements that openly opposed governments, and others support projects that assist those suffering from some of the worst effects of government repression.

One might expect, given these differences, that cooperation between governments and NPOs might break down at both the sending and receiving ends of the international NPO network and that private donors in the north would soon stop supporting organizations that threatened some of their economic interests. What keeps the system functioning, however, are a sufficient number of overlapping interests among all the partners, despite some diverging objectives each espouses. Moreover, the actual projects among the grassroots poor abroad do not threaten either developing country governments or the interests of North Atlantic public and private donors.

Citizens in North Atlantic countries tend to give the most to NPOs during times of well-publicized disasters like famines, earthquakes, migration of refugees in civil wars, and so forth, and the large North Atlantic NPOs still act as major conduits of relief aid to the victims of such disasters when they occur. In spite of the shift to long-term development as the first objective of many North Atlantic NPOs since the 1960s, many still operate as short-term relief agencies — even the Canadian and European NPOs that do not receive substantial food aid from their respective governments. This continued humanitarian focus maintains strong credibility for all NPOs among private donors at home. It also gives them added legitimacy with governments of different ideologies, all of whom need immediate relief assistance whenever natural or human-made crises occur.

Although some North Atlantic NPOs, especially in Canada and Europe, engage in education and lobbying campaigns at home that challenge some of the interests of their governments and private citizens alike, their influence in effecting policy changes in these areas has been minimal (Smith 1990, 215). Their dissent is thus tolerated even by parliaments

dominated by right of center coalitions. Such criticisms actually find some support among leftist parties in parliaments. Whether they wield executive power or not, leftists often favor liberalization of trade, aid, and immigration policies but are not in a position to implement them owing to a lack of public support.

The airing of criticisms by NPOs thus is accepted as part of the political debate in countries with a much wider ideological spectrum than the United States. Citizens in Europe do not view the call for significant political changes as beyond the legitimate purview of NPOs. French NPOs, for example (see Ullman, in this volume), have been significant lobbyists in domestic welfare reform over the past decade.[3]

More so than American NPOs, Canadian and European ones tend to favor political change as a major goal of the projects they sponsor abroad. This is evident in table 15.1, which is based on a survey I conducted in 1982 and 1983 among American, Canadian, and European NPOs.[4] The

3. A sizable proportion of the population in Europe views development problems abroad as requiring political, not merely economic, solutions. This segment is not upset by NPOs that call for major changes in power relations between rich and poor nations and inside poor nations. A random survey of more than 9,700 persons in ten West European countries in 1983 indicated that 60.6 percent believed that rich countries (including their own) exploited poor countries, and 83.3 percent felt that within developing countries a rich minority exploits the rest of the population — in contrast to only 6 percent of Americans who viewed the poor in such societies as victims of unjust systems (Rabier, Riffault, and Inglehart 1985, 81, 84, 92, 93, 96; Contee 1987, 49; Laudicina 1973, 11).

4. In my sample of interviews I included persons in administrative positions in forty-five of the largest American, Canadian, and European NPOs. All respondents were asked to rank order the six goals, and I weighted the priorities according to how often they were mentioned to come up with a composite score: first choice, six points; second choice, five points; third choice, four points; fourth choice, three points; fifth choice, two points; sixth choice, one point; not applicable, or not ranked, no points (Smith 1990, 133–34). Although these data are more than a decade old, the same patterns have continued. American agencies still tend to stress technical and economic issues and shy away from the espousal of confrontation. Canadians and Europeans continue to empha-

Americans rated as their top objectives the improvement of technical skills and the increasing of job opportunities. The Canadians and Europeans ranked their main priorities as the building of institutions run by the poor themselves and empowering of the poor to challenge dominant power structures in their environment.

Notwithstanding this sharp difference of objectives among North Atlantic NPOs, the kind of development projects they sponsor abroad do not differ significantly. These tend to cluster around skill- and resource-enhancement programs that generate *new* income and social opportunities among the poor rather than challenge dominant elites to surrender some of their *existing* privileges or power.

Although intermediary NPOs in developing countries are frequently staffed by persons critical of their governments for not adequately addressing the needs of the poor, they do not normally espouse as part of their goals a redistribution of wealth or political power. Under authoritarian regimes in Latin America in the 1970s and early 1980s some NPOs carried out legal assistance to victims of oppression or offered economic assistance to those ostracized for political reasons, but they did not engage in popular mobilization to thwart government policies or to stimulate open political opposition (Smith 1990, 267–69; Smith 1980). The evidence presented by L. David Brown in his chapter in this book indicates that the development projects of NPOs in military or single-party states in Asia and Africa (including Bangladesh, Indonesia, Pakistan, and Zimbabwe) were also no threat to regime stability. In fact, he shows that some of these governments either sought the cooperation of NPOs or listened seriously to their advice in learning how to provide needed services to the poor in the areas of immunization, irrigation, sanitation, and credit management.

In some democratic countries, NPOs sometimes take more openly critical stances toward government policy. For example, AWARE, an NPO in the state of Andhra Pradesh in India, has orchestrated a series of public demonstrations by grassroots groups it assists to pressure the local government to implement land reform legislation promulgated by the central government but largely ignored thereafter. It has also encouraged members of local groups to run for election to the local parliament, and forty of the two hundred seats are now held by AWARE local groups. NPOs in neighboring Bangladesh have urged the same strategy for landless groups they have been assisting (Clark 1990, 98–99).

NPOs rarely seek, however, to replace political parties or to act primarily as partisan political groups themselves. Some rather tend to use political structures that are responsive to public pressures as conduits for furthering their causes within the rules of the system (Clark 1990, 99).[5]

In democratic regimes throughout Asia, Africa, and Latin America, however, most NPOs focus on supporting economic projects that have some impact on enhancing skills or resources rather than aiming at political participation of the poor (Smith 1990; Fisher 1993; Clark 1990). These national and regional NPOs work closely with self-help organizations (grassroots NPOs) formed by the poor themselves to gain some well-defined improvement in their lives.

Some of the more innovative and extensive activities have been in areas of basic health and family planning, credit and management training for small businesses, small-scale agriculture and water development that is linked with environmental preservation, and production and consumer cooperatives. All of these have included both technical assistance and financial help from intermediary NPOs, but individuals and groups at the local level manage the projects themselves through their local NPOs. These have also been some of the areas in which techniques have been replicated through dissemination of information by intermediary and northern NPOs, and (as Brown also shows in his chapter) sometimes governments have adapted these into their own public service programs (Fisher 1993, 119–28, 202–03; Clark 1990, 86, 110–11; Smith 1990, 241–47).

The poorest of the poor (the landless, the sick, the elderly, the handicapped) usually do not directly benefit from all of these grassroots associations because many grassroots NPOs — especially those that are cooperatives or credit unions — require a minimum of resources and skills to participate. Many local projects tend to miss the poorest 5 to 10 percent in their regions. The reach of grassroots NPOs, however, clearly extends beyond that of most government agencies, which do not go below the bottom 20 percent of the poor in service delivery. Moreover, even the poorest groups benefit from the activities of those grassroots NPOs that are multiservice organizations and include as part of their mission nutrition and health assistance to all in need (Carroll 1992, 67–69; UNDP 1993, 96).

Thus, most governments in developing countries, regardless of their political ideology, find NPOs at the intermediary and local levels useful. Although public officials normally do not have access to NPO funds, NPOs leverage new international resources for their societies not available to the governments themselves. Sometimes local development projects such as those sponsored by private agencies act as surrogates for social services formerly provided by the governments facing shrinking resources; or they pioneer in delivering new cost-efficient services later to be adapted by public institutions (see Brown, in this volume). By acting as important gap-fillers and troubleshooters, NPOs shore up social stability, head off potential unrest, and sometimes pave the way for

---

size in their literature the necessity to change political structures so as to alleviate poverty abroad (Smilie 1993, 18–20; ACVFA 1990, 1993).

5. I found this to be the case in Colombia, where I studied a variety of intermediary NPOs (thirty-six in all) in 1984. Although the activities of

some of their staff included political tactics (e.g., petitioning local government agencies to implement land reform already required by law), the NPOs to which they belonged did not become competitors of political parties in their respective regions (Smith 1990, 255–56).

governments to learn better techniques of reaching isolated regions or marginalized groups. Even authoritarian governments have tolerated NPO activities so long as they operate within the boundaries of relief assistance or economic development — which the vast majority do.

ARE THE POOR EMPOWERED?

In spite of the above caveats and limitations on the *political* power of NPOs in developing countries, there clearly have been some forms of empowerment of the poor as a result of their activities. A United Nations report of 1993 on the work of NPOs in development underscores the *economic* empowerment countless people have experienced because of NPO work:

> Many people judge NGOs [nongovernmental organizations, or NPOs] primarily by their success in improving the living standards of the poor, and there are plenty of individual success stories. The landless have obtained land. Farmers are growing more food. Wells and boreholes have been sunk. Children have been inoculated against killer diseases. In these and countless other ways, NGOs have transformed the lives of millions of people all over the world. (UNDP 1993, 94)

The same report also cites other studies that point to the *social* empowerment of the poor resulting from their participation in NPO projects:

> How far NGOs really enhance participation is impossible to say. But one recent Dutch study [1992] — with evidence from Brazil, Burkina Faso, Chile, Indonesia and Zimbabwe — concluded that NGOs had broadly increased empowerment, even if it could not offer quantitative evidence. It reported that people in target groups now "... act more often as partners in discussions with organizations outside the village, have the courage to lodge complaints with civil servants of the local government, move freer and travel more." These are seemingly small changes but of essential importance for the people themselves. (UNDP 1993, 94)

Grassroots NPOs of all types have been particularly helpful to women in their efforts to advance their social power throughout developing countries. Health and family planning NPOs have not only given women more security and choice, but they have often been run by women themselves, thus enhancing their own self-esteem and their stature in their respective communities. Revolving credit funds have given rise to many new small businesses run by women in regions where such projects have been created. Buying and selling of cooperatives have enabled women to supplement their family incomes through more effective linkages to markets for the labor-intensive goods they produce. Through all of these new roles women collectively have begun to erode some of the stereotypes in their respective countries, stereo-

types that assume that male leadership is essential for the implementation of effective development (Clark 1990, 101; UNDP 1993, 96–97).

Linking all of these dimensions of social empowerment are the new organizations operated by the poor themselves.[6] Although not financially autonomous, thus far they have operated with some autonomy from governments and political and economic elites in their societies. This has given the participants increased control over their immediate environment and a sense of group awareness that they can do things for themselves. Moreover, their benefactors — that is, intermediary NPOs, international NPOs, foreign private donors, and foreign governments — have allowed them a range of freedom to define their own objectives so long as they stay within broad parameters of economic development. If these grassroots NPOs can maintain their relative autonomy and continue to set their own economic goals, the social empowerment of their members is likely to grow.

L. David Brown, building on the work of Robert Putnam, identifies the greatest contribution of NPOs as expanding the "social capital" of the poor — structural arrangements of voluntary cooperation that nurture attitudes of trust, self-confidence, tolerance, and hope for a better future (Brown, in this volume). These new collective experiences and the gradual attitudinal changes they foster do not translate into an immediate increase of political power for the poor — more voice in governments, more parties responsive to their interests, more effective laws protecting their rights, and so on. But the expansion of social capital is laying the groundwork for a different type of future society in which the poor will have enhanced capacities to articulate, pursue, and realize some important interests on their own. Eventually, if such capital continues to accrue it cannot help but have a positive impact on political systems. Growing numbers of the poor are coming to believe that they have a stake in society and that they can make institutions work in their favor and for the good of others — one basis for healthy democratic politics.[7]

Currently, NPOs in developing countries are not a serious threat to established economic and political elites. As indicated above, they serve some important interests of governments in developing countries, and their existence makes it possible for other actors in the transnational NPO network to achieve some of their objectives. In the north and south alike, therefore, NPOs enable groups in both public and private

6. John Friedmann (1990) has defined the social power that is accruing to various low-income groups through grassroots NPO projects as greater control over their "life space," their economic resources, social networks, and autonomous organizations.

7. Daniel Levine makes a similar argument based on behavioral and attitudinal changes he observed among those participating in new local communities sponsored by the Catholic Church in Latin America, many of which function as grassroots NPOs. These organizations foster attitudes of respect and cooperation among their members in carrying out needed social services and act as training grounds for potential new community leaders among the poor (Levine 1992, 319–20, 340–44).

spheres to achieve a variety of objectives that would not be as easily realized if the transnational NPO network were not in place.

CHALLENGES FOR THE FUTURE

Despite overlapping interests in the transnational NPO network, there are some emerging trends that may create serious problems for its future stability. Governmental pressures on northern NPOs to professionalize and specialize, the increasing competence of southern NPOs vis-á-vis their northern NPO funders, the shrinking state in developing countries searching for private contractors for public services, and the latent political potential of grassroots NPOs in poor countries — all of these factors are creating challenges for the transnational NPO network in the future.

Pressures on Northern NPOs to Professionalize and Specialize

North Atlantic governments are beginning to demand higher standards of performance from NPOs to whom they make grants. They are asking for more systematic evaluation procedures to determine conditions of project success and to generate more systematic information on what has been learned from failures. They are also urging NPOs to upgrade their managerial skills and are offering grants for NPO institutional development (Smith 1990, 165–66, 199, 211).

Canadian and European governments have recently created funds for more specialized NPO projects in regions that are foreign policy priorities of home governments (for example, former colonies) or in policy areas of domestic political concern (for example, AIDS prevention, women in development, support for democracy) (Smilie 1993, 12, 20). The U.S. government in the post–Cold War era has become particularly interested in focusing more of its foreign aid on those countries and subregions of nations that have the greatest possibility of expanding markets for U.S. products or providing more needed raw materials for its domestic consumption. The U.S. Agency for International Development (AID) has begun to view American NPOs as contractees performing specific services for clients and in the process is imposing more stringent administrative restrictions on NPO operations. It is also urging them to convince NPOs in developing countries to charge "user fees" for services rendered to the poor as a way of cutting project costs (ACVFA 1993, 13; Smith 1993, 331–32), a trend now also occurring among domestic U.S. NPOs.

These growing pressures for professionalization, specialization, and efficiency can have positive effects in improving NPO project quality and focus. Such demands can also limit NPOs' flexibility in breaking new ground, their autonomy in setting their own agendas in response to developing country needs, and the variety of activities they can sponsor abroad.

Craig Jenkins warns (in this volume) that donor pressures for increased professionalization in NPOs can curtail support

for grassroots movements. This probably will not occur because grassroots NPOs abroad will still be necessary to implement projects. Nevertheless, if these suggestions are implemented they could eliminate some poor people from participating if they do not live within the particular countries or regions identified by foreign governments as priorities, or if they cannot afford to shoulder more of the costs — for example, pay user fees for services received.

Shrinking government budgets for public services in North Atlantic countries are creating demands on state-subsidized private organizations to become more cost-efficient (Hyde 1993). These same pressures to cut and monitor more carefully public expenditures are now beginning to affect North Atlantic NPOs using governmental resources for international development. Responding to these pressures without losing some of their independence and range of action will be a critical challenge for NPOs in the years ahead.[8]

Expanded Capacities of Intermediary NPOs in Developing Countries

Just as increased professionalization may be a mixed blessing for NPOs in North Atlantic countries, expanding institutional capacities of intermediary NPOs which administer the funds in developing countries can create new challenges. Many intermediary NPOs are reaching a stage where they can act as significant agents in the development process — screening and evaluating increasing numbers of projects, assisting in the creation, expansion, and coordination of grassroots NPOs, formulating micropolicy recommendations for their governments, creating consortia among themselves at the regional and international levels to share experiences (Korten 1987; Stremlau 1987).

These growing professional skills are increasing NPOs' capacities to manage more funds, make decisions more effectively, and wield some influence in public policy making (see Brown, in this volume). Intermediary NPOs are also asking northern NPOs for block grants and greater discretion over use of funds; at present, most northern NPOs make all the decisions on a project-by-project basis. They are also approaching northern governments on their own with funding requests, bypassing northern NPOs), and some have had success in leveraging direct government aid from abroad (Smilie 1993, 22–23; Smith 1993, 334–37).

These are signs of institutional maturity and growing professionalization among intermediary NPOs. They may, however, create some serious tensions with northern NPOs who will have to surrender some of their power and deal with

8. An alternative for North Atlantic NPOs would to be expand their sources of private funding and thus cut their dependence on governmental subsidies to maximize their autonomy. Private funding of NPOs, however, is still not increasing except in time of disasters. In 1992, for example, donations for all international causes were a very small part of overall American philanthropy, amounting to only 1.4 percent of total U.S. charitable contributions — $1.7 billion of $124 billion — and that was $40 million *less* for all foreign causes than in 1991 (Teltsch 1993).

southern NPOs more as partners than as clients. This will require some readjustment in attitude and style of operation and a letting go of some northern NPO prerogatives.

Some northern NPOs may have to scale down their operations or expand in other areas to maintain their institutional size — for example, by increasing their advocacy at home for more equitable governmental policies toward developing countries. A time of uneasy readjustment of the relationships among northern and southern NPOs may lie ahead.

Increasing Ties between Intermediary NPOs and Home Governments

A more serious challenge to southern NPOs' professionalization, however, is the increasing incidence of offers from their governments to act as government contractors. As the reputation of intermediary NPOs grows, there is an effort by governments to incorporate them into public social service systems as they privatize their economies and cut back on state expenditures. This trend has existed for some time in parts of Africa and now is expanding rapidly in Latin America.

Newly constituted Latin American democratic governments, some of whose policymakers worked for intermediate NPOs during previous military regimes, are setting up special funds for private service programs (Carroll 1992, 177–78). There are popular expectations that a return to democracy will better the economic situation of the poor, who suffered both political repression and economic austerity under previous military regimes. Newly elected civilians, however, are also under continuing pressures from international lending institutions (to whom large debts still are owed) to continue privatizing their economies. They need to find ways to increase social services for the poor but do not have adequate resources or delivery mechanisms to do so.

The World Bank, the Inter-American Bank, and AID are all providing these countries with additional loans and grants to help meet these service needs. Because NPO administrative costs in Latin America are still lower than those of the state — a situation that does not hold in North Atlantic countries (see Ullman, in this volume) — and because NPOs can leverage additional foreign money on their own through the transnational NPO network, Latin American governments are seeking them out as new partners to meet public needs.[9]

If such funds grow and NPOs take increasing advantage of them, it could help them expand and scale up considerably their service delivery capabilities to meet the ever-growing demands of the poor. Moreover, moving into a closer association with the public sector might result in governments

adopting innovative NPO techniques in their own service agencies (see Brown, in this volume). Some of the recent literature on NPOs in developing countries, in fact, has been urging that they extend their reach, seek to have their projects replicated on a wider scale, and search for more effective ways to impact on public policy making (Fisher 1993, 209; Clark 1990, 78–79; UNDP 1993, 98; Carroll 1992, 179–80).

Developing country governments, however, will likely place more stringent conditions on their contracts with intermediate NPOs than do current international NPOs on their grants. If this occurs, the danger of being co-opted to serve government interests will grow, and NPOs' ability to serve as independent advocates for the poor will decline (Smith 1993, 341). In fact, such co-optation is already happening to those NPOs in advanced capitalist societies that, as government contractors, are suffering the effects of the welfare state crisis (Hyde 1993).

If such controls emerge in developing countries, the credibility of intermediary NPOs in the eyes of grassroots NPOs and the poor whom they now serve could be significantly diminished. They could become parastatal organizations, thus losing their capacity for innovation and flexibility. More research is needed on how local government funding is affecting the autonomy and performance of those intermediary NPOs because the implications of such arrangements have yet to be explored in developing countries.

The Growing Political Potential of Grassroots NPOs

Just as there is a tendency for intermediary NPOs to establish federations, networks among grassroots NPOs are now emerging. Some are regional organizations (cooperatives), some informal economic networks (bartering systems), and other, more heterogeneous groupings combining grassroots NPOs and social movements seeking redress of grievances for their members (for example, peasant unions, tribal organizations, environmental groups) (Fisher 1993, 57–74). As a result of such coordination, the political potential of grassroots NPOs (as discussed earlier) may be increasingly realized in the years ahead. Strategies deployed in India and Bangladesh, where some NPOs are encouraging participants to run for local office, may evolve into trends in other contexts as NPOs become more coordinated.

This scenario is fraught with both positive and negative implications. On the one hand, if grassroots NPOs establish closer bonds with one another at the regional and national levels in their societies and also forge closer links with popular protest movements, they might be able to create new political organizations (or reform existing ones) that are truly representative of the interests of the poor. These, in turn, may then be able to shift some political power away from landed, industrial, and commercial elites in these societies. This would please many European and Canadian NPOs (as reflected in their responses in table 15.1).

On the other hand, greater involvement in politics could divert the energies of grassroots NPOs away from some of

9. The governments of Colombia, Peru, Bolivia, Chile, Guatemala, Honduras, and Mexico all now have social investment funds. These pay private agencies to deliver needed social services to the poor. The funds range in amounts from $20 to $60 million (Colombia, Bolivia, Chile, Guatemala), to $100 million to $200 million (Peru and Honduras), to $2 billion (Mexico). Telephone interview and correspondence with Dr. Charles A. Reilly, Thematic Studies Officer, Office of Learning and Dissemination, Inter-American Foundation, Alexandria, VA, October 1993.

the solid economic and social accomplishments they have achieved thus far and embroil them in debilitating partisan battles. Governments could begin to resent those who link closely with social protest movements and remove their nonprofit status. Others might gradually take on the characteristics of parties, which they currently criticize, if they eventually decide to compete in the electoral arena — exaggerated campaign promises that outrun performance in office, leaders who become enamored of power and lose their interest in caring for the needs of their clientele, compromises with other parties that sacrifice principle for expediency.

In sum, the world of politics could have more of an impact on NPOs than vice versa, and, if so, they would lose some of their comparative advantage in development. Ironically, the closer NPOs come to assisting the poor toward political empowerment, the more jeopardized is their viability. Whether grassroots NPOs can join forces with other social movements of the poor to exert more coherent pressure on governments for equitable public policies while avoiding the debilitating effects of partisan politics remains to be seen.

The choices open to NPOs in the north and south as they face all of these new challenges will not be easy. Managing new opportunities will require adjustments in their interrelationships and in their linkages with public and private donors if the transnational NPO system is to continue to operate as an important instrument for global equity.

REFERENCES

Advisory Council on Voluntary Foreign Aid (ACVFA). 1990. *Responding to Change: Private Voluntarism and International Development.* Washington, D.C.: U.S. Agency for International Development (USAID).

———. 1993 *International Development and Private Voluntarism: A Maturing Partnership.* Washington, D.C.: USAID.

Adelman, Irma, and Cynthia Taft Morris. 1973. *Economic Growth and Social Equity in Developing Countries.* Stanford: Stanford University Press.

Bratton, Michael. 1989. "The Politics of Government-NGO Relations in Africa." *World Development* 17:569–87.

Carroll, Thomas F. 1992. *Intermediary NGOs: The Supporting Link in Grassroots Development.* West Hartford, Conn.: Kumarian Press.

Clark, John. 1990. *Democratizing Development: The Role of Voluntary Organizations.* West Hartford, Conn.: Kumarian Press.

Contee, Christine E. 1987. *What Americans Think: Views on Development and U.S.-Third World Relations.* Washington, D.C.: Interaction and the Overseas Development Council (ODC).

Curti, Merle. 1963. *American Philanthropy Abroad: A History.* New Brunswick: Rutgers University Press.

Durning, Alan B. 1989. "Action at the Grassroots: Fighting Poverty and Environmental Decline." Worldwatch Paper No. 88. Washington, D.C.: Worldwatch Institute.

Fisher, Julie. 1993. *The Road from Rio: Sustainable Development and the Nongovernmental Movement in the Third World.* Westport, Conn.: Praeger.

Fleet, Michael, and Brian H. Smith. 1997. *The Catholic Church and Democracy in Chile and Peru.* Notre Dame, Ind.: University of Notre Dame Press.

Friedmann, John. 1990. "Empowerment: The Politics of an Alternative Development." Graduate School of Architecture and Urban Planning, University of California at Los Angeles. Mimeographed.

Garilao, Ernesto D. 1987. "Indigenous NGOs as Strategic Institutions: Managing the Relationship with Government and Resource Agencies." *World Development* 15:113–20.

George, Susan. 1990. *A Fate Worse than Debt: The World Financial Crisis and the Poor.* Rev. ed. New York: Grove Weidenfeld.

Goulet, Denis, and Michael Hudson. 1971. *The Myth of Aid: The Hidden Agenda of Development Reports.* New York: International Documentation (IDOC) North America.

Hyde, Cheryl. 1993. "Class Stratification in the Nonprofit Sector." Paper presented at the conference Private Action and the Public Good, Indiana University Center on Philanthropy, Indianapolis, November 4–6, 1993.

Korten, David C. 1987. "Third Generation NGO Strategies: A Key to People-Centered Development." *World Development* 15:145–59.

Landim, Leilah. 1987. "Non-Governmental Organizations in Latin America." *World Development* 15:29–38.

Laudicina, Paul A. 1973. *World Poverty and Development: A Survey of American Public Opinion.* Washington, D.C.: Overseas Development Council (ODC).

Levine, Daniel H. 1992. *Popular Voices in Latin American Catholicism.* Princeton: Princeton University Press.

Organization for Economic Cooperation and Development (OECD). 1981. *Collaboration between Official Development Cooperation Agencies and Nongovernmental Organizations.* Paris: OECD.

———. 1988. *Voluntary Aid for Development: The Role of Nongovernmental Organizations.* Paris: OECD.

———. 1989. *Directory of Nongovernmental Organizations in OECD Member Countries Active in Development Cooperation.* 2 volumes. Paris: OECD.

———. 1996. *Directory of Nongovernmental Organizations Active in Sustainable Development, Part I: Europe.* Paris: OECD.

Paddock, William, and Elizabeth Paddock. 1973. *We Don't Know How: An Independent Audit of What They Call Success in Foreign Assistance.* Ames: Iowa State University Press.

Putnam, Robert D. 1993. *Making Democracy Work: Civic Traditions in Modern Italy.* Princeton: Princeton University Press.

Rabier, Jacques-René, Hélène Riffault, and Ronald Inglehart. 1985. *Euro-Barometer 20: Aid to Developing Nations, October 1983.* Ann Arbor: Inter-University Consortium for Political and Social Research, University of Michigan.

Ringland, Arthur C. 1954. "The Organization of Voluntary Foreign Aid, 1939–1953." *Department of State Bulletin* 30: 383–93.

Smilie, Ian. 1993. "Changing Partners: Northern NGOs, Northern Governments." Paris: OECD Development Center. Mimeographed.

———. 1995. *The Alms Bazaar: Altruism under Fire — Nonprofit Organizations and International Development.* Ottawa: International Development Research Centre.

Smith, Brian H. 1980. "Churches and Human Rights in Latin America: Recent Trends in the Subcontinent." In *Churches and Politics in Latin America,* ed. Daniel H. Levine. Beverly Hills: Sage Publications.

——. 1990. *More than Altruism: The Politics of Private Foreign Aid.* Princeton: Princeton University Press.

——. 1993. "Nongovernmental Organizations in International Development: Trends and Future Research Priorities." *Voluntas* 4:326–44.

Stremlau, Carolyn. 1987. "NGO Coordinating Bodies in Africa, Asia, and Latin America." *World Development* 15:213–25.

Teltsch, Kathleen. 1993. "Despite Slump, Giving to Charities Rose 6.4% in '92." *New York Times*, May 26, A8.

United Nations Development Program (UNDP). 1993. *Human Development Report 1993.* New York: Oxford University Press.

United States Agency for International Development (USAID). 1992. *Voluntary Foreign Aid Programs 1992.* Washington, D.C.: Bureau for Food and Humanitarian Assistance, Office of Private and Voluntary Cooperation, USAID.

U.S. Congress. 1973. *Mutual Development and Cooperation Act of 1973: Hearings before the Committee on Foreign Affairs.* 93d Congress, 1st session. Washington, D.C.: Government Printing Office.

16

L . D A V I D   B R O W N

Creating Social Capital: Nongovernmental Development Organizations and Intersectoral Problem Solving

Social capital refers to institutional arrangements — social trust, norms of reciprocity and tolerance, and networks of informal association — that foster voluntary cooperation among individuals (Coleman 1990; Putnam 1993a, 167). Such social capital encourages active civic engagement and cooperative action by citizens and provides a variety of ways to solve social, political, and economic problems. High levels of social capital have been associated with more effective and responsive government institutions, more rapid economic development, and higher levels of citizen well-being (e.g., Esman 1978; Putnam 1993a).

At the heart of social capital is the question of coordinating activity. High levels of social capital provide the institutional context for cooperating to solve problems and manage differing interests; low levels of social capital are associated with Hobbesian competition in which problems are resolved by anarchic struggles or by centralized authority (Putnam 1993a; 1993b). The distribution and use of power in society are intimately related to its stocks of social capital: large stocks enable cooperation and lateral decision making, while the absence of social capital requires hierarchical coordination.

If stocks of social capital are critical to political and economic development, the problem of creating social capital becomes very important. Robert D. Putnam's (1993a) study suggested that levels of social capital may be rooted in hundreds of years of history. On the other hand, recent experience suggests that the bases for cooperative social problem solving can be created quite quickly, even among parties with a history of conflict and antagonism (Gray 1989; Trist 1983) and even in national contexts characterized by relatively low stocks of social capital (Brown and Tandon 1993).

Nonprofit, nongovernmental development organizations (NGOs) have played important roles in promoting cooperative problem solving in some circumstances.[1] The existence of NGOs may reflect the levels of social capital in their societies, because they often grow out of informal associations organized to respond to social concerns. I shall argue that NGOs can play critical roles in fostering cooperation among unequally powerful parties when the aim is to solve social problems, and that such cooperative problem solving can in

The research for this chapter was supported in part by grants from the UN Development Programme and the Joyce Mertz-Gilmore Foundation. The paper has benefited from ideas contributed by colleagues at the Institute for Development Research in Boston, the Society for Participatory Research in Asia (PRIA) in New Delhi, and the Synergos Institute in New York, as well as from feedback of conference participants and the editors of this volume.

1. Organizations referred to as nongovernmental organizations in developing countries are often called nonprofit organizations or private voluntary organizations in the United States. Because the examples in this chapter are all drawn from developing countries, I will use the term most common there.

turn create social capital. I draw on four examples of cooperative problem solving in Asia and Africa by grassroots groups, NGOs, government agencies, and international donors in order to develop preliminary hypotheses about NGOs' roles in bridging power inequalities and building stocks of social capital for their societies.

CONCEPTUAL BACKGROUND

Social capital includes informal associations, institutions that support cooperative action, and norms of tolerance and trust. Informal associations and organizations can train their memberships in effective cooperation while giving them voice in the larger society (Putnam 1993a, 89–91). Studies of grassroots development activity reveal strong relationships between the presence of local organizations and economic and social improvements (Esman 1978; Morss, Hatch, Mickelwait and Sweet 1976). Evaluations of World Bank projects several years after their successful completion indicate that local organizations which take over project activities are essential to sustaining improvements (Cernea 1987; Esman and Uphoff 1984). Local organizations are critical actors in local development success and sustainability.

Norms of trust, tolerance, solidarity, and reciprocity are most likely to emerge when they are embedded in and reinforced by a dense network of associations and organizations (Putnam 1993a, 87–89). Such norms and expectations underpin the expectations of mutual influence that are essential to cooperative action and to democratic and pluralistic governance patterns. Under conditions of distrust, intolerance, and lack of reciprocity, authoritarian hierarchy is often required to police the opportunism and anarchy that prevail.

The notion of social capital focuses attention on the organizations and institutions that underlie economic, political, and social activity. Patterns of hierarchical and authoritarian decision making are associated with institutional arrangements that encourage defection, distrust, shirking, exploitation, isolation, disorder, and stagnation. In these circumstances, rationality requires citizens to compete with and exploit one another. In contrast, where there are democratic and pluralistic patterns of decision making, characterized by high levels of cooperation, trust, reciprocity, civic engagement, and collective well-being, it is rational for citizens to cooperate and make collegial decisions with each other (Putnam 1993a, 177). Strong civil societies foster strong governments and strong markets (Putnam 1992; Bratton 1989a; Esman and Uphoff 1984).

What does it take to create institutional arrangements that support cooperation and civic engagement? How can countries or regions systematically increase their stock of social capital? Putnam's (1993a) analysis suggests that social capital is rooted in hundreds of years of civic association and organization. Indeed, the different regions of Italy invented centralized and democratic patterns of governance appropriate to different levels of social capital a thousand years ago.

For many countries, increasing present stocks of social capital requires altering existing institutional arrangements that may be deeply entrenched. Citizens accustomed to social distrust, intolerance of diversity, and lack of reciprocity may find it difficult to adopt other institutional arrangements, and individuals who hold the centralized power required for social coordination in regions with low social capital may not be willing to give up their power. The kinds of changes required to bring about more innovation and cooperative problem solving may vary considerably across countries: The institutional problems that constrain civic engagement and joint action in Africa, for example, may differ dramatically from those in Asia or Europe (see Hyden 1983, 1992).

Patterns of governance in some circumstances may change over months and years rather than centuries. Jonathan Fox (1994), for example, has argued that in Mexico the transition from autocratic to more democratic patterns of governance occurs through an incremental process based on local and regional negotiations that alter the power relations among elites and grassroots groups. This process appears to replace autocratic with more democratic patterns of decision making as grassroots groups develop political awareness and negotiating capacities. Analysts of recent political changes in Africa have emphasized the role of churches in Kenya, unions in Zambia, and NGOs in Zimbabwe in creating the institutional capacity and the social norms necessary for grassroots voices to be heard in public policy (Bratton and Rothchild 1992). Changes in institutional arrangements that support cooperation and innovation may also be negotiated in more limited contexts. Many social problems are difficult or impossible to solve with the resources available to one organization, yet there has been little institutional infrastructure to support cooperation among organizations or across public and private sectors. A variety of new institutional arrangements for cooperative problem solving among diverse organizations and sectors have been created during the past two decades to engage problems of community development (Trist 1983), education (Waddock 1993), and a variety of other problems (Gray 1989; Weisbrod 1992). These alliances have demonstrated that organizations can work together even if they have long histories of conflict and power struggles. In essence, these alliances have developed the institutional arrangements and attitudes associated with higher levels of social capital in relatively short periods of time.

Such institutional changes often emerge from conflict, contradiction, and ambiguity, and they can be strongly influenced by the distribution and exercise of power among the parties (DiMaggio and Powell 1991; Friedland and Alford 1991). Struggles over power may be particularly difficult in settings in which resources are severely limited and national traditions do not support influence by grassroots groups in key decisions, as is the case in many developing countries (for example, Paige 1974).

At the core of many of these efforts has been the problem of promoting cooperation among parties who are unequally powerful. Power imbalances present problems for cooperation in countries with many local organizations and long traditions of reciprocity, trust, and tolerance (Gray 1989). They are even more serious obstacles to cooperation in regions characterized by low levels of social capital, as in many developing countries. Power imbalances are more extreme and difficult to manage when authoritarian, hierarchical decision making is the norm; efforts to bridge those differences are more likely to fail when relations among parties are characterized by distrust, defection, and deception (Brown 1982). As a result, cooperative social problem solving across power inequalities is rare in many settings—and worth examining when it occurs.

At least three elements affect the ability of participants to influence one another in problem solving: (1) the *resources* they bring that are relevant to other parties (Pfeffer 1981; Pfeffer and Salancik 1978); (2) their capacity to shape *awareness* of interests and alternatives facing the parties (Gaventa 1980; Lukes 1974); and (3) their ability to set and maintain *rules and agendas* by which interaction among the parties is governed (DiMaggio and Powell 1991; Clegg 1989).

I shall focus on several cases of cooperation aimed at solving social problems by diverse and unequally powerful organizations in developing countries. Experience suggests that individuals and organizations willing to act as bridges among the parties play a critical role in the creation and implementation of cooperative interorganizational problem solving (Trist 1983; Gray and Wood 1991). I have argued elsewhere (Brown 1988) that NGOs may be especially suited to act as "bridging organizations" that catalyze cooperative problem solving involving grassroots groups and government agencies. NGOs often gain experience in dealing with diverse and conflicting constituencies by working with such constituencies in carrying out their own programs. They are often skilled in articulating values and visions around which diverse parties can join, given their status as values-driven organizations. Finally, because their own work requires that they deal with unequal constituencies, they have considerable experience in dealing with power differences and in maintaining contact across inequalities (Brown 1988; 1991).

My argument in this chapter builds on an initial analysis (Brown and Tandon 1993) of cooperative interorganizational problem solving in developing countries in Asia. In those cases, NGOs often acted as bridging organizations that brought the different parties involved together. This study examines four cases of interorganizational cooperation from Asia and Africa and develops hypotheses about two questions:

1. How do NGOs help promote cooperation across power inequalities?
2. How does interorganizational cooperation across power inequalities contribute to social capital?

METHODS AND CASES

This analysis seeks to generate hypotheses about how NGOs bridge power differences and how cooperative problem solving contributes to social capital. It draws on past research to identify issues in the development of interorganizational cooperation and uses comparative analysis to generate hypotheses from the cases.

I selected the cases to meet four criteria. First, the cases represent cooperative problem solving in countries governed by military dictatorships or single-party regimes, where hierarchical and authoritarian decision making is common. There is some reason to believe that these countries are relatively low in social capital. These cases were exceptions to the ordinary patterns of hierarchical coordination among government and grassroots actors. Second, the cases involve organizations that were quite diverse, particularly in terms of resources and power. The organizations included government agencies, NGOs, grassroots community-based organizations, and local and international donors—many of them with histories of conflict, distrust, and vulnerability to abuses by more powerful parties. Third, each case continued over several years and markedly improved the lives of thousands of participants, whether by immunizing children, maintaining irrigation systems, improving urban sanitation, or increasing savings to improve village agriculture. The cooperation had substantial regional or national effects. Finally, in each case, an NGO played a key role as a bridge among the parties. NGOs sometimes were called in by other parties; sometimes they initiated the cooperation. In all these cases, they played a critical part in starting and sustaining the cooperation.

Table 16.1 provides a brief overview of the problems, events, and outcomes of the four cases. In each case, NGOs helped define the problem, set directions for problem solving, and implement cooperative action to solve it. The Asian cases were written as part of a larger comparative research project on the problems and potentials of intersectoral problem solving (Brown and Tandon 1993). The African case was developed in studies of relations between NGOs and governments (Bratton 1990). The casewriters all had long histories of involvement and credibility with representatives of the different parties.

ANALYSIS AND HYPOTHESES

Reviews of research on interorganizational problem solving indicate that cooperation evolves over time (for example, Gray 1989; Wood and Gray 1991). In this section, I first examine NGOs as bridging organizations, especially with respect to bridging power differences, at four stages of cooperative effort: (1) convening the parties, (2) framing the problem, (3) setting directions for action, and (4) implementing problem solutions. I then shift focus to the outcomes of cooperative problem solving with respect to (1) solving the initial problem and (2) creating social capital. In each segment, my

Table 16.1. Cases of Cooperation

Problem	Events	Outcomes
Bangladesh Immunization Program: to provide expanded immunization program for children throughout the country. At the start of the program in 1985, only 2% of children were vaccinated.	The government of Bangladesh invited two large NGOs, BRAC (Bangladesh Rural Advancement Committee) and CARE/Bangladesh, to work with Ministry of Public Health and Family Planning staff and representatives of WHO, UNICEF, and the World Bank to plan and implement the first phase of the national Expanded Program of Immunization. In later phases, as many as 1,300 NGOs helped with the vaccination campaign, using their close ties to grassroots groups to mobilize families to bring their children for vaccination (Hussain 1991).	Child immunization coverage increased from 2% in 1985 to 80% in 1990; child mortality down 20%; improved relations between government and NGOs; training for government workers; increased local awareness and action on health issues.
Indonesian Irrigation Program: to turn responsibility for system maintenance over to local farmers. Irrigation systems are vital to small farmers, and government resources for their construction and maintenance were seriously reduced by changes in oil revenues.	LP3ES (The Institute for Social and Economic Research, Education and Information) worked with government departments, universities, the Ford Foundation and water-user associations to develop and implement ways to turn over control of small irrigation systems to the associations. LP3ES helped interpret pilot research on alternative systems, formulate the turnover policy, train government staff to carry it out, create procedures and manuals for program implementation, and provide ongoing consultation to agencies charged with implementation (Purnomo and Pambagio 1991; Bruns and Soelaiman 1991).	New policy adopted for local control of small irrigation systems; new water-user associations organized; substantial reductions in system maintenance costs; improved attitudes in government for local management of systems.
Pakistan Urban Sanitation Program: to build sewage systems in Karachi squatter settlement area, where 100,000 families live with no system for disposing of human wastes.	OPP (Orangi Pilot Project) is an NGO that began by spending six months working with a neighborhood "lane organization" to identify their concerns and then develop an appropriate technology for building the desired local latrines and sewage systems. On the basis of the resident-built systems, OPP then negotiated with local government officials, national government agencies, and international donors to expand the self-reliant sanitation development process to other neighborhoods, cities, and countries (Rashid 1991).	Developed sewage system for a fraction of regular cost; built more than 64,000 latrines, 4,000 sewage lines, and 300 secondary drains; residents contributed 90% of resources required; scores of lane organizations formed and active in many areas; OPP offers technical support for wider replication.
Zimbabwe Village Savings Program: to encourage grassroots savings to improve agricultural productivity in rural villages where most of the potential savers are illiterate.	SDM (Savings Development Movement) created a technology to enable illiterate villagers to save money together in village savings clubs. Then SDM lobbied the Ministry of Agriculture to provide technical support for using the funds to improve agricultural productivity. They also arranged for the Ministry of Community Development and Women's Affairs to train villagers in the savings methodology and for financial support for the training from a fertilizer corporation interested in expanding its village markets (Bratton 1990).	Developed technology for keeping track of club savings; changed Ministry policy to enable village assistance; organized more than 5,000 village clubs to increase agricultural productivity; improved lives of 250,000 rural villagers.

intent is to formulate preliminary hypotheses about cooperative efforts in their social, political, and economic contexts.

NGOs as Bridging Organizations

NGOs have acted as bridges among diverse parties in developing countries in the past (for example, Brown 1991; Brown and Tandon 1993). Although the political aspects of interorganizational problem solving have been recognized in some studies (Gray 1989; Wood and Gray 1993), power differences have not been a primary concern of most investigators. In these case studies, however, power differences are at the heart of understanding both the challenges of enabling mutual influence in problem solving and the impact of that problem solving on social capital.

Convening the Parties. Previous research suggests that efforts to promote intersectoral cooperation are affected by several factors, including the historical and institutional context of the parties, the history of relations among them, and the position and characteristics of the convening or initiating party. Histories of power differences and interorganizational conflict, for example, make cooperation more difficult (Gray 1989; Trist 1983). Sandra Waddock (1993) found that collaborative problem solving to improve urban school systems in a dozen American cities was affected by the local history of intersectoral networking and cooperation. When those histories were marked by lack of contact or by conflict and distrust, cooperation was more difficult. Success is also affected by the power base of the party that initiates problem solving (Wood and Gray 1993; Trist 1983). Waddock (1993) found that the presence of a credible broker or mandate for joint action promoted successful educational collaborations.

The history of intersectoral relations between NGOs and government organizations in military or single-party regimes can be problematic for several reasons. NGOs often distrust governments because of real or perceived histories of abuse of power; governments often see NGOs, especially those that serve large grassroots communities, as potential rivals for political power (Tandon 1989; Bratton 1989b). NGO relations with governments in such settings are often a complex mixture of cooperation, conflict, and avoidance.

NGOs are an active, well-established institutional sector in some countries, such as Bangladesh, where they are major actors in development activity and are seen as a political force by the government. In other countries, Pakistan, for example, they comprise a relatively small and unrecognized political force. More important for the purposes of this analysis, NGOs vary considerably in reputation and relationship with government agencies. Both the Savings Development Movement SDM in Zimbabwe and the Oranji Pilot Project OPP in Pakistan were new agencies, with short institutional track records and histories. In contrast, the Bangladesh Rural Advancement Committee BRAC and the Cooperative for American Relief to Everywhere (CARE) in Bangladesh and the Institute for Social and Economic Research, Education, and Information LP3ES in Indonesia were well known by government agencies and international donors for their work with grassroots populations.

The initiation of interorganizational problem solving reflected differences in the starting positions of the NGOs. In Bangladesh and Indonesia, the government approached the NGOs to mobilize grassroots participation in government programs. The government of Indonesia asked LP3ES to help develop research studies, assess alternative policies, and develop training programs for government officials and water-user associations in the course of government deliberations about turning over control and maintenance of irrigation systems. The government of Bangladesh asked BRAC, CARE, and other NGOs to coordinate and mobilize grassroots groups to participate in the national immunization campaign. When governments ask NGOs to take on such roles, they implicitly recognize the NGOs' access to important resources and, in effect, their legitimacy. They thereby set the stage for mutual influence in social problem solving.

In Zimbabwe and Pakistan, the NGOs initiated cooperation with grassroots groups and then worked with government agencies to expand their programs. In Zimbabwe, SDM invented the savings technology, tested it in the villages, and eventually persuaded government ministries and other donors to support it. OPP in Pakistan worked for six months with one neighborhood organization to define needs, develop appropriate technologies, and demonstrate the possibility of local construction of sewage systems. Then OPP sought support from larger coalitions of grassroots groups, international donors, and government agencies to expand their program. In both cases, a new NGO worked with grassroots groups to develop and demonstrate an innovative solution to a widespread problem. In essence, they used a two-step process, in which the initial alliance proved the utility of an innovation and built the credibility required for initiating a coalition with parties with more power and resources (see Wood and Gray 1991). For NGOs who seek to launch such an innovation, getting initial resources and political space can be problematic, particularly if they are perceived to be a threat to high-power groups who are accustomed to authoritarian decision making.

In short, the convening of parties to initiate cooperative problem solving may take quite different forms, depending on the institutional histories of the key actors. NGOs play different roles in the convening process, depending on their reputations and capacities for influencing the parties. Key elements of this discussion can be summarized in the form of a preliminary hypothesis:

Hypothesis 1: NGOs can bridge power differences to convene unequal parties by:
•working with parties separately to prepare them for engaging with other (particularly high-power) parties;
•piloting innovative solutions to problems to establish credibility for alternative solutions and actors; or
•drawing on reputations and credibility established in past relations to convene otherwise noncooperating parties.

Convening of parties with histories of conflict and power differences often replicates conflicts and abuses of power that make cooperative problem solving difficult or impossible. In the programs initiated by NGOs and grassroots groups, the demonstrated success of NGO-grassroots cooperation in the area of urban sanitation in Pakistan and savings development in Zimbabwe established the credibility for the NGO to convene discussions with government agencies and international donors. That success, in turn, depended on the NGOs' initial work with grassroots groups. In the programs initiated by government agencies, in contrast, the NGOs were invited to convene the parties because they were recognized as having access to grassroots groups essential to accomplishing government goals. The credibility of the NGO with multiple parties was essential to convening of initial meetings—but that credibility had different bases in cases initiated by different parties. In the government-initiated cooperation, the reputations of NGOs with government agencies were important; for cooperation initiated by NGOs and grassroots groups, NGO success in innovative work with grassroots groups was essential to building the credibility of NGOs who were previously unknown.

Problem Framing

The process of framing the problem is central to fostering interorganizational collaboration. Gray (1989, 57–58) suggests that problem framing includes identifying stakeholders and resources, defining the problem in terms that permit participation by all the parties, and developing a commitment to collaborate among stakeholders. The problem-framing phase includes critical decisions about whom to include or exclude and sets precedents for interaction that enable or constrain later participation of various stakeholders (Bingham 1986; Gray and Hay 1986).

In government-initiated programs, NGOs helped reframe initial definitions of problems to emphasize the interests and the participation of grassroots groups. In Bangladesh, for example, BRAC and CARE helped reframe immunization from a delivery of service problem—which emphasized government coverage of poor populations—to a demand problem—which focused on mobilizing grassroots interest in getting their children vaccinated. The second frame led to the organization by a coalition of government agencies, international donors, and NGOss of a mass movement to get children vaccinated. In Indonesia, LP3ES helped government agencies and water-user associations reconceive irrigation system maintenance as a responsibility of farmers rather than government officials. A key issue in reframing problems for government-initiated projects is the amount and kind of participation by grassroots groups in problem solving. These NGOs used their access to and expertise about grassroots groups to reframe problems in the eyes of government agencies to emphasize the need for local resources and the importance of local interests in problem definitions.

In NGO-initiated projects, initial problem framing focuses on the concerns and capacities of grassroots groups. Only after initial problem-solving activities have been successfully implemented do the parties engage other stakeholders in reframing problem definitions. In Pakistan, the OPP and neighborhood organizations reframed local sanitation, initially seen as a problem to be solved by government services, as a target for local action and appropriate technology. OPP and the neighborhood organizations engaged municipal councils and government agencies in discussions of large-scale drains after they demonstrated that latrines and neighborhood sewage systems could be constructed by local groups. In Zimbabwe, SDM initially worked with a few vil-

lage clubs to define lack of capital as a significant problem, then to design and test the savings methodology, and eventually to develop ways to use the resulting savings. SDM then helped government ministries, international donors, and other actors to reconceive the problem of generating agricultural capital in terms of local skills for savings. These NGOs began by working with grassroots groups to frame problems that could be solved by an NGO-grassroots coalition; once successful innovations had been developed and tested, the NGOs helped other stakeholders recognize how their interests and resources might fit with replicating the innovations.

NGOs also can catalyze the reformulation of problem definitions by facilitating information exchange among parties, particularly where power inequalities limited previous communication. In the Indonesian discussions, LP3ES fostered dialogues between government officials and water users. In Pakistan, OPP was an intermediary between government bureaucrats, neighborhood groups, and international donors. In Zimbabwe, SDM staff lobbied government agencies to understand the needs and provide support to village groups. In Bangladesh, BRAC and CARE played key roles in helping grassroots actors, small NGOs, and government bureaucrats engage each other in building better understanding of the forces that inhibited the grassroots vaccination campaigns. NGOs can use their understanding of the different views and capacities of diverse parties to foster interaction and mutual influence in understanding different perspectives on complex problems that enable better understanding and even substantial change in perspectives.

These patterns of NGO influence in the framing of problems can also be summarized in hypothesis form:

Hypothesis 2: NGOs can bridge power differences to foster reframing of problems by:
•helping parties (especially high-power parties) reconceive the problem, its causes, and each others' stakes in it;
•helping parties recognize each others' resources relevant to problem-solving; and
•facilitating interaction and mutual influence in problem definition.

The framing or reframing of the problem is in large part a conceptual task. The reframing task places a premium on the capacities of agencies in bridging roles to understand the problem from multiple perspectives and to synthesize redefinitions that respect the interests and concerns of all the parties. The NGOs in these cases were able to see the problems in a relatively long-term, large-scale perspective that revealed the benefits of multiparty participation and the importance of their diverse resources to problem solutions. In addition, a successful reframing process provides the parties with an initial experience of cooperation and mutual influence. When past experience is dominated by conflict or one-way influence, experiences of cooperation and mutual influence that produce a shared problem definition are often powerful incentives for further contact. By the same token, efforts at problem definition that reproduce past experiences of conflict or dominance are unlikely to lead to future cooperation. Commitment to further participation depends on problem-framing processes that demonstrate the possibilities of cooperation.

Setting Directions

Setting directions for joint action includes establishing ground rules for interaction, setting substantive agendas, organizing subgroups to carry out key tasks, engaging in joint search and analysis of information, exploring options for action, and negotiating agreement on some of those options (Gray 1989, 74–86). Direction setting creates goals to which all the parties are willing to commit and action plans that will mobilize and utilize their resources to solve the problem. The direction-setting process may involve extensive negotiations among the parties about the specifics of problem solving, so that it affords many opportunities for mutual influence or abuse of power inequalities.

Power inequalities can make joint direction setting very difficult: Low-power parties may be apathetic and unaware of their resources or highly sensitive to their vulnerability; high-power parties may be oblivious to their power and its impact or assume that they should be in control (Brown 1982; Gaventa 1980). NGOs can play a critical role in direction setting by balancing power differences and enabling participation of all parties in setting goals and planning joint action.

In government-initiated programs, NGOs invited to participate because of their access to grassroots populations can identify and plan to mobilize grassroots resources for implementing programs of interest to the government. In Bangladesh, the initial involvement of two NGOs in planning and implementing a pilot immunization project eventually led to the inclusion of hundreds of NGOs in the immunization campaign, as it became clear that NGOs could mobilize grassroots participation better than government agencies. In Indonesia, pilot research projects demonstrated that appropriately prepared water-user associations could take over management of small irrigation systems. LP3ES helped develop plans for turnover and then trained government agencies and water-user associations charged with primary responsibilities for implementing the turnover.

For NGO-initiated programs, the resources of grassroots participants are often clearly defined as a prerequisite to convening the other parties, because the influence of the NGOs depends on their ability to demonstrate an effective innovation. In Pakistan, for example, the OPP spent six months working with one neighborhood organization to define goals and pilot test the latrine-building program before they considered expanding the program. They were reluctant to approach government agents, in part because they feared that the innovation would be sabotaged by bureaucrats with financial interests in the existing system. In Zimbabwe, SDM

first demonstrated that their savings development clubs could generate capital for agricultural improvements before they approached government ministries to expand the program. These preliminary coalitions demonstrated that grassroots groups commanded resources that might enhance problem solving by government agencies or international donors.

In each case, NGOs played important roles in negotiations that produced a shared plan of action. In Bangladesh, several NGOs worked closely with Ministry of Health and Family Planning officials to create an elaborate plan to recruit and coordinate hundreds of NGOs and thousands of grassroots groups. The NGOs served as conduits for information and influence among government officials, grassroots groups, and small NGOs, and so brought about a kind of mutual influence rare in their previous contacts. In Indonesia, LP3ES facilitated the interpretation of research on pilot projects, the formulation of policy for turning over system control, and the planning for water-user associations and government agencies to carry out the new policy. The NGOs fostered mutual influence by translating grassroots experience to government policy makers and government policy concerns to grassroots groups.

In some circumstances, NGOs took firm stands to balance power differences in the direction-setting process by establishing and enforcing norms that supported mutual influence. When a government agency threatened to centralize the implementation of an expanded sanitation project in Pakistan, OPP refused to participate until the agency agreed to preserve grassroots influence and participation. This challenge succeeded in part because of support from international agencies funding the project. Sometimes NGOs must be ready to challenge actions of parties, even high-power parties like government agencies, in order to preserve the possibility of mutual influence among unequal parties.

The roles of NGOs in balancing power inequalities during the setting of direction for cooperative action can also be summarized as a hypothesis:

Hypothesis 3: NGOs can bridge power inequalities to foster mutual influence in direction setting by:
•identifying the resources brought by parties that are relevant to problem solving;
•promoting the identification and assessment of alternative courses of action;
•developing plans that utilize the resources of the parties to accomplish joint gains; or
•setting and enforcing ground rules that enable cooperation and mutual influence.

Direction setting involves discussion of concrete details to accomplish shared goals and visions. It calls for assessing proposals and plans, analyzing alternatives, examining action possibilities, and negotiating specific expectations and interests in action plans. NGOs are most effective in this phase when they understand their own resources and those of the other parties and they can negotiate, mediate, and otherwise deal with the inevitable conflicts of interest and perspective that surface in the course of planning activities to accomplish more abstract shared values and visions. Preserving mutual influence in direction-setting discussions may call for active balancing of power inequalities and interventions to prevent high-power participants from taking over the choice of action alternatives and the process of planning implementation.

Implementing Cooperative Solutions

The implementation of joint solutions involves dealing with the constituencies of the parties involved, building support among stakeholders not involved in the planning process, organizing and carrying out programmatic activities, and assessing the impacts of those activities on the problem (Gray 1989, 86–94). It is sometimes a challenge to get agreement from party representatives who sit around the table; it is a much greater challenge to get hundreds or thousands of others to implement that agreement. Implementation is particularly problematic when it must overcome a history of antagonism among the parties (DiMaggio and Powell 1992, 22–25).

Some NGOs support implementation by helping to identify and build capacities to carry out joint activity. At the grassroots level, for example, the savings clubs organized by SDM in Zimbabwe and the neighborhood organizations organized by OPP in Pakistan were essential to implementing cooperative action, making contributions for which no other parties could substitute. Control over essential resources of information and energy — some unrecognized before the projects began — conferred significant power on the grassroots groups and on the NGOs they trusted to work in their interests. NGOs also helped expand the capacities of government agencies: LP3ES in Indonesia, BRAC and CARE in Bangladesh, and SDM in Zimbabwe provided training, technical assistance and capacity-building programs for government officials as well as grassroots groups. Capacity building, a core competence of many NGOs, proved an important contribution in the implementation of these innovative projects.

NGOs also help to reduce power inequalities by organizing implementation activities that depend on the special resources of different parties. In Bangladesh, for example, there was no way to get millions of rural children to vaccination centers without active participation by thousands of grassroots groups and small NGOs. The campaign also required medical expertise to train vaccinators, the Ministry of Health's capacity to transport staff and vaccines, and the resources of national and local media to inform the public. The immunization campaign empowered many groups and organizations by creating roles appropriate to their resources. In Zimbabwe, improving of agricultural productivity required savings by village savings clubs, but it also demanded training and technical support from ministries. SDM created a program that used the resources and served the interests of both grassroots groups and government organizations. When parties depend on each other to carry out a complex plan,

success can reinforce mutual influence and more cooperative attitudes.

NGOs can also help expand activities to affect wider constituencies. SDM in Zimbabwe lobbied over the years to include more ministries, fertilizer corporations, and international donors in supporting the movement, and so facilitated its rapid expansion to affect thousands of villages. In Bangladesh, the initial NGOs helped build a campaign that included hundreds of NGOs and grassroots groups as well as many other sympathetic institutions and individuals. Because many NGOs develop widespread networks of supporters and cooperators, they may be positioned very well to expand programs during implementation activities.

NGOs also serve a training and translating function in implementation activities. LP3ES fostered research, information sharing, and training with different parties involved in transferring control over irrigation systems from government to water-user associations in Indonesia. SDM acted as facilitator and mediator among ministries, international donors, interested corporations, and village savings clubs as the movement expanded in Zimbabwe. NGOs coordinated the activities of more than thirteen hundred organizations participating in the Bangladesh immunization campaign. OPP created a research and training institute to make its programs more widely available. The access and credibility of NGOs with many parties in earlier phases positioned them to be facilitators and translators when needed in later phases and also to be critical resources for enabling grassroots voice in program assessment and modification as they progressed.

The power-balancing work of NGOs is often central to the effective implementation of multiparty, intersectoral problem solving:

Hypothesis 4: NGOs can bridge power inequalities to foster cooperative implementation by:
•identifying and building capacity to carry out program tasks;
•organizing and managing implementation to use the special resources of each party;
•widening the constituencies committed to implementation; and
•translating and troubleshooting to solve problems and ensure widespread voice in program assessment and change.

Implementing of large-scale problem-solving activities requires attention to thousands of concrete decisions, and the differences among the parties — sometimes obscured in discussions of big issues and shared goals — must be dealt with in concrete terms. Organizing and implementing of these activities call for skill in managing differences, organizing joint activities, translating the perspectives of different parties, and coping with inevitable tensions and conflicts in ways that reinforce cooperation and positive attitudes. NGOs can build on the credibility and perspective generated in earlier stages to provide a crucially important mediating and

Table 16.2. Outcomes of Cooperation

Case	Problem-Solving Outcomes	Social and Institutional Changes
Bangladesh Immunization Program	Immunization coverage increased from 2% to 80%; mortality of children under five down 20%; improved health services to grassroots communities.	Encouraged grassroots activism in pursuing health services; improved cooperation of government and NGO field workers; improved relations among NGOs, government officials, and grassroots groups; increased awareness and capacity for large-scale alliances for development purposes.
Indonesian Irrigation Program	Reduced maintenance costs 50–60% for small irrigation systems; trained government staff in working effectively with water users; involved water users in system management and construction.	Accredited 166 water-user associations; improved government officials' attitudes toward water-user participation; increased NGO capacity to play intersectoral mediating role; adopted policy transferring control of small irrigation systems to water users.
Pakistan Urban Sanitation Program	Constructed 64,000 latrines and related sewage systems in Karachi slums; more than 90% of resources provided by slum dwellers; appropriate technology reduced costs to less than 20% of commercial costs.	Organized 4,000 neighborhoods to construct sewage systems; neighborhood organizations undertook other locally defined projects; OPP recognized as research and training center; involved international donors and government agencies to replicate project in other areas.
Zimbabwe Savings Development Movement	Developed low-cost method for capital formation and investment by villagers; organized savings programs, mostly with rural women, affecting 250,000 people; reshaped extension activities of Ministries of Agriculture and Community Development and Women's Affairs.	Created more than 5,000 community savings clubs, mostly women; set precedent for cooperation among grassroots groups, ministries and NGOs; demonstrated possibilities of grassroots capital formation to both villagers and government; involved international donor organizations to promote grassroots savings.

linkage role in the course of implementation. Because most NGOs do not operate on a national scale they may be less equipped than government agencies to administer large-scale programs — but they may be very useful in troubleshooting and problem solving at the interfaces among the participants (see Brown 1991).

CONSEQUENCES OF COOPERATION

Interorganizational cooperation can generate information, mobilize resources, and produce solutions to problems that are intractable to the parties working alone (Bingham 1986; Gray 1989; Wood and Gray 1992). When parties are able to make constructive use of differences in interest, power, and perspective, the results can be impressive. The cases described here created new solutions to very difficult problems and disseminated them widely with important impacts on poor populations.

In the long run, these ventures may have other social and institutional consequences that are less visible but even more important. The experience of cooperation among organizations from different sectors, especially organizations that are unequal in power, status, and resources, is rare in many of these settings, and participation in cooperative problem solving that persists over time and produces outcomes in the interest of all the parties may have effects on attitudes, practices, and institutions that reverberate beyond the immediate problem solutions. Such social and institutional changes may be more important in the long term than the impacts on im-

mediate problems because they can contribute to institutional contexts — to the creation of social capital — that enable wider engagement and more effective problem solving on many problems in the future.

Table 16.2 provides an overview of the impact of these interorganizational problem-solving activities on the problems they were intended to solve and on their social and institutional contexts. Each will be discussed in the following section.

Problem Solutions

These cases were selected because in some way they represented successful responses to complex problems. Thus, the immunization program in fact increased the proportion of immunized children in Bangladesh, and the urban sanitation program built more latrines and sewage systems in Pakistan. What is less obvious from looking at the outcomes alone are the patterns of activity that improved problem-solving performance. Examination of these case studies suggests that at least three factors were important to achieving improvements.

In government-initiated programs, cooperation with NGOs and grassroots groups may *improve utilization* of government programs and agency capacities. In Bangladesh, for example, collaboration with international donors, NGOs, and grassroots groups increased the capacity of the Ministry of Health and Family Planning to deliver child immunization services, enabling a fortyfold increase in coverage. In Indonesia, cooperation with universities, NGOs, international donors, and water-user associations significantly reduced costs of maintaining and rehabilitating irrigation systems. For government agencies, cooperation with other actors enabled wider and more efficient delivery of services.

In NGO-initiated collaborations, successful work with other actors can *enable widespread replication* of projects that have been successful on a small scale — expansion far beyond the capacity of the NGOs by themselves. In Pakistan, OPP and the lane organizations constructed latrines and neighborhood sewage systems, but the expanding of the program to hundreds of communities and to larger sewage systems required cooperation with municipal authorities and international donors. In Zimbabwe, replicating the village savings clubs in thousands of villages required training and technical assistance from the national ministries and outside donors. The NGOs were able to develop and test technologies for grassroots problem solving, but their replication regionally and nationally called for the kinds of resources more often found in government agencies and international donors.

Cooperative problem solving across power and organizational differences in many circumstances also *mobilizes previously unrecognized resources*. In Indonesia, better understanding and cooperation between water users and government officials gradually demonstrated that the water users could manage the small irrigation systems. Previously unrecognized capacities of water-user associations were revealed or developed in the course of the multiparty deliberations over the evolving policy. In Bangladesh, government officials became more aware of the potential contributions of NGOs and grassroots groups to government programs, and so did grassroots groups themselves. On many occasions, grassroots participation in the immunization program catalyzed more interest and activism in health programs in general. In Zimbabwe, the SDM generated previously unavailable village capital for improving agricultural productivity in addition to mobilizing grassroots efforts to use that capital effectively. In Pakistan, the OPP combined appropriate technology with local labor to build dozens of sewage systems for the cost of a single commercially installed system, mobilizing local resources not previously recognized or available. Cooperative problem solving can generate resources — information, energy, ideas, funds — that were not available to prior efforts.

These ideas about the ingredients of improved performance by interorganizational cooperation on difficult problems can also be expressed in hypothesis form:

Hypothesis 5: Cooperative problem solving across power and sector differences can create resources to solve intractable problems by:
•expanding the use, particularly by poor populations, of government programs;
•expanding and replicating successful innovations by NGOs and grassroots groups; and
•creating or revealing new resources that are available only through cooperative effort.

The engagement of diverse parties can improve problem solving in many ways. The parties together may generate new information and perspectives on problems; they may bring together complementary resources for solving them; they may achieve better targeting of key problems or bottlenecks through interactive analysis. It has been widely recognized that ongoing learning is critical for organizations that, like most development agencies, face rapidly changing environments (Korten 1980; Senge 1991). Cooperation across sectors and power inequalities may foster a kind of ongoing learning that is not otherwise available for difficult problems.

Contributions to Social Capital

These cases also illustrate that problem solving across power and sectoral differences can generate outcomes beyond solutions to immediate problems. In social and institutional contexts that favor hierarchical decision making rather than civic engagement and coordination for mutual benefit, cooperative problem solving that spans sector and power differences is rare. Once started, however, the success of such cooperation may contribute to institutional changes — building social capital — that will support improved problem solving in the future. The cases studied took place in countries with relatively few institutional mechanisms for mutual influence between government agencies and grassroots groups. Their success appears to have encouraged several contributions to future social capital.

In many cases, the projects *created new local organizations* that enhanced the capacity of low-power populations to solve their own problems, engage in cooperative action, and influence other actors. The SDM fostered the organization of thousands of women's village savings clubs in Zimbabwe to generate capital and improve agricultural productivity in ways that emphasized cooperation among villagers. The OPP helped organize thousands of urban neighborhood organizations to build sewage systems and latrines in Pakistan, and those organizations subsequently took on a variety of other self-help projects. The Indonesian irrigation policy project organized and trained scores of water-user associations and created the policy base for the development of hundreds of others. Such local organizations can mobilize local resources for solving specific problems; they can also create the institutional base for other activities that require grassroots cooperation (Cernea 1987; Morss et al., 1976). The density of local organizations, a key element of social capital (Putnam 1993a), was significantly enhanced by these cooperative efforts.

These collaborations *increased the capacity of other participating organizations*. Thus, the Bangladesh immunization campaign enhanced the abilities of many small NGOs to deliver rudimentary health services and helped government agencies learn more about how to work effectively with grassroots groups. In Indonesia, LP3ES trained government officials to work more effectively with water users. In Zimbabwe, cooperation enabled the Ministry of Community Development and Women's Affairs to support a successful program for training women's savings clubs and brought the Ministry of Agriculture thousands of clients for technical assistance in improving agricultural productivity. The programs demonstrated that cooperation can have a capacity-building impact at different levels.

Joint work across power and sector differences *built attitudinal and institutional bases for future cooperation*. In the settings studied, cooperation among grassroots groups, NGOs, government agencies, and international donors was rare. Successful joint action created perceptions and precedents to support future cooperation. In Bangladesh, participants reported that the immunization campaign, initially hampered by tensions between NGOs and government organizations, changed attitudes and increased interest in future cooperation on both sides. Indonesian government officials reported more favorable attitudes toward farmer participation in irrigation system management after their experience with pilot projects. The Pakistan sanitation project and the Zimbabwe savings development movement started without government participation or interest but eventually convinced government agencies that they should support program expansion. The experience of cooperation, to some extent, created norms and precedents for future behavior.

This is not to say that cooperation is inevitable: Governments sometimes try to take over or dominate program activities, and a single instance of mutual influence is not likely to overthrow expectations and practices grounded in centuries of experience. But the conspicuous success of these cases and their widespread visibility and impact can be contagious. Indonesian government officials, for example, were substantially influenced by the success of a comparable venture in the Philippines supported by the Ford Foundation.

These examples of interorganizational problem solving also *generated international interest and support* for cooperative problem solving. All these projects received some support from international donors and development agencies, support that in some cases contributed to their legitimacy in the eyes of government agencies. The OPP in Pakistan used foundation support for early program development and then blocked a government takeover by using its credibility with international donors. The SDM used support from international donors to expand its program in Zimbabwe. The role of LP3ES in the Indonesian irrigation policy project was supported by international resources, as were visits to similar programs in other countries. The Bangladesh program drew heavily on support from the World Health Organization, the United Nations International Children's Emergency Fund, and the World Bank to carry out the immunization campaign. International agencies often supported initial innovations as well as encouraged widespread recognition and dissemination of their impact.

In short, the cases studied had social and institutional consequences relevant to future cooperation among the parties and future organized activity by grassroots groups. In hypothesis form:

Hypothesis 6: Cooperation across sector and power differences may increase social capital by:
•strengthening local organizations and capacities for problem solving;
•enhancing the capacities of parties to achieve their goals;
•creating attitudinal and institutional bases for future cooperation; and
•attracting external resources to support cooperative efforts.

The building of social capital is not simple or quick, and none of the results described here automatically translate into widespread civic engagement or norms for social trust and reciprocity or networks of association. To the extent that cooperative ventures succeed as problem-solving innovations, however, they may be seedbeds of organizational and institutional changes that have importance beyond their immediate impact on specific problems.

DISCUSSION: COOPERATION, POWER, AND SOCIAL CAPITAL

NGOs were important actors who served as bridges among unequal parties in these cooperative efforts. At the outset, most were likely to have influence on the basis of access to key actors, such as grassroots groups needed to implement government-initiated programs or governments and donors needed to expand and replicate grassroots successes. They influenced problem definition by facilitating constructive dialogue among diverse parties and reframing initial concepts to account for the interests of many stakeholders. NGOs fostered mutual influence in direction setting by identifying resources brought by diverse parties, developing plans that utilized those resources, and promoting ground rules that supported mutual influence. NGOs organized cooperative implementation activities to build and use the resources of many parties, expand commitment to cooperative problem solving, and translate and mediate to enable mutual influence among a wide range of participants.

One of my initial research questions was, How do NGOs help promote cooperation across power inequalities? Across these phases of cooperation, NGOs appeared to draw on several sources of power to balance inequalities among participants, including controlling important resources, shaping participants' awareness of their own and others' interests, and defining and enforcing rules of the game to promote mutual influence.

Many analysts have focused on the power inherent in control of such key resources as information, authority, funds, material goods, and other items of value to the parties to be influenced (see Pfeffer and Salancik 1978; Pfeffer 1981). The NGOs in these cases typically did not control authority or material resources, but they were influential in their ability to provide *access to resources* controlled by antagonistic or unconnected groups. In government-initiated cooperative problem solving in Bangladesh and Indonesia, by virtue of their access to grassroots groups, NGOs were able to shape events and balance the resources and legitimate authority of government agencies in work on major problems. In NGO-initiated programs in Pakistan and Zimbabwe, NGOs were able to expand dramatically the impacts of grassroots innovations through their credibility with government ministries and international donors. In some circumstances, NGO activities were influential through *creating new resources* that were vital to problem solving. In Pakistan, OPP created new technology and new grassroots organizations to mobilize local energy and materials for creating sewage systems. In Zimbabwe, SDM promoted the formation of village capital and organized savings clubs to carry out improvements in agricultural technology. The ability of NGOs to play a catalytic role in convening joint problem-solving activities owed much to their demonstrated access to and influence over critical resources.

NGOs also wielded considerable influence on the basis of their ability to affect the awareness of various parties and their skill at constructing accounts and rationales for joint activity. In some circumstances, NGOs play critical roles as *articulators of alternatives*. In Zimbabwe and Pakistan, NGOs created innovations in cooperation with grassroots groups and then helped government and international donors recognize their importance. In other settings, NGOs are *facilitators of collective reflections* that produce new perspectives. In Indonesia and Bangladesh, for example, NGOs helped to clarify the possibilities of joint action in discussions with government officials, international donors, and water users. In still other situations, NGOs became *educators* of people charged with carrying out joint activities. In Indonesia and Zimbabwe, NGOs trained government officials to work more effectively with grassroots groups and fostered more awareness and understanding of key implementers about joint action plans.

Finally, NGOs play active roles in defining and enforcing the rules of the game that govern the interaction among the parties. Sometimes NGOs acted as *mediators and translators*, helping small NGOs understand government requirements, as in the Bangladesh immunization campaign, or clarify the concerns of grassroots groups, as in Indonesia. Sometimes NGOs helped to *organize and manage joint activity*, as in designing the support programs for savings clubs in Zimbabwe or in facilitating cooperation among universities, water-user associations, and government officials in Indonesia. In other instances, NGOs acted as *enforcers* to ensure that rules were followed, as in the refusal of OPP to allow a government agency to subvert the participation and mutual influence norms of the sanitation project. NGOs often exercised unobtrusive power in rule making and reinforcing processes that supported continuing mutual influence among

unequal parties. They helped to create and maintain a new "negotiated order" that supported cooperative decision making (Day and Day 1977; Nathan and Mitroff 1991; Strauss 1979).

Although the cases studied offer evidence that NGOs can sometimes balance power differences to foster intersectoral cooperation, they often do so at some risk. These NGO leaders were knowledgeable about and connected to the national power structures. They were careful about relations with government agencies when they were promoting NGO- and grassroots-initiated projects. Both OPP and SDM faced serious challenges from state agencies when they were seen as stepping out of line. Their positions at the intersections of many parties offered NGOs the opportunity to balance power differences and have major impacts on important problems — but they also placed them in positions of significant risk of incurring the wrath of powerful actors.

My second research question was, How does interorganizational cooperation across power inequalities contribute to social capital? I identified four ways in which cooperation appeared to expand social capital in these case studies: by strengthening local organizations, enhancing the capacities of many parties to accomplish their goals, creating attitudes and institutions to support future cooperation, and attracting external resources to support cooperative efforts.

Renegotiation of power relations appears to be critically important in the creation of new social capital. Work within these projects provided concrete experience of pluralistic and democratic decision making associated with relatively high levels of social capital.

Interaction is central to these experiences. The development of local organizations, particularly prominent in the NGO-initiated cases, grows out of extensive interaction among NGOs and grassroots groups intended to identify and solve problems in ways consistent with grassroots concerns and resources. The improvement of government agency programs, particularly likely in government-initiated programs, grows out of engagement between the agencies and grassroots groups that improves the fit between programs and local needs. Social trust is developed and cooperative institutions are created by repeated experiences of joint problem solving and mutual influence. Patterns of joint decision making and effective action, facilitated by the power-balancing roles of the NGOs, are essential to building the norms, attitudes, and institutions that promote expanded cooperation in the future.

These cases illustrate the possibility of cooperative problem solving that produces mutual gains and so fosters a self-reinforcing pattern of interaction that advances the interests of all the parties. The interaction promotes changes in organizational arrangements, norms, and attitudes — increases in social capital — that provide a base to support further cooperative interaction in the future. Patterns of positive-sum interactions that at once produce rapid change and set the stage for future improvements have been remarked in other development projects. Norman Uphoff's (1992) analysis of quantum leaps in the performance of a Sri Lankan irrigation system focuses on the interplay of ideas, ideals, and friendship as they bring about self-reinforcing, positive-sum patterns of interaction that produced spectacular changes in farmer behavior and institutional contexts—but the study could easily have focused on social capital as well. Interaction patterns that reshape institutional arrangements, create contexts for future cooperation, and so foster dramatic changes have been identified in grassroots development projects in many countries and regions (for example, Uphoff 1992, 373). It is not easy to set off such "benevolent cycles," but it is clearly possible.

If social capital grows out of experiences of successful cooperation across differences in sector and power, agencies that can successfully bridge those gaps in order to promote cooperation can play an extraordinarily important role. NGOs (and to a lesser extent, international development agencies) acted as catalysts and guardians of cooperation in these four cases. They made it possible for the parties to experience mutual influence and joint action to solve important problems—experiences like those that may have created high social capital systems in the first place (see Putnam 1993a, 121–62).

The concept of social capital provides an intriguing frame for examining other experience in problems of development and power. Craig Jenkins (in this volume), for example, has noted that foundation grants tend to follow and institutionalize rather than launch social movements. From the perspective of starting social movements, this may seem a disappointing finding. On the other hand, from the point of view of social capital formation, support for building institutional, attitudinal, and normative underpinnings for movement gains may be essential to sustaining and expanding them in the future. Brian Smith (in this volume) has questioned whether nonprofit development organizations, in spite of their empowerment rhetoric, are co-opted by their dependence on government-controlled funds. At the same time, he points out that some organizations encourage "social empowerment" that enables more local organization and cooperation rather than political power. Social empowerment activities may well produce what I have called social capital, and so in the long run be as important as direct political empowerment. The concept of social capital focuses attention beyond immediate social behavior to assess its implications for the institutional context of future action. Investments in building the right institutional contexts today may dramatically reshape social, political, and economic activities tomorrow.

The four case studies described here were selected because they were successes, and successes in economic, political, and cultural contexts ordinarily not hospitable to cooperation across sector and power differences. It is important not to overgeneralize: the solution to all the intransigent problems of development, oppression, and ecological deteriora-

tion is not at hand. Nonetheless, I believe these experiences offer important clues to engendering constructive social change. If we can catalyze self-reinforcing changes in social capital, we may be able to foster rapid and self-sustaining political, economic, and social improvements as well.

REFERENCES

Bingham, G. 1986. *Resolving Environmental Disputes: A Decade of Experience*. Washington, D.C.: Conservation Foundation.

Bratton, M. 1989a. "Beyond the State: Civil Society and Associational Life in Africa." *World Politics* 41(3):407–30.

———. 1989b. "The Politics of Government-NGO Relations in Africa." *World Development* 17(4):569–87.

———. 1990. "Nongovernmental Organizations in Africa: Can They Influence Public Policy?" *Development and Change* 21:81–118.

Bratton, M., and D. Rothchild. 1992. "The Institutional Bases of Governance in Africa." In *Governance and Politics in Africa*, ed. G. Hyden and M. Bratton, 263–84. Boulder: Lynne Rienner.

Brown, L. D. 1982. "Interface Analysis and the Management of Unequal Conflict." In *Conflict Management and Industrial Relations*, ed. G. B. J. Bomers and R. B. Peterson, 60–78. Boston: Kluwer-Nijhoff.

———. 1988. "Private Voluntary Organizations and Development Partnerships." In *Social Development: A New Role for the Organizational Sciences*, ed. P. Khandwalla, 71–88. New Delhi: Sage.

———. 1991. "Bridging Organizations and Sustainable Development." *Human Relations* 44(8):807–31.

Brown, L. D., and R. Tandon. 1993. *Multiparty Collaboration for Development in Asia*. New York: United Nations Development Programme.

Bruns, B., and I. Soelaiman. 1991. "From Policy to Practice: Agency and NGO in Indonesia's Program to Turn Small Irrigation Systems over to Farmers." Paper presented at the Asia Regional Workshop: NGOs, Natural Resource Management and Linkages with the Public Sector. Hyderabad, India. Administrative Staff College, September 1991.

Cernea, M. 1987. "Farmer Organizations and Institution Building for Sustainable Agricultural Development." *Regional Development Dialogue* 8(2):1–24.

Clegg, S. R. 1989. *Frameworks of Power*. London: Sage Publications.

Coleman, J. S. 1990. *Foundations of Social Theory*. Cambridge: Harvard University Press.

Day, R., and J. V. Day. 1977. "A Review of the Current State of Negotiated Order Theory: An Appreciation and a Critique." *Sociological Quarterly* 18:126–42.

DiMaggio, P. J., and W. W. Powell. 1991. Introduction. In *The New Institutionalism in Organizational Analysis*, ed. W. W. Powell, and P. J. DiMaggio, 1–38. Chicago: University of Chicago Press.

Esman, M. J. 1978. "Development Administration and Constituency Organizations." *Public Administration Review* 38(2): 166–72.

Esman, M. J., and N. T. Uphoff. 1984. *Local Organizations:*

Intermediaries in Rural Development. Ithaca: Cornell University Press.

Fox, J. 1994. "The Difficult Transition from Clientelism to Citizenship: Lessons from Mexico." *World Politics* 46(2):151–84.

Friedland, R., and R. R. Alford. 1991. "Bringing Society Back In: Symbols, Practices and Institutional Contradictions." In *The New Institutionalism in Organizational Analysis*, ed. W. W. Powell, and P. J. DiMaggio, 232–63. Chicago: University of Chicago Press.

Gaventa, J. 1980. *Power and Powerlessness: Quiescence and Rebellion in an Appalachian Valley.* Urbana: University of Illinois Press.

Gray, B., and D. J. Wood. 1991. "Collaborative Alliances: Moving from Practice to Theory." *Journal of Applied Behavioral Science* 22(1):3–20.

Gray, B. G. 1989. *Collaborating: Finding Common Ground for Multiparty Problems.* San Francisco: Jossey-Bass.

Hussain, A. 1991. *Collaborative Efforts in Rural Immunization: The Bangladesh Case.* Association of Development Agencies of Bangladesh.

Hyden, G. 1983. *No Shortcuts to Progress: African Development Management in Perspective.* Berkeley: University of California Press.

———. 1992. "Governance and the Study of Politics." In *Governance and Politics in Africa*, ed. G. Hyden and M. Bratton. Boulder: Lynne Rienner.

Korten, D. C. 1980. "Rural Organization and Rural Development: A Learning Process Approach." *Public Administration Review* 40:480–511.

Lukes, S. 1974. *Power: A Radical View.* London: Macmillan.

Morss, E. R., J. K. Hatch, D. R. Mickelwait, and C. F. Sweet. 1976. *Strategies for Small Farmer Development.* 2 vols. Boulder: Westview.

Nathan, M. L., and I. I. Mitroff. 1991. "The Use of Negotiated Order Theory as a Tool for the Analysis and Development of an Interorganizational Field." *Journal of Applied Behavioral Science* 27(2):163–79.

Paige, J. 1975. *Agrarian Revolution.* New York: Free Press.

Pfeffer, J. 1981. *Power in Organizations.* Boston: Pitman.

Pfeffer, J., and G. Salancik. 1978. *The External Control of Organizations.* New York: Harper and Row.

Purnomo, A., and A. Pambagio. 1991. *Fostering Local Management of Small Irrigation Systems.* Jakarta, Indonesia: Pelangi.

Putnam, R. D. 1993a. *Making Democracy Work: Civic Traditions in Modern Italy.* Princeton: Princeton University Press.

———. 1993b. "The Prosperous Community: Social Capital and Public Life." *The American Prospect* (13):35–42.

Rashid, A. 1991. *Self-Financed, Self-Managed, Low-cost Sanitation Development in Orangi.* Karachi, Pakistan: Orangi Pilot Project.

Senge, P. M. 1990. *The Fifth Discipline: The Art and Practice of the Learning Organization.* New York: Doubleday.

Strauss, A. 1979. *Negotiations: Varieties, Contexts, Processes, and Social Order.* San Francisco: Jossey-Bass.

Tandon, R. 1989. NGO-*Government Relations: A Source of Life or a Kiss of Death?* New Delhi: Society for Participatory Research in Asia (PRIA).

Trist, E. 1983. "Referent Organizations and the Development of Inter-organizational Domains." *Human Relations* 36(3):269–84.

Uphoff, N. 1992. *Learning from Gal Oya: Possibilities for Participatory Development and Post-Newtonian Social Science.* Ithaca: Cornell University Press.

Waddock, S. 1993. "Lessons from the National Alliance of Business Compact Project: Business and Public Education Reform." *Human Relations* 46(7):777–802.

Weisbrod, M. 1992. *Discovering Common Ground.* San Francisco: Berrett-Koehler.

Wood, D. J., and B. Gray. 1991. "Toward a Comprehensive Theory of Collaboration." *Journal of Applied Behavioral Science* 27(2):139–62.

Part Five

Making and Maintaining Organizational Mission

17

BARRY D. KARL

Volunteers and Professionals: Many Histories, Many Meanings

Establishing the relation between volunteers and professionals working as staff for charitable organizations is a distinctly modern concern, although the terms themselves go back centuries. Not only do volunteers provide services that are often essential to the daily operations of organizations, but their presence may be important to an organization's economic viability. The recent interest in the role of volunteers is also the product of changes in our understanding of the meaning of professionalism, as well as some important transformations in the idea of the volunteer. The familiarity of these terms may give us the illusion that we understand the history of those changes and conceal some sources of conflict as well

I am happy to acknowledge my indebtedness to the Indiana University Center on Philanthropy and the seminars on Governance of Nonprofits which sponsored the years of stimulating meetings that brought this historian into communication with a remarkable range of skilled social scientists. Professor James Wood, who organized the program, was always supportive, while Robert Payton, then director of the center, was the model of open and healthy investigation that such an enterprise requires. The editors of this volume were more than that title suggests, particularly Elisabeth Clemens, to whom all readers must be grateful for enabling me to give my argument as well as my prose a clarity few of those who have edited me have been able to force into being. I take full responsibility for whatever unclear thought remains; at the same time I take delight in the evidence of her hand on every page.

as cooperation that characterize what have become significant factors in the management of nonprofits.

Like many terms we use to describe our social order, *professional* and *volunteer* have not had the same meanings over time. We use them as though they did, however, and even celebrate the sense of sustained history they give us, in a perhaps unconscious effort to preserve values in the face of changed historical conditions that threaten the stability of institutions. The preservation of the same terms is also a way of transferring values from old institutions to new ones to reduce the dangers of institutional change. Such hidden transformations may pose unexpected problems for historians seeking to explain the process of change. They may also hold the seeds of the disputes that arise when new formulations of issues by participants in institutional reorganizations trigger the very conflicts the reformations were intended to resolve.

The President's Summit for America's Future, a three-day series of hortatory speeches and meetings intended to inspire volunteering nationwide, was held in Philadelphia in late April 1997. The news media fed a sense of drama and urgency that evoked a confidence in renewal but with little or no reference to the history being renewed, let alone what parts of the past were really available for rebirth at the end of the century. It may be useful to look back at some of the

245

issues that would trouble an American historian looking at pictures of President Bill Clinton in bright yellow T-shirt, baseball cap, and jeans embracing the women who were giving their time to painting over graffiti on urban walls. One might wonder whether they were removing a distasteful contemporary art form or providing a clean canvas for future artists. Much of the history of voluntary effort has raised such questions for defenders and critics of both voluntary and professional social reform.

The use of *volunteer* to designate someone who provides unpaid services is part of a language that goes back at least to the sixteenth century in discussions of religious and military obligation. Because such services are, along with medicine and the law, where we look for the origins of the professions, the terms *volunteer* and *professional* have been linked from the very beginning. Religious offices, military service, medicine, and law also distinguished professions from other forms of work by their dependence on specialized knowledge, training, certification, and agreed upon rules and obligations defined within the profession itself rather than by an individual employer whose demands govern work. The standards of professions are thus understood as being objective and rational, as contrasted with the individual, often arbitrary, issuance of orders that govern work. Professionals follow rules. Workers obey commands.

Although it is obvious that professionals and laborers alike may be unpaid or volunteer, unpaid professional service tends to be given a degree of respect that unpaid labor is not. Though we speak of a labor of love to describe some kinds of work done without pay, the *labor* in the phrase is used metaphorically to describe something that might be considered a higher order of labor. Voluntary professional service is given out of altruism and a sense of responsibility to the cause being served. That the service could also be paid for if the giver of service insisted on it and the receiver of the service had no other way of getting it is part of the understanding of the special value of the service and the provider of service. Both agree on the value of the service but have decided that it be given voluntarily.

One can ask why, if some kind of volunteer contract has been agreed upon by both parties, volunteerism should have to be promoted or defended. The answers one can give are complex but can be traced to the fact that the two are not always seen as equivalent in a society that has increasingly measured the value of service and respected those who deliver it according to the fees paid. Where limited budgets force organizations to depend on unpaid services, those services become as essential to the operation of the organization as if they were paid. Because there can be no expectation of profit to pay for services, endowments, contributions to operating budget, fees charged, and volunteer services become the basis for defining the effectiveness of the organization.

The explanation of our need to promote voluntarism may stem from the fact that we have promoted professionalism aggressively in our commitment to modern technological efficiency in all fields in spite of our growing suspicion that some essential social virtues may be missing from our professional ideals. Ethics, for example, may be unrelated to scientific knowledge. Highly skilled professional specialists may have as much difficulty putting moral values in perspective as do the general run of human beings. Their training, if it taught them any ethics at all, did not teach them a special approach to ethics that would be appropriate to their profession. Despite the religious origins of the term, modern professions may not be inherently committed to the good as we understand social good. Professionalism also tends toward bureaucratization in ways that touch on our deepest fears of bureaucratization as the universal threat to free democratic choice. The exercise of one's profession may be surrounded with social and political values in every conceivable way without itself being in the slightest democratic. Surgeons at an operating table do not vote on procedures. Airline pilots do not choose their individual routes, altitudes, and velocities. Volunteers as nonprofessionals in fields we associate with social well-being and improvement seem capable of preserving democratic values by their very presence as nonprofessionals in fields we have defined as specialized professions. Their sustaining of democracy may be as essential in our world as it is anomalous.

Talcott Parsons elaborated what has been for many years now the consummate analytical history of the idea of professionalism, beginning with the specialized knowledge of priesthoods which protected their control of arcane systems and provided techniques for managing the social order. Successive transformations of those primitive origins generated the multiple professions (Parsons 1968). Parsons's history, like Max Weber's account of the origins of bureaucracy, is a history of progress from primitive forms to ever more sophisticated methods of social control resting on knowledge. Both are progressive histories of professionalism. Professionalism is a good, one of the higher essentials in the building of a social order. It rests on ideas of development and a Whig conception of change as change for the better. Modern conceptions of popular democracy, however, raise questions about professions and their tendency to organize life into elite hierarchies; but we seem comfortable putting those questions aside by introducing education into the social order, cutting across class lines by giving opportunity to those who might otherwise be restricted, making their talents the key to their position in society. In medieval society, for example, power could transcend class in such professions as the church and the military, where the need for special talents rewarded individuals for their accomplishments apart from their social origins and economic positions in society. That transcendence of class through professional training, recognized originally in prowess in battle and the ability to read, has been part of the rise of the university and the drive toward universal education.

Modern universities, particularly those in the United States, where universities tended to be less associated with class, religion, and the state than they were in England and Europe, introduced yet another puzzle into the world of professions by creating a multipurpose meritocracy based on knowledge and intellectual talent. In the United States, the dominance of jealously protected local federalism led to a regional dispersion of private sectarian and nonsectarian institutions existing side by side with publicly funded state and city universities and colleges. The resulting collection of places of learning offered an incredible range of options for personal advancement in every profession. The absence of a national university underscored the diversity. The differences in quality of training posed problems for those who chose to examine the system closely, at the same time that its very range supported the democratic commitment to education for all. One could accept a select few universities as sources of elite leadership without criticizing all of them. Graduates of the elite institutions could be recognized in each generation as a sectarian priesthood of the higher learning.

Edward Shils's melding of the religious with the academic, and of both with the emergence of universities and the social sciences brought the historic development of the knowledge professions in line with modern intellectual idealism (Shils 1980). Robert K. Merton's search for the relation between scientific ideas and the growth of modern democracy brought our understanding of the growth of modern science to a special point that fitted all too well into post–World War II questions of the relation between science and a free society (Merton 1942). Herbert Butterfield's *The Origins of Modern Science* captured in its marvelously poetic way the ultimate epic journey that defined the progress of science for humanists, one of the dreams of the beginnings of the modern age, to find the promise of the future in the odyssey of scientific leadership that led from Aristotle to Einstein (Butterfield 1949). The atomic age had created a world newly fearful of the triumphs of scientific research. If one could capture the engine of progress, even those who feared the possibility that it might run away with them could safely lead and be led. It would be the responsibility of those professionals whom social theorists a generation earlier had called engineers and, more broadly, intellectuals to use their knowledge for the more general social good and to organize the state accordingly. Thorstein Veblen and José Ortega y Gassett had urged that new role on their students and disciples, the new professionals, in the years before the Second World War (Veblen 1928; Ortega y Gassett 1944).

In recent years, the reexamination of the meaning of professions and professionalism has taken a new direction. The work of Edward O. Laumann and John P. Heinz in particular has questioned the mystical validity (although that is not their term) of some applications of the idea of profession to fields in which the original ideas of arcane knowledge and specialized expertise no longer apply (Heinz and Laumann 1982). Laumann has been interested specifically in the legal profession, in which certified membership has become much more important than the special character of the knowledge

of the law. Given the public's long-standing ambivalence toward lawyers, this questioning may not be altogether new; but its application in present circumstances does raise some interesting issues about the meaning of professionalism in each of its instances. It might also lead to some puzzlement about the relation between the professions and not only universal education but the rapid growth of computer technology, in which the increasing availability of specialized knowledge once considered arcane and immediate application of it by individuals who require no specialized training, let alone special intellectual insight, suggest a future in which professionalism will again have to be redefined. As programs for computers allow individuals to do everything from preparing their income taxes in ways that satisfy the Internal Revenue Service to writing complex wills and contracts acceptable to the courts, the need for technicians to mediate will decline. Computer medical diagnostics is presently being debated, as are systems of transportation that will operate themselves. It would be hard to think of a field in which the need for experts is not challenged by computer programs capable of assembling data and calculating outcomes far more accurately and quickly than even the best-trained human minds.

More advanced technologies may have caused the most recent explosion in our questioning of the need for experts. A suspicion of the moral responsibility and fundamental humaneness of the professional has been a basic element in the traditional hostility to bureaucracy. Part of the redefinition of professionalism over the last half-century may have to do with a questioning of the inherent democratic sensitivity of the professions as specialized areas of knowledge, at least as Parsons, Weber, and Shils understood them and as Laumann is coming to understand them anew. One can track the breakdown of the post–World War II optimism through the complex years of the 1960s and 1970s, when critics on both the Left and the Right opened their attacks on the managers of the New Deal and its successor domestic reform programs. Some of these critics were questioning whether social scientists and the social programs they recommended were basically good, let alone capable of demonstrating a commitment to the public's need to participate in its own pursuit of happiness. Irving Louis Horowitz attacked the seeming confidence of expert professionals in his *Uses and Abuses of Social Science* (Horowitz 1975). Although "the best and the brightest" of the Vietnam era were the natural targets of such criticism, it has been extended to all of the programs for social reform that began in the Progressive Era and moved through the New Deal into the Great Society. Professionalism was the battle cry of Progressive reformers seeking to replace well-meaning amateurs and do-gooders with trained and experienced workers.

By the end of the Great Society, reaction had set in. That reaction took the form of a general mistrust not only of intellectuals, as leaders of professional bureaucracies were being called, but also of the governments they had helped create for social reform, the bureaucracy that managed them, and the politicians who sought to expand them. Tangled up in the reaction was a search for alternatives to large, centralized reform governments as well as to professions. New normative meanings were attached to the conception of the volunteer and to the organizational systems through which volunteers worked. The ideas of not-for-profit associations and the existence of a so-called third sector were launched to provide institutional structures that served the public but were independent of government.

One could argue that *nongovernmental organizations* would have been a sufficient, even more accurate identification but for the dependence of such agencies on American capitalist enterprise and the society that supported it through its government. After all, in the entire history of capitalist development, business was no more genuinely independent of government than nonprofits were, but the distinction between nonprofit and nonstate was needed to bring back necessary conceptions of citizen responsibility and democratic participation. American society needed such organizations historically to develop stable responses to the major changes caused by the social revolutions of the post–World War II years in race relations, gender equality, and the older, still central problem of ethnic assimilation. Paradoxically, perhaps, such revolutions needed both the agency of state authority and the illusion that it was the public itself that had taken itself by the scruff of its own neck and pulled itself into a new democratic age. The idea of the volunteer took on new meaning, or, more accurately, picked up meanings it had already begun to develop in the years after World War I, when Herbert Hoover and his generation began to use it to call for an American alternative to the centralizing forces of social change they saw developing in Europe. He called his alternative individualism and promoted it through the expansion of voluntary associations that could govern without requiring the intervention of the state (Hoover 1923).

Such historical approaches to volunteerism as we have are, by comparison with those we have taken toward professionalism, crude. The social science literature that deals with the professions did not trouble itself with volunteers even as an alternate part of the picture until very recently. Once one leaves the earlier uses of the term to describe philosophical commitments to free will or military service, one finds an emerging distinction more common to nineteenth-century British than to American usage, namely, a distinction between the support of social or educational institutions required by law and support given to such institutions by individuals acting voluntarily. In societies accustomed to the idea that such institutions should be managed by the state, by local governments, or by a church authorized by the state, the freedom to form associations for such purposes afforded a sharp alternative.

The distinction between state institutions and voluntary associations had less meaning for Americans in the nineteenth century. There was no state church in the United States, let alone any other institutions that provided such professional services as established churches had traditionally provided in Great Britain and Europe. There was no national military service; indeed, the rejection of such service was part of the American democratic tradition. The distinctive American meaning of militia was that such armies were local collections of volunteers locally formed and controlled rather than national engines of professional military power essential for the building of empires. The range of difference in state and local institutions and their very different relations to churches and public governing bodies left the creation of a language for discussing general issues of public versus private for a later era.

Alexis de Tocqueville had noted what he called associations for dealing with community problems of governance in the United States of the early nineteenth century and contrasted them with British and French governmental and bureaucratic systems; but not until after World War II did most American readers seem to notice his discovery (Tocqueville 1966). His descriptions of the use of such associations by Americans have become quite possibly one of the most quoted of Tocqueville's comments on American culture, although by the 1950s American translators and editors felt constrained to add adjectives like *public* and *voluntary* to make his simple reference to associations fit their purposes. They wanted a distinction between public and private that no one in the nineteenth century had needed. The awareness of government as a threat to liberty had become part of a new consciousness produced, in part, by the two world wars, New Deal social and economic reforms, and the development of Nazism and Communism as the Manichean opposition to the various forms of liberalism that had evolved out of two centuries of democratic revolution.

Although it is common to speak of the relation between voluntarism and professionalism as though it were an evolutionary process that begins with voluntarism and ends with professionalism, such a formulation is misleading. The belief that professionalism developed out of voluntarism over time is an American progressive myth that does a great disservice to the complex processes of administrative growth, processes that are centuries older than American progressivism. The American approach to progress asserts that special factors in American history, chiefly the presence of a democratic government that demands endless improvement for the lives of all its citizens, will lead to an endless process of equalization whereby the social and economic benefits produced by scientific and technological advance will be made available to all. The persistence of inequity is counterbalanced by the availability of opportunity.

To call such beliefs myths is nothing more than a commentary on the inequities that seem to persist or to appear anew with each successive drive toward equality. One can argue that such progress is a faulty theory of history that contains dangerous seeds of disenchantment, another consequential aspect of myth. One could argue, nonetheless, that it is an indispensable element in the drive toward equality that all democracies share, however impossible its achievement sometimes seems. The idea of progress is thus a potentially dangerous concept, especially in modern democratic society, in which mobility is restricted by educational opportunities and by a consciousness of the talents and skills that govern advance in the professions.

Professions are protected by barriers that exclude those who do not qualify for admission. They represent protected elites. Admission to a profession may rest on opportunities for education and qualification available to all, but entry is restricted by standards set by the profession itself, not by the larger democratic society. When volunteers engage in activities in a professional world, their relation to the professionals of that world becomes problematic if they see themselves as equal to or superior to the professionals who govern their work. In the history of American philanthropy, for example, the upperclass Americans who ran charitable organizations were volunteers who in turn employed professional social workers, a profession the volunteers had helped create through their founding of schools to train them. That those volunteers saw themselves as providing training for men and women who would serve them, not manage their volunteer services, was a belief that disappeared as professionals moved into positions of control. The distinction between professional social service and the doing of good by well-meaning volunteers moved into place as the dominant model of the relation between professionals and volunteers and became a way of separating knowledge and training from benevolence. The new professionalism improved the old volunteerism, even replaced it, some thought, by making it more intellectually effective. The fact that the old volunteers were still expected to provide economic support for the new professions was perceived initially as less of a problem than it was destined to become. The emphasis on progress as inherently good and as fueled by new knowledge helped ease the transition to professionalism. But a commitment to progress may be linked to two alternative relations between volunteerism and professionalism: either a new, modern professionalism triumphs over an antique voluntarism or a now lost and morally more viable voluntarism must be restored to its rightful place in the order of democratic management.

Cycles in the ways volunteers and professionals relate to one another have been part of bureaucratic and antibureaucratic discussions of the general field of American philanthropy for almost a century. They may describe our ways of talking about reality rather than a genuine historical reality. That may be particularly true in nonprofit organizations before the idea of nonprofit was created to satisfy those who felt the need for a way of dignifying useful organizations in our committedly capitalist world. Even though such organizations violate that commitment by quite deliberately failing to make a profit, the mix of volunteers and professionals has remained a mix. Nonprofits are capitalist enterprises that do not follow capitalist ends, employ essential workers whom

they do not pay, and deliver services whose value they defend. Neither do they tend to consider themselves stopgap services whose functions are temporary. The Red Cross, for example, is a permanent agency for responding to immediate crises that will continue to happen. The most triumphant capitalism will not end that need or, one presumes, turn it to profits that moral men and women would find acceptable. The presence of volunteers as well as their services to the organization justifies its unprofitability and preserves its value.

My analysis thus far has centered on questions of names and categories, whether or not they are adequately descriptive and flexible to help us understand the problems that seem to recur in the management of nonprofits. At their worst, questions of the kind I have been raising could be accused of being Wittgensteinian exercises in the debunking of the meanings of terms, even the meaning of meaning, reducing rational discussion to nonsense. That old Keynesian saw about the power of dead economists to influence history is part of an elegant game we play with the relevance of ideas. Yet ideas do in fact guide in the making of decisions. Whether or not they can be proven to have been true may have nothing to do with the matter. The sky does not fall, we can argue; but if the belief that it is falling ends us in the cave of Foxy Loxy where we are eaten, then the real dynamics of the celestial world are obviously going to be less important than our sadly misbegotten perception of it. Provably incorrect, even foolish perceptions have real effects in history.

By the same token, when our language remains stable but the circumstances of our history change, we may inadvertently generate confusion by concealing from ourselves the problems that arise from our appropriation of old language to describe new circumstances. And when that language is embodied in institutions we are trying to preserve to manage those new circumstances, we may find ourselves coping with conflicts that are the result of our way of describing the problems rather than of the conditions themselves. While it might be pleasant to consider a world in which the language would adjust instantly in some computerlike fashion to meet changes in circumstances, that's not the way it works or, quite possibly, the way it ought to work. We need stable language for describing the world in the same way we need stable institutions for managing that world. The effectiveness of our communication with one another depends on it. The fact that we can become entrapped in language, however, may require us to use caution in accepting the seeming certainties language is designed to produce. Words are not numbers. We may not want to question meaning at every step of the way, but periodic examination of it may help us see problems that might otherwise be obscured.

Let me provide examples of the complexities that grow out of the roles of volunteers and professionals from some of the research projects undertaken by the group of scholars who examined the governance of nonprofits during the multiyear program run by the Center on Philanthropy at Indiana University. Although the relations between professionals and volunteers were not the central issue of anyone's research agenda, it played so significantly at the edges of many of the studies that its presence in our discussions sounded what I felt to be a significantly recurrent note. Whether one looked at the problem from its modern beginnings in the decades following the Civil War or from the perspective of the most recent decades of social reform following the Second World War, one could see both recurrence and transformation in the ongoing problems of modernization and change. At the root of all of the issues was the oldest issue of human civilization: our sense of civil responsibility and our search for ways of giving it institutional form. Western history in general and American history in particular imposed frameworks that shaped our understanding of our responsibilities as well as of the religious, governmental, social, economic, and technological systems we have used for defining the institutions for implementing those responsibilities. The relation between volunteers and professionals in the management of those institutions reflects tensions that may be as old as the institutions themselves. Our reshaping of the language we use in defining those terms can be used to mark both the tensions and our efforts to resolve them.

Margaret Johnson's study of twelve chapters of the International Association of Women (IAW) (a pseudonym) over the years 1974–92 describes a major social transformation by a group not given to looking for social transformation (Johnson 1993). One of many organizations founded in the early years of the twentieth century to give upper-class women opportunities to engage in public service rather than contenting themselves with displays of wealth through coming out parties and other lavish celebrations of the social season, the organization was faced with the demands for inclusiveness characteristic of the past two decades. The membership had to change itself and sought to control not only the breadth and depth of change, but also its speed and ultimate direction. Regulations prohibiting racial discrimination were dutifully introduced by the national board but were vague enough at the national level to allow individual local groups the autonomy to control change in ways appropriate to their communities. (This, parenthetically, was no different from the practices employed by successive federal legislative acts in bringing reform to the states in every field from social security to public housing.) The fact that IAW board membership became relatively more homogeneous as membership in the organization became more diverse suggests that boards solidified their control, perhaps not to prevent change but to determine some essential factors in its speed.

Yet the pool of members itself was changing its character. Upper-class women had always tended to be well-educated. They still were, but now they were being professionally educated as well, not only in traditional fields like elementary education and social work, but in law, medicine, business, and finance, the professions into which they once would have had to marry. Their professions, not their class origins, allied them with potential newcomers. The organization could not

be at the center of their lives as it was for the women who traditionally took on such activities as the major public expression of their family and community responsibility. We still call them volunteers, but their relation to the system of volunteers and professionals is different. Their volunteerism has become part of their professionalism. As a result, the IAW moves from private club with public responsibilities voluntarily chosen to one with a broader set of responsibilities imposed by social change as well as by law; and the intervention of law is a critical fact.

In the aftermath of the civil rights revolution of the sixties, which wrote equality of treatment into laws governing all forms of accommodation, the distinction between public and private could no longer be used to conceal discrimination. Professions might continue to define an intellectual elite, but they could not confuse that definition with social and cultural exclusions. The democratization of knowledge called for the democratization of power. Like all institutions with even a tangential influence on social opportunity, the IAW must reflect — and now include — the society it had traditionally committed itself to serving.

One could still ask what empowered society to exact democratic inclusiveness of private associations. The demand was part of an era. The ability to give it teeth, over and above the moral persuasion that had long been part of the pressure for social change, came from the courts and, where such associations were concerned, from exemptions from taxes some of them claimed because of the charitable services they performed. Whether or not the threat to withdraw exemption would have affected budgets seriously, the change in status seemed a contradiction of purposes for those who had traditionally separated their purposes as charitable from those of other social organizations.

Imposition of outside public standards professionally derived from law, tax policy, and the like on a private organization whose only intersection with public policy is the tax exemption may affect policy, but how much does it actually change it? In the era Johnson is dealing with this becomes a complex problem for any private organization that can be said to have both social and professional advantages for its members and hence disadvantages for those excluded from the organization. And some of those consequences may be symbolic as well as real: for example, membership in golf clubs that restrict their clientele in any way. Those consequences now entitle the public to intervene. As the organizations become more inclusive in their membership, the board's reflection of the social makeup of the organization changes, even though its sense of its responsibility to the values of the organization remains the same. The controlling group reflects the criteria of the older order now determining entry and behavior of the new. The way older professional groups recruit new members and exclude them from control by keeping them at a safe distance may be a new and less obvious form of discrimination. There are some interesting and important historical questions here as one examines the process of control, generation by generation, even as inclusiveness clouds the issue of control.

Mary Jean McDonald's study of the Citizens' Committee for the Children of New York for the years 1945 to 1972 tells about the group's transition from child saving to child advocacy and shows a complex shift in the bodies of language used, from that of social work, in which child saving began, to that of the law (McDonald 1993). Once again, in such a transfer of languages, the terms may remain the same while meanings change or new terms may be introduced to indicate an attempt to transform meaning. The larger context of the creation of rights for those dependent on the state includes not only children, but the poor in general and, in another particular set of cases much dealt with in this same period, accused criminals in courtrooms and prisoners in jails.

The whole idea of civil rights for children is revolutionary. It has been raised in recent legal comments on the placement and potential adoption of children placed in foster homes and under the rubric of the interests of the child. It remains a significant and exciting issue because it indicates an awareness of a need for new understanding of an old issue and the drive to find an acceptable language for dealing with it. "Real" parents may be in for redefinition as the "interests of the child" take precedence over the once overpowering force of biological relationship. Psychological factors are becoming more important than biological in the definition of family. Children are to become independent beings with rights as well as needs rather than chattel whose ownership is shared by families and the state. Under law, now, citizenship is independent of birth.

The redefinition of the family as a social and legal entity independent of biological origins threatens our oldest and most primitive conceptions of the human community. Politicians lamenting the supposed decline in family values are forced to treat the problem as though it could be solved by returning to some hallowed past rather than responding to the need to build new forms of basic social organization to fit the realities of modern life and our more sophisticated understanding of them. The parental child savers who sought to confirm a traditional sense of family they knew even they themselves may have failed to provide for their own children wanted to build something better in the legal system whose operations they worked to improve. Yet, the professionalism they created was destined to become the framework for public bureaucracies in child welfare as complex in their operations and effectiveness as anything they were trying to correct. They believed, nonetheless, that their personal involvement in the building of a new framework would somehow transmit their values to the new professionalism.

The transition from volunteers to professionals in the management of family life required that transmission to justify the independence of the new forms. Child savers were ideally responsible parents sharing their upperclass parenthood with children in need. Eleanor Roosevelt presented herself as wife and mother in her regular newspaper columns.

Her competence was assumed from her roles as First Lady and mother. Yet many autobiographical statements testify to her very real consciousness of her serious weaknesses as mother of her own children. In spite of what could be understood as a significant degree of family dysfunction she saw nothing wrong in presenting herself as unofficial role model — First Mother — for a role she herself had not fulfilled properly. The lack of official status did not touch the reality of implied status, and the tradition of first ladies did not raise the question of professionalism. She could help others learn from her mistakes, from the wisdom she had painstakingly acquired.

The distinction between the personal and official roles may not be easy, above all when one observes the slow transition from Eleanor Roosevelt to Hillary Rodham Clinton. Clinton is a lawyer. She is also a wife and a mother, but none of those roles gives her the status she has as the wife of the elected president of the United States. Her past business and professional mistakes are errors to be criticized, not learning experiences to be passed on. Yet in defending herself against public criticism, she, like Eleanor Roosevelt, uses the same family images even when she responds to charges against her activities as lawyer and businesswoman. Voluntarism and professionalism, private and public, are not judged by the same standards.

The differences between the volunteer child savers and their staffs of professional social workers and today's new professional woman — I think specifically of Marian Wright Edelman and Ruth Bader Ginsburg — raise two interesting aspects of the relationship of volunteers to professionals. The years before 1945 were years of alliance in the field of social work between upper-class women who volunteered their services and the emerging profession of social workers. The law served as the background of that alliance in the development of family and juvenile courts. After 1945, it moved toward the center. The women who had traditionally volunteered became the new legal professionals who took over the management of the change. The relation between the profession of social work and the profession of the law suggests a complex process of expansion in which gender is relevant in some ways, irrelevant in others. Justice Ginsburg cannot confine her role on the Supreme Court to issues of women and children, even if she wanted to; yet her presence on the Court is quite obviously related to her career as a woman in the legal profession of her generation. She and her contemporary women professionals carry an unmistakable aura of civic virtue derived from the earlier public roles defined by elite volunteers. The stories of Justice Ginsburg's career have become a parable of transition as we follow her past the barriers of her battles for recognition and advancement against the sexist academy and legal profession — and marvel at her husband's willingness to subject his career to hers, as though we were witnessing the symbols of a mystical sanctification.

The elements of class and gender are also intertwined in Dawn Greeley's study of the turn-of-the-century scientific philanthropy movement (Greeley 1995). Philanthropy was not controlled solely by economic interests, but by an interesting complication of gender issues and the volunteer/professional dichotomy. Policy making was often dominated by men, delivery of services by women. The separation of policy making from service delivery was an important part of early twentieth-century social philanthropy as some of the leading figures of the era in both philanthropy and politics employed men and women from the service areas they were acquainted with to help them establish policies as well as to carry them out. Herbert Hoover and Franklin Roosevelt depended in part on their wives, Lou Henry Hoover and Eleanor Roosevelt, for their contacts with the reform communities concerned with social welfare, but also with the men and women who had provided those communities with professional services: Harry Hopkins and Frances Perkins being the best-known examples. Although we are accustomed to thinking of both First Ladies primarily as wives of their leader-husbands, wives who seemed somehow to choose voluntarily to meddle in policy making, they also represent the mediation that elite volunteers provided between male policymakers and the growing community of volunteers and professionals forming to establish the new welfare bureaucracy. The implementation of the bureaucratic state in the aftermath of the First World War was dependent on that mediation.

The persistence of shared community values through modern conceptions of voluntarism has been one of the ways of attempting to preserve ideas of participatory democracy in the increasingly complex society reflected in the growth of modern service professions. Self-government is by its very nature personal action. The delegation of one's right to act is a personal act in itself, but it is one that assumes a community of agreement between those who delegate and those to whom they delegate. Factors that inhibit agreement may prevent effective action, and nowhere so seriously as when they are misunderstood or not understood at all in the initial assumption of agreement. Transitions in the understanding of such factors as class, race, and gender have become significant elements in the necessary discovery of mistaken assumptions, but the lessons to be learned from such experiences remain ambiguous. The fact that such transitions in understanding can appear to undermine confidence in the ability of communities to resolve their problems, however well-meaning their intentions, has time and again led to disillusionment with programs of reform. Yet, to turn over the management of such programs to professionals, particularly in the aftermath of failure, can raise serious questions about the continued effectiveness of the self-governing communities on which American democracy has been built.

One can see such troubling transitions in women's clubs, child advocacy groups, and all of modern welfare history. Paul Schnorr takes some of the same problems of volunteerism and professionalism to a level formulated by the ethos of community democratization energetically shaped by the era of the Great Society. The relation between voluntary participation and bureaucratic regulation had begun to reveal new problems as communities tried to act on their own to achieve an integration that the law had been attempting to require in its own piecemeal fashion (Schnorr 1993). Schnorr's communities of suburban whites and urban blacks could not be brought together, even given their common religious confidence and their belief in the traditional dogma of the American democratic community. There were barriers to volunteerism as effective social action. This did not necessarily mean that volunteerism was dead, only that its limits could be pointed out. Yet, the identification of such limits can be threatening to a society committed to judging programs and policies not by the knowledge they enrich but by the effects they produce. Much of New Deal and Great Society reform has been subjected to the same test of effectiveness, as has Progressive reform before the New Deal and all of liberal reform since the Great Society. If one asks if the New Deal ended the Depression or if the Great Society ended poverty, one must also ask if community integration programs work or if any social policy works. Books like Charles Murray's *Losing Ground* attest to the popularity of the negative answers one can give to all such questions as well as to the confusions that can be generated by social science methodology turned cannibal. One can even broaden the range of the questions if one wants to subject historical ideals as they were understood in their day to an accounting. Did the American Revolution produce democratic equality? Did the Civil War end slavery? Did the First World War make the world safe for democracy? The answers seem obvious, even if one asks what data or what technology one would use to prove them one way or another.

It may be that the American language of social reform rests on concepts of homogeneity that do not describe a historic reality. In our world at the end of the twentieth century, such an assumption is a bit like arguing that Catholics and Protestants in Northern Ireland should agree because they are both Irish, that Serbs and Muslims have an old history in common, that two thousand years of Jewish history in Poland should have ended Polish anti-Semitism long ago. A common history may include a history of bitter, unresolvable hostility. Failures to resolve such hostilities imbue human history with the basic tragedies from which we seek to learn. Rather than prove policies right or wrong, they enrich the history of public policy.

As the histories of all of our religions seem to press us to understand, failure is essential to our metaphysical understanding of our lives. The reasons for it, even the reality of it, are never obvious. If we are believers, we may accept the fact that they will never be known. Thus, the belief that conceptions like community, association, professional, and volunteer embody common ideals and produce commonly desired ends may be misguided. Our discoveries of failure may in fact be discoveries of our misunderstanding of the relation of our generalizations to our history. The effort to produce homogeneity is a strong one in American history. The opposition to it in groups now discovering how oppressed by it they have been only raises the question of generalization to a new, more public level. After all, homogeneity was once as politically correct as the hostility to it is today. The common desire for upward mobility assumes cultural integration as a common theme based on common methods. This had been the problem of Progressives in dealing with immigrants. Were they successful? To some extent, yes, but their integration began to fall apart, too. The suppression of cultural identity has been costly and harsh, particularly for groups like Blacks and Native Americans, who can appear to have been written off even by those most committed to saving them. A separation of suburbs and neighborhoods had followed the same lines with ethnics that it has with Blacks.

Robert Chapman's study "Jewish Philanthropy and Social Service in Minneapolis, 1900–1950" raises some questions about the application of traditional conceptions of Jewish philanthropy in twentieth-century American society (Chapman 1993). Classical lines of argument dating back to the thirteenth-century Jewish philosopher Maimonides point to a very internal system of self-support and self-help by a people accustomed to isolation in foreign, often hostile cultures. In the modern American context, multiple groups with different traditions undergo amalgamation within the larger Jewish community as well as within the many Christian philanthropic and secular welfare service communities comprised in American urban life. The professionalization of welfare services becomes an outside, American force changing the internal tradition of the Jews. This is a very interesting example of the kind of cultural impact one sees in so many aspects of the Americanization process, but with an element the usual studies of assimilation don't generally have. Disagreements within the Jewish community itself are as important for documenting the process of change as are the external influences. American Jews came from a wide range of European backgrounds and settled in different American places at different times. They entered communities that included not only other religions but other Jews, which gave their assimilation a dual character — they had to assimilate with others, but also with their own in conflicting ways they could not have anticipated.

Many of the questions raised by Chapman go to the heart of professionalism as an abstraction. Professionals who are not themselves members of the community may run into difficulties that their status as professionals alone cannot be adjusted to cover. Administrators who were not Jewish would quite obviously have been a problem, but so could administrators with different Jewish backgrounds who, in addition, had been educated as social work professionals by the American Protestant profession. The common character of the problems of social welfare may create a relation to other communities outside of the Jewish community. There are many ways of perceiving the relation between outsiders and insiders in a larger community that serves as an umbrella for different communities trying to work together despite differences with one another. Chapman provides us an opportunity to see the Jewish community and its internal differences as part of the larger community with its needs and differences. His examples of conflict between professionals and policymakers help us relate the community he examines with the more general differences that complicate the world of social service. The problems Chapman documents all point to issues of identity that have a direct influence on professional objectivity and the acceptability of professional methods in dealing with community issues. One can extend the general argument to all of the many kinds of community that look to professional management. The community's choice of a professional and willingness to follow his or her lead may well depend on factors that have nothing to do with professional standards but derive from cultural and class acceptability, the very factors that our contemporary concern with the makeup of pools from which job applicants are to be chosen has been intended to go beyond.

There are many reasons for insisting that both professionals and volunteers be selected and judged on the basis of known professional standards; but, as Chapman's analysis makes clear, effectiveness may call for other factors that community needs seem to require. Those factors touch on issues of cultural history that may not be amenable to arguments that stress objective professional standards or the generalizations of the social sciences. Professional knowledge and the intellectual perceptions and particular cultural needs of members of the community who give and receive services as citizens may not be inherently compatible.

Ideas are essentially more troublesome for democratic societies than Merton seemed to want them to be in 1942 or, indeed, than all intellectuals want them to be (Merton 1942). The relation between professionals and volunteers may be one of the ways of looking at the problems produced by ideas of elitism in a democratic setting. For if such ideas are essential to professional knowledge and if their spread is essential to stable democracy, as all of our theorists of professions seem to accept, then the production and distribution of ideas will become either the background or the battleground of a stable social order. There may be a gap or "cultural lag" between knowledge and its acceptable social standing, but the dream of William F. Ogburn's progressive generation of social scientists was the narrowing of the gap, possibly its obliteration. We may be more sophisticated — or more cynical. We are in any case more experienced. The relation between professional knowledge and the institutions that put it into practice is more complex than Ogburn's generation seemed to anticipate it would be; and the role of participants more difficult to define. We may have more respect for the disjunction between theory and practice in the sciences, less willingness to assume the reliability of the imposition of theory on practice than the Progressives did. We are also inclined to be more suspicious of the sources of theory and more conscious of the myriad oppositions that may go into the development of theory.

Although professionalization may itself be treated as theory, within each of the professions and the academic disciplines that control teaching and certification are collections of ideas that govern our definitions of professions. Those ideas are held in custody, so to speak, not only by the individual professionals and volunteers who develop them and use them, but by the institutions that preserve and promulgate them. Universities, museums, and, indeed, all of the corporations that act as repositories of ideas in the arts and sciences are part of a system for perpetuating cultural life that is considered as important to the maintenance of civilization as the traditional charitable and religious organizations we find in the world of nonprofits. Indeed, the three sets of institutions — cultural, charitable, and religious — share with both government and business a concern with bringing younger people into the world of their professionalization. The employment of so-called interns who work as unpaid volunteers in business and government has been justified as a way of supplying apprenticeships for the young who provide useful services as part of a training experience.

The association of such volunteers with the public functions of institutions like art museums, where individuals often called docents are trained to lead tours through galleries, and universities, where alumni are asked to help not only by giving but by raising funds from others, is part of an increasingly complex program whereby professionals engaged to manage the museum and the university and their fund-raising efforts seek volunteers to assist them. Victoria Alexander offers examples of the transformations that have taken place in the museum world in past decades. Professionals who manage museums have come to an awareness of their roles as coordinators of the interests of their donors in the art world and the public who are asked to support museums. As she sees it, the new, multiple constituencies allow museums "to rewrite museum missions, to change the museum's role in the community, and to establish new exhibition formats and subjects" (Alexander 1990).

The involvement of volunteers in the public services that museums provide serves functions that enrich and extend the programs devised by the expanded number and range of professionals in the arts who manage the museums. Volunteers can be trained to explain exhibits to the public in ways that meet the standards used by professionals to set up exhibits in the first place, thereby also assuring understanding by those who funded the exhibit that it will be publicly accepted as a worthwhile contribution to art education. Volunteers as educators of the public mediate between the art professionals and the audience of museum visitors. Donors see active involvement in the enjoyment of art rather than simply passive acceptance. They see the expansion of the audience for art from the knowledgeable and socially defined visitors of the past to new audiences who can be turned into continuing visitors, even contributors. City governments who increasingly come to see museums as part of the attractive culture of the community and contribute tax monies to that end also press museums to see themselves as public, to democratize, and to use their professionals to bring public and private interests together. Art donors have been transformed from private collectors transferring their collections to private institutions controlled by friends and people like themselves into contributors whose gifts are systematically made public by museum professionals and their volunteer staffs.

One can see similar transformations in the field of university education, in which the development of relations between donors and the disciplines they are asked to support shows another side of the relation between the giving of voluntary services and the professions. Stanford, the institution Suzanne Kay Stout studies, is interesting from the perspective of philanthropic funding (Stout 1993). Stout raises some basic questions about the relation between donor interests in the institution the donor is asked to fund and the institution's perception of its financial needs. Taking the academic department as the focus of giving from 1960 to 1990, she charts the separation of donor interests from the institution's needs as a whole. The effort to define elements that lead to the attraction of donor interest and subsequently to the dissolution of that interest gives us a window on an era of remarkable expansion and increasing complexity in the funding of American higher education. Increasingly sophisticated donors, professionally trained themselves, seek to expand knowledge, research, and training in the institutions in which they themselves were trained.

Again, one can ask, Who are the volunteers, who are the professionals? We can no longer assume sharp distinctions between the two or, even within each group, a uniformity of perspective. Our language may assume simplicities that confuse rather than clarify our search for meaningful distinctions. What's interesting from that perspective is that we deal with a complex of professionals: corporate donors; individual large donors, who have their own professional interests in the institution and may be drawn to certain academic groups because of those interests; alumni, who have their college recollections to sustain; foundations, who are programmatic in what they want to support; institutional fund-raisers, who now constitute an individual profession themselves; institutional managers (presidents, department chairs, and whatever other formal positions the institution uses for its management), some of whom are certainly part-time or amateur professionals; men and women who engage in high-level professional management for which they have not been trained. They may control large budgets, select and govern staffs who make critical institutional decisions, and mediate between others like themselves who are not responsible for management and trustees who are managerially experienced but lack the professional credentials to claim control. Such amateur professionals may be academics drawn in to administration for periods of time or on administrative tracks with other institutions in their pasts or futures. Who are the amateurs or part-time amateurs? Alumni are asked to support collegiate recollections by supporting unrestricted funds.

Donors are being asked the same thing, although they are more likely to have institutional interests in particular departments. And then there are the linkages profession to profession as doctors and foundations with medical interests are asked to fund medical research, and other such relationships. When, in the case of the medical profession, one adds the companies whose interest in research is in the creation of profitable products, one sees a modern complex of institutional developments that further complicate the definitions one might want to reach.

Kelly Moore's study of the formation of public interest science organizations in America addresses an important aspect of the problems raised by the examination of university fund-raising, museum development, and indeed any area in which, increasingly, the interaction of professionals and the public begins to affect fundamental issues of influence and funding (Moore 1993). Moore explores the establishment of political action organizations by scientists in the years from 1955 to 1970. Although it is not central to her argument, the scientists she studied were in fact joining a movement that social scientists had begun in the 1920s, when political leaders like Herbert Hoover and Franklin Roosevelt had begun to utilize new policy groups of university social scientists to advise them on the planning of programs for social and economic reform. The seeds of a conflict we recognize today in the various policy think tanks described as liberal and conservative were planted in the New Deal and, after World War II, continued in the years that culminated in the Kennedy-Johnson administrations. Even the revolution against those programs that we associate with the Reagan administration took the form of counterprograms recommended by economists like Milton Friedman and a new generation of social and political conservative theorists funded by what were now being considered conservative think tanks.

The emergence of nuclear physics as a center of political and professional dispute was an immediate aftereffect of the atomic bomb. Physical scientists and the engineers and technicians who gave their theories practical effect were now professionals whose work had dramatically direct effect on public interest. They were thereby drawn into political debate. By 1955, when Moore's study begins, the stage for a new political role for scientists was dramatically set. Conflict between the political action organizations she describes and a federal government that was behind so much of the funding for science set up a whole range of dispute both within the scientific community and outside it. Sophisticated issues about the power of knowledge became part of a literature concerned with basic moral issues. Yet put in terms of our issue here — amateurs versus professionals — the problem opened up a specific set of puzzles. Scientists as scientists are professionals. Scientists as citizens are not. What is the relationship between citizenship and professionalism?

The language of the Cold War and the intensity with which Americans in the fifties debated it seemed to bypass the possibility of so rational a question. The problem remains one of the historic factors behind the question of citizenship today. It is our version of political drama that includes names like Socrates, Galileo, and Lavoisier. The choice between a commitment to intellectual debate within the context of one's own professional specialty and ideological commitment to the state can be a difficult one to make. Does one include the now-famous letter of the Rhodes scholar William Jefferson Clinton criticizing the Vietnam War and refusing to participate in the armed services? But the issue here is one that Moore raises also: Does the scientific standing of scientists as figures the public accepts as professionals reinforce their influence in the public arena? Does it hurt science? The question is at least as old as Socrates. The power of knowledge may be socially dangerous. But was it Socrates' knowledge or his standing as a human being influencing the young that his critics perceived as dangerous? And what is the relationship between the two?

Indeed, the problems Moore raises are fundamental to any analysis of the modern relation between intellectuals and their society and to the potential metaphysics, so to speak, that touches all of the issues of volunteers and professionals. For these terms themselves are part of a language that human beings have created to classify the actors in the organizational world. As that organizational world has grown more complex, it has become possible, even necessary, for given individuals to act in many capacities as they change functions in the worlds they inhabit.

In modern society, *professional* has come to mean someone trained in a recognized discipline in which anyone with sufficient preparatory skills can be trained. Such a person must be willing to submit to three tests: those set by the educational system that trains and certifies professionals, those established by statute defining entry into the profession (or some other selection process instituted by the profession and its managers), and those tests that may be set more informally by the public the profession serves, a public that chooses those services and pays for them, thereby marking the would-be professional for success or failure. In fact, the expanded character of malpractice and its position in the courts suggest that the public tests grow more formal all the time. The legal profession now intersects with the medical, and both with politics as the public seeks to intervene in the programs and laws designed to govern the relation among professions. The moral equivalent of religious commitment plays a considerably diminished role, as the periodic flurries over the teaching of ethics in schools of medicine, law, and business testify. One could argue that my definition of professional is still the old one, that modernity has not changed it, that there are no time boundaries to it at all. After all, Hippocrates asserted an ethic for medicine to fight unethical practices that existed. He did not create the medical profession as the practice of healing, he made it scientific and responsible.

Volunteers choose the action in which they engage or are asked to serve the community without the promise of pay.

They may receive the gratitude of the community for their compensation, or, again, they may be critically attacked or ignored. It could be argued that volunteerism rests on a preexisting professionalism, not the reverse. Perhaps volunteerism is the triumphant counter to the ageold onslaught of professionalism on the freedom of concerned individuals to become involved. It could also be argued that in the absence of a preexisting professionalism, volunteerism will fail as an endless succession of inexperienced amateurs' attempts to substitute personal commitment for expert knowledge and trained skills.

There is now a genuinely modern form of relation between amateurs and professionals in which the two shift back and forth and may become indistinguishable as professionals in one area are called upon to be volunteers in another. For the nation's nonprofits and their relation to the professions and to amateurs, public reality encroaches on once private endeavors controlled by an earlier generation of private funders. All have been forced to accept citizenship, if you will. All have gone public, sometimes happily, as the range of public support enlarged the resources for professional expansion, sometimes less happily, as the seeming costs demanded by the expanded public or its elected representatives had to be met.

It is possible that one can see in these institutions the issues of professionalism and volunteerism in a light that is different from that cast more traditionally on problems of welfare and the culture of ideas. As charity was transformed by philanthropy, so philanthropy was transformed by an expanded sense of cultural need and the acceptance of trained intelligence as the key to meeting that need. The move from private graciousness to public responsibility was as evident in women's clubs, where no public resources were involved, as it was in museums, where new public resources exacted a price. The line between public and private became as unclear as that between volunteer and professional.

The Clinton summit of April 1997 — the President's Summit for America's Future — is the most recent of numerous efforts in the United States to create a restoration of the seemingly lost voluntarism that preceded the government takeovers of public service that began somewhere in the past. It is likely that most contemporary observers would date this takeover to the New Deal. More historically aware commentators might place it considerably earlier, either in the Progressive Era at the turn of the century or even in the Jacksonian Era, when efforts to turn voluntary service organizations into governmental agencies in fields like mental health and education all failed. The point is that reforming elites were demanding federal intervention during much of the national history of the United States. Part of that demand was a recognition by those reformers of the need for more systematic and trained attention to the issues of health and general welfare, an attention that people today would call professional. Voluntary service had demonstrated its amateur inadequacies as far as many of the reformers were concerned. The modern ro-

manticization reflected in such events as the summit cannot deal with issues like the need to manage volunteers to make them effective and to do it without funding. The cost of making helping hands helpful has to be taken into account, along with the very real possibility that professionally trained hands might just be a better bargain in the long run.

Are we reduced again to language? If so, it might be unwise to consider that a reduction per se. For both changes in language and the persistence of old terms despite changes in our conceptions of problems may be the result of a new consciousness of old problems, not the cause of that consciousness, and certainly not a substitute for it. The richness of our search for meaning does not have to be lost in any tangles of linguistic obfuscation. We can continue to search, aware of the fact that the distinctions we use are our creations. They are tools, intended as ways of understanding problems. They may remain the same terms, but our understanding of them has to change to encompass an awareness of new circumstances. If they become the causes of problems, it will only be because we have given them a reality they do not deserve.

REFERENCES

Alexander, Victoria D. 1990. "From Philanthropy to Funding: The Effects of Corporate and Public Support on Art Museums." Ph.D. dissertation, Stanford University.

Butterfield, Herbert. 1949. *The Origins of Modern Science*. New York: Macmillan.

Chapman, Robert M. 1993. " 'To Do These Mitzvahs': Jewish Philanthropy and Social Service in Minneapolis, 1900–1950." Ph.D. dissertation, University of Minnesota.

Greeley, Dawn M. 1995. "Beyond Benevolence: Gender, Class and the Development of Scientific Charity in New York City, 1882–1935." Ph.D. dissertation, State University of New York at Stony Brook.

Heinz, John P., and Edward O. Laumann. 1982. *Chicago Lawyers: The Social Structure of the Bar*. New York: Russell Sage Foundation.

Hoover, Herbert. 1923. *American Individualism*. Garden City: Doubleday, Page.

Horowitz, Irving Louis. 1975. *The Uses and Abuses of Social Science*. New Brunswick: Rutgers University Press.

Johnson, Margaret A. 1993. "Change in a Voluntary Organization, 1975–92: A Consideration of Social Change, Organization Structure, Gender and Class." Ph.D. dissertation, University of Texas at Austin.

McDonald, Mary Jean. 1993. "The Citizens' Committee for Children of New York and the Evolution of Child Advocacy, 1945–1972." Ph.D. dissertation, New York University.

Merton, Robert K. 1942. "Science and Technology in a Democratic Order." *Journal of Legal and Political Sociology* 1:115–26.

Moore, Kelly. 1993. "Doing Good While Doing Science: The Origins and Consequences of Public Interest Organizations in America, 1945–1990." Ph.D. dissertation, Department of Sociology, University of Arizona.

Ortega y Gasset, José. 1944. *Mission of the University*. New York: W. W. Norton.

Parsons, Talcott. 1968. "Professions." *International Encyclopedia of the Social Sciences,* ed. David L. Sills. New York.

Schnorr, Paul S. 1993. "Institutionalization of Racial Integration: From Social Movement Ideology to Organizational Governance." Ph.D. dissertation, Northwestern University.

Shils, Edward. 1980. *The Pursuit of Knowledge and Other Essays*. Chicago: University of Chicago Press.

Stout, Suzanne Kay. 1993. "The Dynamics of Organizational Linkages: The Case of Higher Education and Philanthropy." Ph.D. dissertation, Stanford University.

Tocqueville, Alexis de. 1966. *Democracy in America*, ed. J. P. Mayer and Max Lerner. New York: Harper and Row .

Veblen, Thorstein. 1928. *The Engineers and the Price System*. New York: Viking.

18

C A T H E R I N E   A L T E R

Bureaucracy and Democracy in Organizations:
Revisiting Feminist Organizations

We assume that the bureaucratic form of organization is necessary for the delivery of human services and for reform efforts which aim to change or ameliorate large-scale social problems. Bureaucracy, a hierarchical form of organization, is virtually the only type of organizational form used in the public sector through which health and welfare benefits are dispensed to large populations. Even in the private sector, in which nonprofit organizations are smaller and client populations more localized than in the public sector, hierarchy is the typical form of organizing. Given such widespread use, it is a puzzle, then, why bureaucracies engender widespread dissatisfaction among clients and consumers, staff and administrators.

The bureaucratic form is recognized for its efficiency and ability to formalize and routinize vast amounts of work (Weber 1946); it is also, however, notorious for its negative effects on organizational members—alienation, antipathy, and burnout (Crozier 1964). In the public sector, there have been experiments and much research in the area of organizational development demonstrating alternatives to bureaucracy which draw on contemporary organizational theory and practice. There has been precious little of this type of development among voluntary associations.

The democratic form of organization has always been viewed as appropriate to voluntary associations given their nature and aims but seldom has it been consistently imple-mented in health and welfare organizations. Although historians and students of government have studied democracy in political systems, it has not been a primary focus of those interested in the development and improvement of voluntary associations and welfare systems.

Classical thinking has always assumed the presence of democracy in voluntary associations, however. Alexis de Tocqueville, during his travels in the young America, observed firsthand that *men,* escaping the despot, want to be in control of their social relations and will share power with others rather than return to the tyranny of a king. Of course, in de Tocqueville's age, *all others* were defined as white, landowning males. Nineteenth-century philosophers could not view democratic aspirations as inherent to all human beings, and neither could they foresee the rich variety of organizational forms, processes, and transformations necessary to realize these aspirations. The twenty-six-year-old Comte de Tocqueville during his trip to America in 1831, expressed his contemporaries' concept of democracy: "The principle of equality, which makes *men* independent of each other, gives them a habit and a taste for following in their private actions no other guide than their own will. This complete independence . . . tends to make [man] look upon all authority with a jealous eye . . . and value that government whose head he has himself elected and whose administration he may control" (emphasis added). The principle of equality is the basic concept of democracy, an inherited truth upon which Western society has built its institutions and voluntary associations.

It is ironic, then, that 150 years later, it is feminist organizations that most clearly exemplify democratic principles in their construction and day-to-day operations, in spite of the fact that feminists themselves have seldom used the concept of democracy as the defining variable of their distinctive normative type of organization (one exception is Brown 1992). Feminist and women's organizations were formed and continue to be formed as a democratic alternative to contemporary bureaucracy — an organizational form that, they assert, is hierarchical, authoritarian, and discriminatory.

Although suffrage organizations are credited with achieving significant political, legal, and workplace advances for women, and feminist movement organizations are believed to have been responsible for further pushing gender-based discrimination and oppression into the national agenda, the feminist organization as an ideal type has been ignored, if not discounted.

As an oppositional form, the distinctive characteristic of feminist organizations is that they are collectives, whereby all members have equal voice in the decisions of the organization, and the organization proceeds only after consensus is reached. They are nonhierarchical and function by means of processes that attempt to preserve nondifferentiation, collaboration among all members, and equal attention to means and ends. Because feminist organizations are almost always formed as small, voluntary associations with clearly articulated ideology and member commitment they are an overlooked test case of the iron law of oligarchy.

The question of whether health and welfare organizations can be established and maintained through the democratic form is especially important for nonprofit organizations that are confronted today with increases in the intensity and scope of social problems. The study of feminist organizations shows that the strength of ideological commitment, organizational goals, political resistance, and resource dependency are factors which can inhibit or promote the development of either democratic or bureaucratic processes, depending on how they combine over time. Given that many feminist organizations have survived relatively intact for more than two decades and that the problems of many mainstream nonprofit organizations are reaching crisis proportions, it may be that the lesson learned by feminists in resisting elite rule and hierarchy has application today in a wide range of voluntary associations.

SOCIAL EQUALITY OR TECHNICAL EFFICIENCY

By law, nonprofit voluntary associations must be democratically constituted to be tax-exempt. To obtain status under section 503 of the United States Internal Revenue Code, a voluntary organization must be nonprofit, serve a public purpose, be governed by its membership, and maintain financial records that are open to public scrutiny. These formal requirements are, of course, minimal, but they establish the basic tenet that the public interest, as opposed to private interests, can be achieved only by structures designed to ensure the principle of *social equality*.

Although nonprofits are legally constituted as democratic organizations, Internal Revenue Service regulations do not ensure democracy in organizations in any substantial sense. The basic, or inherent, character of an organization is defined by a much wider range of processes and practices which, by the tenets of substantive democracy, guarantee that all members of the organization be able to hold office and have a voice in all important decisions affecting the organization (Hage 1980). Substantive democracy thus requires additional rules beyond the basic requirements of legal or formal construction. At a minimum, organizational bylaws must establish a rotation schedule for directors, the tenure of directors, the maximum number of consecutive terms that may be served by directors, procedures for election by secret ballot or by mail ballot, the requirement of at least two nominees for each office from a nominating committee, and the election of the nominating committee (Cafferata 1982). All of these rules, established to prevent individual privilege and the development of status groups, are institutionalized by means of the organization's bylaws and serve to maximize *equality of opportunity*.

All nonprofit organizations, then, meet the criteria of social equality by virtue of their Internal Revenue status, and many achieve substantive democracy via bylaws which incorporate the principle of equality of opportunity. Thus, higher levels of democracy are achieved by rules which govern internal processes of decision making and operations. It is perhaps ironic that rules are necessary for preserving democracy; yet, they are a two-edged sword. On one hand, rules protect minority interests and opinion within the organization and ensure the maintenance of social equality and equal opportunity. On the other hand, rules can be used to establish elite governance and bureaucratic processes and, in excess, they can stultify and rigidify an organization. Contrary to what the critics of public bureaucracy (and many feminists) assert, it is not rules themselves that are inherently nondemocratic. It is their number and how they are used by the men and women of an organization that determine whether they yield democratic or bureaucratic governance. Many nonprofit organizations, although democratic in their infancy, tend to become oligarchical and bureaucratic as they develop. The central task of this chapter is to describe the factors which enable organizations to reverse this bureaucratization process.

The term *bureaucracy* generally describes an organization in which all important decisions are made by an individual or small group at the top of a hierarchical, pyramidal structure. The operational definition used here, however, is Max Weber's (1946): a bureaucracy is an organization that maximizes *technical efficiency* through a large number of administrative rules, horizontal differentiation, complexity, span of control, permanent administrators, exclusivity of membership and promotion within the organization, vertical differentiation of the authority structure/centralization of decision making, and specialization of roles/divisions of labor (Cafferata 1982, p. 302). The requirements of technical efficiency also involve a large number of rules which are intended to narrow decision-making authority rather than broaden it.

The relationship between democratic rule and bureaucracy was the essence of the dispute between Weber and Robert Michels (Nyden 1985). The two theorists agreed that bureaucracy always accompanies the struggle to achieve democracy. Further, they agreed that as organizations begin to fulfill their intended purpose, they tend to grow, requiring increased specialization of function and expert leadership and reducing grassroots control of important decisions. They disagreed, however, over the question of whether growth, and its companion, bureaucracy, spells the end of democracy. Whereas Michels believed that "every system of leadership is incompatible with the most essential postulates of democracy" (1959, 400), Weber thought that some level of equality could be maintained via rules which work to prevent the development of an inaccessible status group and to expand the sphere of influence of the total membership (Weber 1968, 985). For Weber, it cannot be assumed that the appearance of elite or expert leadership eliminates all possibility of democracy (Scaff 1981). If we take Weber's view that the "iron law of oligarchy" is not inevitable, then we can view any organization as more or less democratic and bureaucratic. Because of the legal mandates for nonprofits, we also assume that organizations serving the public interest, in comparison with organizations operated for profit, will be more democratic and less bureaucratic — and have more rules ensuring social equality and fewer implementing technical efficiency. This conception of democracy is not that of a static form of organization; rather, it is one that acknowledges democracy as a developmental process which results in a wide range of organizational types with differing degrees of democracy and bureaucratic rule. Nonprofits, starting with the same degree of formal democracy, may take various developmental paths, depending on many internal and external factors.

The relationship of democracy to bureaucracy in nonprofits is of interest not just to academics; it continues to attract public and media attention. The national press in 1992, for example, extensively covered revelations that the United Way of America had for some time been ruled by elites who were serving their own private interests and not fulfilling the public mission for which United Way was created. In spite of its altruistic mission, elitist and autocratic governance in United Way took control, and the organization was severely damaged in the process.

The press is also quick to point out, however, that the process can go in the opposite direction. For example, the Forest Service was described in a recent article as a rule-bound bureaucracy which, thanks to participatory decision making and quality circles, has been transformed into an agency with full worker participation (McKenna 1993). Likewise, the once mob-ruled and highly oligarchical Teamsters union was reported to have been remade by means of court orders which mandated unionwide elections (Bernstein 1991). The point is that nonprofit organizations are perceived as being capable of wide swings between democratic and bureaucratic forms and are not necessarily stuck in unchanging patterns of governance (for a counter view, see Cafferata 1982). This observation concerning the processes of democratization and bureaucratization is illustrated by the theoretical model described below.

Democratic and Bureaucratic Processes

For many decades, the study of organizations has been, in effect, the study of bureaucracy in its many variations. Based on Weber's assertion that hierarchical organizations are the most efficient way to accomplish goals, very little attention has been paid to alternative forms of organization — how they develop, how they maintain themselves in the face of strong and subtle environmental forces, and whether, given different circumstances, they are actually less efficient. Also, for many decades, one of the crucial issues in social development has been the role of voluntary organizations and their ability to adjust to changing organizational conditions while remaining true to their mission (Zald 1970). What has not been explored fully are organizational forms that allow nonprofits to adjust to internal and external forces and yet remain congruent with the values and ideology upon which they were founded. It is often assumed that growth is accompanied by a parallel increase in bureaucratic structure and process, but little attention has been paid to the factors which sustain self-rule against totalitarian incursions and which minimize the degree to which development imposes stultifying rules, processes, and values.

In this section I describe briefly a theoretical model intended to explain why some organizations may be capable of achieving this improbable feat. The model is described first in general terms, with a brief explanation of the factors which push and pull against democratic rule. I hypothesize that four factors can largely explain democratization and bureaucratization in voluntary associations: ideology (Zald 1970), organizational goals (Etzioni 1964; Hage 1980), the need for resources to implement goals (McCarthy and Zald 1977; Benson 1975), and outside oppositional forces (Hyde 1992; Rodriquez 1988). These four factors have direct and indirect effects on the development of both democracy and bureaucracy, and together they have a wide range of consequences for the organization. The effect of these four factors on organizational growth and subsequently on the tendency toward democracy or oligarchy in organizations is illustrated in figure 18.1.

Voluntary associations differ in the nature and strength of their ideological commitment to the mission of the organi-

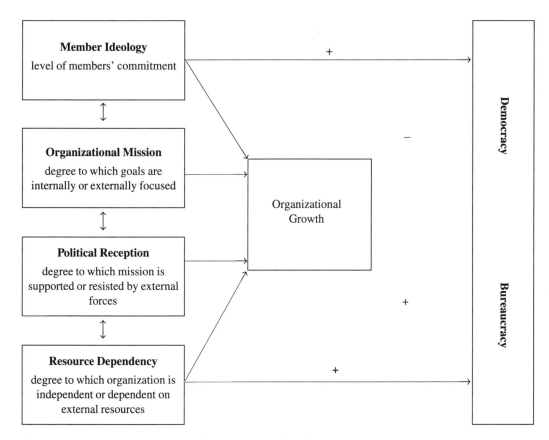

Figure 18.1. Bureaucratization and Democratization in Nonprofit Organizations

zation. The nature of ideology is shaped by many forces, among them the historical epoch and popular culture of the time and the socialization and personal histories of the members of the collective (or dominant group) (Etzioni 1988). The nature of ideology is, of course, based on deeply held cultural and religious values which produce a system of beliefs. A voluntary association, created to be an instrument of collectively held beliefs, develops in direct response to the nature and intensity of the membership's tightly linked beliefs and values. There are many dimensions of ideology which could be cited here; the one most important in terms of organizational development is the level of member commitment (Brown 1992). Commitment determines the persistence and obstinacy with which members pursue the organization's objectives in the face of resource shortages, market changes, and political opposition (Zald 1970). Commitment stems from the degree to which the members' ideological system is clearly articulated and zealously held.

Nonprofit organizations also vary widely in the mission and goals which operationalize their organizational ideologies. As a description of the idealized future which the organization is striving to achieve, goals guide and justify the activities and efforts of the membership. Goals, therefore, have enormous influence on the internal processes of organizations. If they are related to social change and development and are externally focused, then the membership will be

forced, over time, to expand the organization's size in order to achieve its global mission. If, on the other hand, the organization's mission is related to members' self-improvement or to bettering the collective in some way, then members will find it less necessary to become dependent on external resources.

Voluntary associations also differ in the degree to which their goals are supported or resisted by major actors in their environment. If there is widespread approval for the aims, then political and social support will accrue to the organization and it will expand to whatever size is necessary. If, on the other hand, the objectives engender opposition and resistance, then the opposite may well be the case. Opposition, of course, may vary in intensity, ranging from political methods which subtly undermine the organization's ability to function, to extremely acrimonious attacks which wreck havoc. The most visible forms of resistance have been the violent physical acts against women's health clinics, ranging from harassment and blockades to gas and fire bombings. In some cases, attacks against abortion clinics and their physicians have caused the temporary suspension of services, but they have not been successful in permanently closing clinics. It is clear that a high level of commitment by the membership, accompanied by some measure of organizational self-sufficiency and combined with support for the clinic's mission by other external constituencies, has resulted in the survival, if not the growth, of reproductive rights groups and women's health services.

Last, voluntary associations vary in the degree to which they remain independent of external influence (Pfeffer and Salancik 1978). There are social, religious, and special interest organizations which have survived for long periods of time as essentially self-sufficient bodies requiring no resources outside the association — voluntary associations and cooperatives which fulfill a need of their members and which rely solely on the resources and efforts of members. On the other hand, some organizations, in their desire to seek social change and altruistic goals, expand their scope and size so as to reach a greater audience or geographic area or to pursue greater effectiveness and efficiency. In order to acquire the information and technologies needed to achieve these objectives, voluntary associations may become dependent on external public and private resources (Kramer and Grossman 1987). This fourth factor, resource dependency, has a strong impact on the operations of an organization, as has been pointed out by a long line of organizational theorists (Benson 1975; Brown 1992; Smith and Lipsky 1992). When a voluntary association adopts goals whose accomplishment requires concerted action in the larger environment, then the organization becomes necessarily more dependent on its environment for resources because the membership itself does not have the resources necessary to achieve its goals.

These, then, are four potential forces which have a direct effect on growth and which, in turn, drive democratic or bureaucratic processes. The intervening variable, organizational growth, is the strongest force pushing against democratic rule and toward technical efficiency. The effect of an organization's size on the operations of profit-making firms has been widely researched; it has received far less attention in the literature on voluntary organizations.

When it becomes necessary because of increasing organizational size to differentiate between types of members and to control increasingly chaotic organizational activities, then more rules are promulgated to balance power between directors and staff and among staff and the clients, patients, or service consumers. There are two basic dynamics arising out of growth and expansion which tip the balance of nonprofit development toward bureaucracy.

The first is an internal dynamic set in motion by efforts to bring order to out-of-control conditions associated with growth. This balance of power is achieved through requirements that make distinctions between organizational members and by structures that segment members into different operating units — for example, those governing operations, finance, personnel promotion and evaluation, and marketing. The more that organizational members are placed in different roles, with different functions and tasks, the greater the likelihood that status differences will develop and that those in control of the whole will have more power and authority.

The second dynamic is the effect asserted by external forces needed for growth. The bureaucratizing influence of government funding on voluntary associations is well documented (Kramer and Grossman 1987; Morgan 1986; Rodriguez 1988). The quid pro quo of state funding is accountability, which can mean everything from requiring staff to be professionally trained to double entry fund accounting procedures to limitations on the scope and duration of the organization's activities. The potential results of utilizing external resources are incremental steps toward rationalization and formalization of the operations of the organization and of the interactions among its members. Those voluntary associations which abstain or minimize their reliance on outside resources retain a far greater measure of internal autonomy.

Maintaining social equality and equality of opportunity in a nonprofit organization is probably difficult in the best of circumstances. Endurance requires, at a minimum, abiding organizational goals, stable and supportive environments, and abundant internal resources. In less nurturing circumstances, decisions by organizational members can move the organization in opposite directions. In sum, democracy and bureaucracy are opposite poles of the same controlling mechanism, two potentials which exist simultaneously in all organizations and which point toward diverging organizational objectives — social equality or technical efficiency — both of which are necessary if a nonprofit organization is to sustain democratic rule in a turbulent environment and during periods of organizational expansion. Under these circumstances, organizational members are required to make continually occurring choices, each of which nudges or propels the organization in one direction or the other, each of which either resists oligarchical tendencies or sustains democratic rule. If voluntary associations are incubators of democratic rule, as proposed by de Tocqueville, then it is important to understand what factors enable organizational members to withstand nondemocratic forces (and thus prove Weber to be right and Michels to be wrong). The important question here is the membership's ability or willingness to steadfastly pursue its goals in spite of market constraints, regulations, and ideological assault. There are many descriptions in the academic literature as well as in the popular press of organizations that have abandoned their ideology or displaced their goals because of internal change or external pressure. There are also a large number of organizations that have survived for a considerable period of time and been able to resist encroachments upon their autonomy. Feminist organizations are a class of nonprofits which fall into the latter category.

FEMINIST ORGANIZATIONS

Feminist and women's organizations today exist around the world in great profusion. They are created for many purposes and causes and are dedicated to innumerable goals in their attempt to better the lives of women and children. In the West, these organizations had their genesis in earlier suffrage movements, which, after forty years of dormancy, gathered force again in the late 1960s as the women's movement.

These organizations have survived twenty to twenty-five years, and, although they are highly diverse in some aspects, they have much in common. In the mid-1990s, they engender curiosity but to date, little research (exceptions are Bordt 1990; Hyde 1992). In that they represent alternative forms of organizing and that they have survived for a quarter century or more they are useful for investigating the relation between organizational growth and the processes of democratization and bureaucratization. I shall examine these organizations through the lens of the model described above, framing the analysis in terms of ideology, goals, resource dependency, and environmental resistance or support as antecedents of organizational size.

It is difficult to use these organizations as an explicit category of alternative organization because we immediately encounter definitional problems. Although the feminist organization is an ideal type that differs from the traditional organization in very significant ways, it is also, in reality, part of a continuum which displays significant within-group differences. A range of organizations promote the interests of women, reflecting differences in the degree to which their agendas advocate reform of the status quo or more basic structural change in gender and sexual roles. Other women's organizations attempt to co-opt the feminist movement in order to advocate traditional gender role relationships in home, work, and political life. Although these organizations call themselves women's organizations and advance the traditional ideals of "total women" and "feminism" (Kaminer 1994), they are in many cases part of fundamentalist religious movements or radically conservative political parties with broader agendas and therefore cannot be understood as feminist organizations.

Of the organizations that do advocate reform or structural change, the mainline women's organizations were formed to challenge discrimination in a wide range of arenas, and they focus on problems of exclusion of women from political, commercial, social, and artistic life. The oldest of these organizations date from the suffrage movement, and they include such national organizations as the American Association of University Women and the League of Women Voters as well as many state and community voluntary associations which have survived as democratic organizations in which important decisions are made by consensus. The newer of these organizations, those arising out of the women's movement, are national feminist organizations which advocate profound change and community organizations which are collectivist but focused on a narrower set of issues. An example of the former is the National Organization for Women; examples of the latter are battered women's shelters, women's health clinics, and artists' cooperatives. These are explicitly self-styled feminist organizations whose members challenge not only discrimination and exclusion, but the assumptions and personal behaviors which undergird them. They require individual change of both men and women as well as social change in society.

An interesting recent development—on a theme that seems to unite the disparate range of women's and feminist organizations, including perhaps even those I term bogus feminists—is a belief that female-oriented organizations meet female needs better than traditional organizations do. There is a growing sense that assimilation into male-dominated organizations will not advance the cause of women as much as activism within a feminist organization. This is the old separatist versus integrationist argument, but now there is evidence that women in feminist organizations do better than those in male-dominated ones: girls who attend girls' schools score higher in mathematics and science; women who graduate from women's colleges reach higher levels in politics and corporations (Estrich 1994); women who avail themselves of domestic violence shelters and women's health clinics experience more empowerment and have a much better sense of their potential (Rodriguez 1988). To a greater or lesser degree, the belief in the efficacy of women's organizations is based on women's negative perceptions of and experiences in male organizations.

Feminist Critiques of Traditional Organizations

The postmodern feminist critique asserts that modern organizations are dependent upon a specific configuration of gender relations. This assertion is arrived at through historical study, linguistic analysis, and organizational research. Feminist historians, for example, have analyzed the development of bureaucracy in the nineteenth century. The classic case studies are the reform of the British Civil Service (Corrigan and Sayer 1985) and the Post Office (Zimmeck 1988), and they provide specific evidence of the development of the hierarchical distinction between mechanical and intellectual labor (Savage and Witz 1992). These analyses show that the rapid growth of bureaucratic organizations was made possible by the so-called White Blouse Revolution, which employed women for routine work, institutionalizing them as subordinate workers in both white- and blue-collar organizations and freeing men to do the cognitive work. This gendered structure of work within organizations had a series of important effects. First, because they did the commonplace, day-to-day work, women made it possible for organizations to promote male employees more quickly into positions of authority, for male workers to gain the knowledge necessary to do administrative work through education and training rather than by learning the business as they rose through the ranks, and for men to have careers because women, of course, were not eligible for promotion (Compton 1986; Compton and Jones 1984). Thus, as organizations grew larger, differentiation increased proportionately. Women were denied status and power because of their housekeeping roles within organizations and because of their exclusion from the networks through which men gained knowledge and political resources. Rosabeth Kanter (1977) offered this process and its outcome, male homosocial reproduction, as one explanation for the patriarchal culture and structure of bureaucracy. Until very recently, job classification and promotion structures have remained gender-based—women and men recruited into different job tracks, with different salary structures and promotion prospects (Kanter 1977).

More recently, the critique of organizations has been extended by postmodern feminist scholars who analyze the discourse and linguistic patterns of organizations to identify the institutional practices that maintain gender and organizational identity. For example, K. E. Ferguson (1984) described bureaucratic discourse as male-dominated, linking this observation to the historical fact that women have been excluded while men have been included in the public realm. Women's exclusion has enabled them to develop a "submerged" voice, one characterized by expressive modes of action and discourse. When women do enter the public realm, they are disadvantaged, being unfamiliar and unschooled in the "rational" and "instrumental" modes of male discourse.

Focusing on the nature of organizational discourse, feminist scholars postulate that when family ties were completely removed from work and replaced with highly bureaucratic and professional structures, then organizational goals and purposes completely dominated discourse within the organization (Hearn, Sheppard, Tancred-Sheriff, and Burrell 1989). The dominance of bureaucratic and professional culture purged organizational life of all emotional content and strengthened "the process in which men become associated (in location) with rationality/instrumentality and women with emotionality/expressiveness" (Burrell 1984, 104; Miles 1988). If this is the case, then it follows that decision making in organizations separates mind and body by isolating and suppressing the emotional and physical self from the process of organizing (Mumby and Putnam 1992):

> Researchers using the bounded rationality concept treat emotional experience (defined as feelings, sensations, and affective responses to organizational situations) as either a weak and handicapped appendage to reason or as another "means" to serve organizational ends. In the former case, emotions are devalued, trivialized, or treated as inappropriate at work. For example, decisions based on "gut feelings," emotions, or intuition, must be rationalized through satisficing and alignment with organizational values and goals. . . . In the latter case, emotions are ways to achieve such organizational ends as efficiency, profit, and productivity. As such, the emotional realm is co-opted and alienated in a form known as *emotional labor*. (Mumby and Putnam 1992, 472)

Emotional labor is a central concept of postmodern feminist scholars because it is viewed as the means by which organizations remain undemocratic and male-dominated in spite of legislation that equalizes spending by gender in college athletics, affirmative action, and the strivings of individual women. Emotional labor is a form of organizational control of the emotions whereby feelings are treated as organiza-tional commodities, as when employees are forced to be nice, to use phony smiles, to suppress anger, and to tolerate sexual harassment (Hochschild 1989). Thus, feminists see emotional labor as just another means of socially constructing roles which force women to make an unfair choice (Schwartz, Gottesman, and Perlmutter 1988). They can either adopt the role and thus fail to achieve an integrated self or they can differentiate themselves and be seen as not fitting in or as insubordinate (Ferguson 1984).

Other feminist scholars, using standpoint methodology, have extended these ideas to describe the distinctive ways in which women engage in daily life at home and within patriarchal organizational structures. By describing the systematically different structure of male and female life activity, these scholars understand women's lives as being shaped by the sexual division of labor. Dorothy Smith (1987), for example, sees the development of bureaucracy as the emergence of an abstracted conceptual mode of organizing society and rational administrative practice. By making this distinction between the conceptual mode and the concrete mode, she is able to describe the fundamentally relational difference between the male and female mode of action and discourse:

> If men are to participate fully in the abstract, conceptual mode of action, they must be liberated from having to attend to their needs in the concrete and particular. . . . The place of women, then, in relation to this mode of action is where the work is done to facilitate men's occupation of the conceptual mode of action. . . . At almost every point women mediate for men the relation between the conceptual mode of action and the actual concrete forms in which it is and must be realized, and the actual material conditions upon which it depends. (Smith 1987, 90)

Women, then, are concerned with "the concrete underbelly of conceptual activities" (Savage and Witz 1992, 25), whether they are in the organization or in the home, and are ordering and organizing the real world. From standpoint theory emerges the conclusion that men, who dominate the conceptual and thus authoritarian mode, are privileged at the expense of, but only because of, women. In their review of the feminist literature, Savage and Witz (1992) rightly point out that "the whole concept of 'dependency' within the context of gender relations acquires an interesting new twist, for it is men who are dependent upon the concretizing activities of women in order to sustain their involvement in the everyday world of, for example, bureaucratic administration (Savage and Witz 1992, 27).

One current conclusion of this stream of scholarship is that the powerless position of women in bureaucratic organizations is not just an outcome of historical events that can be fixed by reform activity which aims to removes the "glass ceiling." Rather, exploitation based on gender is an inherent property of modern organizations; bureaucracy is possible as a form because of the exclusion of women from the conceptual and symbolic organization of activity and thus from public life altogether. This "sexual division of labor" pushed women outside the realm of authority and *distributed organizational power by gender.*

Most recently, feminist scholars have disagreed with the view that gender and organizational power are inseparable (Pringle 1989a, 1989b). There has been a shift from the gender paradigm to one of sexuality; the root cause of the dispossession of women is believed to be the power of sexuality. In fact, by this view, *sexuality is power is organization* — three properties which are inseparable and intertwined. No longer are male-female differences thought to account for power differentials; rather, organizational structure and discourse account for male-female differences. It is organization itself which rests on sexuality. Seen in this light, the current campaign against sexual harassment in the workplace is the most important step toward equity within organizations that has been taken in decades.

By these views, bureaucratic organizations are the primary means by which women's oppression has been sustained over the past century and a half. Political and sexual domination of females by males is perpetuated by organizational structures which place power and control in the hands of a few male elites. The suppression of emotionality in favor of rationality and instrumentality — or its use only in service of organizational goals — is the means by which oppression of women continues. The continuation of male domination via hierarchical forms and processes, freed from a need to attend to the concrete necessities of daily life at home and work, is made possible by a continued toleration of male use of sex as power. It is to be expected, therefore, that feminists would strive for alternative means of organizing. Although feminists continue to support actions to reform public and private bureaucracies, the separatist orientation has been adopted by many women who wish to live their ideology within their own organizations.

Feminist Ideology as the Basis for Feminist Organizing
Women who experience themselves as different from their socially prescribed roles have always come together to protest and give mutual support. In the nineteenth and twentieth centuries, women have created formal organizations to accomplish these goals, and their organizations were structured and operated as alternatives to what they perceived to be mere extensions of a society that was patriarchal and discriminatory. Feminists, viewing organizations through the lens of feminist ideology, perceive traditional organizations as extending, perpetuating, and strengthening the inequities of male domination — and eventually of such "-isms" as racism, homophobism, capitalism, and imperialism. Unlike social anarchists and other utopian activists before them, feminists have developed their opposition into a clearly articulated belief system which is the basis for an oppositional ideology of organizing (Brown 1990). Feminist organizing, then, is a self-conscious method of protest itself because feminist organizations are an oppositional alternative — based on principles of

social equality, wholism, nondifferentiation, collectivist rule, and, of course, nonhierarchical form. Because of these principles, made explicit by the feminist movement, the ideal of the feminist organization is easily described in terms of a normative model.

At the heart of feminist ideology is the belief that people can work together for common purposes without resorting to a highly structured, pyramidal hierarchy to control internal processes and order decision making. The ideal of cooperation within a collective of like-minded individuals has seldom had as clear, conscious, and long-lasting an expression by a social movement (Bouchier 1983), in spite of the fact that in its application, many differences across the political continuum have appeared (Kaminer 1993).

Feminist organizations, because they share an opposition to traditional power structures, share a commitment to egalitarianism. As a reaction to and cure for the injustices perpetuated by male political domination of organizations, feminist organizations aim to be universally and explicitly egalitarian regardless of the degree to which they have a revolutionary or reformist orientation. Social equality is an intrinsic characteristic which defines the feminist organization.

The capability of feminist organizations to operationalize cooperative collective behavior is due, in part, to their understanding of the interconnection between individuals and the structures within which they exist; or, to put it a different way, the degree to which *the personal is political* (Friedan 1981; Steinem 1982). This concept encapsulates a wholistic approach to viewing organizations, one which stipulates that process and means are every bit as important as ends and that the structure of organizations should be derived from the process of organizing. Thus, another concept of feminist organizations is that both process and form must be congruent with the tenets of the ideology, and the construction of both is a conscious political act. Feminist organizations strive to pay as much attention to the content of everyday life and to the interactions of members as to daily tasks.

Feminist organizations aim not to differentiate between participants; or at the least, differentiation is minimized to the greatest extent possible. Differences between members — for example, in social status, access to information and resources, and skills — are not acknowledged in work processes; thus all tasks are performed by all members through sharing of jobs or job rotation. Having no leaders, who in traditional bureaucracies have authority to make most or all of the important decisions, feminist organizations require the membership to be actively involved in decision making and to make all decisions collectively. Full participation in all aspects of the organization, from decision making to work processes, is believed to be what makes the feminist organization powerful and empowering.

Given their rejection of hierarchy and a wholistic orientation, feminist organizations operate ideally without leadership, which is possible because of widespread agreement about underlying values and principles among members.

Table 18.1. Goals, Resource Dependency, and Political Resistance to Feminist Organizations

	Consciousness-Raising/ Self-Help Groups	*Service Organizations*	*Social Movement Organization*
Goals	To facilitate members' individual change	To facilitate change in specific groups of women and/or to create change in community structures that discriminate or oppress them	To promote change in community or societal structures that discriminate or oppress women
Resource dependency	Isolated from established political and cultural structures Little or no need for financial resources	Moderately interactive with established political and cultural structures Highly dependent for resources Acquisition tactics require professional skill and persuasion	Highly interactive with established political and social structures Ranges from self-sufficient to highly dependent Acquisition tactics include both professional skill and political action
Political resistance	Low	Moderate	High

Collaborative participation is the means by which nonhierarchy is made to work. Because of the existing consensus over organizational processes, feminist organizations can govern either intraorganizational or interorganizational activity with very few rules and methods of coordination. This characteristic was described by Anna Coote and Beatrix Campbell (1987) in their documentation of the dissolution of the National Coordinating Committee, an early women's movement organization in London in 1971:

> Most women were confident that the movement would hang together without a coordinating committee — and it has remained a loose federation of small groups, linked chiefly by a sense of involvement and a common cause. That it has survived nearly two decades was a measure of the strength of the *idea* that held it together. It was also due to the fact that the movement's lack of formal structure was a positive, not a negative feature. (Coote and Campbell 1987, 27, quoted in Brown 1992, 9)

The belief that hierarchies result in self-defeating traps for those at the bottom (women) is a central tenet of feminist organizations. Hierarchies are inimical to women who struggle for autonomy and fulfillment in positions that are subordinate and disadvantaged, and they symbolize all that is discriminatory and unjust in traditional organizations. The feminist movement is noteworthy for its ability to critique hierarchical organizations and for its success in constructing a positive alternative form of organization. That any women's organizations have survived more than a quarter of a century is evidence that they can work effectively.

Feminist Goals, Political Resistance, and Resource Dependency

Although feminist organizations share a core of beliefs and values, their goals and the level of resource dependency necessary for implementing them can vary substantially. To capture these differences one must start with the purpose for which the organizations were formed; their missions are, of course, tightly tied to their ideology (Clemens 1989, 1993; Hyde 1992; Leidner 1991; Rodriguez 1988).

One useful way of classifying the diversity of feminist organizations is in terms of their orientation. At one end of the spectrum are organizations that focus inwardly and aim to change some aspect of their members' lives. At the other end are those that focus outwardly on other groups of women or on changing some aspect of society at large. The table below is inclusive of this variation and describes feminist organizational goals as well as the parallel variation in resource dependency and political resistance.

The cells in this table are not mutually exclusive; many organizations have multiple goals and thus include self-improvement goals as well as service or social action goals or both within their mission. There are innumerable small women's groups, for example, which were formed for social or intellectual pursuits but which eventually adopted service goals. Likewise, there are service organizations that expand the geographic reach of their mission so far beyond their communities that they link or merge with other, similar organizations, become national in scope, and take on additional policy and legislative change goals. For analysis, however, it is useful to distinguish between self-centered and other-centered goals.

When a feminist organization adds an other-centered goal, it expands its mission in terms of scope or geography. Expansion — in response to additional feminist issues or the need to reach greater numbers of women — requires the organization to grow in size, and this it will do unless it meets with resistance either from unresponsive funding bodies or political foes. If there is substantial opposition, its growth may be slowed or halted and its organizational properties may remain unchanged. If, however, this expanding feminist organization overcomes resistance and its growth is bolstered by financial and political support, then its trajectory toward bureaucratization is guaranteed. As described earlier (see fig. 18.1), the coordinating of activities which serve multiple goals or supervising of operations across vast geographic distances makes it difficult to avoid bureaucratic processes and procedures. In these situations, the strength of the members' ideological commitment to egalitarian and collective processes may enable them to avert a bureaucratic outcome.

The hypothesis represented in figure 18.1 is that every time there is a change in any of the four variables that precede growth — member ideology, goals, environmental resistance, and resource needs — the organization will shift toward greater democratic or bureaucratic governance, depending on how the combination has changed. The reason that feminist organizations are a good test of the hypothesis is that when they are founded they are usually small and have a strong ideological foundation. The question, therefore, is whether their members' commitment is strong enough to overcome political obstruction while simultaneously resisting the corrupting influences of success. The answer, of course, is that it depends on what type of feminist organization it is.

Self-Help Groups and Organizations. Women have always formed cells for protest and support, but the late 1960s and 1970s were a time when consciousness-raising, support, and mutual aid groups became vehicles to aid women in developing the personal strength to overcome discrimination and oppression. These groups were purposely focused on the individuals involved, and their mission was to facilitate change in members (Rothschild-Whitt 1979). Most of the groups formed originally for support have survived as collectives which use group process to enable members to meet their personal psychosocial needs. Many, in addition, have expanded their goals in order to meet members' needs for labor and financial resources. Because they are small and devoted almost exclusively to facilitating personal change or meeting their members' needs, they exist independently of other community political and cultural organizations, which they do not need to survive.

These small organizations are so numerous and private, they are almost invisible. Many — for example, support groups for single mothers, childless women, lesbians, displaced homemakers, minority women, union members, businesswomen — are informal and are organized to facilitate individual change through group processes, give friendship and emotional support, and provide peer counseling. But many are formal nonprofit and profit-making organizations which, in addition to carrying out the functions of the informal groups, exchange and sell labor or commodities. There are cooperatives of women artists, quilt makers, and dairy farmers; there are cooperatives for child care, food procurement, and English language tutoring. There are organizational networks of working-class women, businesswomen, and professional women, who together provide mutual support or attempt to create new products or establish new markets. The list is endless, and all have two characteristics in common: they tend to have relatively small memberships and they are self-sufficient. Because their goal is self-centered — personal change, interpersonal support, or financial gain — they usually do not interact with their environment (unless interaction is necessary to market a product).

Feminist organizations that remain small over long periods of time can maintain democratic governance fairly easily as long as this is the will of their membership. Because they do not have to depend on resources other than their own, they do not have to be accountable to anybody but themselves. Because they do not aim to affect anyone other than themselves, they generally do not engender opposition that can threaten their survival.

Service Organizations. Another expression of the feminist movement looks outwardly and provides assistance to the many groups of women who are victimized in various areas of contemporary life. These organizations offer services or interventions which focus on the social, emotional, health, or welfare problems of women, although the problems are viewed as originating in the larger systems and structures of which the women are a part. Such organizations reject theories based on the medical model, which diagnose or label women's problems in terms of mental illness and social dysfunction (individual pathology) or as intergenerational transference (family pathology). Thus, many of these service organizations aim to empower individual women to change their victimizing circumstances, while at the same time they work on behalf of women in efforts to change the informal and formal organizational systems in which the oppression originates.

Medium- and large-size communities typically have many feminist or women's service organizations today. Some of the oldest provide shelter services to battered women and their children. These domestic violence programs (DVPs) tend to limit the use of professional staff, emphasize self-help and peer counseling, and incorporate a political analysis of battering into their programs (Dobash and Dobash 1978). One DVP in Hawaii is typical:

> It has an egalitarian organizational structure run by a non-professional staff of former residents who earn equal pay, make decisions by consensus, and operate a program in which residents actively participate in running the shelter. . . . it prefers an open-door policy, sets no limits on how long residents may stay, and encourages non-professional, egalitarian, and informal relationships within the organization. Because their goal is to have women achieve self-development, politicization, and liberation, they strive to have the battered women actively participate in running the shelter along with the staff and volunteers. (Rodriguez 1988, 236–37)

The goal of this DVP is to help women avoid returning to abusive relationships and enable them to achieve self-sufficiency for themselves and their children. This goal is common to many types of feminist service organizations. There are women's health care organizations that promote self-care within a self-affirming and wholistic lifestyle. There are rape counseling services that support victims so they can confront their attackers and thus regain their self-confidence. There are business training programs that teach welfare recipients the skills and courage necessary to start small-scale enterprises and thus become self-employed. There are substance abuse programs that afford women a safe place to recover while they care for their children.

Feminist service organizations, however, live with a constant dilemma. On one hand, they strive to meet the needs of all the women in their communities needing their service, a goal which, even with participant and paraprofessional staff, requires substantial financial resources. The operation of one shelter for just a dozen women with children or of a health clinic for a few hundred women requires a hundred thousand dollars a year or more. Feminist organizations do not want to seek government funding or even voluntary dollars, however, because they know it will subject them to many regulations and forms of accountability. Funding bodies, especially public ones, often demand professional expertise in the name of effectiveness and accountability. They require an administrative hierarchy, job descriptions, differential salary structures, limits on duration or intensity of service, and extensive financial reporting.

These requirements, however, are not consistent with egalitarian processes, rotation of members, and consensus decision making. When a feminist organization decides to broaden its goals to reach more women or women with different types of problems, it puts its ideology to the test. The challenge becomes finding ways to maintain operating methods consistent with their beliefs and values while at the same time satisfying outside demands. In addition, the maintenance of internal processes is made even more difficult when the organization experiences political or physical opposition from activists with different ideological commitments. Resistance, however, can have a strengthening effect. Some women's health clinics which perform abortions are stronger because their members' resolve hardened as physical violence escalated. Others closed or stopped performing abortions because their physicians were unwilling to risk their physical safety.

Since the 1970s, some feminist service organizations have become moderately self-sufficient (because they have limited the size of their service populations), while others have grown large and become highly dependent on resource allocation bureaucracies. In the latter case, co-optation has pushed some formerly democratic organizations into bureaucratic processes and structures. This fact raises the question of how a highly dependent social service organization can remain democratic with internal egalitarianism. Can it have both formal structures that are highly bureaucratic to satisfy external forces and day-to-day operations that are highly

democratic and nonhierarchical (Bordt 1990)? The model described above suggests that one necessary (but not sufficient) element for overcoming this dilemma is clearly articulated values which govern day-to-day operations. M. Lipsky and S. R. Smith summarize this dilemma: "Ultimately, our argument that developments in government contracting with non-profit organizations vitally affect the future of the welfare state depends upon recognizing that these organizations have traditionally played a role in integrating the individual into community-sponsored activities (as client, donor, or volunteer) and in offering *an alternative* to public policies derived from governmental power and coercion" (Lipsky and Smith 1989–90, 646) (emphasis added).

Social Movement Organizations. The range of feminist social movement organizations is very wide, and they differ in the degree to which they view women's problems through the single lens of gender or through the multiple lenses of gender, class, race, and sexual orientation. They differ also in the degree to which they are reformist or oppositional, using tactics that range from persuasion to confrontation to combat. Finally, they differ greatly in the size of their infrastructure and the resulting level of bureaucracy needed to carry out large-scale public education and political campaigns. They are all at least moderately democratic, however, and usually use memberwide elections, consensus decision making on at least the policy level, and, although they may have to become somewhat hierarchichal, their form is as flat as possible.

Today, it is easy to forget the enormous impact that suffrage movement organizations had on political processes as well as on women's issues, and that their methods — personal discourse, social research, policy advocacy, and lobbying — became standards for all political organizing after 1920 (Clemens 1989, 1993). Also often overlooked is that the suffrage organizations were transformed, after 1920, into a second generation of organizations that survive today in relatively good health: for example, the National Association of University Women, the Junior League, and many national sororities. The League of Women Voters, for example, has chapters that work directly on women's issues in every state and in many cities and towns and well. The league membership, using the methods of its predecessor as well as media and public relations techniques, adopts study items at the local, state, and national levels each year and then reaches a consensus on collective action to be taken to implement its positions. The league is credited with numerous child labor, welfare, environmental, and political reforms. It and other women's membership organizations are self-sufficient but are limited in their reformist agenda by the middle-class values of their members.

There are, of course, more oppositional women's organizations like the National Organization for Women, Title VII monitoring organizations, and the Guerrilla Girls. The latter, an organization of women artists, campaigns to open up the male-dominated art industry through the use of nonviolent guerrilla tactics, including sophisticated graffiti placed in strategic locations, boycotts, and cooperatives. There are local and national organizations that work to end discrimination against lesbians and gays and that demand increased research on HIV and support for its victims.

The factor that differentiates these feminist social movement organizations is the scope and reach of their missions. Those that focus on the discriminatory institutions and structures within their own neighborhoods and communities may use their own labor and resources to achieve their agendas, although if it is an effort that must be sustained for a long time then additional resources are probably essential. Those that go beyond their own reach in attempts to change larger societal systems and structures cannot rely only on what they bring to the effort, but must acquire substantial resources.

The larger the scope and reach, the larger the organization, the more difficult it is to maintain social equality, collectivist rule, nondifferentiation, and nonhierarchical forms. The reasons are many. It is very difficult to achieve and maintain a sense of social equality among members of a group who must live within a broader society in which social equality does not exist. It takes continual face-to-face interaction among members, time to break down social barriers and to construct new ways of relating and doing. Personal interaction among members of a group becomes increasingly difficult as group size gets larger, and impossible as members are physically distant from one another.

Democracy also takes time. Reaching consensus is extremely time-consuming, especially in the beginning, when normative roles and behaviors are being worked out. It is far more efficient for a supervisor to hand down an order or circulate a directive than for a group to reach agreement on an issue. In addition, members have to be willing to give their time consistently or power and status will devolve to those who are constant in their involvement. Further, even if the organization does not need to expand to achieve its mission, it must constantly search for new members to replace those who drop out from fatigue or who leave because of waning interest.

When a single social movement organization expands its scope beyond its community to the state or regional level, it soon bumps into the limits of voluntary association. If there is to be concerted and consistent action across a wide geographic area, then coordination is necessary. Unless volunteers are willing to assume this time-consuming task, then paid staff is necessary, and this introduces differentiation and status differences into the collective based on educational level and technical skill. Further, if the organization must use education and public relations methods to persuade and influence, then professional communication skills and new technologies are needed for the organization to be effective; this acts as another assault upon social equality and non-differentiation. There are many national organizations in which local cells are collectivist in structure, but in which the centralized state or national coordinating unit is staffed by paid professional staff. This arrangement allows the community organization to operate without a hierarchy but is sure to engender tension and conflict between the two levels. An alternative is the British model described above, a network of small local women's groups without a formal structure or centralized coordinating capability (Brown 1992). To effect change in federal legal or administrative systems is difficult, however, without a central coordination.

To return, then, to the central question of this paper: Are feminist organizations especially successful in using democratic forms of governance, and, if so, how have they been able to sustain nonhierarchical forms of organization and resist the encroachment of bureaucracy as they mature through time? One simple answer to the first part of this question is to recount the achievements of the feminist movement since the late 1960s. Most, if not all, of these gains could not have been made by individual women acting alone; concerted actions by voluntary associations over long periods of time have changed American society. Domestic violence, sexual assault and harassment, and women's health problems — to name only a few — are now recognized by large segments of the population as major problems and are now on the nation's agenda; to a lesser extent, child care, equal pay for equal work, and the Equal Rights Amendment have been given the priority they require.

The question, however, is to what extent feminist organizations have been successful *because* they used processes that were true to their original organizing ideology. This question cannot be answered, of course, without more research, but theory and anecdotal evidence provide guidance for that research.

Clearly, the 1960s adage Small Is Beautiful has merit in this context. Small feminist organizations which stay within their own space and do not evolve much beyond their original purposes (either self-centered or other-centered or both) are more likely to remain nonhierarchical if their members are highly committed to the feminist belief system. Even if they meet with political resistance, this experience often strengthens their resolve. For example, members of one well-known women's health cooperative in the Midwest have often responded to actions by Operation Rescue, an antiabortion group, by saying, "The bad news is our entrances were blockaded again last week; the good news is we have twenty-five new members." It is clear that the intensity of members' ideology is the most important variable in resisting the effects of both attack and the more subtle forms of bureaucratic co-optation.

Ideology is easy to espouse; it is very difficult to enact. For two decades, democratic feminist organizations have used many of the practices that are only now being espoused in the for-profit world, and, as a result, their members have a sense of control and autonomy, feel a sense of personal responsibility for their involvement, have an opportunity to develop personally in concert with the group and the organization, and are able to integrate their work and development with other aspects of their lives. As has been pointed out by organizational theorists from Tom Burns and G. M. Stalker (1961) to Thomas Peters (1987), a work group with these qualities makes for an organization that is flexible, innovative, adaptive, and capable of accomplishing its goals. If democratic feminist organizations have survived with nonhierarchical processes intact, then this fact argues for the conclusion that democracy has evolutionary advantages. Democracy may be less efficient than bureaucracy but effectiveness may be more important in the long run for nonprofit organizations.

It is also clear that many service and social movement organizations must go beyond their original space, either in terms of agenda or locality or both. If they are service organizations and wish to increase their service capacity, they obtain financial support from funding bureaucracies and hire paraprofessional and professional staff. If they are social movement organizations and they must compete with oppositional voices and interests, they need to acquire technology with which to reach and influence larger audiences. To withstand invasion and preserve democratic life within their organizations, feminist organizations then need to consciously and explicitly invent two versions of their reality — their internal collective culture and their worldly personae. Successful attempts at sustaining this dual personality should be documented, so that it can become a technology by which increasing numbers of voluntary associations may preserve their commitment to themselves and their communities.

The model described in figure 18.1 suggests that the level of ideological commitment is the most important factor affecting the degree to which an organization will sustain democratic governance because it has both a direct effect of supporting democratic practices and an indirect effect of sustaining goals that are congruent with the internal belief system. It is perhaps an obvious observation, but nevertheless true, that the most potent remedy for drift toward bureaucratic tendencies is a continual clarification of the ideology as well as of the processes which reinforce it. Many feminist organizations consider their belief system to be organic, and in applying themselves to its continual development, they are keeping their organizational life congruent with their values and their changing environment.

REFERENCES

Alter, C., and J. Hage. 1993. *Organizations Working Together.* Newbury Park: Sage.

Benson, J. 1975. "The Interorganizational Network as a Political Economy." *Administrative Science Quarterly* 20(2):229–49.

Bernstein, A. 1991. "The Teamsters Try Something New: Democracy." *Business Week*, December 9.

Bordt, R. L. 1990. "The Diversity of Women's Organizations: A Survey of New York City." Unpublished report of preliminary findings of dissertation research. New Haven: Yale University.

Brown, H. 1992. *Women Organising.* London: Routledge.

Burns, T., and G. M. Stalker. 1961. "The Management of Innovation." London: Tavistock.

Burrell, G. 1984. "Sex and Organizational Analysis." *Organization Studies* 5(2):97–118.

Cafferata, G. L. 1982. "The Building of Democratic Organizations: An Embryological Metaphor." *Administrative Science Quarterly* 27:280–303.

Clemens, E. S. 1989. "Gender, Class and Political Identity: Progressivism and the Politics of Representation." Later version of a paper presented at the Social Science History Meeting, November, Washington, D.C.

———. 1993. "Organizational Repertoires and Institutional Change: Women's Groups and the Transformation of U.S. Politics, 1890–1920." *American Journal of Sociology* 98(4): 755–98.

Compton, R. 1986. "Women and the Service Class." In *Gender and Stratification*, ed. R. Crompton and M. Mann. Cambridge: Polity.

Corrigan, P., and D. Sayer. 1985. *The Great Arch.* Oxford: Blackwells.

Crompton, R., and G. Jones. 1984. *A White Collar Proletariat? Deskilling and Gender in Clerical Work.* Basingstoke: Macmillan.

Crozier, M. 1964. *The Bureaucratic Phenomenon.* London: Tavistock.

Dobash, R. E., and R. P. Dobash. 1978. "Wife Beating: The Victims Speak." *Victimology: An International Journal* 2:608–22.

Etzioni, A. 1964. *Modern Organizations.* Englewood Cliffs: Prentice-Hall.

———. 1988. *The Moral Dimension: Toward a New Economics.* New York: Free Press.

Ferguson, K. E. 1984. *The Feminist Case against Bureaucracy.* Philadelphia: Temple University Press.

Friedan, B. 1981. *The Second Stage.* New York: Summit Books.

Hage, J. 1980. *Theories of Organization.* New York: John Wiley.

Hearn, J., D. Sheppard, P. Tancred-Sheriff, and G. Burrell. 1989. *The Sexuality of Organizations.* Newbury Park, Calif.: Sage Publications.

Hochschild, A. R. 1979. "Emotion Work, Feeling Rules and Social Structure." *American Journal of Sociology* 85:551–75.

———. 1989. *The Managed Heart.* Berkeley: University of California Press.

Hyde, C. 1992. "The Ideational System of Social Movement Agencies: An Examination of Feminist Health Centers." In *Human Services as Complex Organizations*, ed. Y. Hasenfeld, 121–44. Newbury Park, Calif.: Sage Publications.

Kaminer, W. 1993. "Feminism's Identity Crisis." *Atlantic Monthly*, October.

Kanter, R. M. 1977. *Men and Women of the Organization.* New York: Basic Books.

Kramer, R., and B. Grossman. 1987. "Contracting for Social Services: Process Management and Resource Dependences." *Social Service Review* 61:33–55.

Leidner, R. 1991. "Stretching the Boundaries of Liberalism: Democratic Innovation in a Feminist Organization." *Signs: Journal of Women in Culture and Society* 16(2):263–89.

Lipsky, M. and S. R. Smith. 1989–90. "Nonprofit Organizations, Government, and the Welfare State." *Political Science Quarterly* 104(4):625–48.

McCarthy, J. C., and M. N. Zald. 1977. "Resource Mobilization and Social Movements: A Partial Theory." *American Journal of Sociology* 82:1212–41.

McKenna, J. F. 1993. "Empowerment Thins a Forest of Bureaucracy." *Industry Week* 242(7):64.

Michels, R. 1959. *Political Parties*. New York: Dover.

Miles, A. J. 1988. "Organization, Gender and Culture." *Organization Studies* 9(3):351–69.

Morgan, G. 1986. *Images of Organisation*. London: Sage.

Mumby, D. K., and L. L. Putnam. 1992. "The Politics of Emotion: A Feminist Reading of Bounded Rationality." *Academy of Management Review* 17(3):465–86.

Nyden, P. W. 1985. "Democratizing Organizations: A Case Study of a Union Reform Movement." *American Journal of Sociology* 90(6):1179–1203.

Perrow, C. 1961. "The Analysis of Goals in Complex Organizations." *American Sociological Review* 26:854–66.

Peters, T. J. 1987. *Thriving on Chaos: Handbood for a Management Revolution*. New York; Knopf.

Pfeffer, J., and G. R. Salancik. 1978. *The External Control of Organizations: A Resource Dependence Perspective*. New York: Harper and Row.

Pringle, R. 1989a. *Secretaries Talk: Sexuality, Power and Work*. London: Verso.

———. 1989b. "Bureaucracies, Rationality and Sexuality: The Case of Secretaries." In *The Sexuality of Organization*, ed. J. Hearn et al. London: Sage.

Rodriguez, N. M. 1988. "A Successful Feminist Shelter: A Case Study of the Family Crisis Shelter in Hawaii." *Journal of Applied Behavioral Science* 24(3):235–50.

Rothschild-Whitt, J. 1982. "The Collectivist Organization: An Alternative to Bureaucratic Models." In *Workplace Bureaucracy and Social Change*, ed. F. Lidenfield and J. Rothschild-Whitt. Boston: Porter Sargent.

Savage, M., and A. Witz. 1992. "Gender and Bureaucracy." *Sociological Review*. Oxford: Blackwells.

Scaff, L. 1981. "Max Weber and Robert Michels." *American Journal of Sociology* 86:1269–86.

Schwartz, A. Y., E. W. Gottesman, and F. D. Perlmutter. 1988. "Blackwell: A Case Study in Feminist Administration." *Administration in Social Work* 12(2):5–15.

Smith, S. R., and M. Lipsky. 1992. "Privatization in Health and Human Services: A Critique." *Journal of Health Politics, Policy and Law* 17(2):133–253.

Smith, D. E. 1987. *The Everyday World as Problematic*. Milton Keynes: Open University.

Steinem, G. 1983. *Outrageous Acts and Everyday Rebellions*. New York: Holt, Rinehart and Winston.

Tocqueville, A. de. [1835] 1958. *Democracy in America*, ed. P. Bradley. New York: Vintage Books.

Weber, M. 1946. "Bureaucracy." In *From Max Weber: Essays in Sociology*, ed. H. Gerth and C. W. Mills, 196–244. New York: Oxford University Press.

———. 1968. *Economy and Society*, ed. F. Roth and C. Wittich. Reprint. New York: Bedminster.

Zald, M. N. 1970. *Organizational Change: The Political Economy of the YMCA*. Chicago: University of Chicago Press.

Zimmeck. J. 1988. "The New Women and the Machinery of Government: A Spanner in the Works." In *Government and Expertise: Specialists, Administrators and Professionals, 1860–1919*, ed. R. McLeod. Cambridge: Cambridge University Press.

19

VICTORIA D. ALEXANDER

Environmental Constraints and Organizational Strategies: Complexity, Conflict, and Coping in the Nonprofit Sector

As many researchers have pointed out, nonprofit organizations are characterized by complex goals, multiple constituencies, and fragmented environments (Kanter and Summers 1987; DiMaggio 1987). This chapter identifies environmental sources of complexity and traces, in empirical work, how such complexity enters nonprofit organizations. I suggest that environmental complexity leads to goal complexity as well as to conflict over goals. When constituencies, both internal and external, disagree over organizational goals, as is often the case, nonprofits must manage the disparate factions to remain viable.

I suggest that there are three patterns of responses to external complexity — mapping, deflecting, and exploiting. Under some circumstances, nonprofits open themselves to external complexity, and thus their internal structures come to mirror the complexity in their environments (mapping). Other circumstances allow nonprofits to buffer themselves to some extent from complexity, to retain some organizational autonomy and control, and to work toward the organization's goals, however complex or contested (deflecting). Under still different circumstances, nonprofit organizations are able to use the complexity to enhance organizational performance

I would like to thank Elaine V. Backman, John Campbell, Mark Chaves, Elisabeth Clemens, and Walter W. Powell for their helpful comments.

(exploiting). I discuss what circumstances lead organizations to choose each response strategy.

To understand environmental effects on organizations, I use organizational theory, notably neoinstitutional theory (Meyer and Scott 1992; Powell and DiMaggio 1991; Meyer and Rowan 1977). All organizations are subject to external demands that they must meet or manage. Institutional theory views organizations as embedded in environments that carry not only actors with material resources and demands but also institutionalized understandings about organizational behavior. Further, institutional theory suggests that the interests and goals of organizational members are shaped by external, institutionally based factors. In addition, I draw upon the idea of the "institutional cusp" (Backman, forthcoming) as a significant source of environmental complexity for nonprofit organizations.

It is clear from the research that organizations are not directly shaped by their environments. Rather, organizational participants creatively enact and strategically manage their environments in attempts to preserve autonomy, legitimacy, and organizational viability. Organizational participants try to modify the effects of external complexity in ways that will allow them to pursue the organization's goals, as they see them. On a macro level, environmental effects are evident, but the lesson to learn from an overview of the research is that organizations are not passive vehicles of external pressure, and that environmentally driven organizational change is mediated and channeled by individuals acting to achieve their own goals.

ENVIRONMENTAL SOURCES OF COMPLEXITY

Nonprofit organizations are beset by environmental complexity, a factor which often induces complex goals within the organization. Complexity can be seen in several areas of nonprofit environments. The nonprofit status of voluntary organizations places them in a sector in which performance measures are unclear. As a result, nonprofit organizations are judged by various external (and internal) constituents, who may not agree among themselves on effectiveness criteria. This effect is heightened by the fact that most nonprofit organizations pursue very general, social-good goals that are difficult to measure empirically. Nonprofits also face a variety of laws and regulations from different levels of government as well as a fragmented and sometimes difficult or reluctant set of funders. Further, nonprofits are often the site of contests between professionals and administrators who hold disparate views, each believing that their view embodies what is right and proper for the organization. Finally, nonprofit organizations are often located in the intersection of competing institutional spheres, as nonprofits, traditionally steeped in the rhetoric of charity, religion, or democracy, are increasingly governed by the rhetoric of business.

Legal Form

Nonprofit organizations are usually understood to be 501(c)(3) organizations, defined by the Internal Revenue Service (IRS) as organizations that may accept tax-deductible contributions.[1] Those who would organize under 501(c)(3) must apply for a charter and be approved by the IRS as operating genuinely in the public good.[2] In addition, the primary legal consideration for managing nonprofits is the "nondistribution constraint" (Hansmann 1980), which forbids nonprofits to distribute excess revenues as profits to organizational members. These legal mandates assign organizations subject to them to an institutionalized sector with rules quite different from those of the world of for-profit firms.

This is a crucial distinction. Legal definitions sort organizations into different sectors. These sectors have important influences on organizational behavior, especially in defining goals and setting the yardsticks for determining organizational success. The nondistribution constraint suggests

(though does not require) that nonprofit entrepreneurs be more altruistic and uninterested in making money. Further, by their charters, all nonprofits must have public interest goals (though some organizations place more value on this than others).[3] Nonprofits, then, can hold multiple goals, such as the "bottom line goal" traditionally associated with profit maximizers and a "public good goal" which is associated with firms termed "bonoficers" (Weisbrod, in this volume),[4] and indeed, almost all nonprofit firms have both money-making and bonoficing goals (Kanter and Summers 1987). All nonprofits have some form of financial goals. Some are "for-profits in disguise" and focus on maximizing financial returns. More nonprofits, however, attend to bonoficing goals but also pay attention to financial resources to keep the organization viable. More and more often, nonprofits must pay attention to the bottom line as trustees and donors from the business world use financial health as an indicator of nonprofit health and success and as a criterion for philanthropic giving. Thus, nonprofits mimic the for-profit sector in striving for efficiency, but the efficiency criteria for nonprofits is a mere shadow of what it is in the business sector.

In the proprietary sector, everyone agrees that the bottom-line standard for evaluating a firm is profitability. Although there is disagreement over the measurement and acceptable level of profit, if a business earns money it is generally said to be successful. But how do we judge the success of a nonprofit firm? Though continued financial losses can lead a nonprofit to fold, the presence of profit does not equal success, or a lack of profit, failure. Nonprofit firms are not subject to market discipline, which leads them, economists say, to be inefficient. But inefficiency does not necessarily indicate the absence of socially desirable outcomes. We don't really have a good, agreed-upon measure of nonprofit performance (Kanter and Summers 1987) in part because of the large variety of goals both internal and external constituents hold for nonprofit organizations.[5]

---

1. For the most part, this chapter focuses on 501(c)(3) organizations, though some of the research I cite includes political organizations. Interestingly, some other types of nonprofit organizations like small voluntary associations do not have problems of multiple goals, as the personal goals of the members are the organizational goals. As Clark and Wilson (1961) point out, such "purposive organizations" are the only case in formal organizations in which there is no goal dissension.

2. Defining *public good* is difficult, however, and many states (in contrast to the IRS) have dropped this requirement for nonprofit charters.

3. Economists demonstrate that some nonprofit organizations act like firms either by using the bottom line as a criterion for organizational success or by effectively circumventing the nondistribution constraint by paying high salaries or providing plush perquisites (Weisbrod 1988, 118–19; Clarkson 1972).

4. Weisbrod defines *bonoficing* as unprofitable actions for the public good: Bonoficers (including managers of bonoficing organizations) derive greater utility from their personal involvement in "activities that are socially desirable but unprofitable" (in this volume). It is unclear why the second qualifier, unprofitable, needs to be added, as this conflates two variables. The two goals—profits and public good—can be in accord or at odds, but their relationship in any given circumstance should be an empirical question.

5. Similarly, researchers sometimes want to know how well an organization fits its environment. A good fit implies that an organization can gain resources efficiently and produce products or services where they are needed or desired. Profitability indicates good fit for proprietary firms, but, again, this standard does not indicate environmental fit for nonprofit organizations.

Instead of profitability, nonprofits are likely to be judged on effectiveness, which is "[a] standard applied to the output or activities of an organization. It is applied by all individuals, groups, or organizations that are affected by, or come in contact with, the focal organization. Effectiveness as assessed by each organizational evaluator involves how well the organization is meeting the needs or satisfying the criteria of the evaluator" (Pfeffer and Salancik 1978, 34).[6]

The judging of effectiveness always implies an audience because effectiveness is defined in terms of a stakeholder's point of view. The fact that nonprofits are judged on effectiveness has two important implications for nonprofit management. First, judgments of effectiveness from external actors highlight the importance of the environment for nonprofit organizations. Second, effectiveness ratings are likely to be subjective, complicating nonprofit decision making and goal setting. Complexity in organizational environments comes from several sources in the legal sector that nonprofit organizations inhabit: Legal requirements pushing toward multiple goals, unclear guidelines for success, and multiple judges. All three of these factors combine to create conflicting pressures and demands from external constituents.

The Operating Environment

Nonprofit organizations must attend to numerous types of environmental actors. Following Talcott Parsons (1960), Maria Louise Nathan (1992) argues that each of four arenas — social, political, institutional, and economic — provide resources to, make demands on, and judge the effectiveness of organizations.[7] Nathan shows that environmental demands flow in both directions. That is, environmental actors supply resources (such as goods, money, labor, information, prestige, or legitimacy) to the organization, but they expect to receive other resources in exchange.

W. Richard Scott and John Meyer (1992) argue that authority in a sector can be characterized on three axes: (1) centralization-decentralization (hierarchical diffusion), (2) fragmentation-unification (coordination among decision-makers at a given hierarchical level), and (3) federalization-concentration (the extent to which decision making occurs on more than one level). Further, the pattern of centralization, fragmentation, and federalization can vary among various types of decisions. Nonprofit organizations tend to be located in decentralized, fragmented, and federalized — in other words, quite complex — environments. For instance, all nonprofits are affected by both federal and state tax laws, which delimit their behavior (see Simon 1987). And at the federal level, information on mental health facilities is collected by the National Institute of Mental Health, the National Institute of Alcohol Abuse and Alcoholism, the National Institute of Drug Abuse, the Social Security Administration, the Bureau of the Census, and the Health Care Financing Administration, among others (Leaf 1985), a fragmented environment indeed for mental health providers (not to mention the additional complexity added by state and local reporting requirements).

Many nonprofits have intangible goals that cannot be met through readily available methods or techniques. Education, physical and mental health, an end to birth defects or world hunger are objectives which lack easy solutions. In other words, the "technology" of many nonprofit industries is not well understood. Unclear technology makes performance measurement difficult (Middleton 1987; Kanter and Summers 1987) and constrains external and internal functioning (Young 1987). More important, unclear technology, like uncertainty in general, leads organizations to focus on the environment rather than on internal organization, as the environment becomes the source for legitimating structures, procedures, and beliefs (Meyer and Rowan 1977; DiMaggio and Powell 1983).

The Funding Environment

In addition to dealing with complex regulations and unclear technology, nonprofits must obtain funds. Most face an uncertain and complex funding environment, gleaning money from a variety of sources. Nonprofits fall into four types, depending on their income source and their control structure (Hansmann 1987, 28). There are "donative" nonprofits, which receive their income mainly through donations, and there are "commercial" nonprofits, which sell goods or services. These two types of nonprofits can be controlled by a board elected by patrons (donors or clients) or by a self-perpetuating board. The board structure mediates the effects of the funding environment.

Many donative nonprofits facing financial shortfalls are dependent on their funders to the point that funders have a say in the organization's goals and operations (Pfeffer and Salancik 1978; Powell and Friedkin 1987). Commercial nonprofits also face fragmented funding environments. As Grønbjerg (1993a, 22) writes, "Most nonprofit service organizations rely on a bewildering array of funding sources . . . : grants and contracts from government; donations in the form of foundation grants, corporate support, direct individual giving, United Way funds, church donations, federal funding, and bequests; earned income from dues, fees, service charges, rent, and product sales; and other income from endowment, investments, and special events." In some cases, commercial nonprofits may become more attuned to the needs of their customers (Zald and Denton 1963); in others, dependency may lead nonprofits to "skim off the cream," serving only the most desirable clients rather than the most needy (Scott 1969) or to become bureaucratized and to lose their identity to the desires of funding agencies (Stone 1993).

6. Pfeffer and Salancik define effectiveness as an external standard. It is important to recognize, however, that actors within organizations also make effectiveness evaluations, both in official and unofficial capacities.

7. Of these, the economic arena has received the lion's share of research attention because it plays the largest role for the business sector, in which it is institutionalized as the ultimate criterion for judging firms.

Though commercial nonprofits are influenced by their funders in these ways, they sometimes have countervailing influence over their funders: "In the social service field, public funders must ensure the continued availability of legally mandated services, withstand legislative scrutiny, and secure continuing appropriations. These challenges provide nonprofit agencies and their managers with leverage over public funders" (Grønbjerg 1991, 170).

Rational Myths and Normative Sources of Complexity

Many nonprofits define themselves in terms of meeting public needs and providing social goods. Thus, nonprofits are particularly open to ideas from the outside world and particularly concerned with legitimacy. Institutional theory explains that organizational structures are based on institutionalized rules called "rationalized myths" which gives an organization legitimacy (Meyer and Rowan 1977). Rational myths are institutionalized knowledge: "They are *myths* because they are widely held beliefs that cannot be objectively tested: they are true because they are believed. . . . They are *rationalized* because they take the form of rules specifying procedures necessary to accomplish a given end" (Scott 1992, 118). Rational myths can be rules about technology, procedures, or organizational participants and can be based in formal research or in folk wisdom. Rational myths vary as to their cognitive status: some are taken-for-granted assumptions, others are consciously recognized and supported by public opinion. Still others have been embodied in law. Nonprofit organizations are embedded in institutional arenas that specify, implicitly or explicitly, the composition of nonprofit structure and behavior. Managers, volunteers, and other nonprofit personnel draw upon rational myths when they make assertions about how the organization "ought to run."

Similarly, nonprofits are subject to the normative influence of professionals and other groups that are carriers of rational myths for the structure and operation of nonprofit organizations. Nonprofits are particularly likely to be shaped by the normative views held by professionals. As Dennis Young (1987, 173) points out, research shows that "nonprofits tend to be domains in which professionals and professional thinking dominate, and agendas are shaped by a quest for professional excellence and prestige." Professionals are an important source of external influence in organizations, as they carry with them the institutionalized knowledge they have learned elsewhere.[8] Institutional theory recognizes professional influence as an external force (DiMaggio and Powell 1983): Professionals, socialized and trained in universities or other settings external to organizations, usually have quite strongly held notions of the proper ways for them

to do their jobs. They import their ideas into organizations and continue to look outside to their professional colleagues and associations for ideas, validation, and prestige. Though professionals deploy their normative ideas within an organization, the source of these institutionalized normative ideas is external.

The "Institutional Cusp"

The history of nonprofits is rooted in the metaphors and models of philanthropy and charity (Block 1990). In recent years, nonprofits are more and more influenced by business world norms of rationality and efficiency (Bush 1992; Hage, in this volume). Because neither charity models nor business models are fully institutionalized in the nonprofit world, bonoficing and financial goals conflict. Further, nonprofits are often regulated and subject to controls by the state and therefore abide by rules from a third institutionalized sector.

Increasingly, nonprofits operate on what Backman (forthcoming) calls the *institutional cusp*. The term describes organizations that are powerfully pulled between two institutional logics. Roger Friedland and Robert Alford (1991) argue that society is constituted through several overarching and general "institutional logics," with nested subsets of more and more specific institutions comprising both material practices and ideological constructions. These logics — in Friedland and Alford's scheme, the state, democracy, family, religion, and the market — are not mutually exclusive. Rather, they often overlap, and when they do, they can be contradictory, suggesting opposing practices or symbols.

Nonprofit organizations are increasingly likely to experience institutional cusp pressures, as traditional boundaries between the state, the market, and the nonprofit sector blur. Nonprofits are also the site of contests among professionals (for prestige, authority, and how to define the situation), as in the conflicts among psychiatrists, psychologists, and psychiatric social workers (Abbott 1988) or doctors, nurses, and administrators (Freidson 1975). Indeed, all organizations with bifurcated administrative structures (administrators and professionals), no matter what their legal form, are subject to institutional conflicts.

Institutional logics and professionally based institutions pull nonprofits in different directions. As organizations attempt to place themselves to please actors guided by one institutional logic, they can easily violate values that actors adhering to a second logic hold dear. Compromise between two logics is a potential but unsatisfying solution to the pressures of competing institutions. Compromise can leave organizational participants believing that they are being undermined by their own organizations, as goals get "distorted" and the organization stops doing what it is "supposed to do." Selznick's (1949) classic study of the Tennessee Valley Authority showed how the organization survived by co-opting local elites but entered a Faustian bargain which turned it away from its initially primary public interest goals. Similarly, as public television came to pay more attention to such

---

8. This is true for other organizational participants as well, though the effect may be strongest for those we traditionally think of as professionals. But as Karl (in this volume) argues, the relationship of professional and volunteers in nonprofits is cyclical, and, barring strict academic definitions of professionals as credentialed persons, it is often difficult to tell the professionals from the volunteers.

marketing considerations as ratings, some employees felt that it ignored the production of "good, worthwhile shows." These employees deeply believed that making good programs was the core goal of public television, it was "doing God's work"; thus, they felt profoundly betrayed by the organization's shifting focus (Powell and Friedkin 1986, 259). In both of these cases, organization managers attempted to ensure future funding and viability while pursuing goals similar to the original goals. But other stakeholders judged the organization to be ineffective and viewed the new goals as displacing rather than being a theme on the original goals.

NONPROFIT RESPONSES TO ENVIRONMENTAL COMPLEXITY

Nonprofit organizations, then, are subject to complexity that arises from a variety of external sources. It is clear that nonprofits, like all organizations, face not a single, unified environment, but rather multiple — and complex — environments. This section, based on empirical research, shows how these sources of complexity play out inside organizations. Nonprofit organizations often respond to environmental pressures in an attempt to minimize them. Common strategies include loose coupling, symbolic management, buffering, using ambiguity or multiplexity to please a variety of stakeholders, resource shifting, and innovation (Thompson 1967; Meyer and Rowan 1977; Pfeffer and Salancik 1978; Oliver 1991). Legitimacy concerns limit how nonprofits adapt to environmental pressures, as nonprofit managers attempt to maintain their autonomy in a way that is consistent with their vision of organizational integrity. In some cases, however, nonprofits will be unable to minimize external pressures. In such cases, nonprofits' structures and programs will become complex and fragmented, mirroring the environment as myriad facets of the nonprofit each come to serve the demands of just one environmental actor. Nonprofit responses to complexity fall into three categories: Organizations map complexity when they open themselves to it from their environments; they deflect complexity when buffering is possible; and in some cases, they exploit complexity to gain more autonomy or viability than would be allowed in less complex environments.

Mapping Complexity

One common way nonprofit organizations deal with external complexity is to incorporate it into their internal structures and programs. An organization that becomes more internally complex along the lines of existing external complexity can be said to map the environment. The complexity of the environment is translated into the organization's structure, as in an administrative unit articulated along the organization's resource flows or a Janus-faced organization that looks outward to two different institutional logics. Institutional theorists suggest that nonprofit organizations can become isomorphic with their environment (Meyer and Rowan 1977;

Meyer and Scott 1992).[9] Scott and Meyer (1992, 142) predict that organizational structure reproduces environmental complexity, and this complexity can come from funder pressure or from institutional sources like cusp pressures.

There is a good deal of research evidence that complex environments lead to complex administrative structures and programs (Scott 1987, 505–06). One group of researchers (D'Aunno, Sutton, and Price 1991) finds heightened professional and procedural complexity in mental hospitals providing drug and alcohol and addiction treatment along with traditional mental health services. The complexity arises because such hospitals face two distinct professional environments, the first composed of mental health practitioners and the second of experts in twelve-step programs like Alcoholics Anonymous. Similarly, Meyer, Scott, and Strang (1987) show that school districts come to mirror the complexity of their funding environments. Funding seems to be a particularly important factor in nonprofit organizations. Kirsten Grønbjerg (1993b, 11) writes about the impact of the funding environment on nonprofit organizations that receive government contracts for service provision: "To minimize conflicting demands on service staff and to facilitate reporting efforts, most nonprofits . . . adopt a high level of program specialization. They assign service staff members to only one public grant or contract if sufficient funding is available to cover the staff member's salary. As a result, these organizations have very complex structures that largely parallel their public funding streams."

Funding effects are visible not only in commercial nonprofits, but also in donative organizations. In public television stations, for instance, Walter Powell and Rebecca Friedkin (1986) find that external complexity invades these organizations. Dependent on all of their constituencies and unable to effectively buffer themselves, they end up pursuing a strategy of trying to please everybody all the time. WNET, the nation's largest public television station, chose a diversifying program strategy in which each program was geared toward a different funder. One series, *Dance in America,* ranged from classical ballet to jazz and tap to postmodern, experimental works, each of which pleased different funding and audience components in the environment.

Powell (1988) reports that WNET underwent an internal reorganization from a unitary to a multidivisional form, a form which has been institutionalized as a more efficient

9. Meyer and his colleagues (Meyer and Rowan 1977; Meyer and Scott 1992) focus especially on isomorphism between organizations and environments in hierarchically arranged systems. In their model, an organization becomes isomorphic with organizations holding funding or operational authority over it. DiMaggio and Powell (1983) predict that organizations in a field become isomorphic with one another. Because competitors and other similar organizations are part of any given organization's environment, DiMaggio and Powell also predict isomorphism of an organization with its environment; however, their model is one of horizontal isomorphism, whereas Meyer's work focuses more on what could be termed vertical isomorphism.

form for business organizations (Chandler 1962; Fligstein 1990; Palmer, Jennings, and Zhou 1993). The reorganization was a conscious effort by WNET to copy rational myths from the for-profit sector in order to gain legitimacy with business executives. Even though WNET managers were unsure about the technical benefits of the reorganization, they believed that it would send a strong signal to their business patrons that WNET was well managed.

The reorganization caused problems elsewhere, which points to a common cost in the mapping strategy: increased internal conflict. One problem involved board members who, under a logic of democracy, were upset that the plan decreased the number of top positions in the organization and thus the potential number of women and minority managers at the station.

Along the same lines, Melissa Stone (1993) shows that pressures from its location on an institutional cusp led the County Association for Retarded Citizens to split into two loosely aligned, legally distinct organizations, each of which dealt with one dominant external logic. A grassroots, advocacy organization drew its rational myths from the logic of democracy whereas a government contracting organization, effectively an arm of the state of Massachusetts, drew upon the logic of the state. The logic of the state and the logic of democracy "are characterized by different orientations: one that is hierarchically ordered under state contracting agencies and oriented toward conformity with rules and regulations; and another that is more loosely structured around interpersonal relationships among parents and other concerned citizens where member ties express an ideological and emotional orientation" (Stone 1993, 21).

Before the split, the two organizations were merged under one roof, and the clashes within the organization arising from the conflicting logics in their environment made it increasingly difficult for the organization to meet its original advocacy goals. This was especially so because state contracting provided much revenue but made it difficult to advocate on behalf of clients against the state. The split is an example of radical absorption of complexity from the environment, and few nonprofits use this strategy. It is also an instance of what might be called niche jumping. The advocacy organization found the state environment inhospitable and so jumped to another. The contracting organization found the state environment beneficial, so remained where it was.

Niche jumping may not be an uncommon strategy in nonprofit organizations.[10] The research in this chapter concentrates mainly on organizational reactions to environments, but it is also important to recognize that the organization determines its environment by choosing a niche. Manipulating organizational structure has implications for the environments that an organization looks to and is influenced by, even to the extent of changing the organization's focus from one set of environments to another.

A strategy of mapping complexity does not indicate the absence of agency (intentional decision making) in an organization. Rather, organizations are sometimes unable to buffer themselves from external complexity, so pursue a strategy that, in the end, causes them to become more internally complex. This strategy can be a successful one, as in the case of the County Association for Retarded Citizens. Often, however, mapping is a costly strategy, involving increased outlays for personnel, increased internal conflict, a decreased ability to plan for the future, and incoherent goals and structures: "Organizations are constantly in search of external support and legitimacy. When financial support and much needed credibility are provided by a dispersed and fragmented environment, organizations respond with a varied mix of procedures and policies. Each response may in itself be formally rational, but collectively the responses will exhibit little internal coherence" (Powell 1988, 126).

Deflecting Complexity

In general, managers attempt to maintain autonomy and control of their organizations against external pressures (Pfeffer and Salancik 1978). This is true of nonprofit managers as well. Nonprofit managers attempt to strategically manage all environmental pressures, including institutional pressures (Powell 1991; Oliver 1991). The research shows a variety of strategic responses to external pressure that fall under the rubric of deflecting complexity. In such situations, organizations remain viable and are able to buffer themselves to some extent from environmental complexity. Unlike mapping, in which organizations match the environment facet for facet, organizations that deflect complexity limit the amount of external complexity that enters the organization.

Mary Tschirhart (1993) uses a "stakeholder analysis" (Freeman 1984) of arts organizations to document the management difficulties of organizations with multiple constituencies. When organizations do not fit well with the environment—that is, when they are not considered effective by external stakeholders—they must pursue strategies to change either the organization or the stakeholders. Tschirhart is interested in situations of incongruence between an organization and its stakeholders' values, norms, activities, or outcomes. Following B. E. Ashforth and B. W. Gibbs (1990), she argues that organizations use symbolic management to alter the way stakeholders perceive the organization. Symbolic management is a form of impression management that

10. Hyde's (1991) comparative study of feminist social movement organizations suggests that organizations often seek out different, more hospitable niches in the face of hostile environmental pressures. Conservative, antifeminist political demands and outright attacks of the New Right led two of the nine organizations she studied to radicalize, one to stagnate, and the rest to become somewhat more conservative while retaining some vestiges of liberal feminism. All went through major shifts in the environmental niche they filled, as each attempted in one

way or another to find more hospitable environments in which fiscal or direct attacks were fewer and constituent support was greater.

frames organizational acts in the best light. Tschirhart sets out a typology of incongruence and five typical responses: "(1) adapting an organization to be more congruent with a stakeholder; (2) misrepresenting an organization to appear to be more congruent with a stakeholder; (3) manipulating a stakeholder's values or norms to improve the stakeholder's congruence with an organization; (4) compromising with a stakeholder; and (5) cutting or weakening ties to a stakeholder to avoid negative consequences of incongruence" (120–21). The last four of these are deflecting strategies which give the organization more breathing room in the face of external demands. In an analysis of thirty-four nonprofit arts organizations in Michigan, Tschirhart finds that although resource considerations were important, legitimacy concerns overrode them. Managers were likely to adapt to external demands, thus mapping the environment, when resources were important; however, when these external actors challenged the organization's mission or threatened its artistic integrity, managers employed a combination of the four deflecting strategies.

Maria Nathan (1992) focuses on how organizations adapt to their environment through strategic decision making. She shows that the Art Institute of Chicago developed "versatile" strategies. Such strategies can be used in several arenas, a phenomenon she terms "multiplexity." This is similar to results of my study (Alexander 1996a), which demonstrates that museums mount exhibitions that are "multivocal," that is, appealing to a variety of external constituents. The use of multiplex, multivocal strategies deflects complexity, as the organization replaces many strategies for many environments (a mapping response) with one strategy for many environments.

Buffering the "technical core" of an organization from complexity is a common deflection strategy (Thompson 1967). Grønbjerg (1993a; 1991) finds that social service organizations buffer their core activities from fund-raising activities. Since fund-raising involves a great deal of uncertainty, coupled with a high failure rate, fund-raising activities are kept in special subunits at the periphery of many service organizations or are even moved outside the organization and handled by consultants. In this way, the service providers in the organizations can continue carrying out their day-to-day activities without the distractions, pressures, and uncertainties that the funding environment brings to the organization.

Margaret Anne Johnson (1993) demonstrates that the International Association of Women, a pseudonym for an elite organization of female volunteers, used several strategies for dealing with increased pressures for accessibility and diversity in the organization's membership. These pressures came through two environmental sources. First, general societal changes in beliefs about equality and civil rights created a disconnect between the voluntary sector's call for diversity and the organization's elite, lily white membership. This disconnect gave it a public credibility problem. Second, funders made donations contingent on membership selection procedures being more open and the organization more inclusive of nonelite and minority women. During the period of her study (1975–92), Johnson found that these external factors did affect the association, spurring them to discuss membership strategies and to create diversity policies. The diversity debates, however, occurred at the national association level, buffering the local chapters from the issue. The organization also used strategies such as loose coupling to maintain traditional, exclusive membership practices: passing organizationwide bylaws that prohibited discrimination while at the same time institutionalizing the discretion of local chapters to recruit members in elitist, discriminatory, and secret ways. In addition, the association did not keep records of the racial and ethnic composition of members, thus remaining ignorant of possible discrimination in membership recruitment (a strategy suggested by Jeffrey Pfeffer and Gerald Salancik (1978) in dealing with resource pressures).

Exploiting Complexity

The research presented above demonstrates that nonprofit organizations can use a variety of strategies to manage complex constraints and pressures. The research paints a picture of nonprofits as muddling through either by mapping external complexity or deflecting it. Under certain circumstances, however, nonprofit organizations can embrace complexity in a way that allows them to become stronger, more viable organizations that can pursue their primary internal goals. Organizations can be said to exploit complexity when they are more successful in reaching their goals in their complex environment than they would be in a more simple environment.

Kenneth Dauber's work (1994, 1993) shows how the Indian Arts Fund (IAF) was able to gain legitimacy by relying on a diverse group of founders. In bonoficing organizations, the definition of social goods must be divorced from the self-interests of the individuals who determine what constitutes the social good. Thus, claims that are agreed upon by broad coalitions are more likely to be seen as legitimate by external actors than ones resting on just one group. The legitimacy of a nonprofit organization, and therefore its ability to garner resources, rests on the image that it is creating a public good. The apparently selfless nature of the need defined by a coalition masks, though does not change, the self-interest. Through philanthropy, individuals actively construct their identity and status and advance their political interests. Dauber argues that researchers studying philanthropy must recognize "the general principle that people are drawn to particular acts of patronage because of the usefulness of those acts to projects in which they are engaged" (1993, 79).

In the case of the IAF, four coalitions each had its own self-interested goals for the fund. Notably, the four groups were largely made up of people relatively new to New Mexico, people who were in conflict with well-established elites over their rights to participate in the community. The IAF was a form of cultural warfare through which new elites in New Mexico could carve a space for themselves in contrast to older groups.[11] In spite of the demands these philanthropists made on the IAF to provide them with political resources, the IAF was able to give the appearance of being primarily interested in pottery and in the people who made it. The fund successfully exploited the complexity that camouflaged individual self-interest, and the IAF flourished.[12]

This finding has affinities with Elisabeth Clemens's (1993) work, which shows that women were successful in gaining political power precisely because they chose models of political behavior that allowed them to appear disinterested. Clemens's research starts with a puzzling question: How did women's groups with no access to the vote gain entree to the masculine political sphere? The answer is that women's groups, acting strategically, cleverly imported models of political behavior that allowed them to collect and disseminate information — in effect, to lobby — under the beneficent guise of informing citizens. She shows that at the turn of the century, women's groups started to use a model of the educated citizen to get around the exclusively male, fraternal model dominant in nineteenth-century politics. This model, which already existed in spheres other than politics, allowed the women to avoid appearing self-interested, thereby giving them the ability to sidestep closed, masculine, fraternal political organizations. Interestingly, the club women's success with the new model led to the institutionalization of the educated citizen model, which, in the long run, changed the nature of American politics from a partisan system based on party loyalty to an issue-based system based on lobbying, advertising, and pressure tactics.[13]

Clemens suggests a mimetic source of organizational models and structures, borrowing tools from the cultural repertoire and applying them to sectors in which they have not been used before.[14] Women's organizations had no legitimacy, as politics were dominated by men's organizations, which did not acknowledge women's importance. But because there were multiple models of organizing available — multiple rational myths — women were able to position their organizations in such a way as to meet their goals.

Nonprofits can gain autonomy when they "enact" the en-

vironment. Enacting is the process by which managers interact with the environment to actually *create* opportunities or constraints (Weick 1979).[15] For instance, museums have traditionally mounted a variety of exhibition types. To continue mounting such shows, curators and development officers creatively enact the environment to find funding for shows *the museum* wishes to mount. Museum managers

> think of clever ways to attract funding for an exhibition they wish to mount, by appealing to a corporate interest that is not ordinarily associated with art. For instance, the Philadelphia Museum mounted an exhibition of seventeenth century Dutch art sponsored by Mobil Oil which owns off-shore drilling rigs in Dutch waters. Theme exhibitions sometimes have theme sponsorship. For instance, Polo/Ralph Lauren sponsored the show titled *Horse and Man,* filled with hunting pictures and other canvasses of people and horses. (Alexander 1996a, 70)

Multiple funders and constituents can be a source of autonomy for organizational participants, as Powell (1988, 127–28) argues for the programming staff of public television, and I argue for museum curators:

> The existence of many funders allows museum personnel more leverage and freedom to do what they want than a few funders would. Curators creatively use funders, picking and choosing among them when they can easily find overlapping goals, and innovating to find new types of artworks or exhibitions that meet both museum and funder goals when the goals do not immediately mesh. Further, funders can be used to influence one another, as can be seen in the success of matching grant programs, and in research showing that the existence of other corporate arts funding encourages corporations to start or to continue to donate to museums (Galaskiewicz 1991; Useem and Kutner 1986). New funders provide the leverage, and the spur, curators need to bring certain forms of creative expression into museum shows. (Alexander 1996b, 123)

In some cases, managers can control the internal use of externally provided resources, strengthening those parts of the organization that are weak or not attractive to external actors. Suzanne Kay Stout (1993) models linkages between a

---

11. An interesting contrast can be found in the work of DiMaggio (1982a,b) in which elites in Boston use cultural means to defend their legitimacy against newcomers.

12. The IAF continued to be successful in this strategy until the crisis in 1933 that Dauber describes, when attempts at focusing the IAF on the public good failed and constructions of public interest disintegrated into an amalgamation of self-interest.

13. Clemens's work suggests that to understand nonprofit behavior, researchers must understand how people use cultural tools (see Swidler 1986; Sewell 1992; Friedland and Alford 1991; Scott 1991; Jepperson and Meyer 1991).

14. Westney (1987) also discusses borrowing models from other contexts.

15. Enactment blurs the distinction between organizational actors and environments. In Weick's view, environments are not tangible entities to which organizations respond; rather, environments come into organizations only through managerial enactment: "Managers construct, rearrange, single out, and demolish many 'objective' features of their surroundings. When people act they unrandomize variables, insert vestiges of orderliness, and literally create their own constraints. This holds true whether those constraints are created in fantasy to justify avoided tests or created in actuality to explain tangible bruises" (164). Enactment can embody bracketing, deviation amplification, self-fulfilling prophecies, and the social construction of reality. See Weick 1979, chap. 6.

university's departments and external donors. She started with the hypothesis that the presence of donors might cause the organization to change, through mutual adaptation between donor and recipient. Specifically, she expected to find that departments that received a good deal of external money would also get substantial support from the university itself. Departments richer in funders do get more dollars overall; however, Stout finds little evidence of actual adaptation and argues that such adaptation is constrained by such institutional pressures as academic freedom and interdepartmental equity. The university uses internal money to subsidize departments that get few grants and gives the richest departments a lower proportion of university money.

This strategy is similar to the "resource shifting" I find in museums (Alexander 1996c). In museums, external funding is more readily available for some types of exhibitions than for others. Museum personnel, acting to maintain their autonomy and legitimacy, engage in such strategies as resource shifting, innovation, and buffering. While money is obtained for more easily funded exhibits, museums divert internal funds to cover more esoteric shows that are more difficult to fund.

COMPLEXITY AND CONFLICT

A major cost of environmental complexity for nonprofit organizations is goal complexity and organizational conflict. The empirical research shows nonprofits to be an arena in which groups of individuals with varying professional motivations and belief structures mix and disagree. The amalgamation of these diverse groups within nonprofits leads to multiplex goals and to internal conflict, and if these are not kept in check, the organization may fail.

Organizational analysts today often view organizations as coalitions (Pfeffer and Salancik 1978; Cyert and March 1963). These coalitions vie for ascendancy, attempting to define the organization's primary vision (Fligstein 1990). The coalition which succeeds in defining the organization's vision and thus its goals is termed the "dominant coalition" (Cyert and March 1963); however, in many nonprofits, more than one dominant coalition exists, and these coalitions battle for control. Further, coalitions may be quite willing to compromise organizational performance or the performance of other coalitions for the good of its own coalition members (Child 1972).

Participants with Different Professional Motives

Scott (1991) and Powell (1991) both point out that competing professionals increase organizational conflict and dissension. Though this effect plays out within organizations, it is important to remember that professional goals and beliefs are shaped by such environmental factors as professional training and the influence of professional associations and colleagues. Recent research shows that, on a macro level, the interests of professionals and interested decision makers are

important in shaping organizational fields and the conventions embedded in them (DiMaggio 1991; Brint and Karabel 1991; Galaskiewicz 1991; Fligstein 1990). The beliefs of organizational participants are also institutionally composed, and organizational response to environmental concerns are shaped by the goals of the various internal and external constituencies.

Mark Chaves (1993) studies religious organizations in the United States, organizations that are composed of both a religious structure and an agency structure. The major intra-organizational power struggles in Protestant denominations are struggles between two elites, the top of the agency structure and the top of the religious structure. Chaves demonstrates that the degree of power the agency structure has depends on the centralization of agency structure—more centralization equals more power. This finding has important implications for the "internal secularization" of denominations: Since the turn of the century (and as agency structure centralizes), denomination "CEOs"—the primary administrative officer—have increasingly come from the agency rather than the religious structure.

Internal struggles have implications for the organizations' goals. As Chaves writes, "The career backgrounds of the persons selected to [leadership] positions will reflect dominant views concerning the set of skills necessary to run a denomination" (24). For instance, agency leaders are likely to see congregations and individual members as a resource base, either a market or a constituency, and are oriented toward external goals, whereas the religious authorities are oriented toward internal matters and view the congregations as objects for religious control (10). Differences in goals and attitudes which come from different background, training, and professional orientation are sources of normative pressures on organizations.

Interestingly, not all denominations became internally secular, and others have been able to reverse the trend. Some denominations were protected from increasing agency control through a strong religious authority structure which resists internal and external pressures toward agency centralization. In other denominations, the religious elite was able to reverse increases in power gleaned by the agency structure by mounting a highly centralized, religious "social movement" within the denomination. This finding highlights the seemingly contradictory nature of the balance between environmental pressures and organizational agency. External pressures change religious denominations at the same time as some denominations are able to deflect such pressure and resist change. How organizations manage environmental complexity and under what circumstances they are able to duck its effects is an interesting question.

Chaves suggests that his findings have implications for all organizations which are staffed by both professionals and managers. Similarly, in my research on museums (Alexander 1996a), I find that there are struggles within museums between professionals (curators) and administrators (directors and their staff). These two groups have profoundly divergent ideas of what a museum should be, and as with the religious and agency elites, their ideals for museums are rooted in their professional backgrounds. Curators view museums as a scholarly place, whereas administrators increasingly see museums as a business organization that markets products to clients. From the late 1960s onward, museums' administrative component has become more empowered, a change largely the result of external pressures for accountability and an increasingly complex environment requiring additional boundary personnel. This trend is bolstered by changes in museum boards: trustees come increasingly from the corporate elite rather than from local family elites. The administrative presence has changed museums, institutionalizing a more populist and business-oriented model of the museum. Curators, however, keep up a struggle to maintain their own vision of museum goals.

These two studies suggest that organizational goals are shaped through the competition among organizational participants with differing visions for what is best for the organization as a whole. This is an important insight into the behavior of nonprofit organizations. The goals of professionals may clash with bonoficing or financial goals held by other internal and external stakeholders. For instance, curators wish to increase their professional prestige and (in a situation analogous to that in universities which pits research against teaching) push museums toward scholarly judges and elites and away from the philistine targets of museum outreach programs. Curators also wish to mount exhibitions, research art works, and write catalogues and monographs without regard to financial cost. Their professional goals, then, put them at odds with the educational and administrative staff. The debate among these coalitions does not unfold along narrow, self-interested lines, however. Each group maintains that the other groups are undermining what a museum should really be. Along the same lines, members of religious elites may believe that agency CEOs are ignoring the religious aspects of the organization — ignoring, from their point of view, the core functions of a denomination. Agency elites, for their part, probably view the religious elites as ill-prepared to run the complex, national-level denominational organizations, a job that now requires modern management skills.

In addition, these studies suggest that the balance of power between coalitions in organizations — coalitions which embody different normatively shaped views that cut to the essence of the nonprofit form involved — can shift over time. These shifts appear to be spurred by change in the external environment, but they are always accompanied by internal conflict and political struggle as each group works to keep its vision institutionalized in the organization.

Participants with Different Belief Structures
The kind of internal conflict and debates over goals, strategies, and structures found by Chaves and Alexander is endemic to nonprofit organizations. Further, complexity is heightened by ambiguity, as when organizational participants acting on different assumptions do not know that they disagree with one another. These assumptions are institutionally based. Institutions are "both supraorganizational patterns of activity through which humans conduct their material life in time and space, and symbolic systems through which they categorize that activity and infuse it with meaning" (Friedland and Alford 1991, 232). Institutional influences play out not only through institutional logics, rational myths, and the normative beliefs held by professionals but also by institutionalized assumptions about how the world is constituted that all organizational participants carry.

The institutional nature of organizational conflict in nonprofits is most powerfully shown by Paul Schnorr (1993). In a study of various organizations involved in a voluntary resettlement of poor, urban African Americans to a primarily white suburb, he finds that organizational conflict and eventually the failure of the program were attributable to conflicting definitions of community.

Project Neighbors, a consortium of members from mainline white and black churches, sought to bring poor blacks from an inner-city neighborhood to a more "wholesome" upper-middle-class suburb. The effort, founded with good will on the part of all participants, was to help relocated African American families. Within a year of the first relocations, however, the program experienced severe conflict over goals and activities. This led some white sponsors to leave the program, spurred some families to move back to the city, and fostered a decision-making structure that excluded the relocated families, furthering their social isolation and alienation.

At the heart of the program's failure was a lack of shared cultural, cognitive, and experiential frameworks — common institutions — which could have enabled black and white program participants to create a shared community. For the wealthy white residents, community meant being involved in various organizations (church, sports clubs, and children's groups like Scouts and Little League), each taking up only a few hours per week. They saw their friends in this context, spending only a few hours per week socializing. The whites were "busy people" who valued activities by their time cost. African Americans, by contrast, favored deep involvement with community members and defined community as high commitment and daily contact with friends. White sponsors' contacts with resettled black families were goal-directed. For example, a white sponsor would drive a mother and children to a dentist appointment but would not sit and visit in the unstructured way that seemed appropriate to the sponsored family. White sponsors spent time in Project Neighbors the way they spent time in their other social organizations. They participated a few hours a week, in their areas of expertise, in an attempt to create "efficient structures." Whites did not understand blacks' valuation of diffuse sociability and acted in ways that made relocated neighbors feel excluded. Further, although white members of the community truly wanted to increase diversity in the neighborhood, what they looked for were changes in the visible composition of current neighborhood organizations (for instance, whites were happy to see a black child on a sports team), but they did not think that the structure of the community itself should change.

In the end, relocated families were integrated physically into the suburb, but they were not economically or socially integrated. Different frameworks for understanding community and social contact led to the isolation of relocated families, an isolation which was exacerbated by racial hostility, lack of kinship ties and support, and no public transportation. Schnorr's findings suggest that "organizations reflect the cognitive frameworks of participants and that organizations attempting to bridge class and status barriers may encounter problems when these frameworks conflict" (iv). He shows that once conflict arises, people's statements about program goals indicate their understanding of "the way the world should be." Here we can see environmental factors, in this case, constitutive assumptions about sociability affecting organizational goals and leading to organizational conflict.

The lesson Schnorr draws from his study is that "the best intentions can fail." But another lesson, to use James March's terms, is that "ambiguity preserves consensus." Project Neighbors got off the ground and leaders from both black and white churches agreed with the initial goals of the program, until the divergent ideas of community were uncovered. This suggests organizational ambiguity as a strategy for dealing with fundamental conflict.[16]

PREDICTING NONPROFIT REACTIONS

How organizations react to the environment and what responses are possible under given circumstances are complex questions that deserve more research attention. Current research on organizational change gives us some tantalizing clues about nonprofit strategy but no real answers. It suggests that financial considerations play an important role, along with legitimacy concerns and constraining factors in an organization's structure.

The research I shall review here suggests that various constraints, or lack thereof, influence organizational responses to the environment. Access to ample resources, even from a complex and fragmented environment, allow organizations to pursue their chosen goals. But this insight does little to further our systematic understanding of how nonprofit organizations react under adverse conditions. Though we have some insight into why some nonprofits wither or die while others survive and even prosper, we do not have the kind of systematic understanding that would allow us to gauge how organizations will respond to multiple pressures, to predict when organizations will use mapping, deflecting,

16. Chaves (in this volume) also notes the importance of ambiguity in nonprofit functioning. He suggests that the ambiguity of religious goals pushes religious organizations in a "do-gooder" direction.

or exploiting strategies, or to teach nonprofits how to maximize the number of successful responses.

So far I have mostly discussed studies of single organizations. Given the complexity of nonprofit organizations and their environmental relations, however, a case study alone is not sufficient to understand the roots of complex reaction patterns. Comparative research across a number of organizations will allow researchers to disentangle the effects of multiple variables, including environmental constraints, structural constraints, and the luck and skill of individuals.

Ronit Shemtov (forthcoming) studies goal expansion in organizations founded as single-issue protest organizations. She proposes what could be termed a community "embeddedness" argument for predicting goal expansion (see Granovetter 1985): Organizations in which a web of friendships develop are likely to expand their goals in either number or scope. Organizations that do not develop such a network disband when the organization meets or fails to meet its original goal. Friendship networks, Shemtov argues, allow a group to create a sense of identity in a cultural and symbolic sense. Along with elaborating network and cultural influences on organizational change, Shemtov's work highlights the sometimes particularistic nature of change as well as the importance of personal goals, in this case sociability, to the continuation of the organization.

Tschirhart (1993) suggests that resource considerations, legitimacy considerations, and organizational demographics affected whether the thirty-four arts organizations she studied mapped or deflected environmental pressures. When resources were important to the organization, the organization was more likely to adapt to the demands of actors controlling those resources. But when legitimacy issues were considered (pressures that compromised the organization's mission or its artistic quality), the organization was likely to use strategies to deflect the pressure. Organizational age and size also affected strategy choice. Older organizations were more likely to adapt to external stakeholder's demands but were also more likely to cut ties with disagreeing stakeholders. This may indicate a wearing down effect, wherein older organizations succumb to pressures that they have undergone for longer, but may also indicate that older organizations have more secure ties to a variety of stakeholders and can afford to forgo the support of troublesome stakeholders. Younger organizations were more likely to choose the deflecting strategy of trying to change the stakeholder's views when stakeholders and the organization disagreed. Younger organizations may be unable to lose any stakeholder's support but may also hold their organizational missions more strongly than older organizations, leading them to try to maintain resource ties without changing themselves. Interestingly, large organizations were more likely than smaller ones to map environmental pressures. This perhaps indicates that larger organizations have more capacity for internal complexity; or it could indicate that larger organizations have less strongly held missions.

Board structure is also important in organizational strategy (D. Smith, 1993). In hospitals, Pfeffer (1973) finds that the primary function of a board is determined by the environment in which the hospital is situated (indicating that board structure can map the environment): Fund-raising gets more attention in nonprofit hospitals that depend on private contributions, while administrative tasks are of primary importance to hospitals dependent on the government or a religious organization for funds. Rebecca Bordt (in press) also studies board function but finds that function is related to board composition. She argues that boundary spanning (managing the environment) is just one role that boards can take. In women's nonprofit organizations, some boards focus on the organization's internal functions (some of these passively and others actively), and others serve only a symbolic, legitimating function. Internally focused boards and so-called paper boards are made up of nonelites, whereas boundary-spanning boards are made up of community elites or feminist leaders or both. Internally focused boards appear in smaller, poorer organizations but can also be found in larger, more financially secure organizations based on alternative, feminist principles of organization like collective decision making and a nonhierarchical, decentralized authority (see Ferguson 1984; Rothschild-Whitt 1979). In these larger organizations, trustees see their role as counterbalancing the executive director's power and maintaining the influence of the opinions of collective members.

Board structure both determines relevant environments and structures the types of responses an organization can make to an environment. Stone's (1993) study suggests that one type of board structure is appropriate for a grassroots environment and a very different type is necessary for a state contracting environment. The two new organizations she studied each created a board structure which accorded with its primary environment and tasks. The advocacy organization was headed by an "executive director" and had a large board that met frequently, whereas the service organization had a board based on a corporate model — small and headed by a "chairman" — while a "president" ran the organization.

The board structure, in other words, leads organizations to pay attention to particular aspects of their environment. In Stone's case, the board was chosen to match the environment. In other cases, existing board structure leads the organization to the environment. Clearly, grassroots boards and advocacy boards will react differently to similar pressures. Along these lines, Elaine Backman (forthcoming) traces differing responses by organizations facing similar environmental pressures to differences in the legal structure of the boards. She studies nonprofits on the institutional cusp between religious and civil law: social services for women and girls provided by an order of nuns. Backman finds two types of responses, adaption and selection, to the institutional cusp among the five governing bodies in the order (geographically divided into provinces). The fact that she finds different responses to

similar environments points out the constraining forces of organizational structure. In this case, options hinged on a province's civil legal structure, which constrained provinces in various ways, opening up and closing off certain strategies.

In a study of organizational transformation, Powell and Friedkin (1987) find that financial considerations played a major role in change in nine out of the ten detailed case studies they review. In the tenth case, the incorporation of a neighborhood council as a nonprofit spurred goal changes. This incorporation was necessary for the organization to receive grants, so the change was also funding-related, though it was not the same type of direct financial constraint experienced by the other nine organizations. Powell and Friedkin divide their ten cases into three categories, two in which goal change weakened the organization and the third in which change strengthened the organization. The first class of weak responses is internal and occurs when managers decide to keep their organization going even though the goals of the organization clearly will not be met. In these cases, the result is an enfeebled organization. The second class of weak responses results from external pressure and occurs when mangers allow funders, professionals, or standards of accountability to distort the organization's original purpose. The third class of responses is strong responses to external pressures, without goal transformation: "We considered these cases successful because the original goals were pursued more intensely . . . or new, related goals were adopted once the stated goal was achieved . . . or the initial mission was broadened in a manner that led to organizational expansion and enhanced viability" (191).

Two factors seemed to allow a strong response: (1) financial stability — none of the successful organizations was resource poor — and (2) pluralism in governance, with no single constituency or professional group dominating decisions. Though it is useful to distinguish strong and weak adaptations, both of which clearly occur in nonprofit organizations, it is worth pointing out that whether a given shift in goals is a "distortion" (weak response) or a "broadening" (strong response) is a matter of debate in many nonprofit organizations.

Research on social service organizations also shows, not surprisingly, that a resource-rich environment helps nonprofits attain their goals. Lester Salamon (1987) found that nonprofit organizations benefit from government funding, which improved their ability to help the needy, even though it hastened their bureaucratization. But as government funding has become tighter, Stone (1993) points out, nonprofits have undergone rapid goal transformation, becoming more aligned with governmental priorities (Smith and Lipsky 1993; Wolch 1990).

It is clear that the overall amount of funding is important for predicting nonprofit response to complexity, and the ability of nonprofits to deflect and exploit complexity or to manage the costs of mapping complexity. More funds give nonprofits more security; more funders lead to more options and freedom. Grønbjerg (1993a, 24) argues further that the *character* of the funding pattern structures a nonprofit's response:

> Nonprofit revenue sources differ in the nature of the exchange relationships they create (customers versus clients), the degree and type of competition they involve (few versus many competitors, protected versus open competitive systems), the extent to which they provide predictable and controllable funding, and the degree of dependency they encourage (broad versus narrow). These features have important internal consequences for the organizations, particularly for the structure of power and management control, the range of strategies to manage staff, and the extent and nature of planning efforts they pursue.

Kelly Moore (1993) studied three nonprofit political organizations uniting science and the public interest. Following Powell and Friedkin (1987), she finds that the two successful organizations had ample resources and diversified boards, while the unsuccessful organization's board composition had become quite narrow, and the organization was strapped for funds. Moreover, she shows that organizations are constrained by internal organizing decisions made early in the life of the organization.

> An organization's *ability* to respond to changes in its environment is highly dependent on its original collective identity. . . . the mechanism that makes an organization able to respond to a particular environment lies in the rules and routines for action that are structured by the group's shared definition of who they are. These features are set up early in the organization's history. Rules, routines, and the group's shared definition make some kinds of action possible — like hiring full-time staff or working collectively — while rendering others unacceptable. In addition, the group's early activities and actions place the group in a particular "micro-environment" or subculture, which shape the possibilities for the group's action. (Moore 1993, 233)

It is clear, Moore states, that the direct cause of the unsuccessful organization's failure was its inability to garner external support, but she goes on to analyze why this organization did not change so it could take advantage of available resources. The organization, based in radical politics, chose an alternative (democratic, participatory) form of organization. In the end, this form turned out to be weaker than the traditional model, but the form chosen was fundamental to the identity of the founding group. In addition, the organization's collective identity led it to oppose the establishment rather than working with it in order to milk resources from it. The successful organizations, in contrast, initially chose or shifted to more traditional organizational forms that were compatible with their environment of liberal, reformist, pluralist politics. Strategic use of institutions and strategic responses to in-

stitutional pressures is an important part of institutional theory today (Meyer and Rowan 1977; DiMaggio 1988; Fligstein 1990; Oliver 1991; DiMaggio 1991; Brint and Karabel 1991; Galaskiewicz 1991). These ideas focus on the micro level: how managers filter environmental pressures on organizations. It is important to recognize the theory's original contribution was the idea that environments influence and change organizations on a macro level. Institutional theory introduced "organizational fields" as a unit of analysis. Organizational fields are "those organizations that, in the aggregate, constitute a recognizable area of institutional life: key suppliers, resource and product consumers, regulatory agencies and other organizations that produce similar services or products" (DiMaggio and Powell 1983, 148). At this level of analysis, it is clear that organizations in a field undergo environmentally driven, homogenizing — and diversifying — processes.

Chaves (1993) suggests that institutional pressures on the agency structure within Protestant denominations led to increasing isomorphism among denominations (the increasing strength of the agency structure); however, actions on the part of a subset of religious leaders who resisted this institutional pressure maintained a degree of diversity in the organizational field. Chaves suggests that researchers looking at organizational fields should look for patterns of both homogeneity and diversity: "Political dynamics internal to organizations enhance or suppress institutionalization and, consequently, contribute to the overall degree of diversity and homogeneity within an organizational population" (Chaves 1993, 43).

My research also suggests that organizational fields are subject to both homogenizing and diversifying pressures, though my research points to a different mechanism (Alexander 1996a). I argue that as organizational fields become structured, individual organizations are drawn not only into an institutional field in which isomorphic pressures are tantamount, but also into a community ecology in which increasing competition for resources among organizations leads to increasing diversity. This finding is likely to hold especially for nonprofit organizations like museums that share overlapping funding sources. The existence of both homogeneity and diversity in organizational fields points out that organizations do not always react to environments in the same way.

CONCLUSION

In sum, a broad array of research demonstrates that the impact of environmental pressures on nonprofit organizations is forceful. Environmental complexity engenders goal complexity, and internal conflict is a common result. Yet nonprofit personnel work hard to keep their organization's goals in line with their own goals. Nonprofit managers buffeted by extreme complexity employ one or a combination of three strategies as a response: mapping, deflecting, and exploiting.

Organizational theory recognizes that organizational actors are not passive receptors of environmental pressures (Pfeffer and Salancik 1978; Weick 1979; Child 1972). Institutional theory, in particular, has come to adopt notions of agency which balance its previous thrust of environmental determinism, as ideas from institutional theory, resource dependency, and strategic decision making blend (Grønbjerg 1993a; Oliver 1991; Alexander 1996c). The three terms I use to describe organizational responses encompass such concepts expressed by other scholars as buffering (Thompson 1967), strategic management (Oliver 1991; Pfeffer and Salancik 1978), and loose coupling (Meyer and Rowan 1977). The terms I chose emphasize the agency of individual decision-makers who actively choose how to manage environmental pressures. The theoretical lesson is that we must continue to balance our understanding of the effects of environments with a degree of organizational agency.

The research presented here leaves us with two broad areas to rethink and research further.

1. Under what conditions do nonprofit organizations map, deflect, or exploit complexity? What are the costs and benefits of each strategy? It is clear that financial considerations play an important role in nonprofit response, and the obvious condition applies: Rich organizations have more leeway to avoid unwanted external demands. It is also clear that organizations work hard to avoid external demands that actually conflict with the organization's sense of its own goals. Beyond this, however, the research presented in this chapter does not allow us to draw firm conclusions about these questions.

Here, I make some predictions about nonprofit responses to environmental complexity that should be read as hypotheses for future research. Each strategy provides incentives (or disincentives) to managers who are able, given organizational constraints, to adopt that strategy. Mapping is an easy strategy to implement as it can rely on an ad hoc decision style. It can be a successful strategy when it allows the organization to satisfy a multitude of external actors who in turn provide resources. It is a strategy that is likely used when there are tight links between funders and the organization or when, as in service contracting, the external actor has some legal authority or other rights over the organization for accountability or to inspect records. These external actors are likely to penetrate buffering attempts, symbolic management, or loose coupling, reducing the organization's ability to deflect environmental complexity. Mapping is also a strategy used by organizations who do not find external demands distasteful or overly constraining. Therefore, we could expect nonprofit managers to use a mapping strategy when the goals of environmental actors do not differ significantly from their own goals. Mapping may also be a useful strategy when the environment is not so complex that mapping will generate excessive internal conflict. Similarly, nonprofit organizations that rely on client-paid fees are likely to map the de-

mands of those clients when these organizations believe their mandate is to serve clients. In these cases, nonprofits' goals remain intact. When nonprofits' external funding sources are distinct from their client base, mapping funding sources can pull the organization away from its original goals.

Alternatively, mapping is likely to be used by organizations who depend on each and every one of their constituencies and cannot afford to alienate any. In this regard, it is likely to be used by resource-poor organizations. When organizations absorb complexity because of extreme dependency of this sort, they can easily lose sight of their goals.

The costs of a mapping strategy can be high, even when it is generally successful. Costs include increased numbers of personnel, with resulting salary and overhead costs, and heightened internal conflict as the organization becomes more fragmented and complex. Mapping leads to a greater potential for goal displacement, especially for resource-poor organizations and those in which the clients of the nonprofit are not the payers.

Deflecting is a strategy that many ongoing nonprofits will be able to use in one form or another. This strategy requires an overarching managerial unit capable of strategic decision making. More important, it requires some financial slack. It may further require a more shared understanding among its members of the organization's goals, complex and contested though they may be, than in organizations that use a mapping strategy. Therefore, we might expect deflecting to be used by stable organizations with some basic resources. Further, deflecting is useful to organizations that wish to avoid external influence. External influence always constrains organizations in one way or another, so organizations generally attempt to deflect environmental pressures if possible. When the environmental pressures conflict with the goals of organizational members, however, the organization is more likely to divert organizational resources toward deflection. Therefore, we might expect that nonprofits that exist in hostile environments would use deflecting strategies often. More specifically, nonprofits who receive donations from entities like corporations that are rooted in fundamentally different assumptions are likely to attempt to deflect pressures from such donors. Finally, organizations in which members come closer to sharing—and thus to collectively defending—a set of fundamental goals probably use deflecting more than mapping.

There are many benefits to using deflecting as a strategy. Buffering provides stability for the buffered unit; loose coupling and symbolic management do not require organizational change to meet environmental demands. There are some possible drawbacks to this approach, however. These include overhead for management and the parts of the organization that serve as buffers; the risk that misrepresentation and willful loose coupling will be uncovered, tarnishing the organization's reputation; and the potential resentment of personnel relegated to buffered units who resent being taken out of the loop and their concomitant loss of power or influence in the organization.

The exploiting of complexity is the most difficult reaction to predict. Managers who are able to exploit complexity recognize that "each form of constraint is, in varying ways, also a form of enablement. Constraints open up possibilities at the same time as they restrict or deny others" (Powell 1991, 194). Multiple constraints can give managers leeway and freedom to reach their goals by finding a path among constraints to possibilities. These avenues would not be open to managers whose environments are unitary and simple. Or managers with multiple external constituencies can play these actors off one another. Thus, to exploit complexity, managerial skill and creativity is a must.

Organizations that are able to exploit complexity must be additionally privileged. Exploiting requires some financial slack for the organization to be able to make the deals that give it the edge. In order to maneuver among demands, such organizations need a degree of structural flexibility, too. In addition, clever organizational personnel need to have shared goals, if not for every aspect of the organization, then at least in the areas in which the organization can exploit the complexity. We would expect more exploitation of complexity in donative organizations than in service contracting organizations, as donors have less authority and inspection rights than do service contractors. In addition, some strategies like resource shifting require a general operating budget over which the organization has control. Thus, exploiting is most likely in organizations, like universities and museums, that have an endowment. The benefits of exploiting complexity are great, as the organization manages to pursue its goals freer of external constraints than they would be in less complex environments. This approach does have some drawbacks, however. The most notable cost comes down again to the coalitional nature of organizations: not all participants will agree with the organization's fundamental goals or with the goals that are furthered by the exploitation. These personnel may resent or dispute the success of the other, more dominant coalitions.

To gain a more complete understanding of nonprofit reactions, these observations on response strategy must be applied to the various structural units that make up the nonprofit. Each part or level of organizations might use a different strategy to manage environmental complexity. In museums, the curatorial and conservation parts of the museum are sealed off from the environment (Alexander 1996a), a deflecting strategy used by the museum as a whole. Yet curators were able to exploit funding complexity to pursue their own preferences for exhibitions. It is possible that curatorial departments are successful in exploiting complexity precisely because they are buffered from the environment.

Organizational response to environmental pressures is an ongoing process. Nonprofit organizations are unable to completely resolve the contradictory pressures from their environment, and thus they tend toward a state of flux. For instance, organizations that map environmental complexity create internal conflict. The managing of this conflict, however, can push the organization out of alignment with the environment, triggering more adjustments to the environment. Or a strategy that was successful while funds were munificent may not work when funds dry up. Internal adjustments, of course, take place vis-à-vis environments, which are themselves changing, suggesting that we think of nonprofit response as dynamic and ongoing.

2. Does complexity function differently in proprietary firms? We have seen how complexity functions in nonprofits. An obvious question is whether complexity functions differently in the for-profit arena.[17] Proprietary firms have multiple goals, arguments over implementation, disagreements about outcomes, and pressures from the environment, as organizational theorists have long recognized (Barnard 1938; March and Simon 1958; Cyert and March 1963; Pfeffer and Salancik 1978). However, for-profits can also rely on institutionalized forms, such as salary (for participant inducement), the market (for exchange of goods), and profit (as an effectiveness criteria). Indeed, the market is among the most highly institutionalized forms in modern society (Friedland and Alford 1991, 234; Powell 1990, 298). Proprietary firms attempt to prosper, and they are monitored by institutions like the stock market that index and reward profitability, using methods such as hostile takeover to correct misalignments between a company's value and the value of its stock.

Proprietary firms do not face competing pressures to the same extent as nonprofits because they are firmly governed by the highly institutionalized business logic. Outside constituents rarely ask managers to change what managers see as the organization's core function: to turn a profit. And such actors as environmental or political lobbies that do ask firms to give up profits are cast by firms as illegitimate. In contrast, constituents often ask nonprofits to meet goals that do not mesh with the nonprofit's views of its goals. Profitability (efficiency) is different from effectiveness only because the evaluators of proprietary firms agree that it is a valid standard. Nonprofits are at a disadvantage compared with firms because their legal form puts them in a less institutionalized environment.

The usual view of institutional theory is that it applies more to nonprofit organizations than to proprietary ones. This is not true. Contrary to the standard view, which suggests that the nonprofit sector is particularly subject to institutional pressures, for-profits exist in a sector that is *more institutionalized* than the nonprofit sector. The effect of institutional rules is strong. Because the business sector has been institutionalized sufficiently, the institutional rules are taken as the backdrop. Thus, the institutional rules can be taken for granted. In the nonprofit sector, however, institu-

---

17. Many theorists have written about the differences between nonprofit organizations and other types of organizations. For reviews, see DiMaggio and Anheier (1990), Hansmann (1987), and Douglas (1987).

tionalization of background rules is incomplete, is achieved only at the detailed level, or is contested,[18] making conflict over such rules endemic and problematic. Institutions are more visible in the nonprofit sector because there are *more* competing sets of them. This view suggests that institutional theory is more useful for understanding homogenization in the business sector but sheds more light on the heterogeneity in the voluntary sector.

I suggest a rethinking of our view of institutional theory and for-profit organizations. Institutional theory was developed in nonprofit organizations, and some conventional wisdom suggests that it is better there. This is not the case. Both proprietary and voluntary organizations are subject to institutional forces. Importantly, institutional theory leads us to blur rather than reify the distinction between for-profit and nonprofit organizations, as both types of organizations are subject to external pressures mediated by individuals drawing upon external models for organizational structures, goals, and evaluation that will give organizations resources and legitimacy. Further, the concept of the institutional cusp also suggests that we think of organizations as being located in spheres that rest on one or more dominant logics. For-profit firms tend to rest in business logic, though this is not always the case. Backman (forthcoming) suggests that family firms might be pulled between business and familial logics. And Marshall Meyer and Lynne Zucker (1989) show how proprietary firms can become "permanently failing organizations" when buffeted by multiple stakeholders who ignore the efficiency of the organization. Moreover, nonprofits are pulled between logics of business, public good, democracy, and the state. Nonprofit organizations are increasingly governed by business norms and state regulations along with models of charity and democracy. We have asked how proprietary organizations compare with nonprofit organizations. We might as well ask similar questions about government organizations. Indeed, given that the public sector is parceling out more work to proprietary and voluntary organizations and that for-profit firms are entering arenas traditionally covered by church and community groups, we are seeing increasing numbers of organizations from each sector

shading into the other sectors. We can anticipate more blurring in the future.

REFERENCES

Abbott, Andrew. 1988. *The System of Professions: An Essay on the Division of Expert Labor.* Chicago: University of Chicago Press.

Alexander, Victoria D. 1996a. *Museums and Money: The Impact of Funding on Exhibitions, Scholarship, and Management.* Bloomington: Indiana University Press.

———. 1996b. "From Philanthropy to Funding: The Effects of Corporate and Public Support on American Art Museums." *Poetics: Journal of Empirical Research on Literature, the Media and the Arts* 24:87–129.

———. 1996c. "Pictures at an Exhibition: Conflicting Pressures in Museums and the Display of Art." *American Journal of Sociology* 101:797–839.

Ashforth, B. E., and B. W. Gibbs. 1990. "The Double-Edge of Organizational Legitimation." *Organization Science* 1:177–94.

Backman, Elaine V. (forthcoming). "Good Works, Inc.: The Effects of Corporate Structure on the Provision of Private Social Services." Ph.D. dissertation, Stanford University.

Barnard, Chester I. 1938. *The Functions of the Executive.* Cambridge: Harvard University Press.

Block, S. 1990. "A History of the Discipline." In *The Nonprofit Organization: Essential Readings*, ed. David L. Gies, J. Steven Ott, and Jay M. Shafritz. Pacific Grove, Calif.: Brooks/Cole.

Bordt, Rebecca L. (In press). *The Structure of Women's Nonprofit Organizations.* Bloomington: Indiana University Press.

Brint, Steven, and Jerome Karabel. 1991. "Institutional Origins and Transformations: The Case of American Community Colleges." In *The New Institutionalism in Organizational Analysis*, ed. Walter W. Powell and Paul J. DiMaggio, 337–60. Chicago: University of Chicago Press.

Bush, R. 1992. "Survival of the Nonprofit Spirit in a For-Profit World." *Nonprofit and Voluntary Sector Quarterly* 21:391–410.

Chandler, Alfred D., Jr. 1962. *Strategy and Structure: Chapters in the History of the American Industrial Enterprise.* Cambridge: MIT Press.

Chaves, Mark. 1993. "Intraorganizational Power and Internal Secularization in Protestant Denominations." *American Journal of Sociology* 99:1–48.

Child, John. 1972. "Organizational Structure, Environment and Performance: The Role of Strategic Choice." *Sociology* 6:1–22.

Clark, Peter M., and James Q. Wilson. 1961. "Incentive Systems: A Theory of Organizations." *Administrative Science Quarterly* 6:129–66.

Clarkson, Kenneth. 1972. "Some Implications of Property Rights in Hospital Management." *Journal of Law and Economics* 15:363–84.

Clemens, Elisabeth S. 1993. "Organizational Repertoires and Institutional Change: Women's Groups and the Transformation of U.S. Politics, 1890–1920." *American Journal of Sociology* 98:755–98.

18. Institutions are nested, existing at the most general level as the "western cultural account" (Meyer, Boli, and Thomas, 1987) or as "institutional logics" (Friedland and Alford, 1991). Below these very generalized institutional schemes come increasingly specific institutions that at the lowest and most detailed levels resemble "cultural tools" (Swidler 1986) more than constitutive assumptions. Nesting creates levels of institutions. Institutions come in bundles which can conflict with other bundles of institutionalized norms and rules. Actors carrying one set of bundles can contest the institutionalized knowledge of actors carrying different bundles, at a detailed level. At a higher level, institutional logics compete at the institutional cusp. In addition, an idea can be in the process of becoming institutionalized (or deinstitutionalized) and thus exists in a state of weaker or partial institutionalization. Theorists do not agree on when an institution might be a more detailed, lower-level institution rather than a partially institutionalized one.

Cyert Richard M., and James G. March. 1963. *A Behavioral Theory of the Firm*. Englewood Cliffs: Prentice-Hall.

Dauber, Kenneth. 1994. "Contesting Goals, Projecting Power: The Politics of Defining Need." Paper presented at the Conference on Private Action and the Public Good, Indianapolis, November 4–6.

———. 1993. "The Indian Arts Fund and the Patronage of Native American Arts." In *Paying the Piper: Causes and Consequences of Art Patronage*, ed. Judith Huggins Balfe, 76–93. Chicago: University of Illinois Press.

D'Aunno, Thomas, Robert I. Sutton, and Richard H. Price. 1991. "Isomorphism and External Support in Conflicting Institutional Environments: A Study of Drug Abuse Treatment Units." *Academy of Management Journal* 34:636–61.

DiMaggio, Paul J. 1991. "Constructing an Organizational Field as a Professional Project: U.S. Art Museums, 1920–1940." In *The New Institutionalism in Organizational Analysis*, ed. Walter W. Powell and Paul J. DiMaggio, 267–92. Chicago: University of Chicago Press.

———. 1988. "Interest and Agency in Institutional Theory." In *Institutional Patterns and Organizations*, ed. Lynne G. Zucker, 3–21. Cambridge, Mass.: Ballinger.

———. 1987. "Nonprofit Organizations in the Production and Distribution of Culture." In *The Nonprofit Sector: A Research Handbook*, ed. Walter W. Powell, 195–220. New Haven: Yale University Press.

———. 1982a. "Cultural Entrepreneurship in Nineteenth-Century Boston: The Creation of an Organizational Base for High Culture in America." *Media, Culture and Society* 4:33–50.

———. 1982b. "Cultural Entrepreneurship in Nineteenth-Century Boston, Part II: The Classification and Framing of American Art." *Media, Culture and Society* 4:303–22.

DiMaggio, Paul J., and Helmut K. Anheier. 1990. "The Sociology of Nonprofit Organizations and Sectors." *Annual Review of Sociology* 16:137–59.

DiMaggio, Paul J., and Walter W. Powell. 1983. "The Iron Cage Revisited: Institutional Isomorphism and Collective Rationality in Organizational Fields." *American Sociological Review* 48:147–60.

Douglas, James. 1987. "Political Theories of Nonprofit Organizations." In *The Nonprofit Sector: A Research Handbook*, ed. Walter W. Powell, 43–54. New Haven: Yale University Press.

Ferguson, Kathy E. 1984. *The Feminist Case against Bureaucracy*. Philadelphia: Temple University Press.

Fligstein, Neil. 1990. *The Transformation of Corporate Control*. Cambridge: Harvard University Press.

Freeman, R. Edward. 1984. *Strategic Management: A Stakeholder Approach*. Boston: Pitman.

Freidson, Eliot. 1975. *Doctoring Together: A Study of Professional Social Control*. New York: Elsevier.

Friedland, Roger, and Robert R. Alford. 1991. "Bringing Society Back In: Symbols, Practices, and Institutional Contradictions." In *The New Institutionalism in Organizational Analysis*, ed. Walter W. Powell and Paul J. DiMaggio, 232–63. Chicago: University of Chicago Press.

Galaskiewicz, Joseph. 1991. "Making Corporate Actors Accountable: Institution-Building in Minneapolis-St. Paul." In *The New Institutionalism in Organizational Analysis*, ed. Walter W. Powell and Paul J. DiMaggio, 293–310. Chicago: University of Chicago Press,.

Granovetter, Mark. 1985. "Economic Action and Social Structure: The Problem of Embeddedness." *American Journal of Sociology* 91:481–510.

Grønbjerg, Kirsten A. 1993a. *Understanding Nonprofit Funding: Managing Revenues in Social Services and Community Development Organizations*. San Francisco: Jossey-Bass.

———. 1993b. "Transactions Costs in Social Service Contracting: U.S. Lessons in International Perspective." Paper presented at Contracting — Selling or Shrinking? Voluntary and Nonprofit Organizations and the Enabling State in International Perspective: A Conference for Policy-Makers, Scholars, Researchers, and Practitioners. London, July 20–22.

———. 1991. "How Nonprofit Service Organizations Manage Their Funding Sources: Key Findings and Policy Implications." *Nonprofit Management and Leadership* 2:159–75.

Hansmann, Henry. 1987. "Economic Theories of Nonprofit Organization." In *The Nonprofit Sector: A Research Handbook,* ed. Walter W. Powell, 27–42. New Haven: Yale University Press.

———. 1980. "The Role of Nonprofit Enterprise." *Yale Law Journal* 89:835–901.

Hyde, Cheryl Ann. 1991. "Did the New Right Radicalize the Women's Movement? A Study of Change in Feminist Social Movement Organizations, 1977–1987." Ph.D. dissertation, University of Michigan.

Jepperson, Ronald L., and John W. Meyer. 1991. "The Public Order and the Construction of Formal Organizations." In *The New Institutionalism in Organizational Analysis*, ed. Walter W. Powell and Paul J. DiMaggio, 204–31. Chicago: University of Chicago Press.

Johnson, Margaret Anne. 1993. "Change in a Voluntary Organization: 1975–1992. A Consideration of Social Change, Organizational Structure, Gender, and Class." Ph.D. dissertation, University of Texas at Austin.

Kanter, Rosabeth Moss, and David V. Summers. 1987. "Doing Well while Doing Good: Dilemmas of Performance Measurement in Nonprofit Organizations and the Need for a Multiple-Constituency Approach." In *The Nonprofit Sector: A Research Handbook*, ed. Walter W. Powell, 154–66. New Haven: Yale University Press.

Leaf, Philip J. 1985. "Mental Health Systems Research: A Review of Available Data." *American Behavioral Scientist* 28:619–38.

March, James G., and Herbert A. Simon. 1958. *Organizations*. New York: John Wiley.

Meyer, John W., John Boli, and George M. Thomas. 1987. "Ontology and Rationalization in the Western Cultural Account." In *Institutional Structure: Constituting State, Society, and the Individual*, ed. George M. Thomas, John W. Meyer, Francisco O. Ramirez, and John Boli. Beverly Hills: Sage.

Meyer, John W., and Brian Rowan. 1977. "Institutionalized Organizations: Formal Structure as Myth and Ceremony." *American Journal of Sociology* 83:340–63.

Meyer, John W., and W. Richard Scott, eds. 1992. *Organizational Environments: Ritual and Rationality,* 2d ed. Beverly Hills: Sage.

Meyer, John W., W. Richard Scott, and David Strang. 1987. "Centralization, Fragmentation, and School District Complexity." *Administrative Science Quarterly* 32:186–201.

Meyer, Marshall W., and Lynne G. Zucker. 1989. *Permanently Failing Organizations*. Beverly Hills: Sage.

Middleton, Melissa. 1987. "Nonprofit Boards of Directors: Beyond the Governance Function." In *The Nonprofit Sector: A Research Handbook*, ed. Walter W. Powell, 141–54. New Haven: Yale University Press.

Moore, Kelly. 1993. "Doing Good while Doing Science: The Origins and Consequences of Public Interest Science Organizations in America, 1945–1990." Ph.D. dissertation, University of Arizona.

Nathan, Maria Louise. 1992. "A Grounded Theory Account of Strategic Decision-Making as a Key Mediating Mechanism Between Organization and Environment." Ph.D. dissertation, University of Southern California.

Oliver, Christine. 1991. "Strategic Responses to Institutional Processes." *Academy of Management Review* 16:145–79.

Palmer, Donald A., P. Devereaux Jennings, and Xueguang Zhou. 1993. "Late Adoption of the Multidivisional Form by Large U.S. Corporations: Institutional, Political, and Economic Accounts." *Administrative Science Quarterly* 38:100–31.

Parsons, Talcott. 1960. *Structure and Process in Modern Societies*. New York: Free Press.

Pfeffer, Jeffrey. 1973. "Size, Composition and Function of Hospital Boards of Directors: A Study of Organization-Environment Linkage." *Administrative Science Quarterly* 18:349–64.

Pfeffer, Jeffrey, and Gerald R. Salancik. 1978. *The External Control of Organizations: A Resource Dependence Perspective*. New York: Harper and Row.

Powell, Walter W. 1991. "Expanding the Scope of Institutional Analysis." In *The New Institutionalism in Organizational Analysis*, ed. Walter W. Powell and Paul J. DiMaggio, 183–203. Chicago: University of Chicago Press.

———. 1990. "Neither Market nor Hierarchy." *Research in Organizational Behavior* 12:295–336.

———. 1988. "Institutional Effects on Organizational Structure and Performance." In *Institutional Patterns and Organizations*, ed. Lynne G. Zucker, 115–36. Cambridge, Mass.: Ballinger.

Powell, Walter W., and Paul J. DiMaggio, eds. 1991. *The New Institutionalism in Organizational Analysis*. Chicago: University of Chicago Press.

Powell, Walter W., and Rebecca Friedkin. 1987. "Organizational Change in Nonprofit Organizations." In *The Nonprofit Sector: A Research Handbook*, ed. Walter W. Powell, 180–92. New Haven: Yale University Press.

———. 1986. "Politics and Programs: Organizational Factors in Public Television Decision Making." In *Nonprofit Enterprise in the Arts: Studies in Mission and Constraint*, ed. Paul DiMaggio, 245–69. New York: Oxford University Press.

Rothschild-Whitt, Joyce. 1979. "The Collectivist Organization: An Alternative to Rational Bureaucratic Models." *American Sociological Review* 44:509–27.

Salamon, Lester M. 1987. "Partners in Public Service: The Scope and Theory of Government-Nonprofit Relations." In *The Nonprofit Sector: A Research Handbook*, ed. Walter W. Powell, 99–117. New Haven: Yale University Press.

Schnorr, Paul. 1993. "Denied a Sense of Community: Problems of Class, Race and Community Form in a Voluntary Resettlement Effort." Ph.D. dissertation, Northwestern University.

Scott, Robert A. 1969. *The Making of Blind Men: A Study of Adult Socialization*. New York: Russell Sage Foundation.

Scott, W. Richard. 1992. *Organizations: Rational, Natural and Open Systems,* 3d ed. Englewood Cliffs: Prentice-Hall.

———. 1991. "Unpacking Institutional Arguments." In *The New Institutionalism in Organizational Analysis*, ed. Walter W. Powell and Paul J. DiMaggio, 164–82. Chicago: University of Chicago Press.

———. 1987. "The Adolescence of Institutional Theory." *Administrative Science Quarterly* 32:493–511.

Scott, W. Richard, and John W. Meyer. 1992. "The Organization of Societal Sectors" In *Organizational Environments: Ritual and Rationality,* 2d ed., ed. John W. Meyer and W. Richard Scott, 129–53. Beverly Hills: Sage Publications.

Selznick, Philip. 1949. TVA and the Grass Roots. Berkeley: University of California Press.

Sewell, William H. 1992. "A Theory of Structure: Duality, Agency, and Transformation." *American Journal of Sociology* 98:1–29.

Shemtov, Ronit (forthcoming). "Goal Expansion among Social Movement Organizations: The Case of Community-Environmental Groups." Ph.D. dissertation, University of Connecticut.

Simon, John G. 1987. "The Tax Treatment of Nonprofit Organizations: A Review of Federal and State Policies." In *The Nonprofit Sector: A Research Handbook*, ed. Walter W. Powell, 67–98. New Haven: Yale University Press.

Smith, David. 1993. "Trustees and Moral Issues in Nonprofit Governance." Paper presented at the Conference on Private Action and the Public Good, Indianapolis, November 4–6.

Smith, Stephen Rathgeb, and Michael Lipsky. 1993. *Nonprofits for Hire: The Welfare State in the Age of Contracting*. Cambridge: Harvard University Press.

Stone, Melissa Middleton. 1993. "The Future of Advocacy in State-Dominated Environments." Paper presented at the Conference on Private Action and the Public Good, Indianapolis, November 4–6.

Stout, Suzanne Kay. 1993. "The Dynamics of Organizational Linkages: The Case of Higher Education and Philanthropy." Ph.D. dissertation, Stanford University.

Swidler, Ann. 1986. "Culture in Action: Symbols and Strategies." *American Sociological Review* 51:273–86.

Thompson, James D. 1967. *Organizations in Action*. New York: McGraw-Hill.

Tschirhart, Mary. 1993. "The Management Problems with Stakeholders." Ph.D. dissertation, University of Michigan.

Useem, Michael, and Stephen I. Kutner. 1986. "Corporate Contributions to Culture and the Arts: The Organization of Giving and the Influence of the Chief Executive Officer and of Other Firms on Company Contributions in Massachusetts." In *Nonprofit Enterprise in the Arts: Studies in Mission and Constraint*, ed. Paul DiMaggio, 93–112. New York: Oxford University Press.

Weick, Karl E. 1979. *The Social-Psychology of Organizing,* 2d ed. Reading, Mass.: Addison-Wesley.

Weisbrod, Burton A. 1988. *The Nonprofit Economy.* Cambridge: Harvard University Press.

Westney, D. Eleanor. 1987. *Imitation and Innovation: The Transfer of Western Organizational Patterns to Meiji Japan.* Cambridge: Harvard University Press.

Wolch, Jennifer R. 1990. *The Shadow State: Government and Voluntary Sector in Transition.* New York: Foundation Center.

Young, Dennis R. 1987. "Executive Leadership in Nonprofit Organizations." In *The Nonprofit Sector: A Research Handbook,* ed. Walter W. Powell, 167–79. New Haven: Yale University Press.

Zald, Mayer N., and Patricia Denton. 1963. "From Evangelism to General Service: The Transformation of the YMCA." *Administrative Science Quarterly* 8:214–34.

20

J E R A L D   H A G E

Reflections on Emotional Rhetoric and Boards for Governance of NPOS

Some of the more distinctive and interesting kinds of non-profit organizations (hereafter NPOS, see Powell 1987), such as social movement organizations (hereafter SMOS, see McCarthy and Zald 1977), organizations with expressive outputs like music, dance, and art and service or fund-raising organizations that rely upon large amounts of volunteer labor, have generally been ignored in the traditional organizational literature (for example, Hall 1991; Scott 1993; Hage 1980). Although there has been a considerable amount of work on hospitals, schools, and welfare agencies in this literature, the tendency has been to emphasize their bureaucratic aspects rather than the problems created when organizations attempt to change society or rely upon contributions of time and money. Even the relatively recent population-ecology literature (Carroll 1987, 1988; Hannan and Carroll 1992; Hannan and Freeman 1989; Singh and Lumsden 1990), while including studies of labor unions, trade associations, and some voluntary associations, has not devoted as much attention to the problems of survival when there is a need to rely upon donations and volunteers. Only the new institutionalism (see Meyer and Rowan 1977; Meyer and Scott 1983; Powell and DiMaggio 1991; Scott 1987; Zucker 1987) has been critically involved in the study of NPOS, particular expressive organizations, precisely because the problem of social beliefs about the most appropriate form of structure and control is likely to be quite critical within this kind of

governance structure (DiMaggio 1991; Meyer and Rowan 1977; Meyer and Scott 1983).

To rectify this imbalance within the traditional organizational and management literatures, this chapter will focus on NPOS that have at least one of three distinctive qualities: (1) SMOS (Curtis and Aguirre 1993; Diani and Eyerman 1992; Larana, Johnston, and Gusfield 1994; Tarrow 1994) involved in attempting to bring change to the society — whether conservative, populist, or equalitarian; (2) organizations that rely upon a considerable proportion of volunteer labor (Jencks 1987) — whether for fund-raising, board participation, or in provision of services; and (3) organizations with expressive outputs such as art or music organizations (DiMaggio 1987). The emphasis on these dimensions rather than coordination style (Mintzberg 1979), type of paradigm (Scott 1993), or the cross-classification of knowledge inputs and market/strategy context (Alter and Hage 1993; Hage 1980; Hage and Powers 1992) highlights several interesting issues for both the organizational and management literatures. Specifically, these distinctive qualities call attention to the importance of emotional rhetoric or frames and the importance of board involvement. The former concept allows us to unite the sociology of emotions literature in a new way with the study of organizations and social movements, and at the same time synthesize literatures at the micro, meso, and macro levels of analysis. And while the topic of boards has been within the organizational literature for decades, their general importance for NPOs as distinct from for-profit and government organizations has not been stressed.

Both emotional rhetoric and board involvement represent certain dilemmas that illustrate differences between NPOs and particularly SMOs and private, for-profit and governmental organizations. While emotional rhetoric might be effective in mobilizing individuals to protest—and even kill!—and to make quite extreme sacrifices so as to change society, it does not necessarily always provide the financial resources from the general public, which may be necessary for the continuation of the organization. In contrast, emphasis on the kinds of cognitive strategies more typical of business and government organizations can mean a decay in the commitment of individuals to the cause and an unwillingness to adopt the militant strategies necessary for societal change. Similarly, board involvement can provide for a much more dynamic organization but paradoxically it can also prevent the organization from changing when the environment does. These dilemmas need to be considered.

These three distinctive dimensions—societal change, reliance upon volunteer labor, and expressive outputs—associated with some NPOs allow us to expand and develop a taxonomy of organizations, thus continuing the work suggested by B. McKelvey (1982), who argued for a classification system for organizations. The building of the taxonomy requires, however, that we isolate the critical dimensions that are related to various performance characteristics. Therefore, the thrust of this chapter is on the performance implications of these dimensions.

EMOTIONAL RHETORIC AS STRATEGY

What is Emotional Rhetoric?

The term *emotional rhetoric,* especially within the context of NPOs, requires careful definition because it can be interpreted in various ways. Essentially the definition is the use of appeals that arouse deep feelings in individuals. Because all words have some emotional content, a content that can vary by context or situation, it becomes difficult to assess when rhetoric has this capacity and when it does not. Ultimately the test is in the response of individuals to the appeals.

Probably the most equivalent concept is to be found within the social movement literature, in which the idea has been expressed as frames in the work of David Snow and Robert Benford (1988). I prefer to use the term *emotional rhetoric,* however, to emphasize the relative presence (or absence) of the emotional character of the appeals aimed at either or both the members of the organization and the general public from which support (usually financial resources) can be drawn. Appeals for support, that is, the rhetoric, can be entirely rational or relatively devoid of emotional content. The concept of frames is usually discussed as a cognitive strategy, reflecting its origin in the work of Erving Goffman (McAdam

1994, 37; Tarrow 1994, 121–30), and appears too close to the old organizational concept of goals or mission statement (Perrow 1961), that is, the specific reasons for the existence of the organization, including its basis of legitimacy (Parsons 1956). It does not automatically imply the depth of emotional content.[1]

Presumably the frame of the social movement or the goals of an organization receive emotional content when their appeal touches some deeply felt value that frequently has been imprinted at an early age in the individual or collective consciousness. Doug McAdam (1994, 37) calls this cultural resonance and uses the example of Martin Luther King and the civil rights movement, in which the basic emotional appeal is the denial of the right to vote. Clearly, whether or not certain rights have emotional appeals depends upon how we have been socialized. Another, similar example is the National Rifle Association's use of the appeal of people's right to bear arms. This is more than a slogan; it has an emotional appeal because of its role in the history of the United States and the *loss of life* which accompanied the American War of Independence. When a group has had to fight for some right or privilege or when the memory of such a fight has become part of the collective heritage, that right assumes an emotional force. Similarly, many fund-raising organizations provide examples of basic emotional appeals designed to mobilize our pocketbooks. The American Cancer Association can easily raise large amounts of money because its campaign can tap into the pain and hurt of many who have lost a friend or a relative to cancer. The word *cancer* alone has extraordinary emotional meaning.

Perhaps the most dramatic examples of emotional rhetoric are to be found in the debate over abortion. Phrases such as *child murder, control over my own body,* and *a woman's right to choose* illustrate the power of emotional rhetoric and its centrality for both SMOs (for example, the National Organization for Women (NOW) and the conservative right religious movements) and such organizations as the abortion clinics that rely upon volunteer labor (for example, Planned Parenthood). Any time a frame can involve issues that appear to relate to matters of life of children or control over one's own life and death, it assumes enormous emotional power.

Political campaigns, which are quintessential attempts to mobilize people's time and money, furnish a number of examples of how critical emotional rhetoric is. George Bush won in 1988 in part thanks to the successful Willie Horton campaign, which aroused in many people's minds fears of personal safety. Security against rape, particularly by criminals who have been temporarily released from prison, is a

1. Another concept that appears to be similar is ideology. But this means usually the particular justification that is used to support the specific distribution of power and rewards in society; again, this is a cognitive argument and leaves out the emotional appeals that are part of the justification.

powerful symbol. Unfortunately, this particular campaign carried racial overtones as well, thus tapping into the emotion of hate as well as fear.

Another excellent set of examples of the use of emotional rhetoric is provided by development work (Diaz-Albertini 1993) in developing countries, where SMOs emphasize social change and many non-SMOs provide services to the poor. Both are likely to employ emotional rhetoric. NGOs, as they are usually referred to in the development literature, that are not SMOs typically argue for empowerment and the creation of a more equitable society. Javier Diaz-Albertini (1993) observes that emotional rhetorics are particularly critical for winning public support when interventions and actions are needed for social change. Additionally, as he observes in quoting the work of Peter Marris (1982), these rhetorics give meaning to those engaged in development work, rewarding them with an identity and commitment or the élan necessary in SMOs, especially those in developing countries, where the obstacles may seem formidable.

Although the social movement literature (Curtis and Aguirre 1993; Gamson 1990; Larana, Johnston, and Gusfield 1994; Tarrow 1994) contains a number of rich examples of the importance of emotional appeals or rhetoric, this aspect has been ignored in the organizational literature. Yet, one of its concepts is closely related: organizational strategy. In the management literature and particularly in the work of Michael Porter (1980, 1985, 1986, 1990), this concept comes closest to the idea of emotional rhetoric. Certainly NPOs are likely to draw on emotional appeals as part of their strategy for raising funds, as I have already suggested. But even business organizations concerned with profit can employ rhetoric with an emotional content when discussing the distinctive qualities of their product or service. A familiar example is the advertising for Volvo that stresses the safety of the car in accidents. But although emotional rhetoric can be one part of an organization's strategy to gain a market niche, Porter and others have emphasized the rational or cognitive aspects of an organization's attempt to survive. This is particularly striking in several of the typologies of strategy that have been developed, for example, proactive versus reactive (Miles et al. 1978) or cash cows versus dogs.

An examination of the mission statements of some of the leading corporations in the United States, specifically Ford, Texaco, Intel, and Johnson and Johnson, reveals an emphasis on the typical issues that concern business organizations: profit, quality, and effectiveness. Clearly, these words have little emotional content. Yet, as shall be suggested below, the emotional content becomes an increasingly important aspect for business organizations, especially in postindustrial society, in which products are perceived to have consequences for the health and safety of the individual, the purity and integrity of the environment, and the cohesion and viability of the larger society, or what economists might call externalities.

The suggested dichotomy between the cognitive message

and the emotional appeal is, as anyone familiar with advertising knows, a false one. The goal of the hospital may be to save lives, and this quickly assumes an emotional content, just as the goal of schools to develop the whole person does. The same can be said of such organizations as Johnson and Johnson, although this is not what its mission statement says. What is usually absent in the mission statement and its articulation by managers is the continued emphasis on emotional appeals as a way of building support. Many executive directors of NPOs emphasize a rational argument as to why they should receive support rather than a mission statement that has emotional appeal. Furthermore, the management of many for-profit and government organizations assumes their support base is secure and therefore do not perceive the need for sustained emotional appeals. Given the current extent of global competition and fiscal crises of the state, nothing is less certain.

Why Is Emotional Rhetoric so Critical?

The most obvious reasons for employing emotional rhetoric are to gain legitimacy and to mobilize resources, as has been suggested in some of the examples above. But if we return to the three dimensions of NPOs, the relevance of emotional rhetoric becomes much more compelling. SMOs are concerned with changing society. Any attempt to change society, regardless of direction, necessitates much more than the words "to gain legitimacy and to mobilize resources" imply. The crux of the problem of social change is to alter people's worldview, to change their cognitive model and then to give this cognitive model an emotional charge. To convince other people of the correctness of the cause, the rhetoric has to tap into some basic and profound social belief, one that is infused with emotion. It is emotions that make various messages compelling, not logic or reason.

Furthermore, SMOs are different from typical volunteer organizations like the Red Cross, Salvation Army, and Goodwill because they require devotion and sacrifice that go beyond a few hours of volunteer labor or a monthly pay deduction to one's favorite charity. The public demonstrations involved in the civil rights movement are particularly compelling examples, as are the more current attempts to block the building of nuclear reactors. And the dedication of those who work for change in developing countries is also another compelling illustration.

In one sense SMOs have to develop a charismatic relationship with their followers, to use Max Weber's term (1946). Unfortunately, Weber stressed the importance of leaders rather than the rhetoric they use. Although he did argue that charismatic leaders articulated new values, he did not stress the emotional content attached to these values. Because of Weber's work, we equate these issues with the definition of a charismatic leader, but visions of societal change that are well articulated, that is, that involve emotional rhetoric, develop an aura about them that makes their cause itself quasi-charismatic. Furthermore, and this is the important point, once the emotional rhetoric has currency, the social movement can survive without charismatic leaders, at least until the rhetoric loses potency. As a corollary to this idea, once certain words carry the emotional impact, other individuals can employ them and acquire some of the aura attached to them. Many Republican members of Congress are now speaking out against big government, a locution in which the word *big* has assumed emotional content, connoting bad, bogus, and bureaucratic.

When one considers the volunteer organizations that rely upon donations of time and money, other issues are raised that also make the subject of emotional rhetoric an important one for organizational theory. In organizations such as the local church choir, garden society, bridge club, or fraternal order, the problem of motivation is usually solved because the individuals consume at least part of the benefits of their contributions. But in some volunteer organizations — those that are providing public goods such as saving the environment (Greenpeace) or consumer protection groups (Nader's Raiders) or associations that raise money to provide services for various disadvantaged groups like the homeless (Committee for Non-Violence), victims of family abuse (the House of Ruth), or those ill with AIDS — the recipients are not the same as those who are making the contributions. Following the logic of economists such as Mancur Olson (1965), one would not expect many people to make these kinds of contributions. But in fact, recent research (Knoke 1990) indicates that many are willing to make sacrifices for public goods. How does one explain this nonrational behavior, at least from an economist's perspective, on the part of so many people in society? The answer is emotional rhetoric, which provides a justification to making contributions even when we do not directly benefit.

Even when the members of the volunteer organizations consume the benefits, as in the examples of labor unions and trade associations, the problem of motivation remains. Indeed, many of the examples cited by Olson (1965) in his book *The Logic of Collective Action* were labor unions. His reasoning was that workers would free ride on the efforts of others who gained such victories as increased wages. Some of these problems are illustrated in a contrast between the labor movement in France and that in the United States. The French labor movement has been largely a failure because of the difficulty of convincing workers to pay dues and to stay out on strike. In contrast, the American labor movement has been much more successful in motivating its members to participate in strikes for long periods and to pay their dues, which then have been employed as strike funds. The emotional appeal of solidarity has worked much better in the heterogenous United States than in the much more homogeneous France.[2]

Finally, organizations that produce expressive outputs such as dance, music, television, and movies or that store these kinds of cultural products (museums, for example) must rely upon emotional rhetoric as a way of securing legitimacy and resources because they cannot easily point to any rational, that is, measurable reason, to support their particular organization. Indeed, one could go further and suggest that in any organization that does not have an easily measured output either as product or service, emotional appeals become more common and necessary as a way of justifying the existence of the organization and securing support in the larger society (Meyer and Scott 1983). Emotions become a substitute for evidence; they furnish moral authority.

In many of the expressive organizations, the salaries are quite low. Many dance organizations, theater groups, and opera companies live on the dedication of their companies. This is also true more generally for many of the NGOs that provide services. Although the extremely high pay of the executive directors of the National Association for the Advancement of Colored People and United Way during the 1990s drew considerable attention, the reality is that the workers on the front lines providing the services are frequently underpaid. Emotional appeals help us explain the wage and salary differentials between the NPO sector and the private, for-profit sector.

Another theoretical advantage for arguing for the importance for emotional rhetoric is that it allows one to integrate the sociology of emotions into both the organizational literature and social movement literatures in new ways, and in the process unite micro, meso, and macro levels of analysis. Although *The Managed Heart,* a study of airplane attendants, is an organizational study, it has had much more impact in the sociology of emotions than in the organizational literature. Furthermore, its central point, namely, that flight attendants have to manage their emotions, usually by suppressing them, has generated a number of articles about emotional work. In these studies, however, the emphasis is not on emotional appeals but on how to create plastic smiles and suppress anger, not on how to motivate people to make an extra effort, but the suppression of emotions. Instead, the literature on the sociology of emotions should be concerned with their expression as critical to the success of the social movement or volunteer organization, both members and donators.

This quite opposite view of the role of emotion in the success and even survival of SMOs is illustrated in the recent history of the feminist movement within the United States, which since the early 1970s has had a considerable range of emotional appeals associated with particular kinds of tactics (Hyde 1991). The liberation branch wanted a total change

2. To explain why carries us too far afield, but part of the problem in France is that anarchism has an enormous emotional appeal, whereas it does not in the United States. Then, too, the labor force in France has been split among different emotional appeals related to alternative political agendas — communist, socialist, and catholic. Finally, it very well may be the extreme nature of the emotional appeals in the history of the French labor movements that discredited them.

of society, which usually meant the creation of new kinds of organizations — women's banks, health clinics only for women, rape crisis centers, and so on — that would deliver services that women desperately needed but were not provided. The emotional appeal dealt with the problem of oppression from a patriarchal, controlled society that made decisions that only benefited men. Health research is a particularly striking example. In contrast, many chapters of NOW (one must be careful in generalizing in this quite complex movement and even within specific chapters) associated themselves with the strategy of changing the laws of the land, specifically, the Equal Rights Amendment (ERA). Here the emotional appeal was equality or justice. Still a third segment advocated change at the individual level and thus eventually at the cultural level, which espoused the idea of one outrageous act a day as a mechanism for achieving change at the individual or role-relationship level. Although all themes deal with discrimination, how they emotionally wrap it is quite distinct, as are their strategies and tactics of change.

As is apparent in these examples, by focusing on emotional appeals and their relative effectiveness, one can evaluate the success of each of these approaches to the problem of societal change. Furthermore, by doing so one is uniting the meso, macro, and micro levels of analysis in each of these three strategies of societal change.

Emotional rhetoric is relevant not only to NPOS, but also to business and government organizations, who can use it to (1) raise employee morale to a level of dedication and (2) convince the public that their products are morally responsible.

The traditional attitude toward workers has been to provide them with sufficient pay and quality of work life so that they are motivated to remain in the organization, that is, to reduce job turnover. But anyone who has read *The Soul of a New Machine* (Kidder 1979) realizes that in high tech organizations, which are increasingly common, the excitement of being on the frontier — which is an emotional appeal — is what is necessary to produce that kind of employee dedication. One could go further and suggest that in those organizations involved in creating new products or services, there is a golden opportunity to use emotional rhetoric about being in the vanguard or being the first to provide the new products or services. Furthermore, increasingly people want to work in organizations that they perceive as making a difference and bettering society. And good should not be interpreted as simply liberal causes; many in the religious right, including a number of the representatives elected in November 1994, are on a crusade to save the country. This has profound implications for the importance of how the mission and strategy of an organization are articulated. The best people are likely to search for the stimulation of being on the frontier or being actively involved in correcting the evils of society, however these are defined. Emotional appeals for employees and civil servants can produce what the French call élan or esprit de corps. Employees are not excited about producing quality products or making a profit — ideas contained in the typical

mission statements — but they can become enthusiastic about making the world a better place in which to live. But observe that as this becomes part of the appeal of organizational strategy and rhetoric, then the business or government organization is becoming more and more like a social movement organization, at least relative to its claims.

The idea is not farfetched. Irrespective of what one may think about Henry Ford during the 1930s and afterward or of the Ford Motor Company today, the critical fact is that Ford did have a vision: he wanted everyone in the country to have cheap transportation. This is quite distinct from the idea of making a profit (although it does not exclude it). Furthermore, he succeeded and in the process enormously transformed the society, in good ways and bad. The same Ford campaigned for the $5-dollar day for workers during the period of the First World War, another kind of vision. Consider, too, the motivations of an Alexander Graham Bell or, more recently, of Edwin Land (Polaroid camera) or Steve Jobs; these inventors were not motivated by profit or money (one reason they lost control of their companies). Because high tech companies are in the business of producing new products, their purpose is to change the world, if only in some small way. The recognition of this can generate enormous energy among those who heed the appeal, as is apparent in *The Soul of a New Machine*.

The current discussion about how to reinvent government opens many of the same opportunities for organizational innovators with some vision of new ways of providing better and more effective services to enlist the help of many.

The conventional wisdom is that if one produces the better product, that product will triumph in the marketplace. But given the general and expanding concern about what these products do to the individuals who use them or to the environment as they are produced, used, or discarded, organizations that ignore these aspects of their products will lose out. Educated consumers are now aware of the many poisons — fats, sugars, carbohydrates, cholesterol, and so on — contained in food; of the damage done to the environment by cars and plastics; of the growing problem of the ozone hole, the greenhouse effect, and the depletion of the oceans. Implications for the health of the individual, the protection of the environment, or the quality of life more generally are emotional issues for many. Increasingly, companies find it necessary to build into their advertising the fact that they are green, safe, or benign. In Europe, these ideas have given rise to new political parties, whereas in this country they have been associated with several ecological social movements.

The same logic applies to governmental services. All would agree that various welfare programs in the United States have not worked or that the health care system must be rethought. These are only two of the many issues that reflect the need to reconstruct and rethink the relationships between local, state, and federal governments in each of the distinct service areas.

The final reason for being concerned about the emotional

rhetoric is its increasing importance not just for NPOs but for the analysis of society generally. Amitai Etzioni (1968) long ago argued that American society was becoming an active society, meaning that more and more groups were committed to, that is, emotionally engaged in, achieving their goals. Consistent with this, there has been a steady growth in the number of emotional appeals that have been made, quite measurable by counting the demonstrations reported on the Washington, D.C., news each year (and correspondingly a growth in the social movements literature). Annual civil rights, gay, and feminist marches are now part of the calendar in the capital city (and elsewhere as well). The current debate over the appropriateness of emotional rhetoric in the abortion debate and its consequences for human life is another example. The effectiveness of Newt Gingrich in his use of media is still a third illustration of how important emotional rhetoric has become in political discourse.[3]

Perhaps the most interesting debates during this decade will be those over the loss of community and of family values. Communities and families constitute civil society, which is so critical for the continuation of trust in social institutions. Furthermore, it is in communities and families that one learns which values should have emotional content and how to control one's emotions. Civil society is the home of feelings and emotional commitments. Violence comes not only because there is a lack of feeling but because the feelings that are present are not tempered with other ones like compassion, a basic emotion learned in the family.

THE DILEMMAS OF EMOTIONAL RHETORIC

The Cultural Context

Given the argument just presented, one might assume that all that an organization's leaders have to do is to make some emotional appeal and they will automatically have the commitment, legitimacy, and resources that they need. But the various examples of the French labor movement, the American civil rights movement, and the feminist movement worldwide demonstrate that the use of emotional rhetoric is not enough. First, emotional rhetoric has to have an appropriate emotional environment in the society, what McAdam (1994) calls a cultural resonance. Indeed, this is exactly how the concept allows us to relate micro (individual responses to appeals), meso (social movements, SMOs, NPOs, and other kinds of organizations), and macro (societal or cultural) levels. There are moments when particular emotional appeals can be persuasive and then for various reasons lose their currency. I have already suggested that the French labor movement was not able to unite around a single emotional

appeal, and even the three appeals that were current did not resonate with many workers. And while the feminist movement engaged many women during the 1970s and early 1980s, more recently it has lost considerable support (Hyde 1991). Earlier, the same could be said about the civil rights movement, which enjoyed enormous support during the late 1950s until the mid 1960s.

Consistent with this idea is the new concept in the social movement literature of opportunities (Amenta and Zylan 1991), which can be applied to emotional rhetoric. Appeals work at particular moments and not others. A good example is the galvanization of the labor movement in Sweden after the killing of several strikers in 1931, a climactic movement in Swedish labor history. This is an example of what McAdam (1994) calls a suddenly imposed grievance, which can be enormously helpful in generating support, at least for a period of time. The police's treatment of American civil rights workers in the South had the same consequence for the U.S. civil rights movement. One can cite many examples across space and time in which certain incidents generated public outrage.

To have cultural resonance, the emotional appeal must be phrased in the rhetoric that is appropriate to the country. This is what gives so much power to the American National Rifle Association; they have a ready-made emotional appeal. In the United States, guns cannot be taken away from citizens. More generally in the United States, as Tarrow (1994, 129) observes, emotional appeals have to be expressed in terms of basic rights or problems of injustice.

Each country has its own distinctive appeal, as we have seen. The killing of strikers had an enormous impact on the mobilization of Swedish society against the capitalists. In contrast, the much higher levels of violence associated with such strikes as the famous Pullman strike and many of the miners' strikes in the United States have not had — nor would they in the future — the same impact. The answer again relates to the emotional climate. The United States is a violent society, as is indicated in the level of murders, and has had a violent history rooted in both the frontier and the lynchings in the South. Furthermore, the absence of connection between rural and urban populations in the United States, the heterogeneity of both, and basic divisions over race reduce the emotional impact of killings. In contrast, Sweden is much more homogeneous and had a large farm population that identified with the working-class movement, and finally and most critically there was a very strong sense of community. In 1931, the Swedish industrialists violated a fundamental rule of the culture.[4] Similar violations are calls for action today. In December 1992 in Sweden, there were several cross

---

3. Historians might rightly argue that it has always been important. It is difficult to demonstrate that it has become more salient across time, but I believe the spread of SMOs is at least one indication of the growing importance of emotional rhetoric, an importance generated by the omnipresence of media. Certainly, all would agree that the nature of emotional rhetoric has changed.

4. And as always, even these variables do not cover all the many factors that are involved. Another important one is that the Swedish capitalists controlled a much larger proportion of the wealth in the country and thus were a much smaller elite, making it easier for the industrial working class to achieve solidarity.

burnings on the lawns of homes belonging to black immigrants. The next night, 250,000 people held a candlelight parade in downtown Stockholm, and similar marches took place in many other Swedish cities. It is hard to imagine such a reaction occurring in the United States.[5] Again, we see how the nature of a culture influences the appropriateness of the particular emotional appeal.

Many of the points that Weber (1946) made about the fragility of charismatic leadership can also be applied to emotional rhetoric. The appeals are not enough by themselves to sustain a social movement; they need to be sustained by success as well. Major defeats will cause collapses in the participation rates within the SMOs. A number of examples can serve to illustrate this point. When the labor unions in Britain lost the general strike in 1926, there was a considerable drop in union membership. The same thing happened in France in 1948, when the union movement split over the communist attempt to destroy the French state. More recently, membership in NOW has declined since the defeat of ERA.

The policies of the state influence the general climate and feelings about likely success or failure. Certainly Ronald Reagan's firing of the air traffic controllers resulted in a loss of union membership and also encouraged employers to be more resistant to union demands, thus having a double impact. Studies of union membership across time (Rankin 1993; Smith 1994) indicate that the passage of legislation desired by the labor movement leads to continued growth in membership net of other factors.

Victories allow for a replenishing of emotional stock — but only up to a point because victories also lessen the sense of injustice, which is part of the driving force in many emotional appeals (Gamson 1990; Tarrow 1994). This is one of the basic dilemmas in SMOs that employ emotional rhetoric: appeals carry the seeds of their self-destruction. Theda Skocpol (1992) suggests that a number of women's movements in the United States during the first part of this century lost their potency once women gained the right to vote. Certainly, the civil rights movement after the political victories of the 1960s found it difficult to retain much support.

Another dilemma in emotional rhetoric is that as a rule it must be targeted to a particular group — those who are feeling the injustice or who are deprived in some way. In this sense the early history (Robertson 1992) of the YWCA is especially interesting because its emotional appeal was to "sisters under the skin," that is, all women regardless of color or ethnicity. This appeal gradually broke down between the two world wars, again, perhaps because of the granting of political rights to white women. But in general, at least in the United States, emotional rhetoric has been targeted to specific kinds of social groups, making distinctions on the basis of these characteristics. Thus, emotional rhetoric, at the same time it defines who is to be included, also defines who is to be excluded. In the United States, social change has been status-based rather than class-based, a pattern more typical in Europe, where working-class movements have been common. But then this is understandable given the heterogeneity of the United States in comparison to much more homogeneous European societies.

The Emotional Appeals of SMOS versus NPOS

A closely related dilemma is the choice as to whether or not to have the legal status of an NPO, that is, to be eligible for charitable donations. SMOs interested in political change are not allowed this option. Daniel Cress (1994) illustrates this point in his study of the homeless and their alternative strategies. Opting for NPO status usually meant being forced to select a less militant and therefore less emotional appeal because it might affect the flow of resources from the general public.

This leads to the other basic and most profound dilemma facing organizations that use emotional rhetoric: the difference between short-term and long-term survival. Precisely because emotional appeals can lose their currency quite quickly given changes in the society and shifts in prevailing attitudes, many SMOs find themselves gravitating toward mission statements that emphasize efficiency and are designed to reassure the general public and thus gain resources from it. Although emotional rhetoric may be effective in leading some members to make major sacrifices, including even to shoot someone, to lie down in front of police cars, or to stage major demonstrations, it does not necessarily mean that such sacrifices will gain resources. Hence the dilemma.

This dilemma becomes particularly acute precisely as the general culture or climate shifts in new directions. Several recent dissertations (Diaz-Albertini 1993; Hyde 1991) about SMOs and NPOs found shifts in recruitment patterns across generations. One example is the general waning of emotional rhetoric in what Diaz-Albertini refers to as the new generation of development professionals recruited in Peru during the middle of the 1980s. This exactly replicates the problems of SMOs observed by Hyde in the complaints of feminist leaders about the general lack of zeal among younger women in the United States.

Especially difficult to maintain are what might be called extreme emotional appeals that demand militancy. The liberation movement of the feminists, the Black Panthers in the civil rights movement, the communist party in Europe, especially during the 1980s, are all examples. Heightened emotional appeals are the most difficult to maintain precisely because one cannot live at a fever pitch. Then, too, usually some accommodations are made, and this lessens the credibility of the extreme appeal. But interestingly enough, in the research of Diaz-Albertini (1993) and Hyde (1991), it is not the initial founders who lose the faith, but rather the next generation, whose attitudes have been formed in divergent circumstances and who is less interested in making the necessary sacrifices.

---

5. The reader might wonder about the societal reaction to the beating of Rodney King. In this instance the issue was the sense of the violation of an individual's *constitutional rights*.

Another way of phrasing the dilemma is to suggest that in any emotional rhetoric there are internal contradictions. Diaz-Albertini (1993) suggested that development organizations (NPOs in particular) face the following contradictions. The first is to provide demonstration projects and services in the hope that they will eventually be adopted by the state, though that is unlikely. The second is to remain a social movement organization emphasizing lobbying and political action, but in the process frequently losing mass support. Finally, the third is to work closely with the poor and powerless, giving them professional and technical aid, which means administering poverty. This same contradiction, essentially between a social movement strategy and an organizational strategy, was observed above in the discussion of Cress's dissertation on the homeless and the dilemma of being a nonprofit agency.

I may be misinterpreting the work of Diaz-Albertini (1993) and of Cress (1993), but these dilemmas and contradictions may reflect the inherent difficulty of combining social movements and organizations. It seems to me that some of these strategies are appropriate for social movements and others for organizations; the problem is how to combine the two successfully. Hyde's (1991) study of feminist organizations suggests that there is an inherent conflict of interest in pursuing organizational survival strategies and social movement change strategies, between the cognitive and the emotive.

The Maintenance of Emotional Rhetoric

Thus, the maintenance of emotional rhetoric becomes problematic. As I have suggested, the cultural climate changes and no longer resonates. Victories eliminate the force of claims of injustice. The tactics employed can discredit the social movement or its particular organizations. The adoption of cognitive strategies that emphasize efficiency take their toll as well as undermine SMOs' attempts to maintain their emotional rhetoric. For all of these reasons, maintaining the fervor and fire becomes a major issue.

One important, never-changing source—one implicit in various dissertations (Cress 1993; Robertson 1992) attached to the governance project—is the presence of a moral rhetorical frame provided by religion, and perhaps taken for granted in the SMOs and NPOs involved in these studies, which does provide emotional motivation. Religion was the basis for the beginnings of the civil rights movement and generally has been involved in a number of NPOs that provide services for blacks; for example, it was critical in the YWCA (Robertson 1992) during its early history. Many of the organizations attempting to help the homeless (Cress 1993) have a religious basis, as do social service agencies generally.

One way of maintaining SMOs is to find a new emotional rhetoric once the old one loses its currency. A good contemporary example of this comes from France, where the public debate about the need for change in society has been revitalized by terming people such as the homeless the "ex-

cluded members" of society. This represents an enormous shift from the previous discourse about the working class. Both the Left and the Right as well as the Center now accept the necessity of doing something about the excluded members. Why does this have cultural relevance in French society? Precisely because the idea of exclusion strikes not only the French as a whole—a homogeneous group with a strong sense of national cohesion—but also the typical French person as being totally unacceptable; the words have an enormous emotional appeal. This emotional appeal provides the consensus that leads to changes in the laws of the society as well as in individual behavior.

Another way of maintaining the emotional rhetoric is to continue to serve those in desperate need on a local basis. Hyde (1991) found that those feminist agencies that continued to supply critical services were the least likely to alter their emotional rhetoric in favor of a strategy that emphasized efficiency. The same was true in a study of NPOs in Peru (Diaz-Albertini 1993).

Social movements as distinct from SMOs can also more easily maintain an emotional rhetoric because their resource needs are less. Those social movements that create organizations and thus become SMOs by definition have many more difficulties. Thus, the paradox that developed in the case of the feminist movement in the United States (Hyde 1991): The liberation section, which wanted to reconstruct society and thus established alternative services, found itself under the greatest pressure to change its rhetoric so as to obtain support for these services. In contrast, the various chapters of NOW, a social movement primarily concerned with political education and fund-raising and not the direct provision of services, is under less pressure and therefore altered its rhetoric the least.

Finally, another way in which emotional rhetorics can be maintained is to continue to innovate in the kinds of services provided, thus affording continual stimulation to the participants and continued justification for seeking resources. An emphasis on the innovation of services for some declared constituency can avert the dangers of overemphasizing efficiency and its consequences for the choice of emotional appeals. Here is where the organizational literature can offer new insights about how to maintain a vital organization with a focus on social change even when the larger climate might be hostile. Being on the frontiers can be highly motivating, as Kidder's *The Soul of a New Machine* (1978) testifies. The problems of how to motivate people and create an élan are the same across the three sectors, even though NPOs and especially voluntary associations have to be more concerned about this issue.

BOARD-ORGANIZATION RELATIONSHIPS

One of the more interesting problems in the study of SMOs, of organizations that rely upon volunteers, and of organizations with expressive outputs is the nature of the board-organization relationship.[6] The interest flows from the distinctive characteristics of boards in these situations. First, these organizations and NPOS generally rely upon volunteers to serve as board members. This means that the motivation of the board is an issue for the organization. Second, the factors that lead people to volunteer to be members of these boards also lead them to want to control and dominate the organizations for which they have some responsibility. For a variety of reasons, boards of NPOS are likely to have more power than those in the two other kinds of organizations. Thus, there is an inherent dilemma between board motivation and board control which is largely absent in government and private, for-profit boards.

How vital a board can be is illustrated in a study of the Art Institute of Chicago (Nathan 1992) across a century of time. Clearly, the Art Institute has become one of the most successful museums in the country. About one-fourth of the decisions made over this period involved new programs or joint programs, which in turned allowed for the continued mobilization of more support. Thus by following a policy of continued innovation, the museum grew into an extremely powerful force in the cultural community of Chicago, and this was largely owing to the board and its active involvement. The opposite situation is revealed in another study. In one of the agencies that Martha Golensky (1993) studied, the board could not move ahead with a fund-raising campaign because the agency had no visibility in the general community, which suggests that this board had not really been fulfilling its function.

One advantage of studying boards is that it allows us to unite at minimum a meso and a macro level of analysis. Boards generally decide organizational strategy. Thus, by definition, they connect the organization to the larger society. This connection may include only decisions about how to raise funds and attract support but more broadly may involve fundamental approaches as to how to change society. Societal change was the goal of the boards attached to feminist SMOS (Hyde 1991), to the early YWCA (Robertson 1992), and to NPOS in Peru (Diaz-Albertini 1993).

The Determinants of the Power of the Board
One of the reasons boards have not been studied often in the traditional organizational literature, I believe, (Hage 1980) is precisely that except during an organizational crisis — economic, political, or social — the board is fairly inconsequential. Hage (1980) lists the many factors that reduce the relative power of the board, factors that tend to be greater in non-NPOS. These factors include such variables as the size of the organization, its complexity, and the experience of the board members with the specific kinds of products or services that the organization provides. NPOS tend to be small, provide noncomplex services, and typically recruit board

members from the professional community, individuals who have technical expertise relevant to the organizational goals.

Golensky (1993) also argues that boards are critical for stabilizing NPOS, giving them a different function from the one they perform in either the public or private sectors. Certainly, SMOS, organizations that rely upon volunteer labor and financial contributions, and expressive output organizations have to be more concerned about legitimacy and the mobilization of support than organizations in the governmental and business sectors, and therefore the role of the board becomes more critical and thus powerful.

What characteristics of board members increase their power beyond what has already been said? Board members who have large amounts of free time and who enjoy high status are likely to have considerable power. And this leads to a paradox. There may be a glass ceiling in the corporation for women, but in NPOS, the most powerful boards can be composed entirely of women! Such was the case in an agency studied by Golensky (1993); but if the women are housewives as opposed to being professionals and therefore have free time and if their husbands are powerful, wealthy members of the community, then the board's power is considerably increased vis-à-vis the staff in an NPO. Women who have more time become more involved and thus acquire more information about various organizational problems. The board of the Junior League as well as that of the Art Institute had a number of women.

But many NPOS do not have access to this kind of board member, especially those that provide services. These agencies are more likely to rely upon professionals within the community; they do not have the same free time to devote to the cause and therefore the agency suffers.

The Involvement of Boards
How can organizations maintain the involvement of the board? The problem is not discussed in the literature, and in some organizations it is not an issue. Certainly when board members are paid, as they are in many private, for-profit organizations, presumably involvement is not problematic; nor is it necessarily in all NPOS.

SMOS are likely to recruit quite dedicated board members, those who believe in the particular cause and therefore are likely to spend large amounts of time working to further it. As a consequence, SMOS are much more likely to have active boards, an interesting by-product of emotional rhetoric. Because SMOS are concerned with the mobilization of people for some cause, by definition, their board members must be dedicated to the cause, even exemplars of its tenets. In turn, this means that they are likely to become considerably involved in the workings of the organization, influencing the recruitment process. Examples are the NOW chapters studied by Hyde (1991).

The study of the Art Institute (Nathan 1992) indicates a different strategy for the mobilization of boards: board differentiation, that is, the creation of special committees. This

---

6. I find it more useful to perceive the board as a separate entity than as part of the organization in order to make more visible the problematics of the relationship between the board and its organization.

strategy has enormous potential, especially for SMOs and NPOs generally, precisely because it dovetails with a strategy of innovation as a way of maintaining the continued support of both the members of the organization and the public. Organizations that want to innovate — above I suggested why SMOs and NPOs should want to — can do so by expanding their boards via the creation of new tasks related to new organizational programs. Some 14 percent of the decisions made by the Art Institute involved the establishment of new committees and board services. This gave the institute a way of mobilizing more and more people on the board, and in meaningful ways, too, given that they were involved in decision-making activities. The creation of such committees usually led to program innovations within the following five years. We do not know how long each committee was active and whether they still are. But the strategy of the Art Institute in this area would seem to be almost a textbook example of what can be done by NPOs, and it is applicable to the developing world as well.

Another advantage of a strategy of board expansion is that it allows for continued renewal of human resources and also encourages the circulation of elites. Some NPOs and many SMOs become saddled with the board that they had when founded, and this board is reluctant to leave. Also, given its initial involvement in the starting of the NPO, the board is powerful and incapable of being dislodged. Because there is no differentiation of committees or new tasks, the board members are unlikely to be willing to relax control or accept new board members, attempting to continue with the same group long after it is useful to do so. This leads to what might be called the quasi-family board.

There are, then, at least three dimensions to consider when examining board-organization relationships: the relative power of the board, its involvement, and the way in which board involvement is obtained and thus another potential dilemma for organizations.

CONCLUSIONS

Both emotional rhetoric and board involvement would appear to be useful topics for constructing a more extended taxonomy of organizational types and for integrating the organizational literature both with the work in the area of the sociology of emotions and with the social movement literature. Together they allow for an integration of multiple levels of analysis and in particular draw together the themes of societal change and organizational analysis.

Emotional rhetoric allows an organization to increase its élan among its own staff, recruit more dedicated board members, and generate support in the community. The emotional rhetoric, however, must resonate with the larger cultural values and can easily lose its potency.

One way of solving the likely decline in the power of attraction of the rhetoric is to continue to innovate. New services have the consequence of allowing for the recruit-ment of new board members and thus the maintenance of a vital board And the innovations also allow for the continual change of society.

REFERENCES

Alter, Catherine, and Jerald Hage. 1993. *Organizations Working Together*. Newbury, Calif.: Sage.

Amenta, Edwin, and Yvonne Zylan. 1991. "Political Opportunity, the New Institutionalism, and the Townsend Movement." *American Sociological Review* 56:250–65.

Carroll, Glenn R. 1987. *Publish and Perish: The Organizational Ecology of Newspaper Industries*. Greenwich, Conn.: JAI Press.

———, ed. 1988. *Ecological Models of Organizations*. Cambridge: Harvard University Press.

Cress, Daniel. 1993. "Mobilization among the Homeless: A Comparative Study of Organization, Action, and Outcomes in Eight U.S. Cities." Ph.D. dissertation, University of Arizona.

Curtis, Russell, and Benigno Aguirre. 1993. *Collective Behavior and Social Movements*. Boston: Allyn and Bacon.

Diani, Mario, and Ron Eyerman. 1992. *Studying Collective Action*. London: Sage.

Diaz-Albertini, Javier. 1993. "Nonprofit Advocacy in Weakly Institutionalized Political Systems: The Case of NGDOs in Lima, Peru." Ph.D. dissertation, SUNY–Stony Brook.

DiMaggio, Paul. 1987. "Nonprofit Organizations in the Production and Distribution of Culture." In *The Nonprofit Sector*, ed. Walter W. Powell, 195–220. New Haven: Yale University Press.

Donati, Paolo. 1992. "Political Discourse Analysis." In *Studying Collective Action*, ed. Diani and Eyerman, 136–67.

Gamson, William A. 1990. *The Strategy of Social Protest*. 2d ed. Belmont, Calif.: Wadsworth.

Golensky, Martha. 1993. "The Board-Executive Relationship in Nonprofit Organizations: Partnership or Power Struggle?" Ph.D. dissertation, CCNY.

Hage, Jerald. 1980. *Theories of Organizations*. New York: John Wiley and Sons.

———, ed. 1988. *Futures of Organizations*. Lexington, Mass.: D. C. Heath.

Hage, Jerald, and Kurt Finsterbusch. 1987. *Organizational Change as a Development Strategy*. Boulder, Colo.: Lynne Reiner.

Hage, Jerald, and Charles Powers. 1992. *Post-Industrial Lives*. Newbury, Calif.: Sage.

Hall, Richard. 1991. *Organizations: Structures, Processes, and Outcomes*. 5th ed. Englewood Cliffs: Prentice-Hall.

Hannan, Michael, and Glenn R. Carroll. 1992. *Dynamics of Organizational Populations: Density, Legitimation and Competition*. New York: Oxford University Press.

Hannan, Michael, and John Freeman. 1989. *Organizational Ecology*. Cambridge: Harvard University Press.

Hyde, Cheryl. 1991. "Did the New Right Radicalize the Women's Movement? A Study of Change in Feminist Social Movement Organizations 1977 to 1987." Ph.D. dissertation, University of Michigan.

Jencks, Christopher. 1987. "Who Gives to What?" In *The Non-*

profit Sector, ed. Walter W. Powell, 321–39. New Haven: Yale University Press.

Johnston, Hank, Enrique Larana, and Joseph Gusfield. 1994. "New Kinds of Social Movements." In *New Kinds of Social Movements*, ed. E. Larana, H. Johnston, and J. Gusfield, 3–35. Philadelphia: Temple University Press.

Kidder, Tracy. 1979. *The Soul of a New Machine*. Boston: Little, Brown.

Kriesi, Hanspeter. 1992. "Support and Mobilization Potential for New Social Movements: Concepts, Operationalizations and Illustrations from the Netherlands." In *Studying Collective Action,* ed. M. Diani and R. Eyerman, 22–54.

Larana, Enrique, Hank Johnston, and Joseph Gusfield, eds. 1994. *New Social Movements: From Ideology to Identity*. Philadelphia: Temple University Press.

McAdam, Doug. 1994. "Culture and Social Movements." In *New Social Movements*, ed. Larana, Johnston and Gusfield, 36–57.

McKelvey, B. 1982. *Organizational Systematics*. Berkeley: University of California.

Meyer, John, and Brian Rowan. 1977. "Institutionalized Organizations: Formal Structure as Myth and Ceremony." *American Journal of Sociology* 83:340–63.

Meyer, John, and W. Richard Scott. 1983. *Organizational Environments: Ritual and Rationality*. Beverly Hills: Sage.

Miles, Raymond, et al. 1978. "Organizational Strategy, Structure, and Process." *Academy of Management Review* 3:546–62.

Mintzberg, Henry. 1979. *Structuring Organizations*. Englewood Cliffs: Prentice-Hall.

Nathan, Maria. 1992. "A Grounded Theory Account of Strategic Decision-making as a Key Mediating Mechanism between Organization and Environment." Ph.D. dissertation, University of Southern California.

Olson, Mancur. 1965. *The Logic of Collective Action*. Cambridge: Harvard University Press.

Powell, Walter W., ed. 1987. *The Nonprofit Sector: A Research Handbook*. New Haven: Yale University Press.

Powell, Walter W., and Paul J. DiMaggio, eds. 1991. *The New Institutionalism in Organizational Analysis*. Chicago: University of Chicago Press.

Powell, Walter W., and Rebecca Friedkin. 1987. "Organizational Change in Nonprofit Organizations." In *The Nonprofit Sector,* ed. Walter W. Powell, 180–92.

Rankin, Bruce. 1993. "The State and Labor Organization: Explaining Divergent Patterns of Unionization in Canada and the United States." Ph.D. dissertation, University of Maryland at College Park.

Robertson, Nancy. 1992. "Race Solidarity versus a Christian Fellowship of Women: A Voluntary Association Confronts Race and Gender Issues in the 1920s." Paper prepared for the ARNOVA conference, Yale University.

Scott, W. Richard. 1987. "The Adolescence of Institutional Theory." *Administrative Science Quarterly* 32:493–511.

———. 1992. *Organizations: Rational, Natural, and Open Systems*. 3d ed. Englewood Cliffs: Prentice-Hall.

Simon, John. 1987. "The Tax Treatment of Nonprofit Organizations." In *The Nonprofit Sector,* ed. Walter W. Powell, 67–98. New Haven: Yale University Press.

Singh, Jitendra, and Charles Lumsden. 1990. "Theory and Research in Organizational Ecology." *American Review of Sociology* 16:161–95.

Skocpol, Theda. 1992. *Protecting Soldiers and Mothers: The Political Origins of Social Policy in the United States*. Cambridge: Belknap Press of Harvard University Press.

Smith, Lovell. 1994. "Union Mobilization and the State: An Examination of the Political Impact of Social Insurance Legislation on Union Growth in Britain and France, 1885–1975." Ph.D. dissertation, University of Maryland at College Park.

Snow, David A., and Robert Benford. 1988. "Ideology, Frame Resonance, and Participant Mobilization." In *From Structure to Action: Social Movement Participation across Cultures*, ed. B. Klandermans, H. Kriesi, and S. Tarrow, 197–217. Greenwich, Conn.: JAI Press.

Tarrow, Sidney. 1994. *Power in Movement: Social Movements, Collective Action, and Politics*. Cambridge: Cambridge University Press.

Zucker, Lynne. 1987. "Institutional Theories of Organizations." *Annual Review of Sociology* 13:443–64.

About the Contributors

Victoria D. Alexander is the Foundation Fund Lecturer in Economic Sociology at the University of Surrey in the United Kingdom. Her research interests fall in the intersection of the sociology of culture and the sociology of organizations. She is currently studying art museums in comparative perspective. She is the author of *Museums and Money: The Impact of Funding on Exhibitions, Scholarship and Management* (Indiana University Press, 1996).

Catherine Alter is a social worker specializing in the organization and management of human service delivery systems. She has professional experience in urban and regional planning, administration of social service organizations in the fields of child welfare, elderly services, juvenile justice, and policy research and analysis. She was on the faculty of the University of Iowa School of Social Work from 1980 to 1996 and was director from 1988 to 1993. Alter is currently dean of the University of Denver Graduate School of Social Work, and she evaluates state welfare reform programs and school-based interventions for at-risk children.

Helmut K. Anheier is an associate professor of sociology at Rutgers University, and a senior research associate at the Johns Hopkins Institute for Policy Studies. His work has focused on organizational studies and structural and comparative analysis. He is involved in research on a compara-

tive study on the size, scope, and role of the private non-profit sector in more than twenty-five developed and developing countries. He is editor of *Voluntas,* the international journal of research on nonprofit organizations. Anheier's most recent publications include *The Emerging Sector — An Overview* (Manchester University Press, 1996) and *The Third Sector: Comparative Studies of Nonprofit Organizations* (DeGruyter, 1990).

L. David Brown is president of the Institute for Development Research and professor of organizational behavior at Boston University. His research and consulting focus on interventions to strengthen the capacities of social change organizations to build coalitions that promote democratic governance, foster sustainable development, and strengthen civil societies. He is currently working with nongovernmental support organizations in Asia and Africa as well as international organizations and coalitions concerned with these issues.

Craig Calhoun is chair of the Department of Sociology at New York University. His newest book is *Nationalism* (University of Minnesota Press, 1997). He is also the author of *Neither Gods nor Emperors: Students and the Struggle for Democracy in China* (University of California Press, 1995), and *Critical Social Theory: Culture, History and the Chal-*

lenge of Difference (Blackwell, 1995). He is the editor of *Habermas and the Public Sphere* (MIT Press, 1992), *Social Theory and the Politics of Identity* (Blackwell, 1994), and *Hannah Arendt and the Meaning of Politics* (University of Minnesota Press, 1997). Since 1994 he has edited the American Sociological Association journal, *Sociological Theory.*

Mark Chaves is visiting associate professor of sociology at the University of Illinois, Chicago. Much of his work spans the boundary between the sociology of religion and the sociology of organizations. He is the author of *Ordaining Women: Culture and Conflict in Religious Organizations* (Harvard University Press, 1997), a comparative study of women's ordination policies, practices, and conflicts.

Elisabeth S. Clemens is associate professor of sociology at the University of Arizona. Building on both organizational theory and political sociology, her work addresses the role of voluntary organizations and social movements in processes of institutional change. She is the author of *The People's Lobby: Organizational Innovation and the Rise of Interest Group Politics in the U.S., 1890–1925* (University of Chicago Press, 1997), a comparative study of labor, agrarian, and women's groups in American politics at the turn of the century.

Kirsten A. Grønbjerg is professor of public and environmental affairs at Indiana University. She has held faculty appointments at Loyola University of Chicago, SUNY — Stony Brook, and Hofstra University. A native of Denmark, she earned an undergraduate degree in sociology at Pitzer College in Claremont, California, and M.A. and Ph.D. degrees in sociology at the University of Chicago. Her interests focus on the structure of public and private human service systems. Her most recent work includes research on public and philanthropic funding for human services. She is the author of *Understanding Nonprofit Funding: Managing Revenues in Social Services and Community Development Organizations* (Jossey-Bass, 1993).

Jerald Hage is professor of sociology at the University of Maryland. His most recent books in the organizations area are *Post-Industrial Lives,* with Charles Powers (Sage, 1992), and *Organizations Working Together,* with Catherine Alter (Sage, 1993). His current writing interests deal with such topics as adaptive costs and benefits, resource availability and competition, and the role of technology in creating sustainable advantage. He is presently involved in two large-scale research studies, one on the problem of global competition, organizational form, and adaptiveness in the shoe industry, and the second on national and organizational factors that affect the likelihood of winning a Nobel Prize in medicine. Both studies involve long historical periods and attempt to integrate organizational theory with processes of large-scale societal change.

J. Craig Jenkins is professor of sociology and faculty associate, Mershon Center for International Security, at Ohio State University. He has taught at the University of Missouri and held appointments at the Program on Non-Profit Organizations, Yale University, and the Center for Policy Research, New York. He is the author of *The Politics of Insurgency: The Farm Worker Movement of the 1960s* and the coeditor (with Bert Klandermans) of *The Politics of Social Protest: Comparative Perspectives on States and Social Movements* (University of Minnesota Press, 1995), and numerous articles on political power, social movements, and comparative politics. He is currently completing a book on social movement philanthropy and working on a global analysis of political violence and humanitarian crisis.

Barry D. Karl is the Norman and Edna Freehling Professor Emeritus of History and the Social Sciences at the University of Chicago. He is now Bloomberg Visiting Professor at the John F. Kennedy School of Government at Harvard University. Most of his writing and teaching has been in the interrelated fields of twentieth-century American government and the impact of the social sciences on policy making. He is the author of *Executive Reorganization and Reform in the New Deal: Charles E. Merriam and the Study of Politics* and *The Uneasy State: The United States from 1915 to 1945.* He is presently completing a book on the impact of private foundations on twentieth-century social and cultural policy.

Michael Krashinsky graduated from Yale University with a Ph.D. in economics in 1973 and joined the faculty at the Scarborough Campus of the University of Toronto, where he is now professor of economics. His research is principally in the area of social policy. He has written two books, one on day care policy in Ontario and the other on user charges in the social services. He has also written numerous articles on day care, nonprofit institutions, housing, mandatory retirement, welfare policy, public education, and Canadian elections.

Jane Mansbridge is a professor at the John F. Kennedy School of Government at Harvard University and a member of the American Academy of Arts and Sciences. She is the author of *Beyond Adversary Democracy* (University of Chicago Press, 1983) and *Why We Lost the ERA* (University of Chicago Press, 1986) and editor of *Beyond Self-Interest* (University of Chicago Press, 1990), and coeditor, with Susan Muller Okin, of *Feminism* (Edward Elgar Publishing, 1994).

Elizabeth Mauser is an economist in the Office of Research and Demonstrations at the Health Care Financing Administration. Her current research interests include comparative behavior of for-profit and nonprofit organizations, long-term care, integrated health care delivery systems, and substance abuse treatment programs. She received her Ph.D. from the University of Wisconsin.

Walter W. Powell is professor of sociology and director of the Social and Behavioral Sciences Research Institute at the University of Arizona. He has previously taught at MIT and Yale. He is the editor of *The Nonprofit Sector* (Yale University Press, 1987) and coeditor with Paul DiMaggio of *The New Institutionalism in Organizational Analysis* (Univ. of Chicago Press, 1991). He is currently studying the role of interorganizational collaborations, particularly those between universities and science-based companies, in the development of the biotechnology industry. A companion project examines the causes and consequences of changes in the division of labor in the life sciences between the academy and industry.

Nancy Marie Robertson completed her doctorate in history at New York University. This article draws on her dissertation " 'Deeper Even Than Race'?: White Women and the Politics of Christian Sisterhood in the Young Women's Christian Association, 1906–1946." She was an Indiana University Fellow in Nonprofit Governance from 1989 to 1991. She has also held a Charlotte W. Newcombe Fellowship for the study of ethical and religious values. Robertson has taught courses in U.S. history and women's studies and served as assistant editor for the Margaret Sanger Papers. She has also worked on historical research projects for the YWCA of Eastern Union County (New Jersey), the David Rockefeller Papers, and the 92nd Street Y.

Lester M. Salamon is a professor at Johns Hopkins University and the director of its Center for Civil Society Studies. Previously, he was director of the Center for Governance and Management Research at the Urban Institute in Washington, D.C. Between 1977 and 1980, Salamon served as deputy associate director of the U.S. Office of Management and Budget. Before that he taught at Duke, Vanderbilt, and Tougaloo College. Salamon received his B.A. degree in economics and policy studies from Princeton University and his Ph.D. in government from Harvard University. His recent work has focused on alternative instruments of government action and the scope, structure, and role of the private nonprofit sector in the United States and around the world. His recent books include *Partners in Public Service* (Johns Hopkins University Press, 1995), *The Emerging Nonprofit Sector,* with Helmut Anheier (Manchester University Press, 1996), *Defining the Nonprofit Sector: A Cross-National Comparison,* with Helmut Anheier (Manchester University Press, 1997), *America's Nonprofit Sector: A Primer* (Foundation Center, 1992), and *Beyond Privatization: The Tools of Government Action* (Urban Institute Press, 1989).

Mark Schlesinger is associate professor of public health and fellow of the Institution for Social and Policy Studies, Yale University. He is also a visiting associate professor at the Institute for Health, Health Care Policy and Aging Research at Rutgers University. Schlesinger was previously on the faculty at the Kennedy School of Government and Harvard Medical School and received his graduate training in economics at the University of Wisconsin. His health policy research includes assessments of federal programs for children and the elderly, studies of the growth of for-profit enterprises in health and mental health care, investigations of the scope and consequences of various forms of managed care and utilization management, including their application to managed competition, and analyses of public attitudes toward health care reform. His research on other aspects of social policy includes studies of government contracting for services from private agencies, public perceptions and attitudes shaping intergenerational tensions and age-targeted social programs, and the comparative performance of private nonprofit, for-profit, and public agencies.

Wolfgang Seibel is a professor of political science at the University of Konstanz, Germany. He graduated from the University of Marburg and the Graduate School of Administration Sciences, Speyer, and holds a doctorate in economics and social science. His most recent book in English is *The Third Sector: Comparative Studies of Nonprofit Organizations* (coeditor with Helmut Anheier, DeGruyter 1990).

Brian H. Smith holds the Charles and Joan Van Zoeren Chair in Religion, Ethics, and Values at Ripon College in Ripon, Wisconsin. His advanced degrees are in political science (Yale, 1979), religion (Master of Divinity, Woodstock College, 1970), and ethics (Master of Sacred Theology in Ethics, Union Theological Seminary, 1971). He has taught at Fordham University, Georgetown University, and the Massachusetts Institute of Technology. His books include *The Church and Politics in Chile: Challenges to Modern Catholicism* (Princeton University Press, 1982), *More Than Altruism: The Politics of Private Foreign Aid* (Princeton University Press, 1990), and *The Catholic Church and Democracy in Chile and Peru,* coauthored with Michael Fleet (University of Notre Dame Press, 1997).

Claire F. Ullman is a former fellow at the Brookings Institution's Center for Public Management. She received a Ph.D. in political science from Columbia University in 1995 and has taught at Barnard College and the Wharton School. Her research focuses on the growing political importance of the nonprofit sector in France and the United States and on the evolution of the welfare state in the United States and Western Europe.

Burton A. Weisbrod is John Evans Professor of Economics and former director of what is now the Institute for Policy Research at Northwestern University. Prior to his appointment at Northwestern University in 1990, he was Evjue-Bascom Professor of Economics, founder and director of the Center for Health Economics and Law, and director of the NIMH Training Program in Health and Mental Health Economics at the University of Wisconsin — Madison, where he had been a member of the faculty since 1964. A native of Chicago, Weisbrod received his undergraduate degree in management from the University of Illinois, and his M.A. and Ph.D. degrees in economics from Northwestern University. He has held visiting faculty appointments at Brandeis, Harvard, Princeton, and Yale universities as well as at the Australian National University and the Universidad Autónoma de Madrid. He also served as a senior staff member of the Council of Economic Advisors to Presidents John F. Kennedy and Lyndon B. Johnson. Weisbrod is the author or coauthor of nine books, editor of five, and author or coauthor of more than 160 published articles and papers. His research has focused on public policy analysis of the economics of education, health, medical research, manpower, public interest law, the military draft, and benefit-cost analysis. Most recently, he has been engaged in research into the causes and consequences of, and the impact of health reform on, technological change in health care; the comparative economic behavior of for-profit, governmental, and private nonprofit organizations; and the causes and consequences of the growing commercialism of nonprofits. His latest book is *The Commercialization of the Nonprofit Sector,* to be published by Cambridge University Press in 1998.

Alan Wolfe is university professor and professor of sociology and political science at Boston University. He is the author of numerous books, among them *Marginalized in the Middle* (Chicago University Press, 1996) and *Whose Keeper?: Social Science and Moral Obligation* (University of California Press, 1989). Besides his scholarly writings, he writes essays and reviews that appear regularly in the *New Republic,* the *Wilson Quarterly, Harpers,* the *Washington Post,* and the *New York Times.* His book about middle-class morality will be published in 1998.

Index

Accountability, 160

Administrators of nonprofit organizations: nonpecuniary incentives for, 87, 90, 95–96; organizational conflict faced by, 280–82; professionalization of, 90–91, 253

Advocacy organizations, 208

African Americans: internal diversity of, 27; and the mammy cult, 197–98; and the problem of community and difference, 21–22, 28–34; settlement houses, 56, 57; in the women's voluntary association movement, 194–203

African nonprofit organizations, 217, 229, 231–40

Alexander, Victoria, 254

Alford, Robert, 275

Alternative foundations, 210–11

Altruism: behavioral, 37–39; conformist dimension of, 38; demagogic appeals to, 4; environmental, 41–42, 43, 63, 125; and justice, 202, 202*n*23; motivational, 39–41; nested in self-interest, 14–16, 210, 212; social scientific studies of, 36–37, 43

Anderson, R. Wayne, 62

Anheier, Helmut, 54, 56*n*8, 63

Aquinas, Thomas, 7*n*10, 8, 13

Archambault, Édith, 165

Aristotle, 7, 7*n*9, 8

Arrow, Kenneth, 10, 70

Art Institute of Chicago, 299–300

Ashforth, B. E., 277

Asian nonprofit organizations, 217, 222, 231–40. *See also* Bangladesh Immunization Program; Indonesian Irrigation Program; Pakistan Urban Sanitation Program

Assistance. *See* Developing countries, nonprofit assistance to

Association for the Development of Progressive Associations (DAP), 167, 168, 172

Atomism, 24

Augustine, 7*n*10

Auspice, 114–15; and Canadian day care policy debates, 115–17; and consultants' opinions of day care quality, 117–18; distribution of day care centers according to, 116; and government preference, 120–22; and parents' opinions of day care quality, 119–20. *See also* Institutional form

Autogestion, 167–68

Axelrod, Robert, 13*n*24

Backman, Elaine V., 275, 283

Bakker, Jim, 72

Bangladesh Immunization Program, 231; direction setting in, 234; intersectoral relations in, 232; problem framing in, 233–34; social

capital increased by, 237–38; solution implementation in, 235–36, 237

Bar-Tal, Daniel, 37

Barnard, Chester, 50

Barry, Brian, 7*n*8, 9, 9*n*20

Batson, Daniel, 14, 39, 40, 42

Beard, Charles, 27

Beckford, James, 50

Bellah, Robert, 23, 24

Ben-Ner, Avner, 54

Benford, Robert, 292

Benn, Stanley, 10*n*22

Bentham, Jeremy, 9*n*20, 10, 24, 32

Berger, Peter, 23

Berry, Wendell, 25*n*11

Beuttler, Fred, 49–50

Biddle, Jeff E., 51

Bloch-Lainé, François, 166–67, 170, 172

Block, S., 275

Boards, nonprofit, 291–92, 298–300; and complexity, 283; corporate participation in, 140–42; parent boards in day care centers, 122

Bonoficer organizations, 72, 73–74, 75, 273, 273*n*4. *See also* Nonprofit organizations, bonoficing.

Bordt, Rebecca L., 268, 283

Bowles, Eva, 197

307